EATING
ITALY

© 1998 Jeffrey L. Ward

EATING IN ITALY

A Traveler's Guide to the Gastronomic Pleasures of Northern Italy

FAITH HELLER WILLINGER

photographs by FAITH ECHTERMEYER

WILLIAM MORROW AND COMPANY, INC.

NEW YORK

Text copyright © 1989, 1998 by Faith Heller Willinger
Photographs copyright © 1989, 1998 by Faith Echtermeyer
Maps copyright © 1998 by Jeffrey L. Ward

It is the policy of William Morrow and Company, Inc., and its imprints and affiliates, recognizing the importance of preserving what has been written, to print the books we publish on acid-free paper, and we exert our best efforts to that end.

Library of Congress Cataloging-in-Publication Data

Willinger, Faith Heller.
  Eating in Italy : a traveler's guide to the gastronomic pleasures of Northern Italy / [Faith Heller Willinger]. —Rev. and updated.
    p.   cm.
  Includes index.
  ISBN 0-688-14614-7
  1. Cookery, Italian—Northern style. 2. Gastronomy. 3. Wine and wine making—Italy, Northern.
  I. Title.
TX723.2.N65W55   1998
641.5945—dc21   97-24707
                                                                          CIP

Printed in the United States of America

8   9   10

www.williammorrow.com

Italia, ti voglio bene assai

FOR MAX, MASSIMO, AND DAD

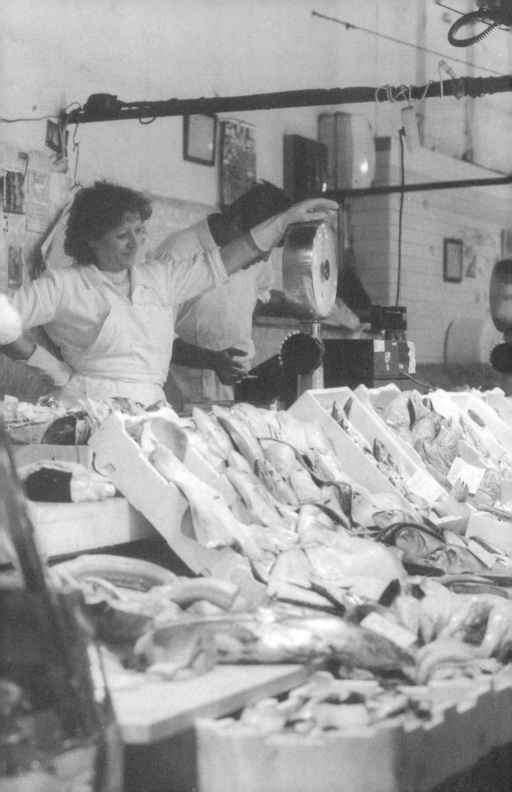

Grazie
and thank you

This book took many years to write.
I began to amass the information without a specific plan, just because
I wanted to know everything about Italian regional *cucina*. The inspiration
to round up my accumulated knowledge, and to learn more, straight
from the source, came from Annie.

Thanks to Ann, Gail, Paul, and Jen, who became instant believers.
It frequently worried me to work
with the positive people at Morrow, who found no fault with my obsessions.

Thanks to Faith, who read computer
printouts and photographed with style and taste buds.

And finally, thank you and *grazie*
to the people who fed me food, wine, information, and
encouragement, who took the time to explain, who directed
me down some fine roads. To
Angelo, Annie, Ann, Ampelio, Annalisa, Adriana, Alvaro, Antonio, Andrea, Alfredo,
Arlette, Aurelia, Arturo, Aimo, Afra, Alan, Beatrice, Barbara, Bruno, Bruce, Burt, Bert,
Bertha, Betta, C., Carmen, Carol, Cristina, Cesare, Clara, Claudia, Carlo, Claudio, Corby,
Dina, Dania, Dario, Duccio, Enzo, Ezio, Elda, Enrico, Edoardo, Enza, Emiliana, Ettore,
Eugenio, Elisabetta, Elio, Faith, Fiametta, Fabio, Fabrizio, Fran, Franca, Franco, Fausto,
Francesca, Francesco, Fred, Girolamo, Gualtiero, Gianna, Giuliana, Gianfranco,
Gianpaolo, Giovanni, Giannola, Giacomo, Giorgio, Giuliano, Gioacchino, Gloria, Herb,
Henry B., Judy, Julia, Joan, Ken, Kyle, Lisa, Laura, Laurie, Livio, Lucio, Lydie, Lucia, Luigi,
Lou, Mario, Massimo, Matteo, Maurizio, Maggie, Marco, Marvin, Marie, Marcella,
Marion, Molly, Nancy, Nuccio, Nerio, Neil, Nadia, Osvaldo, Piermario, Pierangelo, Paolo,
Paula, Primo, Patrizia, Philip, Paola, Rinaldo, Realmo, Roberto, Rose, Rosy, Roccaldo,
Rory, Romano, Stefano, Sally, Silvano, Scott, Sabine, Sauro, Sergio, Sandro,
Schultzy, Silvana, Suzanne, Tonino, Torquato, Tobia, Ugo,
Umberto, Vanna, Vasco, Victor, Vittorio, Vittorio Fiore,
Walter, Wayne, Wendy, and especially
the Wags!

Contents

Introduction

Being an American in Italy has its advantages for me. My attachment to the traditional foods of the various regions of the country doesn't go back to my infancy, isn't tied emotionally to my family history. Rather, it has been formed with the help of Italians who do have these ties, whose palates have helped me develop a sense of the flavors of each province. Traveling in the eleven regions of the north that are covered in this book, I began to grasp the nature of the foods and wines of each area, unencumbered by the roots that in some cases bind Italians to their own regional traditions to the exclusion of all others—and in others stir a rebellion against anything local.

I learned that Italian regional cooking, *la cucina tradizionale,* is defined by geography, climate, and conquest. Natural boundaries—the mountains, lakes, rivers, and seas—divide the land into a patchwork of microsystems where soil and climate determine the main ingredients. The olive tree thrives in the meager rocky soil of Toscana, and olive oil is dominant in kitchens there. The fertile plains of the Po Valley provide pasture for the livestock that produce the meat and cheese for the recipes of Lombardia and Emilia-Romagna. The tasty vegetables that grow in the rich alluvial soil of Venezia's lagoon, and the fish from her waters, are the basis of that region's specialties.

Italy's northern mountain ranges block off the Nordic cold, and the lakes and seas temper the winter weather. New York and Napoli may be on the same latitude, but lemon trees grow in Napoli. So are Boston and Firenze, but the sight of a snowflake brings traffic to a halt around the Duomo. Palm trees and olives unexpectedly flourish in the foothills of the Alps.

As for conquest—every populace bent on conquest, or escape from conquest, seems to have passed through the Italian peninsula. Some never left, and were assimilated into this Mediterranean melting pot. *Farro,* a barleylike grain found today in parts of Friuli, Umbria, and parts of Toscana, fed the Roman legions. And some pastries served in Veneto, Friuli, and Lombardia are remnants of Austrian domination of the eighteenth century. But while eddying political powers engaged the city-states in a game of musical boundaries, life in the countryside was relatively unaffected. The church defined the boundaries of the village, and many never ventured beyond the sound of its bell, or perhaps beyond the provincial capital. (*Campanilismo,* from "campanile," means an almost claustrophobic localism—the negative aspect of this provincialism.)

With the advent of the bicycle, then the Fiat 500, and now highways, television, and jet travel, this localism appears to be fading fast. But there are still gastronomic traditionalists, tenaciously clinging to the past, reinterpreting and adapting it to suit the present. My contact with these exceptional devotees has been an amazing experience for the palate, eye, and intellect. It was a joy to track down both native and "born again" winemakers, restaurant owners, cooks, bread bakers, *grappa* distillers, coffee roasters, vinegar makers, pastry chefs, farmers, cheesemakers, pasta rollers, butchers, truffle hunters, rice growers, millers of every imaginable grain, meat and fish smokers, candy makers, tableware artisans.

I fell in love with Italy as an adult. In an unfamiliar language, I had to learn how to carry out simple everyday tasks. Shopping for groceries, ordering a coffee or a meal or a glass of wine, reciting my choice of three flavors for a *gelato*—all took practice. I had to learn about the regions of the country, each with its own unique dishes and wines. I studied with my son, Max, read his Italian schoolbooks, and learned about the geography of rivers, mountains, and seas, the names of the winds, and about the waves of influence that make up each region's history. I learned the language, traveled, asked questions, and listened (one of the few calorie-free aspects of studying Italian cookery!).

The answers, which have been acquired over twenty-five years of living in Italy, are all here in this guide. The first part of the book explains basic, everyday Italian gastronomic behavior, and includes introductions to the country's special foods, the tools for making and serving them, and the cooking experience itself. The second part deals with the eleven regions that make up northern Italy (the southern border of Toscana, Umbria, and Le Marche represents a Mason-Dixon line for me, dividing the more formal restaurant and winemaking traditions of the north from the south, with its simpler, more Mediterranean approach to food and wine). Each chapter reveals the character of a different region (a unit similar to one of our states), starting with a brief geographical and historical introduction. "The Menu" explains local foods in the order they appear on a menu: appetizers, soups, main courses, cheese, fruit, dessert. "The Wine List" describes some of the best local selections. In "Regional Specialties" you'll read about local products for the kitchen or table, many of them unavailable outside the area. The creators of these products are masters at their work, passionate monomaniacs who are interested in excellence and are excited about

what they're doing, which makes their products such a pleasure to use.

Under the "Guide" for each region, you'll find an alphabetical listing, by location, of the sources of this distinctive regional *cucina* and special food-related products: restaurants, markets, specialty food shops, bars, housewares, stores, bakeries, wine shops, ice cream stores, cheesemakers. I've mentioned some hotels and inns convenient for touring, because people always ask me where to stay. This is not a hotel guide, though. For a complete list with prices, head for the local E.P.T. office (Ente Provinciale di Turismo), often in the center of town.

All geographical names are in Italian (Firenze, not Florence; Torino, not Turin) because that's the way they appear on the best maps. (Check the index if you're not certain.) Because of the fluctuating exchange rate, prices are broadly categorized: Restaurants are listed as inexpensive (under 30,000 lire per person), moderate (30,000 to 60,000), and expensive (over 70,000). Hotel prices are inexpensive (less than 100,000 for a double), moderate (around 150,000 lire), expensive (around 250,000), and luxury (over 300,000). Due to ever-fluctuating exchange rates, prices are given in lire. Banks give the best rate of exchange. At the time this book went to press, one American dollar was worth about 1,700 lire. The Italian government has been threatening for years to knock three zeroes off the present monetary system, an effort at simplification known as the "heavy lira." Its acceptance is probably far in the future, although Italians are full of surprises.

Special tips are scattered throughout: a vocabulary list of *gelato* flavors, a key to opening and closing hours, types of pasta, wine terminology. At the back of the book you'll find a food glossary and an index.

EATING IN ITALY

The Restaurant

Before I start to tell you when and how and what to eat, and where, it's only fair to let you know what I look for in a restaurant. The first requirement, more important than anything else, is good food that relates to the area. It pleases me to find regional specialties on the menu, but even if the food isn't traditional, it should be made with the best, freshest seasonal produce. I like food to look like food. I am not impressed with braided, curled, tied, or sculpted arrangements on my plate—I dislike the idea that someone has been playing with my meal. Some Italians, uninterested in dining out on the same food they eat at home, appreciate this *new wave* cooking more than I do.

Fine wine makes any meal better, and I love to drink interesting regionals, usually the best complement for the local *cucina*. Although I may opt for the locally produced house wine in an inexpensive country *trattoria,* I won't accept a poor selection in an expensive restaurant. I enjoy efficient service but will accept a lot less if there's good food to be found. I don't like to be hurried through a meal. I love a family restaurant with tradition and roots, especially one with three generations in the kitchen.

Although I have eaten some wonderful meals in large and medium-size cities, in Italy the best food is generally found in rural areas, in towns without much of a cultural or artistic patrimony. Just getting to them may be a lesson in local geography. The Touring Club Italiano's *Atlante d'Italia*—a soft-covered atlas of Italy—is essential for getting around in the countryside. It's easy to read, with no folding and unfolding required, and equipped with an index, indispensable for locating some of the obscure villages mentioned in this book.

"Why are you here in the middle of nowhere?" I frequently asked restaurant owners after an extraordinary meal in a village that none of my Italian friends had ever heard of.

"Because this is where I'm from" was invariably the answer. It's not only a question of roots, however, but of raw materials, of friends and neighbors who produce the best wines, cheeses, and *prosciutto,* of knowing who has the early-ripening cherries, or the sweetest butter or tastiest olive oil. Many of these restaurant owners have worked in the big cities; some have studied in France; most have traveled extensively in Italy to see what their colleagues are up to. But invariably the most profound influence comes from the local gastronomic heritage, from their own memories of mouth-filling flavors and regional tastes, always sharper and more intense in their native habitat than when transported elsewhere.

A trip to the village market is the ideal way to find out what's local and what's in season. Look at "The Menu" in this book for the region in which you'll be eating, and check the menu posted outside most restaurants for signs of traditional cooking. While you're examining the menu, look at the diners if you can: They should be mostly Italian (local customers won't come back if the food isn't good). Tourist centers tend to have the worst restaurants, since patrons are unlikely to return; they take advantage of a captive audience with food that is better left undescribed. It may be difficult to get a good meal in Venezia or

Firenze, but it will probably be impossible in Siena, San Gimignano, or Assisi, where most visitors spend only a few hours and therefore don't concentrate on the food. An empty restaurant at mealtime is a poor sign, naturally—except during soccer championships, when most of the country is glued to the TV set in the local bar. Skip all restaurants with a German tourist bus parked in front. Beware of restaurants with waiters in costume, and don't place too much importance on decor; at times I welcome a sincerely ugly restaurant. As a general rule, avoid restaurants near train stations or major tourist attractions, which cater to the unwary and the rushed. I tend to distrust a restaurant that displays a menu translated into four languages.

the menu

Navigating an Italian menu takes practice. A typical meal consists of four courses, although some can become marathons of eight or more tastes.

The *primo,* or first course, is pasta, either sauced or in broth, rice or *risotto,* or soup.

The *secondo* is usually fish, meat, or poultry, although *frittate* (pan-fried flans), mushrooms, and substantial vegetable dishes may also be listed. Meat and fish are frequently priced by weight: 100 grams (*un'etto,* or 100 gr) is about 4 ounces.

Italians like their fish cooked simply, so the fresh tastes of the sea stand out, unhidden by sauce and undamaged by overhandling. Fish may be brought to the table in its entirety, complete with head, tail, and fins, to be examined for freshness. Grilled, boiled, or baked fish may be served whole, presenting a project that do-it-yourself surgeons will relish. Italian waiters make a wonderful drama of deboning fish with a fork, a spoon, and a flourish, dividing it up into individual portions and leaving

behind an intact skeleton of head, bones, and tail.

Next is a *contorno,* a side dish of vegetables at room temperature (and often overcooked) or a green salad dressed at the table with olive oil and vinegar.

Most Italians end their meal with fruit, considered a palate refresher. Unwashed fruit is served with a bowl of water for a rinse, and is then peeled—with the exception of cherries, grapes, plums, and apricots. Ripe peaches are one of the great joys of the summer in Italy. Some Italians have perfected the art of peeling fruit to the point that they can carve without picking the fruit up in their hands, a treat to watch. Fresh fruit salad, called *macedonia,* is made daily in many restaurants.

A more elaborate repast will begin with an *antipasto* (appetizer), usually based on local *salumi* (a general term for cured meats like *prosciutto* and salami), often served with fresh figs or cantaloupe in season. Some restaurants display a platter-filled table (frequently self-service; watch other diners for a clue), others wheel a cart to your table, displaying assorted marinated vegetables, olives, fish, and salads, listed as *antipasto misto.* Its price is indicated by the letters p.v., which stand for *prezzo da vedere* ("price to be seen"), determined by what and how much you eat; or s.q., *secondo quantità* ("according to the quantity"). Your menu may also list cheeses and fruits with the same indication.

Dessert is looked upon as a special treat, not an everyday finish to the meal. *Torte* (cakes), *crostate* (jam or fruit tarts), and *gelato* (ice cream) are found on most menus, as is *tiramisù,* a rich *mascarpone* dessert originally from Veneto, which seems to be a favorite everywhere. Fancy restaurants serve *piccola pasticceria,* little pastries or cookies, after dessert. *Panna cotta,* a lightly gelatinized cream dessert is

WHEN YOU'RE ORDERING

I'd like to eat something traditional.
Vorrei mangiare qualcosa di tradizionale.
Voh-RAY mahn-JAR-ay kwal-COH-za dee tra-DITS-yah-NAH-lay

I'd like to eat something light.
Vorrei mangiare qualcosa di leggero.
Voh-RAY mahn-JAR-ay kwal-COH-za dee lay-JAIR-oh

I'd like to eat a half portion of . . .
Vorrei mangiare mezza porzione di . . .
Voh-RAY mahn-JAR-ay METS-zah portz-YOH-nay dee . . .

We'd like to split a portion of . . .
Vorremo dividere una porzione in due di . . .
Voh-RAY-mo dee-VEE-dah-ray OON-ah ports-YOHN-ay een DOO-ay dee . . .

I'd like to eat fish.
Vorrei mangiare pesce.
Voh-RAY mahn-JAR-ay PEH-shay

I'd like to eat meat.
Vorrei mangiare carne.
Voh-RAY mahn-JAR-ay CAR-nay

Can you cook without salt?
Può cucinare senza sale?
Pwoh koo-chee-NAH-ray SEN-zah SAH-lay?

I am a vegetarian.
Sono un vegetariano [una vegetariana].
SOH-noh oon veh-jeh-tah-ree-AH-noh [OON-ah veh-jeh-tah-ree-AH-nah]

usually served with a fruit or chocolate sauce.

Many restaurants offer a tasting menu (*menu degustazione*), a series of samples of their regional or seasonal best, often matched with appropriate wines.

The Italian menu is flexible enough to satisfy carnivore and vegetarian alike. If you want to keep it light, order the *antipasto* and skip the main course, or skip the *antipasto* and *primo*, concentrating on meat and vegetables, choosing the regional dishes that seem the most interesting. But ordering pasta and a salad is poor form—three courses is the minimum for a meal in Italy.

Time has eroded the clear distinction in style and price between an *osteria* or *locanda*, a *trattoria*, and a *ristorante*. Often an *osteria* will serve more elegant and expensive food than a *ristorante*.

reservations, service, and tipping

Reserving a table in a restaurant is a sign of respect, and Italians are pleased by the commitment. Reservations for dinner in small restaurants may be hard to come by, especially during trade fairs. But it is usually not necessary to make a reservation for lunch, except in the most formal restaurants. Do call to cancel one if you can't keep it. Someone at your restaurant will probably understand English; in any event, Italians are great communicators and will try to figure out what you want even if they don't understand what you are saying. Many country restaurants don't take credit cards, so be prepared to pay in lire. (If you can supply the exchange rate from a newspaper or bank, you may be able to pay in dollars or traveler's checks.)

The tip should be left in cash. How much depends on the quality of the service, the type of restaurant, and the size of the cover and service charges. Most restaurants charge a fixed cover charge for occupying a set table, listed on the menu as *coperto*. This varies with the type of restaurant—linens, crystal, silver, and flowers on the table will mean a higher *coperto*. The *servizio* is a percentage for service, automatically added to the total cost of your meal. The higher the cover and service charges, the lower your tip should be. If the *servizio* is more than 15 percent, the tip should be reduced to a gesture—one small bill per person. There is no excuse for poor or surly service, which should never be rewarded with a tip.

When to Eat

There is no shortage of occasions for eating in Italy, both during and between meals, and there is no shortage of vocabulary for any of these occasions!

You can have breakfast (*la colazione* or *la prima colazione*) at your hotel or in a *bar-caffè*. Hotels and *pensione* usually offer a continental breakfast: a choice of coffee, tea, hot chocolate, or *caffè latte* (small pitchers of American-style coffee and milk), plus fresh rolls, rusks, butter, preserves, and maybe fresh croissants.

Breakfast in a *bar-caffè* —usually served between 7:00 and 10:30 A.M.—is a far better choice: The coffee will be richer, the pastry fresher, and the scene worth watching. However, if you sit at a table, prices may increase anywhere from 50 to 300 percent. Most Italians stand at the counter for their breakfast. The procedure may seem confusing at first: You look over the pastries, then go to the cashier (*cassa*),

state your order, and pay for it. You'll get a receipt, which you give to the barman or place on the counter as you restate your order. Weight down your receipt with a 50- or 100-lire coin, the correct tip for all this confusion. The coffee choices in a *bar-caffè* may seem endless, but the classic breakfast drink is a *cappuccino*.

Around 10 A.M., light breakfasters may be ready to "put something under their teeth," as the Italian expression goes. Order a *panino* (sandwich), *toast* (a grilled ham and cheese on American-style bread), a *pasta* (pastry), or a quick shot of caffeine— all of which are always available at the *bar-caffè* for between-meal hunger.

Lunch (*pranzo* or *colazione*) starts at 12:30 or 1:00 and lasts from thirty minutes to three hours. Time, cost, calories, and hunger may be factors in what you decide to do for this meal on any given day. A stand-up snack or self-serve lunch is a possible alternative to a restaurant meal. Sandwiches with a wide variety of fillings are available in a *paninoteca,* a bar specializing in sandwiches, either made to order or ready-made (the latter found under a napkin in a self-service display case of pastry and rolls). Grocery stores will split a roll and sell enough *salumi* to fill it. Most bread bakeries sell freshly made flatbreads, called *focaccia* or *schiacciata,* and pizza, sold by the slice or weight. (Avoid pizza shops displaying gaudily garnished pizza; they're exclusively for tourists and the pizza is indigestible.)

If you're staying in a city or town for a few days, one way to make your visit especially pleasant is to become a "local." Choose a small, simple neighborhood restaurant that looks interesting, and eat lunch there every day. The second day, your waiter will be pleased to see you, and on the third you'll receive a generous welcome. A relaxed lunch can begin with an aperitif accompanied by salty snacks, and end with a long lingering *caffè* in the sunshine— one of the great joys of mealtime in Italy.

Dinner (*cena* or *pranzo*) is served from 7:30 on, although most Italians dine around 8:30. The before-dinner *aperitivo* can be taken in a bar. On the coast in the summer, where life is less formal, dinner often starts after 9:30. Italians dress casually, yet with great elegance, when they dine out. Restaurants require neither jacket nor tie—but no athletic attire, please.

The Bar-Caffè

Many restaurant meals are prefaced with a drink and postscripted with a coffee at a *bar-caffè,* one of the best places to observe the natives and partake of their rituals. An Italian bar isn't only for the consumption of alcoholic drinks: You can also get breakfast, make a phone call, take a coffee break, grab a snack or *gelato,* check out the poster of what's playing at the movies, flip through the local newspaper, or listen to a soccer match. Most of these activities are done standing up, since sitting down,

inside or out, means higher prices with a surcharge for table service. Bear in mind that Italians think cold beverages are bad for the digestion. If yours isn't cold enough for you, ask for *ghiaccio* (ice)—*con molto ghiaccio* if you'd like more than two or three cubes.

If there's a big navy or black and white "T" (for *tabacchi*) displayed outside, you can also buy cigarettes, three different kinds of matches, salt, stamps, and bus tickets at the *bar-caffè.*

The Picnic

Italians love to eat outdoors. However, their idea of a picnic isn't a light meal on a blanket—it's closer to a five-course Sunday lunch, complete with collapsible chairs and table, tablecloth, refrigerated beverages, and an umbrella for shade. Making a modest version of this is simple, however,

thanks to grocery stores and specialty shops (*alimentari, salumeria,* or *gastronomia*) that will sell enough cold cuts for a sandwich, a wedge of cheese, a handful of olives or artichoke hearts, and a chilled bottle of wine or mineral water.

Most grocery shops also have take-out

The Bar Menu

Caffetteria

Caffè or espresso: Italian espresso coffee, served in a demitasse cup

Caffè freddo: iced coffee, usually served highly sugared

Caffè d'orzo: an ersatz coffee, made from barley (*orzo*)

Camomilla: camomile tea—a relaxing, diuretic infusion

Cappuccino: literally, "the little hood" or "the little monk." Espresso topped with foamy steamed milk, the colors of Capuchin monks' robes. Often called *cappuccio* in some areas.

Cioccolata calda: at its best, a cup of hot, thick, almost black bitter hot chocolate. *Con panna:* topped with unsweetened whipped cream.

Latte: milk. Served hot (*caldo*), steamed, in a glass; or if you insist, cold (*freddo*).

Thè or tè: tea: usually a little pot of hot water with a tea bag. Served *al latte* (with milk) or *al limone* (with a slice of lemon)

Tè freddo: iced tea, usually served highly sugared

Tisana: an herbal infusion (tea)

Aperitivi

Aperol: Orange-colored and -flavored, usually served in a glass with a sugar-coated rim

Biancosarti: yellow, all natural, vague flavor

Campari: this famous cherry-red aperitif is made from herbs, bitter orange peel, and soaked quinine bark, among other ingredients, and is said to be stimulating and habit-forming

Campari bitter: 25 percent alcohol, is served plain, with a twist of lemon, or on the rocks. *Campari soda,* 10 percent alcohol, is a Campari-flavor carbonated beverage

Carpano: brownish-red bitters

Cinzano: a famous brand of vermouth, this is a fortified wine flavored with herbs and roots. The *rosso* (red) and *bianco* (white) are sweet; the *secco* is white and dry.

Cynar: dark brown, distilled from artichokes. Also used as a digestive.

Martini: a famous brand of vermouth, a fortified wine flavored with herbs and roots. The *rosso* (red) and *bianco* (white) are sweet; the *secco* is also called dry.

Milano-Torino: a cocktail of Campari and Carpano

Negroni: a cocktail of Campari and gin

Punt e Mes: brown bitters

Riccadonna: a brand of vermouth, a fortified wine flavored with herbs and roots

Bibite

Acqua minerale: mineral water. Either *gassata* (fizzy) or *naturale* (still)

Aranciata: orange carbonated beverage

Aranciata amara: bitter orange carbonated beverage

Birra: beer, which may be *nazionale* (from Italy) or *estera* (imported). *Alla spina* means draft, or on tap.

Crodino: nonalcoholic fizzy bitters, in a cute little bottle

Spremuta: freshly squeezed juice: *di arancia* (orange), *di pompelmo* (grapefruit), or *di tarocchi* (blood oranges)

Succo di frutta: fruit juice, usually pear, peach, or apricot, bottled in single portions

Gassosa: sweetened mineral water, sometimes with a slight lemon flavor

San Pellegrino Bitter: also nonalcoholic fizzy bitters, in a cute little bottle

---

TRAVEL FOOD

Eating in the dining car of a train conjures up images of the *Orient Express,* of the Grand Tour, of a time when people traveled with trunks. Times have changed. The self-service car serves some of the most unattractive, indigestible food in all of Italy. Dining-car offerings are prepared on the train and are usually overcooked; the wine bottles have aluminum screw tops. Occasionally the Italian State Railway chooses to honor (or promote) the cooking and wines of a particular region, and the results are a bit more interesting—the level rises to mediocre. The best bet is to provide your own self-catered lunch or dinner.

The same holds true for airline food. I don't know why the food in planes is so horrible. The names they give the dishes on airline menus are entertaining enough, but the reality is as close to cuisine as Musak is to music. Especially offensive is the attempt to serve pasta, usually overcooked beyond belief. Airline meals are pre-cooked or browned and then baked—not microwaved—on board, to finish the cooking. As anyone who has ever reheated a meal knows, there is no excuse for the food baked in flight. The salad, although not particularly exciting, is the only item consistently worth eating. The added space in business class is a pleasure but the food and wines aren't much of an improvement, although I do appreciate eating on a real dish and drinking out of glass, not plastic. Eating in first class is a big improvement, but the simple things are the best. The wine selection, even in first class, and even on Alitalia, isn't very good, and I suggest that you bring your own, which is permissible on all international flights.

My favorite food to bring along on a flight to Italy is Chinese takeout. If I can't get that, I like delicatessen or anything I might miss eating in Italy. Coming from Italy I purchase *l'ultima,* the last picnic of the trip, in the best *alimentari* or *gastronomia* the day before departure. Peck in Milan, and Fior Fiore or Volpi in Rome are my favorite shops for airline picnics.

---

containers of prepared foods and salads, which can be ordered by the portion (*porzione*) or by weight (*un'etto* is 100 grams, around 4 ounces). You can buy basic picnic equipment at one of the lower-priced department stores—UPIM, Standa, Coin, Rinascente—or in a housewares store.

Choose inexpensive equipment that will last through your trip or more expensive ware that can serve as a memento when you return home—local pottery, designer flatware, brightly colored plastic picnic sets, elegant Richard Ginori china. Whatever you choose, don't forget the *cavatappi* (corkscrew)! Wine always tastes better from a glass, with or without a stem, and inex-

PICNIC SUPPLIES

cavatappi corkscrew	**cucchiaio** spoon
apribottiglia bottle opener	**bicchieri** glasses
posate flatware	**tovaglioli di carta** paper napkins
forchetta fork	**piatto** plate
coltello knife	**sale e pepe** salt and pepper

pensive *osteria* glasses (short and squat, without a stem) are almost unbreakable, and easy to tuck into a lunch basket.

A do-it-yourself meal may also be the ticket to train and plane travel. Italian train and airline food at its very best is mediocre; you'll do much better with a picnic—and this is true if you're traveling the *autostrade* as well (the food in the Autogrill restaurants along the Italian highways seems to have been inspired by airline food).

Logistics

getting around

Theoretically it is possible to reach most of the villages mentioned in this book via the Italian State Railway *(Ferrovie dello Stato)* and/or local intercity bus companies. The trip could, however, take a few days. Public transportation may work well locally (Firenze to Pisa or Siena or Lucca), but it becomes complicated when crossing regional frontiers. Those willing to tackle the railway should purchase the paperback schedule for all of northern Italy's trains, sold at newsstands. Watch out for seemingly insignificant symbols (which are explained in the complex key) that denote special holiday trains. Service to the hinterlands is slow, tourists are rare, and the trains stop at every station, but this can be fun if time is of no concern. Cross-referencing to the Touring Club Italiano's road atlas (see page 28) would probably be helpful.

The Italian government has clearly chosen to strengthen the highway system rather than the railroads, and although the *autostrada* isn't the most beautiful way to see the countryside, it is the fastest way of getting around most of Italy. The toll roads with the worst reputation (clogged with traffic or slowed by geography or weather) are those of the Padana Valley and the plains of the river Po, which get blanketed by a fierce fog in the winter; the Bologna–Firenze, which crosses the Apennine Mountains and is under constant construction; and the road that hugs the Ligurian coast, plowing through mountains and hovering over the city of Genova on stilts.

weather

From a gastronomic point of view, the best season for a visit to Italy is winter. The weather is cold, crisp, with snow in the mountains and in some northern cities. Seasonal dishes become richer, more complex, and respond to Italy's wonderful regional red wines.

Spring begins in March in most of northern Italy, but it is occasionally completely rained out. Baby lamb, the season's first tender green vegetables, field greens, and ripe strawberries and cherries add a fresh, light touch to the *cucina.*

Italian summers are hot, and un–air-conditioned for the most part. Most Italians take the month of August to cool off and head for the seaside or the mountains, which will be crowded and expensive. Summer herbs, tomatoes, eggplants, sweet peppers, melons, and peaches compensate for the excessive heat, and white wine seems to evaporate from the bottle.

The Italian autumn feels like summer with naturally air-conditioned nights. The *vendemmia,* the harvest of wine grapes, is the season's greatest event. Ripe figs, grapes, peaches, and the last memories of summer tomatoes and peppers grace the table in the sweetest of the Italian seasons. Olives are pressed in the late fall, producing pungent, fresh extra virgin olive oil.

The only constant for Italian winter is its unpredictability. Sometimes spring never comes and summer emerges directly after a long, wet, chilling winter. Snow can appear as far south as Roma, causing total chaos in cities unused to the complications of slippery cobblestone. Winter can also include spells of weather that seem like a close imitation of spring.

"chiuso"

Chiuso (closed), often accompanied by a vacillating upraised index finger, a "no-no"

gesture, is probably the most disappointing word in the Italian language. Due to a different cultural timetable, holidays of dubious nature, local customs, the dreaded strike, and the even more dreaded restoration, the place you felt was going to be the highlight of your trip may be shut.

All restaurants and bars have a regular *giorno di chiusura,* one or two days a week when they are closed. Fish restaurants are almost always closed on Mondays, since Sunday is the fisherman's day off and many fish markets are closed on Mondays.

Banks, stores, offices, and many restaurants close for *feste nazionali,* the national holidays on January 1, New Year's Day; April 25, commemorating the liberation of Italy in 1945; and May 1, Labor Day. They also close for *feste religiose* (religious holidays): *Pasqua* and *Pasquetta,* Easter Sunday and "little Easter" Monday; All Saints' Day on November 1; Immaculate Conception on December 8; *Natale,* Christmas; and *Santo Stefano,* December 26. The entire country closes tighter than a clam on *ferragosto,* August 15. Many Italians lengthen a one-day holiday into a minor vacation by combining it with the nearest weekend.

Every village in Italy has a hometown patron saint's day, a holiday that many consider sacred, even if the banks aren't always closed.

Banks are open Monday through Friday from 8:30 A.M. to 1:30 P.M. and from 2:45 to 3:45 P.M., or from 3:00 to 4:00 P.M.

Shops are normally open Monday through Saturday, 9:30 A.M. to 1:30 P.M. and from 3:30 to 7:30 P.M., closed Monday mornings year-round and Saturday afternoons in the summer. Bakery, fruit and vegetable, and other food shops are closed on Sunday, and each town has one afternoon a week when food stores close, although in the summer they may also shut down on Saturday afternoon.

Markets are open Monday through Saturday mornings from around 8:30 A.M. until 1:30 P.M. After 1:00, when the vendors are dismantling their stands, great bargains can be found on unsold produce.

Chiuso per ferie ("closed for vacation") shuts down many restaurants for an entire month, at times in July, but more often in August—when it may be almost impossible to find a good restaurant open, except on the coast or in major summer resort areas where they close during the winter off-season.

Unless you read the Italian newspapers, watch the TV, or listen to the radio, you'll probably be unaware of an upcoming *sciopero* (strike). At times a form of national protest, or a union display of strength to help in contract bargaining, or a sign of solidarity among workers, most strikes don't last more than four or five hours, but this can be enough to foil your plans for a trip to the museum, the post office, or the bank. Transportation strikes will delay the arrival of planes, trains, and ferries. City transportation, buses, and cabs will be unavailable, and every native with a car will try to squeeze his vehicle into a town designed for the horse and carriage. It always rains, of course, during a transportation strike.

Chiuso per restauro ("closed for restoration") means that you'll arrive only to find an intricate web of netting or bamboo mats draped from a Tinkertoy scaffolding totally obscuring whatever it is you've come to see. Buy the postcard and wait for your next trip, forgiving the Italians, because their attention to restoration is the reason why so much is still there for you to see.

OPEN . . . CLOSED

The long midday break is still the rule in Italy, although it is becoming less so in the large cities. In general, business hours are as follows:

Restaurants: Open at 12:30 for lunch, at 7:30 for dinner
Fish restaurants are usually closed on Monday.
Banks: Open Monday–Friday 8:30–1:30, 2:45–3:45
Shops: Open Monday–Saturday 9:00–12:30 or 1:00, 3:30–7:30
Usually closed Monday morning; Saturday afternoon in the summer.
Food shops are closed Sunday, one afternoon a week, and Saturday afternoon in the summer.
Markets: Monday–Saturday 8:30–1:30
(Great bargains on unsold produce can be found after 1:00.)

HOLIDAYS

Banks, stores, offices, and many restaurants are closed on these national holidays:

January 1—New Year's Day
April 25—Liberation Day
Easter Sunday
Easter Monday
May 1—Labor Day

August 15—Assumption Day
November 1—All Saints' Day
December 8—Immaculate Conception
December 25—Christmas
December 26—Saint Stephen's Day

Special Foods and Beverages

Italy presents the serious eater with a wealth of unusual foods and beverages that can be very different from products of the same name at home. Many of these specialties are easy to find, once you know what you're looking for, and are well worth seeking out. (See the Glossary for a more complete listing.)

arriving home

Many of my friends—and I—have, over the years, devised ingenious schemes to lead U.S. Customs astray. So it was with great surprise that I learned, from the United States Department of Agriculture, that most Italian foods can be brought into the U.S. if you declare them. You can even bring back some fruits and vegetables. They'll be inspected and returned to you if found pest-free. Truffles and mushrooms can be brought in if they're completely free of soil. Dried foods like beans, rice, grains and flours, and all baked goods are okay. Cheese must be fully cured; fresh cheese like mozzarella, *toma*, and ricotta are not allowed. Roast coffee (not green), either whole or ground, is fine, as are all canned or jarred products.

The big surprise is that seeds are on the list of approved products; the only exceptions are corn, cotton, cucumber, lentil, melon, pearl millet, potato, pumpkin, rice, squash, and wheat seeds. No meat products, either fresh or cured, can be brought into the United States.

One word of caution: The Beagle Brigade, an eager squad of canine sniffers, is on guard at international airports, just waiting for a whiff of forbidden *prosciutto* or truffle dirt. Watch out!

wine

Italy was called Enotria, or "land of the vine," by the ancient Greeks, and over four million acres of vineyards dominate the Italian landscape today. The grape varieties and winemaking styles vary with the geography, climate, and customs of the individual areas. Many fine wines are easiest to find in their native regions, and are best tasted with the local *cucina*. But they don't remain in the provinces forever, as wine stewards, restaurant owners, and importers attend tastings and scour the countryside for lesser-known quality wines.

Italian wine consciousness ranges from the "red or white?" mentality to cork-sniffing wine stewards swirling long-stemmed crystal goblets the size of a football. The only point of agreement is that wine is the best complement to Italian food. Traditionally, most Italians order red wines in the winter with its hearty cold-weather dishes, and white wines with the lighter foods of summer. Residents of some areas that produce mostly red wine tend to drink it all year round, and white-wine–producing areas may be equally loyal. The house wine, called *vino della casa* or *vino sfuso*, is sold in quarter-, half-, and one-liter carafes, and may not be a bad choice in countryside restaurants that produce their own wine, but in a city the house wine will most likely turn out to be mediocre at best. In simple restaurants one wine will ably accompany a meal, but in more wine-oriented establishments, two or more wines may be served, and a tasting menu may feature a different glass of wine with each course. Fine wines are one of Italy's great bargains, and discovering and drinking them in Italy is just part of the experience, since many can be found in the U.S., inspiring gastronomic memories of meals past.

Bottled Italian wines can be divided into two main groupings. Wines labeled with the letters DOC, which stand for *Denominazione di Origine Controllata,* or DOCG, *Denominazione di Origine Controllata e Garantita,* are controlled (and guaranteed with the "G") by laws determining geographic origin, grape variety, character or taste, yield, and aging requirements. These laws have, in most cases, contributed to an improvement in the general quality of wine, but there are gaping loopholes: Permissible grape yields per acre are often too high for quality production; rigid traditionalism dominates the choice of grape varieties; and wine or concentrates from outside the DOC growing zone may be used to "correct" a wine, not exactly a "controlled" origin.

The law also gives individualist Italians something to rebel against, a chance to make a unique statement about what a wine should be. The wines in this second grouping are sold as unclassified table wine, *vino da tavola,* and may range from banal to divine. Winemakers striving for excellence may want to grow nontraditional grapes, and thus be excluded from the DOC classifications. Their *Vino da Tavola* represents a personal commitment not dictated by law. But much table wine is inferior and to be avoided.

The regional wine lists in this book represent a limited selection, an orientation toward drinking-quality Italian wines. For a complete listing of all regional wines and vintage information, see Burton Anderson's *Pocket Guide to Italian Wines.*

WINE TERMS

abboccato   slightly sweet

amabile   semi-sweet

annata   vintage year

asciutto   dry

barrique   225-liter oak barrel, used for aging

bianco   white

brut   dry sparkling wine

dolce   sweet

enoteca   wine store

frizzante   effervescent, slightly bubbly

metodo classico or metodo champenois   the classic Champagne method of making bottle-fermented sparkling wines

passito   wine, usually sweet, made from semi-dried grapes

produttore   producer

riserva   reserve, a special selection DOC or DOCG wine with longer aging requirements

rosato   rose

rosso   red

secco   dry

spumante   sparkling

vendemmia   harvest, vintage year

mineral water

Over 180 companies in Italy bottle *acqua minerale* as it gushes forth from more than 250 springs. Subject to frequent bacteriological analyses to ensure purity, mineral water must be bottled as is, as it comes from its source, as *acqua minerale naturale* (natural mineral water) or with the addition of CO_2, as *acqua minerale gassata* or *frizzante* (sparkling mineral water). Fizzy *gassata* is preferred by most Italians and is considered a better thirst quencher. The phrase *addizionata di gas acido carbonico* will appear somewhere in the jumble of information printed on the label—including analysis results, bottling date, and a list of minerals that looks like a big chunk of the periodic table, followed by decimals with as many zeroes as an Italian banknote.

Mineral water is classified by the quantity of minerals measured in milligrams per liter after evaporating the water at 180°C. The water with the lowest mineral content, from 0 to 50 milligrams (mg) per liter, is called *minimamente mineralizzata*, minimally mineralized. Low mineral content, from 50–500 mg per liter, is defined *oligominerale*. *Minerale* contains 500–1,500 mg, and anything above that is considered *ricca in sali minerale*, rich in mineral salts, probably tasting like a salt lick. For the exact mineral-salt content, check out the *residuo secco* on the bottle label. *Acqua minerale* must, by law, have therapeutic or sanitary properties, which are also stated on the bottle's busy label: aids digestion; beneficial for kidney stones, liver function, gout, and corelated unhealthy conditions; is a diuretic; or recommended in the diet of suckling babies. An instant spa in your glass!

Fine mineral water, like wine, is sold in glass bottles, not plastic, which alters the taste slightly, according to mineral water mavens. The most popular brands of low-mineral waters are Fiuggi (99 mg per liter), Levissima (66 mg), Lora Recoaro (158 mg), Apejo (85 mg), Panna (125 mg). Minimally mineralized waters include San Bernardo (43 mg), and my favorite, Surgiva (38 mg), clean, light, refreshing. I'm not wild about San Pellegrino, with a fixed residue of 1,120 mg. Widely distributed Ferrarelle, known for being neither fizzy nor still, is rich in mineral salt, 1,596 mg per liter. Local brands of water can also be tasty. Your waiter will ask if you'd like your water *gassata* or *naturale* when he brings your menu or when you order.

Most Italians drink *acqua minerale* because it tastes good and is supposed to be good for you, but there is nothing wrong with the tap water, *acqua del rubinetto*, except that it may have a slightly chemical flavor. Tap water in Roma is excellent. The sign *Acqua Non Potabile*, usually seen on fountains, means the water isn't fit for drinking, although if you see Italians filling up plastic containers it means that the water hasn't undergone chemical analysis, but is considered okay to drink by the locals.

the aperitif

The *aperitivo* is an appetite-stimulating beverage, sipped during a ritual loiter preceding meals. Italy has many unusual aperitif liquors that are laced with essences of herbs and bark and are supposed to prepare your digestive tract for the upcoming assault of a meal. An aperitif can be consumed in a bar, restaurant, or even self-catered in your hotel room, although it's at its best in an outdoor *caffè*. Few restaurants have a full bar or make cocktails, although they may serve a glass of *spumante* or a mixture of fruit juice and *spumante* as an *aperitivo*. Bars will probably have an *aperitivo della casa*, a house cocktail, usually made with white wine, bitters of some kind, and a mystery ingredient, and they

BREAD

pane bianco white bread

pane nero or **pane integrale** whole-wheat bread

pane francese French bread

pane con le olive bread flavored with olive paste

pane ai cinque cereali five-grain bread (rice, rye, oat, wheat, and barley flours)

pane di mais cornmeal bread, sometimes made with walnuts

pane di noci walnut bread

carta da musica "sheets of music": unleavened, wafer-thin, large flat disk of traditional Sardinian cracker bread

ciabatta "slipper": low flatbread

panini rolls

rosette "little roses": hollow, all-crust rolls

grissini breadsticks

pane casereccio or **pane casalingo** home-style coarse-textured bread

focaccia, schiacciata, or **pizza bianca** freshly baked pizza crust, plain or with sliced potatoes, onions, or eggplant, depending on the season and the bakery, brushed with olive oil and sold by weight, per slice

---

may also offer white wine by the glass, in addition to the usual aperitifs (see the list on page 7). Nonalcoholic carbonated bitters (*analcolico*) are also served. Most Italians don't drink cocktails before a meal, and they tend to savor Scotch whisky, aged rum, or *grappa* after a meal, not before.

bread

It's hard to realize, when faced with the numerous regional breads available in Italy today, that before World War II white bread was eaten only by the wealthy and the sick. Most rural Italians lit their wood-burning ovens once a week to make bread with flour that was frequently mixed with inexpensive grains, producing a darker, coarser, less palatable loaf. In the city, bread bakeries and ovens catered to both classes, selling white bread and rolls, and darker, more economical *pane nero.* (City dwellers would bring a Sunday chicken or roast, or a dish of *lasagna,* to their neighborhood

forno [bread oven] to be cooked in the still-hot ovens after the baking was done, since most homes had no oven.)

White bread was a sign of wealth, something to be aspired to, and with the postwar economic prosperity, Italy was swept up in a wave of tasteless, anemic, industrially produced breadsticks and crackers. Even tan, soft-crusted, presliced packaged white bread appeared. But some traditional breadmakers, working with flour, water, starter, and salt, and clad year-round in shorts, rubber sandals, undershirt, and a heavy dusting of flour, kept baking. And in the past ten years a new interest in bread and grains has created a marketplace for shops selling all kinds of bread, traditional and innovative, local and from other regions. But the basic *pane* that graces most tables is white, with a crust that can range from crisp and flaky, to a heavy country crunch, to a disappointing stale, soggy has-been. *Pane nero* or *pane integrale* (whole-wheat bread) is common. The *ciabatta*, a crusty flat "slipper" of a loaf, has become popular throughout Italy. Each region sticks staunchly to its traditional breads, from the saltless Tuscan *filone* to the golden-crusted *biove* of Piemonte to the phallic *banane* of Lombardia. And every region seems to love the hollow, crispy *rosette*, popular throughout the country.

"Three lackeys in green, gold and powder entered, each holding a great silver dish containing a towering mound of macaroni. . . . The appearance of those monumental dishes of macaroni was worthy of the quivers of admiration they evoked. The burnished gold of the crusts, the fragrance of sugar and cinnamon they exuded, were but preludes to the delights released from the interior when the knife broke the crust; first came a mist laden with aromas, then chicken livers, hard-boiled eggs, sliced ham, chicken, and truffles in masses of piping-hot, glistening macaroni, to which the meat juice gave an exquisite hue of suede."
—Giuseppe di Lampedusa, *The Leopard*

pasta

It's hard to imagine a world without pasta—freshly rolled, leathery, egg-yolk orange, or dry, toothsome, wheaty, hugging its sauce. Who invented it? Pasta, like the wheel, was a product of necessity, an inexpensive solution to hunger using readily available ingredients: water and wheat. Many historical references to pasta exist: fourth-century Etruscan frescoes and implements; the Roman cookbook of Apicio, *De re coquinaria,* with a chapter devoted to pasta; Abu Abdallàh Muhammad ibn Muhammad ibn Idris's travel guide, written in 1154, with its mention of food made from flour in the form of strings, in the Palermo area of Sicily; and

the inventory of Ugolino Scarpa, a meticulous Genovese accountant, dated February 2, 1279, which includes a "case filled with macaroni," bequeathed by Ponzio Bastone to his heirs. All this before Marco Polo came back from China! But no matter where it came from, it is in Italy that pasta has become an art form, a local gastronomic expression that magically changes form with the variables of climate, creativity, and myriad seasonal sauces. The result may be down-to-earth food to feed the hungry or subtly spiced creations to tantalize the jaded palate.

Pasta can be made with flour of wheat, wheat bran, whole wheat, buckwheat, cornmeal, emmer, or chestnut. It may contain whole eggs, egg yolks (duck eggs are reputed to be best), or water. There are three basic categories of pasta: dry, which is industrially produced by extrusion through bronze or Teflon dies and dried; fresh, which is hand- or machine-rolled; and stuffed, which ideally is handmade and filled. The names, shapes, flours, and fillings may change from village to village. In general, the smaller and lighter the pasta, the lighter the sauce should be. Stuffed pasta should be sauced as simply as possible or served in broth, so the subtle flavors of the filling can be tasted.

Long strands of pasta, whole and uncut, are twirled around the tines of a fork (without the assistance of a soup spoon). If you're not up to fork-twirling, ask for the easier-to-manage *pasta corta* (short lengths of pasta): *penne* ("quills"), *fusilli* ("spirals"), or *rigatoni* ("big stripes").

risotto

Italians use many varieties of rice, in four main size categories. *Originario* is the shortest grain, followed by *semifino, fino,* and *superfino,* the largest (longer than ¼ inch). Vialone Nano, Arborio, Carnaroli,

THE MARKET

The local outdoor markets, a cornucopia of seasonal plenty available six days a week from early morning to 1:30 P.M., provide the fresh raw ingredients that are the backbone of all quality Italian cooking. A ten-minute stroll through a market provides a timeless experience—a panorama of fruit and vegetables, the hustle of commerce, an unguarded view of the Italians engrossed in their daily shopping ritual, and an idea of what's in season. *Primizia,* the produce anticipating the season, tiny and expensive, is preciously displayed, out-of-town vegetables and fruit are neatly packed in wooden crates, and freshly picked local bounty is piled up in mounds. The selection may range from hand-picked mountain blueberries to South American exotics cradled in Styrofoam. The color and flavor of the market change with the seasons—wild mushrooms with moist dirt clinging to their stems, asparagus tied together with a supple twig, baskets of field greens, vegetables with tops and roots that have just recently been in touch with the earth. In other market sections the poultry has feathers and claws, the wild boar's head leaves no doubt about the identity of nearby slabs of maroon-colored, black-bristle–covered meat. Whole fish are lined up on crushed ice on slanting marble counters. Nothing is prepackaged or processed. This is primal shopping, guided by the senses.

Although they may appear similar (eight lettuce specialists?), each stall has its faithful customers, and vendors are quick with greetings, recipes, advice, and a piece of fruit for a toddler. Some stands sell a wide range of produce; others focus on one strictly local seasonal item—a mountain of fragrant strawberries piled on fern fronds, or potatoes dusty with earth, or shiny red and yellow peppers, or long-stemmed green and purple artichokes.

The larger markets usually have butchers, fishmongers, bread, cheese, and cold-cut vendors, as well as housewares stands that sell a wide range of reasonably priced items—cheese graters, pasta strainers, plastic containers and bowls, espresso makers, and every possible replacement part for the various sizes of the classic *caffettiera,* the Model T of Italian coffeepots.

Smaller towns have a weekly market day, when a major piazza is crowded with wide umbrellas shading stands of inexpensive shoes, clothing, army surplus, wicker furniture, plants, linens, and sewing supplies in addition to the food.

Medium-size cities have a central market, permanently or semi-permanently installed, usually selling vegetables, fruit, and flowers and surrounded by complementary grocery stores, bakeries, and fish and butcher shops.

The big cities usually depend on small neighborhood markets, tucked into small piazzas or at various intersections, disappearing without a trace in the afternoon.

The market experience is a vital Italian tradition, a physical involvement with fresh food and people intent on purchasing the seasonal best. It's an important key to understanding the *cucina regionale.*

and Baldo are all perfect for *risotto*—with enough starch to enrich and thicken the cooking liquid and enough hardness to remain firm.

Risotto can be one of the world's finest dishes. The rice is barely toasted in butter over low heat, and then broth is added, a bit at a time during a slow cooking process, until almost all liquid is absorbed. Grated Parmesan and butter are mixed in before serving. Seasonal vegetables, fish, seafood, meat, herbs, or spices may be added to flavor the *risotto* during cooking. Frequent stirring with a wooden fork is necessary throughout the cooking process, to prevent sticking and to keep the grains of rice separate. Although some chefs parboil the rice and finish cooking it when it's ordered, the very best *risotto* is prepared to order. Many restaurants insist on cooking at least two portions (they say one portion doesn't come out well, but I suspect that the logistics of dozens of single-portion pots of *risotto* demanding constant stirring may be the determining factor), but they may make an exception if they're not too busy. *Risotto* shouldn't be a mass of rice stuck together in a blob. Cooked to perfection with first-rate rice, it should be creamy, not quite liquid and not quite solid—individual short, rounded grains cooked *al dente* and generously coated with a translucent sauce. The mixture should slowly slip across a tilted plate or soup dish. This consistency is known as *all'onda*, wavy.

extra virgin olive oil

Extra virgin olive oil is the first-pressing, lowest-acidity, and best of the oils. (Any oil with the word "virgin" is obtained without chemical solvents.) Like all olive oils, it is cholesterol-free. At its best it is produced from hand-picked olives that are quickly transported to the olive mill, where they are washed, picked over, and crushed with millstones. The resulting pulp is smeared on woven straw disks, which are piled up on a spindle like a stack of records, and then pressed. The liquid that runs off is separated, by centrifuge or by removing the floating oil, and the vegetable water discarded. The resulting olive oil is always green, although some producers filter theirs to create a more transparent product. Extra virgin olive oil is at its most flavorful in the early winter, when it is freshly pressed—dense and murky green, with a peppery bite. Olive oil doesn't go bad if stored in a cool dark place (a producer I know stores all his in grottoes; mine seems to do okay in a closet), but the flavor will slowly deteriorate, and the oil should be consumed within eighteen months. Umbrian, Ligurian, and most of all, Tuscan extra virgin olive oils are popular in Italy, but lesser-known oils from other regions, notably Le Marche, Veneto, Romagna, and Lombardia, can frequently be of high quality. The best extra virgin olive oil will have the words *prodotto e imbottigliato*, meaning it is produced and bottled by the same company, printed on the label; or *selezionato*, meaning it was chosen and milled under the guidance of an olive oil expert. Otherwise the olives may have been grown in areas outside the production zone.

the truffle

According to folklore, truffles are the result of lightning striking a tree or the ground. In actuality, truffles are a fungus that grows four to eight inches below ground in parasitical symbiosis with the roots of oak, poplar, chestnut, hazelnut, willow, and walnut trees. Supposedly, the harder the wood of the tree, the better and the more intense the perfume and flavor of the truffles.

There are two types of truffles. Black truffles, *Tuber melanosporum*, are found from December through May throughout Italy.

They are usually served cooked. *Tuber magnatum*, white truffles, are found from late September through January in northern and central Italy. The best white truffles are from Piemonte and are eaten raw, sliced paper-thin. (Most Piemontese feel that black truffles are little more than garnish, not at all in the same league as the white variety.)

Aphrodisiacs? Scientists claim the distinctive truffle perfume resembles the smell of pigs in rut. Porcine exploitation may be the perverse truffle-hunting technique favored by the French, but the Italians, rather than trying to control sex-crazed pigs, use dogs to hunt their truffles. Selectively bred and fed an occasional taste of truffle, these hounds are worth quite a bit, since truffles can be sold for 3,000,000 lire per kilo and a skilled hunter can dig up to two kilos in an evening. It is said that the best *trifulaû*, or truffle hunter, can detect the presence of truffles by beating the ground with a special stick, feeling the vibrations and listening to the sound of the thud. The best truffle locations are a closely guarded secret, handed down in the family, known only to *trifulaû*, dog, and stick.

A perfect truffle should be compact and comparatively smooth. Excess convolutions hold dirt and increase the weight. Tiny holes in the surface indicate the presence of worms. Smaller truffles are supposed to be more intensely flavored than the big ones. The fresher the better.

fruit

During one of his first trips to Italy, my brother ordered an orange for dessert. He deftly peeled the fruit, only to find a bloody red, pulpy mass of stuff, looking nothing like any orange he'd ever seen, which he proceeded to cut up, toy with, and finally abandon. He'd been given a *tarocco*, a blood orange.

Some varieties of fruit that you'll find in Italy's markets will be new to you, a special treat, but even the familiar fruits will bear a nose-prickling perfume unlike many in this country. Most fruit in Italy has never seen the inside of a refrigerator and is often sold with its leaves attached, a proof of freshness. In the Italian fruit calendar, spring comes in with *fragoline*, tiny wild strawberries that taste like delicate, perfumed flowers; the loquat (*nespola*), a small tart orange fruit that looks like a bruised apricot; and cherries (*ciliege*), pale and sour or deep purple-black. Summer brings in golden, lightly fuzzed, blushing *albicocche*, apricots; *susine* and *prugne*, purple and red plums; and best of all, the tiny greenish-blue *claudia* plum. Peaches (*pesche*) surely never tasted sweeter or juicier than on a hot summer day. Ripe, musky, orange-colored *melone* (named cantaloupe after the papal estate of Cantalupo, the first grower of this luscious fruit in Europe) is paired with *prosciutto*, a strange but successful combination. Fresh figs (*fichi*), green- or purple-skinned, filled with seed and sweet, fragrant pulp, are served with *prosciutto* or *salame*. Late summer sees the ripening of grapes (*uva*), either green (*bianca*) or purple (*nera*), served in a bowl of water. Prickly pears (*fichi d'India*) come from the south—thorn-covered, with a sweet, musky flavor. Fall, with its cooler weather, is the time of the pomegranate (*melagrana*), the deep orange, tart, mushy persimmon (*cachi*), and the fruit of the Mediterranean strawberry tree, *Arbutus andrachne, corbezzolo*. And a sure sign that winter has arrived is the smoky scent of chestnuts (*castagne*) roasting in the street-vendors' braziers.

vegetables

Vegetarians and vegetable lovers, rejoice! Italians eat many vegetables that you've probably never seen, even if they do tend to overcook them a bit. Most are highly seasonal, usually perishable, and at times regional (Tuscan black cabbage is unknown by the nearby Ligurians, who have kept their wonderful white and purple asparagus a secret from everyone). Spring is the greatest of the Italian vegetable seasons. Artichokes (*carciofi*) can be conical, with purple thorn-tipped leaves, or green-leafed cones on long stems, stacked in sheaves, both served either raw or cooked. *Agretti*, called "barilla" in English, looks like an antlered relative of the chive family and has a pleasant sour taste with no hint of onion. Wild field greens with tongue-twisting names, too young and tender to be bitter, are dressed with extra virgin olive oil. Asparagus can be spaghetti slim and dark green, or the size of cigars, either white fading to a purplish tip or the more common green, and can be eaten with your fingers. Baby zucchini end in a bright yellow flower, a sure sign of freshness, and cases of zucchini flowers are destined for deep-fryers that will turn them into crunchy bites. Summer is the reign of the tomato (*pomodoro*, literally "golden apple," because tomatoes from the New World were yellow). Tomatoes are often served green in salads, a good treatment when they are tart and crisp. But the ripe red plum tomato, the *san marzano*, tastes of summer sun and achieves glory as the perfect sauce for pasta. Glossy dark purple or lilac and white eggplant (*melanzane*) and ripe yellow or red bell peppers (*peperoni*) are important summer flavors. Wild mushrooms have a brief but intense season in the fall, and sometimes in the spring when the weather is right. Imperial agaric mushrooms (*ovoli*) are eaten raw in salads; *porcini* are eaten raw or cooked; morels (*spugnoli*) and chanterelles (*galletti* or *finferle*) are eaten cooked and are at their best with fresh pasta. Italy's most important winter vegetables are beans and grains, the protein of the poor. Lentils (*lenticchie*), bar-

ley (*orzo*), ground cornmeal (*polenta*), rice (*riso*), beans (*fagioli*), and emmer (*farro*), an ancient Roman grain with a wheaty taste, are winter favorites. Three main varieties of red radicchio appear on the winter table, both raw and cooked; *treviso*, with its elongated white-ribbed red leaves, often cooked with about three inches of its root; *castelfranco*, with pale green and red marbleized leaves; and *verona*, a small purple lettucelike head. Anise-flavored fennel (*finocchio*) is eaten raw or cooked.

wild greens

Italians eat plenty of wild greens. They change names from region to region, but are found in salads and cooked in *frittate*. Italians stalk greens in the countryside, mostly in the spring and fall. Field greens are sometimes found in markets, and are almost always expensive, paying for someone else's labor.

herbs and spices

Pungent green herbs are a note that echoes throughout regional Italian cooking. They are sold fresh at vegetable markets and produce stores, in any quantity desired, from a few leaves to a massive bunch. Fruit-tree leaves may also be used like herbs in the preparation of preserves or fruit desserts. Bay leaves (*alloro* or *lauro*) are usually not sold at the market, but the plant is used as a hedge all over Italy. I pick my bay leaves in Firenze's Boboli Gardens. Basil (*basilico*), the perfect companion to the tomato, is delicate when green and tender, and the small-leafed Ligurian type is strong enough to stand up to garlic and aged *pecorino* cheese in the classic *pesto*. The Ligurians, great herb lovers, also liven up many dishes with marjoram (*maggiorana*), and stuff pasta, or flavor its dough, with borage (*boragine*). Trendy tarragon (*dragoncello*) is traditional only in the Siena area. Fennel (*finocchio selvatico*) grows wild throughout much of Italy; its green leafy fronds, which resemble dill, are used in the spring, and its seeds, sometimes still attached to the pistils of the flower, gently spice winter dishes. Gnarled, bushy evergreens spiked with deep green needles and tipped with lilac flowers in the spring, rosemary (*rosmarino*, or *ramerino* in Toscana) is a major Italian flavor. Sage (*salvia*), with large gray-green, slightly fuzzy leaves, is another important herb available all year round. But the most popular of herbs is parsley (*prezzemolo*). The bright green, flat, three-sectioned leaves are minced, and impart a distinct flavor to the dishes where they appear, unlike their wimpy curly relative, which is unknown in Italy.

Spices have been a symbol of wealth ever since Italian navigators expanded the world's horizons and returned with pungent seeds and barks—expensive exotic imports used in minute quantities to perfume or disguise the flavor of food. But pepper is the only spice commonly used throughout all of Italy. Each region's attitude toward spices is different, based on availability and cultural influences. Wealthy Emilia; Austria-influenced Lombardia; and Veneto, whose capital, Venice, was home of the Rialto market, a stock exchange for the republic's spice trade—all take their spices more seriously than do the more herbally oriented Toscana, Umbria, Le Marche, and Liguria. Spices are also known as *droghe* (drugs) and are often sold in *drogherie* (drugstores).

meat and game

The Mediterranean diet, a regime forced by poverty on much of Italy, calls for lots of pasta, grains, and fresh vegetables, and limited amounts of animal fats, dairy products, and meat. Italians don't eat large portions of meat. After an *antipasto* of thinly sliced *salumi* or a portion of pasta has taken the edge off your hunger, you probably won't want to eat a big chunk of meat either. Traditionally, beef or veal rarely found its way to the average Italian's daily table, and even courtyard animals (chickens, rabbits) were considered food for festivities. Fresh pork was eaten when the yearly pig was slaughtered, but most of it was destined to be preserved as sausage (*salsicce*), *salame*, and *prosciutto*. Spring is the season for lamb (*agnello*), a tiny newborn animal with chops the size of a quarter. Game is known as *cacciagione* and is hunted in the cooler winter months, after the fall harvest. Some markets sell a variety of small feathered birds that can include lark, woodcock, partridge, and thrush. Plumed pheasant, wild rabbit with its fur still on, and hairy, black-bristled wild boar are also found in the fall game season. Courtyard animals, known as *animali da cortile*, are available all year round and include chicken (*pollo*), squab or pigeon (*piccione*), quail (*quaglia*), and guinea hen (*faraona*). Chicken may be sold with its head, feet, and feathers, and filled with unborn eggs in the spring. Eggs (*uova*) are graded by freshness; best of all are the *uova da bere*, eggs fresh enough to be sucked raw from the shell. Rabbit (*coniglio*), if you can overlook cultural prejudices, is quite a tasty bite. A butcher displaying a large poster of a horse isn't an equestrian fan, but sells horsemeat (*cavallo*), darker and a bit sweeter than beef and said to give strength to the ill. Tripe (*trippa*), looking like a faded beige latex bathing cap, is an Italian favorite.

fish and seafood

Most Italian seafood, if it is local and fresh, will probably be unfamiliar to you. Italians eat a wide variety of fresh- and saltwater fish from the surrounding seas (only five

FISH AND SEAFOOD

acciuga, alice anchovy	**palombo** "smooth hound," a member of the shark family
anguilla eel	
baccalà salt cod	**polpo, polipo** octopus
bianchetti, gianchetti larval anchovies	**rombo** turbot
branzino sea bass	**san pietro** John Dory
calamari, calamaretti squid, squidlet	**sarago** sea bream
cappone gurnard	**sardine, sarde** sardines
cernia grouper	**seppie, seppioline** cuttlefish
dentice sea bream	**sogliola** sole, the finest flatfish
merluzzo hake	**spigola** sea bass
moscardini curled octopus	**stoccafisso** air-dried cod
orata gilt-head bream	**tonno** tuna
parago sea bream	**totani** flying squid
pesce persico perch	**triglia** red mullet
pescespada swordfish	**trota** trout
pescatrice, rana pescatrice monkfish	

CRUSTACEA AND MOLLUSKS

aragosta spiny lobster (this term is often misused)	**gamberi** shrimp
	gamberoni big shrimp
astice lobster (this term is often misused)	**granchio** crab
	mazzancolle shrimp
capesante scallops	**ostriche** oyster
canocchia mantis shrimp	**riccio di mare** sea urchin
cannolicchio razor-shell clam	**scampi** Dublin Bay prawns
cozze mussels	**tartufo** warty venus clam
dattero di mare sea date	**vongola verace** carpet-shell clam
gamberetti little shrimp	

regions of the country have no coast) and inland lakes and rivers. Stiff, yellowed, cardboardish, seemingly inedible salt cod (*baccalà*), sold dry or, on Fridays, reconstituted, is imported from Nordic countries. But most other seafood is Italian, from tiny larval anchovies, known as *bianchetti* or *gianchetti* or *schiuma di mare* and not much bigger than worms, to imposing swordfish (*pescespada*), complete with sword. Most of the quality fish and seafood caught in Italian waters are directed to the major market in Milano, although fresh fish can be found throughout Italy, especially by the sea. Eel (*anguilla*) is sold live and squirming, and has a nervous system that just won't quit. Newborn elvers (*cee* or *cie*) are found only in the spring. Squid

PIZZA

marinara classic, minimalist: with tomatoes, garlic, and oregano

Napoletana with tomatoes, garlic, and anchovy fillets

Margherita classic: tomatoes, mozzarella, and basil. My son likes a *margherita* livened up with *aglio e peperoncino*—garlic and an unpredictable amount of chile pepper.

Capricciosa "capricious" pizza, depends on the caprice of the *pizzaiolo* but usually includes artichoke hearts, mushrooms, olives, ham, and hot dog slices.

Quattro stagioni the "four seasons," divided into quadrants of artichoke hearts, mushrooms, olives, and ham

Prosciutto with ham

Funghi with mushrooms

Cipolla with onion

Salsiccia with sausage

Con frutti di mare with seafood

Calzone classic folded half-moon pizza with filling inside and tomato sauce on top

Calzone al prosciutto calzone stuffed with mozzarella and ham

---

(*calamaro*) is sold, black with its ink, in Styrofoam cases. Flying squid (*totano*) is twice the size of the *calamaro*. Octopus, with its mottled gray skin and lots of suction cups, is called *polipo* or *polpo*. The *moscardino* is a smaller curled version of the octopus. Cuttlefish (*seppie*) are often sold black with their ink, and contain an internal bone, the cuttlebone, known to pet bird owners. The fish that Alan Davidson's *Mediterranean Seafood* calls "smooth hound" is the Italian's *palombo*, a tasty medium-size sharky-looking fish. Clams come in a variety of sizes and colors, from the tiny purple and grayish-yellow wedge shells, called either *arsella* or *tellina*, to the tube-shaped razor-shell *cannolicchio*, or the warty venus (*tartufo di mare*), a ridged clam with a tightly pleated shell. The best clams to grace a strand of pasta are the *vongola verace*, the "true" carpet-shell clam, grayish yellow and medium size, and the brownish date-shell clam (*dattero di mare*), looking very datelike. Scallops, called *capesante*, are often cooked in their shells. As usual, Italians on each coast feel that their own fish and seafood are the best—the sandy, shallow Adriatico, whose fish is said to be more delicate; the deeper, rockier Tirreno and Ligure seas, with their tastier, more flavorful fish.

pizza and flatbreads

Simple rustic flattened breads of flour and water, baked in the ashes or on the stone floor of the hearth, must be almost as old as man. Pizza, or *focaccia*, is the original takeout food, an inexpensive edible plate awaiting the artistry that embroiders the wheat-and-water crust with local tastes of *prosciutto*, herbs, greens, tomatoes, or cheese. The *torta al testo, focaccia, schiacciata*, and *piadina* are all traditional flatbreads from different regions. Pizza achieves glory in Napoli (is it the water? or the sea air? or the humidity?), a gastronomic siren whose fresh, straightforward song will never be as sweet when heard elsewhere.

The best pizza is made to order. It should be deftly stretched or rolled out into a perfect circle, sauced, and slipped on a long-handled paddle into a wood-burning brick oven, its dome-shaped ceiling redistributing the dry heat produced by burning embers, its porous brick walls absorbing the moisture given off by the cooking pizza. The T-shirted *pizzaiolo* performing these acts is an exhibitionist, his marble work station a stage in front of the brick oven backdrop. He may feign indifference to your interest in his crisp, precise movements, but his performance improves with admiring spectators.

Most popular of all *pizze* is the *margherita*, made with tomatoes, mozzarella, and basil—the red, white, and green of the Italian flag—named after Queen Margherita, who had this unusual street food brought to her during a visit to Naples in 1889. The *napoletana* is a purist's pizza of tomatoes, garlic, and oregano. The *marinara* adds garlic and anchovy fillets to the classic uncooked tomato base. The *capricciosa*, or "capricious," pizza's contents depend on the caprice of the chef, but will probably include artichoke hearts, mushrooms, olives, ham, and hot dog slices. The "four seasons" of the *quattro stagioni* are usually quadrants of artichoke hearts, mushrooms, olives, and ham. The *calzone* is a folded half-moon pizza with filling inside and tomato sauce baked on top. Most *pizzerie* have a house pizza, named after either the restaurant or an explosive device, which will usually contain everything the *pizzaiolo* can fit on the crust, including a fried egg or sliced hot dogs *(wurstel)*, and will be the most expensive item on the menu. Some creative chefs are experimenting with a wide range of ingredients, and you may find Gorgonzola cheese, eggplant, red radicchio lettuce, artichokes, ripe bell peppers, zucchini, or even fruit toppings offered.

Brightly colored precooked vegetable-and-cheese–topped rectangles in the windows of snack bars in tourist areas or around train stations may resemble, or even be identified as, pizza. Don't believe it. This is food for the unwary, or for those with superior digestive systems.

gelato

Anyone who has ever dug a short plastic spoon into a squat paper cup of Italian *gelato* knows that ice cream and *gelato* are not the same thing. Ice cream—iced rich cream—turns most flavors into pastels. *Gelato*, a combination of whole milk, eggs, sugar, and natural flavoring—or fresh fruit and sugar in the fruit flavors—is a less firmly frozen, softer, more intensely flavored and colored creation, essential to the Italian summer. Arabs brought what came to be known as *sorbetto* to Sicily; but *gelato* is said to have been first created by Bernardo Buontalenti for the court of Francesco de' Medici in 1565. In a recent region-wide competition, Tuscan *gelato* artisans came up with a delicately perfumed, egg-yolk–rich, almost orange-colored velvety flavor called *Buontalenti*, homage to a Renaissance artist.

Although *gelato* is available all year, the sunny spring and summer months are the season when it becomes a driving force in the Italian culture, an excuse for an expedition into the cooler night air, a chance to hang out, something to meet over, a preface or postscript to the evening's activities, Italian air-conditioning. Many *gelato* shops *(gelaterie)* stay open until 1 A.M. or even later in the summer.

The best *gelaterie* will display a sign, *Produzione Propria, Nostra Produzione,* or *Produzione Artigianale*—all indicating that their *gelato* is homemade. The best fruit *gelato* is made from crushed fresh ripe seasonal fruit. Although freezing should diminish flavors, somehow *gelato* winds up tasting more intense than the fruit from which it has been made. The best milk-based *gelato* is flavored with all-natural

GELATO

albicocca apricot	**mirtillo** blueberry
amarena sour cherry	**more** blackberry
ananas pineapple	**nespola** medlar, loquat
arancia orange	**nocciola** hazelnut
bacio chocolate with hazelnut pieces	**noce** walnut
banana banana	**panna** whipped cream
caffè coffee	**pera** pear
castagna chestnut	**pesca** peach
ciliegia cherry	**pescanoce** nectarine
cioccolato chocolate	**pistacchio** pistachio
cocco coconut	**pompelmo** grapefruit
cocomero or **anguria** watermelon	**ribes** black or red currant
crema egg-yolk custard	**riso** rice pudding
datteri dates	**stracciatella** chocolate chip
diaspora or **caco** persimmon	**stracciatella di menta** or **after eight**
fico fig	mint chocolate chip
fragola strawberry	**tarocchio** blood orange
fragoline wild strawberries	**tartufo** chocolate chip truffle (usually
frutti di bosco wild berries	a lumpy-looking hunk of
gianduia milk-chocolate hazelnut	bittersweet-chocolate–studded dark
cream	chocolate *gelato* with a candied-
lampone raspberry	cherry center)
limone lemon	**tiramisù** triflelike
macedonia fruit salad	**torroncino** nougat
malaga raisin	**uva** grape
mandarino tangerine	**vaniglia** vanilla
mela apple	**viscole** or **marasche** black sour
melone cantaloupe	cherries
menta mint	**zuppa inglese** trifle

ingredients and has a silky consistency. They will all melt faster than ice cream does. Colors should seem natural, not too intense. If the pistachio is bright green, it's been artificially colored and probably artificially flavored. Fruit flavors should reflect seasonal fruits. *Gelato* sitting in plastic bins is industrially produced; homemade *gelato* is always stored in stainless-steel bins, which can be sterilized and reused.

Semifreddo, literally "half cold," is made from the same base as *gelato* but has whipped cream folded in. It vaguely resembles a mousse, which is what the chocolate flavor is called.

Sorbetto (fruit sorbet) has become popular in many Italian restaurants and is often served halfway through the meal to separate the fish and meat courses and act as a palate cleanser, but instead it anesthetizes the mouth in time for the arrival of the red wine. I feel that the *sorbetto* belongs at the end of the meal, not in the middle.

Granite, slushy grainy water ices, usually come in lemon or coffee flavors, are normally found in bars, and are more common in southern Italy.

Gelato is purchased with the same receipt system as *caffè* in a bar. If you want a paper cup (*coppa*), check out the sizes, usually displayed prominently with prices printed on the sides. If you want a cone (*cono*), there will probably be a choice of sizes as well. March up to the cashier and ask for either a *coppa* or a *cono,* state the price (size) that you want, and pay. Take your receipt to the counter after having worked out your selections (more than four per serving is considered poor form) and restate your order with your choice of flavors. If you have ordered chocolate, you may be asked if you'd like some *panna,* unsweetened whipped cream.

coffee

A perfect cup of thick rich espresso or a foamy brown and white *cappuccino* may be worth the trip to Italy. The flavors are intense, harmonious, and stimulating. Italians drink *caffè,* espresso coffee, all day long in its various forms. *Cappuccino* is consumed at breakfast or instead of a meal, and it's considered poor form—a social gaffe akin to finishing a fine meal with a milkshake—to order *cappuccino* after a meal. Go native and ask for a *caffè macchiato,* espresso coffee "stained" with a little milk. Coffee will always be at its best in a busy bar because the coffee beans are freshly ground as needed, in a machine that shrieks like a buzz saw, invariably whenever you try to use the public phone. The con-

stantly maintained steam pressure of a frequently used coffee machine is a crucial factor in the production of rich brown *caffè.* Sugar is served in individual packages, from a collective self-service sugar bowl with long-handled spoons, or from a shaker that, with luck, spits out a portion of sugar at a time. Italians seem to be capable of dissolving large quantities of sugar in a tiny demitasse cup.

Caffè, the basic unit of the bar, is made in a machine that forces steam through freshly roasted and ground coffee beans, and served in a small demitasse cup. Properly made from quality coffee beans, *caffè* will be topped with a burnished golden foam, known as *crema.* There are numerous varieties of the *caffè,* which can be served stronger (*ristretto,* made with less water), weaker (*lungo,* made with more water), "corrected" with a shot of brandy or liquor (*corretto*), or "stained" with a bit of steamed milk (*macchiato*). *Cappuccino,* called *cappuccio* in some parts of Italy, is made of espresso and foamy steamed milk, and is the color of the Capuchin monks' robes. The stronger, darker *marocchino* is made with less milk; the lighter *caffè latte,* made with more milk, is served in a bigger cup. Decaffeinated coffee is usually called *Hag,* the brand name of Italy's most popular decaf. All variations of *caffè* can be made with *Hag.*

Italian coffee can easily be brought home from your trip. Master coffee roaster Andrea Trinci recommends having the coffee ground, since most home grinders don't get an even grind, and vacuum-sealed in small 250-gram packages, if possible. Once opened, keep coffee in an airtight container.

After discovering the glories of an Italian *caffè,* you may want to buy an espresso maker. The *macchinetta da caffè,* simple, inexpensive, and easy to use, is available at all housewares stores, along with spare parts for every possible eventuality. (The most famous model, a classic, is the Bialetti Moka, but lots of less expensive copies are available.) From a pure modern design standpoint, Alessi's coffee makers by Aldo Rossi and Richard Sapper, and Girmi's linear electric *caffè concerto* (make sure you get the 110-volt USA model), are probably the most attractive choices. I love the Euromatic electric model. See page 258 (Illy in Trieste) for more information. And for those who can't be without a *caffè*, the individual-size demitasse-cup–shaped coffee thermos may be just what you're looking for, and can be found at most well-equipped housewares stores.

digestive liquors

Digestivi (digestive liquors, also known as *amari*) are mostly alcohol infusions or distillates made from herbs, barks, and roots. They are consumed at the end of a meal, after coffee is served, to aid and stimulate digestion, a process of great interest to Italians. Many unwritten laws that govern eating habits (regulating food and beverage temperature, use of spices, cooking methods, and after-meal activities) are dictated by an obsession with the functions of the liver, the body's filter, an organ not to be taken lightly. Americans are thought to be concerned only with the stomach, a rather simplistic approach to digestion. Fernet Branca, made from a blend of herbs, roots, and alcohol, is the most famous *digestivo*— and the bitterest, a punishment for overworked taste buds, an acquired taste and said to be slightly habit-forming. Fernet is available in regular and mint flavors, the latter an unsuccessful attempt at palatability. Another popular after-dinner drink is Sambuca, an anise-flavored liqueur, served *con le mosche* (with coffee bean "flies" floating in the glass). Homemade infusions of

herbs, spices, or fruit in alcohol are occasionally found in country restaurants. Spirits—such as Cognac, *grappa,* or whiskey (served without ice)—are considered a more sophisticated conclusion to a meal.

grappa

Grappa is distilled from pomace, the grape skins and pits left over after the winemaking process. It has long been a traditional drink and source of warmth in Italy's colder northern regions. Aggressive, alcoholic, and raw, like whiskey in the cowboy movies, *grappa* was tossed down in shots, a peasant painkiller for the physical and spiritual aches of poverty, a breakfast rinse for the coffee cup. Children were given a shot of *grappa* before heading out in the cold for school.

Giannola Nonino's distillery in Friuli has been making *grappa* for almost a century, but fifteen years ago she started producing *grappa monovitigno,* each distilled in modern custom-made copper stills from a single grape variety, using fresh pomace from fine wineries. The bottles are wonderful to look at. A simple chemistry-lab look, with a silver-topped stopper and a label hanging from a colored string, doesn't interrupt the clean lines of the clear *grappa* in its glass globe. This *grappa* is perfumed, 50 percent alcohol, intense, and the price is elevated. Nonino also makes *ùe,* a distilled grape must that is more delicate than *grappa,* made from seven varieties of grapes. The *ùe* made from *picolit,* a Friulano dessert wine grape, is sold in a hand-blown bottle made by Venini of Murano. The latest Nonino product is *le frute,* distilled from local mountain strawberries, raspberries, blackberries, pears, and apricots.

Other makers, following the lead of Giannola Nonino, have vastly improved the quality of their *grappa*. Elegant packaging has contributed to the new image for this former rustic "schnapps," which is now considered a sophisticated choice to conclude a fine meal.

Romano Levi is a poetic Hobbitlike spirit who assures me that he completes Piemonte's life cycle and will therefore live forever. He gets his grape pomace from Angelo Gaja and other outstanding wine producers and then distills it over direct fire in his Rube Goldberg-like copper maze, pressing the distilled grape skins into bricks, drying them to use as fuel to feed the fire of the still. The ashes are then given back to the wine producer from whence the seeds and skins came, to fertilize the vineyard soil. The labels of Levi's potent *grappa*—up to 60 percent alcohol—are handwritten in black and red ink on torn paper, and the names are graceful poetry: "Dear Maria, I have to talk to you," "A dream I have dreamed," and "Grappa of the wild women who scale the hills."

Completing the Picture

The food experience in Italy does not stop at the table, but extends to the kitchens, back roads, festivals, newsstands, bookstores, and housewares shops.

reading material

I love to read, to learn something about the region I'm in, and I always have a *Blue Guide* with me when I travel; it lists monuments and museums and also usually includes the address of the E.P.T., the local tourist office, which provides travelers with free maps, information about local events, and a list with prices of all hotels in the province. (Someone there will speak English.) I also always travel with Burton Anderson's *Pocket Guide to Italian Wines*, a slim, informative book, indispensable for anyone who wants to know more about Italian wines. The Touring Club Italiano's *Atlante d'Italia*—a soft-covered map book, easy to read, extremely detailed, and equipped with an index—are essential for anyone traveling by car with the intention of abandoning the main highway, and can be purchased in most bookstores in Italy. For big-city shopping I refer to *Made in Italy* by Annie Brody and Patricia Schultz, an introduction to the shopping experience in Roma, Firenze, Milano, and Venezia. And for a feel of the provinces I love to read Italo Calvino's *Folk Tales*, fables from all regions of Italy. It provides a link to the rich regional folk tradition—a wealth of kings, queens, knights, trolls, trapdoors, dragons, thieves, witches, and spells embroidered on the everyday fabric of life in the provinces.

cooking schools

Learning to cook at one of Italy's many schools can be an interesting experience, as varied as the regional *cucina*, with classes taught by a housewife in her home kitchen, by a titled hostess teaching from the kitchen of a country estate, or by the elegant hotels of Venezia. Most courses are created for the American home cook who has some culinary skills and would like to participate in a gastronomic vacation. A selection of schools is listed here by region.

Piemonte

The Scavi family are from the Gavi area of Piemonte—their daughter Pia lives in London but comes back a few times a year, organizing culinary workshops at her family's country home as well as programs in other regions. Taste truffles and prepare regional Piemontese cooking at a restored monastery. Participants of other programs are based at hospitality farms (see Agritourism, page 33). Pia's courses are inexpensive by American standards, but don't expect private bathrooms, phones, or hotel service. Contact Tasting Italy, 97 Bravington Road, London, England W9 3AA, tel. 0181.964-5839, fax 0181.960-3919.

Emilia-Romagna

Margherita and Valeria Simili are gifted teachers. They specialize in baking (bread, puff pastry, cookies, and more), and have guest chefs who teach sessions on regional cooking or focused topics like *gnocchi*, fish, meat, appetizers, preserving, or Christmas specialties. Prices are low and participants arrange accommodations in Bologna. Contact Margherita and Valeria Simili, via S. Felice 166, Scala G, Bologna, tel./fax 051.523-771, for information and dates.

Toscana

The Capezzana Wine and Culinary Center focuses on the food and wines of the Carmignano area, west of Firenze. The estate has been making wine and oil since A.D. 804, according to a document dating to the time of Charlemagne. The estate is owned and run by Count Ugo Contini Bonacossi and his family. His wife, Countess Lisa, is one of the best home cooks in the region. The estate's kitchens and facilities are used in the spring and fall for their

Culinary Center, a six-day program that visits the area's best restaurants and food artisans, and includes cooking demos, hands-on cooking sessions, do-it-yourself pizza in a wood-burning oven, and a day devoted to tasting Tuscan wine and extra virgin olive oil. For information and dates contact Tenuta di Capezzana, via Capezzana 100, Carmignano 50042, tel. 055.870-6005, fax 055.870-6673, or Marlene Levinson, 55 Raycliff Terrace, San Francisco, CA 94115, tel. 415.928-7711, fax 415.928-7789.

Peggy Markel fell in love with Italy and decided to create a program at the Fattoria degli Usignoli, a farm in the countryside outside Firenze. Her program, La Cucina al Focolare ("Hearth Cooking"), combines excursions to Firenze and the Regello area and cooking lessons with a professional chef. For information and dates contact Peggy Markel, La Cucina al Focolare, P.O. Box 646, Boulder, CO 80306-0646, tel. 800.988-2851, fax 303.440-8598.

Judy Witts has been teaching Tuscan cooking since 1988. Her school is in the center of Firenze, convenient for a lesson or two during a stay in the city. Judy is *simpatica* and a gifted teacher, works with small groups and private students, and gives lessons most of the year. Contact Judy Witts, via Taddea 31, Firenze 50123, tel./fax 055.292-578, for more information and dates.

Also see page 326 (Montefiridolfi) and page 349 (Villa a Sesta).

Giuliano Bugialli's Cooking in Florence

P.O. Box 1650
Canal Street Station
New York, NY 10013–1650
☎212.966-5325
Fax 212.226-0601

Culinary star Giuliano Bugialli hosts a one-week total immersion in Florentine gastronomy, with demonstrations, lessons, historical lectures, slides, market visits, and dinners in his favorite restaurants. Giuliano has kitchens in the city of Florence, but now teaches mostly in his self-restored farmhouse in the Chianti Barberino area. Many of the recipes covered in class are complicated and contain hard-to-find ingredients, but they are generally faithful to the local tastes and traditions. No food processors allowed! Giuliano's most dramatic moment is the pasta demonstration, where he cranks yards of fresh egg pasta from his machine, flipping festoons in the air, a feat that would leave a less dexterous demonstrator wrapped up like a mummy. The wines served are not up to the rest of the experience.

The Villa Table

Badia a Coltibuono
Gaiole in Chianti
☎0577.749-498
Fax 6577.749-235

Ms. Judy Ebrey

7077 Willow Vine Court, Apt. 219
Dallas, TX 75230
☎214.373-1161
Fax 214.373-1162

Badia a Coltibuono, an eleventh-century abbey, villa, and winery, is the setting for "The Villa Table," where up to twelve houseguests share Lorenza de' Medici's heritage and style for a week of cooking lessons. Lorenza, who has published many cookbooks in Italy and has given demonstrations in Europe and America, is a gifted teacher, and her uncomplicated fresh Italian cooking, based on produce from the Coltibuono estate, is tasty and practical. Participants cook with Lorenza in the morning, tour the Tuscan countryside in the afternoon, dine in the evening in important private villas and castles, and taste the Coltibuono wines, extra virgin olive oil, vinegar, and honey. Guests experience the Tuscan lifestyle, lolling in the frescoed fifteenth-century drawing room, reading from the extensive library, strolling through the Renaissance gardens or the estate's woods, enjoying the swimming pool or sauna.

Umbria

Le Tre Vaselle

Via Garibaldi 48
Torgiano
☎075.988-0447
Fax 075.988-0214

Le Tre Vaselle, a five-star Relais & Chateaux hotel, offers cooking classes taught by the chef of their restaurant, one of the best in Umbria. A bilingual guide will translate as well as escort participants through the Umbrian countryside to unknown hill towns, a chocolate factory, or special restaurants. A visit to the Wine Museum, the best of its kind in Italy, and a wine tasting of Lungarotti wines highlight the sessions, custom-tailored to the schedule of the group. Contact the hotel for information.

Friuli

Gianna Modotti

Via Palmanova 133 Udine
☎0432.602-766

Gianna Modotti, who teaches at the Cipriani school in Venezia, also gives lessons from her kitchen in Udine, featuring the cooking of her native Friuli, one of Italy's most interesting and unknown regional *cucine*. Gianna and her stylish daughter-in-law Anna teach practical, everyday traditional cooking and entertaining. A true sense of hospitality and warmth makes these lessons a treat. Gianna teaches in Italian, but services of a translator are available. Courses can be specially scheduled with advance notice.

Veneto

Natale Rusconi, the managing director of the Hotel Cipriani in Venezia, is a culinary expert and has always hosted cooking programs at the hotels he has been connected with. Marcella and Victor Hazan have taught at the Cipriani for years, a far less intense version of their program at home, set in luxurious accommodations. Julia Child spends a week at the Cipriani, taking participants to dine at Venetian noble palaces. I work with the Cipriani culinary program and teach a session for them each year in the spring. These programs are a relatively inexpensive way to stay at one of the world's most luxurious hotels, since most meals are included. For information contact Hotel Cipriani, isola della Giudecca 10, Venezia, tel. 041.5207744, fax 041.520-3930.

Hotel Gritti Palace
Campo Santa Maria del Giglio 2467
Venezia
☎041.520-0942
Fax 041.794-611
or Contact

CIGA Hotels
745 Fifth Ave.
Suite 120
New York, NY 10151
☎800.221-2340
The Hotel Gritti Palace has been holding cooking courses every summer since 1974. Many of Italy's best cooks and restaurant owners, like the chef of the Peck restaurant of Milano and Gianfranco Bolognesi of the highly rated restaurant La Frasca in

Romagna, have taught at the Gritti. All participants lunch on dishes prepared during the lesson, accompanied by two wines chosen by the Gritti's wine steward. An American translator is on hand to explain and interpret. Each course consists of five lessons, and you can choose to take some or all of them, to suit your schedule. Hotel package rates are a bargain.

Fulvia Sesani
Castello 6140
Venezia
☎/Fax 041.522-8923
Fulvia Sesani, a kind of Venetian Martha Stewart, teaches food for entertaining out of her patrician palace. The oval dining room, the table settings of heirlooms, the comfortable terrace overlooking a canal, are impressive. Fulvia's high-tech home kitchen is equipped with everything, a collection that she's amassed in her world travels.

housewares
If you enjoy cooking or eating Italian, you're probably interested in the special tools used to prepare or serve regional food. Most are sold in tempting shops known as *casalinghi*, "domestic goods" emporiums: combination houseware-hardware stores with stocks of soap, wax, paint, mothballs, plastics, cooking utensils, storage containers, glassware, picnic equipment, and more—a vast array of wares for the house displayed in an almost overwhelming wall of floor-to-ceiling open shelves in an invariably tiny shop with barely enough room to turn around in. They always seem to have everything, sometimes even a choice of different models of a wide selection of household items, some unique to Italy. Housewares sections in department stores seem to have a less extensive selection but better prices at times, with self-service displays that simplify shopping, and they accept credit cards. In the neighborhood

shops you'll have to ask for or point to what you want, and pay in cash. Most outdoor markets have at least one housewares stand, with a limited but interesting selection of necessities, reasonably priced.

The section devoted to coffee and its accessories in a *casalinghi* or department store will be large. The classic coffee maker, *la macchinetta,* is a three-part traditional home espresso pot, and comes in sizes from 1 to 22 espresso cups. All parts are replaceable, from the *filtro* (filter), *manico* (handle), *contenitore per il caffè* (the part that holds the coffee), to the *guarnizione* (rubber gasket that holds the filter in place). An unusual accessory sold for the *macchinetta* is called *il rompigetto;* a shower-cap–like device, it fits inside the top section, where the coffee bubbles out, to prevent spattering. The Neapolitan-style coffee maker, *la napoletana,* makes drip espresso coffee (water is boiled in the bottom section, the pot is turned over, and the water filters through the coffee) and is the choice of some purists. It is sold in sizes from 1 to 20 espresso cups, although the larger sizes are hard to find.

Parmigiano fans may be on the lookout for the special knife, *coltello per parmigiano,* with its short teardrop-shaped blade—not for cutting or slicing but for breaking off a chunk of the cheese. The *gratella* or *griglia* is a rectangular cast-iron pan with a ridged surface for stovetop grilling of vegetables, meat, poultry, and fish; a personal favorite, this is a tool I wouldn't like to be without. The most practical cheese grater, *grattugia,* will have a section to collect the grated cheese. The rolling pin (*mattarello*) with zero, one, or two handles, depending on use and local custom, has no moving parts. The long-handled pins are for pasta making, the short ones for shaping pizza dough. Some cooks wonder how they ever lived without the *mezzaluna,* a crescent-shaped double-

handled rocking knife, used by practically every Italian housewife. Chestnuts can be roasted over a stovetop burner in the *padella per castagne* (chestnut-roasting pan), which looks like a long-handled frying pan with holes in the bottom. The *piastra di terracotta refrattaria* (terra-cotta pizza stone) stimulates an Italian brick pizza oven in your own home oven. Most shops have a large selection of sifters (*setaccio*), with circular bentwood frames, metal mesh screens, and no moving parts. The screen comes in different gauges, including a silk screen for sifting ultrafine flour. Probably my favorite Italian utensil is the *tostapane,* a cordless Italian toaster. It consists of a hole-punctured stainless-steel square topped with a wire grid screen, and a U-shaped metal handle (no moving parts). It's used for toasting bread of any thickness over a gas flame, an essential tool in the preparation of *fettunta,* Tuscan garlic bread, always on the menu in my kitchen.

slow food

Fast food has invaded the entire world, Italy included. But Italians are putting up a fight, defending their culinary and cultural traditions through an organization known as Slow Food, or *Arcigola* ("Big Gluttony"). Their logo is a snail, national headquarters are in Piemonte, but there are chapters throughout Italy. Arcigola and its local chapters sponsor events, tastings, seminars, and publish books and magazines about food and wine. I'm crazy about their guide *Osteria d'Italia,* probably the first Italian guide to focus on reasonably priced traditional regional cooking. Contact Carmen Wallace at Arcigola Slow Food, via della Mendicità Istruita 14, Bra CN 12042, tel. 0172.411-273, fax 0172.421-293, for information about how to join, to learn of upcoming events, or to purchase their fine publications.

"GOOD MEMORY PLATES"

Collectors of gastronomic memorabilia may be interested in the *Unione Ristoranti del Buon Ricordo*. Sponsored by the Touring Club Italiano, an automobile club serving the motorist, this association was created in 1964 to stimulate an interest in traditional foods. Each member restaurant features a regional specialty, and clients ordering this dish are given a hand-painted ceramic *Piatto del Buon Ricordo* (literally "Good Memory Plate") as a souvenir of the meal. The name and locality of each restaurant is printed around the circumference of the plate, and a drawing representing the specialty or relating to the restaurant decorates the center. Over 200 different plates have been issued. Some members have dropped out, closed, or changed specialty, and collecting and trading the memento plates from the past or from the ninety-eight current members has become a pastime, like gastronomic stamp collecting. The hardest to find, from the Taverna della Giarrettiera in Milano, in production for only one year, may sell for more than $1,000. The *Collezionisti di Piatti del Buon Ricordo*, a club in Torino with a membership of over 5,000 collectors, can track down hard-to-find memento plates, and plate vendors and traders can often be found outside food and wine shows, swapping away. Some of the *Ristoranti del Buon Ricordo* are among my favorites, most serve above-average food, but some are inexcusably inferior and deserve to be kicked off their plates.

winery visits

Most wineries in Italy enjoy visitors but don't have regular schedules and can be seen by appointment only. Donatella Cinelli Colombini heads an association, *Movimento per il Turismo di Vino,* to encourage wine tourism. Regional chapters of the *Movimento* sponsor events periodically and publish guidebooks with culturally interesting itineraries and names of wineries that welcome visitors. In May the *Movimento* organizes *Cantine Aperte* ("Open Cellars")—over 500 wineries throughout the country are open to the public. Contact Donatella Cinelli Colombini, c/o Fattoria dei Barbi, tel. 0577.849-421, fax 0577.849-356, for information or names of regional organizations.

agritourism (agriturismo)

Working farms offer rural hospitality that ranges from no-frills to fully restored

apartments and a swimming pool. Credit cards aren't usually accepted, but the price is generally modest, an inexpensive alternative to hotels. Meals are sometimes available, and by law must utilize products grown or raised on the farm. There are many regional *agriturismo* associations. One called *Agriturist* publishes a yearly guide, often found in Italian bookstores, of farm hospitality throughout Italy. For more information or to order the guide, contact Agriturist, Corso Vittorio Emanuele 101, Roma, tel. 06.685-2397, fax 06.686-1726.

farmhouse and villa rentals

Renting a home in Italy can be a wonderful experience. The following agencies handle rentals. Contact them for catalogs and more information.

THE PROVINCIAL FEAST

Adventurers curious about local cooking should attend a feast, called a *sagra*. For every regional, seasonal specialty in Italy, there is probably a feast somewhere to honor it: Winter festivals feature wild boar, sausage, truffles, and chestnuts and chestnut desserts; in spring homage is given to the strawberry, cherry, asparagus, and artichoke; summer festivals honor melons, peaches, hazelnuts; and in the fall freshly made olive oil, mushrooms, garlic bread, and the grape harvest are celebrated. Some feasts aren't tied to any specific season, but exist to heap praise on fried fish, snails, frogs, chickens, pasta, *polenta*, or whatever strikes the fancy of local residents. To recognize a feast in the making, look for signs posted on provincial roads, or festoons over the roadway, with the name of the town, the designated honoree, and the dates, usually two or three days that include a weekend. There will probably be music on Saturday night. It's considered bad luck not to stop for a *sagra del vino*, a wine festival. Food may range from inexcusable to sublime, with local volunteers dishing out plastic plates of overcooked flavorless greasy pasta; pink and green crescents of sun-ripened watermelon; crunchy fried whitebait, which look like guppies, served in a paper cone that absorbs the excess oil; or a three-course dinner with wine, all costing next to nothing. To connect with this bounty you may need to use the *scontrino* system, paying a cashier for a slip of paper which is then presented to the people dispensing the meal. You may pay a blanket fee to get into an area where each family unit fends for itself, its members standing on various lines and reserving places at the long communal tables. Observe the locals and act accordingly.

Salogi
Via Fatinelli 11
Lucca 55100
☎0583.48717
Fax 0583.48727

Solemar
Via Cavour 80
Firenze 50100
☎055.239-361
Fax 055.287-157

Cuendet
Il Cerreto
Strove, Monteriggioni
☎0577.301-100
Fax 0577.301-149

chinese restaurants
It's sad but true. Many of Italy's small, inexpensive *trattorie* have been taken over by Chinese restaurants. And the even worse news is that they haven't discovered fresh vegetables and are preparing almost everything from a can or frozen. This is Chinese cooking at its very worst, seemingly from the province of Canton, Ohio. Proceed at your own risk.

THE REGIONS

The northwest corner of Italy, Piemonte (from *pie*, "foot," and *monte*, "mountains") is separated from France by the Alps and from Liguria by the Apennines, which slope into hills as they stretch east to the alluvial plains of the Po Valley.

Piemonte

Ruled by the Roman Empire and then the medieval Longobards and Franks, split into dukedoms, earldoms, and marquisates, bound to the royal House of Savoy in 1045, Piemonte expanded and contracted with the political power plays and trades of European nobility. French was the language, and France the primary influence.

Hot summers, cold winters, and lots of fog make up the climate necessary for this unique *cucina*. For the Piemontese, dining seems more a procession than a meal. The traditional appetizers of marinated meats, vegetables, and mushrooms change with the seasons and may seem like a meal in themselves. *Bagna cauda,* available only in winter, is a variety of raw vegetables dipped in a "hot bath" of oil, anchovies, and garlic in a ceramic fondue-type arrangement. *Fritto misto* here consists of deep-fried meats, poultry, vegetables, fruit, and fritters.
The first course might be *agnolotti* (pasta stuffed with meat, egg, and cheese), or shoelace-size, irregularly cut *tajarin* pasta, simply sauced; or *risotto* made with rice from the lowlands, flavored with seasonal vegetables.

Meats are stewed in rich red wines. Accompanying these full-flavored dishes are some of Italy's finest red wines, hearty and spirited to drink young, or complex, intense, and elegant with aging.

Traditional sweets feature a rich-tasting hazelnut in simple cookies, *torrone* (a honey-and-egg-white candy), and cake often accompanied by *zabaione.*

White truffles from other regions are a treat, but they will never touch the glory of those born under a cold moon in Piemonte. They are sold almost furtively in the markets at dawn—whole and in pieces, from marble- to baseball-size. Piemontese truffles are intensely scented, intoxicating, allegedly aphrodisiac, and addictive, I'm sure—why else would one sniff of their unmistakable odor set me to scheming for a trip to Piemonte?

The Menu

Salumi

Salame al barolo *or* **salsicce al barolo:** pork and veal, marinated in rich red Barolo wine, spiced, and cured

Salamin d'la duja: soft mild salami, preserved in lard in a terra-cotta pot *(duja)*

Antipasto

Bagna cauda *or* **calda:** raw vegetables dipped in a "hot bath" of olive oil, anchovies, and garlic. A winter-only appetizer that can also be a main course.

Capunet: small, finger-size stuffed cabbage leaves. In the summer, zucchini flowers are used instead of cabbage.

Insalata di carne cruda: a ground lean beef marinated with oil and lemon, topped with truffles in season

Insalata di pollo: chicken salad dressed in oil, lemon, and truffles

Vitello tonnato: roast veal with a tuna sauce

Antipasto piemontese: marathon of appetizers, usually including all of the above plus salami, sausage, and marinated vegetables—a meal in itself

Subrich: vegetable and egg fritters

Primo

Agnolotti *or* **agnellotti:** meat-stuffed miniature ravioli

Aia *or* **agliata:** ribbon pasta with walnut garlic sauce

Cisrà: chick-pea soup

Fonduta: Fontina-based cheese fondue, served over toast or as a sauce, topped with truffles in season

Gnocchi di patate: potato *gnocchi*

Panissa *or* **paniscia:** a *risotto* with beans

Polenta cunsa: *polenta* sautéed in butter with cheese

Ris an cagnon: soup with rice and Fontina cheese

Risotto alla piemontese: simple *risotto,* with onions, butter, and cheese

Tajarin: homemade egg noodles

Tofeja: bean and pork rind soup

Zuppa canavesana: turnip soup garnished with gratinéed bread and cheese

Secondo

Anatra farcita: duck stuffed with rice and sausage

Bollito misto: mixed boiled meats; served with *bagnet,* a green or red sauce

Brasato al barolo: beef braised in Barolo wine

Camoscio alla piemontese: chamois stew

Finanziera: a stew of leftover meat, chicken livers, and sweetbreads; favored by the high-finance wizards of the 1800s

Fritto misto *or* **fricia:** intricate progression of deep-fried foods: lamb chops, chicken, sausage, sweetbreads, brains, zucchini, eggplant, zucchini flowers, mushrooms, cubes of sweet semolina, peaches, and almond cookies

Lepre al sivè: wild hare, marinated in red wine and stewed

Puccia: stewed cabbage and pork, mixed with *polenta* and served with Parmesan. The next day, may be cut into slices and fried.

Tapulon *or* **tapulone:** mule or donkey, stewed with wine and spices

Contorno

Cipolle ripiene: baked onions, often stuffed with cheese

Funghi: mushrooms, served grilled, stewed, or as a salad

Formaggio

Bra: cow's milk cheese, either young or aged

Bross *or* **bruss:** bits of leftover cheese, mashed and marinated in *grappa*

Castelmagno: unique, pungent, rare

Formaggetta: small, soft, tasty white round, made from a mixture of cow's and ewe's milk

Gorgonzola: rich, creamy, blue-veined, pungent

Raschera: hearty, smooth

Ricotta *or* sairas: soft, mild fresh cheese made from whey, at its best when freshly made

Robiola: soft, creamy, rich, delicate; from cow's or ewe's milk

Tome, tomini: smooth, firm, fresh cheese

Dolce

Amaretti: almond cookies made from regular (sweet) almonds and a few bitter ones

Baci di dama: chocolate-covered almond cookies

Bonet: custard pudding containing chocolate, rum, and *amaretti*

Krumiri: *polenta* butter cookies

Panna cotta: rich, elegant reduced cream or gelatin-thickened dessert with burnt-sugar topping. Makes crème caramel seem like diet food.

Pere (*or* ciliege) al barolo: pears or cherries cooked in Barolo wine

Torta di nocciole: hazelnut cake

Zabaione: egg yolks whipped with sugar and Marsala until thick and golden, served with dry

cookies or as a dessert sauce; named for San Giovanni Bayon, patron saint of pastry chefs, venerated in Torino at the church of San Tommaso

The Wine List

Most Piemontese wines are made with grapes found only in this region. Arneis, Dolcetto, Freisa, Grignolino, but most of all, Nebbiolo grapes are frequently grown on small single-owner plots, and transformed into some of Italy's finest wines. Barolo and Barbaresco, ample and elegant, get most of the attention, but Barbera and Dolcetto are perfect for everyday drinking and stand up well to the gutsy, flavorful regional foods. Don't forget to end your meal with a glass of Moscato d'Asti, a delicate, barely alcoholic dessert wine that tastes like a combination of flowers and fruit.

Arneis a soft, dry white, is best with fish and seafood. Top producers are Castello di Neive, Cornarea, Bruno Giacosa, Malvirà, Vietti, Gianni Voerzio, and Ceretto, who calls his Arneis, with its distinctive cutout label, "Blangè."

Barbaresco is one of Italy's truly great wines, a dramatic, elegant dry red. Made from the Nebbiolo grape and aged for at least two years—four for a *riserva*—Barbaresco is at its best after four to eight years, served with roast meat and fowl. The following fine producers make some special single-vineyard wines (listed in parentheses): Cantina del Glicine (Marcorino), Castello di Neive (Santo Stefano), Ceretto (Bricco Asili and Asij), Gaja (Costa Russi, Sorì San Lorenzo, Sorì Tildin), Bruno Giacosa (Santo Stefano), I Paglieri (Crichet Pajè), Giuseppe Mascarello (Marcarini), Moccagatta (Bric Balin), Marchesi di Gresy (Camp Gros), Produttori di Barbaresco, Prunotto (Montestefano), Vietti (Rocche di Castiglione Falletto).

Barbera a rustic, hearty dry red, not intended for aging, is made in many areas of Piemonte. Drink this high-spirited wine with meat and fowl.

Barbera d'Alba a rich, smooth dry red, is made from Barbera grapes in the area outside Alba, and is paired with meat and fowl. The following top producers make Barbera d'Alba and special single-vineyard wines (listed in parentheses): Cantina del Glicine (Curà), Castello di Neive, Ceretto (Piana Brunate), Aldo Conterno, Giacomo Conterno, Clerico, Fratelli Cigliutti (Serraboella), Giacosa, Gaja (Vignarey), Podere Rocche dei Manzoni, Prunotto, Renato Ratti, Vietti Batasiolo, Corino, Paolo Scavino, Luciano Sandrone, Aldo Vajra, Matteo Corressia, and Giuseppe Mascarello.

Barbera d'Asti a full, dry red, is made in the area outside Asti by top producers Scarpa Rivetti, Luigi Coppo, Marchesi Alfieri, Bertelli, Cascina Castlet, Il Mongetto, and the wines of Braida, especially single-vineyard Castlèt Ai Suma, Bricco della Bigotta, and La Monella, to be drunk young.

Barolo ruby colored, complex, rich, and long-lived, is called "the king of wine and the wine of kings" by the Piemontese. Made from the Nebbiolo grape, aged at least three years and at its best after eight, Barolo is served with meat, fowl, and game. The following quality producers also make special single-vineyard wines (listed in parentheses): Ceretto (Bricco Rocche, Brunate, Prapò, and Zonchera), Clerico (Ciabot Ginestra), Aldo Conterno (Bricco Bussia), Giacomo Conterno (Monfortino), Paolo Cordero di Montezemolo (Monfalletto), Bruno Giacosa (Collina Rionda), Mascarello (Monprivato), Bartolo Mascarello, Prunotto (Cannubi), Elio Altare (Vigna Arborina), Batasiolo, Pio Cesare (Ornato), Gaja (Sperss), Sandrone (Carnubi Boschis), Aldo Vajra (Bricco delle Viole), Paolo Scavino (Caunubi), Corino (Vigna Giachini),

Gianni Voerzio (La Serra), Roberto Voerzio (Cereguio), Conterno-Fantino (Sorì Ginestra), Podere Rocche dei and Manzoni, and Vietti (Bussia).

Brachetto d'Acqui is a light, sparkling semisweet red wine made from the Brachetto grape, served with *salumi* and desserts. At its best when produced by Braida and Villa Banfi.

Cortese di Gavi also known as **Gavi,** is a rich, dry white made from the Cortese grape near the village of Gavi. It is a perfect companion to fish and seafood in all forms. Top producers are La Battistina, La Chiara, La Scolca, Tenuta San Pietro, Constellari Bergaglio, La Giustiniana, Villa Sparina, and Castello di Tassarolo.

Dolcetto made from the Dolcetto grape and, in spite of its name (which seems to imply sweetness), is a dry, fruity red. It is made in seven different DOC areas, often paired with fowl and hearty regional cooking.

Dolcetto d'Alba is a balanced, grapey, dry red. The following quality producers make Dolcetto as well as special single-vineyard wines (listed in parentheses): Castello di Neive (Basarin), Ceretto (Rossana and Vigna), Aldo Conterno (Cascina Favot), Paolo Cordero di Montezemolo (Monfalletto), Dogliotti (Campo Rosso), Gaja (Vignabajla), Bruno Giacosa (Basarin), I Paglieri, Marchesi di Gresy (Monte Aribaldo), Podere Rocche dei Manzoni, Renato Ratti (Colombè), Luciano Sandrone, Vietti (Bussia and Castelletto), Roberto Voerzio. Aldo Vajra (Coste and Fossati) Domenico Clerico, Luciano Sandrone, Conterno, Fantino, Batasiolo, Gianni Voerzio, Roberto Voerzio, Elio Altare (La Pria), Moccagatta (Vigneto-Buschet).

Dolcetto di Dogliani is a well-balanced dry red made from three different vineyards of Chionetti (Briccolero, San Luigi, and La Costa).

Dolcetto di Ovada is a dry red of quality as produced by Dott. Pino Ratto (Vigneti

Scarsi) and the wonderful wines of Abbazia di Vallechiara.

Freisa delle Langhe is a ruby-red still or slightly sparkling wine made from the local Freisa grape, and is served with poultry or hearty regional dishes. Top producers include Fratelli Cigliutti, Aldo Conterno, Caudrina, Gaja, Scarpa, and Vietti.

Gattinara is an ample dry red made mostly from Nebbiolo grapes near the village of Gattinara, and served with roast and sauced meat, fowl, and game. Quality wines are produced by Antoniolo, Travaglini, and Nervi.

Grignolino d'Asti made from the local Grignolino grape, is a delicate, pale-colored, dry red, to be drunk young and fresh, at the beginning of a meal. Quality wines are produced by Braida, Bruno Giacosa, Incisa della Rocchetta, Rivetti, Villa Fiorita, and Scarpa.

Moscato d'Asti is a delicate, slightly sparkling, floral-scented white wine, a perfect accompaniment to fruit, dessert, or cookies, especially when made by Bera, Rivetti, La Spinetta, Caudrina, Braida, I Vignaioli di Santo Stefano, Saracco, and Vietti.

Nebbiolo d'Alba is a full, dry red made from the local Nebbiolo grape, served with roasted and grilled meats, poultry, and cheese dishes. Quality producers, who also make single-vineyard wines (listed in parentheses) include: Ceretto (Lantasco), Gaja (Vignaveja), Bruno Giacosa (Valmaggiore), Malvirà, Marchesi di Gresy, Mascarello and Figlio (San Rocco), Prunotto (Ochetti), Vietti (San Michele) Correggia, and Conterno-Fantino.

Roero a DOC from the same growing area as Nebbiolo d'Alba, is an ample, dry red, at its best made by Malvirà, Prunotto, and many of the Nebbiolo d'Alba producers.

Spumante sparkling wines of high quality, some made according to *méthode champenoise*, are produced in Piemonte. Marone Pas Dosè is made by Cinzano; Banfi Brut is made by Villa Banfi; Bruno Giacosa Extra Brut is made by Bruno Giacosa; Riserva Privata Angelo Riccadonna is made by Riccadonna; Gran Cuvé Carlo Gancia and Crémant Riserva Vallarino Gancia are made by Fratelli Gancia; Contratto Brut and Riserva Novecento are made by Contratto; Riserva Montelera is made by Martini & Rossi; and Valentino Brut is made by Podere Rocche dei Manzoni.

Exemplary reds and whites classified as Vino da Tavola are made by some of Piemonte's finest winemakers. Rich red Bricco dell' Uccellone is produced by larger-than-life Giacomo Bologna. Chardonnay Gaia & Rey, an elegant white, and Darmagi, a rich, full red cabernet, are both made by Angelo Gaja, Piemonte's leading winemaker. Elio Altare's Barbera-based Vigna Larigi, and Nebbiolo-based Vigna Arborina barrel-fermented Chardonnay from Bertelli Coppo's mostly Chardonnay Monteriolo, Ceretto has planted nontraditional varietals like Chardonnay, Cabernet Merlot Viognier, and Pinot Nero at the new Bernardina estate. Opera Prima, a ripe, elegant red, is made by I Paglieri. Bricco Manzoni, a deep red, is made by Podere Rocche dei Manzoni. Villa Pattono, a rich red aged in wood, is made by Renato Ratti.

Regional Specialties

Hazelnuts. The *tonda gentile delle Langhe*—the round gentle hazelnut of the Langhe region—is unique: rich, intense, smoky, with a skin that slips off more easily after roasting than the skin of regular hazelnuts. These special local hazelnuts appear in many sweets—combined with chocolate in *giandujotti*, suspended in honey and meringue *torrone*, or ground in the heady *torta di nocciole* (hazelnut cake), a world-class dessert when prepared with the *tondo gentile*.

For sources of *torrone*, see page 73.

Chestnuts. Although both *marroni* and *castagne* are called "chestnuts" in English, they are not the same. Fans of what was once known as "poor man's bread" (an accessible form of protein in the diet of poor Piemontese farmers) can easily tell the difference. *Castagne* grow inside a green, sea-urchin–like spiked husk, which always contains an odd number of chestnuts (either three, five or seven), each with one flat surface. *Marroni* always contain three nuts in each husk, but two of them atrophy and the remaining fruit fills the entire space, resulting in a rounder, bean-shaped chestnut. *Marroni* are richer, more flavorful, and are a specialty of the Val Susa, outside Torino. They are preserved in sugar syrup and made into *marrons glacés*, a local invention in spite of its French name (most of France's *marrons glacés* come from Piemonte or Campania, in the south). Chestnuts were traditionally preserved in the cellar under sand or in the woods under a pile of chestnut husks; or they were slightly fermented in water for nine days to enrich their flavor, then stored in stone grottoes.

For the best in *marroni*, see page 51.

Truffles. The *tartufo* is a fungus that grows four to six inches below ground in parasitical symbiosis with the roots of walnut, oak, poplar, chestnut, hazelnut, and willow trees. Supposedly the harder the wood of the tree, the better and more intense the truffle's perfume. There are two distinct kinds of truffles. *Tuber melanosporum*, the black truffle, is found from December through March in much of Italy. It is usually served cooked and is almost tasteless. The black truffle owes its reputation to its kinship with the higher-priced, highly scented *Tuber magnatum*, the white truffle, which is found from late September through January in northern and central Italy. Pungent, gassy-scented, intense, and haunting, it is at its best in Piemonte, fresh out of the ground, shaved on a special truffle slicer. The white truffle reaches stratospheric gastronomic heights when combined with eggs.

The search for white truffles involves stealth and secrecy. Selectively bred hounds help their masters find up to five pounds of truffles in an evening. This bounty is sold by the gram (at over $1,000 a pound), almost furtively, wrapped in wrinkled handkerchiefs or paper towels, at dawn in the markets in Nizza Monferrato, Canelli, Asti, and Alba, a cash-only ritual with its own style and pace, conducted in dialect. Unscrupulous truffle vendors will fill in wormholes, adding grams of high-priced dirt, or will toothpick together a broken truffle. The largest truffle market takes place in Alba (see page 46); smaller markets are in other villages.

Chocolates. Piemonte is a region that takes its chocolate seriously. Locals don't let you forget that they were the chocolatiers of the royal House of Savoy, and that the Swiss came to Torino to learn the arts of blending, roasting, tempering, and forging the exotic import from the New World. Chocolates are frequently sold by the piece, and gift boxes are assembled according to the whim of the buyer. Chocolate hazelnut creams (*giandujotti*) are the specialty of Torino, but local *grappa, marroni* chestnuts, walnuts, and other natural ingredients flavor rectangles, leaves, truffles, barrels, hearts, shells, and snails of glossy dark or light brown chocolates.

Peyrano (page 68) makes sublime chocolates.

Gianduja: The Marriage of Chocolate and Hazelnut. How typical of the practical Piemontese to combine the expensive, exotic, imported cocoa bean with the smoky local hazelnut, cheap and abundant. The bitter intensity of chocolate is tempered by the nutty richness of the hazelnut, for a taste far more complex than the wimpy Swiss invention, milk chocolate. Almost all the great Torinese chocolate makers produce *giandujotti*, chocolate hazelnut creams, made with ground hazelnuts, sugar, and chocolate. With a slightly sticky texture, like peanut butter, this confection is piped (not molded) into traditional chubby wedge shapes and individually wrapped in foil.

Peyrano and Caffarel produce excellent *giandujotti*.

Many chocolatiers also make a soft chocolate hazelnut spread, *crema gianduja*, a Piemontese response to peanut butter and jelly, which is applied in a thick layer on freshly made bread—a taste trio of nuts, chocolate, and bread that isn't taken as seriously as it should be. See page 47 for the world's largest producer of chocolate hazelnut spread.

Vermouth. Vermouth has been a Piemontese tradition since the 1700s, created by a type of shop no longer in existence—a cross between the candymaker, *bar-caffè*, and pharmacy. Each store had its own special recipe, blending herbs, spices, and

wine. In the 1800s vermouth became a commercial product, no longer artisanal but made in quantity by companies using traditional formulas of herbs, spices, roots, and barks (especially absinthe, or wormwood) infused in a neutral, nonaromatic wine and sweetened with sugar. The so-called medicinal function of vermouth was to prepare the stomach for the onslaught of a meal, a digestive call-to-arms. The classic vermouth, either white or red, is consumed before lunch or dinner: *liscio* (neat), *con ghiaccio* (on the rocks), with a splash of *seltz* (soda water) and *con una scorza di limone* (a twist of lemon peel).

To visit the Cinzano cellars or the Martini & Rossi Museum, see page 63.

Grissini. Yard-long breadsticks—gold and tan, hand-rolled and slightly knobby, sprinkled with pale semolina—frequently form the centerpiece of the Piemontese table setting. These are *grissini*, slim, featherweight, and all crunch. According to a recent conference on the history and nutritional value of this illustrious form of bread, in 1668 the Savoia court doctor, Don Baldo Pecchio, had the court baker whip up some crunchy, thin, and easily digestible breadsticks for the sickly Prince Vittorio Amadeo II, who suffered from "intestinal fevers." He ate his *grissini*, "miraculously" recovered, and went on to govern as the first Savoyard king.

The packaged commercial breadsticks found in other regions of Italy are barely related to the glorious fresh *grissini* of Piemonte. At least twice the length of breadsticks found in other regions, they are served whole, tied in a bundle with a napkin, or simply placed on the tablecloth. They also appear in unlabeled waxed-paper envelopes.

See page 50 for fine *grissini*.

Piemontese Beef and Wine-Flavored Salame. It's difficult to find locally produced meat in Italy and lots of upscale restaurants serve imported Angus beef. But not in Piemonte, where a local breed, called *fasson* in dialect, is protected by law and certified as raised locally and classified as *Carni Bovine Certificate*. Meat from the Piemontese breed is lower in cholesterol than most beef and can be found in butcher shops that display the *Carni Bovine Certificate L.R. 28/88* or *CO.AL.VI.* logo. Many regional restaurants proudly list Piemontese beef on their menus.

The village of Carrù holds the *Fiera del Bue* ("Beef Fair"), the Thursday before Christmas. More than 500 examples of *fasson*, scrubbed and polished, some weighing in at over 2,500 pounds, compete for the *gualdrappo*—a white drape embroidered with gold, which goes to the butcher who purchases the animal; the cup and medallion are awarded to the breeder. The categories are harmonious structure and muscle mass, far more prestigious than the prize for size. The *muscarola d'oro,* a golden rendition of a no-frills object that kept the flies out of cows' eyes, is awarded to the breeder who wins for two years. Silvio Brarda of Cavour (see page 55) frequently buys the winning beef and there's always a *gualdrappo* or two hanging in his shop.

Lusty red Barbera wine flavors the *salame* of many butchers in Piemonte, but Silvio Brarda uses Italy's finest wines to enhance the flavors of his first-class beef. Look for Piemontese *salame* in restaurants and food shops, or make a pilgrimage to Macelleria Brarda in Cavour to taste the best of kind and check out the beef.

Cookies. Lots of towns in Piemonte claim to make the true hazelnut chocolate cookie flavored with wine, *grappa,* or rum. Bakers in La Morra make *lamorresi,* those of Alba make *albesi,* Cuneo makes *cuneesi,* Bra has *braidesini. Krumiri,* rich, buttery, moustache-shaped cookies, are a specialty of

Casale Monferrato and found throughout Italy. See page 54 for more information.

Cugnà. In the late fall when grapes have been pressed for wine, some of the must is reserved to make a chutneylike condiment called *cugnà* in dialect, or *mostarda d'uva.* Grape must is cooked in a copper kettle with quinces, figs, *martin sec* pears, pumpkin, and hazelnuts, utilized with *polenta,* boiled meat, cheese, or snow. La Contea in Neive, I Bologna in Rocchetta Tanaro, and many other restaurants serve *cugnà,* and are willing to sell a jar to diners who fall in love with its rich caramelized fruit flavors. Il Mongetto in Vignale Monferrato produces a *cugnà* that's sold throughout Italy. See page 73 for more information.

Stuffed Peperoncini. I first ate tasty small round peppers, not excessively spicy, stuffed with an anchovy-wrapped caper, and preserved under extra virgin olive oil, at the home of winemaker Giacomo Bologna. His wife, Anna, prepared dozens of jars of this specialty each year, a zesty bite to accompany the winery's lusty young Barbera, La Montella. Anna didn't have the time or desire to commercialize the peppers. So Giacomo encouraged his friends Roberto and Margherita Santopietro, who made wine and preserves at their farm, Il Mongetto in Vignale Monferrato, to produce Anna's irresistible *peperoncini,* and now I don't have to wait for a trip to Piemonte for a taste. See page 73 for more information on Roberto and Margherita's products.

Rice. The Vercelli area of Piemonte is an important rice-growing region. The low flat fields are flooded to grow Arborio, Vialone Nano, Carnaroli, and Baldo rice, all varieties that are well suited for *risotto* making.

Castelmagno. Piemonte produces lots of kinds of cheese, but the one with the cult following is Castelmagno, rare, almost impossible to find outside the region, not a cheese for the faint of heart, intensely scented with a piquant flavor, white, dry, and slightly crumbly with a rusty or amber-brown rind. It's a cheese with a long history, as attests a document from 1277 that determines the yearly rent for a few pastures, paid in Castelmagno to the Marchese of Saluzzo. Castelmagno was declared a DOC cheese in 1983, and is produced in the *comunes* of Castelmagno, Pradleves, and Monterosso Grana, although the Castelmagno area is said to produce the finest cheese. Only 14 producers make around 4,000 wheels of Castelmagno each year, from the milk from 1,000 cows that graze on grass and wild herbs in high-altitude pastures. The milk is heated, the curd is broken, drained, placed in wooden containers to rest for a few days, broken up with a meatgrinder, pressed with wooden bands, and weighed down with a stone for three days until the cheese is shaped. The 3- to 7-kilo wheel of Castelmagno is then salted and aged for two to five months in a damp but well-aired cellar (or cave) with an earthen floor. Fifty liters of milk produce 5 kilos of cheese. The best Castelmagno is made from the summer milk. See page 55 for more about this rare but exceptional cheese.

Terra-cotta Bean Pots. *Tofeja*, the elliptical terra-cotta clay bean pot, is one of the last vestiges of the Piemontese traditional crafts, still made in Castellamonte, north of Torino. The pots can be found at the exciting Porta Palazzo market in Torino. Artisanal and semi-industrial models can be found at La Mezzaluna in Torino (see page 70) and at most housewares stores in the region.

The Silversmiths of Savoy. Piemonte is a region of contrasts, from the poverty of Cesare Pavese's *The Moon and the Bonfire* to the splendor of the Savoy palace. The tradition of court artisan has almost completely disappeared, but Piemonte is still an important center for crafted silver. Moving into the twenty-first century, some companies have chosen to work with silverplate, or even stainless steel, combining technology with tradition. Design may range from Piemontese baroque to Milanese postmodern, but the emphasis is on quality.

Cities & Towns

Alba

Nestled in the valley of the Tanaro River, amid grapevine-covered hillsides parceled into single-owner plots, Alba is a charming town of medieval towers, medieval pageantry, and a sunset that stretches to the Alps.

HOTEL

Hotel Savona
via Roma 1
☎0173.440-440
Fax 0173.364-312
All credit cards • moderate

INN

Cascina Reiné
Localitá Altavilla 9
☎/Fax 0173.440-122
No credit cards • inexpensive

Too good to be true is the only way to describe Cascina Reiné, a villa in the hills overlooking the city of Alba and the Tanaro Valley, and on a clear day, with a view of the Alps. Signora Giuliana Giacosa has opened a part of her home—three rooms, each with private bath, and one two-bedroom apartment—and her guests are in for a real treat of country-style hospitality on this working farm. An ample American-style breakfast is included. Reserve in advance and Signora Giacosa will prepare a meal for you, of her own farm-fresh poultry, fruit, and vegetables, and even homemade *gelato*.

BAR-CAFFÈ

Caffè Calissano
Piazza Risorgimento 3
☎0173.442-101
Closed Wednesday

The Caffè Calissano is a place to spend time in, for people-watching and for enjoying the decor of marble, brocade, and lace. The bar dates from the turn of the century, and there is a back room with sofas, a fireplace, and frescoed ceilings. The pastry and *gelato* are first-rate, and the selection of *grappa* and wine is impressive.

TRUFFLES

Piemonte's largest truffle market, and the most accessible to the nonprofessional, non-Piemontese buyer, takes place on Saturdays in October, November, and December, along via Maestra or via V. Emanuele, under the arcade, and in Palazzo Maddalena.

BAR-GELATO

Bar Roma
Corso Coppino 3
☎0173.442-127
Closed Monday

The Bar Roma makes the best *gelato* in Alba, a city that takes this frozen confection seriously. Fruit flavors are made with strictly fresh fruit, custard flavors taste of real eggs. First-rate sandwiches are also available for those with savory palates.

PASTRY

io ... tu ... e i dolci
Piazza Savona 12
☎0173.441-704
Closed Monday

"You and I and the desserts" is the name of Beppe Scavina's *pasticceria*, and it reflects his point of view. Beppe is involved with each item that comes out of his minute kitchen, and he practically custom-makes desserts for his clients. The cakes are meant to be eaten and aren't excessively decorated, although some of Beppe's more unusual custom Easter eggs and special orders are fanciful and imaginative. *Torrone, albesi,* chocolate hazelnut truffles, and chocolate-covered *goffi* ("clumsies") are all delicious. Beppe's enthusiasm for life is expressed in his desserts and in his attire—so don't be surprised if you find him behind the counter sporting a bow tie made of mirror or marble, or a skirt, or a pair of transparent nylon pants.

HAZELNUT CREAM
Ferrero
Piazza Ferrero 1
☎0173.3131
Fax 0173.363-034

Ferrero is the world's largest producer of chocolate hazelnut cream spread; Italy accounts for half their total yearly output (55,000,000 pounds) of Nutella, probably the most popular snack for school-age children. Not all their hazelnuts are local, and Nutella also contains powdered skimmed milk, cocoa, palm oil, and emulsifiers. It's kids' stuff and doesn't have much appeal for postadolescent palates, but isn't too bad warmed up with a shot of rum and served over ice cream. To visit the factory, a hygienic high-tech production-line behemoth, fax Dott. Ravera, c.o Ferrero, Pino Torrinese 10025, for an appointment.

FOOD SHOP
Gastronomia Petiti
Via G. Alberione 3
☎0173.440-934
Closed Sunday afternoon and Monday
No credit cards

This is the kind of take-out I wish was around the corner from my home, with a selection of at least ten different components of *antipasto piemontese* and hot baked pasta dishes, stuffed vegetables, roast chicken, and meats that change daily. Purchase food for a picnic.

WINE
Il Crutin
Via Cuneo 3
☎0173.293-239
Closed Monday

Il Crutin, "the wine cellar" in Piemontese dialect, has a vast assortment of local wines, *grappa*, and distillates, and quality regional products. Wine tastings can be arranged.

RESTAURANT
Osteria dell'Arco
Vicolo dell'Arco 2/6
☎0173.363-974
Closed Sunday
All credit cards • moderate

Osteria dell'Arco has white stucco walls, archways, and is decorated with beautiful color photographs of the graceful local countryside. The menu is limited (not particularly regional) and changes daily. Pasta and desserts are homemade, portions are generous, the ambience is informal, and the wine list, of regional Piemontese and Italian offerings, is formidable for a restaurant of this size. Alberto Gallizio will make you feel welcome.

ENOTECA-OSTERIA
Caffè Umberto
Piazza Savona 4
☎ Fax 0171.441-397
Open evenings only, closed Monday
MasterCard, Visa • low moderate

Ignore the drinks, music, and young crowd and head toward the back of the room and down the stairs to the old brick and stone-walled cellars decorated with prints of the Langhe and bottles of fantastic wine, a suitable setting for the classic cuisine of the Langhe. *Salumi, vitello tonnato*, peppers in tuna sauce, homemade pasta, *gnocchi* sauced with *raschera*. Boiled, roasted, and braised meats. You'll understand why the *osteria* is called Enoclub when you read the extensive wine list that focuses on, but isn't limited to, the wines of the zone, all well priced, tempting diners to drink something really fantastic.

RESTAURANT
Il Vicoletto
Via Bertero 6
☎/Fax 0173.363-196
Closed Sunday evening, Monday
All credit cards • high moderate

Victor Hazan recommended that I try Il Vicoletto and, as usual when Victor makes a suggestion, I wasn't disappointed. Small, warm, and elegant, Il Vicoletto serves classic Piemonte cuisine with style, paying great attention to the best regional products available. Owners chef Ilvia Bonino and Bruno Boggione in the dining room have everything under control, and diners are never disappointed by homemade pasta, or Piemontese beef served raw or braised with Barolo. Cheese is local, worth saving room for, worthy of the well-chosen wine list of regional and Italian gems. Desserts, especially the apple tart served with Moscato *zabaione* sauce and anything with local hazelnuts, are fine conclusions to a meal at Il Vicoletto, a favorite of Victor Hazan's.

RESTAURANT
Vigin Mudest
Via Giacosa 4
☎0173.43921
Closed Monday and August
No credit cards • moderate

Vigin Mudest serves traditional, predictable Piemontese *cucina*. But the listing, printed in red at the bottom of the menu, for their *antipasti misti freddi* doesn't convey the excitement of fifteen different offerings of cold marinated salads, meats, vegetables, cheeses, and egg dishes. The locals always seem to be enjoying the homemade pasta, hearty meat and game dishes, and house desserts, but I have never been able to get past the *antipasto*. In season, truffles are served over fresh pasta—priced, according to a cardboard sign, by the grating, or *grattata*. The wine list offers some gems under the heading "Others" (*Altri*).

Albaretto della Torre

HOTEL
Albergo Bellavista
Via Umberto I 10
Bossolasco (close by)
☎/Fax 0173.793-272
Visa • low moderate

RESTAURANT
Da Cesare
Via Umberto 12
☎0173.520-141
Fax 0173.520-147
Closed Tuesday, Wednesday, January, and August
No credit cards • expensive to very expensive

Da Cesare is the gastronomic version of a one-man band. Although daughter Elisa and son Filippo all work in the dining room, the heart and soul of this restaurant is Cesare Giaccone. His eyes light up when he discusses his food, a moody vision of regional dishes, at times inspired, at times bizarre, created with the finest local ingredients, extravagantly presented on large leaf-covered trays, but not decorated or fussed with. Hiding behind a huge, handsome, chestnut-colored moustache, but cooking in sight of some diners through the glass kitchen door, Cesare skillfully prepares a personal, masculine *cucina*. Meats are roasted whole on a spit in the fireplace, or in a bread crust, or wrapped in foil, then surrounded by a layer of earth and baked. Woodsy mushrooms, truffles, and game appear in season, and the pasta is hand-rolled and delicate. The hand-whisked *zabaione* is a poem in body language, a thrill to watch and taste, especially with the plate-size buttery hazelnut cookie. Excited hordes of noisy German and Swiss gastronomic tourists flock to Da Cesare during truffle season, and you may be hard-pressed to hear a word of Italian. But I'd risk it for a taste of Cesare's *cucina*. The wine selection is splendid.

Asti

Asti is a pleasant city featuring medieval monuments and in September, a historic procession dating from 1275, a horse race, and a wine fair called the *Douja d'or*.

HOTEL
Palio
Via Cavour 106
☎0141.599-282
Fax 0141.530.223
All credit cards • low expensive

HOTEL
Cavour
Piazza Marconi 18
☎0141.530-222
Fax 0141.530-223
All credit cards • low moderate

AGRITOURISM
Azienda Agricola Persenta
Via Serra di Variglie, 2 km from Asti
☎0141.208-179 or 0337.362-998
No credit cards • inexpensive
Attractive, inexpensive rooms on a working farm outside Asti are charming alternative accommodations; open April through October, but guests are required to stay for at least three days.

BAR–TRUFFLE MARKET
Caffè San Carlo
Via Cavour 142
☎0141.30249
Closed Tuesday
This nondescript bar is the unofficial site of Asti's truffle market, which takes place

before dawn on Wednesdays and Saturdays during truffle season from late October through January. The scent of white truffles is overwhelming; all transactions are conducted in local dialect for cash without receipts. Photographers aren't welcome, but those who want to do so can observe the action.

RESTAURANT
Gener Neuv
Lungo Tanaro 4
☎0141.57270
Fax 0141.436-726
Closed Sunday night, Monday, and August
American Express, Diners Club,
Visa • expensive
It seems that some of the greatest expressions of traditional *cucina piemontese* are turned out by women, and Gener Neuv is a classic example. The success of this fantastic restaurant is due to the hard work of the Fassi family—Piero offering selections from a splendid wine list to go with the *cucina* of his wife, Giuseppina, and daughters Maura and Maria Luisa. Local ingredients are wisely combined, perfectly executed, and simply placed on the plate. I can't imagine a better *finanziera* (lightly stewed cockscombs, sweetbreads, and mushrooms), and the rabbit dishes are exceptional. During their glorious season, Piero skillfully slices wafers of intensely perfumed truffles with abandon. Save room for a taste of ripe regional cheeses paired with intense Piemontese red wines, and don't skip the dessert plate, decorated with a cocoa-dusted stencil of the restaurant's logo, a cavalier.

RESTAURANT
Da Dirce
Via Valleversa 53, Caniglie
☎0141.272-949
Closed Monday, Tuesday lunch
No credit cards • moderate
The hyper-typical Trattoria Da Dirce is out-

side the city of Asti, not too easy to find but definitely worth the search for the well-priced homestyle cooking. Three small dining rooms are filled with furniture that have the feel of someone's home; there's no written menu and dishes change daily. Diners will be pleased with a partially fixed meal that offers a few choices, beginning with a five-part *antipasto* that always includes *vitello tonnato*. Homemade pasta is first-rate, *tajarin* are served with a roast-meat sauce, *maltagliati* pasta and beans are drizzled with Ligurian olive oil. It's hard to choose between the roast kid and the beautifully prepared *finanziera* of chicken innards. Cheese is local and worth saving room for. Traditional desserts like *bunet, panna cotta,* and *crostata* are joined by chocolate mousse for locals bored with the same old sweets. The wine list is short but sweet, and offers some well-priced wines from small local wineries.

Barolo

HOTEL

Barolo
Via Lomondo 2
☎0173.56191
Fax 0173.56354
MasterCard, Visa • low moderate

ENOTECA

Enoteca Regionale del Barolo
Piazza Falletti
☎0173.56277
Closed Thursday, January, and the first half of February; Open 10:00 A.M.–12:30 P.M., 3–6 P.M.
The Enoteca Regionale, which shows around 120 different labels of Barolo, is housed in the old cellars and eighteenth-century upstairs rooms in the Castle of Barolo, which itself dates from the tenth century. More than eighty different Barolos are for sale. Fans should call to find out the dates of spring and fall tastings, which focus on the latest vintages.

HOTEL-RESTAURANT

Del Buon Padre
Via delle Viole 30, Vergne
☎/Fax 0173.56192
MasterCard, Visa • low moderate
The Viberti family, with three generations of experience, has perfected the quintessential home-style Piemontese dining experience. Giovanni provides for the restaurant, supplying his wife, Maria, with first-rate ingredients. She rolls out the pasta, stuffs and "pinches" the *agnolotti,* braises local beef with Barolo, artfully turning out Piemontese classics without a hint of pretension. Their son Gianluca, with an enology degree from the University of Alba, has improved the quality of the Viberti wines, which are now organic. Giovanni's brother owns the grocery-bakery next door, closed on Thursday and Sunday afternoons, a good source for first-rate *grissini, salumi,* cheese, and cookies.

BREAD

Panettiere Cravero
Piazza Castello 3
☎0173.56134
Closed Sunday afternoon and Thursday
Panetteria Cravero, across the street from the Castello di Barolo, makes splendid hand-rolled *grissini* and also sells an incredible goat's milk *robiola* cheese.

MEAT

Macelleria Canonica Pier Carlo
Via Roma 43
☎0173.56131
Closed Sunday afternoon and Monday and Thursday afternoons
Rosanna and Pier Carlo Canonica sell quality meats in their tidy butcher shop, and they make their own sausage and salami, a zesty blend of garlic, spices, pork, and veal, marinated in son Giovanni's Barolo wine. This is an example of the creative Piemontese *cucina,* combining local ingredients, mundane and sublime, to produce an

improved version of a familiar food, in this case salami and sausage.

Borgomanero

HOTEL
Albergo San Francisco
Via Maggiate 109
☎0322.845-860
Fax 0322.846-414
MasterCard, Visa • low moderate

RESTAURANT
Ristorante Pinocchio
Via Matteotti 147
☎0322.82273
Fax 0322.835-075
Closed Monday
All credit cards • expensive
Ristorante Pinocchio, once a place to go for a family outing, almost impossible for non-natives to find, seems to be suffering from delusions of nouvelle cuisine. Two different *degustazione*, each for a minimum of two diners, and selections from the somewhat fancy nonregional menu are nothing to write home about, and the wine list also has its highs and lows. But the *paniscia* (rice and vegetables) and *tapulon* (stewed minced donkey) served with *polenta* may be worth the trip. The eclectic decor of plaid wall-to-wall carpeting, wood paneling, and hanging lamps matches the menu.

Borgo San Dalmazzo

HOTEL
Oasis Hotel
Via Po 28
☎0171.262-121
Fax 0171.262-680
MasterCard, Visa • low moderate

CHESTNUTS AND CANDIED VIOLETS
Agrimontana
Borgo San Dalmazzo
☎0171.261-157
Fax 0171.261-670
Brothers Cesare and Enrico Bardini own this state-of-the-art factory, which produces the world's finest-quality *marroni* chestnuts preserved in syrup, as well as *crema di marroni*, a cream of riced chestnuts and cane sugar, and *marroni* in Cognac. They are responsible for the production of genuine candied violets (not the colored and sugared blobby-looking acacia flowers often passed off as violets). Each flower, grown outdoors, is hand-harvested. Its petals are individually coated with gum arabic, dusted with superfine sugar, soaked in sugar syrup for two days, and then dried in a warm oven. A drop of all-natural violet essence in the pale bentwood oval box delicately perfumes the candied flowers—a dainty pale mauve piece of romance.

MUSHROOMS AND TRUFFLES
Clemente Inaudi
Shop: via Garibaldi 69
☎0171.269-047
Closed Sunday afternoon, Monday morning, Thursday afternoon
MasterCard, Visa
Factory: Corso Mazzini 148
☎0171.266-189
Fax 0171.262-822
Closed Sunday
Porcini and other wild mushrooms are processed by hand at the Inaudi factory and sold in the shop in town in all preserved forms—dried, under oil, in jarred pastes. Mushroom lovers can visit the factory, which works with wild mushrooms all year long. Inaudi also processes black and white truffles and those who want to observe the

production should plan to visit in October through December. Clemente Inaudi has promised all readers of this book a tasting after the factory visit—fax to let him know you're coming.

Boves

RESTAURANT-INN
Rododendro
Frazione San Giacomo
☎0171.380-372
Fax 0171.387-822
Closed Sunday night, Monday, Tuesday lunch, Christmas, and August
American Express, MasterCard • expensive

Mary Barale has a permanent place in the pantheon of female Piemontese chefs, having transformed her country-style *trattoria* into one of Italy's most illustrious two-star restaurants. Much of the regional *cucina* has disappeared from her kitchen, and many of the basic ingredients are French, but the Piemontese in her is irrepressible, especially in her abundant use of the local white truffle. Mary's pastry work is among the finest in all of Italy. I stopped eating other croissants after I tasted her elongated twists of featherweight puff pastry. I watched Marco Valinotti, able director, carve and serve a banana to a client with such grace and style that I wound up liking this restaurant in spite of its Frenchness. The wine list concentrates on fine Piemontese and French wines. The breakfast is reason enough for an overnight stay in one of the Rododendro's few rooms.

BREAD, SWEETS
Forno Bruno Baudino
Piazza Garibaldi 8
☎0171.380-208
Closed Sunday afternoon and Monday
If the Rododendro experience and its superior breakfasts aren't enough to lure you to

end-of-the-road Boves, probably the eighty-six different breads including fig, hazelnut, leek, chestnut, rye, Carlo Alberto (with walnuts, anchovies, and pepper—served to the soldiers when King Carlo Alberto came to review the troops), and the hand-rolled *grissini*, all baked in a wood-burning oven, will be of no interest to you either. But who can resist Bruno and Piera Baudino's homemade chocolates—pralines and liquid centers—and jellied candies made with over forty varieties of fresh fruits?

Bra

Bra is the hometown of Arcigola, which can be translated as "Superlative Gluttony" or "Extra-Large Throat." It's a gastronomical recreational club with over 15,000 card-carrying members, with political ties to the Italian Communist Party.

HOTEL
Nuovo Hotel Giardini
Piazza XX Settembre 28
☎0172.412-866
Fax 0172.432-661
All credit cards • low moderate

RESTAURANT
Osteria Boccondivino
Via Mendicità Istruita 14
☎0172.425-674
Closed Sunday
All credit cards • low moderate

Walk through the courtyard, up the stairs past the Arcigola Slow Food offices and around the balcony to the entrance of this rustic *osteria* that's always filled with Slow Food staff members feasting on the traditional cooking of Maria Pagliasso. The menu is simple, changes daily, and offers a limited selection of well-prepared dishes. Interesting starters include warm vegetable flans, raw-meat salad, pickled eel. Handmade *tajarin* are always on the menu, topped with truffles, by reservation in season. Rabbit cooked with Arneis, tripe, and beef braised with Barolo are tasty main-dish possibilities. Save room for the terrific local cheese selection, and conclude with featherweight *zabaione* flavored with Moscato, served with cornmeal cookies, a wonderful dessert for those who have eaten one too many *panna cotta* or *bunet.*

PASTRY
Pasticceria Arpino
Via Cavour 36
☎0172.412-951
Closed Monday
Local legend Carlo Arpino founded this *pasticceria,* which still makes the best desserts in town, including Montebianco, *panettone* with Moscato wine, and *braidesini* cookies flavored with rum. A wide selection of mignon pastries is tempting.

Canelli

HOTEL
Asti
Viale Risorgimento 44/B
☎0141.824-220
Fax 0141.822-449
No credit cards • moderate

AGRITOURISM
La Luna e i Falò
Regione Aie 37
☎0141.831-643
No credit cards • inexpensive
One apartment and two rooms on a working farm of vineyards, fruit, vegetables, and courtyard animals in the hills outside Asti. There's a two-day minimum stay.

RESTAURANT
San Marco
Via Alba 136
☎/Fax 0141.823-544
Closed Tuesday
All credit cards • high moderate

Mariuccia Ferrero in the kitchen, husband-sommelier Piercarlo in the dining room. Classic and innovative Piemontese cooking is served in the elegant modern dining room. Truffles abound in the late fall, although Mariuccia's cooking deserves a visit during the rest of the year. Pasta is homemade, the regional cheeses are first-rate, a great excuse to drink a fantastic red. Simple desserts are perfectly paired with the local Moscato, the most enticing dessert wine in the world, not to be missed. The wine list is wonderful, with a fine selection of wines from Piemonte, the rest of Italy, and beyond.

GELATO
Gelateria Ezio
Piazza Carlo Gancia 18
☎0141.835-273
Closed Monday
Visitors to Canelli will want to stop at Ezio Parodis' *gelateria* to taste his Moscato-flavored creations. *Gelato, semifreddo,* and the Moscatella *torta* are scented with the local Moscato. Classic Piemontese hazelnut cookies and cake and cornmeal cookies made with stone-ground grain are also worthwhile.

Cartosio

HOTEL-RESTAURANT
Cacciatori
Via Moreno 30
☎0144.40523
Fax 0144.40524
Closed Thursday
No credit cards • moderate
Generations of the Milano family have perfected the Piemontese country dining experience. Giancarlo and sons Massimo and Carlo in the dining room, wife Carla Chiodo in the kitchen. The setting is elegant, service is professional, and the food is superb and shows signs of nearby Liguria.

Start with vegetable *frittatine* or peppers with anchovy dressing. Handmade pasta, fantastic *risotto,* and potato *gnocchi* are tasty. Main-dish boned and stuffed rabbit, baked kid, beef braised with red wine, or flawlessly executed greaseless *fritto misto* are among the more interesting offerings. The incredible wine list focuses on Piemontese wines—check out the Grandi Rossi pages for some big red temptations.

Casale Monferrato

H O T E L

Garden

Viale Montebello 1/H

☎**0142.71701**

Fax 0142.77267

All credit cards • moderate

Castello di San Giorgio

Via Cavalli d'Olivola 3

San Giorgio Monferrato

☎**Fax 0142.806-203**

American Express, Diners Club, Visa • high moderate, not bad for a real castle

C O O K I E S

Krumiri Rossi

Via Lamza 19

☎**0142.453-030**

Closed Sunday and Monday

Rich golden-brown, crisp, buttery vanilla cookies, two-inch handlebars shaped like the moustache of King Vittorio Emanuele of Italy, are called *krumiri,* a specialty of the Casale Monferrato area. The best *krumiri* are made by Rossi, founded in 1878, and still made with local first-rate eggs and butter. A Rube Goldberg–like machine extrudes the dough, but the rest of the work is done by hand, and the cookies are cut on wooden boards, hand-shaped, and baked in a special formation that produces a deep golden color. Krumiri Rossi can be found in food shops throughout Italy in an old-

fashioned red tin that will appeal to box collectors. *Krumiri* fans should visit the shop at eight in the morning when the first batch exits the ovens and is sold still warm, an entirely different taste sensation from the tinned cookies. Call Signora Portinaro if you'd like to visit the bakery, but don't expect her to reveal the secret of this tasty cookie.

Caselle Torinese

H O T E L - R E S T A U R A N T

Jet Hotel

Via della Zecca 9

☎**011.991-3733**

Fax 011.996-1544

All credit cards • expensive

Ristorante Antica Zecca

☎**011.996-1403**

Closed Monday • low expensive

Conveniently located across from the Torino airport, the aptly name Jet Hotel is the home of Antica Zecca, a wonderful restaurant that doesn't get the credit it deserves, probably due to the proximity of the airport. But frequent fliers and savvy gastronomes find excuses to fly into Torino for the thrill of what surely must be the best closest-to-airport restaurant experience in Italy. Owners chef Bruno Libraron, pastry chef Roberto Vai, and his brothers Renato and Sergio in the dining room have created a restaurant that serves innovative but well-thought-out creations using the best, freshest local ingredients. Black and white truffles are found in season, but it would be a shame to miss the beautiful food served during the rest of the year. Desserts are world-class, cheese is well chosen. The wine list is simply fantastic, with lots of relatively unknown Piemontese wines. Rooms at the hotel are soundproofed so the jet noise doesn't disturb guests.

Castello di Annone

HOTEL
See Asti

RESTAURANT
Ristorante La Fioraia
Via Tagliata 26
☎**0141.401-106**
Closed Monday
No credit cards • high moderate
Ornella Cornero runs the kitchen while her husband, Mario, is out in the markets, hunting down fine ingredients, bringing his personal selection of local wines to his wife's daily menu. Most dishes are traditional, well prepared, and interesting. The pasta is homemade, the *grissini* are crispy, the service is efficient. But the true star of this restaurant is the *brasato*, beef braised in Barolo and Barbera wines, served with silky mashed potatoes, crispy chunks of *polenta*, and one of the brownest, wine-rich sauces I've ever encountered. Worth a detour for braised-beef fans.

Castelmagno

HOTEL
See Pradleves

CHEESE CONSORTIUM
Consorzio per la Tutela del Formaggio Castelmagno
Piazza Caduti 1, Campomolino
☎**0171.986-190**
Almost always open
Castelmagno, whose origins date from the thirteenth century, is a hard cheese to find, produced in small quantities in the *comunes* of Pradleves, Monterosso Grana, and Castelmagno from the milk of cows that have grazed in high-altitude pastures. The cheese is aged in cool, damp mountain caves for two to five months. The consortium, based at the cooperative La Poiana,

governs eighteen producers and sells first-rate Castelmagno.

Cavour

HOTEL
See Torino

BUTCHER
Macelleria Brarda
Via Peyron 28
☎**0121.6295**
Closed Sunday, Monday, and Wednesday afternoons
I was introduced to the *salumi* of Silvio Brarda by the late winemaker Giacomo Bologna, who wanted me to taste everything extraordinary that Piemonte had to offer. His spirit and fine example still guide me on my travels throughout Italy. Meat fans traveling in Piemonte should definitely plan a pilgrimage to the Macelleria Brarda, where Silvio raises or buys prize-winning Piemontese beef at the competion in Carrù. Silvio's beef salami is flavored with first-rate Piemontese wines. The shop also sells a fantastic selection of excellent Italian food products. The fresh lard seasoned with rosemary (less than half the cholesterol of butter) is worth a voyage.

Cherasco

HOTEL
See Bra

PASTRY
Sorelle Barbaro
Via Vittorio Emanuele 74
☎**0172.488-373**
Closed Wednesday
My son Max is gastronomically spoiled, constantly surrounded by the bounty of my field work—samples of pastries, chocolates, cheese, *salumi*, breads, and more. Most desserts languish on our table, barely tempting Max to a second taste. But he

went through an entire box of Sorelle Barbaro's exceptional Baci di Cherasco, chocolate and local hazelnut kisses. The chestnutty *marrons glacés*, chocolate-covered chocolate loaf, *pane di cioccolato*, and small pastries are also tasty, but I head straight for the Cherasco kisses, gastronomic light years beyond generic kisses with no zone of origin. They're expensive and addictive, sold in a terrific, old-fashioned, fake-crocodile–patterned brown and black box with gold writing and medallions won in competition by Marco Barbaro, who founded the bakery in 1881.

Cioccaro di Penango

H O T E L
Locanda del Sant' Uffizio
☎0141.916-292
Fax 0141.916-068
All credit cards • high moderate

Beppe Firato and his wife, Carla, who own and run the restaurant Beppe (see below), have beautifully restored a nearby seventeenth-century church complex. The Locanda del Sant' Uffizio has eighteen suites, large communal living rooms, a billiard room, gardens, tennis, and swimming, all set amid the tranquillity of the Monferrato countryside, north of Asti.

R E S T A U R A N T
Beppe
Via Piano 11
☎0141.916-292
Closed Tuesday, the first half of January, and 10 days in August
All credit cards • expensive

A meal at Beppe starts off with the house aperitif (local white wine and peaches) and light and crispy fried pastry, to take the edge off your hunger before proceeding to the Piemontese marathon of an *antipasto*. Homemade pasta and typical Piemontese dishes like *fritto misto* and *panna cotta* (cus-

tard) are well prepared, and the house wines, produced in Beppe's nearby Sant' Uffizio vineyards, are pleasant. Be sure to dine in the garden in summer.

Cossano Belbo

H O T E L
See Canelli or Alba

R E S T A U R A N T
Trattoria della Posta da Camulin
Via Negro 3
☎0141.88126
Fax D141.88559
Closed Sunday evening, Monday
American Express, Diners Club • moderate

I adore Camulin. It's one of my favorite restaurants that I just missed including in the first edition of this book, and I'm thrilled to remedy the omission. Although its official name is Trattoria della Posta, everyone calls it Camulin, a diminutive nickname for the Giordano family men, who originated from the village of Camu and were short, related Cesare Giordano who came up to my chin. Giorgio Giordano and his enthusiastic son Cesare bustle through the dining rooms packed with locals who know just what they want— anything prepared by Giovanna, hyper-Piemontese. Sit down, let Cesare suggest a wine from the fantastic, well-chosen, well-priced list, but try to pace yourself through the *antipasto*, which includes most of the classics like raw meat, chopped with a knife and not ground, peppers, *vitello tonnato*, stuffed vegetables, *cotechino* sausage served with rich *fonduta* sauce. Save room for the *tajarin*, hand-rolled, said to be the best in Piemonte, and I agree. Second-course offerings include perfectly prepared *fritto misto* with *porcini* mushrooms in season, braised or roast meat like kid, hare, rabbit, and chicken. Will anyone have the energy to taste the wonderful *mattone al caffè*? I had to go back three times to get through the menu, but it was worth the calories.

PASTRY

Pasticceria Cardino

Via Fratelli Negro 17

☎0141.88152

Closed Monday

This *pasticceria* is next door to Camulin, and they are famous for their *amaretti Carla,* lighter with egg white than traditional *amaretti,* a perfect culinary souvenir of a meal in Cossano Belbo.

Costigliole d'Asti

HOTEL

See Isola d'Asti

HOTEL

Hotel San Giacomo

Via Arulla 4, Agliano d'Asti (nearby)

☎/Fax 0141.966-012 or 954-178

American Express, Visa • expensive

RESTAURANT

Guido

Piazza Re Umberto 127

☎/Fax 0141.966-012

Closed Sunday

American Express, Visa • expensive

The location (in the basement of what looks like a bank), the stuffy formal ambience (paneled walls, Oriental rugs, draperies, heavy Piemontese antique reproductions), and the high ratings in most guidebooks had me worried that Guido was going to "nouvelle" out on me. Wrong. In spite of its appearance, this is a family affair: Lidia Alciati in the kitchen with her son Ugo, husband Guido in the dining room with sons Andrea and Piero. Their professionalism and commitment are overwhelming. The *cucina* is all Piemontese, with some of the most attractive and tasty dishes in the region. Mushrooms and truf-

fles are used to perfection in season; all pasta is homemade and hand-rolled; the *stinco* (veal shank), baked for six hours, is tender, rich, and meaty; the local cheese is splendid; and the *piccola pasticceria* (small pastries) are not to be skipped. The mostly Piemontese wine selection is excellent, although other regions and countries are also represented.

Cuneo

HOTEL

Royal Superga

Via Pascal 3

☎0171.693-223

Fax 0171.699-101

All credit cards • low moderate

ENOITECA-RESTAURANT

Osteria della Chiocciola

Via Fossano 1

☎0171.66277

Closed Sunday

All credit cards • moderate

The letter "i" in the *enoteca* is no typographical error, but means that Osteria della Chiocciola belongs to a group of wine shops committed to serving great wine by the glass, accompanied by some kind of food, with the greatest sense of hospitality. Owner Gigi Riva succeeds in all *enoiteca* ideals, both on the ground floor, with its welcoming bar with wine by the glass, small snacks, and bottles to go, and upstairs dining room for more serious eating and drinking at moderate prices. Gigi beams when he hands over the wine list or glances at the shelves filled with Italy's finest wines, well priced, an invitation to drink big. Chef Beppe Lucia uses local ingredients with a creative twist, perfect for anyone who's had one too many raw-meat salads. The menu changes daily, with a comfortable selection of dishes. *Risotto,* homemade pasta, braised meats are among the traditional offerings.

Truffles are used with abandon in season, but it's a shame to limit a visit to this charming *osteria* to the winter months. Three different economical tasting menus at lunchtime are geared to small, medium, and large appetites, while two moderately priced dinner tastings are more of a meal.

PASTRY

Pasticceria Arione
Piazza Galimberti 14
☎**0171.629-539**
Closed Monday

Is the Pasticceria Arione caught in a time warp? And am I pleased? Stucco, mirrors and dark wood, and fine pastry that hasn't changed since Airone copywrited the recipe for their *cuneesi al rhum* in 1923. They're confections of meringue, liqueur, a heart of chocolate cream, all enveloped in first-rate bittersweet chocolate. In the winter meringues, vanilla or chocolate, are stuffed with flavored whipped cream, a tasty bite.

GELATO

Bar Corso
Corso Nizza 16
☎**0171.602-014**
Closed Wednesday

Piero Basso makes superb *gelato*, worth a voyage in Michelin terms. It's easy to find the Bar Corso because of the crowds of happy *gelato* fans milling outside, even in the winter. The selection isn't huge, but all flavors, expecially those made with fresh seasonal fruit, are fantastic. Even the *pinguino* ("penguin"), a rectangular vanilla *gelato* on a stick coated with bittersweet chocolate, evolved from the Piemontese tradition of *pezzi duri* ("hard pieces") frozen confections, is a thrill.

Desana

HOTEL

Hotel Il Giardinetto
Via Sereno 3, Vercelli
☎**0161.257-230**
Fax **0161.259-311**
All credit cards • moderate

RICE AND CORNMEAL

Tenuta Castello
Piazza Castello 8
☎**0161.253-352**
Fax **0161.257-778**
Closed Sunday

Tenuta Castello, owned by Mamma Vercellone and her seven children, plus their husbands, wives, in-laws, and offspring, produces first-rate Arborio, Carnaroli, Vialone Nano, and Baldo rice and hard-to-find *marano* cornmeal (stone-ground, of course). They also have a line of organic, hand-harvested (and more expensive) Arborio, Carnaroli, and Vialone Nano cultivars grown without herbicides. Tenuta Castello also grows red-speckled *saluggi* beans and makes pasta from emmer (*farro*).

Dogliani

PASTRY

Pasticceria della Ferrera
Via Vittorio Emanuele 18
☎**0173.70587**
Closed Wednesday

Hazelnut fans should flock to this simple bakery for the intensely nutty *torta di nocciole* (hazelnut cake) made with local hazelnuts; it's heavenly when eaten fresh. The pound cake with raisins (called *plum cake* in Italian) and the *baci di Dogliani,* two chocolate hazelnut cookies glued together with a chocolate filling, are also tasty.

Garessio

HOTEL
Italia
Viale Paolini 28
☎/Fax 0174.81027
Visa • inexpensive

MINERAL WATER
Fonti San Bernardo
Via O. Rovere 41
☎0174.803-398
Fax 011.562-5647
Closed Saturday, Sunday
San Bernardo water from the Rocciaviva fount is fantastic, minimally mineral (*minimamente minerale*), with a fixed residue of 43, one of the lowest in Italy. Rocciaviva is a high-altitude source, 1,300 meters, of pure glacial water from the Maritime Alps. Designer Giorgetto Giugiaro has designed a new 1-liter transparent bottle with eighty-eight clear droplets, a stylish, clean look for a light, clean-tasting mineral. Look for this tasty water in Piemonte and throughout Italy as well as in the U.S. Fax if you'd like to visit the source.

Isola d'Asti

RESTAURANT-HOTEL
Il Cascinale Nuovo
Strada Statale Asti–Alba
☎0141.958-166
Fax 0141.958-828
Closed Sunday night, Monday, and August
All credit cards • high moderate
The only farmlike part of Il Cascinale Nuovo ("The New Farm") is the freshly picked vegetables. Tennis courts, a swimming pool, four fully equipped suites with Jacuzzis and linen sheets, and one of Piemonte's rising stars in the restaurant scene are not what Old MacDonald was ee-

ay-oh-ing about. Two Ferretto brothers, Walter in the kitchen and sommelier Roberto in the dining room, have teamed up to create a new-wave Piemontese *cucina*, aided by old-wave Piemontese women (Mamma Silvana and two grandmothers) who speak up if a dish doesn't work out. The food is traditional but lightened up, and takes advantage of first-rate fruit, vegetables, eggs, and poultry raised by the family. The decor in pale wood, gray, and white, the elegant silver, the large white dinner plates, and the breadstick bundle wrapped in a napkin are as refreshing as the food. The Langhe salad of *porcini* mushrooms, Roccaverano cheese, and duck with balsamic vinegar is a winner, and desserts are beautifully presented. If you spend the night, breakfast is a treat of fruit nectar, pound cake or croissants, and preserves, all homemade.

Momo

RESTAURANT-HOTEL
Ristorante Macallè
Via Boniperti 2
☎0321.926-064
Fax 0321.962-828
All credit cards • moderate
Sergio Zuin is in the kitchen with his mother, Speranza, and his wife, Silvana, runs the dining room of Macallè, one of the few traditional restaurants in the area that haven't gone nouvelle. The menu features regional specialties: homemade *salumi*, *risotto*, hard-to-find *paniscia* (vegetables and rice), donkey stew, game, homemade desserts, and rich *zabaione*. Fresh fish is served on Friday and Saturday. The wine list offers some pleasant surprises.

Monforte

HOTEL
Grappolo d'Oro
Piazza Umberto 1
☎/Fax0173.78293
No credit cards • inexpensive

RESTAURANT
Della Posta
Piazza XX Settembre 9
☎0173.78120
Closed Thursday
MasterCard, Visa • moderate

Run by the Massolino family since 1975, the Della Posta is a fantastic *trattoria*. I love to walk through the tiny spotless kitchen, where Gianfranco Massolino, with the help of his mamma, Elvira, prepares first-rate *cucina* of the Langhe to the cozy dining rooms, where Sabino Massolino greets clients and helps them with the extensive, well-priced wine list studded with gems. The menu, which offers few surprises and no disappointments, begins with the flawlessly prepared usual appetizers, like raw beef, chopped with a knife as tradition insists; *vitello tonnato;* game pâté; and vegetable flans. First-course options include homemade *tajarin* and *agnolotti,* tripe and chick-pea soup, *risotto al barolo* or with mushrooms in season. Braised, roast or boiled meats, or a marathon *fritto misto* are among the main-dish selections. Cheese is strictly local, worth saving a glass of red wine for. Simple desserts and tasty small pastries conclude the meal. Truffles grace all the usual dishes during their glorious season.

Montemagno

HOTEL

See Asti, Vignale Monferrato, or Cioccaro di Penango

RESTAURANT
La Braja
Via San Giovanni Bosco 11
☎0141.63107
Fax 0141.63605
Closed Monday and Tuesday
All credit cards • high moderate

Brothers Antonio (in the dining rooms) and Giuseppe Palermino aren't Piemontese, and their elegant restaurant will probably come as a relief for those who have tired of traditional regional cooking. Giuseppe uses to advantage the finest local ingredients, like Piemontese beef, first-rate rice, cheese, and *porcini* mushrooms. Pasta is homemade, *risotto* is always on the menu. Flavored breads and three different kinds of *grissini* are fresh and tasty. Desserts are worth saving room for, and the wine list is a jewel, a joy to drink from. Two tasting menus offer a well-priced dining experience for small or large appetites.

La Morra

INN

See Alba, Barolo, or Verduno

CULTURAL CENTER
Ca' dj'amis
Via Vittorio Emanuele 8
☎0173.509-225
Fax 0173.509-283
Local artist Claudia Ferraresi's "Friends' House" is a cultural center dedicated to tradition. It's like a living room open to the public, where Claudia and her friends have expositions, drink a glass of wine, and hang out. There are spring and fall book festivals, culinary events, tastings, encounters, and more. Phone or fax for details.

FLOUR MILL
Mulino Artigiano Sobrino
Via Roma 108
☎/Fax 0173.501-118
Closed Thursday afternoon and Sunday

The Sobrino family have been millers for four generations. Renzo Sobrino works in a wooden mill with stone grinders built over 100 years ago. He grinds organic grain—strictly local, first-class wheat, corn, oat, rye, and buckwheat cultivars—producing whole-grain flours and cornmeal, old-fashioned since they contain the entire kernel. The chestnut flour is made from local white chestnuts called *garessine,* grown and dried whole by small producers, milled with stone. All flours are sold in 500-gram and 1-kilo pressure-sealed bags or in larger sizes for serious bakers. Renzo also sells toasted *tondo gentile delle Langhe* hazelnuts and dried chestnuts. Fax ahead if you'd like to visit the mill.

ENOTECA
Enoteca Comunale di La Morra
Piazza del Municipio 2
☎0173.509-204
Closed Monday and Tuesday, open all of
September and October
Open from 11 to 12:30 P.M., 2:30 to 6:00 P.M.

Some of the best wine in Piemonte is made in the *comune* of La Morra, a terrific reason to make an *enoteca.* Nebbiolo, Dolcetto, Barbaresco, and Barolo from thirty-eight producers are displayed and for sale. Claudio Silvestro will open a bottle or two for tastings. The Compagnia dei Vignaioli, an association of producers based at the *enoteca,* organizes a yearly Mangialonga (literally "eat long," a spoof of the *Marcialonga,* a 70-kilometer cross-country ski race) on the last Sunday in August, an enogastronomic hike through the countryside, with five stops for sustenance, one course of a traditional Langhe lunch, and local wines poured by producers at each

stop. The event is limited to 3,000 participants—reserve in advance since places aren't easy to come by.

PASTRY
Pasticceria di Giovanni Cogno
Via Vittorio Emanuele 18
☎0173.509-192
Closed Saturday and Sunday

Giovanni Cogno is a passionate baker. His plain hazelnut cake, and a version with chocolate chips, are more cookielike than most, but both are clearly made with freshly toasted local hazelnuts. Chocolate hazelnut cookies (*lamorresi*) are given an adult treatment with Barolo, rum, or *grappa.* Whole-grain cornmeal cookies (*biscotti di meliga*) are delicately perfumed with lemon peel. All natural ingredients, no preservatives added, and Gianni Gallo's charming drawings on the labels are other good reasons for a visit to Giovanni Cogno's *pasticceria.*

RESTAURANT
Belvedere
Piazza Castello 5
☎/Fax 0173.50190
Closed Sunday night, Monday, January,
and February
MasterCard, Visa • moderate

The Belvedere, true to its name, has a view that will make you yearn to come back, a kind of visual and gastronomic *Three Coins in a Fountain* effect. Gianfranco Bovio is a winemaker, and ably takes care of provisions and the dining rooms, while his sister Maria Vittoria reigns in the kitchen. The simple, clean lines of her traditional *cucina* never fail to ring true. Game pâté, mushrooms, and truffles in season, hand-rolled and cut *tajarin* pasta, *agnolotti,* and richly flavored whole-grain cornmeal *polenta,* served with stewed or braised meats or game, are well prepared. Local cheeses are carefully chosen, and the wine list offers many pages of well-priced regional gems that will make enophiles go crazy. Finish your meal with a *grappa* and a lingering glance at the countryside, and you'll vow to return.

Neive

RESTAURANT-INN

La Contea

Piazza Cocito 8

☎**0173.67126**

Fax 0173.67367

Closed Sunday night and Monday

American Express, MasterCard • high moderate

Every time I come back to Piemonte, I feel like a homing pigeon, heading for Neive, which has always been my local point of reference. Claudia and Tonino Verro's sense of warmth and hospitality creates the mood in this enchanting restaurant, with its patterned wallpaper, terra-cotta floors, wood-burning fireplaces ablaze, and Piemontese villa feeling. La Contea's front room has few tables and a bar, where someone always seems to be drinking a *caffè* or a glass of wine or a *grappa*. Jars of homemade preserves and *bross* (cheeses mashed in *grappa*) sit on the shelves of large antique cupboards. Claudia has endured my questions and let me watch the action in her kitchen; she is a combination of traditional talent, professionalism won by pure hard work, a heart as big as all of Piemonte, and a vocabulary of Tuscan obscenities that makes the Florentine in me smile. Tonino has taken me to taste *grappa*, to market for truffles at dawn, and we have all sat up drinking Barbaresco and talking *cucina* until 3 A.M. What do I think of La Contea? I am moved by the *cucina*, by the strength of the traditional food that Tonino, Claudia, Gianni, and Maurizio offer in the three intimate dining rooms. I have never ordered anything, but have always let Tonino and Claudia put whatever they

want on my plate. Their choices have never been disappointing. What a treat! Tonino's pairing of local wines with Claudia's cooking is an act of love. Spend the night in one of the charming guest rooms upstairs, and breakfast on hazelnut cookies and cake.

Pallanza

Pallanza is a small, elegant tourist village on Lago Maggiore, a perfect base for exploring the area's ornate villas with their immense, well-planned, Italianate terraced gardens adorned with tropical, exotic, and local plants and trees. Villa Taranto, Villa Borromeo, and the Giardino Botanico of the Isole Borromee are settings that seem to call for white flannels, blazers, and linen lawn dresses.

HOTEL

Europalace

Viale delle Magnolie 16

☎**0323.556-441**

Fax 0323.556-442

All credit cards • high moderate

HOTEL

Castagnola

Via al Collegio 18

☎**0323.503-414**

Fax 0323.556-341

Diners Club, MasterCard, Visa • low moderate

RESTAURANT

Il Torchio

Via Manzoni 20

☎/**Fax 0323.503-352**

Closed Monday and the second half of June

All credit cards • moderate

Restaurants cater to tourists in this area—not the best climate for traditional *cucina* and attentive service. But Il Torchio, run by brothers Vittorio (in the kitchen) and Franco Gurian (sommelier) and their wives has concentrated on fine local lake fish and the bounty of the Milano market, transforming quality ingredients into fine food. The Piemontese wine selection is superb, with some great vintage wines for enophiles and Italian and French wines for locals bored with the fantastic regional reds.

Pessione di Chieri

MUSEUM

Martini & Rossi

Museo del Vino

Piazza L. Rossi

☎011.947-0345

The Martini & Rossi Museum, in the original Martini & Rossi cellars in Pessione, houses one of the world's most important collections of winemaking artifacts and traces the history of wine from the seventh century B.C. through its 3,000-year evolution. Apulian, Attic, Corinthian, Etruscan, and Roman objects, grape presses, carts, and.vats are beautifully displayed in the vaulted brick cellars that still retain some of the scent of wine.

Piobesi d'Alba

TRUFFLES

Tartuflanghe

Via Provinciale 9

☎/Fax 0173.619-347

Always open in season

Tartuflanghe wholesales truffles—fresh or processed as paste—throughout Italy, and exports their wares all over the world. The office and warehouse are well guarded. You can purchase truffles in season, truffled pâté, and other jarred truffle products.

RESTAURANT-INN

Le Clivie

Via Camoreto 1

☎/Fax 0173.619-261

Closed Monday

MasterCard, Visa • moderate

Caterina Clivio has turned her nineteenth-century villa, surrounded by manicured gardens, into a charming seven-room inn. The dining room has vaulted frescoed ceilings, marble columns, and service by a uniformed "butler" in grand Piemontese style. Carlo Cracco is in the kitchen preparing traditional seasonal dishes like meat-stuffed *caponet,* done in the summer with zucchini flowers and in the winter with cabbage, *bagna cauda,* and hand-rolled pasta. Truffles are served in season, fine local cheese is available, breads are homemade, and the cellar holds some fine Piemontese wines.

Pradleves

RESTAURANT

Tre Verghe d'Oro

Via IV Novembre 131

☎0171.986-116

Closed January and Tuesday in winter

No credit cards • inexpensive

The Tre Verghe d'Oro is tucked in the Valle Grana, close to the village of Castelmagno, a mecca for lovers of full-flavored cheese. Seven generations of the Durando family have run this mountain lodge serving traditional Piemontese *cucina,* seasonal mushrooms, marinated meats, a lengthy but tasty *antipasto* series, potato *gnocchi* sauced with Castelmagno cheese, and a *fritto misto piemontese* (order in advance) of fifteen delicately fried meats, vegetables, fruit—even *amaretti* cookies. Save room for a taste of hard-to-find fresh and ripe Castelmagno cheese, and conclude with a glass of Ginepy, an herbal digestive. The wine selection has its highs and lows. Spend the night in one of the thirty slightly seedy rooms and wake up to the music of the Grana River.

Priocca

HOTEL

See Asti, Alba, or Santa Vittoria d'Alba

RESTAURANT

Centro

Via Umberto 5
☎/Fax 0173.616-112
Closed Tuesday
All credit cards • moderate

In the center, hence its name, of the village of Priocca, this *trattoria* with a restaurant in the back has now converted to all restaurant, and I can't blame them since the cooking is so good. I miss the workers' dining room in the front, but could never resist the restaurant owned by Enrico Cordero, sommelier, and his wife, Elide, who both preside in the dining room while Mamma Rita rules the kitchen preparing some of finest cooking in the region. Classic appetizers include *frittate*, chopped raw meat, and *vitello tonnato;* pastas like *tajarin* and *agnolotti* filled with guinea hen are homemade. Rabbit and game are wonderful main-course options, but *fritto misto* fans should reserve in advance for an impeccably fried mixture of meat, vegetables, and mushrooms that is cooked one ingredient at a time in a black iron pan in fresh oil, the way tradition dictates. Cheese is strictly local, served with *cugnà,* desserts feature the local hazelnut, and I love the *zabaione* made with Moscato d'Asti. The wine list is well chosen, well priced, and Enrico's suggestions are worthwhile.

Rocchetta Tanaro

Rocchetta Tanaro is a gastronomic destination, home of the winery of the late Giacomo Bologna, ably run by his family. Relatives own the wonderful Trattoria I Bologna. Singer-winemaker Bruno Lauzi hangs out at the Bar Coffibon. And Mario Fongo bakes tasty *grissini* and crispy long

flatbreads. All good reasons for a visit to Rocchetta.

HOTEL

See Asti

BAKERY

Panificio Mario Fongo

Via Nicola Sardi 48
☎0141.644-604
Closed Sunday and Thursday afternoon

Everyone in Rocchetta has a nickname and Mario Fongo is known as Patilli. Although he makes traditional *grissini* and bread, his *lingue di suocera,* or mother-in law's tongue, a crispy, thin two-foot flatbread, gets all the attention. The flatbreads are sold by weight or in a wooden crate, which may not appeal to those who like to travel light.

RESTAURANT

I Bologna

Via Sardi 4
☎0141.644-600
Fax 0141.644-197
Closed Tuesday
No credit cards • moderate

The stables were simply restored, turned into two attractive rustic dining rooms, where the cooks, mother and son Mariuccia and Beppe Bologna, offer traditional and innovative views of local cooking. The menu changes weekly and offers a limited selection of well-prepared dishes. Pasta is always homemade, but lighter dishes like rabbit, poultry, and vegetable sauces take over in the spring and summer from the heartier roast and braised meats and stuffed pastas of the fall and winter. Local *formaggette* are served with *cugnà,* desserts are nontraditional but worth saving room for. The entire range of superb wines from Braida, owned by another part of the Bologna family, as well as fine regional, Italian, and non-Italian wines are all well priced. This restaurant was totally destroyed in the devastating floods of 1994 in the Asti area, but the stubborn Bologna family has cleaned up and found the strength to continue. Hooray!

Santa Vittoria d'Alba

HOTEL
Hotel Santa Vittoria
Via Cagna 4
☎**0172.478-189**
Fax 0172.478-465
All credit cards • low moderate

VERMOUTH
Cinzano
Via Statale Santa Vittoria
☎**0172.47041**
Cinzano makes one of the more popular vermouths. For an appointment to visit their cellars, call 011.57401.

Torino

On the banks of the Po River, in sight of the Alps, stands Torino. The Roman colony of Augusta Taurinorum, the capital of Savoia, the center of the Italian Risorgimento, and the first capital of the newly united Italy, it is clearly a city of noble aspect, with spacious piazzas, elegant shops in covered arcades, and turn-of-the-century architecture. Its castles and palaces are a reminder of over 600 years of rule by the important and powerful family monarchy of Savoy. Great wealth and power in Torino is now clearly represented by Fiat, but gastronomic trends last longer than politics. Traditional bars in the city are always crowded, each filled with its own partisans, who stop in for a coffee, pastry, chocolate, cocktail, aperitif, or even a *marron glacé*. The Fiat plants have brought immigrants in from the south, and many restaurants offer *cucina Toscana*, frequently cooked by southern chefs who prepare pasta to perfection (unlike the way it's done in Toscana). Chocolates, tiny pastries, and the *bicerin*, a shot of coffee, sweetened hot chocolate, and whipped cream served in a special glass, are all part of the special Torinese gastronomic tradition, among the most interesting in Italy.

HOTEL
Villa Sassi
Strada al Traforo del Pino 47
☎**011.898-0556**
Fax 011.898-0095
All credit cards • luxury

At the gates of the city of Torino, Villa Sassi has seen the passage of royalty and local luminaries for over 200 years. It has been turned into a luxury hotel, with ten rooms and two suites, overlooking magnificent gardens and huge trees. This is what living like a king is all about.

HOTEL
Hotel Victoria
Via Nino Costa 4
☎**011.561-1909**
Fax 011.561-1806
American Express, MasterCard, Visa • high moderate

The eighty-room Victoria, located in the center of Torino, is a perfect hotel. All rooms are fully equipped; some are furnished in charming flea-market antiques, others in simple modern. The staff is friendly and helpful, and parking is available nearby.

BAR-CAFFÈ
Caffè San Carlo
Piazza San Carlo 156
☎**011.515-317**
Closed Monday

The Caffè San Carlo, which bills itself as "the living room of Torino," features gilt columns, mirrors, green-and-rust–veined marble tables, and a massive Murano glass chandelier, all authentic 1800s decor on the corner of piazza San Carlo. Another smaller, frescoed tearoom and a more modern no-nonsense bar handle the stand-up business.

BAR-CAFFÈ
Caffè Torino
Piazza San Carlo 04
☎011.545-118
Closed Tuesday

Behind the old-fashioned bar, in a scallop-shell shrine, stands the rampant bull, symbol of Torino from the Roman colony of Augusta Taurinorum. The ambience of this local institution is classic.

BAR-CAFFÈ
Al Bicerin
Piazza Consolata 5
☎011.436-9325
Closed Wednesday

Although some other bars in Torino make the *bicerin*—a hot chocolate, coffee, and whipped cream beverage served in a glass—this is the bar to head for if you want a taste of the most authentic version in town. Watch out for the hordes of Torinese out for a Sunday afternoon stroll and a *bicerin,* and look for the *toro* water fountain in the corner of the piazza.

BAR-CAFFÈ
Antica Dolceria Baratti
Piazza Castello 29
☎011.561-3060
Closed Monday

Baratti is a nice place to rest while you gawk at the vast assortment of wrapped candies and tiny pastries. The small turn-of-the-century bar is a gem.

BAR-CAFFÈ
Platti
Corso Vittorio Emanuele 72
☎011.511-507
Closed Friday

Platti seems to have the best sandwich selection of the Torinese bars. All the bread is homemade, the little pastries are attractive, and they make their own *marrons glacés* and *giandujotti* (chocolate hazelnut wedges).

MARKET
The Porta Palazzo market must be one of the largest food markets in Italy. Meat, poultry, and perishable goods are sold in pavilions, but the excitement and hustle of this market is outdoors, amid piles of fruit and vegetables—local bounty bartered, traded, and sold with a flourish. Fresh hazelnuts, real *marroni* chestnuts, fantastic ripe peppers, and chains of braided garlic, along with a treasure of organic and synthetic goods—all are cleared away at 1:30 P.M. Lunch around the corner at San Giors or Tre Galline, both typical Torinese *trattorie.*

MARKET
Via Lagrange is Torino's gastronomic Fifth Avenue, the food street, with a fine selection of cheese, pastry, meat, produce, and some fancy take-out. Fine wine is available around the corner.

SPECIALTY FOODS
Salumeria Rosticceria Castagno
Via Lagrange 34
☎011.544-350
Closed Wednesday afternoon

Torino's Castagno shops are a local version of the Peck empire in Milano (see page 221), three high-quality specialty shops selling a beautiful selection of meat, cheese, and take-out. The salads in the windows of the corner shop, simply placed on trays and in baking dishes, are fresh-looking and attractive. *Nervetti* (calf's-foot salad), peppers with *bagna cauda* sauce, *tavola calda* (hot table) items, and roast meats are sold to go.

M E A T

La Bottega del Maiale

Via Lagrange 38

☎**011.519-934**

Closed Wednesday afternoon

"The Pork Shop" seems to sell every cut of pork, and a wide selection of *prosciutto* and *salumi* as well.

C H E E S E

La Baita del Formaggio

Via Lagrange 36/A

☎**011.547-257**

Closed Wednesday afternoon

All the special regional cheeses of Piemonte, like Castelmagno, *toma, ricotta piemontese, robiole,* and *tomini* are sold here, as well as quality *parmigiano* and *provolone* produced in other regions.

P A S T A

Pastificio Defilippis

Via Lagrange 39

☎**011.542-137**

Closed Wednesday afternoon

Fresh and dry pasta, and flours and beans of all kinds, are the specialty of the Pastificio Defilippis. It'll make you wish you had a pot of boiling water waiting at home.

P R O D U C E

Scanavino Due

Via Lagrange 36

☎**011.547-257**

Closed Wednesday afternoon

Fruit and vegetables, local and imported exotics, and dried fruit and nuts are all attractively displayed in this chic modern produce shop on via Lagrange.

T R U F F L E S   A N D   G A M E

Ottino

Via Lagrange 36

☎**011.544-928**

Closed Wednesday afternoon

Founded in 1919, Ottino sells truffles, mushrooms, game, poultry, eggs, and meat. In the fall this shop is in full bloom, with an array of feathered game birds and hairy animals, and the perfume of truffles in the air.

S P E C I A L T Y   F O O D S

Steffanone

Via Maria Vittoria 2

☎**011.546-737**

Closed Wednesday afternoon

The salads, especially the aspics, at Steffanone are special, made with homemade mayonnaise and aspic. The Ligurian-style stuffed vegetables and *torta pasqualina* (vegetable tart) make a pleasant picnic lunch.

C H E E S E

Toja

Via Torino 48

☎**011.910-1271**

Closed Wednesday afternoon

Toja doesn't always have all the great local cheeses, but when they do have them, the quality is high. *Brus, robiole* made from goat's or cow's milk, Gorgonzola from Novara, and squashed mountain *tomini* can sometimes be found.

W I N E

Enoteca Casa del Barolo

Via Andrea Doria 7

☎**011.532-038**

Closed Wednesday afternoon

Gigi Molinaro has a splendid, vast selection of Piemontese wines, as well as a personal, more limited but nevertheless splendid selection of wines from other regions, and *grappa*. Chilled whites are always available.

W I N E

Il Salotto dei Vini

Via San Massimo 12

☎**011.830-418**

Closed Wednesday afternoon

Franca Ferraro's one-room wine shop has a good selection of wines and hides, down a spiral staircase, a comfortable wine cellar where she holds interesting tastings.

PASTRY

Pasticceria Falchero

Via San Massimo 4

☎**011.817-3077**

Closed Monday

No smoking allowed in Signor Falchero's pastry shop, where the air is brought in from the roof because it's better than street air for his pastry, the best in Torino. The miniatures are smaller, more original, and the selection is wider; the puff pastry is light and flaky; cookies, warm *cornetti*, mini-pizzas, custom cakes, and chocolates of the highest quality are made fresh daily.

PASTRY

Pfatish

Corso Vittorio Emanuele 76

☎**011.568-3962**

Closed Monday

A complete line of Peyrano chocolates and fine pastries are specialties of this pastry shop, which starts with a silent "P."

CHOCOLATES

Peyrano

Corso Moncalieri 47

☎**011.660-2202**

Antonio Peyrano founded his chocolate shop in 1915 in the chic suburbs of Torino. Giorgio and Bruna Peyrano run the family business today, with total control over every phase of the chocolate-making process. A blend of nine different cocoa beans is toasted over heat produced by burning olive wood, then ground with a porphyry stone mill. After aging for three months, the ground beans are melted, "slapped" (stirred and beaten) for seventy-two hours at 45°C (113°F), tempered, and molded into ingots, awaiting transformation. A visit to the factory is a chocoholic's dream

come true, surrounded by Willie Wonka machinery all devoted to the worship of the cocoa bean. The tan gift boxes are simple and sturdy, the type you never throw away, and a numbered edition of 5,000 beautiful handmade layered wooden boxes, designed by Ettore Sottsass, is available to those of discriminating taste with money to burn.

GELATO

Pepino

Piazza Carignano 8

☎**011.542-009**

Closed Monday

Pepino was founded in 1884, across the street from Palazzo Madama, site of the first Italian senate. Did Cavour send someone across the street for one of Pepino's wrapped ice cream bars, the classic chocolate-dipped *pinguino* ("penguin") in either mint, custard, chocolate hazelnut, or hazelnut, or the chocolate *tartufi*, or candied-fruit–studded *cassate*, or *amaretti*-flavored *spumoni*, or truncated *pezzi duri* in chocolate or vanilla, or the up to twenty fruit-flavored *gelati* offered in the summer? I like to think he did.

RESTAURANT

Ristorante del Cambio

Piazza Carignano 2

☎**011.546-690**

Fax 011.543-760

Closed Monday and August

American Express, MasterCard,

Visa • expensive

The Cambio has been a classic in Torino since 1757. Crystal chandeliers, plush red velvet seating, a small entranceway bar with marble-topped and pedestaled tables—the onetime elegance of Torino has been preserved like an Egyptian mummy. The *cucina* doesn't seem to have changed much since then either, with its emphasis on Baltic sturgeon, Strasbourg foie gras, and other continental favorites. But the traditional dishes are nicely cooked; try the homemade pasta, *finanziera* (chicken liver and sweetbread stew), Barolo-braised beef, and the Barolo-flavored *zabaione* served with cornmeal lemon cookies and *amaretti*-and-cocoa–stuffed peaches. Reserve the table where Cavour liked to dine, backed by a banner of faded green, white, and red bunting. On Friday evenings in the spring, the spirit of Old World Torino is re-created with chamber music and royal family menus—six- or seven-course meals—accompanied by local wines. The Cambio's wine list, with its vintage Barolo and Barbaresco going back to the 1960s, will please enophiles even more than the *cucina*.

RESTAURANT
C'era una volta
Corso Vittorio Emanuele II 41
☎**011.655-498**
Fax 011.650-5774
Open evenings only, closed Sunday and August
All credit cards • moderate
"Once upon a time" is the name of this restaurant, one flight up, where you'll be served a traditional Piemontese dinner: one sitting, a fixed menu of eight *antipasti*, two first courses, *sorbetto*, two meat dishes, vegetables, and a taste of three desserts. Owner-sommelier Piero Prete welcomes all diners and selects interesting, reasonably priced wines that go well with his procession of a meal, served by waiters in red-and-white–checked shirts and blue V-neck sweaters. Conclude your dinner with a *grappa*, served from a cute little cask. The dining room, with its frescoed ceiling and ornate cornices, makes you feel like a guest at a private party.

RESTAURANT
Gatto Nero
Corso Turati 14
☎**011.590-414**
Fax 011.590-477
Closed Sunday and August
American Express, Diners Club • expensive
The owners of Gatto Nero are from Montecarlo, a walled village outside Lucca, and produce their own extra virgin olive oil and splendid wines for their Tuscan restaurant, the city's oldest. The restaurant is modern, with a brick-wall rustic ambience and built-in shelves holding a large selection of wines. The *cucina* is a blend of Toscana, Piemonte, and fresh fish and vegetables prepared by their able cooks. The menu is quite large; the *degustazione* tasting of Gatto Nero's specialties includes a lightly dressed seafood salad, *melizza* (a mini-pizza on a slice of eggplant), homemade pasta with seafood, cooked to almost crunchy perfection, mushrooms in season, grilled meats, fish, or a *fritto misto* marathon. The house wines are wonderful, especially the white and the red reserves that the family makes in Toscana.

RESTAURANT
Tre Galline
Via Bellezia 37
☎**011.436-6553**
Closed Sunday, Monday lunch, and August
No credit cards • low moderate
Around the corner from Porta Palazzo, Tre Galline ("Three Hens") is one of the oldest restaurants in Torino. Marble-chip floors, painted wainscoting, coat hooks, typical high-hung *trattoria* paintings, and an all-local clientele set the mood. The menu features some fine local specialties—a variety of appetizers, *bagna cauda* (anchovy-garlic dip with raw vegetables), Barolo-braised beef, and mixed boiled meats served with four kinds of sauce. In season, truffles are sold by the *grattata*, or grating. The chef is from the south, and his pasta is perfectly cooked. Cheese lovers will want to try the *tomino elettrico* ("electric") cheese marinated in oil and spicy chile peppers. The house wine is without character, and wine

bottles are displayed rather than listed on the menu. Coppo's Barbera or Grignolino goes nicely with the *cucina* of this classic gem of a *trattoria*.

RESTAURANT

San Giors

Via Borgo Dora 3
☎011.521-1256
Closed Monday and Tuesday
MasterCard, Visa • moderate

Around the corner from the Porta Palazzo market, up a flight of stairs in a seedy hotel, the San Giors (San Giorgio in Piemontese dialect) serves traditional Torinese *trattoria* food. The house specialty is *bollito misto*—mixed boiled meats served with a variety of sauces (including ketchup!)—and hard-to-find hearty *tofeja*, a bean and pork rind soup. The strictly local crowd seems to contain a high proportion of smokers in all three dining rooms of this no-frills authentic *trattoria*. A personal favorite!

RESTAURANT

La Smarrita

Corso Unione Sovietica 244
☎011.317-9657
Fax 011.317-9191
Closed Monday and most of August
All credit cards • expensive

La Smarrita is the name of the bell that rang out for lost travelers, rung by the cavaliers of Tau, a chivalrous order that provided hospitality to stranded knights in central Italy in the 1300s. Waiters at the restaurant are garbed in the tunics of the cavaliers of Tau and provide succor to victims of the Torinese work ethic with the best food and wine in town. The decor is modern, the colors subdued, the lighting soft, and the acoustics better than in most restaurants. The *cucina* isn't particularly regional, although the Tuscan background of Moreno Grossi and his sister Franca shines through in the use of extra virgin olive oil.

Fresh fish and vegetables are lightly cooked, barely sauced, treated with respect, and individual flavors and textures stand out. Mushrooms in season are a special treat. There's no printed menu or wine list, but Moreno will discuss your meal and help you to decide, and his sommelier, Antonio Dacomo, will choose a wine from their wonderful selection to complement your meal. The waiters are a bunch of cuties.

PIZZERIA

Spacca Napoli

Via Mazzini 19
☎011.812-6694
Closed Tuesday
American Express, Visa • moderate

Fine pizza is sold individually or by the meter, crafted in wood-burning ovens in the Neapolitan style. Spacca Napoli offers an outer-regional culinary experience for those who have eaten too much traditional Piemontese cooking.

HOUSEWARES

La Mezzaluna

Via Lagrange 2/D
☎011.557-5181
Closed Monday morning
American Express, Diners Club, Visa

Torino's best housewares shop is named after the two-handled rocking knife that most Italian housewives use. The shelves are neatly arranged with the finest names in Italian products—Alessi, ICM, and Sambonet stainless, IVV glassware, Guzzini plastics, and Montana knives—as well as English jar labels, French pottery, German baking tins, and traditional terra-cotta bean pots. Owners Anna Calcagne and Paola Giubergia are passionate about cooking and equipment and are friendly and helpful. They'll wrap and send your purchases home if you want.

CANDLES

Colenghi

Piazza Solferino 3
☎011.512-550
Closed Monday morning
No credit cards

All sizes, lengths, and colors of candles, from birthday-cake size to decorative holiday tapers, spirals, fruit, vegetables, a sandwich on a realistic roll, and even custom-designed candles, are the specialty of Colenghi. They also make soap, including some serious-looking detergents and blocks of no-nonsense *Sapone Marsiglia* for removing oil-based stains from washables.

BAKERY EQUIPMENT

Siccardi

Via Principe Amadeo 22/B
☎011.839-7210
Closed Saturday
No credit cards

Siccardi is a bakery equipment shop for professional or ambitious bakers, and their selection of utensils is a joy to behold. Boards to shove bread into the oven; cake molds in chestnut, mushroom, pine-cone, corn-cob, and shooting-star shapes; cutters, molds, sifters in all sizes and meshes, pizza accessories, rolling pins, hand-carved wooden spoons, bowls, strainers, a pantographic seven-bladed crimped or straight-edged pastry cutter, and *rosetta* stamps that look like a cross between knuckle-dusters and an Oriental martial-arts weapon.

BOOKS

Luxemburg Libreria Internazionale

Via Cesare Battisti 7
☎011.532-007
Closed Monday morning
No credit cards

The Luxemburg Libreria Internazionale has a large collection of Judaica, as well as a nice assortment of cookbooks in both Italian and English. They will send your books home if you wish.

BOOKS

Bloomsbury Books and Arts

Via dei Mille 20
☎011.839-8989
Closed Monday morning
American Express, Visa

Bloomsbury Books and Arts has a good selection of Italian cookbooks, literary and art books in English and Italian, and local pictorials. The ambience is inviting. They will send, a plus since books are heavy.

MUSEUM

Egyptian Museum

Via Accademia delle Scienze 6
☎011.537-581
Closed Monday

Housed in the Science Academy, the Torino Museo Egizio, the oldest Egyptian museum in the world—founded even before Cairo's museum—is breathtaking, and you don't have to suffer Egyptian hotels and food to see it. A vast collection of everyday Egyptian relics from daily life, from inkwells to pawns for an unknown board game, are displayed in case after case of fabulous and amazing objects. Cairo on the Po, open from 9 A.M. to 2 P.M.

FLEA MARKET

Balon

Porta Palazzo Market
Open Saturday

The Porta Palazzo market hosts the Balon flea market on Saturdays. Although the best stuff is snapped up early, and most interesting items are too big even to consider purchasing, I can always find something fun to bring home—tableware, glasses, old linens.

MUSEUM

Museo dell' arredamento

Palazzina di Stupinigi
☎011.598-844
Closed Monday and Friday

Built by famed architect Juvara in 1730 as a hunting lodge for Vittorio Amadeo II, rococo

Villa Reale now houses the Museo dell'arredamento, a unique glimpse into noble Piemontese taste and lifestyles. The portraits, especially those of the small children, evoke another time and a different world.

Torre Pellice

RESTAURANT-INN

Flipot
Corso Gramsci 17
☎0121.953-465
Fax 0121.91236
Closed Tuesday, 2 weeks in March, 2 weeks in October
American Express • moderate

Torre Pellice, in the Valle del Pellice, is gastronomically closer to Switzerland and France. The *cucina* at Flipot is based on regional traditions and the season, and offers fresh field greens and wild herbs cooked up in *frittate*, homemade pasta, local goose (in November), wild boar, chamois, deer, and trout, Sanato Piemontese veal, and farm-raised poultry. Cheese is purchased directly from the dairy; taste the seirass, a fresh ricotta with herbs that I've never found elsewhere. Walter Eynard, his wife, Gisella, and maître d' Marco Fornarone seem to have thought of everything, and the selection of fine Piemontese—and French and Californian—wines is impressive. Spend the night in one of the seven simple, clean rooms.

Treiso

HOTEL
See Alba or Neive

RESTAURANT
Osteria Unione
Via Alba 1
☎0173.638-303
Closed Sunday evening, Monday, and Tuesday
No credit cards • low moderate

Pina Dongiovanni and her family have created the quintessential *osteria* of the Langhe area. Six tables in the simply appointed dining room are always filled with locals and superstar winemakers who are never disappointed with the predictable but perfectly executed home-style traditional cooking. *Grissini* are fantastic. The menu changes in the spring and fall, and features a typical marathon of appetizers that includes salami, *frittatine, vitello tonnato,* raw-beef salad, and *toma d'Alba* served with green sauce. Tiny "pinched" *agnolotti* or *tajarin* served with a delicate meat sauce are tasty first-course options. Rabbit, prepared with Barolo and peppers in the winter, wild herbs in the summer, is worth a voyage. Sit outside under the grape pergola when the weather is nice. Let Beppe suggest a wine from the large well-chosen selection of superior reds.

Vercelli

HOTEL
Il Giardinetto
Via Sereno 3
☎0161.257-230
Fax 0161.259-311
All credit cards • moderate

RICE
Acquarello
Tenuta Carpo
Livorno Ferraris
☎/Fax 0161.477-832
The Rondolino family have cultivated rice on their land since 1612, following traditions but utilizing the best cultivars and avoiding chemical treatments. Acquarello, as their Carnaroli is called, is certified organic, cultivated in small quantities, irrigated with spring water in fertile fields, aged at a low temperature for a year before being milled. The rice, once milled, is packaged in pressurized cans to maintain flavors at their maximum. Michele Rondolino

claims that his rice is perfect for almost all preparations, holds up well under cooking, and can even be reheated successfully. If you're planning to visit, fax to let them know you're coming.

TABLEWARE

Sambonet (factory)
Via XXVI Aprile 62
☎0161.5971
Fax 0161.251-812
Founded in 1856, this company makes high-quality silverplate. Designs for their tableware are classic as well as modern, and are found throughout Italy. Call Dott. Bruno in Milano, 02.668-00293, for an appointment.

Vignale Monferrato

FARM-INN
Mongetto Drè Castè
Via Piave 2
☎/Fax 0142.933-469
Meals on Friday evening, Saturday evening, and Sunday lunch, or by reservation
No credit cards • moderate
Brothers Carlo and Roberto Santopietro and Roberto's wife, Margherita, are the powerhouse family behind Il Mongetto, a farm that casually produces wines in the mostly unsung Monferrato area. Encouraged by the late winemaker Giacomo Bologna, who incited anyone interested in quality and tradition, Roberto hired a top enologist who improved the wines dramatically. With his wife and brother, he created a line of jarred products, including Giacomo's wife Anna's famous stuffed peppers (see page 44). Other specialties include local fruit preserves, peaches poached in Moscato, *martin sec* pears poached in Grignolino, and *cugnà,* cooked grape must and autumn fruit preserves, the traditional

Piemontese condiment for *polenta,* boiled meats, cheese, or snow. Il Mongetto's *bagna cauda* set, a jar of garlicky anchovy-flavored sauce used as a dip for raw winter vegetables, is sold with a traditional terra-cotta warmer, making this classic festive Piemontese dish almost effortless, eliminating the need to hunt down first-rate anchovies and peel heads of garlic. The Santopietro family restored a farmhouse on the property, dividing it into two one-bedroom apartments—bedroom, bathroom, and small kitchen, and three frescoed double rooms, each with private bath. They serve meals on the weekends or by reservation that include tastings of Il Mongetto's fine products as well as those of their friends, a lesson they learned from Giacomo. Mamma Carla supervises her sons Carlo and Roberto in the kitchen. It's impossible to find a room in late June, July, and the first week in August, during the Vignale Dance Festival.

Visone d'Acqui

HAZELNUT CANDY
Canelin
Via Acqui 123
☎0144.395-285
Closed Sunday afternoon, Monday
There are no secret ingredients in *torrone,* according to Giovanni Verdese, a fourth-generation maker of this nougat hazelnut candy. Honey, sugar, and egg whites are cooked for eleven hours (instead of the three or four hours of other candy makers), lots of toasted local hazelnuts are folded in, and the mixture is poured into molds of 200-, 300-, 400-, and 500-gram blocks as well as a jumbo 1-kilo size. It's not difficult to find good *torrone,* but Canelin's is probably Piemonte's finest.

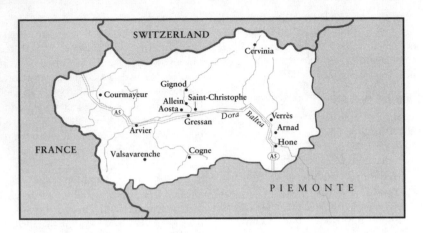

The character of Valle d'Aosta, Italy's smallest region, has been formed by mountains, valleys, and rivers. The Aosta Valley is separated from Switzerland and France by towering Alps, western Europe's tallest mountains, and bisected by the main valley of the Dora Baltea River, fed by torrential tributaries coursing down through smaller valleys.

Valle d'Aosta

The Valle d'Aosta is dotted with archeological excavations, Roman monuments, medieval castles, Gothic churches, slate-tiled stone cottages, ski resorts, and grazing cows that outnumber the inhabitants of this bilingual (French and Italian) region.

The *cucina* is dominated by animal protein—meat and dairy products. Game comes from the mountain forests, cheese and butter from the cows that have summered in the high alpine pastures. Venison and chamois, a small goatlike antelope, are stewed or salt-cured and dried. *Mocetta,* traditionally a chamois *prosciutto,* is now more commonly made of beef. The local bread—called "black," *pane nero*—is made from rye flour and is the main ingredient in most of the traditional first-course soups. Pasta is nowhere to be found, although rice, *gnocchi,* and *polenta* appear as first courses. Many dishes are enriched with butter and

Fontina cheese, a hallmark of the *cucina valdostana.* Meat is stewed with red wine and spices and served with *polenta;* trout is cooked in butter or red wine.

Regional cheeses can be exceptional. Fontina, made from whole unpasteurized milk, is still produced by small artisanal dairies, stored and aged by cooperatives, and stamped with the seal of the Consortium of Fontina Producers to guarantee quality. *Toma,* made from spring, summer, or fall milk, is found in varying degrees of ripeness ranging from delicate to putrid.

The dramatic finale to a typical meal is *caffè valdostano,* a mixture of coffee, lemon or orange peel, *grappa,* and sugar, sipped from the spouts of a *coppa dell' amicizia* ("friendship cup"), a steaming, squat wooden pot to be passed around among friends at the table.

The Menu

Salumi

Boudin: potato-based blood pudding or sausage
Lardo: salt-cured lard streaked with pork
Mocetta: leg of chamois or ibex, cured like *prosciutto*

Primo

Fonduta: creamy melted Fontina, milk, and eggs, served with *polenta* or toast rounds
Gnocchi alla valdostana: potato *gnocchi* with Fontina sauce
Polenta concia: *polenta* cooked with butter and Fontina
Riso alla valdostana: rice cooked with onion, broth, butter, and Fontina
Seupetta di cogne: rice cooked with broth, Fontina, butter, and stale rye bread
Zuppa alla ueca: soup of vegetables, pork, barley, stale rye bread, and Fontina
Zuppa alla valpellinentze, *or* **alla valdostana:** soup of cabbage, stale rye bread, Fontina and broth, sometimes topped with nutmeg

Secondo

Trota al vino rosso: trout cooked in red wine
Boudin: sausage served with potatoes
Camoscio e polenta: chamois stew, cooked with red wine and spices, served with *polenta*
Carbonada: beef stew cooked with red wine and spices
Costoletta alla valdostana: veal chop stuffed with *prosciutto* and Fontina

Formaggio

Fontina: large reddish wheel, delicate buttery flavor, compact and smooth
Reblec: fresh curdled cream cheese
Robiola: soft, creamy, rich, small round
Toma: medium-size flat round, ranging from bland to feisty
Tomini: small rounds of fresh goat or mixed-milk cheese or coated with herbs (*alle erbe*)

Dolce

Frutta cotta: seasonal fruit, especially the *martin sec* pear, cooked with red wine and spices
Tegole: literally "roof tiles," round curved hazelnut cookies

The Wine List

Italy's smallest region also has the smallest wine production; there's not much space for growing grapes between the Alps and the valleys traversed by torrential mountain streams. However, the people "of the valley," as they refer to themselves, ever industrious, have terraced south-facing slopes for growing limited quantities of native grapes. The wine that these dedicated winemakers produce is barely enough to fill the regional need, and is rarely found outside the Valle d'Aosta. Valle d'Aosta is a new DOC that covers fifteen different wines in almost all of the Aosta Valley's vine-growing territory. Among the best are:

Blanc de Morgex is a delicate dry white made from the local Blanc de Morgex grape, served with first-course dishes and fish. Costantino Charrere and Alberto Vevey are quality producers.

Chambave Rouge is a full dry red, made from Petit Rouge blended with other local grapes, served with meat and game from the mountains. Top producers are La Crotta di Vegneron and Ezio Voyat.

Enfer d'Arvier, the "Arvier Inferno," is a rich dry red made with the Petit Rouge grape, served with meat and regional *cucina,* produced by Co-Enfer.

Passito di Chambave is a sweet, aromatic golden wine, made from the Moscato grape, served with simple desserts or between meals, and at its best produced by Ezio Voyat and La Crotta di Vegneron.

Petit Rouge is a purplish, intense, dry red made from the Petit Rouge grape, served with meat, fowl, and regional *cucina.* Top

producers are Institut Agricole Régional Aoste and G. Gabriele.

Pinot Noir is a lively, purplish, dry red, made from the Pinot Noir grape, produced by the Institut Agricole Régional Aoste, and served with sauced meats and stews.

Torrette is a robust, dry, ruby-red wine made from the Petit Rouge and a blend of local grape varieties. It is served with meat and hearty regional dishes, and produced by Filippo Garin and Les Cretes.

Vin du Conseil is a straw-colored, rich, dry white made from the Petite Arvine grape, served with light first-course dishes and fish. It is produced by the Institut Agricole Régional Aoste.

Regional Specialties

Fontina. Almost all the milk produced in the Valle d'Aosta, from a local breed of over 20,000 cows, is used in the production of Fontina cheese. Cows are trucked from their farms to alpine mountain pastures for a summer of grazing on grass and herbs. Modern-day shepherds, milkers, and cheesemakers use essentially the same techniques that have been used for seven centuries. Fresh whole unpasteurized straight-from-the-cow milk is partially cooked, drained, dry-salted, and aged for at least three months in a cool, humid room. The best cheese is made with milk from cows that have been grazing in high mountain pastures on spring's tender alpine grass and herbs. The Cooperativa di Produttori Latte e Fontina, a cooperative of milk producers and cheesemakers, guarantees the quality of each rust-colored wheel, which may weigh anywhere from seventeen to forty pounds. They seem to have some kind of secret numbering system for coding the valuable high-altitude spring-milk Fontina. I have recently discov-

ered that cheese numbers 10 through 453 indicate high-altitude grazing lands. Will I ever figure out the code for spring milk?

For more information about the cooperative, see page 83.

Lard. Lard (*lardo*), the subcutaneous fat from the dorsal, flank, or shoulder area, is probably the most flavorful part of the pig. The lard from the village of Arnad is cut into chunks, marinated in brine with mountain herbs and spices, and sold in jars that can keep—stored in a cool, dark, well-aired pantry—for a year or two. At its best, it has a rich, complex, buttery sweetness. It is *not* like eating raw bacon.

See page 79.

The martin sec pear and the renetta apple. The *martin sec* pear and the *renetta* apple are typical products of the Aosta Valley culture, with its emphasis on preserving food for the long, hard winters. The small, rough-skinned, rust-colored pear with gray freckles isn't eaten fresh, but preserved—or it is cooked with wine, a typical mountain dessert. The apple is a lumpy ovoid, rough-skinned, straw-colored, with red sun-spot "cheeks." The pulp is white, juicy, and sweeter than most apples.

For apples and apple products, see page 82.

Crafts. The isolation of Valle d'Aosta's mountain winters has inspired one of Italy's finest craft traditions. Five regional I.V.A.T. shops (Institut Valdtain de l'Artisanat Typique) sell handmade lace, hand-loomed woolen blankets, wrought-iron fireplace tools, and beautiful hand-carved wooden objects. Butter molds, graceful scoops, bowls, friendship cups for coffee,

the *grolla,* a chalicelike cup for wine whose origin dates from the Crusades, and other artfully created items are far superior to the junk displayed in most tourist souvenir shops. The Aosta store (via Xavier de Maistre 1) has the largest selection and is open year-round (tel. 0165.40808). The smaller shops in village locations (Cogne, Valtournenche, Gressoney, and Antagnad) are open only during the summer and winter tourist seasons. They have no telephones and may lack a specific street address, but they aren't hard to find. No credit cards are accepted.

See also the Foire de Saint-Ours, page 79.

Cities & Towns

Allein

AGRITOURISM

Lo Ratelè

Frazione Ville 2

☎**0165.78265**

Open Saturday and Sunday by reservation

No credit cards • low inexpensive

Lo Ratelè is a working farm outside Aosta with cows and courtyard animals, with three no-frills rooms, one double and two triples for guests. Meals are served by reservation in the restored stables on the weekends, but guests staying at the farm can dine on weekdays. The Conchatre family works hard, and their food is simple, genuine, traditional. Begin with blood sausage, *prosciutto,* or lard, served with boiled chestnuts. *Polenta* with melty cheese and *seupa valpellinentze* are always on the menu. Nettle *gnocchi* are sauced with butter and cheese. Braised chicken or rabbit, kid or

duck with cabbage from the farm are served with *polenta.* The Conchatres also make fine cheese—Fontina, *caprini* goat cheese. Even the whipped cream for desserts is from their farm. Wines are local.

Aosta

Aosta, situated along the strategically important road to the alpine passes of the Grande and Piccolo San Bernardo, was founded by the Romans in 25 B.C. The Roman and medieval monuments, wide piazzas, and small-town feeling in the center make this city a fun place to visit.

HOTEL

Hotel Europe

Via Ribitel 8

☎**0165.236-363**

Fax 0165.40566

All credit cards • expensive

HOTEL

Rayon de Soleil

Viale Gran San Bernardo
☎0165.262-247
Fax 0165.236-085
All credit cards • moderate

MEAT

Salumeria Anselmo

Via de Tillier 50
☎0165.40187
Closed Thursday afternoon

Salumeria Anselmo has the best selection of meat and *salumi* in town. Their local homemade products—lard (*lardo*), sausage (*boudin*), cured chamois *prosciutto* (*mocetta*), and goose salami (*salame d'oca*)—are first-rate. A few take-out dishes are prepared daily. French, Italian, and a local dialect unlike both languages are spoken here.

CHEESE

Palmira Olivier

Via E. Aubert 36
☎0165.34495
Closed Thursday afternoon

The small, crowded grocery store of Palmira Olivier has the best selection of Val d'Aosta's cheeses, in varying stages of ripeness, made from the milk produced in different months and from different pastures. Spring cheese, made from the milk of cows grazing on tender young wild herbs and grass, is said to be the best. Fontina and *tome* range in taste from delicate to decidedly pungent; freshly curdled *roblec* is more like a custard than a cheese; and *seras* is a kind of ricotta made with the whey left over after making Fontina. These fine and hard-to-find cheeses are available at Palmira Olivier's shop.

WINE

Enoteca La Cave

Via Sestaz 53
☎0165.44164
Closed Monday morning in winter
American Express

La Cave is a family operation, with Mamma Piera and her son Guido selling a surprising selection of quality wines and *grappa*. All the best local, limited-production, hard-to-find wines are usually available, as well as a wide choice of fine Italian wines from almost every region. Swiss enophiles come to La Cave to stock up on their favorites. Informal wine tastings are held on Saturday afternoons.

CRAFTS

Foire de Saint-Ours

January 30–31

The Foire de Saint-Ours, an amazing crafts fair held on the last two days of January, is a 1,000-year-old tradition in the city of Aosta. Hand-fashioned articles are displayed in the streets and piazzas, and prizes are awarded to local craftsmen celebrating their folk art traditions: carved wooden objects—butter molds, scoops, bowls, friendship cups for coffee, *sabots* (wooden clogs), woven baskets, buckets—along with tools, wrought iron, and lace items that are a pleasure to own. Animal sculptures, especially rabbits with graceful upright ears, are special. The yearly poster competition, open to all comers, has resulted in some stunning artwork, displayed during the fair in the Torre dei Signori di Porta S. Orso.

For more information, call the Assessorato Industria, Commercio e Artigianato (tel. 0165.303-523).

Arnad

MEAT

Marilena Bertolin

Via Nazionale 11
☎0125.966-127

"Lard?" my friends said to me when I proposed a taste of the barely pink-streaked, creamy-white *lardo*, a specialty that I had brought back from Arnad, a tiny village on the banks of the Dora Baltea River. "What about the cholesterol?" was the question I encountered most often when I pulled out my jar of Marilena Bertolin's lard. The cholesterol in a thin slice of lard is less than half the equivalent amount of butter, and lard contains fewer calories per gram than olive oil. And it is tasty. Sliced wafer-thin, on a slice of warm bread, slightly melty, lightly perfumed with herbs, and no tough muscular meat to chew, it can be exquisite. If you get hooked on lard, you'll probably be interested in the commemorative festival, with lots of tasting, that takes place at the end of August in Arnad.

Arvier

HOTEL

Le Clou

Via C. Gex 22
☎**0165.99004**
Fax 0165.99323
MasterCard, Visa • low moderate

ENOTECA-RESTAURANT

Café du Bourg

Via Lostan 12
☎**0165.99094**
Open evenings only, closed Thursday
No credit cards • low moderate

The Café du Bourg is close to Courmayeur and merits a visit for the simple food and wonderful well-priced wine selection, chosen by Claudio Jonini. He pairs wines from all over Italy with local lard, Fontina, and his mother's cooking, regional dishes like *carbonada,* blood sausage, *la fonduta, zuppa valpellinese.* Simple pastas, soups, grilled meats, and simple desserts like *crostata* and *tiramisù* round out the menu.

Cervinia

RESTAURANT-INN

Les Neiges d'Antan

Località Perrères

☎**0166.948-775**
Fax 0166.948-852
Closed Monday, and May through July
American Express • high moderate

Situated three kilometers (less than two miles) south of the center of Cervinia, tucked in a ring of hills, Les Neiges d'Antan is a perfect stop for skier-gastronomes. The small hotel has thirty-two simple, functional rooms, plus a large living room with a fireplace and an impressive seven-speaker stereo system and collection of tapes. Husband-host Maurizio and wife-chef Carmen Bich, and their son, sommelier and *tisane* expert Ludovico, all unique individuals, run the hotel and the restaurant in personal style. The *cucina* is mostly regional, hearty mountain food like local *salumi,* wonderful hard-to-find cheeses, grilled meats, *polenta,* fruit cooked in wine and spices or preserved in alcohol, and homemade *gelato.* Wines are mostly Piemontese.

Cogne

HOTEL

Hotel de la Tor

Via Dr. Grappein 76
☎**0165.749-190**
Fax 0165.749-196
All credit cards • moderate

HOTEL

Hotel Sant'Orso

Via Bourgeois 2
☎**/Fax 0165.74821**
MasterCard, Visa • moderate

RESTAURANT

Lou Ressignon

Rue des Mines 92
☎**/Fax 0165.74034**
Closed Monday evening, Tuesday, and September 15–30
All credit cards • low moderate

Skiers and hikers have always come to this typical Valdostano restaurant around midnight for a snack, or a *ressignon*, in the dialect of Cogne. Arturo Allera, ski instructor, sommelier, owner, and *simpatico* host, will welcome you into a cozy room with a blazing fireplace and walls decorated with mountain scenes and antlers. The so-called snacks are partially traditional, with some concessions to tourism (pasta, fondue, Swiss raclette, hot dogs). Stick with the *salumi*, especially the lard and *mocetta*, and first-course *soupetta* (a cheesy Fontina *risotto*) or perhaps *polenta alla valdostana* (*polenta* baked with butter and Fontina). Chamois or veal is stewed in red wine and spices and served with *polenta*. Conclude your meal with Arturo's fine local cheeses. The wine list offers some fantastic local wines as well as a small, personal selection from other regions. A few weeks after we first met, I bumped into Arturo leading a group of restaurateur-bicyclists, pedaling and tasting in the wine country of Friuli, searching for wines to send home.

Courmayeur

Courmayeur, once famous for its mineral waters, was the chic 1800s vacation spot of the royal Savoia family and the Piemontese nobility. It has always been a favorite of skiers and, especially, mountain climbers.

HOTEL

Palace Bron
Via Plan Gorret 37
☎0165.846-742
Fax 0165.844-015
American Express, Diners Club, Visa • expensive

HOTEL

Hotel La Brenva
Entrèves (close by)
☎0165.869-780
Fax 0165.869-726
American Express, Visa • high moderate

CHEESE

Le Bien Faire, La Maison du Fromage
Via Roma 120
☎0165.844-634
Closed Thursday afternoon
No credit cards

A nice selection of regional cheeses can be found at Le Bien Faire, on via Roma, the main drag of Courmayeur.

WINE

Goio
Avenue Mont Blanc 18
☎0165.84282
Closed Thursday afternoon
No credit cards

Goio has a good wine selection and an impressive collection of *grappa*, arrayed in an almost dizzying floor-to-ceiling display.

RESTAURANT

La Maison de Filippo
Entrèves
☎0165.89968
Closed Tuesday, May, and November
American Express • moderate

This is a quintessential rustic mountain restaurant, with attractive prints and paintings, cascades of red geraniums in the summer, a cozy fire in the winter, and a procession of a meal that seems endless. The fixed-price marathon includes an eight-course *antipasto* of bowls, platters, and trays of marinated cheeses, vegetables, anchovies, and cooked ham and sausage with boiled potatoes and cabbage, plus a cutting board of at least six slice-it-yourself *salumi*. Pace yourself to be ready for the first-course choices (try the *zuppa alla valdostana*) and a second course of traditional meat or game dishes. The onslaught continues with the cheese selection; marinated fresh, cooked, and dried fruit; homemade *gelato;* and if you still haven't had enough, a *caffè alla valdostana*. The house wine is pleasant, but a few quality bottles from local producers are also available. This restaurant is used to hungry skiers, and the service is swift and courteous. Dine outside in the summer under the Cinzano umbrellas.

BOOKS AND PRINTS

Leo Garin
Scorciatoia La Palud
☎0165.89164

If you fall in love with Courmayeur and the warmer southern slopes of the mountain you used to think of as Mont Blanc, head for Leo Garin, who sells a lovely selection of prints, paintings, and books of the Valle d'Aosta and Monte Bianco. Call for an appointment.

Gignod

RESTAURANT-INN

Locanda La Clusaz
Frazione La Clusaz 32
☎0165.56075
Closed Tuesday and lunch
No credit cards • moderate

This wonderful home-style Valdostano restaurant, in its farmhouse dating from 1040(!), offers simple heart-and-soul–warming *cucina*. Maurizio Grange serves the same food that his grandfather, who founded the restaurant in 1925, dished out. Homemade sausages (*boudins*), butter, cheese, their own farm-raised beef, pork, vegetables, and honey are the raw materials with which Mamma Vittorina Fiou prepares her traditional dishes. Try the grain soup, *polenta* cooked over a wood-burning fireplace, salt cod (*merluzzo*) on Friday, and *carbonada* (veal stew). Salads are dressed with Maurizio's own walnut oil. The fine selection of regional, Italian, and even French wines is a pleasant surprise in this rustic restaurant.

Gressan

FRUIT

Rodolfo Coquillard
Agrival
La Tour de Villa
☎0165.552-363
Closed Saturday afternoon and Sunday

Rodolfo Coquillard organically grows apples on his seven-acre farm and sells the very best as fresh fruit, mostly to a list of friends who beg for a few kilos each year. The rest of the crop is pressed, and the juice is turned into sweet fermented cider, apple gelatin, and special apple vinegar. The vinegar, called *agro di mele*, is made from the cider of organically grown apples, aged for eighteen months, and bottled in attractive glass bottles. The flavor is fruity, intensely appley, without the aggressiveness of most vinegars.

Hone

HOTEL

Ponte Romano
Piazza IV Novembre 14, Pont St. Martin (nearby)
☎0125.804-320
Fax 0125.807-108
All credit cards • inexpensive

RESTAURANT

Osteria della Società Cooperativa
Via Colliard 77
☎0125.803-241
Closed Monday
No credit cards • inexpensive to low moderate

This is a quintessential *osteria*, with local cardplayers tossing back glasses of wine. Check out the blackboard that lists the daily specials, like cabbage soup, *risotto*, braised beef served with *polenta*, as well as dishes from nearby Piemonte, like *bagna cauda* and boiled meats. *Salumi*, especially lard and *mocetta*, are first-rate. Vegetarians may actually be able to find something to eat here, but it's wise to call and let them know. The wines are local and from Piemonte.

Saint-Christophe

RESTAURANT-HOTEL

Albergo Ristorante Casale
Regione Candemine 1
☎**0165.541-203**
Fax 0165.541-962
Closed Sunday evening, Monday, and December
American Express • high moderate

Brothers Fulvio and Ugo Casale and their wives, Mafalda and Chiara, prepare and serve a fixed menu at their hotel restaurant, an abundant review of the entire *cucina valdostana*. Start with rye bread, butter, and local honey; continue with *salumi*, soups, *polenta*, meats, trout, cheese, and dessert. A fun meal in the antiminimalist style. Fulvio and Ugo are both sommeliers and pair quality local wines with their regional *cucina*. Drink a *grappa* from the wide selection, and when you can feast no more, trudge upstairs to one of Casale's simple rooms.

CHEESE

Cooperativa Produttori Latte e Fontina della Valle d'Aosta
Croix Noire
St. Christophe
☎**0165.40551**
Closed Monday morning

You can buy Fontina directly from the cooperative five days a week.

Valsavarenche

HOTEL-RESTAURANT

Hostellerie du Paradis
Località Eau Rousse
☎**0165.905-972**
Fax 0165.905-971
Always open
All credit cards • moderate restaurant, inexpensive hotel

In the valley that leads to Gran Paradiso, the Hostellerie du Paradis is a wonderful hotel for skiers and hikers. The restaurant serves supertraditional cooking created with local ingredients. Dine on *salumi* or game pâté, *polenta alla valdostana*, or *fonduta*. The selection of artisanally made cheeses is fine, the house wine is worth drinking, and they've got some outer-regional wines too.

Verrès

RESTAURANT-INN

Hotel Ristorante da Pierre
Via Martorey 43
☎**0125.929-376**
Fax 0125.920-404
Closed Tuesday, except in July and August
American Express, Diners Club • high moderate to expensive

Da Pierre has two warm rooms for winter dining—decorated with pewter plates and hand-carved wooden crafts on the walls—and for the summer, a patio with huge pine trees and pots overflowing with geraniums. The *cucina* is seasonal, and takes a more creative look at regional ingredients than do most restaurants: *salumi*, homemade pasta, salmon trout, game, and wonderful cheeses, especially the *bichette dans le nid* (baked goat cheese served on a bed of chicory lettuce). Enjoy one of the fine regional wines. Spend the night in one of the twelve fully equipped rooms, and visit the nearby castles of Verrès and Issogne. And if castles don't appeal to you, you can dance until dawn at the hotel's disco, Crazy Things.

Liguria is a narrow arc of land stretching from France to Toscana. It is backed by the Alps and Apennine Mountains, which form a barrier against the cold northern winds, and fronted by the *Mar Ligure*, whose sea air mitigates the winter weather—southern Mediterranean palms, giant oleanders, and orange and lemon trees thrive here, at the same latitude as Maine.

Liguria

The western coast is known as the Riviera di Ponente, "the coast where the sun sets," and the eastern coast as the Riviera di Levante, "the coast where the sun rises." Historically, Liguria's contacts with the outside world were primarily by sea. The region was originally populated by the ancient Ligure and later ruled by the Greeks, Saracens, Romans, Venetians, Lombards, French, and Piemontese, and influenced, through trade, by Sicily, Spain, and northern Africa.

The cuisine of the seafaring Ligurians is dominated by the color green. Products of this warm Mediterranean climate include fresh herbs, tasty early-ripening vegetables, and delicately perfumed, sweet extra virgin olive oil—perfect with fish and essential to the preparation of *pesto*, the crushed basil sauce that put Liguria on the gastronomic map. *Focaccia*, a flatbread sprinkled with herbs and olive oil, or stuffed with cheese, is sold at most bakeries and may be offered along with bread in some restaurants. *La farinata*, a chick-pea-flour crepe baked in a pizza oven, may be more difficult to pin down, because it's usually sold only in the morning. The *torta pasqualina*, a vegetable tart with thirty-three paper-thin layers of pastry, shows clear signs of northern African or Greek influence. *Cappon magro*, literally "lean capon," is a Christmas Eve tradition for a meatless dinner, a counterpoint to the next day's real capon and an architectural triumph; a pyramid of layered shrimp, lobster, oysters, fish, boiled vegetables, and sea biscuits, flavored with a sauce containing pine nuts, anchovies, and capers. Pastureless Liguria depends on courtyard animals, mostly chicken and rabbit, for its meat. Vegetable stuffings (*ripieni*) are piped into hollowed-out vegetables or simply baked and cut into squares. Pastry shops sell *torta genovese,* a yellow, egg-rich sponge cake (mysteriously known throughout the baking world by its French name, *genoise*) rarely found in restaurants. Most Ligurian meals end with fruit or nontraditional desserts.

It seems that the *cucina* of Liguria was styled for its navigators who, nauseated by the ever-present perfumes of the spices they traded, sought the fresh-tasting herbs and vegetables they missed during their long, dangerous sea voyages. Or was it formed by the Genovese, with their reputation for extreme parsimony? In any case, the Ligurian table is a palette of greens and a wealth of pungent herbal flavors.

The scenic panorama that has made the Ligurian Riviera famous has attracted hordes of tourists, and restaurants on the coast frequently cater to unsuspecting travelers, serving mediocre food at best. Beware!

The Menu

Salumi

Salumi di suino:　salami or sausage, usually found inland

Salami di Sant'Olcese: pork and beef salami

Antipasto

Acciughe marinate:　fresh anchovies marinated in lemon juice

Acciughe sotto sale:　salt-cured anchovies

Farinata:　large chick-pea-flour crepe, baked in an oven, served in wedges

Panissa or paniccia:　chick-pea-flour *polenta,* served with onions

Sardenaira or pissadella: anchovy, olive, onion, and tomato pizza

Torta pasqualina:　"Easter tart," with thirty-three paper-thin layers of pastry, stuffed with chard, artichokes, ricotta, and whole hard-cooked eggs. (Cooks in a rush make do with eighteen layers of pastry.) Everyday versions—only four layers of pastry—of this vegetable tart are made with zucchini, peas, fava beans, or winter squash.

Primo

Ciuppin:　fish stew

Corzetti:　hand-rolled pasta cut into disks with a wooden stamp that embosses a pattern, usually star-shaped, on the rounds

Corzetti alla polceverasca: figure-eight–shaped pasta served with butter, pine nuts, and herb, meat, or walnut sauce

Mesciua:　soup of chick-peas, wheat, and beans, served with pepper and olive oil

Minestrone col pesto: thick vegetable soup containing pasta, served with *pesto, pecorino sardo* (sheep's milk cheese to be grated), and Parmesan

Pansoti or pansotti:　ravioli stuffed with cheese and borage or chard, served with a creamy walnut sauce

Pesto:　a sauce made of fresh basil, pounded in a stone mortar with pine nuts, garlic, *pecorino sardo,* Parmesan, and olive oil

Riso col preboggion:　soup made with rice and field greens, *pesto,* and grated Parmesan

Trenette col pesto:　thin strips of pasta served with *pesto.* The authentic version should contain string beans and pieces of boiled potato.

Trofie *or* troffie al pesto: homemade lightninglike squiggles of pasta, served with *pesto,* potatoes, and string beans

Tuccu (*or* tocco) de nuxe: creamy paste of walnuts, garlic, bread, and at times, *prescinsoea,* a yogurtlike cheese

Tuccu (*or* tocco) di carne: meat sauce, used with pasta

Tuccu (*or* tocco) di funghi: mushroom sauce, used with pasta

Secondo

Baccalà alla genovese: strips of salt cod in a tomato sauce

Bollito freddo: cold salad of boiled beef, sea biscuit, anchovies, capers, and olive oil and vinegar

Buridda: fish stew prepared with salt cod and dried mushrooms or with fresh fish

Cappon magro *or* cappun magru: layered pyramid of mixed fish, sea biscuits, and vegetables, garnished with lobsters, shrimp, oysters, clams, mussels, and olives, in a sauce containing anchovies, garlic, and capers

Cima alla genovese: veal breast stuffed with veal pâté, brains, sweetbreads, peas, pine nuts, Parmesan, and eggs, wrapped in a cloth, boiled, chilled, and sliced

Condion *or* condiggion *or* condijun: salad of sea biscuits, tomatoes, cucumber, lettuce, and thinly sliced dried tuna or pressed mullet roe, dressed with olive oil and vinegar

Coniglio in umido: rabbit cooked with rosemary, bay leaves, white wine, pine nuts, and nutmeg

Frittata di bieta: pan-fried flan with chard

Frittata di carciofi: pan-fried egg and artichoke flan

Frittata di gianchetti (*or* bianchetti): pan-fried egg flan made with tiny sardines or anchovies

Frittata di zucchini (*or* fiori di zucca): pan-fried egg and zucchini (or zucchini flower) flan

Lattughe ripiene: braised lettuce stuffed with eggs, vegetables, fish, ground meat, or chicken

Scabecio: fried fish, marinated in vinegar, onions, garlic, sage, and rosemary; similar to the Venetian *saor*

Scorzanera: salsify (oyster plant) root, served braised or deep-fried

Stecchi alla genovese: either a mixture of veal sweetbreads, brains, breast, and mushrooms; or an artichoke wrapped with a dense béchamel sauce; both skewered and deep-fried

Stoccafisso in tocchetto: salt cod cooked with tomatoes, and dried mushrooms

Tomaxelle: braised veal rolls stuffed with ground meat, mushrooms, and potatoes or beans, served with Parmesan

Triglie alla genovese: red mullet baked with a sauce of fennel seeds, white wine, capers, and tomato paste

Formaggio

Formaggella *or* formagetta: fresh cheese found inland, rarely ripened

Dolce

Castagnaccio: flat, unleavened chestnut-flour cake with raisins

Pandolce genovese: Christmas yeast bread with candied fruit and pine nuts

Pasta genovese: the original *genoise:* yellow egg-rich sponge cake

The Wine List

A rocky coast backed by steep mountains isn't the most hospitable environment for grapevines, and Liguria's small production of quality wines is destined to be consumed locally. Few restaurants on the much-touristed coast emphasize quality wine, and the house wines you find will probably be nothing special.

The DOC **Cinque Terre** wine, made with the Bosco, Vermentino, and Albrola grapes, can be a dry delicate white, perfect with fish and seafood; produced by Cooperative Agricola di Cinqueterre. Or with a stroke of luck you may find **Sciacchetrà**, a legendary amber dessert wine that can also be served as an aperitif. Liana Rolandi is the top producer.

Granaccia di Quiliano is a non-DOC rich dry red made from the local Granaccia grape, served with meat and cheese. Scarrone is the best producer.

The **Riviera Ligure di Ponente,** a DOC area along the western Riviera, produces the following wines: **Pigato di Albenga,** a full dry white, and **Vermentino,** a delicate, fresh dry white, both served with fish and seafood; **Pornassio Ormeasco,** a rich spicy red; and **Rossese,** a soft dry red, served with fowl, rabbit, and regional *cucina.* Top producers are Anfossi, Bruna, Cascina Feipu dei Massaretti (Parodi), Colle dei Bardellini, and Lupi.

The DOC **Rossese di Dolceacqua,** made of local Rossese grapes, is a lush dry red, best when paired with meat, game, fowl, and rabbit. Croesi, G. B. Cave (Mandino), and Guglielmi are the best producers.

Regional Specialties

Extra Virgin Olive Oil. Ligurian extra virgin olive oil, made from a local olive called *la taggiasca,* is delicate, sweet, more golden than green. Some of Italy's largest commercial manufacturers of olive oil, usually labeled "pure" olive oil in the United States and simply "*olio di oliva*" in Italy, are located in this region. Their oils are made of olives imported from Spain, Greece, or northern Africa and refined in Liguria, and are to be avoided. Read the label carefully and look for *olio extra vergine di oliva,* which is made with the first "soft" pressing of olives.
Chick-pea Crepes. La *farinata* is a flat crepe made of chick-pea flour, water, and salt, drizzled with olive oil and a sprinkle of black pepper, and ideally baked in a wood-burning pizza oven. The best *farinata* is sold in *friggitorie* (fry shops) or in restaurants with pizza ovens, and is usually found in the morning, around 10 A.M. Some restaurants, rediscovering a neglected traditional gem, are serving slices of *farinata* covered with fresh rosemary as an appetizer with a glass of sparkling wine, a splendid idea.

Fine chick-pea flour (*farina di ceci*) is produced by the Mulino di Pegli. For the tastiest *farinata,* see pages 98 and 100.

Local hardware stores in Liguria sell

shallow round baking pans—in tin-lined copper or in less expensive aluminum—for making *farinata.*

Pesto. Does the basil in Liguria really taste better than that grown in any other region of Italy, as locals claim? Is the small-leafed basil with a cult following really in an entirely different league? I'm not quite sure, but I do know that *pesto,* the sauce that placed Liguria in the Culinary Hall of Fame, made of basil, garlic, olive oil, pine nuts, and grated cheese, tastes better in Liguria than it does anywhere else. It's not an ancient dish, documented only from the early nineteenth century, but based on crushed nut or seed sauces, a tradition that dates from the medieval era.

Pesto mavens mash garlic and salt in a marble mortar with a wooden pestle, adding a few basil leaves at a time, rotating the pestle to pulverize the basil, adding pine nuts, which soak up the basil liquid, crushing the whole mass, adding grated *pecorino* and *parmigiano* to form a thick paste, which is transferred to a bowl and thinned with Ligurian extra virgin olive oil. Although most restaurants nowadays use a food processor or blender, *pesto* purists would never submit their special basil to a blade.

Pesto sauces handmade pasta or *trenette,* flat strands that in the classic preparation are cooked with potatoes and green beans. The additional starch of the potatoes helps the *pesto* stick to the pasta. I have no idea what the green beans do. You can purchase seeds for Genovese basil (*basilico*), but bear in mind that the *pesto* will never taste the way it does in Liguria.

Herbs. It's claimed that Ligurian mariners, who sailed great distances in spice-filled ships, longed for the fresh herbal flavors of the land when they came home. Spice is rarely found in the *cucina* of Liguria, but intensely perfumed herbs

abound. Although basil gets better press, the region's herb of choice is marjoram (*maggiorana*), present in far more dishes than basil. Marjoram flavors chick-pea fritters; walnut *pesto; pansotti,* herb-and-cheese–stuffed triangles; *torta pasqualina; cima,* stuffed veal; *tomaxelle;* stuffed meat rolls; and more. Marjoram is sold fresh in most markets and produce shops.

Preboggion ("cooking greens" in dialect) are a combination of wild greens, an important element paired with rice or in the stuffing of *pansotti,* which traditionally called for seven wild greens and herbs. Swiss chard has become the domesticated substitute for some cooks, although *preboggion* can be found in Ligurian markets and produce shops.

Primizie (Early Vegetables). Liguria, with its mild coastal climate, was once a major citrus-growing area, supplying much of northern Europe with oranges, lemons, and citrons before the late eighteenth-century construction industry began to carpet the coast and harbors with buildings. Terraced gardens and valleys, graced by the favorable climate, yielded the season's first examples of eagerly awaited produce, called *primizie,* now grown in terraced greenhouses packed along southern slopes and inland valleys throughout the region.

Pale-skinned, trumpet-shaped *trombette* zucchini, white-stalked purple-tipped asparagus, green beans, and most spring vegetables are consumed locally as well as exported throughout northern Italy and Europe. One of the vegetal glories of Liguria is the artichoke that French chef Parmentier called "Genovese sugar"—he had them brought to Paris in a carriage. The farm of Mario Anfossi grows the *violetto spinoso di Albenga,* a local purple and green variety of artichoke with thorn-tipped leaves, grown with minimal chemical intervention far from the time of harvest. They're sold fresh from November to March, or preserved under olive oil, or ground into a paste, sold in jars along with extra virgin olive oil, *pesto,* olives, olive paste, and more at the Anfossi farm outside Albenga (via Pacini 39, Bastia). Call or Fax Mario (tel. 0182.20024, fax 0182.21457) to arrange a visit and tasting of his fine products.

Chestnuts and Chestnut Flour. Chestnuts from the mountains were often the mainstay of a diet imposed by poverty, a cheap source of protein and carbohydrates known as "bread of the poor." Chestnuts are dried and ground to produce chestnut flour, once used to make chestnut *polenta,* a dish so austere that it's never found on menus. Chestnut flour is combined with summer wheat flour, utilized to make pasta, usually *piccagge,* strips like *fettuccine,* with a barely sweet and smoky flavor, often paired with *pesto.* I couldn't find a commercial source for chestnut flour, but Franco Solari of Ca' Peo, gets his chestnut flour from a nearby farmer and is willing to sell some to those who are interested. See page 100. Fausto Oneto of Trattoria ü Giancu (see page 101) serves chestnut pasta.

Focaccia. Don't bother eating regular bread in Liguria. This is the land of *focaccia* (foh-CAH-cha), the flatbread drizzled with extra virgin olive oil that's sweeping American bakeries. It's found throughout the region of Liguria plain, herbed, or studded with olives, and is always the best choice in bakeries or breadbaskets.

Manuelina in Recco invented the *focaccia al formaggio* at her stage-post *trattoria* founded in 1885. This *focaccia* is two flattened layers of bread dough with a mild cheese filling, drizzled with local extra virgin olive oil, baked in a wood-burning oven. See page 102 for the original source or look for it in Ligurian bakeries.

Salame di Sant'Olcese. The Ligurian *salame* from the Sant'Olcese in the province of Genova is familiar to most Americans as Genoa salami; a finely ground combination of pork and beef, spiced, packed into casing, and lightly smoked before aging. One of the best producers is Federico Parodi (via Sant'Olcese 63, tel. 010.709-827, closed Monday morning and Wednesday afternoon). He's a fourth-generation salami maker, but has made a few concessions to modern taste, which prefers a less smoky, less aged product. "One slice was eaten with a loaf of bread, now people have a slice with a *grissino* and want a more delicate flavor," says Federico. He barely smokes his fine *salame* with slow-burning hardwood, then ages them for around a month. The results are worth a detour.

Anchovies and Cod. The Ligurian Sea is deep, with tricky currents and winds, without a great variety of fish. However, anchovies abound and are eaten fresh, one of the great bites of the Mediterranean, or preserved, layered whole with salt, in wooden barrels in the past but now in glass or clay containers. Carts from Liguria used to travel north to Piemonte, exchanging their cargo of cured anchovies for barrels of wine, which they brought back to Liguria.

Genova was one of the most important ports of the Mediterranean for cod—salt-cured *baccalà* or air-cured *stoccafisso.* With over 100 fast days, the regional reputation for parsimony, and a limited supply of local fish, cured cod became an important part of the Ligurian diet. The best quality is known as *ragno,* from Ragnar, the name of the original Norwegian exporter. Cod can be frequently found on *trattoria* menus, especially on Fridays. It's sold already soaked in groceries or dried, at fish markets, in the preserved-fish section along with jars of salt-cured anchovies and frozen

REGIONAL PRODUCERS

These are some of Liguria's quality producers of extra virgin olive oil and olive paste.

Dino Abbo
Via Roma 2/bis
Lucinasco
☎ 0183.52411

Benza e Lupi
Via S. Lorenzo 1
Dolcedo
☎ 0183.280-132

Nanni Ardoino
Via Torino 156
Imperia
☎ 0183.279-717

Laura Marvaldi
Mulino aldilà dell'acqua
Borgomaro
☎ 0183.54031

---

fish. Don't even think about taking cured cod home to the U.S.—it's illegal. And it has an almost indelible, highly unpleasant odor. But cured jarred anchovies are legal and make a fine culinary souvenir.

Cookies. *Amaretti* cookies made with almonds, egg whites, honey, and flour are a tradition imported to Liguria from nearby Piemonte, but the Ligurian interpretation is different, softer and moister. Many towns make *amaretti*, but the most famous ones come from Sassello; wrapped in waxed paper and a layer of brightly colored, fringed paper, they are far more attractive than conventional *amaretti*. Amaretti Virginia (buy them at Bar Jole in Sassello, piazza Rolla 11, tel. 019.724-136) have been making their cookies since 1860; the artisanal *amaretti* of Pasticceria Rossi (via Badano 28, tel. 019.724-101, closed Saturday and Sunday) come in an attractive Art Nouveau tin; both producers have their fans. Many pastry shops sell cookies that resemble the *baci* of Piemonte, sometimes called *baxin* in Ligurian dialect.

Sciacchetrà Dessert Wine. This excellent legendary dessert wine—rich, amber, semi-sweet—is almost impossible to find, especially outside of the Cinque Terre, an isolated, inaccessible necklace of five small villages strung along the Ligurian coast north of La Spezia. Terraced vineyards on cliffs overlooking the sea are difficult to harvest, and ensure a small production.

The best examples I've found are produced by Liana Rollandi, available at the Enoteca Internazionale (see page 95) by the bottle or the glass.

Wooden Pasta Stamps. Wooden stamps are used to cut and emboss a pattern, usually star-shaped, on hand-rolled pasta. The resulting silver-dollar–sized pasta rounds are known as *corzetti*. The symbol, like a watermark or designer's initials, identifies its creator. The attractive stamps are handmade and can be used to emboss a decorative pattern on cookie dough or butter if you're not interested in making *corzetti*.

See page 94.

Cities & Towns

Ameglia

RESTAURANT-HOTEL
Locanda dell'Angelo-Paracucchi
Via XXV Aprile
☎0187.64391
Fax 0187.64393
Always open
All credit cards • expensive restaurant, moderate hotel

Not far from the Roman ruins of Luni, the Locanda dell'Angelo is one of the gastronomic high points of Liguria. Owner-chef Angelo Paracucchi works magic with coastal ingredients. Fish and seafood taste of the sea, and tender early vegetables are flavored with herbs, extra virgin olive oil from his native Umbria, and an occasional dash of balsamic vinegar. Light sauces enhance, never overwhelm, their dishes. The wine list is excellent, although local wines are mostly ignored. Desserts range from refreshing to decadent, and the after-dinner pastries are irresistible. Paracucchi is a true professional, and he has brought his personal vision of Italian *cucina* to Carpaccio, his restaurant in Paris. The Locanda dell'Angelo isn't the same when he's not in the kitchen. The restaurant, and the thirty-six-room hotel, designed in the late 1970s by architect Vico Magistretti, could use some touch-ups.

Angelo Paracucchi has created a line of jarred products that capture the elusive flavors of Ligurian food. Artichokes with marjoram; Bacchus sauce in balsamic and raspberry flavors; sauces for pasta flavored with vegetables, meat, or fish; vegetable sauces for meat and fish; and preserves are all prepared with Angelo's recipes. The sauces are perfect for lazy cooks, and the Locanda will mail them home for those who don't love to schlep heavy glass jars around.

Bogliasco

HOTEL
See Genova

RESTAURANT
Il Tipico
Via Poggio Favaro 4
☎010.347-0754
Fax 010.347-1061
Closed Monday
All credit cards • high moderate

Il Tipico, a *trattoria* grown into restaurant, has a handsome view of a not-so-handsome coastline. The Paoloni brothers, Angelo and Aldo, and their wives, Graziella and Silvana, serve "typical," as their name proclaims, Ligurian *cucina* with an occasional hint of their Tuscan origins. Fresh fish, local seafood, and seasonal vegetables are flavored with a wide variety of herbs. *Risotto* is nicely prepared, and carnivores will enjoy the grilled *Fiorentina* (steak) or *capretto* (kid). Ligurian wines, mostly quality, are served by sommelier Marco Farnè. Service and *cucina* deteriorate on Sundays and holidays, when Il Tipico fills to capacity with Genovese families escaping the city for lunch.

Borgio Verezzi

HOTEL
Villa Rose
Via Sauro 1
☎019.610-462
Fax 019.610-461
All credit cards • inexpensive

RESTAURANT
DOC
Via V. Emanuele 1
☎/Fax 019.611-477

Closed Monday, but not from June to September
American Express, MasterCard, Visa • low
expensive

Chef Paolo and sommelier Cinzia Alberelli's restaurant is aptly named DOC, a synonym for first-rate in Italian. This enthusiastic husband-and-wife team have created a charming restaurant in a turn-of-the-century villa. Paolo defines his cooking as creative Mediterranean, but a few Ligurian classics are always on the menu. All cooking is based on the best local ingredients that Paolo can get his hands on. Look for anchovies and *ciuppin* (fish soup), homemade pasta, grilled or sauced fish, mushrooms and black truffles in season. Breads flavored with walnuts or olives and featherweight *focaccia*, plain or with herbs, are baked daily at the restaurant, and all desserts, including *gelato*, are homemade. Check out the fantastic Ligurian extra virgin olive oils. Cinzia's selection of regional and national wines, *grappe*, and distillates is a gem-studded pleasure.

Camogli

HOTEL

Casmona
Salita Pineto 13
☎0185.770-015
Fax 0185.775-030
All credit cards • moderate in season,
inexpensive the rest of the year

RESTAURANT

Rosa
Largo F. Casabona 11
☎0185.773-411
Fax 0185.771-088
Closed Tuesday and November to January
All credit cards • high moderate

Large windows overlook the port, and a holm oak grows in the middle of the dining room of this classic seaside restaurant with a view. Chef Giovanni Bocchia has cooked

for two generations of Costa owners and works closely with Maria Rosa Costa, who is passionate about marine biology and picky about fish. The menu features classic Ligurian cooking and superfresh fish, especially "blue fish" like anchovies, sardines, and mackerel. Warm seafood salad is fresh and lively, traditional pasta like *pansoti* with walnut sauce and *trofie* with *pesto* are always on the menu along with pasta sauced with fish or seafood. Fine main-course options include *frittura mista* with larval fish and baby squidlets that are all crunch, "drowned" *moscardini* (curled octopus), grilled whole fish, and crustacea. Conclude with *camogliesi* (almond-paste cookies), or the simple homemade desserts. The wine list is ample and well priced.

Castelnuovo Magra

Castelnuovo Magra, on the border between Toscana and Liguria, has the air of another era, with its castle ruins and views of vineyards, olive trees, and the not-too-distant coast.

AGRITOURISM

Cascina dei Peri
Via Montefrancio 71
☎/Fax 0187.674-085
No credit cards • low inexpensive

HOTEL

Villa Irene
Via delle Macchie 125
Ronchi (close by)
☎0585.309-310
Fax 0585.308-038
No credit cards • low expensive

RESTAURANT

L'Armanda
Piazza Garibaldi 6
☎0187.674-410
Closed Wednesday
MasterCard, Visa • moderate

The perfumes and flavors of the food at this simple restaurant are straightforward, with no pretense. Carolina Ponzanelli, known as Armanda, presides in the kitchen of her *trattoria* with daughter-in-law Luciana, and son Valerio is in the dining room. *Salumi* are local. Essential dishes of the inland *cucina*—stuffed vegetables, *polenta* with cabbage and beans, and lamb, rabbit, tripe or *baccalà*—are all beautifully prepared and tasty. The herbs that grow in this unforgiving meager soil are almost grayish, less lush-looking than hothouse herbs, but intense. They enhance all the dishes that are served in this rustic restaurant. The wines, a fine selection of local and Italian gems, are a joy to drink, an added dimension to a wonderful meal. Reservations are a must.

Chiavari

HOTEL

Monte Rosa
Via Marinetti 6
☎0185.300-321
Fax 0185.312-868
All credit cards • moderate in season, inexpensive the rest of the year

RESTAURANT

Luchin
Via Bighetti 53
☎0185.301-063
Closed Sunday
No credit cards • low moderate

This is one of the oldest authentic *osterie* in Liguria, tucked under a portico in the heart of medieval Chiavari, founded in 1907 by Luca Bonino (nicknamed Luchin), the grandfather of current owner Toni Bonino. Everyone who eats at this popular *osteria* begins with *farinata*, prepared to perfection in a wood-burning oven. Pasta or *minestrone* with *pesto*, vegetable *torte*, *cima* (stuffed veal), salt cod, anchovies, and simple homemade desserts are among the

choices on the hyper-traditional menu. The house wine isn't bad, but Toni has a small selection of Ligurian wines for more exigent palates. Eat at big tables or outside under the portico in the summer.

CRAFTS

Franco Casoni
Via Bighetti 73
☎0185.301-448
Franco Casoni, woodcarver and sculptor, makes pasta stamps for *corzetti* (see page 91) at his workshop in Chiavari. He also carves female figures that grace the prows of Ligurian ships, and statuettes for traditional Ligurian crèche scenes.

Cinque Terre

The Cinque Terre, the "five lands" (Monterosso, Vernazza, Corniglia, Manarola, Riomaggiore), is an isolated necklace of five small villages strung along the coast north of La Spezia, linked only by the railway and a footpath along the cliffs overlooking the sea. Their culinary claims to fame include Sciacchetrà, a legendary, hard-to-find dessert wine, and *pesto*. Natives insist that their basil is sweeter and more aromatic than any other and that their delicate golden olive oil is the best suited to the lively green fresh-tasting sauce. During the summer, beaches are dotted with umbrellas, and hotel rooms may be scarce, although an easily infiltrated network of boardinghouses provides rooms for those drawn to the blue water and picturesque rocky coastline. The twisting road to the Cinque Terre is hazardous at best, a real "cliffhanger." The train from La Spezia may be faster and less harrowing, as mountain tunnels occasionally open for a few seconds of bright, breathtaking sea views.

HOTEL

Porta Roca
Monterosso

☎**0187.817-502**
Fax 0187.817-692
American Express, MasterCard, Visa •
expensive

HOTEL
Baia
Via Fegina 88
Monterosso
☎**0187.817-512**
Fax 0187.818-322
MasterCard, Visa • moderate

RESTAURANT-ROOMS
De Mananan
Via Fieschi 117
Corniglia
☎**0187.821-166**
Closed Tuesday, always open in summer
No credit cards • low moderate, inexpensive
rooms

This typical *trattoria* hasn't been ruined by the flocks of tourists that visit the Cinque Terre every year. Vegetarians will have an easy time, with stuffed herbed vegetables, vegetable appetizers, *mesciua* (legume and grain soup), pasta with *pesto* or walnut sauce, homemade ravioli. Everyone else should opt for fresh anchovies in any form, especially marinated, one of the tastiest bites in Liguria. Off-season visitors will find rabbit or wild boar and mushrooms on the menu. Husband Agostino Galetti and wife Marianne Pfeifer are teamed in the kitchen, sister-in-law Sondra Rigelli waits on tables and helps Marianne with desserts like the simple *ciambella*, fruit tarts, *mascarpone* custard, and fig gratin. The house wine is decent, inexpensive, but bottled wines from the local Cantina Sociale cooperative are also available. Agostino and Marianne rent inexpensive studio apartments that sleep two to four in their attractive farmhouse, a five-minute walk from town, overlooking vineyards, flanked by pine trees.

WINE
Enoteca Internazionale
Via Roma 62
☎**0187.817-278**
Closed Tuesday
All credit cards

Francesco and Laura Giusti's wine shop in Monterosso, the largest of the Cinque Terre towns, has an excellent selection of Ligurian wines, sold by the glass or the bottle. They sell authentic Sciacchetrà, the dessert wine, produced by Liana Rollandi, and quality extra virgin olive oil and local honey. The bench in front of the Enoteca Internazionale, always well populated by natives, is the best place to find out about rooms or apartment rentals. In fact, finding a place to stay may be the highlight of your trip!

PASTRY
Pasticceria Laura
Via Vittorio Emanuele 59
Monterosso
No phone
Closed Monday except in summer

If you need a dessert more substantial than *gelato* or fruit, stroll to Laura Desimoni's *pasticceria* for a taste of *la monterossina*, her layered chocolate cream tart.

RESTAURANT
Al Carugio
Via San Pietro 9
Monterosso
☎**0187.817-453**
No credit cards • moderate

Al Carugio serves regional *cucina* as straightforward as its nautical decor. The menu features marinated fresh anchovies, potato *gnocchi* sauced with *pesto*, nicely cooked *risotto*, homemade ravioli, and best of all, fresh seafood and fish from the Ligurian Sea—simply prepared, deep-fried, grilled, or baked. Finish with fresh fruit or *macedonia* (fruit salad). The wines are local, light, and go well with the simple menu.

RESTAURANT

Gambero Rosso

Piazza Marconi 7

Vernazza

☎0187.812-265

Closed Monday, November, and weekdays December through March; open every day in summer

No credit cards • moderate

Vernazza, a sleepy fishing village awakened to the music of tourism, is probably the most characteristic of the Cinque Terre. The Gambero Rosso, with its maritime look, serves fine local cooking. Lemon-marinated anchovies are well prepared, and will keep you busy while you wait (longer than you expected in the height of the tourist season) for tasty traditional first-course *primi* like *troffie al pesto, pansotti al timo,* and *ravioli di pesce* (fish-stuffed ravioli). Main-course options include stuffed mussels, *acciughe alla vernazzina* (anchovies baked with potatoes and onions), or the day's catch, lightly grilled with fresh herbs, served with a wedge of local lemon. Olive oil and wine are also local, although quality wines from other regions also are available. Reserve a table outside in the summertime.

RESTAURANT

Gianni Franzi

Via Visconti 2

Vernazza

☎0187.812-228

Closed Wednesday, January, and February

No credit cards • moderate

Chef Gianni, his wife, Dea, sister Lina, aunt Maria, and other assorted family members run the restaurant Gianni Franzi, and have since 1960. Dine outdoors overlooking the harbor, or in the main dining room with its rough rock walls, on authentic *trenette al pesto, acciughe al forno* (anchovies baked

with potatoes and tomatoes), *acciughe ripiene fritte* (stuffed fried anchovies), *zuppa di datteri* (clam stew), or stuffed mussels. Desserts are simple and homemade; wines are mostly local.

Garlenda

RESTAURANT-HOTEL

La Meridiana–Il Rosmarino

Regione San Rocco 15

☎0182.580-271

Fax 0182.580-150

Closed November and December

All credit cards • low expensive for the restaurant, luxury for the hotel

Il Rosmarino, the Hotel La Meridiana's restaurant, has set out to prove that hotel dining doesn't have to be horrible or outrageously expensive. The *cucina* is predominantly Ligurian, utilizing locally grown vegetables, extra virgin olive oil, fish from the coast, and lots of herbs. At times the results may seem a bit nouvelle, but if you've eaten one too many *ripiene* or *farinate* and crave a bit of lighter cooking, you'll enjoy the food at Il Rosmarino. Flavors are basic, all ingredients are of the highest quality—fresh and local—and owner Edmondo Segre's passionate interest in food and wine seems to have inspired the kitchen staff to greater heights. The wine list has been carefully chosen and includes fine regional, Italian, and even Californian wines. The luxurious hotel La Meridiana, part of the Relais & Chateaux group, is splendid, with a swimming pool, eighteen-hole golf course, riding, tennis, sauna, and service with a capital S. Reservations are required for the restaurant.

Genova

Genova, Italy's most important port, sprawls along thirty kilometers (nineteen miles) of coast, from Voltri to Nervi, hiding its medieval origins in one of the nation's largest historic centers. Bombed heavily during World War II, parts of Genova still seem to be awaiting repair. The area along the port is seedy-looking, but the narrow lanes called *carugi* and the impressive Renaissance and baroque palaces give Genova a unique charm. Beware of August, when it seems that the entire city—for the most part without air conditioning—closes, probably due to the excessive heat.

HOTEL
Bristol
Via XX Settembre 35
☎010.592-541
Fax 010.561-756
All credit cards • expensive

HOTEL
Agnello d'Oro
Vico delle Monachette 6
☎010.262-084
Fax 010.262-327
All credit cards • moderate

BAR-CAFFÈ
Klainguti
Piazza Soziglia 102
☎010.296-502
Closed Sunday

Klainguti is one of Genova's best bars, even if its name doesn't sound very Italian. It was founded in 1828 by Swiss pastry chefs who emigrated to Italy at the turn of the century, and the pastry work has always been fine. Giuseppe Verdi—and "Sir John Falstaff," according to the handwritten note on a framed calling card—were great fans of this Genovese bar/pastry shop.

BAR-CAFFÈ
Romanengo
Via Orefici 31
☎010.203-915
Closed Sunday

Romanengo
Piazza Soziglia 74/R
☎010.297-869
Closed Monday

There are two Romanengo shops on via Orefici. The original, at via Orefici 31, is Genova's oldest bar, founded in 1805. One room is lined with glass jars of colorful candy called *goccie al rosolio*, pastel beads of sugar enclosing a rose liqueur center; bottles of naturally flavored syrups including barley, tamarind, sour cherry, rose, and citron; and pots of honey, preserves, and fruit jellies. The old-fashioned wood-trimmed display counters contain trays of neatly aligned rows of hand-dipped chocolates, *marroni* chestnuts, and at Christmas, a major selection of whole, shiny, translucent, hyper-sweet preserved fruits. I was puzzled by a jar of thick white cream labeled *manna* (not to be confused with the food the Israelites ate in the desert). The salesperson described it as a *rinfrescante*, which means refresher, but Romanengo's *manna* is a sweet syrup, known for its mild laxative powers, made from the sap of a native ash tree.

The owner of the original shop sold it, then regretted his choice and founded a second Romanengo store, uphill from the original. Both have more or less the same selection of old-fashioned bottles, jars, and candied fruits, but some say that the second store's products are superior.

MARKET
Mercato Orientale
Via XX Settembre, next to the church of Santa Maria della Consolazione
Open Monday through Saturday mornings

The name of Genova's market, the "Oriental Market," evokes images of exotic bazaars, silks, and spices, of the days when the Genovese explored the unknown seas. It is the prototypical market, a bit more "oriental" than most, and a perfect stop for picnic supplies. Flower vendors spill out onto the sidewalks of via XX Settembre, backed by a wall of plants and greenery, with buckets of fresh flowers at hard-to-resist prices. Vegetable, fruit, and fish stands are in the middle of the market, ringed by an arcade containing *alimentari* (groceries), meat, poultry, tripe stalls, bread bakeries, and *casalinghi* (housewares shops). The produce inside is impressive, choice, just picked, firm, and scented with garden loam. The fresh fish (the signs say *Nostrane*—"Local") are lively-looking and clear-eyed.

At Stand 181, Francesco Abis has an impressive selection of olives from the Riviera, and sun-dried tomatoes ready to be preserved under olive oil, sold by weight.

At Stand 186, Benedetta Dolcino's display of vegetables and herbs, a study in the color green, is a thriller. Artichoke and asparagus fans should plan a spring visit.

Gino and Sergio, Stand 100–101, have the freshest-looking fish.

Stand 176, Lo Chalet, offers exotic fruit, mushrooms, and a vast variety of shelled nuts.

Al Mulino, a bread bakery at Stand 34, makes a good *focaccia alla salvia* or *alla cipolla* (sage or onion flatbread) and interesting leaf-shaped whole-wheat breads.

At Stand 251, Ermanno Ubaldi sells housewares, including tin-lined *farinata* pans.

FRY SHOP

Antica Sciamada
Vico San Giorgio 14/R
No phone
Closed Sunday

Antica Sciamada
Via Ravecca 19/R
☎010.280-843
Closed Sunday

Genova is the *farinata* capital of Liguria, and two of the best shops for this tasty crepe are both called Antica Sciamada. The original, owned by Ornella Capra, is on vico San Giorgio. The second Antica Sciamada, on via Ravecca, is owned by Viviana Sturla.

GELATO

Cremeria Augusto
Via Nino Bixio 5
☎010.591-884
Closed Saturday and August 10–31

The unassuming sign says *Illy Caffè Cremeria*, and the ambience is archetypal busy bar, but the Cremeria Augusto serves the best *gelato* in Genova. The stainless-steel counter next to the door is punctuated with lids of inset *gelato* containers, and the pink granite bar holds a carousel of fresh ice cream cones. The list includes classics and seasonal fruit flavors, but the true stars are the custardy egg-yolk–rich *crema* (custard cream) and *panera*, which tastes like *cappuccino*, worth a detour for coffee fans. Sunday crowds confirm my enthusiasm for this tasty *gelato*.

SWEETS

Rosella
Via Berghini 59/r
☎010.503-843

Soft, snow-white sugary rectangles of fondant—creamy candies made of water, sugar, and cream of tartar, cooked, then kneaded like dough and flavored—are created by the artisans of Rosella, using Santo Rosello's recipe from the 1800s. Fringed pastel papers are wrapped around the eight flavors: pale pink for raspberry, yellow for lemon, green for apricot, orange for orange, white for mint, blue for anise, light brown for coffee, and dark brown, almost black, for chocolate. For a factory visit, contact Mr. Pallavicini.

PASTRY
Pasticceria Villa
Via Portello 2/R
☎010.277-0002
Closed Monday

I met Marco Profumo in Piemonte in one of my favorite restaurants where both our tables lingered after a meal that included an almost indecent amount of truffles. The Pasticceria Villa has been making pastry and cookies, many made with almonds, since 1827. They produce *pandolce* in both forms, dense and flat, called the *Antica Genova* version, as well as the more modern raised and softer version.

WINE BAR–RESTAURANT
Enoteca Bar Sola
Via Barabino 120/r
☎010.594-513
Fax 010.561-329
Closed Sunday and August
All credit cards • low moderate

A local crowd streams through the Enoteca Bar Sola to drink a glass of wine or beer, purchase a bottle of wine or olive oil or imported gourmet items, or to taste some of the specialties of the Sola family. Rita is in the kitchen, and her brothers Luigi and sommelier Pino are at the counter of their friendly bar. Stop in for a glass of fine local Vermentino and a taste of the fresh *focaccia* with sage or onion. The dining rooms, with dark wood trim, overhead fans, leather banquettes, and director's chairs, combine English and maritime styles. The *cucina* is pure Ligurian, however, with a large selection of regional cured meats, as well as imported products for locals bored with tradition, like caviar, Russian crab, and canned lobster bisque. Pasta, *minestrone*, vegetables, and *cima alla genovese* (veal stuffed with a tasty forcemeat) are beautifully prepared, speckled with fresh green herbs. All cooking is done with local extra

virgin olive oil. Hooray for one of Liguria's best wine lists, with wines priced by the bottle or glass.

RESTAURANT
Antica Osteria dei Bai
Via Quarto 12
☎010.387-478
Fax 010.392-684
Closed Monday
All credit cards • expensive

I hated most of the fancy restaurants that I went to in Genova and many of the *trattorie* as well. But I wasn't disappointed by Antica Osteria del Bai. Garibaldi ate here before embarking for Sicily, but he wouldn't recognize the restaurant today—modern, elegant, fairly formal for Italy. The service is professional, tables are graced with fine linens and silver service plates. Owners chef Gianni Malagoli and Renata Luppi run a tight ship where fish and seafood, all impeccably fresh, dominate the Mediterranean-inspired menu. Pasta is homemade, seasonal vegetables like Albenga artichokes and *porcini* mushrooms are paired with fish and pasta. Save room for cheese, either first-class Italian or imports from Europe. Well-chosen wines are treated with respect, served in large crystal wineglasses, a great excuse to drink a big red. The dessert menu pairs fine dessert wines with all offerings.

RESTAURANT
Toe Drüe
Via Carlo Corso 44
Sestri Ponente
☎010.671-100
Closed for lunch; Saturday and Sunday; and August
All credit cards • high moderate

Don't attempt to drive to Toe Drüe in Sestri Ponente, because you'll never find it. Take a cab (your driver will probably have to ask for directions in Sestri) to this restaurant with its unpronounceable name, which means "thick-topped tables" in Ligurian dialect. The *cucina* is local, tavern-style, based on a knowledge that goes beyond the kitchen to the seas, tides, vines, and the phases of the moon. Alessandro and Andrea Zane dish out food that looks and tastes the way it should—real, not dressed up. Toe Drüe has no black-tie waiters, cork-sniffing sommeliers, china, crystal, or silver, and the acoustics are horrible, but it serves the best, most genuine *cucina* in Genova, accompanied by a selection of wines from the vineyards of Liguria and Piemonte. I have never seen a printed menu in this restaurant, or a wine list, and I doubt that they exist. I leave my choices to them and I've never been disappointed. If the wood-burning oven is lit, you'll get a taste of one of Genova's best *farinate*. Desserts are Piemontese, either *panna cotta* (a rich cream confection) or *bonet* (chocolate almond custard). Reservations are hard to come by at times, and are a must since the restaurant often closes unpredictably.

RESTAURANT

Bruxiaboschi
Via F. Mignone 8
San Desiderio
☎010.345-0302
Fax 010.345-1423
Closed Sunday evening, Monday, and August
All credit cards • moderate

Located in one of Genova's anonymous and not-too-easy-to-find suburbs, Trattoria Bruxiaboschi is staffed by the Sciaccaluga family and serves classic home-style Ligurian *cucina*. Along with the usual stuffed vegetables, flatbreads, and *minestrone* (vegetable soup), the menu offers homemade chestnut pasta, tasty mushroom dishes, lamb, tripe, and a varied *fritto misto* that changes with the seasons but always includes *cuculli* (potato fritters). Conclude your meal with the *latte dolce fritto*, a cinnamon-spiced deep-fried cus-

tard. The lovely local and Italian wines complement the simple menu.

Leivi

RESTAURANT-INN

Ca' Peo
Strada Panoramica 77
☎0185.319-696
Fax 0185.319-671
Closed Monday, Tuesday lunch, and November
All credit cards • expensive

Six kilometers (four miles) of winding country road lead to Ca' Peo, an isolated restaurant immersed in the olive-tree–covered hills above Chiavari. The *cucina* and wines are well worth the trip. Franco and Melly Solari's restaurant, tucked away in a town that none of my Italian friends had ever heard of, is an expression of devotion to Ligurian tradition. Vegetable fans will appreciate Melly's ethereal cooking, especially the homemade pasta stuffed with fresh fava beans and sauced with leeks, and the crispy wide deep-fried strips of zucchini. Fish from the nearby coast, local lamb, and fresh woodsy mushrooms are skillfully prepared. The dining room has an impressive view of the countryside and the distant coast. Tables are carefully set with service plates, crocheted doilies, and simple low flower arrangements. Sommelier Franco is determined in his quest for fine wines, and hosts a yearly competition for the best Ligurian wine, chosen by a panel of experts. Spend the night in one of Ca' Peo's modern rooms or two-bedroom apartments with terraces and a view of the sea, and you can taste all the winners without worrying about driving. The sunset and the *pesto* are worth a detour.

Lerici

HOTEL
Il Nido
Via Fiascherino 75
☏0187.967-286
Fax 0187.964-225
Closed November through mid-March
American Express, Diners Club, MasterCard •
moderate

RESTAURANT
Conchiglia
Piazza del Molo
☏0187.967-334
Fax 0187.966-085
Closed Wednesday and December
All credit cards • high moderate

Small and cozy in the winter, the Trattoria Conchiglia doubles in size in the warmer months with terrace dining. Start your meal with a varied *antipasto*, prepared by owner Massimo Lorate with whatever came in on the fishing boats, lightly dressed with local extra virgin olive oil. Fresh fish is grilled, skewered, or slowly deep-fried to a crunch. Chocolate sauce will probably cover your dessert of ice cream or nut cake. House wines are basic.

Portofino

HOTEL
Splendido
Viale Baratta 13
☏0185.269-551
Fax 0185.269-614
All credit cards • ultra-high luxury in season, low luxury the rest of the year

HOTEL
Piccolo Hotel
Via Duca degli Abruzzi 31
☏0185.269-015
Fax 0185.269-621
All credit cards • high expensive in season, moderate the rest of the year

RESTAURANT
Taverna del Marinaio
Piazza Martiri dell'Olivetta 36
☏0185.269-103
Closed Tuesday
MasterCard, Visa • high moderate

After gazing at the megayachts in the port, food lovers will understand who's patronizing the expensive restaurants in town. Their food's not bad, but prices are for those who don't count the zeroes on Italian banknotes. I prefer the low-key Taverna del Marinaio, under a portico facing the port, for its simple ambience and Ligurian menu that features marinated anchovies, baked mussels, fish soup, potato *gnocchi* or *trenette* dressed with *pesto*, stuffed squid, simply prepared fish, and an occasional meat dish for fish haters. Conclude with *panna cotta* or a slice of a homemade tart. The Ligurian olive oils are choice, the wine list small but well priced.

Rapallo

HOTEL
Rosabianca
Lungomare V. Veneto 42
☏0185.50390
Fax 0185.65035
All credit cards • low expensive

HOTEL
Cuba e Milton
San Michele di Pagana
☏0185.50610
Fax 0185.58422
All credit cards • moderate

RESTAURANT
Trattoria ü Giancu
Via San Massimo 78
☏/Fax 0185.260-505
Closed Wednesday, Thursday lunch, November, and December
No credit cards • low moderate

Mamma Pasqualina in the kitchen and her son Fausto Oneto in the large dining room of ü Giancu ("white" in dialect, the nickname of the original owner) serve *cucina ligure* that will thrill vegetarians and traditionalists alike. The food is home-style, the wines are simple, and on Fridays the menu features vegetarian dishes so varied you won't miss the meat. The *formagetta* cheese is homemade and tasty. Charming Fausto's English is perfect, learned from friends, he says. During the off-season they are closed early in the week; call to be sure.

Recco

HOTEL
Elena
Via Garibaldi 5
☎0185.74022
Fax 0185.721-295
All credit cards • moderate

RESTAURANT
Focacceria
Via Roma 278
☎0185.75364
Closed Wednesday; open evenings only mid-January to mid-February
No credit cards • low moderate

The Focacceria is owned by the same family as, and shares its kitchen and street number with, the famous restaurant Manuelina. Manuelina is coasting along on its past glories—it is credited with inventing *focaccia col formaggio*, flatbread stuffed with melty *stracchino* cheese. The Focacceria's *cucina* is traditional, with all the classics, but stick to the *focaccia*, the house specialty, oozing cheese out of the tasty thin bread-dough crust. Prices are modest, and there's always a crowd waiting to be served.

San Remo

HOTEL
Royal
Corso Imperatrice 80
☎0184.5391
Fax 0184.61445
All credit cards • luxury in season, low expensive the rest of the year

HOTEL
Parigi
Corso Imperatrice 66
☎0184.505-605
Fax 0184.533-020
All credit cards • low expensive in season, low moderate the rest of the year

RESTAURANT
Paolo e Barbara
Via Roma 47
☎/Fax 0184.531-653
Closed Sunday evening, Monday
All credit cards • low expensive

I had to be convinced by a friend to dine at chef-owner Paolo Masieri and wife-sommelier Barbara Pisani's, restaurant, which was called Din-Don, the Italian equivalent of Ding Dong, probably the worst-named restaurant in Italy, mercifully changed to Paolo e Barbara shortly after my visit. It may not be original but defines exactly what makes this restaurant work. Paolo buys the best, freshest fish, seasonal produce, extra virgin olive oil, and utilizes his prime materials with restraint. Anchovies and air-dried cod are treated with respect; mushrooms are available in season. Hard-to-find regional cheeses are difficult to resist. Desserts feature local flavors like chestnuts, lemons, candied fruit, and hazelnuts. The wine list has an impressive selection of regional, national, and French wines, *grappe,* and distillates.

RESTAURANT
Carluccio–Osteria del Marinaio
Via Gaudio 28
☎0184.501-919
Closed Monday and from October to December
No credit cards • low expensive

Tiny, on a street that leads to the port, this genuine *trattoria* was opened in 1948 by Gianni Locatelli's father, Carluccio, who sold *focaccia* with anchovies. The ambience is original—ceilings painted with maritime themes and dancing straw-covered wine bottles by Florentine painter Gino Mugnai in 1951, walls of portrait paintings, shelves of wine bottles. The restaurant closes when Gianni can't get fresh fish, so when it's open, diners can expect to find the freshest, sweetest fish and seafood that money can buy. Don't expect anything fancy, just simple classics perfectly executed. Conclude with homemade *gelato* or wild berries. Gianni will recommend something from his choice wine list of terrific regional, national, and international gems.

ENOITECA
Bacchus
Via Roma 65
☎0184.530-990
Open 10 A.M.–8:30 P.M., closed Sunday
All credit cards • low moderate, drink big

This wine bar is the perfect place to stop off for a snack, light meal, gastronomic shopping spree, or simply to worship the Roman god of wine and revelry. Giovanni Fabris's *enoteca* has an all-star Italian selection of wine, distillates, and nonperishable foods. Visit the *enoteca* in the basement, scope out the upstairs shelves of their own extra virgin olive oil, *taggiasca* olives, olive paste, jarred *pesto*, and a good selection of nonlocal *balsamico*. Sit on the modern barstools at the counter in the front room for snacks and fine wine by the glass, or take a table in the back room, dig deeply into the wine list of regional and Italian

gems, well chosen, well priced. Lunch or snack on plain or herbed *focaccia, focaccia di formaggio*, vegetable tarts, air-dried cod cooked with tomatoes and olives, Ligurian-style or *alla Vicentina* or *mantecato*, both tipoffs of Giovanni's roots from Veneto. Giovanni's father, Mario, makes all the desserts.

Sestri Levante

HOTEL
Hotel Bardilio
Via C. Colombo 54, Riva Trigoso
☎0185.480-725
Fax 0185.481-159
All credit cards • moderate

RESTAURANT
Fiammenghilla dei Fieschi
Via Pestella 6, Riva Trigoso
☎0185.481-041
Open evenings, Sunday, and holidays for lunch; closed Monday, January, and October
All credit cards • low expensive

This restaurant, on a tiny, twisting road off the via Aurelia, is almost impossible to find and not too easy to pronounce, but lovers of Ligurian cooking will find the effort worthwhile. Look carefully for the sign for the turnoff, follow the arrows, and be rewarded with a fantastic dining experience, set among olive trees, in a stunning red eighteenth-century villa, one of the summer residences of the noble Genovese Fieschi family. Chef-owner Gabriella Paganini transforms seasonal, regional fish and produce into Ligurian classics that her husband, sommelier Giancarlo Rezzano, ably pairs with regional or Italian wines. The ambience is elegant, understated with wooden chairs, framed mirrors. There's a written menu, but Giancarlo recites the daily specials that Gabriella has prepared. Stuffed *totanetti* (baby flying squid), *cappon magro, ciuppin*, artichoke ravioli, chestnut pasta with ricotta, baked or sauced fish are among the specialties. Hope that the *gallinella* (tub gurnard), a fish worth tasting, is available. Desserts are based on seasonal fruit—summer diners shouldn't skip the figs with custard *gelato*. Giancarlo's local cheese from artisanal producers will thrill cheese lovers, creating a valid excuse to drink red from the impressive wine list. *Grappe* and distillates will tempt all but the designated driver.

Ventimiglia

RESTAURANT-INN

Baia Beniamin

Corso Europa 63

Grimaldi Inferiore

☎0184.38002

Fax 0184.38027

Closed Tuesday evening, Wednesday, and October

All credit cards • expensive

Baia Beniamin, a restaurant-inn with elegant service and eight rooms, is one of the places people begged me not to include in my book, for fear of never again finding a table in this almost unknown gem. But it didn't seem fair not to mention the hardworking partners, Oscar Falsirolli in the dining room and Carlo Brunelli in the kitchen, dedicated to light, mostly fish, partly Ligurian, *cucina*, beautifully prepared, nicely presented. The wines are excellent and carefully selected. The diners are mostly French, out for a splendid bargain at such an elevated gastronomic level. This is one of the most promising restaurants on the coast, a rising star.

HOTEL

La Riserva

Castel d'Appio

☎0184.229-533

Fax 0184.229-712

All credit cards • low moderate

GARDEN

Hanbury Botanic Garden

Cape Mortola, La Mortola

☎0184.39507

Open 10 A.M.–4 P.M. in the winter; closed Wednesday, 9 A.M.–6 P.M. in the summer

Thomas Hanbury bought an estate that covered the Cape Mortola promontory in 1867, and, with the help of his brother David, created a garden of exotic plants. Four editions of *Hortus Mortulensis* document the increasing size of the garden, which had over 5,800 species of plants at its most glorious. The place was damaged heavily in World War II, sold to the Italian state, fell into disrepair, and was eventually taken over by the University of Genova. Subtropical fruit trees, African and American species as well as Mediterranean classics, are set along paths that wander down to a small temple with a millstone from an olive oil mill. Check out the cyprus lane, dragon and mermaid fountains, mausoleum of Sir Thomas and Lady Catherine, as well as the plants and trees. The roses are at their best in May.

CACTUS GARDEN

Giardino Esotico Pallanca

Via Aurelia 1, Bordighera

☎0184.266-347

Fax 0184.266-345

Closed Monday morning

Cactus fans will go wild in the Giardino Esotico Pallanca, with over 3,250 species of cactus and a view of the coast that can't be beat. Call or fax Dott. Pallanca for an appointment.

Voze

Voze, almost 4 kilometers (2½ miles) inland from the coastal village of Noli, is a pleasant detour into olive country.

HOTEL

Punta Est

Via Aurelia 1
Finale Ligure (close by)
☎/Fax 019.600-611
American Express, Visa • expensive,
moderate off season

HOTEL

Hotel Corallo

Via Aurelia 143
☎019.745-583
Fax 019.745-582
MasterCard, Visa, American Express •
moderate, inexpensive off season

RESTAURANT

Lilliput

Regione Zuglieno 76
☎019.748-009
Closed Monday, January, and weekday lunch
No credit cards • moderate

The *cucina* of Lilliput is Ligurian, reexamined by Carlo Nan with patience and intelligence, and nicely prepared. The *farinata* sprinkled with rosemary and black pepper is served with a glass of *spumante* (sparkling wine) for openers. Warm vegetable *antipasti* and cold fish salads compete for the appetizer course. Pasta, potato *gnocchi*, and *risotto* are sauced with seafood, mushrooms, or herbs. Fish are grilled to perfection, and the wines are of equally good quality.

Zuccarello

HOTEL

See Garlenda

HOTEL

Ondina

Viale Italia 41
☎0182.51334
Fax 0182.554-538
American Express, MasterCard, Visa • high
inexpensive

RESTAURANT

La Cittadella

Via Tornatore 62
☎0182.79056
Closed Monday
Mastercard, Visa • high moderate

La Cittadella is in the medieval inland village of Zuccarello, in the restored twelfth-century stables of the Marchese del Carretto. Chef Mirella Porro and her husband, Angelo Bani, in the dining room propose a five-course fixed menu that changes every few weeks, featuring the best and freshest fish and produce that Angelo can get his hands on. The *cucina* is creative, with Ligurian flavors if not tradition. *Focaccia* is homemade, pasta sauced with seafood and vegetables. Local deep-water *bezugo* (bronze bream)—according to Angelo, the best fish in the Mediterranean—is on the menu. Otherwise look for sea bass with artichokes or *trombette* zucchini, or turbot with balsamic vinegar. Vegetarians should warn Angelo when reserving to have an all-vegetal dinner. Fruit desserts tempt, but chocoholics should hope that Mirella has prepared hot chocolate *sformatino* with mint sauce. The house extra virgin olive oil is from Laura Maravaldi, one of the finest in the region. The wine list is contained, personal, choice, intelligently paired with Mirella's cooking.

Trentino and Alto Adige are geographically united by mountains, by deep valleys cut by streams coursing down from towering peaks; they are separated from Veneto by the dramatic Dolomite mountains and linked to the rest of Europe by the Brenner Pass. But the hyphen between Trentino, the southern half of this fraternal—not identical—twin region, and northern Alto Adige (the South Tirol, the southern side of the Austrian and Swiss Alps) separates two distinct cultures. All street signs in Alto Adige are in both Italian and German, but the dominant language and culture in this region is Teutonic.

Trentino-Alto Adige

Interwined histories account for Alto Adige's traditional attachment to Austria. Trentino, which was governed for almost 800 years by the ecclesiastic principality of Trento, preceded and followed by brief periods of Austrian and Tirolian domination, is far more Italian.

The *cucina* of Trentino is decidedly Venetian in spirit, with *polenta* playing an important role, frequently accompanied by mushrooms. In Alto Adige, regional dishes have German names, translated into Italian on most menus. Bread there is usually white or rye, often flavored with caraway or fennel seeds. Ham is the most likely appetizer, either cooked and served with freshly grated horseradish or marinated in brine with aromatic herbs and spices, then cold-smoked and aged to produce *Speck*. No traditional pasta is found; dumplings and soup are the usual first courses. Meats are roasted or stewed; game is often cooked with fruit. Cabbage, sauerkraut, and potatoes are the traditional vegetables. Strudel, a sure sign of Austrian influence, is frequently found, made with a regional speciality of great importance, the apple. (Vast apple orchards carpet the fertile valleys of Trentino and Alto Adige.) Grapes for the crisp white and fruity red wines cover the hills, and German-speaking tourists in hiking boots and red knee socks dot the mountain paths. At times the tension between the Italian majority and a vocal minority of German separatists flares up in Alto Adige, but signs of strain are rarely evident in the velvety green pastures with their grazing cows, haystacks, and split-wood fences.

Watch out for off-season closings here; many hotels and some resturants close down for a month or longer in the winter.

The Menu

Salumi

Speck: brine- and smoke-cured pork

Primo

Canederli: bread dumplings that can be plain or flavored with meat, liver, or brown bread

Minestrone d'orzo: barley soup

Ribel: buckwheat fritters

Smacafam: buckwheat *polenta,* baked with sausage

Spaetzle: flour and egg dumplings

Zuppa acida or **sauerkrautsuppe:** sauerkraut soup

Zuppa di terlano: white-wine–based cream sauce

Secondo

Anguilla: eel

Biroldo: blood sausage with walnuts, pine nuts, and chestnuts

Camoscio alla tirolese or **Gemsenfleisch:** chamois cooked in vinegar, spices, and sour cream

Capriolo in salsa: venison cooked in red wine

Gulasch di manzo or **Rindsgulasch:** beef stew with herbs and spices

Lumache: snails

Tortino di patate e carne or **Grostel:** cake of leftover boiled beef, potatoes, and onions

Trota in blu or **Blau Forelle:** alpine trout cooked in white wine vinegar, wine, herbs, and spices

Contorno

Crauti or **Sauerkraut:** sauerkraut

Gnocchetti or **Spaetzle:** potato or flour and egg dumplings

Verdura ripiena or **Gefultes gemuse:** tomatoes, zucchini, or peppers stuffed with ground meat and rice

Formaggio

Puzzone di Moena: soft, intense, piquant

Formaggio grigio: grainy, grayish, piquant

Dolce

Frittelle di mele or **Apfelkuchel:** apple fritters

Krapfen: fried sweet dough, filled with preserves

Strudel: strudel

Torta di grano saraceno: buckwheat-flour cake served with whipped cream

Zelten: Christmas cake of rye flour, nuts, candied fruit, and cinnamon

The Wine List

More than half the wine produced in Trentino and Alto Adige is DOC. Much of it is exported to Germany and Austria, and wine labels in Alto Adige are frequently in German. The crisp, dry white wines are more widely known than the light fruity reds. The dessert wines can be hard to find, but worth the effort.

The Südtiroler or **Alto Adige,** DOC zone, in the province of Bolzano, includes nineteen different types of wine. Crisp, dry whites **Müller-Thurgau, Chardonnay, Pinot Bianco, Pinot Grigio, Riesling Renano, Sylvaner,** and **Traminer Aromatico** are served with appetizers, pasta, and fish dishes. Dry red **Cabernet,** made from Cabernet Franc and Cabernet Sauvignon grapes, and fruity **Pinot Nero** are good choices with meat or regional cooking. Native red grapes are used to produce full-flavored **Lagrein Dunkel;** light, young **Schiava;** and fragrant rosé **Lagrein Kret-**

zer—all paired with sauced meat dishes. Semi-sweet golden **Moscato Giallo** and rosé **Moscato Rosa,** made with the flowery scented Moscato grapes, are fine with simple desserts and pastry. Top producers are Bellendorf, Cornell, Gojer, Girlan, Schreckbichl (also called Colterenzio), Tiefenbrunner (also called Schloss Turmhof) Brigl, Grai, Kuenburg, Laimburg, Baron Widmann, Franz Hass, J. Hofstätter, Kossler, Produttori Cornaiano, Produttori San Michele Appiano, Niedrist, and the exceptional wines of Alois Lageder.

The Caldaro, or **Lago di Caldaro,** a DOC wine from the province of Bolzano, is made from the Schiava Grossa, Gentile, and Grigia grapes. This native light, winy dry red is served with meat and fowl, and is produced by Bellendorf, Girlan, Kuenburg, Schreckbichl (also called Colterenzio), and Tiefenbrunner (also called Schloss Turmhof).

Light, crisp, dry, non-DOC white **Chardonnay** is paired with appetizers, fish, and seafood, and produced by Maso Cantanghel, Pojer e Sandri, J. Tiefenbrunner, and Zeni.

Müller-Thurgau is a dry, aromatic, fruity white made with the Müller-Thurgau grape, and served with appetizers, fish, and seafood. Top producers are Pojer e Sandri, J. Tiefenbrunner, and Zeni.

Pinot Nero is a warm, fruity red, served with meat and fowl, and produced by Maso Cantanghel, Zeni, and Pojer e Sandri with their special reserves.

Santa Maddalena, a dry red with a bitter finish, made from local Lagrein and Schiava grapes. It is at its best served with meat, fowl, and regional *cucina*, and is produced by Bellendorf, Gojer, J. Hofstätter, Kettmer, and Lageder.

The grapes for many quality **Spumante** (sparkling wines), produced locally and outside Trentino–Alto Adige, are grown in this region. Both *champenois* and *charmat*

methods are used with great success on Chardonnay, Pinot Bianco, Pinot Nero, or Pinot Grigio grapes. These delightful sparkling wines are served with appetizers or light first-course dishes. Top producers are Arunda, Équipe 5, Ferrari, Frescobaldi (Toscana), Antinori (Toscana), Marone Cinzano (Piemonte), Vivaldi, and the wonderful wines made by Haderburg.

Teroldego Rotaliano is a rich, full, dry red made from local Teroldego grapes, grown on the Rotaliano plain of alluvial soil in the province of Trento. It is served with meat, game, and richly sauced dishes and produced by Barone de Cles, Conti Martini, Foradori, Istituto Agrario Provinciale San Michele all'Adige, and Zeni.

The **Trentino** DOC zone makes wines from twenty different grape varieties. Whites **Chardonnay, Müller-Thurgau, Pinot-Bianco.**

Riesling, Nosiola, and Traminer are crisp, dry and fruity—served with appetizers, fish, and seafood. Reds **Cabernet,** made with Cabernet Franc and Sauvignon, and **Marzemino** and **Lagrein,** both made from local grape varieties, are served with meat, fowl, and regional dishes. Top producers are Barone de Cles, Conti Martini, De Tarczal, Foradori, Istituto Agrario Provinciale San Michele all'Adige, Poli, Simoncelli, Bolognani, Pojer e Sandri, and Vallarom.

Nontraditional Wines. Some of Trentino–Alto Adige's finest winemakers produce *vini da tavola*—exemplary reds, whites, and rosés produced outside DOC zones. Pojer e Sandri make fruity white Nosiola; delightful Schiava di Faedo and Vin dei Molini, full-flavored rosés; and rich red Cabernet. De Tarczal makes red Pragiara, a rich barrel-aged blend of Merlot and Cabernet. The Istituto Agrario Provinciale San Michele all'Adige makes a barrel-fermented Chardonnay, Portico dei Leoni and fine experimental wines, including Castel San Michele, a rich Cabernet-Merlot blend. Pojer e Sandri make Roso Faye, a Cabernet-Merlot blend. J. Hofstätter makes elegant white De Vite with a hybrid of Riesling and Schiava grapes. Tiefenbrunner makes Goldmuskateller, a rich dry white Moscato Giallo; Feldmarschall, a fruity white Müller-Thurgau. San Leonardo makes elegant Cabernet, and Peter Dipoli makes an outstanding Sauvignon called Voglar, hard to find but worth the search.

Grappe and Fruit Distillates.   A wide variety of single varietal *grappe* are made by the following producers, although unlabeled *grappa* offered at the end of a meal at a *maso* (farm) may range from rustic to refined: Istituto Agrario Provinciale San Michele all'Adige, Guerrieri Gonzaga, Pojer e Sandri, Giovanni Poli, Segnana, and Zeni.

Pojer e Sandri make the region's finest fruit distillates from local fruit and berries. Look for apricot, cherry, quince, black currant, plum, elderberry, blackberry, raspberry, sorb apples: other producers include Giovanni Poli and Pilzer.

Regional Specialties

Apples.   Fruit trees fill the valleys of Trentino and Alto Adige, endless orchards that supply more than 30 percent of Italy's apples. Production is all in the hands of regional cooperatives, and apples with international appeal and maximum storage life have almost totally replaced traditional varieties. I asked everyone I met in both Alto Adige and Trentino if they had any traditional apple trees, and they all shook their heads sadly, remembering the impractical but flavorful fruit that has totally disappeared. Almost all production focuses on the Golden Delicious, available year round. The Val di Non, which looks like a massive orchard, has trademarked their Golden Delicious, commercialized as Melinda, each apple with a distinctive blue sticker. For more information on Trentino's fruit production, see page 127. The experimental agricultural center of Laimburg in the village of Ora in Alto Adige (tel. 0471.978-402, fax 0471.913-193) has saved around forty varieties from extinction, and sells their apples in the fall through the cooperative Dodiciville in Bolzano. In Trentino apples were traditionally sliced and dried,

called *persecche*, to be eaten as a snack or for baking in the winter. Maso del Gusto, outside Nave San Rocco (tel. 0461.870-666) grow their own apples, pears, plums, and persimmons, all certified organic, and dry them in a low-temperature oven.

Berries.   My favorite dessert in both Trentino and Alto Adige is a bowl of *sottobosco* ("under woods"), a mixture of blueberries, raspberries, and blackberries, served plain or with whipped cream. Once upon a time the berries were tiny, wild, picked in the woods and fields, but they've been replaced by cultivated specimens. High labor costs and the rational regional deforestation program have made harvesting wild fruit expensive and impractical. Local farmers of the Associazione Produttori Agricoli San Orsola in Pergine Valsugana (via Lagorai 131, tel. 0461.534-488, fax 0461.530-505) sell just-picked cultivated berries—blueberries, raspberries, blackberries, gooseberries, currants, and both "woods" and regular strawberries from June to October. Their fruit is widely distributed throughout Italy, but is at its very freshest when purchased from the cooperative. Wild blueberries are often preserved in a light syrup or under *grappa*.

Speck. *Speck* means "lard" in German, but in Alto Adige it's boned pork flank, soaked in brine flavored with garlic, pepper, juniper berries, and sugar for around two weeks, dried, smoked, and aged for at least four months. Unfortunately, most *speck* found in the region is industrially produced, with the soaking, smoking, and aging process reduced to weeks. Pigs are raised on small farms, and the local production isn't sufficient to satisfy *speck* makers, who have to look elsewhere for their pork. The best *speck*, almost impossible to find, has a thick layer of pork fat covering an equal layer of meat. Never remove the fat from *speck*, since it's considered the best part and is lower in cholesterol than butter. Purists cut a thick slice of *speck*, which is then cut into strips and eaten with bread, although it is usually sliced wafer-thin, like *prosciutto*. Those who are passionate about *speck* should plan to snack on super *speck* at Panholzerhof in Caldaro—see page 117.

Cheese. Just like a scene from *Heidi*, cows graze in alpine pastures in Trentino and Alto Adige, producing milk for a wealth of local cheeses. Many are simply referred to as *nostrano* ("ours"), although an Italian Cheese Atlas mentions Puzzone di Moena, Solandro, Spressa, Pusteria, Tirolese, Dobbiaco, and Vezzena. Most of the cheese from Alto Adige goes by both German and Italian names. Cheese lovers should look for *formaggio grigio* or *Graukäse* ("gray cheese"), one of the oldest of traditional cheeses, like a sort of aged, pressed cottage cheese, grainy and pungent, served with raw onion or radishes, available in some fine restaurants although rarely in stores. Goat cheese is traditional, undergoing a comeback due to the efforts of Hans Baumgartner and Peter Kantioler. Even

cheese maven Alberto Marcomini was knocked out by their selection.

Trentino's *Carne Salada* Salt-Cured Meat. *Carne salada*, beef cured in a brine of salt, herbs, garlic, and spice for a month, like a preserved *carpaccio*, is found in Trentino most of the year. It's served thinly sliced like *prosciutto*, accompanied by salad greens, dressed with a little extra virgin olive oil.

Grain. Almost every valley in Trentino and Alto Adige with a stream once had its own mill to grind wheat, corn, and rye, grown in the fertile valleys. Although most of the mills are gone and the valleys are planted with apples, grain is still an important element in the cooking of these two regions. Cooks utilize barley in soup. Summer wheat, rye, and buckwheat are common, used in bread and cakes. *Schüttelbrot*, a rustic, round crispy rye flatbread and rye rolls flavored with cumin are found throughout Alto Adige, and also in Trentino, which doesn't seem to have much of a bread tradition. Check out the ethnographic museum in Teodone near Brunico (via Duca Diet 24, tel. 0474.21287) to see a genuine mill, or visit the Mulino Schmiedhofer in Villabassa Niederdorf, via Santo Stefano 69, tel. 0474.75007, where rye, wheat, and barley are milled by Alois Schmiedhofer. And look for the traditional buckwheat-flour cake, filled with berry preserves and served with whipped cream.

Polenta. Cornmeal is an important element in the cooking of Trentino, revealing its contact with Veneto. Corn for meal was also grown widely in southern Alto Adige valleys after eighteenth-century floods until the 1950s, when apple orchards and vineyards took over almost completely. Those who'd like to purchase first-rate local cornmeal should visit the mill of Paolo Pisone in Calavino, via Garibaldi 12, tel. 0461.564-126. Most of the corn comes from Veneto and Fruili. The mill is electric and is utilized to grind the meal for *polenta* fine, medium, or coarse. Paolo also makes a limited production of whole-kernel *polenta integrale* made with local *marano* corn, a low-yield cultivar that has practically disappeared in the area.

Water. Few regions of Italy have water as wonderful as Trentino and Alto Adige, possibly because it's melted from Alpine glaciers. Drinking fountains in the countryside or city spout delicious water that's safe to drink. My favorite mineral water, Surgiva, comes from Trentino, bottled from waters that flow from a rock vein at an altitude of 1,134 meters at Pra dell'Era in the unspoiled Nambrone Valley in the Adamello Brenta Park. It's classified as minimally mineralized, with a fixed residue of 38, one of the lowest in Italy. The water tastes clean, pure, without any unpleasant mineral or salty flavor. It's easy to spot with its elegant, transparent 3/4-liter bottle, attractive label with a vivid purple scribble graphic for sparkling, navy blue for still. Surgiva water is found in Italy's finest restaurants, but rarely sold in stores outside Trentino. Visit the source and the bottling plant that processes 40,000,000 bottles a year, or look for this wonderful water in restaurants.

Grappa and Distillates. A source of calories and warmth for the cold northern winters, distilled from the leftovers of winemaking and therefore an economical product to make, *grappa* is traditional in both Trentino and Alto Adige. Illegal *Schnappstuifl* stills in Alto Adige were once hidden in laundries, which called for some of the same equipment. Modern distillers are making new-style *grappe,* often single native varietals that are smoother, more elegant than the firewater of the past. Giovanni Poli's fine single varietal and herb-infused *grappe* are worth looking for.

Contact Giovanni Poli, via Vezzano 37, San Massenza di Vezzano, tel./fax 0461.864-119, if you'd like to visit.

Fruit distillates or fruit-infused *grappe* are also made in fruit-rich Trentino and Alto Adige. Pojer e Sandri make the region's finest fruit distillates from local fruit and berries. Look for apricot, cherry, quince, black currant, plum, elderberry, blackberry, raspberry, sorb apples, and more, distilled to perfection. And for their Acquavite di Vino, just released after ten years of aging. Call or fax Pojer e Sandri, Molini 4–6, Faedo, tel. 0461.650-342, fax 0461.651-100, to arrange a visit and tasting.

See Trento, page 126, for a shop with a fine regional *grappa* selection.

Vinegar. Winemakers once produced vinegar artisanally throughout Italy; a barrel was set aside with a *madre,* vinegar culture to ferment and acidify wine. Italian bureaucracy has put an end to this practice with a hornet's nest of rules that require a separate building, stringent sanitary conditions, and plenty of paperwork. First-rate winemaker Andreas Widmann has persisted and creates wonderful full-bodied red wine vinegar with 10 percent acidity, quite high for a wine vinegar but worth seeking out. For a taste of his vinegar and fine wines, contact Andreas Baron Widmann, via Piana 3, Cortaccia, tel. 0471.990-092, fax 0471.880-468. And Alois Lageder, Alto Adige's finest winemaker, is about to begin producing vinegar, assisted by vinegar expert Maurizio Castelli, and should have a product by the time this book comes out. Contact Alois Lageder, viale Druso 235, Bolzano, tel. 0471.920-164, fax 0471.931-577, for more information.

Crafts. The royal blue apron called a *grembiule,* which is worn by farmers in various parts of Italy, is practically a uniform in Trentino–Alto Adige, and the locals even wear them to church. You can buy simple or embroidered versions of this sturdy canvas apron in notions stores (*mercerie*) throughout the region.

Archeological excavations in the Val di Cembra have uncovered antecedents, over 2,000 years old, of the *situla,* a container that has been adapted as an ice bucket for chilling wine. The *spumante* producers of Trentino have adopted the *situla* as their symbol.

Cities & Towns

Appiano

HOTEL

Schloss Korb
Missiano (close by)
☎0471.636-000
Fax 0471.636-033
No credit cards • low expensive

HOTEL

Schloss Englar
Piganò 42, San Michele
☎0471.662-628
Fax 0471.660-404
No credit cards • moderate

RESTAURANT

Zur Rose
Josef Innherhoferstrasse 2
☎0471.662-249
Fax 0471.662-485
Closed Sunday, Monday lunch
All credit cards • low expensive

Although the front dining room of Zur Rose looks rustic, small touches like modern flower arrangements, bottles of world-class wines, and a larger room in the back with a central island of impressive distillates attest to the transition from *trattoria* to full-fledged restaurant. Chef-owner Herbert Hintner prepares both creative and traditional dishes with great skill, using first-rate ingredients to great advantage. His wife, sommelier Margot, makes sure everything runs smoothly in the dining rooms. Rustic food like veal head are elevated to elegance. Featherweight *gnocchi* of ricotta, herbs, or freshwater fish are delicately sauced. Pasta is homemade. Mushrooms are stuffed into ravioli, paired with pigeon breast, rolled into strudel. Meat and fresh fish are well prepared. Leave room for the exciting selection of local cheeses. Desserts are elaborate presentations, but the seasonal fruit strudel and homemade sorbet selection are simple and satisfying. The wine list is a thrill, well priced, concentrating on the best local wines, although the rest of Italy is well represented for those who want to drink something from another region.

Bolzano

HOTEL

Figl
Piazza del Grano 9
☎0471.978-412
MasterCard, Visa • inexpensive

HOTEL

Città Hotel

Piazza Walther 21
☎0471.975-221
Fax 0471.976-688
All credit cards • moderate

HOTEL-RESTAURANT

Park Hotel Laurin–La Belle Epoque

Via Laurin 4
☎0471.311-000
Fax 0471.311-148
All credit cards • luxury hotel, high moderate restaurant

The Laurin is, without a doubt, the best hotel in Bolzano. Rooms have been spiffed up, and the manicured lawn and tall trees in the garden are an unexpected treat in the center of the city. The restaurant is still making a big effort with successful results, executing both local and international dishes with skill. The dining room is elegant, well appointed, service is professional. The wine list offers a great selection of regional wines as well as Italian and international wines of note. Dine in the garden when the weather warms up.

BAR-CAFFÈ

Edi Bar

Piazza Walther von der Vogelweide-Platz
☎0471.978-330
Closed Sunday except in summer

Giorgio Grai, the wizard of wine (an enologist known as *l'ombra*, "the shadow," because he's so difficult to get to), can sometimes be found at his bar in piazza Walther. Recently restructured by Afra and Tobia Scarpa, the "new" Edi Bar has a wine-tasting area and a room upstairs where quality products are presented, tasted, and compared, with results that are often surprising. The coffee is excellent, and you can sip a glass of one of Giorgio's hard-to-find wines at an outdoor table in the piazza.

MARKETS

Piazza delle Erbe
Closed Sunday

Piazza Vittoria
Saturday only

The daily Bolzano market has attractively displayed fruit and vegetables, stacked and piled, irresistible to purchase or photograph. Berries, cherries, jumbo Delicious apples, and in- and out-of-season produce look too good to be true. But the farmers at the weekly market in piazza Vittoria on Saturday sell their own produce, fruit is picked ripe and bursting with flavor, and, with a little luck, late summer to early winter visitors may be able to find traditional apple varieties.

APPLES

Cooperativa Frutticoltori Dodiciville

Via di Mezzo ai Piani 12
☎0471.978-402
Fax 0471.973-193
Closed Saturday, Sunday

This cooperative sells traditional apple varieties grown at Laimburg in the late summer through early winter.

GELATO-PASTRY
Streitberger
Via Museo 15
☎0471.978-303
Closed Sunday

All the *gelaterie* of Bolzano failed the *pistacchio* test—too green (evidence of food coloring) to be taken seriously except for Streitberger, so I decided to taste it and was impressed with the results. When I asked to speak to the *gelataio* I was introduced to Elmer Streitberger, who speaks English better than Italian, has traveled extensively in the U.S., apprenticed at pastry legend Demel in Vienna, and loves country-and-western music. Eat anything in this shop with a seventy-five-year-old tradition. A visit during the Christmas season is a thrill.

BAKERY
Panificio Franziskaner
Via Francescani 3
☎0741.976-443
Closed Saturday afternoon, Sunday

Franziskaner, a few minutes from the piazze delle Erbe market, sells dozens of different breads made with wheat, rye, oat, emmer flour, and more. The selection is large and first-rate. Look for flat rounds of crispy *schüttelbrot*, rye rolls with cumin and fennel, and simple baked goods like apple or poppy-seed strudel, *krapfen, torta Lintz* with nuts and red gooseberry preserves.

WINE SHOP
Vinoteque di Alois Lageder
Viale Druso 235
☎0471.920-164
Open 9 A.M.–1 P.M., 3 P.M.–8 P.M.; closed Saturday afternoon, Sunday
MasterCard, Visa

Alois Lageder, Alto Adige's leading winemaker, has a fantastic *enoiteca* outside the historic center of Bolzano. The shop sells all twenty of Alois's wines, including many that are hard to find, and has a fine selection of wines from France, the U.S., and Australia. Single-malt whiskey, *grappa*, extra virgin olive oil, and balsamic vinegar are also for sale. At least six wines from other regions, as well as many Lageder wines, are available for tasting by the glass.

HOUSEWARES
Zimmermann
Portici 21
☎/Fax 0471.976-746
Closed Saturday afternoon
All credit cards

Lovers of Alessi's line of modern housewares will enjoy the huge selection at Zimmermann's, even if they don't mail purchases.

TIROLEAN CHIC
Oberrauch Zitt
Portici 67
☎0471.972-121
Fax 0471.970-603
All credit cards
Closed Saturday afternoon, Sunday

Fall in love with the Tirolean look? Head straight for Oberrauch Zitt for loden coats, jackets with horn buttons, hats with feather plumes, and more. A huge selection of classic and innovative designs in traditional gray, green, or new-wave red. Ask for the catalog in case you want to order by mail.

Bressanone

HOTEL-RESTAURANT
Elefante
Via Rio Bianco 4
☎0472.832-750
Fax 0472.836-579
All credit cards • high moderate

I was charmed by the Hotel Elefante with its façade frescoes of an Indian elephant, a gift from King John III of Portugal for the menagerie of Emperor Ferdinand of Vienna. After a long sea voyage and a big uphill hike from the port of Genova, the elephant was exhausted and its keepers decided to rest in Bressanone. The only stable large enough was that of an inn outside the city walls. Visitors came from afar to view the elephant during its two-week rest. The clever innkeeper had a fresco painted on the façade to commemorate the 1551 event and changed the name of his inn. Antique Tirolean furniture, down-duvet–covered beds, fresh fruit in all rooms, efficient service, and a large garden with a pool are among the Elefante's assets. The restaurant serves both traditional and innovative cooking—many hotel guests stay for an entire month and want variety on the menu. Fresh fish is a specialty, a nice relief from traditional meat-based cooking. Pasta is homemade, mushrooms and wild berries are available in season, the cheese selection is wonderful, desserts like homemade *gelato*, fruit terrines, or first-rate strudel are tasty. The wine list is pricey, with few local bargains. I wanted to see the *PIATTO ELEFANT*, listed on the menu in capital letters to hint at its size and importance, served for a minimum of two diners with hearty appetites. Elephantine only begins to describe this house specialty: a platter piled high with cured meats; rice; boiled vegetables; boiled, roast, or grilled meats like tongue, oxtail, pork chops, beef, veal, chicken, and more. No one had the courage to order it when I visited. I wasn't even tempted. Maybe next time.

HOTEL

Cavallino

Via Brennero 3
☎0472.35152
Fax 0472.38235
MasterCard, Visa • moderate

HEALTH SPA

Casa di Cura Dr. von Guggenberg

Via Terzo di Sotto 17
☎0472.355-525
Fax 0472.34014
No credit cards • expensive, but not for a diet spa

Interested in losing weight with a rather severe, unattractive diet in a Tirolean-style setting? Check out this somewhat scary Casa di Cura.

RESTAURANT

Oste Scuro

Vicolo Duomo 3
☎0472.835-342
Fax 0472.835-642
Closed Sunday evening, Monday
All credit cards • moderate

Oste Scuro is, without a doubt, the best restaurant with the best wine list in Bressanone. The upstairs entrance has a counter where locals stop off for a glass of fine wine, a tradition that dates from the eighteenth century, since this was once a wine bar. A series of intimate dining rooms with stained-glass windows and authentic Tirolean decor—antlers, portrait paintings, city prints, wrought-iron lamps. Chef Herman Mayr's menu is mostly traditional, based on interesting local ingredients like deer, goat, freshwater fish, seasonal mushrooms, first-rate cheese, and wild berries; portions are large, plates well presented. Begin with buckwheat *spaetzle* dumplings, dressed with mountain goat, creamy white wine soup, or *knodel* (also called *canederli*) made with spleen or mushrooms. Second-choice offerings include *speck*-wrapped quail, mountain goat with *marasca* cherries, or *testina di vitello* served with a vinaigrette or breaded and deep-fried — traditional but hard to digest. Dessert lovers will have a hard time choosing from homemade *gelato* sauced with berries, ricotta *Knodel,* individual warm buckwheat cakes served with tart berry sauce and unsweetened whipped cream, or fine strudel. The wine list offers both first-rate local and Italian varieties, with many bargains including a special bottling of Pinot Nero from Lageder. *Grappa* and fruit distillates are served by the glass. Reservations are a must in season.

GROCERY

Enoteca Gastronomia Franzelli

Via Santa Croce 9

☎**0472.832-086**

Closed Saturday afternoon in the winter

In a town with lots of touristy food shops with cute packages of not necessarily first-rate products, Franzelli has the best selection of local products, likes *speck* aged for five or seven months, local honey, berry preserves, *salumi,* flat rounds of dark bread, and strudel from a bakery in the nearby mountain village of Luson. Lorenzo Franzelli is a sommelier and has a nice selection of wine and distillates.

CHEESE

Casa del Formaggio

Vicolo Duomo 14

☎**0472.836-068**

Closed Sunday

Over 100 kinds of local cheese are sold in this tiny shop in the center of Bressanone.

ENOTECA

Vinissimo

Via Porta Sabiona 1

☎**/Fax 0472.833-636**

Open 9:30 A.M.–1 P.M., 3:30–8 P.M.; closed Sunday (and Saturday afternoon in the winter)

American Express, MasterCard, Visa

There are lots of wine shops in Bressanone that sell attractive bottles of *grappa* and run-of-the-mill regional wines, but this is *the* place to go for serious enophiles. Christian

Mitterrutzner has an exceptional selection of wines from his region, as well as Italian national and international wines, fruit distillates, and *grappa.* He'll open almost anything for tasting in an appropriate glass.

HOUSEWARES

A. Constantini

Portici Maggiore 10

☎**0472.836-139**

Closed Saturday afternoon

Visa

In a town filled with touristy trinket shops, this is a real country-style hardware shop, with big wooden storage systems that have lots of drawers and an old-fashioned cash register. Look for tools, housewares, hunting and fishing equipment, accessories for dogs, and even winemaking apparatus like a small press or bottle-capper. I was tempted by cowbells in all sizes (after seeing a cowbell concert in piazza Duomo), and the stone cooking griddles, perfect for those who want to schlep home a heavy souvenir.

Caldaro

AGRITOURISM

Kreidhof

Between Caldaro and Ora

☎**0471.960-025**

No credit cards • low inexpensive

Not too easy to find, but worth the hunt, Verena Nicolussi's bed-and-breakfast, neat as a pin, is on a working farm set amid vineyards and apple trees. Eggs for breakfast come fresh from Verena's chickens and have bright orange yolks and big flavor.

RESTAURANT

Panholzerhof

Lago 8

☎**0471.960-259**

Open from 5 P.M. to midnight; closed Sunday; closed October to May

No credit cards • inexpensive

Set in the midst of Caldaro's vineyards, Luis Adergassen and his wife, Marianne, offer simple snacks, worth a detour for the area's best *speck*. The menu is limited, with *speck*, smoked deer sausage, and homemade salami—order the *panholzer teller* mixed plate for a tasting. Cheese is a fresh, mild goat- and cow's-milk combo, bread is made of rye, either crisp rounds of *schüttelbrot* or cumin-flavored rolls. Pickles or radishes are the vegetables of choice. The ambience is rustic but real in a *maso* farmhouse. Two cozy dining rooms, outdoor tables on a verandah, amusing house wine (10,000 lire a liter), but Luis also serves Panholzer Kalterersee (Lago di Caldaro) Vernatsch, Terlaner Sauvignon, and Südtiroler Cabernet. *Grappa* made from pomace from the vineyard of Keil, said to be the oldest in the region, is too much fun. Reserve in advance and beg Marianne to prepare something hot.

Carisolo

HOTEL-RESTAURANT

Cascata Nardis

Val di Genova

☎0465.501-454

Open April to October

No credit cards • low moderate

There are only three inexpensive double rooms at the hotel, and the bathroom is shared, but the lure of staying in the Adamello Brenta Park next to the spectacular Nardis waterfall, one of Italy's highest, may tempt hikers not concerned about accommodations. Alpine waterfall fans should definitely plan to have lunch at the restaurant for the view from the terrace. The dining room is genuinely rustic, as is the simple, no-frills, home-style cooking prepared by Bianca Fostini and her daughter Nadia. Springtime diners should ask for the unlisted wild asparagus and *radicchio del orso*, said to be the preferred greens of

bears awakening from hibernation, although Bianca preserves both under oil and serves them until they run out. *Speck* is served in thick slabs on a wooden board, to be cut into strips. Pasta or *risotto* with mushrooms, *minestrone* with barley, and *canederli* in broth or with melted butter are good first-course choices. Armando takes care of the trout in the chilly Nardis River behind the restaurant, and it is simply prepared by Bianca. Rabbit, mountain goat, or wild boar are braised with wine, herbs, and juniper berries, served with a dome of *polenta*. Wild blueberries preserved in a barely sweetened syrup are served with *gelato*. The wine list is simple but offers a few good choices. Only 200 visitors are admitted into the park daily, but those with reservations to stay or dine at Cascata Nardis can always get in.

Castelbello Ciardes

AGRITOURISM

Hochhuebhof

Tschars-Freitenweg 11

☎0473-624-138

No credit cards • moderate

Six double rooms at a working farm with fruit trees, pigs, sheep, and a swimming pool.

RESTAURANT

Osteria della Buona Frasca

Località Juval

☎0473.668-238

Closed Wednesday

No credit cards • low moderate

Reinhold Messner, legendary mountain climber from Alto Adige, has restored a farmhouse near the Juval castle, turning it into a simple *osteria*. Souvenirs of his high-altitude exploits decorate this typical south Tirol eatery, which features simple, classic regional cuisine. *Canederli, Speck, Schüttelbrot*, local cheese, and the estate's wine,

Riesling, light white Fraueler, and Pinot Nero. Messner shows up occasionally, but mountain-climbing fans will probably want to visit even if he's not around.

Civezzano

HOTEL

Villa Madruzzo

Cognola di Trento (close by)
☎0461.986-220
Fax 0461.968-361
All credit cards • moderate

RESTAURANT

Maso Cantanghel

Via Madonnina 33
☎0461.858-714
Fax 0461.859-050
Closed Sunday and August
MasterCard, Visa • high moderate

Maso Cantanghel is the name of Lucia Gius's working farm, which produces vegetables, fruit, wine, and even a little *grappa* for its restaurant. The dining room is tastefully furnished with prints, antiques, a collection of soup tureens, and six tables simply but elegantly set with linen, Ginori china, and stemware. The *cucina* is home-style, a fixed menu that wisely uses seasonal home-grown products. Mushrooms are a regional specialty and often accompany silky homemade pasta, or are cooked with tender boned rabbit. Lucia outdoes herself with the homemade *gelato* and a tray of dessert pastries that may include *torroncino* nougat (made daily), candied orange peel, meringues, buttery crumbly *sbrisolona*, and sugar-coated grapes. The wine list offers a splendid personal selection of local, Italian, and some French wines, but the house wine is wonderful.

Cornaiano

HOTEL

Schloss Korb

Missiano (close by)
☎0471.636-000
Fax 0471.636-033
No credit cards • low expensive

RESTAURANT

Marklhof-Bellavista

Via Belvedera 14
☎0471.662-407
Fax 0471.661-522
Closed Monday
American Express, MasterCard, Visa •
moderate

The Marklhof is a typical Tirolean *trattoria*. Its hunting-trophy decor and bilingual menu appeal mostly to German and Austrian tourists. Order, from the more exciting menu of daily specials, the home-smoked *prosciutto* served with horseradish and butter, game, or *grostel* served with a cabbage and *speck* salad. The buckwheat *torta* with whipped cream and the fruit desserts are tasty. The house wines are adequate. In the summer, dine on the terrace overlooking some of Alto Adige's choicest vineyards.

Egna

HOTEL

Schloss Korb

Missiano (close by)
☎0471.636-000
Fax 0471.636-033
No credit cards • low expensive

RESTAURANT

Enoteca Johnson e Dipoli

Via A. Hofer 3
☎0471.820-323
Closed Monday
No credit cards • moderate

The Enoteca Johnson e Dipoli has one of the most interesting wine lists in all Italy, a product of the intelligence and palate of Peter Dipoli, once the guiding light of this wine bar forced to become a restaurant, but he is no longer actively involved with this wine bar. The original decor, with floors, table, and curved bar of marble, and surprise frescoes in the bathrooms, is refreshing in the midst of this Tirolean village. More than twenty fine wines are served by the glass—in addition to milkshakes, fresh juice, and sandwiches—at the bar or in the adjacent no-smoking room on the ground floor. The upstairs dining room, complete with ceramic stove, seats eighteen and serves a reasonably priced six-course fixed menu in the evening. The wines—local, Italian, French, and even Californian—are splendid, too.

M E A T
Macelleria Kofler
Piazza Umberto 132
☎0471.812-130
Closed Thursday and Saturday afternoon
The Macelleria Kofler makes a fine artisanal speck, beautifully smoked and spiced.

Merano
H O T E L
Castel Labers
Via Labers 25
☎0473.230-630
Fax 0473.211-335
Closed November to mid-March
American Express, Diners Club, MasterCard •
moderate

R E S T A U R A N T
Andrea
Via Galileo Galilei 44
☎0473.237-400
Fax 0473.212-190
Closed Monday, January, and February
All credit cards • expensive

Walter Oberrauch is the heir to Andrea Hellrigl, who left Ristorante Andrea to found Villa Mozart, in turn abandoned for the bright lights of Palio in New York. Walter, who worked with Andrea for many years, quietly absorbing the style and grace of his *cucina,* faultlessly prepares traditional dishes as well as those created by Andrea, efficiently served in a small, elegantly appointed dining room. Snails, wine soup, *canederli* (bread dumplings served in broth), game, parsley purée, and dessert ricotta *gnocchi* with fruit sauce are some of the specialties of this restaurant serving Alto Adige's most professional *cucina.* The wine list concentrates on quality regional, Italian, and French selections.

H O U S E W A R E S
Brugnara
Via Roma 31/A
☎0473.232-755
Closed Saturday afternoon
No credit cards
The housewares stores of Merano—there are three big ones under the arcades on via Portici—offer a wealth of items for the kitchen and the table. But my favorite place to shop in Merano is this hardware store on via Roma, with its unexciting window display of rakes, hoses, lawn mowers, and picnic equipment. Walk to the back of the store, past bolts of chain and displays of tools, and up the stairs, and you'll find yourself surrounded by an unbelievable selection of utensils, a maze of tiny rooms filled with everything from milking pails to four sizes of melon ballers, *Spaetzle* makers, olive pitters, a variety of potato peelers, burner covers, toothpick holders, pastry brushes, and more. Expect to find something you can't live without.

Renon

HOTEL

Hotel Post-Victoria
Paese 1, Soprabolzano
☎**0471.345-365**
Fax **0471.345-128**
MasterCard, Visa • inexpensive

AGRITOURISM

Weisshauserhof
Signat 168
☎**0471.365-285**
No credit cards • low inexpensive
Three inexpensive double rooms on a
working farm.

RESTAURANT

Patscheider Hof
Post Oberbozen, Signat
☎**0471.365-267**
Closed Tuesday, Wednesday lunch, and July
No credit cards • moderate
It won't be easy to find Patscheider Hof, a
genuine *maso* (farm) on a twisting dirt
road overlooking Bolzano, but it's worth
the hunt, as it's one of the most charming
eateries in the region. The dining room is
typical Tirolean, with hand-hewn wooden
floors, ceramic stove in one corner, local
ceramics on the walls, cozy. Chef Alois Rot-
tensteiner has lightened up traditional
cooking without any pretension, and the
results are splendid. Fantastic *speck* or
smoked beef is served with horseradish for
a starter. Choose between the *gnocchi* plate,
a tasting of traditional bread or ricotta
canederli and wonderful beet *canederli* that
I've never found anywhere else, or the
savory spinach strudel. Main-dish choices
include baked pork ribs, *bollito misto, grostl,*
and homemade sausage, accompanied by a
shredded cabbage salad. Conclude with
apple strudel, poppy-seed or buckwheat
cake or, best of all, *stranben,* fried dough
served with thickened cream and red

gooseberries. The house wine is quaffable,
but they sometimes have a few bottles of
Alois Lageder's fine wines, a far better
choice for the first-rate cooking. Dine outside overlooking vineyards, mountains,
and Bolzano in the summer. Finish with a
homemade *grappa* that slips down the
throat with ease, but may make standing up
after your meal a difficult task.

Rio di Pusteria

HOTEL
See Bressanone

HOTEL
Kandlburg
Via del Giudice 61
☎**0472.849-792**
Fax **0742.849-650**
Diners Club, MasterCard, Visa • moderate

AGRITOURISM
Anratterhof
Spinges 26
☎**0472.849-574**
No credit cards • inexpensive
Four apartments sleep from two to six peo-
ple at this modestly priced mountain farm.

RESTAURANT
Pichler
Via K. Lanz 5
☎**0472.849-458**
Closed Monday, Tuesday lunch
All credit cards • high moderate
It's impossible for me to hide my enthusiasm for Pichler, one of Italy's greatest
restaurants, with master chef Hans Baumgartner in the kitchen and sommelier Peter
Kantioler in the dining rooms. The ambience is refined *stübe,* typically Tirolean,
with wooden wainscoting, booths with
padded benches, huge tiled heater, beautifully set tables with a goblet of herbs as a
centerpiece. The *cucina* bridges tradition

and innovation, utilizing the finest local ingredients with artistry and restraint. The five-course traditional tasting menu is a bargain, featuring dishes like featherweight *canederli*, lamb shanks crusted with herbs, stuffed guinea hen, elegantly sauced deer or kid. The vegetable side dishes are fantastic, innovative, unexpected in a region that doesn't really take vegetables seriously. Chanterelles, called *finferle*, are used in many dishes. The wine list is wonderful, well priced, with regional and Italian gems. Hans and Peter have revved up the local cheese production, and the artisanal output is available in their restaurant as well as those of friends throughout the region. Save room for desserts like figs with custard *gelato*, white and bittersweet chocolate terrine, or anything with berries. Conclude with a taste of fine fruit distillates or *grappa*.

Rovereto

HOTEL
Leon d'Oro
Via Tacchi 2
☎**0464.437-333**
Fax 0464.423.777
All credit cards • moderate

RESTAURANT
Ristorante Al Borgo
Via Garibaldi 13
☎/**Fax 0464.436-300**
Closed Sunday evening and Monday
All credit cards • expensive

Al Borgo is run by the Dalsasso family— chef Rinaldo in the kitchen, with wife Daniela, mother Rosa, and brother Carlo in the dining room. The *cucina* isn't traditional, and some dishes seem contrived, but the food is well prepared. All breads, including the appetizer flatbread with thinly sliced potatoes and herbs, are home-

made. Mushroom dishes are a specialty, and fresh fish is nicely underdone. Wild berries and fruit bavarians are often served for dessert. The well-priced wine list, with local, Italian, French, and Californian wines, is a treat.

RESTAURANT
Mozart 1769
Contrada dei Portici 36
☎**0464.430-727**
Closed Tuesday, Wednesday lunch, and in August
All credit cards • high moderate

In 1769 Mozart performed his first Italian concert in Rovereto, and this intimate, attractive, elegant restaurant's name calls attention to the event. The *cucina* is as light, innovative, and creative as Mozart's music must have seemed in 1769. Husband and wife Ezio and Erika Filizola, with chef Claudio Agostini, combine efforts, and the result, although it has almost nothing traditional about it, is simply delicious. Breads are homemade, fish and seafood are cooked to perfection, flavors are delicately balanced. There's even a selection of olive oils, almost unheard of in this northern region. Save room for the tasty desserts. The wine list is a thrill.

REGIONAL PRODUCTS
L'Arcobaleno
Via Spiazze 21, Volano
☎**0464.419-091 or 0337.454-769**
Closed Sunday

Aurelio Brussich and his wife make the region's best preserved-fruit products. Preserves come in classic fruit, berry, and unusual flavors like rhubarb-strawberry and carrot. Blueberries, raspberries, blackberries are sold in light syrup or without sugar, and there's a nice selection of honey including chestnut and acacia. Aurelio also sells dried fruit, a dried apple stick called

Sfizy, müsli with dried berries, buckwheat flour, barley, and regional desserts prepared by artisans like *zelten* (a cake) and a buckwheat cake filled with fruit preserves, packaged in a box or with a cutting board. Check out the first-rate dried *porcini* mushrooms and the mushrooms preserved in oil.

San Cassiano

HOTEL-RESTAURANT

Ciasa Salares–Ristorante La Siriola

☎0471.849-445

Fax 0471.849-369

All credit cards • expensive (in the high season, otherwise moderate) hotel, high moderate restaurant

In the ski resort of Armentarola, the Ciasa Salares has everything a vacationer needs. Tennis courts, indoor swimming pool, gym, playground, and the best restaurant in the area, all in a beautiful setting in the Badia Valley. The restaurant, La Siriola (local Ladino dialect for "nightingale"), is cozy, comfortable, attractive. Owners Stefan Wieser, sommelier, and his wife, Wilma, are perfect hosts and will guide weary diners through the extensive wine list and simple menu. Start with fantastic *speck* and game *salumi* like deer *prosciutto*. Pasta is homemade, soups are hearty and often contain barley, mushrooms are featured in season. Braised game is always a good choice. The fantastic selection of cheeses, both local and French, is a perfect excuse to order an important red wine from Stefan's well-chosen list of local, Italian, and international wines of note. Those lucky enough to stay in the hotel will have a good time with the extraordinary choice of *grappa*, distillates, and Cognac.

San Michele all'Adige

HOTEL

Villa Madruzzo

Cognola di Trento (close by)

☎0461.986-220

Fax 0461.986-361

All credit cards • moderate

HOTEL

Drago Hotel

Piazza San Gottardo 46, Mezzocorona (nearby)

☎0461.603-824

Fax 0461.601-940

All credit cards • inexpensive

ENOLOGICAL INSTITUTE, MUSEUM, LIBRARY

Museo degli Usi e Costumi della Gente Trentina

Via Mach 2

☎0461.650-314

Open 9 A.M.–12 noon, 2:30–6 P.M.; closed Monday

San Michele, with its castle and convent, was the southernmost point of the Tirolean Hapsburg culture. It is home to one of the most important enological institutes in Italy, and also to an interesting museum of folk traditions, devoted to the rural technology of the mountain, preserved until recently by the isolation of most valleys. The museum is divided into sections dedicated to daily agricultural labors. Farm tools, a water-powered mill from 1836, winemaking (check out the huge eighteenth-century winepress), metallurgy, animal husbandry, spinning, weaving, cheesemaking, carpentry, nuptial traditions, ceramic heating stoves, folklore, and hunting are thoroughly documented in attractively installed rooms. The library, open from 1:30 to 5:30 P.M. weekdays, contains over 4,000 volumes on alpine and Trentino ethnology and history. The Istituto Agrario, open from Monday to Friday, sells wine of their own production.

RESTAURANT
Da Silvio
Via Brennero 2
☎0461.650-324
Fax 0461.650-604
Closed Monday
All credit cards • high moderate

In the land of Tirolean village–style construction, Da Silvio, built and frescoed by modern painter Riccardo Schweizer, combines modern design with a traditional Italian family unit, the Mannas: four brothers, a sister, two in-laws, and Mom. The *salumi,* brine-cured *carne salada,* and breads are homemade, and the *degustazione trentina* offers a tasting of traditional dishes. The *piatto Schweizer,* a heated block of granite on which meat, fish, vegetables, mushrooms, cheese, or fruit is grilled, can be purchased here, a weighty but useful souvenir. The wine list concentrates on quality local wines and distillates.

Trento

Trento, with its Romanesque Duomo, Gothic Castello del Buonconsiglio, and *rinascimento* palaces with frescoed façades, a traditional meeting place between the Latin and Germanic cultures, makes a pleasant base for touring the province of Trentino.

HOTEL
Accademia
Vicolo Colico 4/6
☎0461.233-600
Fax 0461.230-174
All credit cards • expensive

HOTEL
America
Via Torre Verde 50
☎0461.983-010
All credit cards • moderate

HOTEL-RESTAURANT
Villa Madruzzo
Via Ponte Alto 26, Cognola (3 km from Trento)
☎0461.986-220
Fax 0461.986-361
All credit cards • moderate

Villa Madruzzo, a fifteenth-century villa, was the summer home of Cardinal Madruzzo, a mover at the Council of Trent. It's set in a park with incredible trees and gardens in the hills just outside Trento, furnished with antiques, and makes a perfect base for touring in Trentino. The restaurant has opened since my last visit, three elegant dining rooms with outdoor dining on the covered terrace when the weather is nice. The menu is a blend of Italian classics and a few local specialties, and mushrooms are used with abandon. *Carne salada* is served over a bed of tender salad greens, topped with wafer-thin slices of apple; rye bread *gnocchi* are dressed with cabbage, smoky *pancetta. Polenta* is paired with wild mushrooms and a selection of melted local cheeses. Desserts are homemade and tempting, although I can't resist the seasonal fruit. The well-priced wine list emphasizes Trentino and Alto Adige, although a small selection of wines from other regions is also available. Service is professional.

RESTAURANT
Ristorante Chiesa
Via San Marco
☎0461.238-766
Fax 0461.986-169
Closed Wednesday evening, Sunday
All credit cards • high moderate

I was never too enthusiastic about Chiesa, thought their idea of the Mela Party, a six-course meal featuring the apple, silly, their fifteenth-century menu not my style. So I was delighted with the changes made by Alberto and Alessandro, sons of owner Sergio Chiesa. The dining room is spacious

but cleverly divided, large modern inter-
pretations of the apple paintings on the
walls, track lighting, comfortable chairs,
well-appointed tables, professional service.
The menu has enough traditional dishes to
satisfy, along with well-prepared Italian
classic or creative dishes. Vegetarians will be
pleased. The four-course chef's special is a
bargain. Diners choosing the Buon Ricordo
menu of *carne salada; talleri,* rounds of
pasta sauced with meat sauce and poppy
seeds; lake trout; and a perfectly executed
shaped-like-a-cut-apple tartlet will be
rewarded with a wonderful meal and a souvenir Buon Ricordo plate. The wine list is a
joy to drink from, greatly improved, well
priced, including most of Trentino–Alto
Adige's wines of note, as well as a lovely
selection from the rest of Italy.

RESTAURANT
Osteria Il Cappello
Piazzetta Anfiteatro 3
☎0461.235-850
Closed Sunday evening, Monday
All credit cards • high moderate
Tucked away on a quiet piazza in a building
that dates from 1400, Osteria Il Cappello is
a restaurant frequented mostly by locals
who want a break from traditional cooking.
Chef Mark Corner is English, worked at
Spago in Los Angeles, met a woman chef
from Trento, and decided to stick around.
His partner, Luca Carraro, is a perfect host
with a keen knowledge of local wine. Their
restaurant is beautifully restored, with
stone columns and vaulted ceilings downstairs, the original ground floor of the
building. Start with a flute of Ferrari
sparkling wine, paired with first-rate
salumi. Vegetable appetizers and anything
with mushrooms will probably please diners. Grilled meat and fresh fish are always
on the menu, more elaborate second
courses change weekly. Chocoholics should
prepare for the gooey chocolate *torta cre-*

mosa, served with cinnamon-flavored
sauce. The wine list is studded with gems.

LOCAL SNACK
Birreria Forst
Via Oss Mazzurana 38
☎0461.235-590
Closed Monday
All credit cards • inexpensive
Locals stop in for a glass of beer, a *wurstel*
(hot dog), and homemade sauerkraut.
Don't bother eating or drinking anything
else.

MARKETS
Piazza A. Vittoria
Piazza delle Erbe
Closed Sunday
Piazza Lodron has been made into a playground, and the market has moved. Official
produce and mushroom vendors and three
cheese stands are in piazza Vittoria; farmers
sell their own fruits, vegetables, and flowers
in piazza delle Erbe. The mushroom selection begins in late June with Yugoslavian
chanterelles, which are replaced later in the
season with local mushrooms. The season
peaks in the fall, when over forty mushroom
varieties are sold. A traffic cop–mycologist
examines the mushrooms to make sure
they're comestible. In September, lessons on
how to recognize and find mushrooms are
given in nearby piazza Lodron, from around
8:30 to 11:00 A.M. Farmers at the piazza
delle Erbe market sell traditional apple varieties from August to October.

GROCERY
Salumeria Polla
Via Oss Mazzurana 33
☎0461.982-405
Closed Saturday afternoon, Sunday
Founded in 1902, this classic shop has their
own production of first-rate sausage,
cotechino, and salami. Regional and Italian
cheese and foods are also sold.

GROCERY

La Gastronomia

Via Mantova 28

☎0461.235-217

Closed Saturday afternoon, Sunday

MasterCard, Visa

Wonderful *speck*, *bresaola*, cheese, bread, and prepared foods, perfect for one-stop shopping for a picnic in the countryside. Outer-regional products like *bottarga* (pressed dried roe), Illy coffee, extra virgin olive oil, and Iranian caviar are also for sale. The sauerkraut is homemade, available when the weather is cool.

GELATO

Torre Verde–Gelateria Zanella

Via Suffragio 6

☎0461.232-039

Open 10 A.M. to midnight, closed Wednesday

Claudio Zanella makes the best *gelato* in Trento. He uses local milk, freezes fresh local fruit in season. Classic flavors include local blueberry, raspberry, and apple, as well as the regional pride, Trento *spumante gelato*. The house specialty is *stracchino*, a coffee *semifreddo* with chocolate bits and hazelnuts, topped with whipped cream, a candied cherry, and a crispy wafer cookie. Claudio also prepares elaborate creations—"eggs in a frying pan," hazelnut, custard, and vanilla *gelato* topped with whipped cream and two apricot halves; "spaghetti," of hazelnut and custard *gelato* topped with strawberry sauce and coconut, or even a banana split. Eat at tables outside under a shaded pergola in the summer.

WINE AND GRAPPA

Enoteca Lunelli

Largo Carducci 12

☎0461.982-496

Closed Monday morning

Founded in 1929 by Bruno Lunelli, this historic *enoteca* introduced the idea of selling wine by the liter, eliminating the local custom of making it at home with purchased grapes and little artistry, a messy inaccurate procedure. Lunelli and his wife also sold sparkling wine made by Ferrari, a local producer who created one of Italy's first high-quality sparkling wines. Lunelli eventually purchased the company. The wine shop prospered under the direction of Bruno's son Franco, who made all bottled and bulk wine available for tasting by the glass. And although wine is no longer available for tasting at the Lunelli *enoteca*, the selection of wines from Trentino simply can't be beat. The entire range of Ferrari sparkling wines is sold in sizes from half bottles to Methuselahs. Surgiva mineral water and Segnana *grappa* are also for sale. Dozens of single-varietal *grappe* from local producers, as well as a fine selection of wines and *grappe* from other regions of Italy and beyond, are displayed on the floor-to-ceiling shelves. First-rate extra virgin olive oil, bottled by È from Liguria, Umbria, and Toscana is also sold as well as the È coffee, produced with the consultance of Andrea Trinci, master coffee roaster from Tuscany who sold his artisanal company to Ferrari a few years ago. The staff is helpful and friendly, they take credit cards and, miraculously, they will send wine to the U.S.

WINERY

Ferrari

Via Ponte di Ravina 15

☎0461.972-311

Fax 0461.913-008

Open Monday through Friday

Sparkling-wine fans should plan a visit to the Ferrari winery, which will arrange for a tour of their cellars and a tasting of their fine wines for readers who fax a month in advance.

TRENTINO FRUIT ORGANIZATION
Associazione Produttori Ortofrutticoli Trentini
Via Segantini 10
☎0461.986-972

This is the center of the fruit-growing strategy of Trentino. A.P.O.T. is an umbrella marketing association of four fruit-growing poles, and it governs more than 10,000 producers in 37 cooperatives and has 150 individual members. Visit the office for information about Melina apple growers from the Non and Sole valleys; La Trentina apples, kiwis, and traditional cherry and plum varieties from the Valsugana and Basso Sarca; the small fruits and vegetable growers of Trentino, over 1,500 farms that grow berries, potatoes, and corn for *polenta*; and the single producers, whose members don't belong to cooperatives. Many members are organic growers, or use organic or integrated defense strategies, avoiding chemical treatments whenever possible.

TIROLEAN CHIC
Oberrauch Zitt
Via Mantova 12
☎0461.981-290
All credit cards
Closed Saturday afternoon

Val di Vizze
HOTEL
Lamm
Via Città Nuova 16, Vipiteno (nearby)
☎/Fax 0472.765-127
All credit cards • low moderate

RESTAURANT
Pretzhof
Tulves 259
☎/Fax 0472.764-455
Closed Monday, Tuesday
MasterCard, Visa • high moderate

The road to Tulves looks like a driveway, winding through the Vizze Valley outside the city of Vipiteno, flanked by pine trees, pastures, wooden fences, farms, and mountains. The reward at the end of the road is the restaurant Pretzhof, where owner Karl Mair presides in two dining rooms, assisted in the kitchen by his wife, Ulli. The restaurant is rustic, with wooden walls, low-beamed ceilings, lots of antler decor, wooden tables, and important wineglasses, a hint that the enological experience here is going to be a thrill. All food comes from their farm—lamb, goat, mushrooms, deer, suckling pig, all produce seasonal. Bread is among the best I've had in the region, flat rounds and thinly sliced whole wheat served with coin-sized slices of flavored butter. Begin with the house *antipasto* of marinated salads or mushrooms, a tasting of cured deer products, and *formaggio grigio*. Continue with vegetable strudel, first-rate *canederli*, buckwheat *spaezle* sauced with deer *ragù*. Carnivores will be thrilled with the pork or lamb shanks, offal with *polenta*, veal or pork ribs or tripe. The cheese plate is worth a journey—everything is homemade, including cow, goat, and mixed milk and butter cheeses. Even desserts make splendid eating, either a fine version of *foresta nera*, chocolate cake; buckwheat-flour *torta saracena* or *krapfen;* lightweight fried ravioli filled with blueberries, dusted with powdered sugar. The wine list is a joy, and although the house wine is pleasant, the list offers a wide selection of bargains, fantastic regional wines that are hard to find elsewhere, well priced, just begging to be uncorked—Karl will, of course, have some worthy suggestions.

The map shows the following labels:

SWITZERLAND
AUSTRIA
TRENTINO ALTO ADIGE
FRIULI-VENEZIA GIULIA
Pieve d'Alpago
Puos d'Alpago
A27
Feltre
Follina
Solighetto
Col San Martino
Conegliano
Cavaso del Tomba
Lago di Garda
Romano d'Ezzelino
Asolo
Giavera del Montello
Bassano del Grappa
Treviso
Lovadina
A4
A22
Montecchio Precalcino
Trissino
Marostica
Rosà
Castelfranco Veneto
San Giorgio di Valpolicella
Montecchia di Crosara
Loreggia
Piave
Sant'Ambrogio di Valpolicella
Caldogno
Vicenza
Mogliano Veneto
Jesolo
Verona
A4
Venezia-Tessera Airport
Castelnuovo
Arcugnano
Rubano
Mira
Venezia-Torcello
Ospedaletto di Pescantina
Monteforte d'Alpone
Padova
Venezia-Cavallino
Montegrotto Terme
Valeggio sul Mincio
Arquà Petrarca
Venezia
Isola della Scala
Bagnoli di Sopra
Venezia-Lido
LOMBARDIA
Adige
Lusia
Adriatic Sea
A13
Po
EMILIA-ROMAGNA

Veneto, in northeastern Italy, is a
topographical four-layer cake. The Alps,
flanked by their foothills, separate it from the
Tirolean culture. Fertile alluvial plains to the
south are divided by the rivers Piave, Brenta,
Adige, and the mighty Po, the Mississippi of
Italy. Along the coast, lowlands and lagoonal
islands rim the Gulf of Venezia and the
Adriatic Sea.

Veneto

Historically, *Venete* tribes, Roman colonization, barbaric invasions, Longobards, and subdivision into fiefdoms and dukedoms kept the mainland busy. Political refugees from all of the above fled to the lagoon, which looked eastward to the Byzantine Empire and to the Orient, with its spice and silk trade. The boundaries of the area that was once known as the *Tre Venezie*—comprising Veneto, Friuli–Venezia Giulia, and Trentino–Alto Adige—are roughly the same as they were in the fifteenth century, when it was a powerful, wealthy, expansionist maritime nation that had ruled for almost 400 years.

Politics ceded Veneto to Austria twice during its history, and signs of that dominion fill the shelves of pastry shops in much of this region. The *cucina* of Veneto is founded on rice and corn. *Polenta* (ground cornmeal) is cooked in a rounded cooking pot (*paiolo*), ladled into bowls, and sauced with hearty game stews; or cooled, sliced, and grilled or fried. It is present on almost every main-course plate in the region. Rice is served as a first course—as *risotto*, cooked with almost everything the countryside and lagoon have to offer, from field greens to baby peas, wild asparagus, fish, shellfish, and game. Lagoon menus feature fish and vegetables, whereas inland, game and poultry are more common—all times spiced with a hint of the Orient, of the power of the *Repubblica Veneziana*. Cheese is found in the mountains, but rarely turns up on the coast. The traditional sweet that seems to have taken Veneto, and the rest of Italy, by storm is *tiramisù*, a rich cocoa-dusted dessert flavored with *mascarpone* cheese and coffee.

The countryside of the Treviso area offers a number of possibilities for living like a doge in a Venetian country villa, with only a ten-minute commute by train to Venezia.

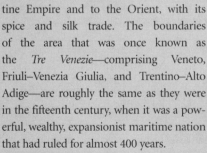

The Menu

Salumi

Salumi di cacciagione: various cold cuts made with game

Antipasto

Granseola: crabmeat dressed with oil, lemon, and parsley

Pesce (or **sarde** or **sogliole**) **in saor:** fish (or sardines or sole) sautéed and marinated in a sauce of cooked onion, vinegar, pine nuts, and raisins

Primo

Bigoli: homemade pasta (with or without eggs), made with a special kind of spaghetti press

Bigoli con l'anatra: cooked in duck broth, sauced with duck

Bigoli in salsa: sauced with oil, onions, and anchovies

Casunziei: ravioli stuffed with ricotta, beets, winter squash, or spinach

Pasta e fagioli: bean soup with homemade pasta

Pastissada de manzo con gnocchi: potato dumplings served with byzantine-spiced meat sauce

Polenta: cornmeal pudding, as a side dish cooled, sliced, and either grilled or fried, served with butter and cheese

Risi: rice

Risi e bisato: cooked with eel, bay leaves, oil, and lemon

Risi e bisi: cooked with peas and *pancetta,* served with butter and grated Parmesan

Risi in cavroman: with a cinnamon-spiced lamb sauce

Riso con i bruscàndoli: rice cooked with tender shoots of wild hops; found only in the spring

Risotto: rice, sautéed, then cooked with broth and any number of enrichments

Risotto di mare or **di pesce:** cooked with mixed seafood

Risotto nero: cooked with cuttlefish and its black ink

Risotto primavera: "springtime rice," cooked with tender spring vegetables: asparagus tips, baby peas, string beans, artichokes

Zuppa coada: baked squab, boned and layered with toasted bread, broth, and Parmesan cheese

Secondo

Anatra col pien: stuffed duck, traditionally boiled, but sometimes roasted

Baccalà alla vicentina: salt cod, cooked with onions, milk, anchovies, and Parmesan cheese, served with *polenta*

Baccalà mantecato: poached salt cod, puréed with olive oil and parsley

Bisato alla veneziana: eel sautéed in olive oil, with bay leaves and vinegar

Bisato sull'ara: eel baked with bay leaves

Capesante alla veneziana: sautéed scallops

Fegato alla veneziana: calf's liver cooked with onions, served with *polenta*

Gamberetti: tiny cooked shrimp, dressed with oil, lemon, and parsley

Moleche col pien: fried soft-shelled crabs

Polenta e osei or **polenta e ucelli:** polenta served with skewered small birds and their roasting juices

Pollastro (or **faraona**) **in tecia:** chicken (or guinea hen) cooked with onions and cloves, served with *polenta*

Seppie alla veneziana: cuttlefish cooked with its black ink and white wine

Torresani allo spiedo: bacon-wrapped spit-roasted pigeons flavored with rosemary, juniper berries, and bay leaves, served with *polenta*

Contorno

Asparagi in salsa or **alla bassanese:** steamed asparagus served with sauce containing hard-cooked egg, vinegar, and olive oil

Fagioli: beans

Radicchio: red chicory, eaten both raw and cooked

Formaggio

Asiago: hard, sharp, cow's milk
Montasio: smooth, mild; sharper and harder when aged
Pecorino: fresh or aged, sheep's milk, distinct
Vezzena: smooth, fatty, bland

Dolce

Baicoli: simple small cookies dipped in dessert wine

Forti: almond spice cookies from Bassano del Grappa
Fregolotta: crumbly almond cake
Frittole: round fritters containing raisins, pine nuts, and candied citron, found at Carnival time
Pandoro: eggy, rich, sweetened yeast bread, found at Christmastime
Tiramisù: *mascarpone, eggs, ladyfingers, and coffee combined in a rich cocoa-dusted dessert*

Zaleti: cornmeal raisin cookies

The Wine List

Veneto is Italy's largest producer of DOC wine. **Soave** from the Verona area is the most popular Italian white wine in the U.S., but **Prosecco** is a local winner, light, sparkling, ethereal, served almost everywhere by the glass, pitcher, or bottle, and consumed almost like a soft drink. At times, some of Veneto's finer wines seem to be easier to find outside the region.

Amarone, also known as **Recioto della Valpolicella Amarone** is a powerful dry red with a bitter finish, a DOC made in the province of Verona with semi-dried Corvina, Rondinella, and Molinara grapes. It is served with red meats and game. Top producers are Allegrini, Le Ragose, Masi, Giuseppe Quintarelli, Serègo Alighieri, Acordini Brigaldara, Brunelli, Dal Forno, Fratelli Speri, and Fratelli Tedeschi.

Bardolino is a DOC from the Lago di Garda area. The **Rosso,** a blend of Corvina, Rondinella, Molinara, and Negrara grapes, is a light, dry red, served with meat, poultry, and rabbit. The **Chiaretto,** a rosé made from Corvina, Rondinella, and Molinara

grapes, is lighter and more delicate, and is served with appetizers and first-course dishes. Top producers are Fratelli Tedeschi, Guerrieri-Rizzardi, Cavalchina, and Le Vigne di San Pietro.

Bianco di Custoza is a soft, dry white, a DOC from the Lago di Garda area, an aromatic blend of Trebbiano, Garganega, Tocai, and other white grape varieties. It is served with fish and seafood. Cavalchina and Le Vigne di San Pietro are the top producers.

Breganze, a DOC area north of Vicenza, produces seven different wines. The Bianco, made with Tocai, Pinot Bianco, and Pinot Grigio are fruity, elegant whites. Vespaiolo, made from the local Vespaiolo grape, is a dry, fresh white. All are served with appetizers, fish, and seafood. Rosso, a blend of Cabernet Franc, Sauvignon, and Merlot, aged in oak, and Cabernet are rich and elegant dry reds, served with meat and sauced dishes. Ruby Pinot Nero is light, fruity, and delicate, served with poultry. Non-DOC Torcolato, a semi-sweet golden dessert wine, is a rare treat, and costly. Maculan is the Breganze's top producer.

Elegant dry red **Cabernet** produced outside the DOC zones is usually a blend of Cabernet Franc and Sauvignon. It is served with meat and regional *cucina*, and is well made by Lazzarini's Villa dal Ferro and by Afra and Tobia Scarpa.

Non-DOC **Merlot,** a dry, elegant red, is produced by Lazzarini's Villa Dal Ferro, Col Sandago, and Afra and Tobia Scarpa.

Prosecco di Conegliano – Valdobbiadene, a DOC from northwest of Treviso, made of the Prosecco grape, is a light, fruity sparkling white that can be dry, semi-sweet, or sweet. **Cartizze** is a sparkling white made from the same grape, from the small microclimate within the **Prosecco** DOC area. Quality producers are Cantine Nino Franco, Gregoletto, Carpenè Malvolti, Le Groppe, Ruggeri, and Pino Zardetto.

Recioto di Soave made from semi-dried Garganega and Trebbiano grapes, is a golden, smooth, delicate, flowery, and sweet dessert wine. It is best produced by Anselmi and Pieropan.

Soave a delicate, dry white DOC produced east of Verona, is made with Garganega and Trebbiano grapes. It's Italy's second most exported DOC wine—more than 52 million liters yearly, most of it not worth drinking. The following winemakers prove that Soave can be a wine of class, a perfect companion to appetizers, pasta with light sauces, vegetables, fish, and seafood: Anselmi—with his special cru, Capitel Foscarino—Guerrieri-Rizzardi, Masi, and Pieropan.

Valpolialla a dry red made from Corvina, Rondinella, and Molinara; the best wines are from the Valpolialla Classico area. Top producers are Acordini, Allegrini, Brigaldara, Brunelli, Dal Forno, Fratelli Speri, Le Ragose, Masi, Quintarelli, Serego Alighieri, and Fratelli Tedeschi.

Spumante made with charmat or champenoise methods, is well produced by Nino Franco and Zardetto.

Regional Specialties

Polenta. *Polenta* is the Italian version of cornmeal mush, a cheap starch that, when served with a bit of sauce, keeps the pains of hunger at bay. Historically, it was probably much coarser than the modern cornmeal, which is called *bramata.* (The outer 40 percent of the kernel is used for animal feed and the remaining 60 percent, the heart of the kernel, is ground to make the cornmeal.) *Polenta* is cooked with salt and water, stirred constantly for a long time, until it becomes a cohesive mass with the consistency of breakfast cereal. It is served freshly made as a side dish (like mashed potatoes) or cooled, sliced, and reheated

with a sauce. In Veneto it is frequently grilled, and accompanies most main dishes. White *polenta* is more delicate, and usually accompanies fish or seafood. Two fine producers of hard-to-find, low-yield, traditional *marano* cornmeal are Lorenzo Borletti (see page 138 for more information about this farm) and the fantastic winery Allegrini (Corte Giara 7, Fumane di Valpolicella, tel. 045.770-1138, fax 045.770-1774), whose *polenta* is commercialized as Cortegiara, distributed in the U.S.

Extra Virgin Olive Oil. The region's best oil comes from olives grown on the southern exposures of the eastern shore of Lake Garda, an area known as the Olive Riviera. Climate is mitigated by the lake and palm trees; lemons and olives grow in one of their more northern settings. Olive cultivars include traditional *Casaliva*, rapidly disappearing *Trepp, Razza, Lezzo, Favarol,* and *Fort*, newer plantings of frost-resistant Tuscan *Leccino*. Extra virgin olive oil is produced in November when the olives turn from green to red to purple to black. Since some olives are picked green, the resulting oil is greenish, fruity yet delicate, without the aggressiveness of Tuscan oil, well matched with fish and seafood. Contact Luigi Quintarelli at the Consorzio di Tutela di Olio Extra Virgine di Oliva del Garda "Riviera degli Olivi" (piazza Matteotti 8, Bardolino, tel./fax 045.721-0820) if you'd like to purchase oil or to see it being pressed in November.

Asiago. The cheese known as Asiago has a history that dates back almost 1,000 years. It was originally made from the milk of sheep that grazed on the high plains, but around 1500, with the advent of animal husbandry, cows were substituted for sheep. Cheesemakers, *casari*, replaced sheep's milk with cow's, but continued using traditional methods. This is the cheese known as *asiago d'allevo* or *stagionato*, destined for ripening. Three different ages of this kind of Asiago are available in fine cheese shops. Look for *mezzano*, aged three to eight months; *vecchio*, aged nine to eighteen months, or *stravecchio*, aged for more than two years. The crust is dark, reddish to brown; straw-colored cheese has small and medium holes, tastes full flavored to piquant. *Stravecchio* from the Passo Vezzena area is said to be the finest, made from the milk of cows that graze in pastures over 1,500 meters. *Asiago pressato*, created for modern palates, is meant to be eaten fresh, weeks after its production; it has a thin, elastic crust, is soft inside, pale straw–colored, light, buttery, and delicate. To taste world-class Asiago, see Bassano del Grappa, page 139, or Marostica, page 148. For more information contact the Consorzio Tutela Formaggio Asiago (corso Fogazzaro 18, Vicenza, tel. 0444.321-758). To visit a dairy cooperative, contact Douglas or Flavio at Cooperativa Latte Alto Vicentino, via Vicenza 145, Bassano del Grappa, tel. 0445.360-666, fax 0424.501-159.

Lamon Beans. Did Pope Clement III give beans he'd received from the New World via Spain to humanist Piero Valeriano from Belluno? According to legend, Valeriano gave them to the farmers of Lamon, who planted the New World beans with most favorable results. Two of the four classic Lamon beans have names that indicate their Spanish origins—the *spagnol* is kidney-shaped, has a dirty white background with wine-red speckles, *spagnolit* is smaller, rounder, with lighter markings. The other two varieties are *caronega*, which looks squashed, with wine-red splotches, and *canalino*, kidney-shaped with dark, reddish-black markings. No matter where they originally came from, the starchy, thin-skinned speckled beans of Lamon have a cult following in Veneto. You'll probably never find the real thing, since production is limited. True bean freaks should plan to visit Lamon for the three-day festival in mid-September, with cultural, folkloristic, and gastronomic events, and three stands that serve Lamon beans in every course of the meal, including dessert. Write, call, or fax the Pro Loco (via Resinterra, Lamon 32033, tel./fax 0439.96393) for the exact dates. Contact president Piero Gaio at the Comunità Montana Feltrina (viale Rizzarda 21, Feltre, tel. 0439.303-210, fax 0439.302-630) for more information.

Bassano White Asparagus. White asparagus grown in the Bassano area has a cult following. Locals go wild from the end of April until June 13, Saint Anthony's Day, after which the asparagus are *never* picked. At the height of the season the city of Bassano has a festival dedicated to their DOC turion (edible shoot). A series of restaurants host special asparagus dinners. Interested in attending? Contact Severino Castellan, tel. 0424.533-043, for more information.

The classic method of eating white asparagus is hands-on, with a do-it-yourself sauce. Each diner is served two hard-boiled eggs, cruets of extra virgin olive oil, vinegar, salt, and pepper. Diners mash the eggs with a fork, add oil, mash, add vinegar, salt, and pepper, and mash to desired saucelike consistency. Dip boiled asparagus in the sauce.

Bellini. I can't imagine Veneto in the spring and summer without the Bellini, a refreshing combination of sparkling fruity Prosecco and white peach purée. It was originally created by Commendatore Giuseppe Cipriani, the founder of Harry's Bar, in the late 1950s, probably to take advantage of the tasty, intensely perfumed white peaches of the Venetian lagoon. It can be found throughout the region, but is at its best in Venice, in the spring and summer months when the peaches are fresh. The quintessential Bellini is prepared at the Cipriani Hotel bar (see page 137) in the summer only.

Radicchio. Radicchio is a winter vegetable, widely grown in Veneto in four major varieties. *Radicchio di Castelfranco* and *radicchio di Chioggia* are leafy heads with green and red marbleized leaves. *Radicchio di Verona* is a small purple lettucelike ball. But best of all is *radicchio di le Treviso*, subjected to a complicated forcing-blanching-sprouting technique that results in elongated, sun-starved, spider mum–like spears of purple red with an impressive

pearly white central rib, held together by a pointed peeled root. If there were a vegetable rights movement, Treviso growers would surely be accused of vegetal molestation. Selected seeds are planted in early summer, reddish-green leafed heads are harvested in the fall with intact root systems, packed tightly in long furrows in a plastic tunnel, removed to low cement pools, where the roots absorb warm spring water (once, this process was done in stalls with roots immersed in manure) and the plants begin to sprout. Looking pretty sad, with rotting outer leaves and a long hairy taproot, the plants are moved indoors to a warm, wet environment, draining onto sawdust, forcing the development of the sprout. Then plants are removed, trimmed of their rotten outer leaves to expose the heart, tender etiolated white and red leaves, and the hairy taproot is carved to one third of the length of the head. This is clearly an expensive process, and real *radicchio di Treviso* costs more than the other varieties. True *Treviso* fans should plan on visiting the Treviso Radicchio Fair, held under the sixteenth-century arcade of the Palace of the Three Hundred in the center of Treviso in late December.

Castelfranco Veneto, with its green-and-red-marbleized–leafed heads of radicchio known as "edible flowers," holds a festival of its own, usually the week before Christmas, although dates sometimes change. There's a big tent in piazza Giorgione that seats up to 1,200 diners and serves meals based on Castelfranco's radicchio, utilized in every course of the meal. Around twenty-five to thirty local producers, compete for the *crigola d'oro*, a golden reproduction of an old-fashioned basket in which radicchio was once sold. Contact the president of the Castelfranco growers, Dott. Battistel, piazzetta Guidolin, Castelfranco Veneto, tel. 0423.490-907, for more information. Radicchio fans should plan to visit Da Domenico in Lovadina (page 147) or Tre Panoce in Conegliano (page 144) where homage is paid to this local specialty during its cool weather season.

Vialone Nano and Carnaroli Rice. Two rice varieties of Veneto are deemed by knowledgeable cooks to make the best *risotto.* The most traditional is Vialone Nano, a short, fat, almost oval kernel with a small chip at one end that makes it look like a tiny tooth. It's widely grown, perfect for making *risotto,* and holds up well to cooking, leaving a firm, al dente core when properly prepared. Carnaroli is harder to find, more sought after, more expensive. Carnaroli was developed in 1945 in Lombardia, holds up even better to cooking, and has enough external starch to thicken *risotto* perfectly. Rice paddies, flooded rectangular fields bordered by an intricate system of irrigation canals, are also home to carp and frogs, and Jerusalem artichokes grow by the banks. All three are often paired with rice in *risotto.* See Bagnoli di Sopra (page 138) and Isola della Scala (page 145) for information about two rice growers. Or contact Marisa at the fantastic winery Allegrini (Corte Giara 7, Fumane di Valpolicella, tel. 045.770-1138, fax 045.770-1774). They grow and sell quality Vialone Nano and Carnaroli rice, commercialized as Cortegiara and distributed in the U.S.

Castraure Artichokes. *Castraure,* tiny, bitter artichokes, usually boiled whole, are a seasonal springtime treat, found in wine bars and *osterie,* one of the *cicchetti* ("little bites") that accompany a glass of house wine. In May the first tightly closed central artichoke on each plant is "castrated," dug out of its tightly closed unformed flower, to give strength to the lateral buds. The *castraure* were once considered too bitter to eat, but are sought after by local gastronomes, who enjoyed the palate-zapping flavors of this tiny artichoke with a cult following. The gardens of Malamocco on the island of Lido are legendary for their *castraure,* said to be the finest due to the salty alluvial soil of the lagoon. Look for *castraure* in May.

Grappa. Veneto isn't the region with a pre-Alp called Monte Grappa for nothing. It's the land of the Alpini, a heroic military corps created in 1871 to guard and defend the northern Alps and valleys. They're known to be big *grappa* drinkers, as anyone who has ever bumped into one of their annual conventions can attest. The epicenter of *grappa* production is in Bassano del Grappa, on the covered wooden bridge spanning the Brenta River, at the Nardini shop. Once upon a time, rafters transported wood to Venice and stopped off for a shot of *grappa* at Nardini, which is still open for *grappa* sampling (see page 140 for more information). To visit a first-rate *grappa* distiller, contact Bonollo, via Padova 74, tel. 049.900-0023. Or visit fruit distiller Vittorio Capovilla (see Rosà, page 154).

Ceramics. Veneto is an important ceramics center. The area around Bassano is rich in clay and the material known as "white earth of Vicenza," utilized for porcelain and pottery. The Brenta river made transportation easy. In the eighteenth century the Antonibon factory in the village of Nove rose to prominence, making *maiolica* and porcelain tableware, apothecary jars, tiles, and statuettes. Pottery fans should plan to visit the Ceramics Museum in Bassano (open 9 to 12), or the newly founded Ceramics Museum in Nove (open Monday to Saturday, 8 A.M. to 1 P.M. or by appointment, tel. 0424.590-022) to see fine examples of local ceramics. Dr. Barettoni is the current owner of the Antonibon factory, and readers can visit the factory (via Mulini

7, tel. 0424.590-013, fax 0424.590-181). Or try Ceramica Stringa (via Munari 19, tel./fax 0424.590-084) for a smaller production of modern and classic ceramics as well as antiques.

I'm wild about the ceramics produced in Este. Their tradition is older than that of Bassano or Nove, but also flourished in the eighteenth century. Check out the Museo Nazionale Altestino for the whole story. And visit the factory of Este Ceramiche Porcellane (via Sabine 31, tel. 0429.2270 or 3064, open from 8 A.M. to 12 P.M., 2 to 6 P.M.). Their ceramics are wonderful, produced for Tiffany, Christian Dior, Valentino, Fauchon, and others. I love the *trompe l'oeil* plates with olives, a large ripe pear, hard-boiled eggs, or peas in pods, and the Aunt Jemima cookie jar. The factory sells perfect pottery as well as seconds, and will ship. They don't take credit cards, so bring cash or traveler's checks.

Cookware. *Bigoli* freaks might want to look for a *torchio*, the press used to make this hearty extruded pasta. They can be found in housewares shops throughout the region.

Cities & Towns

Arcugnano

HOTEL

Villa Michelangelo
Via Sacco 19
☎0444.550-300
Fax 0444.550-490
All credit cards • expensive in season,
moderate off season

HOTEL

See Vicenza

RESTAURANT

Da Zamboni
Via Santa Croce 14, Lapio
☎/Fax 0444.273-079
Closed Monday evening, Tuesday
All credit cards • low moderate

In the hills south of Vicenza overlooking Lake Fimon, this large countryside *trattoria* serves traditional *cucina* with a twist of fantasy. Chef Alfredo Zamboni spent time in France, but it hasn't changed his idea of simple, home-style food. Start with fresh porky *salame*, smoked pork jowl, or vegetable *frittate*. First-course possibilities include *bigoli* dressed with braised duck, wintery cabbage and smoked pork soup, or *risotto* with seasonal vegetables like *bruscàndoli* (wild hops), asparagus, mushrooms, radicchio, or peas. Game or pigeon is braised; kid roasted in the oven; *baccalà* is cooked Vicenza-style with milk, onions, and spice; and everything is served with *polenta* made from *marano* cornmeal. Local goat cheese is worth saving room for. Alfredo's desserts show a bit of French influence, a relief after too much *tiramisù*. The wine list is vast, well priced, with something for every budget.

Arquà Petrarca

HOTEL
Majestic Hotel Terme
Viale delle Terme 84, Galzignano Terme
(nearby)
☎049.525-444
Fax 049.526-466
No credit cards • moderate

RESTAURANT
La Montanella
Via Costa 33
☎0429.718-200
Fax 0429.777-177
Closed Tuesday evening and Wednesday
All credit cards • high moderate

Located in the hills above the village of Arquà Petrarca, La Montanella is a large, modern, comfortable restaurant, surrounded by lawn, gardens, and olive trees, that serves well-prepared food ranging from rustic to sophisticated. The dining rooms have beamed ceilings and are well lit with modern lighting, tables are nicely set, armchairs are comfortable. Service is professional; waiters wear yellow shirts and black ties, and bustle efficiently between tables. The menu is large, divided between *cucina padovana* and classic Italian dishes. Pasta like *tortelloni, tagliatelle, pappardelle,* and *bigoli* are homemade, delicious, sauced with vegetables, game, or *porcini* mushrooms in season. Braised meat and game, meat grilled over wood coals are nicely prepared—*torresani* (squab) are cooked to order, partially boned guinea hen is flavored with bay leaves. Waiters will prepare salad from a cart laden with bowls of lettuce, radicchio, shredded carrots, dressed with one of La Montanella's selection of extra virgin olive oil, including their own production. Four different tasting menus will suit a wide range of diners—I loved the well-priced "Eat and Learn Menu," featuring seasonal traditional Padovana cooking.

There's a large well-chosen list of wines, distillates, olive oils, and vinegars, with a section on local Colli Euganei wines, winefood pairing advice, and a glossary of wine terms in Italian. The dessert (and dessert wine) list is tempting, with homemade *gelato, sorbetto,* pastry, and fresh fruit. Finish with a glass of *grappa* and magnificent *brutti e buoni* cookies studded with big chunks of almond.

Asolo

HOTEL
Villa Cipriani
Via Canova 298
☎0423.952-166
Fax 0423.411-060
All credit cards • luxury

HOTEL
Duse
Via Browning 190
☎0423.55241
Fax 0423.950-404
All credit cards • low moderate

RESTAURANT
Ca' Derton
Piazza D'Annunzio 11
☎0423.529-648
Closed Monday
American Express, MasterCard,
Visa • low moderate

Owners chef Nino Baggio and his wife, Antonietta's restaurant is in an elegant eighteenth-century palace with wooden beamed ceilings, decorated with anonymous paintings and prints, plants in stone pots, a table in the middle of the dining room with digestives and *grappe.* Begin with *polenta* and melty cheese or *soppressa* cooked with balsamic vinegar. *Pasta e fagioli; gnocchi* with wild mushrooms; braised and boned squab soup (*sopa coada*), layered with crispy bread, *parmigiano,* and broth, baked in the oven: or *risotto* are the usual starters. Continue with guinea hen in *peverada* sauce, goose, rabbit stuffed with mushrooms, mixed boiled meats. Game is served in season, vegetables are featured in the summer when it's too hot to think about meat. Desserts are simple, like *zaleti*, fruit tarts, or ricotta mousse flavored with coffee, or *amaretti*. The well-priced wine list emphasizes regional wines, but there's also a good assortment of Italian and international wines.

ENOTECA

Enoteca in Asolo
Via Browning 185
☎**0423.952-070**
Open 9 A.M.–12:30 P.M., 3–8 P.M. weekdays
(3 P.M.–1 A.M. weekends); closed Monday
All credit cards

Vincenzo Rudente is passionate about wine, and it shows in his large first-class selection. Wine is available by the glass or bottle. Snack on *soppressa, salame, pancetta,* or *mortadella.* Cheese like aged Asiago or *morlacco* from the mountains will tempt guests to drink big, well-priced reds. Simple desserts are from Bianchin (see below).

BAKERY

Bianchin
Via Canova 344
☎**0423.529-857**
Closed Wednesday afternoon

Pierluigi Bianchin's bakery, with beamed ceilings, marble-chip floors, and an authentic old-fashioned ambience, makes all cookies and breads in a wood-burning oven. Look for *cantucci*, almond cookies; *zaleti*, cornmeal raisin cookies; round loaves of *cioppa*; and *focaccia.*

GROCERY

Salumeria Bacchin di Ennio Sgarbossa
Via Browning 151
☎**0423.529-109**
Closed Wednesday afternoon

Robert Browning once lived in the building that now houses Sgarbossa, with its windows a jumble of regional and national products, impossible to resist for anyone interested in food. Check out the fine cheese, *salumi,* desserts, honey, dried mushrooms, quince paste, preserves, wine, *grappa*, and more, stacked from floor to ceiling. Buy a chunk of *pinza*, a rustic cornmeal cake studded with raisins and bits of fig, lemon, and orange.

Bagnoli di Sopra

HOTEL

See Padova

HISTORIC RICE AND CORNMEAL ESTATE

Tenuta di Bagnoli
Piazza Marconi 63
☎**049.538-0008**
Fax **049.538-0021**

The first traces of the Borletti family's huge estate (over 3,000 acres) date from the year 954 when Duke Almerigo donated the feudal Dominio (estate) to a Benedictine monastery. It was purchased in 1657 by Count Ludovico Widman who, in typical noble Veneto style, hired a big-name architect (probably Baldassare Longhena) to build a grand palace, an artistic white stone well, and a small theater, since the count was wild about theatrical productions. Carlo Goldoni, illustrious Venetian playwright, visited the Dominio twice, acted in his own plays in the theater, and even dedicated a comedy, *The Coffee Shop*, to the count. In 1742, Widman commissioned sculptor Antonio Bonazza to created a series of statues for the garden depicting characters from Goldoni's plays. The estate was eventually purchased by the Borletti family, who produce first-rate Carnaroli, Arborio, and Vialone Nano rice, yellow *marano* and white *perla* cornmeal, wine, *grappa*, and wine vinegar made from the Friularo grape. The Borlettis are planning to open a simple *osteria*, open on weekends, but it still hasn't happened as this book goes to print. Fax Lorenzo Borletti if you'd like to visit, purchase some of the estate's fine products, and check out the fantastic formal gardens with the Bonazza statues.

Bassano del Grappa

HOTEL

Villa Palma

Via Chemin Palma 30, Mussolene (nearby)
☎**0424.577-407**
Fax 0424.87687
All credit cards • expensive

RESTAURANT-HOTEL

Belvedere

Piazzale Generale Giardino 14
☎**0424.529-845 (hotel)**
☎**0424.524-988 (restaurant)**
Fax 0424.529-849
Restaurant closed Sunday
All credit cards • high moderate

The restaurant, which is located next to the Hotel Belvedere, serves regional, national, and creative cooking based on local ingredients with great success. Bassano's exceptional white asparagus and local truffles and mushrooms flavor many dishes on the menu in season. Begin with classic appetizers like sole with onions, pine nuts, raisins, and vinegar; homemade sausage; aged cheese and *polenta; rusticata* salad of radicchio, shrimp, and *porcini* mushrooms or warm pork cracklings on a bed of wild greens; and *la fondutella tartufata*, truffled fondue. Tripe and bean soup, *pasta e fagioli*, pigeon or wild asparagus soup; pastas like *bigoli* with duck *ragù*, *pappardelle* with truf-

fled hare sauce or *porcini* mushrooms; or seasonal vegetable *risotto* are among the first-course possibilities. There's a large selection of simple or elaborate meat preparations like veal fillet with foie gras and morels, as well as local specialties such as snails with *polenta*, pigeon (*torresani*), "little birds" (*osei*), or hare with wild mushrooms, stewed eel, or Venetian cuttlefish. Diners who opt for the *baccalà* Vicenza-style will be presented with a souvenir Buon Ricordo plate. Conclude with desserts from the cart, wild berries or *sgroppino*, a slushy mixture of lemon sorbet and Prosecco wine. The wine list is large, and owner-sommelier Vanni Bonotto will help diners choose something interesting. Enophiles should ask to see his cellar. Dine in the garden in the summer. The hotel, recently remodeled, is the oldest in Bassano and makes a perfect base for touring the area.

Spicy goulash, Vicenza-style cod, stewed black cuttlefish, braised roe deer, and pork ribs are all served with *polenta;* tripe is always on the menu. Sunday-lunch diners can choose *bollito* (boiled meats) and begin their meal with homemade *tagliolini* in broth. Look for Bassano's white asparagus in season. Desserts are homemade, with seasonal fresh, dried fruit, or nuts. The wine list is short but sweet, with the entire selection of Vittorio Capovilla's wines and lots of his fruit distillates.

ENOITECA

Bar Breda

Vicolo Jacopo da Ponte 3
☎**0424.522-123**
Closed Sunday
All credit cards • inexpensive

Stop in for a glass or bottle of wine, with simple snacks of *salumi* and cheese. Hang out with local enophiles and swirl big reds in big crystal glasses.

RESTAURANT

Alla Riviera

Via San Giorgio 17
☎**0424.503-700**
Closed Monday evening and Tuesday
MasterCard, Visa • low moderate

Alla Riviera used to be an *osteria* where locals played cards and sucked up the house wine, with some food offered since Italians don't drink without eating something. Sandro Ceccon always dreamed of owning an *osteria* and convinced his wife, Carla Frigo, to quit working at a local bookstore. Their *osteria* is a new favorite, charming, with old prints, marble-chip *graniglia* (pressed chips of marble) flooring, old-fashioned lighting, blue-and-white–striped tablecloths, and an attractive display of seasonal fruit and vegetables. I can't imagine Titian-haired Carla, who speaks a blend of rapid-fire Venetian dialect and Italian, working anywhere else. She powers her way through Sandro's menu of traditional Veneto cooking that utilizes seasonal vegetables to great advantage. Appetizers are tempting, like chunky chicken-liver *crostini*, grilled peppers with *bagna cauda*, beans with celery, seasonal *frittate*, marinated veal's foot (*nervetti*), boiled octopus, *sarde in saor*, *baccalà mantecato* (whipped cod), and more. Save room for the soup of the day or homemade pasta.

GRAPPA BAR

Ditta Bortolo Nardini

Ponte Vecchio 2
☎**0424.227-741**
Fax 0424.220-477
Open 8 A.M.–8 P.M., closed Monday in the winter

The Nardini *grappa* bar is on the corner of the covered wooden bridge that spans the Brenta River. Rafters who transported wood to Venice used to stop off for a shot of *grappa* at the Nardini shop, and it's still going strong. Order at the wooden bar in the front room, decorated with an old copper *grappa* still and shelves of *grappa* bottles large and small, hang out in front of the bar on the bridge or in the back room with windows overlooking the river. Go native and ask for *rosso nardini*, an attractive aperitif made with Nardini's red liqueur (only available locally; secret formula), a twist of lemon peel, and a shot of seltz.

GROCERY
Gastronomia Venzo
Via Jacopo da Ponte 14
☎0424.522-229
Fax 0424.518-866
Closed Wednesday afternoon
MasterCard, Visa

Founded in 1911, remodeled many times, Antonia Santi's shop is the place to go for a fantastic selection of local *salumi*, all ages of Asiago, pasta, pastry, wine and *grappa*, and practically every Italian gastronomic product of note. Look for *ventresca* tuna, single-wheat-cultivar Senatore Capelli pasta from Latini, fantastic dried *porcini* mushrooms and much, much more. This is the perfect place to pick up fine culinary souvenirs; they've even got Cryovac (*sottovuoto* in Italian) so that cheese won't smell up your suitcase. Picnic fans should plan to buy some of the take-out foods like whipped or Vicenza-style cod or *sarde in saor.*

Caldogno

HOTEL
Ai Pilastroni
Via Marosticana 2, Povolaro di Dueville
☎0444.595-003
Fax 0444.596-078
All credit cards • low moderate

HOTEL

See Vicenza

RESTAURANT
Molin Vecio
Via Giaroni 56
☎/Fax 0444.585-168
Closed Monday evening, Tuesday
All credit cards • moderate

As its name indicates in dialect, Molin Vecio is an authentic water mill from the sixteenth century, restored in 1984 by Sergio Boschetto and his wife, Leda,

and turned into a charming *trattoria.* Leda's in the kitchen with chef co-owner Amadeo Sandri; Sergio's in the dining room. Their menu is in dialect and may be difficult to understand. The cooking is strictly regional, with *polenta* made with *marano* corn a major element on the menu. For an overview of tradition, order the "authentic Vicentina tasting menu" of potato *gnocchi, risotto* with lake fish and beans, barley soup, *polenta* and *baccalà,* a fried skewer of mushrooms and Asiago sauced with *pearà,* and a *semifreddo* ("half cold") wine dessert. Vegetarians can order the inexpensive *proposta verde* of squash and red cabbage terrine, barley soup, and *polenta* with melted cheese and mushrooms. Or venture into the dialect of the à la carte menu, choosing braised snails, or fried fish and scallops, or stewed chicken, all accompanied by *polenta.* Conclude with *pinza,* apple strudel, or local cookies, accompanied by a glass of Fragolino dessert wine, thus named because it tastes like strawberries. The house wine is amusing, but serious enophiles should probably dine elsewhere.

The Mulin Vecio holds traditional food festivals once a month, the most important being the *Festa della Rua,* on September 8, commemorating the date in 1428 when Vicenza was saved from the plague. A 26-meter-tall tower (Rua) decorated with columns, flags, and 18 people, the symbol of the local notary guild, was carried through the streets of Vicenza by 80 bearers. Unfortunately for lovers of processions, electrical wires drastically abbreviated the route, the custom fell into disuse, and the Rua was burned for firewood during World War II. Reasonably priced fixed meals are served at Molin Vecio's festivals on outdoor tables, re-creating the feeling of a village celebration—call or fax Sergio or Amadeo to check on the dates.

Castelfranco Veneto

HOTEL-RESTAURANT

Fior
Via dei Carpani 18
☎0423.721-212
Fax 0423.498-771
All credit cards • moderate

I was distressed on my last visit to Castelfranco to find my favorite restaurant, Osteria ai Due Mori, closed and chef-owner Danilo Carrano transferred to Germany. I was staying at the Hotel Fior, an over-restored Veneto villa on the outskirts of Castelfranco, a perfect base for touring the area. What the hotel lacked in charm it made up in service and efficiency. The menu displayed in the lobby seemed interesting enough to warrant a meal. The restaurant Fior is downstairs, modern, with curtained glass walls, Murano chandeliers, local ceramic centerpieces on the tables, frequented by locals for classic Veneto and Italian dishes. Pasta is well executed, *al dente,* sauced with seafood or tomato; ravioli and *gnocchi* are homemade, *pasta e fagioli* is always on the menu, *risotto* is prepared for a minimum of two diners. Mushrooms are a big deal in season, turning up in many courses. Fresh-fish specials change daily, meat preparations are less exciting. Salads are composed from a cart with bowls of fresh vegetables and lettuces, dressed tableside with a selection of extra virgin olive oils and vinegars. The *Maestro del Dolce* award in the entrance attests to the importance of dessert at the Fior. Homemade *gelato,* mousse, *semifreddo, tiramisù, panna cotta,* or individual fruit tarts served with *zabaione* are among the tempting choices. Service is professional, and swift, green-jacketed waiters are attentive. The wine list includes some unexpected pleasures.

GROCERY

Favoretto
Piazza Giorgione 53
☎0423.722-078
Closed Wednesday afternoon

Favoretto, hidden in a courtyard behind piazza Giorgione, sells the best cheese and *salumi* in Castelfranco. Look for extra virgin olive oil, wine, *grappa,* and fine Italian and imported foods in this shop.

Castelnuovo

HOTEL

See Padova or Montegrotto Terme

RESTAURANT

Al Sasso
Via Ronco 11
☎049.992-5073
Closed Wednesday
MasterCard, Visa • moderate

Cheese maven Alberto Marcomini introduced me to this wonderful country-style *trattoria,* a new favorite on a rural road bordered by dozens of lesser-quality restaurants that look cute enough. Don't bother stopping anywhere but Al Sasso, where Lucio Calaone, assisted by his mother, wife, and sister in the kitchen, is responsible for one of the great dining experiences in the region. Look for enlightened versions of traditional dishes, prepared with impeccable ingredients, like local poultry, super-fresh seasonal produce and herbs, first-rate *salumi,* excellent cheese. The ambience is carefully restored rustic, with wooden beamed ceilings, a brandy glass of herbs in the center of the table. I wouldn't think of not beginning with a plate of deep-fried zucchini flowers, sage leaves, and mushrooms for a hint of what perfectly fried food is all about, although the bean and potato salad studded with tasty anchovies was difficult to resist. *Pasta e fagioli,* homemade pasta like *tagliolini* with mushrooms or *bigoli* sauced with a terrific chicken *ragù* are among first-course options. Wild seasonal greens like *bruscàndoli* (wild hops), *ortica* (nettles), or *rosole* (poppy greens) appear in different courses. Continue with guinea hen braised with chanterelles or pheasant cooked with Cabernet, but don't miss Al Sasso's justly famous superior fried chicken served with crispy fried potato chunks. Leave room for some of Alberto's impressive cheeses, paired with wines from the simple inexpensive regional list or the bigger, deeper Italian-and-beyond selection with justifiably higher prices. Seasonal fruit desserts—I'm wild about the summery medley of fried peaches, peach tart, and sliced yellow Monselice peaches. Dine under the portico in the summer.

Cavaso del Tomba

HOTEL

See Asolo or Bassano del Grappa

RESTAURANT

Al Ringraziamento
Via San Pio X 107
☎**0423.543-271**
Closed Monday
American Express, MasterCard,
Visa • high moderate

"To give thanks" is what the name of this restaurant means, and many diners are thankful for the hard work of owners chef Mauro Fumei and Emanuela Bedin. Their restaurant isn't easy to get to, but local friends told me it was worth the schlep and they were right. The setting is elevated rustic, with understated decor, low lighting, framed prints, and well-appointed tables. Mauro's *cucina* is seasonal, creative, more territorial than traditional. The menu changes daily—recent appetizers include eggplant confit with a salad of cured

tongue, herbed snails, barley-and-quail salad. Sea bass ravioli with herbs and *bottarga*, winter squash *gnocchi* with smoked ricotta. Tiny lamb chops in an herb crust, rare pigeon sauced with cassis and mushrooms. Dessert offerings are tempting—look for individual blackberry tarts, fruit bavarians, crème brûlée. The wine list focuses on Veneto, Trentino–Alto Adige, and Friuli, with a smaller selection of important reds from Piemonte and Toscana, and even some French wines. Tasting menus are reasonably priced, but must be ordered by all diners at the table.

Col San Martino

HOTEL

Pieve di Soligo
Via Corte della Caneve
Pieve di Soligo (nearby)
☎**0438.980-435**
Fax 0438.980-896
All credit cards • moderate

HOTEL

See Follina

RESTAURANT

Locanda da Condo
Via Fontana 69
☎**0438.898106**
Closed Wednesday
No credit cards • low moderate

The Locanda da Condo looks like a typical provincial family *trattoria,* complete with a bar in the downstairs entrance and a smattering of tables occupied by old men smoking strong-smelling cigarettes. However, the *cucina* has been renewed by Condo's son Enrico, who has blown his redecorating budget on studying with the great chefs of Italy and France. The *trattoria* decor hasn't been abandoned, and neither has the regional *cucina,* although there are plenty of creative, fresh dishes using seasonal local products. Ultratraditional specialties—white *polenta* sauced with mushrooms, bean soup, cooked sausage and smooth mashed potatoes, and boned guinea hen served with liver-anchovy sauce (*peverada*)—are nicely presented. Nontraditional but delicious: homemade vegetable pasta flavored and sauced with the same vegetable, and grilled meats. Conclude your meal with a selection of hard-to-find regional cheeses, like *taleggio di soligo* and *carnia vecchio*, or with homemade desserts. The wine list is wonderful and includes many regional, and reasonably priced, gems as well as wines from other regions of the country. In the summer, dine outside on the terrace, under a cane mat ceiling that conceals the corrugated plastic roof.

Conegliano

HOTEL
Sporting Ragno d'Oro
Via Diaz 37
☎0438.412-300
Fax 0438.412-310
All credit cards • low moderate

RESTAURANT
Tre Panoce
Via Vecchia Trevigiana
☎0438.60071
Fax 0438.62230
Closed Sunday evening, Monday, and August
All credit cards • moderate

Drive through lush vineyards to get to Tre Panoce, a restored farmhouse with a decor somewhere between country and kitsch. Armando Zanotto, looking more like a ship's captain than a chef, will welcome you to his restaurant, and you'll be served a glass of the house Prosecco and a bowl of fresh raw vegetables with a mustard dip. Armando offers a moderately priced tasting menu which I find large—nine courses plus small pastries—and not traditional

enough for my taste. Homemade bread and herbal *grissini* are crispy; local *salumi, polenta,* and *chiodini* mushrooms, splendidly cooked *risotto,* eel with sour cherries, and duck with Prosecco grape sauce are all winners. The cheese selection is local and first-rate. A separate menu for homemade desserts should hint at the importance of this course: vanilla *gelato,* served plain or topped with fruit or chocolate sauce; fresh fruit ices; pastries; *tiramisù;* or refreshing sliced fresh fruit. Armando's wife, sommelier Ave, will help you choose a wine from their impressive list of regional and nonregional selections. Radicchio freaks will wonder how they survived without Armando's book *Il Radicchio in Cucina,* 617 recipes featuring the radicchio of Treviso and Castelfranco Veneto.

ENOITECA
Due Spada
Via M. Beato Ongaro 69
☎0438.31990
Open 9:30 A.M.–2:30 P.M., 6 P.M.–2 A.M.; closed Tuesday, Wednesday
MasterCard, Visa • inexpensive

Stop in at this wine bar in the heart of Conegliano for the ambience, fantastic selection of wines, and something small to eat like *panini caldi, crostini, soppressa, salame prosciutto, speck, formaggi.*

Feltre

GRISTMILL
Molino Stien
☎0439.2321
This modern mill produces quality *farina per polenta bramata* (cornmeal), both white and yellow. The corn is local because, as they informed me, it's the earth that gives the flavor to the corn, and the tastiest corn for *polenta* is, clearly, grown in this area of Veneto. The Molino Stien also makes flour from rye, barley, and oats.

Follina

HOTEL

Abbazia

Piazza IV Novembre
☎0438.971-277
Fax 0438.970-001
All credit cards • moderate

RESTAURANT

Al Castelletto

Via Castelletto 15, Pedeguarda
☎0438.842-484
Closed Tuesday
No credit cards • moderate

Although it's called Al Castelletto, everyone refers to this fantastic *trattoria* as Clemy, after owner-chef Clementina Viezzer. It's in a rustic pink building next to the road, with two cozy dining rooms with linen curtains, beautiful dried-flower arrangements, and a large fireplace for spit-roasting and grilling. Rustic soups like *pasta e fagioli* or bean and barley or homemade pasta are among the first-course offerings. Grilled, spit-roasted, or boiled meats are on the winter menu; fresh *burrata* cheese from Puglia is served in the summer; vegetables are treated with respect, especially mushrooms from the nearby chestnut woods of Madean, worth a detour for *porcini* lovers. Conclude with cornmeal *zaleti* cookies and a glass of dessert wine. The wine list is simple, mostly local but there's something for those who want to drink big.

Giavera del Montello

HOTEL

See Conigliano

HOTEL

Bellavista

Mercato Vecchio, Montebelluna (close by)
☎0423.301-031

Fax 0423.303-612
All credit cards • moderate

RESTAURANT

Agnoletti

Via della Vittoria 131
☎0422.776-009
Closed Monday, Tuesday, and the first half of July
No credit cards • low moderate

Agnoletti has been a *trattoria* since 1780, a stopping-off place for changing carriage horses and having something to eat. The ambience is pure Veneto country, the waiters are surly, the menu is limited, and the wines are nothing special. Local *salumi* are good, but the reason for a visit to this restaurant is for a taste of mushrooms (*funghi*), preferably in every course. First-course soups, grilled meat, game, and anything with *polenta* are all good choices. Finish with local cheese and home-preserved figs with spices, honey, and alcohol, served with or without homemade *gelato*. Avoid this restaurant on Sunday, when, due to the weekly invasion of city folk, the quality of the cooking deteriorates.

Isola della Scala

RICE MILL

Riseria Ferron

Via Saccovener 6, Pilavecchia
☎045.730-1022

The Ferron family has been growing quality rice for *risotto* in their rice paddies and refining it in their mills outside Verona since 1650. They grow mostly Vialone Nano *semifino* (*semifino* refers to the size of the rice kernel, in this case large). The Ferron rice mill, or refinery, is a frenzy of activity, of cogged wheels, machine belts, tubes transporting the rice, wooden trays rocking back and forth to separate grain from chaff, a centrifuge grating the outer husk of the kernel, leaving a dusting of rice flour on the grains that will eventually thicken some-one's *risotto*. In the back of the *riseria* stands an even more astounding object, looking distinctly like a Leonardo da Vinci invention; a series of large wooden metal-tipped pestles driven by wheels off a central axle, pounding into corresponding wooden bowls, each containing a few handfuls of rice. This amazing machine is powered by a seventeenth-century waterwheel, and the rice it produces is extremely rare, marked *Lavorato con pistelli* on the package, and impossible to find outside the area.

Isola della Scala holds a *Fiera del Riso,* a three-day festival held after the rice harvest, during the first weekend in October, with gastronomic competitions—a *"risotto*-off" for the best *risotto,* for professional chefs and for dilettantes. The contest for the restaurant chefs is called *Chicco d'Oro* (Golden Kernel). Finals are held in the old movie house, the Cinema Alba, decorated for the event with a huge poster of a grain of rice looking like a huge tooth. The jury is served a bit better than the public, but tastes of competing *risotti* are available to all comers. *Risotto* with Taleggio cheese and field greens, *risotto* with winter squash and white truffles, and *risotto* with red radicchio and Jerusalem artichokes were past win-ners. Contact Diego Zarantonello (tel. 045.730-0130) for more information about the festival.

Jesolo

HOTEL

Udinese Da Aldo
Via C. Battisti 25
☎0421.951-407
Fax 0421.951-711
All credit cards • inexpensive

ENOITECA

La Caneva
Via Antiche Mura 13
☎0421.952-350

Open 6 P.M.–5 A.M., closed Sunday in the winter
American Express, MasterCard,
Visa • inexpensive

I'm wild about this *enoiteca,* run by leather-aproned, mustachioed wine maniac Mauro Lorenzon. He founded the *enoiteca* associa-tion, is currently its president, has a stupen-dous wine list, enjoys quantity as well as quality, and knows how to wield a cham-pagne saber. It's worth ordering a bottle of *spumante* or champagne just to see him in action. Visit for more than one glass of wine and hope that he's got oysters, other-wise opt for *salumi* like *soppressa, carne sa-lada, pancetta,* marinated anchovies, or first-rate cheese. The pace at La Caneva picks up after midnight.

Loreggia

RESTAURANT-ENOITECA-HOTEL

Locanda Aurilia
Via Aurelia 27
☎049.930-0677
Fax 049.579-0395
Closed Tuesday
All credit cards • low moderate

I'm in love with this *trattoria-enoiteca*-hotel in spite of its mismatched decor of diagonal wooden wainscoting and beaded shade lamps hanging from coiled wires. The estab-lishment is powered by the De Marchi fam-ily—Osorio in the kitchen with his mother, Antonietta, brother Ferdinando (stellar sommelier), and wives Illena and Lucia in the dining rooms and *enoiteca-bar* in the entrance. The clientele is local, the *cucina* based on quality regional ingredients, the cooking traditional. For starters, *salumi* are a good choice, especially *soppressa* and *salame,* served with *polenta* and salad greens. Two or three filled pastas, *tagliatelle* and *gnocchi* are made fresh daily, fillings and sauces chang-ing with the seasons. *Risotto* has the custom-ary two-portion minimum. Main-dish possibilities include Vicenza-style *baccalà, polenta* with melted cheese, tripe, mallard with Calvados, or grilled meats. The cheese board is laden with artisanally crafted local cheeses, a perfect excuse to drink an older vintage red from the absolutely amazing wine cellar, one of the best I've ever seen in a *trattoria*. The wine list has a vintage chart on the inside cover to help diners, since all wines that deserve aging get it here. Young local wines are available, but many usually unaffordable bottles of superior Italian wines are simply impossible to resist. Desserts are simple, home-style, like the bright yellow, made-with-real-eggs *torta margherita*. Spend the night in one of the Locanda's ten clean inexpensive rooms and indulge in an in-depth after-dinner *grappa* tasting in the *enoiteca*.

Lovadina

HOTEL

See Conegliano or Treviso

RESTAURANT

Da Domenico

Località Grave, via del Fante 23
☎**0422.881-261**
Fax 0422.887-074
Closed Monday evening and Tuesday
All credit cards • moderate

Anyone obsessed with red radicchio lettuce from Treviso, mushrooms, or asparagus should jump for joy and head for Lovadina during their respective festivals at this simple country restaurant: Domenico Camerotto, his wife, Sonia, and their children prepare and serve a meal of pure monomania—ten different dishes focused on a single vegetable. Serious asparagus worshipers will enjoy a procession of this relative of the lily, cultivated or wild, raw, fried, baked with eggs, wrapped, minced in *risotto*, puréed, julienned, in soup, or sauced with hard-cooked eggs. Mushrooms and Treviso lettuce get the same respect. Each dish is garnished with a little dyed

mashed-potato flower. The wine selection is interesting and unusual. Da Domenico's decor is unstudied peculiar.

Lusia

HOTEL

Villa Regina Margherita

Viale Regina Margherita 6, Rovigo
(nearby)
☎**0425.361-540**
Fax 0425.31301
American Express, MasterCard, Visa •
moderate

RESTAURANT

Al Ponte

Via Bertolda 1, Bornio
☎**0425-69890**
Fax 0425.69177
Closed Monday
All credit cards • low moderate

It's not easy to find, tucked away in the flatlands northwest of Rovigo, but Luciano Rizzato's *trattoria*, over a bridge on the banks of a canal, is worth the search. His mother, Margherita, and wife, Giuliana, rule in the kitchen, drawing on regional, seasonal ingredients. Begin with their vegetable strudel, timbales, or *frittate*. First-course pastas are homemade, flavored with seasonal herbs, wild greens, or mushrooms. Classics like *pasta e fagioli, risi e bisi* (rice and pea soup), or wintery *malafanti* (pork broth with cabbage and cornmeal), a stick-to-your-ribs kind of dish, are well made. Look for freshwater bounty like catfish, frogs' legs, or eel. Or *baccalà* Vicenza-style, boned braised pheasant, or tripe. Even American sausage maven Bruce Aidells was impressed with Luciano's homemade sausage. Desserts like fruit bavarians and mousses may tempt. Sommelier Luciano has a truly impressive wine list with all the greats of Veneto and beyond, and he has just created a small *enoteca*, where shelves of fine wines are displayed. Stop for a glass of wine and a snack if you're traveling on the *autostrada* that goes south from Venice, even if you don't have time for a meal.

Marostica

Marostica is known for chess and cherries. The city holds a chess match, with Renaissance-costumed locals standing in for chess pieces, and there's always a chess game going under the *loggia* next to the square. Local cherry fanatics look for early varieties like *sandra* and *marosticana*, and attend the annual cherry festival the last Sunday in May in piazza degli Scacchi. The piazza is filled with stands of cherries, cherry desserts, wine, and *salumi*. There's an orchestra in the evening and country-style dancing (*ballo liscio*). Cherry lovers will want to travel the *Strada delle ciliegie* that goes from Bassano to Breganza, overlooking hills and valleys covered with cherry trees. For a road map or information about the festival, contact the Pro Marostica Association, tel. 0424.72127, fax 0424.72800.

HOTEL

See Bassano del Grappa or Vicenza

GROCERY

Casa del Parmigiano
Piazza Castello 25
☎/Fax 0424.75071
Closed Wednesday afternoon
MasterCard, Visa

It's a safe guess that the *parmigiano* at the Casa del Parmigiano is superb, but Luigi Gastaldello's fine shop is worth a visit for much more. Luigi and his sons Erasmo and Corrado have sought artisans who make the finest products of Italy. They sell all ages of Asiago, as well as first-rate cheese from other regions, even France, local and national *salumi*, and prepared dishes that will thrill picnic lovers. The shop is a must for cheese fans. And they'll Cryovac purchases to take home.

BAR

Osteria della Madonnetta
Via Vaienti 21
No phone
Closed Wednesday, open 8:30 A.M.–12:30 P.M., 4–8 P.M.
No credit cards

The Osteria della Madonnetta is a local hangout on a back street in town, owned by Toni Guerra with two seedy dining rooms filled with flea-market clutter, wooden tables, and a courtyard in the back with a few oil-clothed tables. Toni's mother used to cook a few simple dishes in a tiny kitchen that didn't meet the health board standards and so it's been closed. Come to this *osteria* for the ambience. And to visit the back room, beyond the courtyard, with a reproduction of the walls and castle of Marostica that Toni carved from an ancient pine tree felled by a storm. There's a bench inside the city walls and a chess table in the middle instead of a piazza.

ENOTECA–WINE BAR

La Pergola
Via Tempesta 10
☎0424.780-613
Closed Monday, open 9:30 A.M.–2 P.M., 5 P.M.–2 A.M.
No credit cards

Exigent enophiles will have a hard time in Marostica and should head for La Pergola. Roberto Ambrosi has assembled an impressive selection of wines, many available by the glass. Snack on *bruschetta*, cheese, and *salumi*.

Mestre–Marghera

Ugly Mestre and Marghera, Venezia's vital mainland link to the rest of the world, are the best places to leave your car before continuing on to the waterways of Venezia. Mestre's parking lots are less expensive, less chaotic, easier to execute, than Venezia's overcrowded lots at Piazzale Roma, which never seem to have room until a tip is pulled out. Trains leave Mestre every five minutes for Venezia. The food in the following two restaurants, frequented by locals and businesspeople, is better than almost anything in Venezia; the fish is fresher and the bill will be lighter.

HOTEL
Lugano Torretta
Via Rizzardi 11
Marghera
☎**041.936-777**
Fax 041.921-97
Closed November through February
All credit cards • moderate, inexpensive off season

RESTAURANT
Autoespresso
Via Fratelli Bandiera 34
Marghera
☎**041.930-214**
Fax 041.930-197
Closed Sunday and August
All credit cards • low expensive

Autoespresso, across the train tracks from Mestre, started out as a truck stop, serving simple food and lots of it. Then owner Franco Semenzato decided there was more to the restaurant business than feeding large numbers of people, fast. He removed tables, creating a more spacious environment, and added an impressive list of local and Italian white wines. Mother Savina and wife Luciana work together in the kitchen, preparing a minimalist *cucina* of grilled or lightly deep-fried fish, with no sauce. *Polenta* is white, more delicate than yellow, and better with seafood, Franco assured me, as he served a slice of it covered with minute pale pink shrimp coated with olive oil. Spaghetti is perfectly cooked, salads are dressed with your choice of extra virgin olive oil from Liguria, Toscana, or Lazio. A few meat dishes are available for fish haters. The wine list is wonderful, and distillates like *grappa*, Armagnac, and malt whiskey are a specialty.

RESTAURANT
Valeriano
Via Col di Lana 18
Mestre
☎**041.926-474**
Closed Sunday evening, Monday, and August
All credit cards • high moderate

Valeriano's restaurant, a few steps from the train station, serves interesting, well-prepared food. The fish *antipasto* is varied, and large enough to be a whole meal for some. Try to save room for the nicely cooked *risotto*, spaghetti, and simple fresh fish, prepared by Valeriano's wife, Maria, known as Gerry. The restaurant is always packed with locals, and reservations are a must. Not all the wines are thrilling.

ENOITECA
La Vinoteca
Via A. Costa 21/L
☎**041.983-345**
Closed Sunday
MasterCard, Visa • inexpensive

Irma and Graziano Mason are both sommeliers and their centrally located wine bar is a tangible sign of their devotion to wine. They have an impressive selection of Italian and French wines, grappe and distillates, extra virgin olive oils and, in the best Veneto tradition, serve tasty food with their wines. La Vinoteca is air-conditioned, allowing enophiles to drink big reds in the sweltering Venetian summer.

CHEESEMASTER
Alberto Marcomini
Via della Industria 29/D
☎**049.880-4111**
By appointment only

Alberto Marcomini is the Blues Brother of Cheese, with red hair, Ray-Ban sunglasses, and the finest palate for cheese that I've run across. He hunts down artisanal producers in Europe and distributes their cheeses in northern and central Italy. They can be found in many of the country's finest *enoteche* and restaurants, and are well represented in Veneto. Alberto speaks Italian and French and often does tastings. I've been privileged to attend quite a few, a cheese thrill beyond compare. Superfresh buffalo mozzarella; *burrata,* the hyper-rich, clotted-cream–stuffed inflated mozzarella; Castelmagno; tomini; outrageous Taleggio—all among the best versions of these cheeses I've ever tasted. Call to see if he's got a tasting going on anywhere or to find out who carries his cheeses.

CHOCOLATE
Chocoart
Via Vallon 1/E
☎**041.534-0673**
Closed Monday

Young chocolatier Luigi Biasetto is one of the rising stars of the Italian chocolate scene. He studied for seven years at Wittamer in Brussels and learned his lesson well. Stop in his shop for a taste of his fine chocolates made with first-rate cream and butter.

COOKWARE
Luciano Preo
Via Col di Lana 14/4
☎**041.926-451**

Barbecue fans may want to contact Luciano Preo for information about his amazing patented Turn-grill, a vertical rotating charcoal barbecue grill, especially adapted for cooking fish.

Mira
HOTEL
Villa Margherita
Via Nazionale 416, Porte
☎**041.426-5800**
Fax 041.429-728
All credit cards • expensive in season, high moderate off season

HOTEL
Riviera dei Dogi
Via Don Minzoni 33
☎**041.424-466**
Fax 041.424-428
All credit cards • moderate

RESTAURANT
Da Conte
Via Caltana 133, Marano Veneziano
☎**041.479-571**
Closed Monday
No credit cards • inexpensive

I love this restaurant, out of the way but definitely worth the navigational problems. Hyper-hospitable Giorgio and Manuela Zampieri have restored an old-fashioned *osteria* with taste and style and serve both traditional and lightened-up dishes, all based on impeccable ingredients. Manuela prepares the food on the small menu, which changes daily; Giorgio pairs her cooking with world-class wines that invite enophiles to drink big. First-rate *salumi,* pâté, *sarde in saor,* and smoked swordfish are among the starters. Seasonal vegetables like *castraure,* the first artichokes of the season, red radicchio, asparagus and wild greens are treated with respect, served in *frittate* and *risotto.* Hope that Manuela has made her fantastic pork shin, or opt for grilled meat or squid cooked in its ink, served with *polenta.* Save room for the *zabaione,* made with Moscato, served with cookies. Diners with small appetites can choose the one-course meal, a tasty and inexpensive option. Dine outside in the summer.

Mogliano Veneto
HOTEL
Villa Condulmer
☎**041.457-100**
Fax 041.457-134
All credit cards • expensive in season, moderate off season

RESTAURANT
Enoiteca La Sosta
Via Marconi 14
☎041.590-1428
Closed all day Monday and Tuesday lunch
American Express • moderate

Directly on the Terraglio, the main drag from Venezia to Treviso, Enoiteca La Sosta has a large selection of fine Italian wines and *grappa*. The menu is limited to a few simple dishes, but good cheese and *salumi* are always available. The service is friendly, and wine is also sold by the bottle or case.

Montecchia di Crosara

HOTEL

See Verona

HOTEL
Relais Villabella
Via Villabella 72, San Bonifacio (nearby)
☎045.610-177
Fax 045.610-1799
American Express, Visa • expensive

RESTAURANT
Baba-jaga
Via Cabalao
☎045.745-0222
Closed Sunday evening, Monday, January, and the first half of August
All credit cards • high moderate

Chef Piero Burato's wife was studying for an important Russian exam. He was looking for a name for his about-to-open restaurant, and liked the sound of Baba-jaga, a Russian witch. But the magic at this countryside restaurant is in Veneto's dialect, with many creative dishes for locals tired of tradition. *Salumi, risotto,* and homemade pasta are stellar. Fish and meat are grilled over olivewood charcoal. Some creative sauced dishes seem a bit trendy.

Fresh black truffles are used with great abandon in season. Desserts are homemade, and wines are a pleasure. Dine outside on the shaded terrace in the spring and summer.

Monteforte d'Alpone

HOTEL

See Verona or Montecchia di Crosara

RESTAURANT
Riondo
Via Monte Riondo
☎045.761-0638
Closed Monday
American Express, Diners Club • high moderate

Riondo, perched on a hilltop in the middle of Soave vineyards, is a *trattoria* that has kept pace with the times. The *cucina,* mostly traditional—*salumi* served with *polenta,* homemade pasta, nicely done *risotto,* grilled Sorana beef, regional cheese, and *tiramisù*—is well prepared and accompanied by quality local wines. Drink a glass of Recioto di Soave by Anselmi for dessert. Dining on the terrace overlooking acres of grapevines is a treat in the spring and summer.

Montegrotto Terme

HOTEL
Terme Neroniane
Via Neroniana 21
☎049.793-466
Fax 049.795-331
American Express, Visa • moderate

RESTAURANT
Da Mario
Corso Terme 4
☎049.794-090
Closed Tuesday
All credit cards • moderate

I learned about this restaurant from the region's best winemaker, Lucio Gomiero. It was founded by his uncle Mario—son Diego's in the kitchen. The restaurant is modern, with well-lit food-related prints and paintings on the walls, Thonet chairs. The menu is small, with a few traditional dishes and seasonal preparations. Begin with *orzo mantecato*—barley treated like *risotto*—or pasta sauced with fresh herbs. Main courses include beef; *anatra frasena* (crispy duck); boned guinea hen with wild mushrooms; fish like Vicenza-style cod or swordfish *carpaccio*. Conclude with local cheese or desserts: *tiramisù*, pear tart, or *zaleti* cookies. The wine list is well chosen, with Lucio's help—all his Vignalta wines are available at bargain prices—I can't imagine drinking anything else.

Ospedaletto di Pescantina

HOTEL

Villa Quaranta

Ospedaletto di Pescantina

☎045.676-7300

Fax 045.676-7301

All credit cards • expensive

HOTEL

See Verona

RESTAURANT

La Coà

Via Brennero 70

☎045.715-0380

Closed Sunday and Monday

MasterCard, Visa • moderate

La Coà is a quintessential *trattoria* with two cozy dining rooms, enlightened regional cooking, superb wine list. Lovers of horse meat, traditional in this area, will have a good time, but everyone else will have nothing to complain about. Begin with a plate of mixed *salumi* of *prosciutto*, lard, and cured and shredded horse. Or proceed to first-course pastas, sauced with mushrooms or herbs, classic soups like *pasta e fagioli*, or stuffed crepes. Steaks of beef or colt; *pastissada de caval* (stewed horse with *polenta*); boned braised rabbit; or sweet-and-sour capon breast, for squeamish diners, are well prepared and satisfying. Local cheese and simple homemade desserts or cooked fruit from the cart conclude the meal. The wine list is splendid, with world-class wines and a fantastic selection of local gems.

Padova

Padova is a charming city of Roman origins, with its university founded in 1222, Giotto frescoes, Donatello sculpture, and Veneziana attitude. Its gastronomic center is located in the piazze delle Erbe and della Frutta—twin piazzas, with produce in one and dry goods in the other, linked by a passageway of stalls selling cheese, meat, *salumi*, and fish.

For the area's best restaurant, see Rubano, page 155.

HOTEL

Leon Bianco

Piazzetta Pedrocchi 12

☎049.875-0814

Fax 049.875-6184

All credit cards • moderate

HOTEL

Villa Ducale

Via Martiri della Libertà 75, Dolo (close by)

☎041.420-094

Fax 041.420-094

All credit cards • luxury in season, expensive off season

WINE BAR

Enoteca Angelo Rasi

Riviera Paleocapa 7

☎049.871-9797

Closed Sunday lunch, and August

No credit cards • moderate

Enoteca Angolo del Sommelier–Bar Bologna
Piazzale Santa Croce 13
☎049.38993
Closed Wednesday
No credit cards • moderate

Padova's restaurants are disappointing, but simple food like *salumi* (local and from other regions), a wide variety of *prosciutto*, goose salami, an array of cheeses, a choice of extra virgin olive oils, *grappa*, Cognac, whiskey, and, most important, wine are easy enough to find at these two non-restaurants. Both the Enoteca Angelo Rasi and the Enoteca Angolo del Sommelier have splendid selections of local, Italian, French, and Californian wines, a commitment to quality drinking.

Pieve d'Alpago

RESTAURANT-INN
Dolada
Località Plois, via Dolada 9
☎0437.479-141
Fax 0437.478-068
Closed Monday except July and August, Tuesday lunch
All credit cards • expensive

From the Lago di Santa Croce, follow the signs with the stylized snail to a very special inn run by very special people. The chef, Enzo Pra, and his wife, sommelier Rossana, have thought of every possible component of a fine dining or overnight experience, and have set about including them all at Dolada. Small two- or three-table dining rooms expand as needed by a clever system of sliding doors, but the mood is always intimate, elegant, studied. The decor is understated, the flower arrangements are low, the menu is embossed with the snail that helped to guide you to Dolada. Enzo's *cucina* is strong and masculine, contrasting flavors as opposed to blending them. Very few dishes are traditional, other than the *broet de s'cioss e polenta*

(snails cooked with celery, served with *polenta*), which may make snail haters change their minds. The marinated and home-smoked sturgeon may not be traditional, but it is tasty. Some dishes show signs of trendy ingredients like raspberry vinegar, but generally the menu is professionally executed with intelligence, moderation, and style. Save room for the splendid desserts. Rossana will help you choose a wine from her fine selection, which she ably pairs with Enzo's *cucina*. After a *grappa*, if you're lucky you'll head upstairs to one of seven rooms, each a different color, with bathroom tiles, carpet, and bed linens of the same hue, equipped with TV, radio cassette player, refrigerator with splits of Ca' del Bosco *spumante*, cocktail-table photography books to leaf through, and a bathroom with magnifying mirror, towel warmer, and even a Band-Aid. If you're truly lucky, you'll have a view of the full moon illuminating the entire valley, reflected in Lago di Santa Croce. Breakfast, served any time after eight, is world-class, and includes a local version of French toast, and butter so wonderful and sweet that you may eat it without bread.

Puos d'Alpago

RESTAURANT-INN
San Lorenzo
Via 4 Novembre 79
☎0437.454-048
Fax 0437.454-049
Closed Wednesday
All credit cards • moderate

San Lorenzo is a simple inn (*locanda*) where Renzo Dal Farra, his wife, Mara, and his brother Aldo and their mother prepare traditional *cucina*. They have all clearly been influenced by nearby master Enzo Pra and his personal professional style. Local *salumi*, marinated fish, homemade pasta, and some nontraditional but interesting dishes are served with an eclectic wine list that places little emphasis on Veneto. The seven-course tasting meal offers a lot of food for the money.

Romano d'Ezzelino

RESTAURANT

Ca' Takea

Via Col Roigo 17

☎/Fax 0424.33426

Closed Tuesday

MasterCard, Visa • high moderate

It's called Ca' Takea, "House of Trouble-makers" in local dialect, for the habits of previous inhabitants, but the only trouble with Maurizio Maino's restaurant is its difficult-to-find location. Ring the bell at the gate, follow the path to the cozy entrance with a fireplace and a few tables, a small dining room, and a glassed-in verandah filled with diners being rewarded for their navigational skills with an incredible experience. Maurizio's passionate about wine, has a phenomenal cellar, and his list concentrates on older vintage wines, including many historic years of Toscana and Piemonte—enophiles will be truly excited by the wine list. Maurizio draws on the finest ingredients he can get his hands on, treated with the greatest restraint, all the better to showcase his wine. Look for local wild mushrooms, white or black truffles, Bassano asparagus, local fruit and nuts during their seasons. Pasta is homemade, simply sauced with mushrooms or fish and vegetable combinations. Roast kid, hard-to-find Sorana beef *tagliata* flavored with rosemary are two reasons to drink an important red, although Maurizio does a good job with Adriatic fish. *Polenta* accompanies most dishes. Finish with local cheese or seasonal fruit desserts like chestnut mousse with persimmon sauce, cooked pears served with homemade *gelato, sorbetto,* and a nice assortment of cookies pre-

pared by Maria Luisa Leoni. Maurizio is wild about Vittorio Capovilla's fruit distillates and serves them by the glass. Somehow, the road back from Ca' Takea always seems shorter.

Rosà

FRUIT DISTILLER

Vittorio Capovilla

Via Gardini 12, Ca' Dolfin

☎/Fax 0424.581-2220

Fruit distillates are elegant, the nobility of distillation, made with whole fruit, not winemaking leftovers the way *grappa* is. Vittorio Capovilla is Italy's finest distiller of both cultivated and wild fruit. He hunts for wild plums, apples, apricots, cherries, rose hips, sloe, rowanberries, and cornelian cherries in Veneto, Trentino, Austria, and Yugoslavia, smaller, less attractive, more flavorful than most cultivated varieties. He also distills cultivated apples, plums, cherries, pears, blackberries, raspberries, black currants, and three hybrid grape varietals. Fruit is crushed, fermented, then distilled with a bain-marie technique instead of the more usual steam process, and the lower temperature and far slower, less violent process yield a more flavorful product. It takes up to 40 kilos of fruit to make 1 liter. Vittorio's fruit distillates are then aged up to four years, diluted with pure spring water (instead of the demineralized water that most distillers use) to 41 percent alcohol and then bottled. At the 1995 Austrian Destillata Fair, the Olympics of fruit distillates, where 300 producers entered 1,250 fruit distillates, Capovilla was awarded 5 gold, 2 silver, and 4 bronze medals to place second overall in the competition, unheard of for an Italian in this Austrian-dominated event. He even earned two perfect scores for his cornelian and sloe distillates. The Capovilla distillates are found in fine restaurants in the Bassano area, but can be purchased at the distillery. Write or fax if you'd like to see the distilling process in the late summer through fall.

Rubano

HOTEL-RESTAURANT-PASTRY

Le Calandre
Via Liguria 1, Sarmeola
☎**Hotel: 049.635-200**
Fax 049.633-026
☎**Restaurant: 049.630-303**
Fax 049.633-000
All credit cards • inexpensive hotel, expensive restaurant

I'm crazy about the culinary enclave outside Padova created by the Alajmo family. Rita Alajmo and her husband have left Le Calandre in the hands of their capable sons, and are cooking at the restaurant of the Golf Club Montecchia. Massimiliano Alajmo is a chef with a brilliant future, a rising star, only twenty-one but with lots of experience at the stove; sommelier Raffaele rules the dining rooms and hunts for exceptional ingredients and wines between meals. The *cucina* is creative, conceived with intelligence, executed with skill. Beet *gnocchi* sauced with Roquefort, ravioli with spinach and raisins. Vegetarians will have an easy time; carnivores will be pleased with the herbed veal kidneys, boned squab with *porcini* mushrooms and *polenta*, guinea hen coated with herbs; and fish lovers will also be happy with seafood from the nearby coast, like spider crab, turbot steamed with verbena. Save room for cheese such as the exceptional Taleggio or *pecorino* served with pear preserves. Rita still supervises all dessert preparations for both the restaurant and pastry shop next door. Anyone planning to take the road from Padova to Vincenza should stop at the pastry shop for practically anything, either sweet or savory, that comes from Rita's kitchen.

San Giorgio di Valpolicella

RESTAURANT-INN

Della Rosa Alda
Strada Garibaldi 4
☎**045.770-1018**
Fax 045.680-0411
Closed Monday
American Express, MasterCard, Visa • inexpensive rooms, moderate restaurant

Alda Della Rosa is a fantastic cook, the guiding force behind this classic *trattoria*. Expect perfectly executed supertraditional cooking and local specialties of impeccable quality. The decor is understated, well lit, with wooden wainscoting, large pink and white marble–tiled floors. Alda is joined in the kitchen by her daughter Nori and daughter-in-law Severina. Sommelier Lodovico Testi mans the dining room and a wine list that concentrates on the Verona area. Begin your meal with *soppressa* or mule *salame*. Or head straight to the fantastic first-course offerings like seasonal *risotto;* pasta in broth with chicken livers; hand-rolled pasta with black truffles, *porcini* or bean sauce. *Polenta* is the side dish of choice and accompanies stewed horse, donkey, or snails, as well as more conventional roast meats. Save room for the *pissota con l'oio*, a cake flavored with local olive oil baked in a copper container. Dine on the terrace overlooking Lake Garda when the weather is nice.

Sant'Ambrogio di Valpolicella

HOTEL

See Ospedaletto di Pescantina, San Giorgio di Valpolicella, or Verona

AGRITOURISM
Cooperativa 8 Marzo
Ca' Verde
☎045.686-1760
Closed Monday

Fresh and ripened cheese, yogurt, ricotta, and organic fruit and vegetables are produced by this cooperative. Stay in one of the reasonably priced rooms, but bring earplugs so the morning milk-delivery trucks don't disturb. The simple restaurant is fun, filled with locals, the menu is limited but the wines are nothing to write home about.

RESTAURANT
Groto de Corgnan
Via Corgnano 41
☎/Fax 045.773-1372
Closed Sunday
All credit cards • high moderate

Giorgio Soave in the kitchen with his wife, sommelier Assunta Forlin, and sister Elsa. Expect to find perfectly prepared regional cooking and simply spectacular ingredients, treated with restraint, respect, and skill. The ambience is comfortable, rustic but elegant, with a well-laid table. This is a fine dining experience without pretension. Start with goose *salame* paired with *mostarda;* classic *polenta, soppressa* and radicchio; warm onion tart; or the fine lard. It's hard to choose between *pasta e fagioli,* always on the menu; *bigoli* sauced with *pancetta* and beans; *tortelli* stuffed with nettles and ricotta; or seasonal *risotto.* Main-course possibilities include lamb sauced with Amarone and almonds, pheasant in grape sauce, slow-braised beef with *polenta,* or incredible *porcini* baked in a pastry envelope. Anyone who has ever thrilled to the taste of a real chicken should hope the *cacciatora* with mushrooms, served with *polenta,* is on the menu. Black truffles from the Lessina area are used with abandon in season. Save room for first-rate cheese. Fin-

ish with desserts like homemade *gelato* with chestnuts, chocolate mousse, or cookies with a glass of Recioto dessert wine. The wine list is well chosen, with a fantastic selection of Veronese as well as Italian and foreign wines.

Solighetto

RESTAURANT-INN
Da Lino
Via Brandolini 1
☎0438.842-377
Fax 0438.840-577
Closed Monday and August
All credit cards • high moderate

Da Lino is an immense, typical Veneto countryside restaurant with a successful formula that it's been repeating for years, to the point of tedium. Service is swift, but most of the dishes taste precooked and reheated. Mushrooms in season are a specialty, and fish is served on Thursday. The best choice is whatever you see turning on the spit in the fireplace. Jovial groups of celebrants pack this restaurant, and tapping on one's wine glass with a knife in unison seems to be a native custom.

Treviso

Treviso, with its medieval and *rinascimento* palaces, arcade-lined streets, cobblestone lanes, and waterways coursing in and around the city, is a jewel. The area's Palladian-style villas-turned-hotels offer a peek at a former era, and are perfect to use as a base for visiting the Venetian countryside.

HOTEL
El Toulà
Via Postumia 63
Paderno di Ponzano (close by)
☎0422.969-191
Fax 0422.969-994
All credit cards • luxury

HOTEL
Villa Corner della Regina
**Via Corriva 10, Cavasagra di Vedelago
(nearby)
☎0423.481-481
Fax 0423.451-100**
All credit cards • luxury in season, expensive off season

HOTEL
Villa Condulmer
**Zerman (close by)
☎041.457-100
Fax 041.457-134**
All credit cards • expensive in season, moderate off season

HOTEL
Villa Revedin
**Via Palazzi 4
Gorgo al Monticano (close by)
☎/Fax 0422.740-669**
American Express, MasterCard, Visa • moderate

MARKET

The *pescheria* (fish market), located on the *isoletta,* the "little island" on the Botteniga waterway, is a typical daily Veneto market selling the bounty of the Adriatic.

GELATO
Gelateria al Duomo
**Piazza Duomo
☎0422.542-902**
Closed Monday and November through February
Many *gelaterie* in Treviso display five-foot-tall cones with four balls of *gelato,* an irresistible photo-op for *gelato* fans. It's a sign that this city takes *gelato* seriously. After checking out lots of *gelaterie,* I focused on the Gelateria al Duomo, attracted by the pale color of the hazelnut, clearly not made with prepared mixtures, which are always coffee-colored. *Gelato* maker Rosangela and her partner, Anna, explained that they

use only the legendary and more expensive Piemontese hazelnut (see page 42) in their superlative rendition of this classic flavor. All *gelato* is made from raw ingredients— fresh milk and eggs, ripe fruit. Since local *gelato* consumption is greatly reduced in the cold Treviso winter, the Gelateria al Duomo closes during the winter months.

GROCERY
Cacciolato
**Vicolo Rialto 25
☎0422.545-971**
Closed Wednesday afternoon
Luciano Cacciolato has the finest selection of gourmet groceries, cheese, *salumi,* and culinary souvenirs in the city. Look for Illy Caffè, *grappa,* and much, much more.

RED RADICCHIO FAIR
Loggia dei Trecento
☎0422.547-632
The Radicchio Fair, a ninety-five-year-old tradition in Treviso, is held yearly in mid-December, under the *loggia* in the center of town, open from 9 A.M. to 1 P.M. Producers compete for prizes for the best radicchio, and the *loggia* is aswirl with displays of baskets of Castelfranco radicchio and wooden crates of perfectly formed and trimmed heads of Treviso radicchio. Regional restaurants prepare menus that feature this tasty vegetable in *every* course of the meal, from appetizer to dessert.

CRAFTS
Manu Fatti
**Via Barberia 29
☎0422.579-887**
Closed August
No credit cards
Lucia Tessari's lovely shop sells artisanal products, although not all her wares are Italian. Tuscan baskets and linens from Romagna are attractive and well priced.

RESTAURANT

Toni del Spin

Via Inferiore 7

☎0422.543-829

Closed Sunday, Monday lunch, and August

American Express, MasterCard, Visa •

inexpensive

I like the genuine *trattoria* ambience of Toni del Spin—the wooden floors, marble bar, beamed ceilings with large-bladed fans, the feeling that regulars are stepping up to the bar for their daily glass of wine. The blackboard menu features typical *cucina veneta*, such as *pasta e fagioli*, seasonal *risotto, bigoli, baccalà*, and poultry. The back room is lined with generally crummy wines, so Scarpa's fine wines look almost out of place here.

RESTAURANT

El Toulà da Alfredo

Via Collalto 26

☎/Fax 0422.540-275

Closed Monday and August

All credit cards • expensive

This restaurant is the original El Toulà, founded by Alfredo Beltrame, who helped spread the message that regional *cucina* can be elegant as well as tasty. It became the first link in a chain of El Toulà restaurants. All feature the classic *cucina veneta*, with interregional and seasonal dishes on their interesting menu. Traditional *sarde in saor*, perfectly cooked *risotto* or *riso e fegatini* (rice and chicken-liver soup), and the *frittatina con bruscàndoli* (pan-fried flan with wild hops) are splendid, although Italians seem to prefer gazpacho, homemade pasta, marinated swordfish, or grilled vegetables. The Art Nouveau frescoes, pink tablecloths, and formal service are all part of the legacy of Alfredo Beltrame. Drink the Nino Franco Prosecco, one of Veneto's loveliest wines.

Trissino

RESTAURANT-INN

Ca' Masieri

Via Masieri 16

☎0445.490-122

Fax 0445.490-455

Closed Monday lunch and Sunday

American Express, MasterCard, Visa • high moderate

What a joy to find a restaurant like Ca' Masieri, especially since it's become an inn. The *cucina* reflects the charming decor, a blend of clean modern design combined with the traditional country style. *Salumi* are tasty, *risotto* is beautifully prepared, pasta and *bigoli* are homemade. Meat, fowl, and fish are lightly sauced. Pastry and *gelato* are fresh and homemade. The wine list, studded with local and nonregional wines, is worth a detour. A welcoming fire burns in the hearth in the winter, and summer dining is on the terrace.

Valeggio sul Mincio

HOTEL

See Verona

RESTAURANT

Antica Locanda Mincio

Borghetto

☎045.795-0059

Closed Wednesday evening in winter, and Thursday

All credit cards • high moderate

On the banks of the Mincio River, immersed in the greens of ivy and weeping willows, the Antica Locanda Mincio (which dates from the 1700s) serves the traditional *cucina* of the area. Specialties include homemade *salumi*, hand-rolled pasta, freshwater fish, grilled chicken, and the homemade preserved peaches of Valeggio. The wine selection has its highs and lows.

Venezia

"Venezia": the sound of those three musical syllables, so different from the harsher English "Venice," won't prepare you for the fascination of this meeting place/port/Oriental bazaar where natives in costume seem to have been replaced by tourists in sneakers. Waterways are filled with the urban traffic of water buses and barges, but the back lanes are reserved for motorboats and gondolas, gracefully rowed by skilled *gondolieri*, a tradition passed down from father to son. Venezia is divided into six *sestieri*, or neighborhood districts: Cannaregio, San Marco, Castello, Santa Croce, San Polo, and Dorsoduro. Main routes (marked with yellow street signs pointing the way to major destinations), narrow passageways, and unexpected squares are numbered in zigzag or snail-shaped patterns, and make up a uniquely Venetian landscape where the vocabulary is a local dialect—*calle* or *ramo* means street; *fondamenta, rio, riva* are streets on a canal, and *campo*, literally "field," is a square, what the rest of Italy calls a *piazza*. The *cucina* of this once-great maritime nation is based on the fruits of the sea and the bounty of the rich alluvial soil of the Venetian lagoon. *Risotto*, made with locally grown rice, is a specialty, sauced with delicate seafood or tender greens. Fish is simply cooked—sautéed, grilled, fried. Cuttlefish (*seppia*) is stewed in its own ink. Calf's liver is transformed into *fegato alla veneziana*. The Cannaregio and Rialto markets display piles of fruit and vegetables from the lagoon and beyond. Quality wine served with reasonably priced food is hard to find in Venezia, a city with no wine cellars.

HOTELS

Cipriani
Isola della Giudecca 10
☎041.520-7744
Fax 041.520-3930
All credit cards • ultra luxury

Gritti Palace
San Marco 2467,
Campo Santa Maria del Giglio
☎041.794-611
Fax 041.520-0942
All credit cards • ultra luxury

Monaco e Grand Canal
San Marco 1325, Calle Vallaresso
☎041.520-0211
Fax 041.520-0501
All credit cards • high expensive

Santa Marina
Campo Santa Marina 6068
☎041.523-9202
Fax 041.520-0907
All credit cards • high moderate

Bel Sito
Santa Maria del Giglio 2417
☎041.522-3365
Fax 041.520-4083
All credit cards • moderate

Serenissima
Calle Goldoni 4486
☎041.520-0011
Fax 041.522-3292
American Express, MasterCard, Visa • moderate

Locanda ai Santi Apostoli
Strada Nuova 4391
☎041.521-2612
Fax 041.521-2611
American Express, MasterCard, Visa • high moderate
A personal favorite, rooms on the Grand Canal in a Venetian palace with views of the Rialto market.

RIALTO MARKET

Anyone interested in food should plan a visit to the Rialto market, around the corner from the Rialto bridge. Fruit and vegetables come from the mainland, and a few stalls specialize in produce from the island gardens of the Venetian lagoon. Sant'Erasmo and Malamocco are two areas of legend. Their bounty is said to be slightly salty, from the sea-flooded alluvial soil of the lagoon. Look for vegetables like *radicchio di Treviso* and warty-skinned *zucca barucca* winter squash, *chiodini* and *porcini* mushrooms in the fall and spring, and artichokes in the spring. Spring visitors should search out wild greens like *carletti* and *bruscàndoli,* tender peas called *bisi,* asparagus from nearby Bassano. Check out the fish stalls and note the clean scent of the area, a sure sign of freshness. Look for mollusks: *caparozzoli,* carpet-shell clams; *capelunghe,* razor clams; *peoci,* mussels; *capesante* and *canestrelli,* scallops; *bovoletti* and *garusoli,* snails; *seppie* and *seppioline,* cuttlefish in two sizes; *calamari* and *calamaretti,* squid; *polipi* and *folpeti,* octopus; and *latte di seppia,* a mysterious white gland that looks like a scallop. Venetian crustacea include *gamberi, gamberetti* shrimp, and shrimplets; *schie,* tiny gray shrimp, still squirming; *scampi,* Dublin Bay prawns; *granceole,* spider crabs with spiky legs; and live *canocie,* mantis shrimp. Fall and spring visitors should look for *moleche,* just-molted softshell crabs, tasty bites that are worth a trip to Venice for crab lovers. *Mazanete* are thumbnail-size, thin-shelled females, crunched on shell and all. *Sfogi,* flatfish, are sole unlike any you've probably ever seen— small, ten inches long, and fresh from the sea. Look for *branzino,* sea bass; *gò,* black and yellow goby, used in *risotto; sarde,* superfresh silvery, navy, and turquoise sardines, one of the great treats of Venice. *Bisati,* eels, swim in tubs or trays. Although they call it *baccalà* (salt cod), the Venetians are wild about air-dried *stoccafisso,* which is saltless, brownish, and extremely smelly.

BAR · CAFFÈ

Harry's Bar

San Marco 1323, Calle Vallaresso
☎041.528-5777
Fax 041.520-8822
Closed Monday, January, and February
All credit cards • expensive

Harry's Bar has been a classic in Venezia since Giuseppe Cipriani opened its doors in 1931. Although some consider it a fine restaurant, I'd rather dine elsewhere—but I can't think of a better place to stop off for a world-class Bellini. The nautical–private club ambience, tables with yellow cloths, and barstools are a favorite with Italians and tourists, although you'll be hard-pressed to hear Italian spoken in the summer. The waiters are efficient, but for the 20 percent service charge they should be.

BAR · CAFFÈ

Florian

San Marco 56/59
☎041.528-5338
Closed Wednesday in winter • expensive

Venetians hang out at Florian, located in one of the world's most wonderful squares, with an unbeatable view. In a local version of musical chairs, if you order your drink while the orchestra is playing, a service charge will be added to your bill.

BAR · CAFFÈ

La Boutique del Dolce

San Polo 890, Fondamenta Rio Marin
☎041.718-523
Closed Wednesday

Gilda Vio and Gino Riviani's little stand-up bar may not be in the same league as Harry's or Florian for most people, but it's my favorite spot in Venezia for breakfast. The *cappuccino* is well prepared, and they serve just-baked crispy croissants (called *brioche*), fresh fruit tarts, cookies, and pastry. Sandwiches and savory pastry are of the same fine quality.

VENEZIA

I'm in love with Venezia, I spend weeks on end in the city, since I direct the culinary program at the Hotel Cipriani. The fish market is world-class, and the city's great fish restaurants serve some of the finest fish and seafood I've ever eaten. The lows of Venetian cooking are achieved by restaurants and *trattorie* catering to unsuspecting clients, passing off frozen fish for fresh. A clam sauce without shells is a poor sign. Don't expect fish restaurants to be cheap. Venetian dialect may be difficult to understand. Eliminate the letter "l" from words, and you'll begin to get part of the accent.

WINE BAR
Cantina Do Mori di Roberto Biscontin
San Polo 429
☎**041.522-5401**
Closed Sunday
No credit cards

The Do Mori is my favorite place for an *ombra* (or *ombretta*, "little shadow"), offering a close-up view of the real Venezia. Roberto Biscontin has his own boat for the *Festa del Redentore*, a festival of thanksgiving that takes place on the third Sunday in July. (The night before the festival there are fireworks, and the Veneziani picnic on their boats and stay up all night.)

WINE BAR
Vino Vino
San Marco 2007/A
☎**041.523-7027**
Closed Tuesday
No credit cards

Another fine choice for wonderful *cicchetti*. The food comes from the kitchen of the Ristorante Antico Martini, and some of Italy's finest wines are sold here, by the bottle or by the glass. To make a special reservation, call the Antico Martini (tel. 041.522-4121).

WINE BAR
Ca' d'Oro
Cannaregio 3912, Calle Ca' d'Oro
☎**041.528-5324**
Closed Thursday and August
No credit cards

The Ca' d'Oro, in the untouristed Cannaregio neighborhood, is a local hangout. The wine list has evolved. The Ca' d'Oro is near one of my favorite hotels (Ai Santi Apostoli), and close to the Rialto market. Everyone here seems to be smoking.

WINE BAR
Vini da Pinto
San Polo 367, Campo delle Beccarie
☎**041.522-4599**
Closed Monday
No credit cards

Da Pinto, with its no-nonsense decor of blond wood Formica, is one of my favorite places for *cicchetti*. Don't miss the tripe or the *baccalà*. Sit at tables squeezed in the back or in the piazza when the weather is nice.

WINE BAR
Cantina già Schiavi
Dorsoduro 992
☎**041.523-0034**
Closed Sunday
No credit cards

Locals stop off in this authentic Venetian bar for a glass of wine on the way home from work.

WINE BAR
Capitan Uncino
Santa Croce 1501, Campo San Giacomo dell'Orio

☎/Fax 041.721-901
Closed Wednesday
No credit cards

Located in a wide, tree-lined square, Capitan Uncino ("Captain Hook") draws a neighborhood crowd. Go native and dawdle over a glass of the house wine.

BREAD AND GRISSINI BAKERY

Claudio Crosara–L'Arte del Pane
Fondamenta Sant'Eufemia 655, Giudecca
☎041.520-6737
Closed Wednesday afternoon

Adriana Scarpa and Claudio Crosara make the best bread in Venice. It's hard to make great bread in a damp city—most of the stuff winds up tasting like cotton candy. So it was love at first sight when I visited the laboratory of Claudio Crosara on the Giudecca. The front-room shop is perfumed by freshly baked bread and the superior hand-rolled *grissini* and simple Venetian cookies. Claudio's wife, Adriana Scarpa, is behind the counter, selling her husband's just-baked bounty. Buy a still-warm roll and ask Adriana to fill it with *soppressa salame* for one of the great culinary bargains of an expensive city. Or purchase a bag of skinny crispy breadsticks or a sampling of Venetian cookies. Regulars or big spenders may be rewarded with a *l'Arte del Pane* cloth shopping tote.

PASTRY
Marchini
Ponte San Maurizio, San Marco 2769
☎041.522-9109
Closed Tuesday

Marchini has, without a doubt, the best pastry in Venice, due to the efforts of hard-working Giancarlo Vio. Stand on the bridge to watch him at work in the laboratory behind the shop, then check out the attractive windows crammed with candies, chocolates, cookies like *baicoli, buranelli, focaccia veneziana,* and Giancarlo's prize-winning *torta del Doge*. The *zaleti* are a worthy culinary souvenir of this fantastic shop, a must for lovers of pastry.

PASTRY
Giancarlo Vio
Dorsoduro 1192
☎041.522-7451
Closed Tuesday

Near the Accademia, *bar-caffè* Vio is a perfect stop for a coffee and a tempting pastry in the best Venetian and Austrian tradition. Go for the *sacher torte*.

TRADITIONAL JEWISH PASTRY
Giovanni Volpe
Cannaregio 1143
Ghetto Vecchio
☎041.715-178
Closed Wednesday afternoon

The word *ghetto* derives from *getar,* "to throw or cast" in Venetian dialect. The Cannaregio area, where the Jews were confined, was at one time the site of a foundry. Giovanni Volpe is the only permanently established baker in Venezia's Jewish ghetto who is turning out traditional pastry. Pointy *asime dolce* (fennel cookies), *zuccherini* (sugar cookies), S-shaped *bisce,* almond and almond paste *impade* cookies, and *tortiglione* (almond "snake") are sold in this grocery-bakery. The Italian matzoh (*pane azimo*) looks very different from the commercial American version. Signor Volpe learned to make the desserts from a Jewish baker, but isn't kosher or Jewish himself.

TRADITIONAL JEWISH FOODS

Comunità Ebraica

Cannaregio 1189, Ghetto Vecchio
☎041.715-012

The Jewish Center has a community baking oven—open one month a year, from the festival of Purim through Passover—for authentic *pane azimo* and traditional desserts. They send matzoh all over northern Italy and Europe, make essentially the same desserts as Volpe, and also organize fixed-price communal Passover dinners, usually attended by up to 200 people, where traditional Venetian Jewish *cucina* is served.

GELATO

Gelateria Nico

Zattere 922, Dorsoduro
☎041.522-5293

Closed Thursday and December 20–January 20

Soaking up the afternoon sun on the Zattere, overlooking the Giudecca, while eating one of Nico's tasty *gelati,* is the essence of life in Venezia. There are other *gelaterie* on the Zattere, but Nico is the best.

GELATO

Paolin

San Marco 2962/A, Campo Santo Stefano

☎041.522-5576

Closed Monday, always open in summer

Paolin makes what many locals feel is Venezia's finest *gelato.* There are only twelve flavors, all creamy and naturally flavored. Outdoor tables in the campo Santo Stefano provide a ringside seat for some of Venezia's best people-watching, all for the price of a *gelato.* It's open till midnight in the summer.

ENOITECA-ROOMS

Aciugheta

Campo SS. Filippo e Giacomo, Castello 4357
☎041.522-492
Fax 041.520-8222

Closed Wednesday in the winter

All credit cards • inexpensive

Aciugheta is a *bacaro-pizzeria,* an unusual combination, but has one of the best wine lists in Venice. Wines served by the glass are chalked on a slate behind the bar, toothpicked rolled-up anchovies sit in oil, waiting to be tucked into bite-size sandwich rolls. There's a fine selection of cheese and tasty bites like stuffed red peppers and mini-pizzas to snack on at the counter or at a free table in between meals. Sitting at a set table means you're having a real meal, not recommended. But this is a perfect place to stop for a snack or fantastic glass of wine. They've got a tiny *pensione* upstairs with the least expensive rooms in Venezia.

RESTAURANT

Altanella

Giudecca 268, Rio de Ponte Lungo
☎041.522-7780

Closed Monday, Tuesday, and August

No credit cards • low moderate

Across the Canale Grande on the Giudecca, one of the last strongholds of a Venezia without mass tourism, Altanella is a favorite for its pure ambience and traditional *cucina.* The stained trilingual menu is filled with funny English typos, but the *cucina* makes no errors with simple boiled baby octopus, *sarde in saor* (marinated fresh sardines), well-prepared *risotto,* spaghetti, and deep-fried or grilled fish. Don't be put off by the inky, purply black sauce of *seppie in umido con polenta* (cuttlefish cooked with its ink, served with *polenta*)—it's one of the most glorious dishes of Venezia. The prices are miraculously low for Venezia. In fact, everything about Altanella is wonderful—except the wine.

RESTAURANT
Le Carampane
San Polo 1911
☎041.524-0165
Closed Sunday evening, Monday, and August
No credit cards • moderate
Le Carampane is named after the neighborhood's "house of the Rapanti family," where in the fifteenth century prostitutes exposed their breasts to attract customers. Chef Gianni Bartolozzi's local clients pack this *trattoria* for the tasty, typical *cucina* of *sarde in saor,* and spaghetti sauced with fish or mussels. Fish and shellfish are simply stewed, grilled, or fried. Finish with homemade cookies and *crostatine* (tarts). The house wine is nothing to write home about. Dine outside in the summer.

HOTEL-RESTAURANT
Cipriani
Giudecca 10, Fondamenta San Giovanni
☎041.520-7744
Fax 041.520-3930
Closed November through early March
All credit cards • ultra luxury
Arriving at the Cipriani in the hotel's private launch, with a view of the Venetian skyline, San Giorgio Maggiore, and the lagoon, is a special thrill. Rooms and suites are individually decorated, prices are for those who don't count the zeros on Italian banknotes. Omnipotent Gigi, Gianni, and Gastone are probably my favorite concierges in Italy, capable of arranging almost anything. The Cipriani dining room is the only elegant restaurant in Venice, with swift professional

service, beautifully appointed tables, Fortuny fabric draperies, Limoges dishes. Chef Renato Picolotto's menu offers Venetian classics, like perfectly prepared *risotto,* sole *saor* style, beef *carpaccio* or liver, and innovative dishes that make sense, like black pasta with seafood sauce; crispy, semolina-coated deepfried Dublin Bay prawns; lightly sauced fish dishes. Chocoholics should plan to sample the almost black, deep dark chocolate *gelato,* a world-class treat. *Tiramisù* is served in a bitter-chocolate shell, topped with a bitter-chocolate gondola. Pastry and homemade sorbet are also worthy finales for a meal. The wine list is fantastic, with unusual selections that should thrill enophiles. The bar serves the best Bellinis in Venice, available in peach season only, joined on the menu by drinks made with Prosecco and the juice of strawberry grapes, raspberries, pomegranate seeds, or strawberries, also named after Venetian artists. Lunch is served by the largest pool in Venice, when the weather is nice. Calorie-conscious guests will appreciate the sauna, tennis courts, and fitness center. The Cipriani launch is on call from piazza San Marco twenty-four hours a day. Travelers looking for the ultimate in luxury should book a suite at the Palazzo Vendramin, a tiny jewel of an annex behind the Cipriani with heart-stirring views of San Marco and the Grand Canal, open year round.

HOTEL-RESTAURANT
Club del Doge–Gritti Palace
San Marco 2467, Campo Santa Maria del Giglio
☎041.794-611
Always open
All credit cards • ultra luxury
The fifteenth-century palace of magistrate Andrea Gritti, turned into a hotel, was the residence of Dickens and Hemingway (writers must have made more in the old days) during sojourns in Venezia. The luxury of being an honored guest in an actual

palace is an unforgettable experience. Dine on an open-air terrace overlooking the Grand Canal, or in the antique-filled restaurant. Service is splendid, swift, and efficient. Skip the continental cuisine and concentrate on regional *cucina*. The wine list should be better. The cooking school (see page 31) offers some interesting classes.

RESTAURANT

Corte Sconta

Castello 3886, Calle del Pestrin
☎041.522-7024
Fax 041.522-7513
Closed Sunday, Monday, often in July
American Express, Diners Club, MasterCard • expensive

What a wonderful treat it used to be to eat under a grape arbor in the slightly squalid "Hidden Courtyard," sitting on wooden folding chairs and dining with paper napkins and place mats on stone tables. But the thrill, at least during the tourist season, is gone. Hordes of diners, famished for food of quality, descend on this ten-table restaurant and seem to have changed the perspective of the *cucina*. Successful dishes can be outstanding, like the *calimaretti con nero* (tiny tangles of squid in an inky sauce) served with grilled white *polenta*, but many dishes are less than perfect, and the summertime service can be surly. Finish your meal with lemony raisin polenta cookies (*zaleti*) or chocolate nut meringues (*brutti ma buoni*), accompanied by a glass of their mediocre dessert wine. Skip the house wines and ask for some of the gems from Friuli. In the summer, English seems to be the only language spoken in this courtyard that didn't remain hidden for long.

RESTAURANT

Al Covo

Campiello della Pescaria, Castello 3968
☎/Fax 041.522-3812

Closed Wednesday, Thursday
No credit cards • moderate at lunch, low inexpensive at dinner

No visit to Venice is complete for me without at least one meal at Al Covo. Handsome, *simpatico* chef-owner Cesare Benelli and his *simpatica* wife, Diane Rankin, from Texas are close friends. I've peeled *schie* with the staff, shopped with Cesare to check out Venetian seafood, and learned about local ingredients and traditions. Cesare is excited about cooking and it shows. He works with superfresh fish, the best Latini pasta, fantastic extra virgin olive oil which, he correctly insists, is better suited to seafood than butter. Start your meal with a selection of appetizers like mantis shrimp or *schie*, gray shrimplets that are simply dressed with extra virgin to appreciate fully the unadorned grace of Venetian seafood preparations—no sauce or lemon to interfere with the sweet, fresh flavors. Boned *sarde in saor*, ethereal whipped cod, stuffed mussels are usually part of the course. Pasta with carpet-shell clams; light fish soup; potato *gnocchi* sauced with tomato; *pasticcio*, baked pasta with a creamy yet creamless fish filling are among the fantastic starters. Deep-fried, crispy, greaseless bites of Dublin Bay prawns, soft-shelled crabs, tiny cuttlefish are first-rate. Monkfish is baked with mushrooms, radicchio, or artichokes, depending on the season. Diane's desserts, chocolate cake, pear tart with *grappa* sauce, and cookies are worth saving room for. The wine list is spectacular, well priced, studded with bargains that invite enophiles to drink big. Check out the lesser-known wineries that Cesare discovers at the yearly VinItaly wine fair. At lunchtime there's a short menu of *cicchetti*, a wonderful option for those who don't want two full meals a day but would like to sit down for something tasty.

RESTAURANT

Da Fiore

San Polo 2202, Calle del Scaleter

☎041.721-308

Fax 041.721-343

Closed Sunday, Monday, and August

All credit cards • high moderate

Da Fiore serves some of the best food in Venezia. The *cucina* is based on the finest-quality fresh fish and vegetables, given the simplest possible treatment. The flavors are sweet and direct. Chef Mara Zanetti and host Maurizio Martin's idea of a condiment is a drop of extra virgin olive oil and some chopped parsley. *Risotto*—made with special Vialone Nano rice and fish, shellfish, *porcini* mushrooms, or delicately perfumed local vegetables—is perfectly undercooked. Fish is fried with attention, and the results are almost greaseless. Seasonal soft-shelled crabs and baby cuttlefish are sensational. Save room for the S-shaped cookies from Burano, served with a glass of amber-colored Recioto di Soave. The wine list is well chosen, heavy on fine whites from Friuli and Veneto. Fax ahead for reservations because it's not easy to get a table at Da Fiore.

RESTAURANT

Fiaschetteria Toscana

San Giovanni Crisostomo,

Cannaregio 5719

☎041.528-5281

Fax 041.528-5521

Closed Tuesday

All credit cards • high moderate

The name of this restaurant is totally deceptive—it's not a Tuscan wine bar, but one of the best restaurants in the city. Owner Albino Busatto serves classic Venetian cooking, prepared by his son Stefano. *Risotto* made with seasonal vegetables is flawlessly prepared; the pasta with clam sauce, *tagliolini* with spider crab are superb. Baked monkfish or sea bass or the *fritto misto* are tasty. Grilled radicchio or mushrooms in season will please vegetable lovers. Albino's wife, Mariuccia Amato,

makes fine desserts, like fruit tarts and featherweight *zabaione*, whipped custard made with aged Marsala, served with cookies. The wine list is well priced and wonderful.

RESTAURANT

La Furatola

Dorsoduro 2870, Calle Lunga Barnaba

☎041.520-8594

Closed Wednesday evening, Thursday, July, and August

No credit cards • moderate

Reservations are a must in this small out-of-the-way restaurant serving *cucina veneziana*, because it's hard to get a table and if the fish isn't fresh enough, they won't open. The *spaghetti alle vongole* (with clam sauce) is exquisite, main-course fish is simply cooked, and the dessert cookies served with hot *zabaione* are a fun conclusion to your meal. It seems strange that a restaurant that cares so much about its basic ingredients doesn't have wines that are better than the simple house Pinot Bianco and Cabernet from Veneto. Ask for one of the two tables on the terrace overlooking the canal.

RESTAURANT

Alla Madonna

San Polo 594, Calle della Madonna

☎041.522-3824

Fax 041.521-0167

Closed Wednesday and part of August

All credit cards • high moderate

Alla Madonna looks like yet another seedy tourist trap—it's within a stone's throw of the Rialto bridge, known for its views and knickknacks. Instead, this *trattoria* is packed with regulars, locals who lunch here daily on classic *cucina veneziana*. The menu is translated into English, with a few endearing typographical errors, although the most interesting dishes are laid out in a refrigerator case of fresh fish and a two-tiered unstyled display of the day's specials. The owner of Al Graspo de Ua, a famed restaurant across the Rialto from Alla

Madonna, eats here on Monday and Tuesday, when his restaurant is closed. Wine, once again, is unfortunate.

RESTAURANT

Mascaron

**Calle Santa Maria Formosa,
Castello 5225**
☎041.522-5995
Closed Sunday
No credit cards • moderate

WINE BAR

Mascareta

Calle Santa Maria Formosa 5138, Castello
☎041.523-0744
Closed Sunday • open evenings only
No credit cards • inexpensive to low moderate

Mascaron was a popular wine bar that has evolved into a full-fledged restaurant and has spawned a new wine bar, Mascareta, down the lane. Locals used to stop at Mascaron for a glass of wine and a bite to eat, often sitting at the tables in one of the three small dining rooms. They started to prepare hot dishes like pasta with fish or seafood, *risotto* or *gnocchi* at lunchtime, in addition to such snacks as whipped cod, boiled octopus, mantis shrimp, and *sarde in saor,* served at brown paper place-matted wooden tables. Finish with traditional cookies and a glass of dessert wine. There's no written wine list, but Gigi or Davide will recommend something for those who want something more important than the house wine. There's even a nonsmoking dining room, a rare find in Italy. Stop in at night at Mascareta, the new wine bar just a few doors away, for a glass of wine and some fine *cicchetti,* to feel like a native.

RESTAURANT

Ai Mercanti

Calle dei Fuseri, San Marco 4346/A
☎/Fax 041.523-8269
Closed Sunday, Monday lunch
American Express, MasterCard, Visa •
expensive

Ai Mercanti has moved but Bruno Paolato's cooking is unchanged, new-wave Venetian, making optimum use of first-rate ingredients in nontraditional combinations. Mushrooms are on the menu most of the year. Begin with scallops and raw-mushroom salad or spider crab with asparagus tips. Homemade ravioli stuffed with seafood and zucchini flowers. *Fritto misto,* fried fish and seafood, is well prepared, greaseless; tasty white-fleshed *san pietro* is baked with vegetables. In the winter diners tired of fish can enjoy lamb, rabbit, or waterfowl. Desserts will please those with a sweet tooth, the wine list is small but well chosen, and the coffee is Illy.

HOTEL DINING

Monaco e Grand Canal

San Marco 1325, Calle Valleresso
☎041.520-0211
Closed Tuesday in winter
American Express, Visa • expensive

Is the Monaco e Grand Canal Hotel the least expensive one in Venezia that provides linen sheets? The furnishings are elegant, the location is ideal, and the restaurant, overlooking the Canale Grande and the Palladian façade of Le Zitelle on the Giudecca, serves some of the best hotel food in Venezia. The *cucina* is mostly traditional, service is efficient, and the fine wine list is a pleasure.

RESTAURANT-*BACARO*

Osteria da Alberto

Calle Giacinto Gallina, Cannaregio 5401
☎041.523-8153
Closed Sunday
No credit cards • moderate

Alberto Ferrari has moved his *osteria* to a new location, twice the size of his old place, with a real kitchen. There's an ample selection of *cicchetti* that happy locals snack on from 9 A.M. until lunchtime, accompanied by a glass of local plonk. Displayed in the front room are boiled octopus, *nervetti* salad, Ascolano fried olives, hard-boiled eggs, grilled vegetables, crab claws, *salumi,* whipped cod, and more. Full meals or *cicchetti* are served at mealtimes, with all pasta cooked to order and traditional fish preparations now expanding the menu. I'm praying for the wine selection to improve.

WINE BAR–*BACARO*

Osteria al Portego
Calle Malvasia, Castello 6015
☎**041.522-9038**
Closed Sunday
No credit cards • inexpensive to low moderate

Osteria al Portego is hard to find, tucked away on a tiny lane between campos Santa Marina and Santa Maria Formosa. Recognize it by the lantern with the word OSTERIA, on the corner of the *calle.* The selection of *cicchetti* is one of the best in Venice, with fried stuffed olives, meatballs, sausage, hard-boiled eggs with pickled onions and anchovies, fried crab claws, octopus, *nervetti,* and more. Show up at mealtime when two or three hot *primi* like *risotto, gnocchi,* pasta, or soup are served. Customers eat standing at the bar or at one of the tables in the back. The house wine is nothing to write home about. Al Portego closes early, around 9:30 P.M.

RESTAURANT

Paradiso Perduto
Cannaregio 2540,
Fondamenta della Misericordia
☎**041.720-581**
Closed Wednesday
No credit cards • moderate

Large, lively, and open late, "Paradise Lost" serves a typical *cucina veneziana* of sautéed seafood appetizers, fish pasta, and grilled or fried fish. The cover charge doubles on Sunday evenings, when there's live music. The wines of Collavini, especially the sparkling Il Grigio, are a pleasure to run into.

TABLEWARE

Rigattieri
San Marco 3532/35
☎**041.523-1081**
Closed Monday morning
All credit cards

It's impossible for anyone interested in food presentation not to stop at the Rigat-

---

BACARO
CICCHETTI E L'OMBRA
(Pick-Me-Ups and the Shadow)

The tradition of *cicchetti* "pick-me-ups"—little snacks in the style of Spanish tapas, something to munch on while drinking a glass of wine—is still strong in Venezia. They're consumed in a *bacaro*—not really a restaurant, but there's more food than in a regular bar—a Venetian custom that visitors may find addicting. *Cicchetti* (or *cicheti*) may range from a slice of bread and *prosciutto* to walnut-size meatballs, fried vegetables or zucchini flowers, whipped salt cod, or marinated sardines. The glass of wine is known as *l'ombra* ("the shadow"), since in the summer *gondolieri* used to grab some "shade" in the shadow of the *campanile* in Piazza San Marco. Although Veneziani might be horrified, *cicchetti* and a couple of *ombre* could easily substitute for lunch.

VENETIAN COOKIES

Venetian pastry chefs, influenced by the East, are said to have invented marzipan in 1500, created as a tribute to their city; *pane di San Marco* is *marci pan* in Latin, and *marzapan* in Venetian dialect. Cookies seem to be a local specialty, and they come in many shapes and flavors—S-shaped *buranelli* sugar cookies; light, delicate *baicoli;* cornmeal raisin *zaleti;* peppery cornmeal *peverini;* pine-nut *pignoletti.* Both *pan dei Dogi* and *torta dei Dogi* are rich with honey, dried fruit, and nuts. The *fregolata* is a buttery crumble of cornmeal and almond shortbread.

tieri shop's windows and doorways, with an extensive display of objects from miniature copper molds to wonderful, huge, simple white serving pieces. Their Bassano ceramics are better than anything in Bassano (unless you're looking for ceramic-turbaned Indians holding telephones) and include beautiful centerpieces and ceramic tureens shaped like vegetables. The cabbage and squash are especially attractive. I love the specialized service pieces, like the goose platter, the asparagus dishes, the poultry terrines, and anything for game. Liliana and Massimo Rigattieri are friendly, helpful, and will ship your purchases home for you.

GLASSWARE

Industrie Veneziane
Calle Vallaresso 1320
☎**041.523-0509**
Closed Monday morning
All credit cards

If Harry's Bar is your favorite place in Venezia, why not purchase their carafes at Industrie Veneziane, which also sells a wide selection of traditional eighteenth-century Veneziano blue, red, green, and pink gold-trimmed glassware, or the more contemporary designs of Nason-Moretti.

GLASSWARE

Barovier e Toso
Fondamenta Vetrai 28

☎**041.739-049**
Closed Saturday and Monday morning
All credit cards

Barovier e Toso is one of the oldest glass-making firms of Venezia. Their modern serving pieces and glasses are mostly made to order, and many examples of their work are in the Murano Glass Museum.

GLASSWARE

L'Isola
San Marco 1468, Campo San Moisè
☎**041.523-1973**
Closed Monday morning
All credit cards

L'Isola looks more like an art gallery than a glass shop, with its dramatic lighting and sense of display. They have a complete line of the modern glassware by Carlo Moretti, who uses traditional Venetian glass-blowing techniques to create objects of great style. The simple elegance of his designs contrasts with the baroque intricacies of more classic local artisans.

GLASSWARE

Venini
San Marco 314, Piazzetta dei Leoncini
☎**041.522-4045**
Closed Monday morning
All credit cards

Venini is probably the most famous of the modern glassmakers, and the most innovative. This shop is the only place that sells

---

VENETIAN GLASS

The Veneziani rediscovered the art of making glass in the late 1200s, and maintained a monopoly on production through the sixteenth century. The glass produced on Murano is known for its color, intricate patterns, and light weight. Modern pieces with sleek lines and little decoration are created by the artisans of Murano, as are delicate, twisted, gold-trimmed pieces and reproductions of antiques from periods of former glory. Handmade artistry of this order is never inexpensive, so don't expect a bargain. All shops listed here are used to dealing with tourists and are thoroughly familiar with shipping procedures. Glass lovers visiting Murano will want to see the Museo dell'Arte Vetraria, where examples of historical Egyptian, Roman, Venetian, and European glass and modern pieces are displayed.

---

their decorative pieces, bottles, and vases (some designed by Laura di Santillana and Gio Ponti), which are a joy to look at and justifiably expensive.

GLASSWARE

L'Ixa
Campo San Stefano 2958
☎**041.522-9656**
Closed Monday morning
No credit cards

Tempting Murano glass pieces created from 1870 to 1960 are attractively priced and displayed in this wonderful antiques shop in Campo San Stefano. A window-shop here is a perfect excuse for a Paolo *gelato* (see page 174).

LINEN AND LACE

Jesurum
Merceria del Capitello, San Marco 4857
☎**041.520-6177**
Fax 041.520-6085
Always open
All credit cards

In 1868 Michelangelo Jesurum reestablished the lace industry with a core of artisans who remembered the traditional skills. His original shop, in the spectacular 1150 Church of Sant'Apollonia, has moved—but the new location, on two floors, still has the same splendid selection of antique and

modern lace tablecloths and contemporary, brightly colored table linens. I could get lost staring at the incredible antique lace cloths of a quality usually found in museums. Director Eugenia Graziussi will help you if you'd like to order something special. Prices are justifiably steep.

LACE AND LACEMAKING

Scuola dei Merletti
Piazza B. Galuppi, Burano
☎**041.730-034**
No credit cards

The Burano Lace School, founded in 1872, closed on its one hundredth anniversary due to a lack of interest in the painstaking work necessary to produce fine handmade lace and embroidery. It was reopened in 1981 with the help of the Burano Lace Consortium, and offers free courses taught by eleven master lacemakers. Modern and traditional lace or open-work embroidered table linens can be purchased or made to order.

LINEN AND LACE

Maria and Lina Mazzaron
Castello 4970, Fondamenta dell'Osmarin
☎**041.522-1392**
By appointment only
No credit cards

Before World War II, all proper young women in Italy knew how to make lace and

THE LACE OF VENEZIA

The arts of lacemaking and embroidery were brought to Venezia from the East, and the Venetians incorporated lace in royal, clerical, and aristocratic attire, creating a market for the delicately stitched or intricately manipulated threads, handcrafted by nobles, nuns, and common women. The lace "schools" of the lagoon, each with its own special stitch or technique—the bobbin lace of Pellestrina, the Venice-Burano stitch of Burano, the net stitch of Chioggia—practically disappeared with the advent of machine-made lace.

embroider. When they were fourteen, the Mazzaron sisters were sent to study lace-making with the nuns, and they obviously learned their lessons well. Their private shop, on the first floor of a noble Venetian palace, offers linens that look and feel like heirlooms.

STATIONERY

Legatoria Piazzesi
San Marco 2511, Santa Maria del Giglio
☎**041.522-1202**
Closed Monday morning
All credit cards

The Legatoria Piazzesi, the "bookbindery" of the Piazzesi family, sells beautiful paper, hand-printed from a large collection of antique blocks. Directories, recipe files, table place cards, photo albums, stationery, covered boxes, and other items are made from or covered with this traditionally patterned paper.

STATIONERY

Paolo Olbi
San Marco 3653, Calle della Mandola
☎**041.523-7655**
Closed Monday morning
All credit cards

Paolo Olbi sells handmade paper and leather notebooks with blank pages, photo albums, diaries, and stationary.

PRESERVES

Convento degli Armeni
Isola di San Lazzaro

The tiny island of San Lazzaro degli Armeni, close to Lido in the Venetian lagoon, was donated to Armenian refugees, who founded a convent with a printing house, a library of over 50,000 books, some dating from A.D. 900, cloisters, and rose gardens where petals and hips are collected to make rose preserves, which are available at the convent.

Venezia-Cavallino

HOTEL

See Venezia or Jesolo

RESTAURANT

La Laguna
Via Pordelio 44
☎**/Fax 041.968-058**
Closed Thursday
All credit cards • high moderate

The island of Cavallino is accessible by land from Jesolo or by sea, and is definitely worth the voyage for fish and seafood lovers. The ambience of La Laguna is rustic, the dining rooms large, presided over by Olindo Ballarin, with his son Alvise in the kitchen. Start with their own smoked fish—tuna, sturgeon, or eel—or classic Venetian seafood like spider crab, mantis shrimp, minuscule shrimp, hard-to-find baby-pink scallops called *canestrelli*. I can never resist the fresh pasta served with the pan juices of braised scorpion fish (*scorfano*), followed by the boned fish. Grilled eel is spectacular; sea bass, bream, or bogue are baked in a salt crust, moist and tasting of the sea; deep-fried squidlets are served in summer months, greaseless, crunchy little bites. Desserts are worth saving room for, especially those with wild berries, and the tiny pastries that seem to mysteriously disappear from the plate. The wine list focuses on regional whites, with a fine selection of wines from other regions, *grappe*, and distillates. This world-class restaurant merits a visit.

Venezia-Lido

PASTRY-ORGANIC GARDEN
Maggion
Via Dardanelli 48, Lido
☎041.526-0836
Closed Monday, Tuesday

Sergio Maggion grows most of the fruits and vegetables utilized by his son Matteo and wife, Leonide, at their pastry shop on the island of Lido. The garden is in the area known as Malamocco, said to yield spectacular produce due to the slightly salty alluvial soil of the Venetian lagoon. Sergio harvests the first artichoke of each of his plants in May, and Italian-speaking gardeners and gastronomes who want to learn more about *castraure* should contact Sergio. The specialties of the Maggion pastry shop are simply superb. Check out the *focaccia veneziana*, sweet or savory tarts made with Sergio's organic fruit and vegetables, and traditional cookies like *zaleti, busolai*, and *amaretti* that look like little breasts, piped onto *ostie* wafers.

GELATO
Gelateria da Tita
Gran Viale 61, Lido
☎041.526-0359
Closed in the winter, open daily the rest of the year

Gelato lovers should consider a pilgrimage to this out-of-the-way *gelateria* for the legendary egg-yolk–rich custard *gelato*. Nut and fresh fruit flavors are also worthwhile.

Venezia–Tessera Airport

ENOTECA
Mangilli
Aeroporto Marco Polo
☎041.541-6210
Open 8 A.M.–8:30 P.M.
American Express, MasterCard, Visa

Enoteca Mangilli, open seven days a week, is a perfect stop for anyone flying out of Venice to pick up a bottle of fine wine, *grappa*, a wide range of extra virgin olive oils, balsamic vinegar, Latini pasta, and nonperishable culinary souvenirs of your Italian stay. Save room in a tote for some of these well-priced products. Owner-sommelier Lorenzo Menegus or one of his assistants (Eva, Giorgia, or Chiara) will help you select something worth schlepping home. Those landing in Venice may want to purchase a bottle of wine here to celebrate their arrival in one of the most wonderful cities in the world.

Venezia-Torcello

HOTEL
See Venezia

RESTAURANT
Ponte del Diavolo
☎041.730-401
Fax 041.730-250
Closed Thursday and all evenings except Saturday
American Express, MasterCard, Visa •
high moderate

Take the water bus from Fondamenta Nuova to Torcello, a forty-five-minute boat ride through the lagoon, to visit the cathedral and museum, and to lunch at this rustic *trattoria*. Chef Renato Ceccato prepares classic Venetian dishes with great skill. The dining rooms are cozy, filled with vacationing gastronomes onto a good thing. Appetizers like deep-fried *schie*, eaten shell and all, mantis shrimp, spider crab are worthwhile. Homemade ravioli stuffed with spinach and ricotta, sauced with seasonal vegetables, or fish soup lightly flavored with curry are among the house specialties. Baby sole with bright green zucchini sauce, garnished with deep-fried zucchini, grilled fish, or eel are prepared in the fireplace. Conclude with a tasty fruit tart or the irresistible *sgroppino*, a slushy mixture of lemon *gelato* with vodka whisked over ice, said to have wonderful digestive effects. The house wine is fine, although there's a small but interesting wine list. If you fall in love with the attractive wine carafes, they will tell you where he got them. Eat outside in the garden in the spring, summer, and early fall.

Verona

Verona, a city of Roman origin, is located on the banks of the Adige River—hometown of Romeo and Giulietta, of the exciting open-air opera performed in a Roman arena, and of VinItaly, the most important wine fair in Italy, held in the early spring.

HOTEL
Gabbia d'Oro
Corso Porta Borsari 4/A
☎045.590-292
Fax 045.590-293
All credit cards • high expensive

HOTEL
Vittoria
Via Adua 8
☎045.590-566
Fax 045.590-0155
All credit cards • expensive

HOTEL
Aurora
Piazza delle Erbe
☎045.594-717
Fax 045.801-086
No credit cards • inexpensive

HOTEL
Antica Porta Leona
Corticella Leoni 3
☎045.595-499
Fax 045.595-499
All credit cards • moderate

RESTAURANT
Locanda di Castelvecchio
Corso Cavour 49
☎045.803-0097
Fax 045.801-3124
Closed Tuesday, Wednesday lunch
All credit cards • moderate

I've been following Armando Bordin's restaurant career in Verona, and am pleased that he owns the Locanda di Castelvecchio, a small, comfortable *trattoria* across from the Castelvecchio Museum. His wife, Licia Agostini, is in the kitchen preparing classics like *pasta e fagioli* and *tagliatelle*, served in broth with chicken livers or brought to the table plain, to be dressed with meat sauce, chicken-liver *ragù*, or tomato sauce. Boiled or roast meats are the traditional main-course offerings, served with *salsa verde*, *pearà*, *mostarda*, or horseradish. Vegetables are simply prepared; desserts are standards like *tiramisù* and fruit tarts. The wine list is small but well chosen, well priced.

RESTAURANT
La Fontanina
Piazzetta Portichetti Fontanelle 3
☎045.913-305
Closed Sunday, Monday lunch
American Express, MasterCard, Visa • high moderate

La Fontanina, across the Adige River, not in the center of town but worth the search, is a *trattoria* aspiring to something more. The ambience is rustic-cute, with lace-trimmed windows, antique clutter, well-lit tables. The menu changes daily and offers a few regional preparations as well as inventive cooking for those who want to escape home-style *cucina*. *Gnocchi* are sauced with house *ragù*, fresh pasta is sauced with vegetables or fish; second-course offerings are divided between meat and fish preparations. At lunchtime La Fontanina serves reasonably priced fixed menus of meat, fish, or vegetable dishes. The wine list is small, with a few choice wines.

E N O T E C A

Al Carro Armato
Vicolo Gatto 2/A
☎**045.803-0175**
Visa, MasterCard • inexpensive
The wine selection is wonderful in this traditional Veronese *osteria* in a building that dates from the fourteenth century. Munch on *salumi*, cheese, veal's-foot salad, and simple dishes, or stop in late for a glass of wine.

G E L A T O

La Boutique del Gelato
Via Carlo Ederle 13
☎**045.830-1113**
Closed Monday
Paolo, one of Italy's finest *gelato* makers, has closed his shop and moved to South America to be closer to the exotic fruit he adores, but his kids, Angela and Roberto, have opened their own *gelateria* nearby. They learned to make first-rate *gelato* from their father and apply the same passion for *gelato*, combined with the same scrupulous search for seasonal ripe fruit, that made Paolo's products so superior. Look for delicious classics like chocolate, hazelnut, and custard. Fruit flavors are, in the language of guide books, worth a detour: mango; real, pale-colored *pistacchio;* pink grapefruit; passion fruit; strawberry; raspberry;

banana; and practically every flavor of fruit prepared in its season. There are around thirty varieties to choose from at the height of the summer fruit season, less in the winter, when Italians don't eat so much *gelato*.

M A R K E T
Piazza delle Erbe
The central outdoor fruit and vegetable market, in piazza delle Erbe, takes place six mornings a week. The light in the piazza, reflecting off the pastel rust- and apricot-colored brick buildings, is best in the early morning, before nine, when the produce stands are stocked with crisp-looking vegetables and lively fruit, and the perfumes in the air make your nose prickle. The evening light is also wonderful, but the food stands will be closed, leaving only stalls selling touristy trinkets.

R E S T A U R A N T
Il Desco
Via dietro San Sebastiano 7
☎**045.595-358**
Fax 045.590-236
Closed Sunday
All credit cards • expensive
The golden apricot marbleized stucco walls, beamed wooden ceilings, patchwork-inspired tapestries by Missoni, subdued lighting, and warm welcome by host Natale Spinelli set the stage for dining at Il Desco, one of Italy's most attractive restaurants and a rising star on the gastronomic scene. The *cucina*, guided by Elia Rizzo, has little to do with tradition but uses a wide range of not-strictly-local meat, poultry, fish, and vegetables to great advantage. Tastes are balanced, herbs are used wisely, pasta is homemade, and cheese is served with fig bread. Desserts are glorious and have a separate menu. The wine list is splendid and clear, with a great selection of local and Italian wines.

HOUSEWARES

Casa mia di Montaldo
Via IV Novembre 17
☎**045.914-362**
Closed Monday morning
No credit cards

This small maze of rooms with what looks like at least two of every houseware known to man, stacked on floor-to-ceiling shelves, is worth a slight detour—it was on the way to a now-defunct *gelateria*. One room contains all-plastic toys and is especially strong on Lego. I can always find something of interest.

Vicenza

HOTEL

Hotel Giardini
Via Giurolo 10
☎**/Fax 0444.326-458**
All credit cards • moderate

BED-AND-BREAKFAST

Vicenza Hills
Viale 10 Giugno 133
☎**/Fax 0444.543-087**
No credit cards • low inexpensive

American Janice del Prà runs a wonderful bed-and-breakfast in her home outside Vicenza. The price is right, and Janice is extremely knowledgeable about the area, its villas and restaurants.

HOTEL

See Arcugnano

RESTAURANT

Lo Scudo di Francia
Contrà Piancoli 4
☎**0444.323-322**
Closed Sunday evening, Monday
All credit cards • high moderate

The Fanton family's elegant restaurant, in the center of town in a Gothic Venetian palace, feels like a visit to a noble home, with three beautifully appointed dining rooms, suffused lighting from chandeliers, attractively set tables. Begin with local *soppressa*.

Pasta is homemade, ravioli are stuffed with red radicchio, rustic pasta, barley and bean soup is ladled from a terrine. Venetian-style liver, stewed cuttlefish, and roast meat (choose *capretto*, kid, when they've got it) are usual second-course options. *Polenta* is the side dish or garnish, depending on your point of view. Desserts are simple, like crème brûlée or fresh berries. The wine list is small but interesting, and it isn't too hard to find something terrific to drink.

ENOITECA

Bere Alto
Via Pedemuro San Biagio 57
☎**0444.322-144**
Closed Monday, Tuesday morning and, in the summer, also Sunday evening

Daniele de Zotti and Giancarlo Guidolin abandoned their office jobs to start this *enoteca*, and it is a joy. Drink from the well-priced and incredible selection of regional, national, and international wines served by the glass or bottle. Cheese and *salumi* accompany the wine. Swirl it in big glasses as the natives do.

RESTAURANT

Da Remo
Via Caimpenta 14
☎**0444.911-007**
Fax 0444.911-856
Closed Sunday evening, Monday, and August
All credit cards • high moderate

Da Remo is a rustic farmhouse decorated in typical *trattoria* style. The *cucina* is also typical, featuring simple regional food of the Breganze area. Owner Mario Baratto is interested in hard-to-find traditional dishes, and it's a pleasure to find them on his menu. The rice and hops (*riso e bruscàndoli*) may be worth the trip. Mushrooms are served in season. Wine is mostly local. Sunday lunch is a mob scene, interesting from a cultural point of view but not for the food, which is better when the kitchen isn't so stressed.

AUSTRIA

Paluzza • Paularo
Sauris
• Tolmezzo

Villa Santina

• Chianzutan
• Verzegnis • Tricesimo

SLOVENIA

Tavagnacco •
Leonacco
di Pagnacco • Zompitta
Spilimbergo
San Quirino
Lavariano • Sant'Andrat A2
del Judrio
Remanzacco • Stregna

San Daniele del Friuli
Godia • Cividale del Friuli

Rauscedo
Udine • Dolegna del Collio
Manzano •
San Giovanni Cormons • San Floriano del Collio
Al Natisone Corona • Gradiscutta
• Porcia A23 Percoto• Gorizia
Gradiscutta Gradisca d'Isonzo • San Michele del Carso

A4 Cervignano• A4
•Aquileia

VENETO

Trieste
Muggia

Adriatic
Sea

"There," pointing eastward, **"over those mountains is the country formerly known as Yugoslavia,"** the Friulani never fail to let you know. It's a boundary that most people aren't too happy about, since in the early 1950s a whole section of this region, Istria, was ceded to Yugoslavia in exchange for Trieste.

Friuli-Venezia Giulia

Friuli–Venezia Giulia is a land of Alps, hills with some of the best wine-growing areas in Italy, plains, and lagoons, wedged between the Adriatic Sea, former Yugoslavia, Austria, and Veneto. They all played musical chairs with this region after the rule of Romans, Longobards, Franks, the bishops of Aquileia, the dukes of Friuli, and the counts of Grado.

The traditional open hearth (*fogolar*) is an invitation to come in and warm up, an essential element in both restaurants and homes and an expression of the Friulani sense of hospitality and warmth. The *cucina*, influenced by many cultures but above all by poverty, is flavored by original combinations of spices, sweet and sour, and smoke. *Brovada*, its recipe dating from Roman Apicio's *De re coquinaria*, is usually offered with misgivings and apologies in case you don't appreciate turnips, fermented with the dregs of pressed grapes for a month, then grated and cooked. Roman legions were fueled by grain and beans, found here in the form of barley and bean soup. Dumplings (*gnocchi*) may be made of potatoes, winter squash, or stale bread, and the traditional pasta (*cialzones*) may be stuffed with smoked ricotta, herbs, or even sweet-and-sour combinations. *Polenta* may appear as a first or second course, or as a side dish. Meats, mostly pork, game, and courtyard animals, are usually grilled in the *fogolar* or roasted. Field greens and herbs flavor the *cucina friulana* of the hills and plains. Restaurants on the lagoon serve simply prepared Adriatic seafood to summer tourists. Cheese made by individuals who graze their herds in the mountains rarely reaches the city, and never leaves the region. More easily found *latteria* cheese is used to create *frico* or *fricco*, a tasty cheese fritter. It is made, I have been informed many times, by frying a bit of *latteria* until it's done, and then turning it over to complete cooking. Mine has never come out right. Strudel-type desserts reflect the Austrian influence in this region. The Friulani are *grappa* drinkers, not sippers, and even rinse their coffee cups with a shot of *grappa*, known as a *resentin*.

This is the region of Italy where I left my heart. Most tourists seem to have overlooked Friuli's Roman outposts; the star-shaped Venetian fortress of Palmanova; Villa Manin, the country estate of the last Doge of Venezia; the synagogue of Trieste; Udine, with its Venetian piazza and hilltop castle in the middle of town; Aquileia, with backyard Roman columns and a fourth-century mosaic the size of a football field. But could they all have overlooked the Friulani, the warmest and most hospitable of the Italians?

The Menu

Salumi

Muset *or* **musetto:** cooked sausage made with ground pork and spices that may include coriander and cinnamon

Prosciutto affumicato: raw ham smoked with juniper and fir, a specialty of the village of Sauris

Prosciutto crudo di San Daniele: raw ham cured in the hills of San Daniele, thought to be the best in Italy

Salame friulano: cured pork sausage

Antipasto

Cvapcici: unpronounceable meatballs from Trieste, made with veal, pork, and beef

Frico *or* **fricco:** fried cheese fritters

Salame cotto nell'aceto: fresh salami cooked in vinegar, served with *polenta*

Primo

Brodeto *or* **brodetto:** fish soup

Cialzone: pasta stuffed with spinach and candied citron, or potatoes and cinnamon, or herbs and smoked ricotta, served with melted butter

Gnocchi: potato dumplings

Gnocchi di pane: made of stale bread

Gnocchi di susina: stuffed with a prune

Gnocchi di zucca: made with winter squash, served with grated smoked ricotta

Jota *or* **iota:** bean, cabbage, or *brovada* and *polenta* soup

Lasagne ai semi di papavero: sweet poppy-seed *lasagna*

Minestra d'orzo e fagioli: bean and barley soup

Paparot: spinach and cornmeal soup

Ravioli di zucca: squash-filled pasta, at times made from a potato dough

Ris e fasui: rice, bean, and potato soup

Zuppa di pesce alla gradese: soup of local Adriatic fish, made with vinegar and garlic

Secondo

Baccalà alla capuccina: salt cod cooked with anchovies, raisins, pine nuts, and spices

Brovada: turnips marinated with grape skins left over from winemaking, cooked with pork sausage

Capriolo in salmi: venison stewed in a sauce of wine, herbs, and spices

Costine di maiale: roast pork ribs

Fasui cul muset: beans with pork sausage

Frittata alle erbe: pan-fried flan of eggs and field greens

Granzevola alla triestina: crab baked with bread crumbs, garlic, and parsley

Gulyas: (goulash) beef stew cooked with onions, herbs, and paprika

Toc de purcit: pork stewed with white wine, cloves, cinnamon, and other spices

Contorno

Radichietto: tender salad greens, sometimes served with beans

Formaggio

Formaggio di malga: cheese found only in the mountain districts, made from the milk of cows grazing in alpine pastures

Latteria: mild when fresh, more intense when aged, made from cow's milk

Montasio: mild, smooth, made from cow's milk

Ricotta: soft, mild, fresh, or smoked (*affumicata*)

Dolce

Esse di raveo: S-shaped sugar cookies

Gubana: light, flaky pastry stuffed with nuts and candied fruits, or in its more authentic form, a puffy spiral-shaped yeast bread

filled with nuts, cocoa, candied fruit, and liqueur

Presnitz: roll stuffed with raisins, nuts, and candied fruit

Putizza: similar to *gubana*, but moister and containing chocolate pieces

Strucolo: ricotta-raisin strudel

The Wine List

Six major DOC production zones of Friuli, each producing wines named for up to thirteen different grape varieties, plus personal non-DOC wines labeled *vino da tavola*, may contribute to some confusion about the wines of this region. A Pinot Grigio or Tocai from Latisana or Aquileia won't have the same style as the wines of the same name from Colli Orientali dei Friuli and Collio Goriziano, also known as Collio. The flowery whites and rich reds are meant to be drunk young, although some producers seem to be coming up with wines, both red and white, of more lasting promise. Wineries are experimenting with native grape varieties, at times clonally rescued from near extinction, and the resulting lusty reds are worthy of their effort.

Wines from the **Colli Orientali dei Friuli,** an area that stretches along the Slovenian border to the foothills of the Alps, are among the best in the region. The reds, especially elegant **Cabernet,** smooth **Merlot,** and hearty native **Refosco,** are fine with meats and game. **Pinot Bianco, Pinot Grigio, Riesling Renano,** and **Sauvignon** are delicate, fruity, dry whites that go well with *antipasti,* pasta, rice, and fish. **Tocai** is soft, aromatic, and dry, in no way resembling the Tokay of Hungary and Austria. For dessert, **Verduzzo** and **Picolit,** both made from native grapes, are delicately perfumed and semi-sweet. Quality wines are produced by Abbazia di Rosazzo, Dorigo, Giovanni Dri, Livio Felluga, La Viarte, Rocca Bernarda, Ronchi di Cialla, Ronco del Gnemiz, Vigne dal Leon, Le Due Terre, Torre Rosazza, Petrussa, Rodaro, Specogna, Zamò e Palazzolo, and Volpe Pasini.

Some of Italy's finest white wines are made in the area known as **Collio** or **Collio Goriziano,** outside the city of Gorizia, along the border of Yugoslavia. Whites are dry and fruity and are served with *antipasti* and fish dishes: **Pinot Bianco, Pinot Grigio, Sauvignon,** and **Traminer. Collio** is a delicate blend of Tocai, Malvasia, and Ribolla white grapes. Aromatic **Tocai,** at its best from this area, is served with fish and regional *cucina.* Reds **Cabernet** and **Merlot** are dry, light, and fragrant; they're perfect with meat and game. Quality producers include Borgo Conventi, Borgo del Tiglio, Ca' Ronesca, Livio Felluga, Gradimir Gradnik, Francesco Gravner, Jermann, Doro Princic, Puiatti, Radikon, Russiz Superiore, Sfiligoi, Edi Keber, Venica, Vidussi, Villa Russiz, La Castellada, and Mario Schiopetto.

The **Isonzo** area, which follows the Isonzo River from the plains to the hills near the Yugoslavian border, produces fragrant dry reds **Cabernet** and **Merlot,** often paired with meat dishes. **Pinot Bianco, Pinot Grigio, Sauvignon, Riesling Renano,** and **Tocai,** all fine, crisp whites, are also produced in the Isonzo area by Francesco Pecorari, Ronco de Gelso, Vie di Romans, and Pier Paolo Pecorari. They're at their best with antipasti, first courses, and fish.

Fine **Chardonnay,** an elegant dry white served with fish, is produced by Abbazia di Rosazzo, Borgo Conventi, Stelio Gallo, Gravner, Puiatti, and Jermann's amazing "Where Dreams have no end."

Müller Thurgau, an elegant, fruity, dry white, splendid with fish and seafood, is produced by Ronco del Gnemiz, Mario Schiopetto, and Marina Danieli.

The **Grave** Area, a high plain above the Tagliamento River produces reds, **Cabernet, Merlot, Refosco,** and whites **Chardonnay, Pinot Bianco, Pinot Grigio, Tocai, Sauvignon,** and **Verduzzo.** Look for wines by Borgo Magredo, Vistorta.

Pignolo, a uniquely Friulan grape, has been rescued from extinction (clonally!) and is now the basis for a robust, hearty red that pairs well with meat, fowl, and local rustic country cooking. It is ably produced by Abbazia di Rosazzo and Girolamo Dorigo.

Schioppettino is a ruby-colored full red from the native Ribolla Nera or Schioppettino grape. It is usually served with meat, fowl, and game and is produced by Ronchi di Cialla and Vigne dal Leon.

Tacelenghe or **Tazzelenghe,** literally "tongue-cutter" in dialect, is a direct reference to the tannic "bite" of this purple-ruby, lively red table wine made from a local grape variety. It is at its best with meat, fowl, and game, and produced by Girolamo Dorigo and Vigne dal Leon.

Exemplary red, white, and sparkling *vini da tavola* table wines are produced by some of Friuli's finest winemakers. Dorigo makes white Ronc di Juri and Monsclapade, a blend of red grapes aged in wood. Mario Schiopetto produces Rivarossa, a red, Riesling Renano, and Blanc des Rosis, Borgo del Tiglio makes Rosso della Centa from Cabernet and Merlot. Abbazia di Rosazzo makes Ronco delle Acacie and Ronco di Corte, both blends of white grapes, and Ronco dei Roseti, a blend of mostly local reds, aged in new oak barrels. Livio Felluga's son Maurizio has created Terre Alte, a flowery blend of white grapes, and a personal favorite. Jermann makes Vintage Tunina, Vinnae, and Engelwhite, elegant whites, and Moscato Rosa, a rosé dessert wine, with great success. La Viarte ages its white Liende and red Roi in new oak barrels. Volpe Pasini makes Zuc di Volpe, a blend of red grapes. Applause, Il Grigio, and Ribolla Gialla are sparkling whites made by Collavini.

Regional Specialties

Grappa. *Grappa* is made from pomace, the grape skins and pits left over after the winemaking process. It anesthetized generations of Friulani against cold and poverty. Local custom calls for rinsing the after-dinner coffee cup with a shot of *grappa*, thus adding a bit of leftover sugar and coffee to the aggressive alcoholic taste of this potent liquor. For more *grappa* information, see page 183; for a source of Friuli *grappa*, see page 190.

Gubana. *Gubana* is a spiral-shaped yeast dessert cake, originally a specialty of Cividale but found throughout Friuli. There are two basic versions—one made with puff pastry and the other with yeast dough, both with essentially the same filling of nuts, cocoa, candied fruit, spice, and liqueurs. It is eaten sliced and sprinkled with *grappa* for dessert, but is delicious plain for breakfast. See page 184 for sources. Fear not if you fall in love with *gubana*—Carol Field's recipe for this traditional cake in *The Italian Baker* is a gem.

Prosciutto Crudo di San Daniele. It's easy to recognize a San Daniele *prosciutto*—it's the violin-shaped ham complete with hoof, which is never removed from the *prosciutto* that many feel is the tastiest in Italy. But what makes the *prosciutto* from the village of San Daniele so special? The procedure is practically the same one used to make the more famous Parma version. But there are differences. The raw hams, called *coscie* (thighs), are flattened and massaged with salt. The larger surface and thinner ham produced by flattening takes less salt and less time to cure. The hams are hung to age in well-ventilated temperature-controlled rooms, with windows that open to expose the hams to gusts of a cold northern wind known as the *bora*. The great news about

prosciutto di San Daniele is that as of the end of 1996, it can now be imported into the U.S., boned and with hoof removed. It was previously excluded by the F.D.A. because of its supposedly unhygienic hoof, which never hurt anyone in Friuli. *Prosciutto* lovers may want to visit the *prosciutto* festival in San Daniele the last weekend of August. For sources see page 192, and for more information see page 191.

Smoke It! Prosciutto, Trout, and Ricotta. Smoke is an important flavor in the *cucina* of Friuli. *Prosciutto* is cured, then smoked with aromatic wood and spices, once by individuals in the hood of the *fogolar* fireplace, but now in larger smokers by more commercial producers. Everyone told me that the accumulated soot, formed over decades, is a determining factor in the flavor of perfectly smoked *prosciutto*. Smoked *prosciutto* is a specialty of Sauris, and is found throughout the region and even beyond. See pages 185 and 195 to check out two fine producers of smoked *prosciutto*. The same treatment is applied to trout by Friultrota. See page 192 for more information. Smoked ricotta is often grated on pasta or *gnocchi* in Friuli. It can be found in most groceries and restaurants in the region and makes a wonderful culinary souvenir, since it's almost impossible to find elsewhere.

Montasio. Montasio was once produced with milk from cows grazed in the alpine pastures of Mount Montasio. Although local milk is still utilized, the production area has enlarged to the plains of Friuli and eastern and central Veneto. The Consorzio per la Tutela del Formaggio Montasio regulates production, and each form of cheese is branded on the side with a stylized mountainous-looking "M" with the word MON-

TASIO below. Fresh Montasio, with small random holes, sweet, elastic, straw-colored, is ripened for two months. Piquant, crumbly *stagionato* is aged for over a year, often used grated. *Semistagionato*, between fresh and aged in flavor and aspect, is ripened for four to eight months. For more information on Montasio, contact Dott. Loris Pevere at the Consorzio, S.S. Napoleonica, Rivalta di Codroipo, tel. 0432.905-317, fax 0432.908-471.

Muset.   *Muset* in Friulan dialect, *musetto* in Italian, "little face" in English is a cooked sausage like *cotechino*. After being boiled slowly for hours, it's sliced and served with mashed potatoes, sauerkraut, or *brovada*, found in many traditional restaurants.

Asparagus.   White asparagus is one of the glories of spring in Friuli, a great reason for true asparagus lovers to visit the region. The epicenter of asparagus obsession is in Tavagnacco. See page 196 for information about eating and buying white asparagus and for attending the festival.

Wild Greens.   Wild greens abound in the spring in Friuli, utilized in *risotto, frittate,* and salads. *Sclopit* are called "silene" in English; *bruscàndoli* are hops; *ardelut* looks like corn lettuce, tastes like rucola, and is eaten raw in a salad with beans. Look for these wild greens throughout the region.

Cookies: The "S" of Raveo.   This crispy S-shaped butter cookie is a specialty of the town of Raveo, at its best made at home. If, however, you don't know any locals who love to bake, the cookies can be found in groceries. Those who want to go to the source should plan to visit Emilio Bonanni at the factory founded by his father (Biscottificio Aldo Bonanni, zona Artigianale 3, Raveo, tel./fax 0433.746-030).

Mountain Cheese.   Cheese production in Friuli is the antithesis of big business. There are no cooperatives, no standardization,

and the only way to sample the best is to head for the mountains and valleys of Carnia, to the wiggly back roads on the Touring Club map, on the lookout for signs that say *Formaggio.* Country restaurants may have the cheese of a neighboring producer. See below for one source.

The Friulan "Pantry."   *Cjabot,* Friulan dialect for "pantry," isn't a store. It's a kind of collection agency that sets standards of excellence and seeks out the best traditional products from the Carnia, an area known for its genuine, simple mountain *cucina.* *Grappa,* honey, cookies, smoked mountain trout, aged smoked *speck,* cheese, and stone-ground *polenta* are elegantly packaged with attractive graphics. Almost all products have unrecognizable names— *flum, fumat, gust zintil*—that don't even sound Italian, and all are of the highest quality. For more information, contact Gianni Cosetti, the world's greatest Carnia expert (see page 197) or call tel. 0481.80328.

Coffee.   Trieste has always been an important port, which may begin to explain why there's so much fine coffee roasted in Friuli. Almost all decaffeinated coffee in Italy is processed in Trieste. The best coffee in the region (and in Italy in my opinion) is all *arabica,* imported, roasted, and packed in Trieste by Illy Caffè. See page 199 for more information.

Crafts.   Attractive, reasonably priced traditional baskets and shopping bags called *sporte* are woven from corn husks. They are sold at markets and in shops throughout the region.

Copper Pots and Pans.   Tin-lined copper pots and pans were preferred by Renaissance chefs in the noble kitchens of Italy, but the tradition of crafting copper cookware has almost died out. Luckily, Nico Marin has re-created, with the help of artisans and professional chefs, a line of excellent copper pots and pans. Each, according to Marin, is a piece of culinary history. Copper conducts heat far better than stainless steel, and those who can afford copper cookware should consider ordering a few pieces from this artisanal company. For more information contact Nico Marin, Corso Roma 90, Spilimbergo, tel. 0427.50550.

Brovada. You probably won't like *brovada;* the Friulani will tell you when and if it's offered to you. Turnips that have been exposed to a cold autumn moon are submerged for thirty days under the leftovers of the winemaking process, a treatment not unlike the one that turns cabbage into sauerkraut. Then they are sold, grated by produce vendors, to be cooked with local sausage (*muset* or *musetto*). If you fall in love with *brovada,* the regional dish of Friuli, made only in the fall or winter, you might want to purchase a traditional wooden turnip grater, although the food processor works better. Getting the grape pomace will be the hardest part.

Cities & Towns

Aquileia

DISTILLERY
Distilleria Aquileia
Via Julia Augusta 87/A
☎**0431.91091**
Closed Sunday except July and August
No credit cards

If the Roman ruins or the football-field–size fourth-century mosaics aren't enough to lure you to Aquileia, stop in for a taste of *Sgnape dal Checo* and the pear cream produced by the Distilleria Aquileia, sold in the store outside the distillery. (Go easy on the free samples!) If you'd like to see the *grappa*-making process, visits to the distillery are possible Monday through Friday and on Saturday mornings.

Cervignano

GELATO
Gran Gelato
Via Udine 47
☎**0431.34923**
Closed Monday and weekdays 12:30–3:00 P.M.

Benito Nonino of the Nonino distillery (see page 190) is wild about *gelato,* and this is his favorite *gelateria* in Friuli, worth a detour in guidebook language. Milk-based flavors taste rich and creamy. Look for pure white *fior di latte, pinolato,* studded with pine nuts, and honey-flavored *San Ambrosino.* Anyone who plans to visit Acquileia should stop in at Gran Gelato on the way.

Chianzutan

CHEESE
Cocco Carnelus
Chianzutan
No address
No phone

Cocco Carnelus is passionate about two things: goat cheese and vintage Harley Davidson motorcycles. After Cocco left his native Friuli to work in Paris, city life became too much for him and he moved to Provence, where he tended sheep and goats and discovered his craft. He married and moved to the almost abandoned village of Chianzutan, where he and his wife raise and milk around 100 goats and make 2 cheeses from their milk. One is a fresh ricotta that bears absolutely no relation to the insipid curd sold in plastic containers in the U.S. It has the pungency of goat cheese, with the sweetness of fresh country milk. Cocco's other cheese is a delicate, lightly smoked goat cheese. Both, in guidebook terminology, are worth a detour. The 1936 "Knucklehead" Harley rounds out the experience.

Cividale del Friuli

HOTEL
Locanda al Castello
Via del Castello 20
☎0432.733-242
Fax 0432.700-901
All credit cards • moderate

HOTEL
Locanda al Pomo d'Oro
Piazza San Giovanni
☎/Fax 0432.731-489
All credit cards • inexpensive

RESTAURANT
Zorutti
Borgo Ponte 9
☎0432.721-100
Closed Monday
MasterCard, Visa • moderate
The Boccotti family restaurant is large, but don't be put off, because Claudio, with his son Marco in the dining room, daughter Elena and son Luigino in the kitchen, have everything under control. The menu features both regional and national dishes, which change with the seasons. Mushrooms are offered in most courses in season. Portions are massive. The wine list focuses on Friuli.

BAR-CAFFÈ
Caffè San Marco
Largo Boiani 7
☎0432.71001
Closed Thursday
The Caffè San Marco in Cividale has good

coffee, a clean bathroom, and a row of phone booths in the back. The friendly cashier will supply directions with a smile.

PASTRY-GELATO
Pasticceria Gelateria Ducale
Piazza Picco 18
☎0432.730-707
Closed Sunday afternoon, Monday
The best place for *gubana* also makes the best *gelato*. Pine nut *(pinolato)* is rich and nutty, meringue *(meringhe)* with a hint of lemon peel is tasty, and the fruit flavors, made with seasonal fruit, are delicious. The miniature *gubane* (see page 181) are irresistible, if you don't want to commit yourself to a full-sized one.

PASTRY
Vogric
Via Libertà 136
☎0432.730-236
Closed Saturday and Sunday
Vogric's makes a high-quality commercial *gubana* that seems to last longer than artisanal versions. It is found throughout the region and can also be purchased at the bakery.

Cormons

RESTAURANT-INN
La Subida
Località Subida
☎0481.60531
Fax 0481.61616
Closed Tuesday, Wednesday, and February
No credit cards • moderate
Josco and Loredana Sirk's La Subida is a rustic vacation center with seven apartments, some with *fogolar* hearths, in the woods outside Cormons. Tennis courts, swimming pool, and stables make this a perfect base for a family vacation. Their attractive restaurant, Al Cacciatore, serves simple, traditional *cucina,* nicely prepared. The all-Friuli wine list is carefully chosen

and reasonably priced, and offers some gems.

RESTAURANT

Al Giardinetto

Via Matteotti 54

☎ **0481.60257**

Closed Monday evening, Tuesday, and July

All credit cards • moderate

The Zoppolatti family—mother Mariuccia and son Paolo in the kitchen, father Ezio and son Giorgio in the warm, rustic dining rooms—serve up some of the finest food in Friuli. Menus change monthly and offer traditional Austrian-inspired dishes like smoked pork loin served with grated horseradish, ricotta strudel with poppy seeds, prune-stuffed *gnocchi*, and goulash with *polenta*. Desserts are skillfully prepared and presented. The wine list offers a wide range of quality local wines. A monthly *menu degustazione* features a tasting of seasonal traditional dishes. Reserve in advance for a table near the hearth.

SALUMI

Lorenzo d'Osvaldo

Via Dante 40

☎ **0481.61644**

Lorenzo d'Osvaldo hand-cures and smokes 1,500 hams from little black Friulan pigs with a blend of juniper, bay, and fruitwood. The resulting *prosciutto affumicato*, produced from November to April, is lighter and more delicate than the more traditional and much smokier Sauris ham (see page 195).

ENOTECA

Enoteca di Cormons

Piazza XXIV Maggio 22

☎ **0481.630-371**

Closed Tuesday, Wednesday lunch

No credit cards • low inexpensive

This *enoteca* is run by the municipality of Cormons and twenty-five wine producers, and the emphasis is on local wines. Wine is available for tasting by the glass or bottle, accompanied by first-rate *prosciutto, speck,* and cheese, with *gubana* paired with the region's fine dessert wines.

Corona

HOTEL

See Gradisca d'Isonzo or Cormons

RESTAURANT

Trattoria Al Piave

Via Cormons 6

☎ **0481.69003**

MasterCard, Visa • low moderate

Al Piave is a classic *osteria*, with a bar in the front room crowded with locals drinking shots of the house white. Fabrizio Fermanelli prepares typical Fruilan dishes with simplicity and style. He's spent time in the kitchen with Josko Sirk (see Cormons, page 184) and serves the same kind of unfussy food made with first-rate local ingredients. Mom Annamaria will bring a menu if you insist, but she likes to explain what her son has prepared. Begin with *prosciutto* and home-cured *salame*. Barley and bean soup, crepes stuffed with seasonal vegetables, and *gnocchi* of potatoes, eggplant or squash, topped with smoky ricotta are always on the menu. Pasta is homemade, dressed with rich meaty sauces. Roast veal shin, game like deer or wild boar, rabbit with wild fennel are among the main-dish offerings. Conclude with *gelato* sauced with wild blueberries or homemade strudel. The wine list is small, but it's easy to find something wonderful to drink that's moderately priced. Eat in one of the cozy dining rooms or outside in the courtyard when the weather is nice.

Dolegna del Collio

HOTEL

See San Giovanni al Natisone

RESTAURANT

Al Castello dell'Aquila d'Oro

Via Ruttars 11

☎**0481.60545**

Closed Monday, Tuesday, and most of August

American Express, Diners Club, Visa •

moderate

The Aquila d'Oro ("The Golden Eagle") situated in a castle of Roman origin, was probably Friuli's most attractive restaurant, but it's been drastically restored. The food is still good, if not quite as traditional as it used to be. Dine in one of the modern dining rooms in the winter, or on the shaded terrace overlooking gentle hills and vineyards in the spring and summer. The seasonal menu features creative, well-prepared, beautifully presented *cucina*. The desserts are all homemade and delicious, and the wine list offers a nice selection of fine local wines.

AGRITOURISM-RESTAURANT

Venica & Venica

Via Mernico 42

☎**0481.61264**

Fax 0481.639-906

Restaurant closed Monday evening, Tuesday

All credit cards • inexpensive rooms, moderate

restaurant

Ornella and Gianni Venica make fantastic wine. They've also got a working farm with courtyard animals, an herb and vegetable garden, fruit trees, and six rooms with private bathrooms above the winery. They even have a swimming pool and tennis courts, all amid their splendid vineyards. The restaurant is modern, with a display of the Venica & Venica wines and local crafts in the entrance. The food is simple, well prepared by Gianni's mother, Gina, with products from the farm. Homemade bread, *salumi*, and pasta are always on the menu. *Boccoli* crepes and wide strips of *bieki* pasta are sauced with rich meat *ragù* or seasonal vegetables from the garden. Vegetarians can

actually survive here, while pork and rabbit dishes flavored with fresh herbs will satisfy carnivores. Choose from the delightful Venica & Venica wines. The restaurant is open by reservation to those not staying at the winery. Ornella will suggest restaurants and interesting places to visit nearby and make appointments at other wineries.

Godia

HOTEL

See Udine or San Giovanni al Natisone

RESTAURANT

Trattoria agli Amici

Via Liguria 250

☎**0432.565-411**

Closed Monday

All credit cards • moderate

Trattoria agli Amici was founded in 1887, but don't expect a rustic look or rustic food at this family restaurant. The decor is modern, the tables are well appointed with important wineglasses and attractive dried-flower centerpieces. Ivonne Bodigoi is in the kitchen, utilizing local ingredients with a light hand and a creative touch. The menu is divided between fish and meat preparations. Look for pasta like *pappardelle* and ravioli, homemade and simply sauced, or seasonal *risotto*, perfectly prepared. Sea bass baked in salt, bream baked with herbs, beef with a Refosco sauce are among the second-course offerings. Save room for apple tart with custard sauce, simply presented, simply wonderful. Ivonne's son Emanuele is obsessed with wine, and so the list is impressive, emphasizing local, well-priced wines, including hard-to-find older vintages.

Gorizia

RESTAURANT-INN

Locanda Sandro

Via Santa Chiara 18
☎**0481.533-223**
Closed Wednesday and holidays
No credit cards • inexpensive

Elsa Peilizzon, who speaks Italian, German, English, Friulano, and Sloveno, runs this eight-room inn with its "visit to Grandma" feeling. The *cucina* is Gorizia family-style, and features hearty soups, stews, and a local version of hash-brown potatoes. The homemade desserts, especially the *sacher torta*, are delicious. The house wine is horrid. Bring your own, or drink the beer.

HOUSEWARES

La Casalinga di Paolo Ciampi
Piazza Vittoria 54
☎**0481.533-216**
Closed Monday
No credit cards

Paolo Ciampi's housewares shop seems to sell at least one of every houseware invented. His father used to make and sell his own turnip graters for *brovada* (see page 183), which may explain the presence of this hard-to-find item in Gorizia.

Gradisca d'Isonzo

HOTEL

Franz
Viale Trieste 45
☎**0481.99211**
Fax 0481.960-510
All credit cards • low moderate

RESTAURANT

Mulin Vecio
Via Gorizia 2
☎**0481.99783**
Closed Wednesday, Thursday
No credit cards • low inexpensive

This huge *osteria* is right outside town, an old mill with high ceilings, copper pots hanging from beams, is a wonderful stop for a snack or light meal. Locals drop in for a glass of house wine and first-rate *pro-sciutto*. There's no menu—check out the long bar in the main room to see what they've got, usually *salumi*, pickled *sottaceti* vegetables, cheese, a giant *mortadella*, possibly calf's-foot salad (*nervetti*). Soups are available on the weekend. Dine outside in the garden when the weather is nice.

Gradiscutta

HOTEL

Villa Giustinian
Via Giustiniani 11, Portobuffolè (nearby)
☎**0422.850-244**
Fax 0422.850-260
All credit cards • moderate

RESTAURANT

Toni
Via Sentinis 1
☎**0432.778-003**
Fax 0432.778-655
Closed Monday
All credit cards • moderate

Aldo Morassutti has upgraded the simple *osteria* founded by his parents, Toni and Palmira, to a wonderful restaurant that respects tradition. His wife, Lidia, is in the kitchen with chef Roberto Cozzarolo, preparing some of the finest cooking in the area. The restaurant is in a modern building that has a rustic feeling, with beamed ceilings, terra-cotta floors, *fogolar* fireplace, and hundreds of Buon Ricordo plates lining the walls. The menu is in Friulan, mercifully translated into Italian for nonlocals. *Prosciutto*, both San Daniele and smoked Sauris, polenta *crostini* with *pancetta*, melted cheese, and *porcini* mushrooms are among the interesting appetizers. First-course offerings include homemade squash pasta dressed with butter and smoked ricotta; *risotto* with seasonal vegetables like squash, silene, radicchio, asparagus, or mushrooms; and the Buon Ricordo *minestra contadina*, a meat and barley soup. Mallard ducks (*masorini*) turn on a spit roaster and are served with *polenta* and drippings. Aldo grills meat and vegetables in the fireplace. Desserts are mostly traditional and first-rate, like strudel or apple *gnocchi*. The fine wine list focuses on Friuli, but includes national and international wines. There's a good selection of *grappe* and distillates, including single-malt whiskey.

Lavariano

HOTEL

See San Giovanni al Natisone or Udine

RESTAURANT

Blasut–Gnam Gnam Bar
Via Aquileia 7
☎/Fax 0432.767-017
Closed Sunday evening, Monday, and most of August
Diners Club • moderate

Since around 60 percent of the population of Lavariano is named Bernardis, most of them have distinguishing nicknames. Dante Bernardis is *Blasut*, "Shorty," which barely begins to describe the Tweedledee-like owner of this restaurant who propels himself through the dining room with contagious enthusiasm. Blasut and chef Andrea Bordignon search out the best local ingredients—delicately smoked *prosciutto*, farm-raised duck and goose, fresh herbs and vegetables, aged *latteria* cheese—and combine them with style and taste. The menu, which changes monthly, is presented with a glass of sparkling wine and a ruffle of cheese on a piece of whole-wheat bread, topped by a walnut, a meal opener of great charm. Winter dishes are generally more exciting; summer dining takes place on a canopied patio with naïf frescoes. Fish is served on Fridays. The wine list offers a personal selection of quality, mostly Friulano wines. Ask to see the wine cellar and Blasut will jump for joy.

Leonacco di Pagnacco

HOTEL

See Udine

RESTAURANT

Da Toso
Via Pozzuolo 16
☎0432.852-515
Closed Tuesday evening, Wednesday
Visa • moderate

Don't let the lively bar scene, the coat rack and poster decor, or the marble-chip floor that looks like the original prototype for linoleum distract you from the hearth, which is what Da Toso is all about. This ultratraditional *fogolar* fireplace, a low table with four legs (not the more modern brick constructions found in many homes and restaurants), is presided over by Giancarlo Toso and his wife, Alida. The menu never varies much, the pasta isn't very good, the soups are plain home-style, but the grill work is superb. White-aproned Toso pampers homemade sausage, veal, beef, pork, or liver, each cooked to perfection over the embers of a charcoal and wood fire in his *fogolar*. The house wines are decent, but they also have a limited selection of fine, fairly priced, quality local wines. Da Toso is always crowded, so be prepared for a wait if you haven't reserved in advance.

Manzano

HOTEL

See San Giovanni al Natisone

RESTAURANT

Da Romea
Via Divisione Julia 15
☎0432.754-251
Closed Sunday
MasterCard, Visa • inexpensive

Behind the nondescript façade and dining rooms of Da Romea, in a small, pine-paneled rustic dining room with a fireplace, Leda della Rovere prepares, with great skill, dedication, and passion, some of the finest *cucina* in Friuli. The strictly local clientele lunch in the main dining rooms, returning daily for Leda's light-handed treatment of quality ingredients combined with fresh herbs from the garden out back. The regular menu features a few traditional specialties, along with dishes from other regions. Reserve, at least a day in advance, the *Gusta' Furlan*, an inspired tasting menu of regional dishes rarely found elsewhere—best in winter or spring—and hope that it includes deep-fried sage leaves, featherweight ricotta-filled *gnocchi*, winter-squash bread, and Leda's apple, nut, and spice cake. The small, well-priced wine list offers some local gems. The bar and front dining room have been redecorated. I miss the old-fashioned attic furniture, and I dine only in the back room whenever possible.

OLIVE OIL
Abbazia di Rosazzo
Manzano
☎**0432.759-693**
Fax 0432.759-884
Extra virgin olive oil isn't widely used in this northern region today, but historical documents that refer to olive cultivation on the Abbazia di Rosazzo's lands prompted the owners to have the remaining olives analyzed. Pleased with the results, he worked with a nursery in Toscana to repropagate his native trees. They won't produce much oil for a few more years, but it's only a matter of time until extra virgin Friulian olive oil becomes a reality once again.

Muggia

RESTAURANT-INN
Taverna Cigui
Via Colarich 92/D

☎**040.273-363**
Fax 040.273-983
Closed Wednesday
MasterCard, Visa • moderate
I loved Stelio Cigui's tiny restaurant in Trieste, and now that he's moved to the country, surrounded by vineyards, fruit trees, and a vegetable garden, the restaurant's better than ever. The kitchen is still run by his wife, Anny, with the help of her son Paolo. Don't expect creative cuisine, just classic preparations made with superfresh fish. Look for mussels, almost-impossible-to-find sea dates, and supersweet spider crab. Sea bass or bream is baked in a salt crust. The menu features regional classics like *jota* and *bobici* (sauerkraut and corn soup); *gnocchi* with a plum center; vegetable or fish *risotto;* and vegetable *frittate* as well as traditional desserts like strudel, *pinze,* and *palacinche* (crepes filled with homemade preserves, walnuts, or ricotta). Mushrooms and white truffles are served in season, raising the price of a meal considerably. The house wine is worth drinking, although there's a fine list of wines from Collio and local *grappa*. Spend the night in one of Stelio's rooms for the total experience.

NATURAL EXTRACTS– DIGESTIVE LIQUEUR
Janousek Industriale–Amaro Praga
Strada per Laghetti 3
☎**040.232-691**
Fax 040.232-698
Janousek Industriale was founded in 1883 in Prague by Josef Janousek, specializing in the extraction of natural plant essences. The company, intent on expanding its market, created a factory in Trieste in the beginning of the twentieth century, later transferred to Muggia, utilizing modern technology to produce natural extracts. The most important product is a digestive liqueur known as Amaro Praga, originally created by Janousek for his friends, a bitter-

sweet *amaro* of forty plant and spice extracts macerated in alcohol. Look for the beautiful, faceted crystal bottle in fine restaurants or *enoteche*. Contact Francisco Riccardi at the factory for information about natural extracts and flavorings. Or Dott. Noacco at Camel, in Povoletto, tel. 0432.664-144, fax 0432.664-147 for information about Amaro Praga.

Paluzza

TABLEWARE

Ceramica Dassi
Via Nazionale 44
☎0433.775-414
No credit cards

Rustic dinnerware of *graffito*—scratched-in patterns revealing the clay beneath the white glaze—and dishes with designs of local flowers are all hand-formed and -decorated by these traditional artisans of the Carnia, who make terra-cotta, majolica, and ceramic crafts. Shipping must be separately arranged.

Paularo

CRAFTS

Diomiro Blanzan
Via Roma 56
☎0433.70078
Closed Sunday

Genuine *scarpets*, made of many layers of pressed fabric (not velvet), can be found at Diomiro Blanzan's shop, which sells native costumes for women and children, and wooden crafts of the Carnia.

Percoto

HOTEL

See San Giovanni al Natisone

AGRITOURISM

Le Piargule
Via Aquileia 69, Pavia di Udine
☎/Fax 0432.676-000
Closed Monday and Tuesday • moderate

Oscar Filiputti and Loretta Romanutti's *osteria*, Le Piargule ("The Pergola" in dialect), serves classic regional cooking and their own wine. The *fogolar* fireplace is, as usual, the center of the dining room, utilized to grill meat and sausage. The ambience and cooking are home-style; large communal tables are filled with locals dining on *gnocchi*, vegetable strudel, asparagus in season, pork ribs, stewed rabbit, fruit or ricotta tart, or apple cake. There are a few rooms for overnight guests, and the breakfast is fine.

GRAPPA

Nonino Distillery
Via Aquileia 140
☎0432.676-331

Founded in 1897 by Orazio Nonino with a mobile still on wheels, the Nonino distillery, under the direction of Benito and Giannola Nonino and their daughters Betty, Cristina, and Antonella, produces some of Italy's finest *grappa*. Known for its elegant packaging and high-quality products, Nonino was the first to popularize the idea of *monovitigno*, one-grape-variety *grappa* distilled from the leftovers of the winemaking process, which they procure from some of the region's finest wineries. They also produce *ué*, distilled from grape must or juice, and *le frute*, distilled from fruits and berries. Visits to the distillery can be arranged.

Porcia

HOTEL

Hostaria Vecchia Cecchia
Via San Antonio 9
Cecchini, Pasiano di Porcia (nearby)
☎0434.601-668
Fax 0434.620976

INN

See San Quirino

RESTAURANT

Da Gildo

Via Marconi 17

☎0434.921-212

Closed Sunday evening, Monday, and August

Diner's Club, MasterCard, Visa • moderate

You'll be hard-pressed to recognize any of the people in the photographs covering the walls of various dining rooms in this thirteenth-century palace. A menu exists, but no one orders from it. Gildo and his wife, Annamaria, serve a twelve-course marathon of nontraditional dishes. "If you don't like it, I'll take it away and give you something else," Annamaria will tell you. Dramatic presentations like the tower of *prosciutto* or the bouquet of seasonal fruit, complete with butterflies, make this restaurant a favorite with local families. On Sundays music from a wedding or first-communion celebration in one of the large private dining rooms may serenade your meal. In the summer, dine under a canopy in the lush garden. The house wines are mediocre; ask to see the wine list if you're interested in quality.

Rauscedo

GRAPE NURSERY

Vivai Cooperativa di Rauscedo

Via Udine 39

☎0427.94022

Some of Italy's finest vines come from the Cooperativa in Rauscedo, whose 250 nurseries produce 20,000,000 grape plants yearly—half the Italian production. A wide range of varieties and clones are grafted into over 1,000 combinations by this unique nursery. If you'd like to visit, write or call director Dott. Sartore at least one week in advance.

Remanzacco

FOGOLAR

L'Ottagono di Franco Pianalto

Via Ostelin 91

☎0432.667-598

Closed Sunday

No credit cards

The *fogolar* is the heart and hearth of the Friulan home, the center of the regional experience. It's for warming up, socializing, grilling, and much more.

Franco Pianalto specializes in the construction of the traditional *fogolar Friulano* hearth and the *spolerts*, a wood-burning brick oven with iron finishings.

San Daniele del Friuli

HOTEL

Alla Torre

Via del Lago 1

☎/Fax 0432.954-562

All credit cards • low moderate

PROSCIUTTO CONSORTIUM AND FESTIVAL

Consorzio di Prosciutto di San Daniele

Via Andreuzzu 8

☎0432.957-515

Fax 0432.940-187

The San Daniele *prosciutto* consortium sponsors a festival, *Aria di Festa,* the last weekend in August that attracts a few hundred thousand visitors who come for *prosciutto,* wine, music, dancing, and fun. *Prosciutto* fans and lovers of vintage airplanes should plan to visit for free tastes of *prosciutto* and wine at *prosciutto* factories, or in the main piazza of San Daniele, and to check out the air show. The festival begins Friday evening from 6 P.M. to midnight, continues from 10 A.M. to midnight on Saturday and Sunday, and from 6 P.M. to midnight on Monday. Contact Mario Cabai at the consortium for more information.

RESTAURANT

Antica Osteria
Via Tagliamento 13
☎0432.954-909
Closed Monday evening, Tuesday
American Express, MasterCard, Visa • low moderate

Visit the Antica Osteria for its supertraditional ambience with a *fogolar* in the middle of the dining room. Check out the blackboard menu for regional specialties like *salame* cooked with vinegar, barley and bean soup, goulash, baked pork shin, boned roast rabbit, grilled meats. Conclude with classic Italian desserts like *tiramisù*, strudel, or cookies. The house wine is worth drinking, although fine local wines and *grappe* are available for exigent palates. Dine outside under the wooden gazebo in the summer.

SMOKED TROUT

Friultrota di Dario Pighin
Via Aonedis 10
☎0432.956-560

Although smoked fish is not traditional, it certainly is tasty, and since the Friulani smoke meat and cheese, it seems like a logical extension of the regional palate. Dario Pighin raises salmon trout and trout, and smokes them with a special blend of beech and juniper. The flavor is smoky and complex, a treat to eat even if it isn't traditional.

PROSCIUTTO

Prolongo
Viale Trento 117
☎0432.957-161
Closed Saturday and Sunday

The artisans at Prolongo make only 7,000 *prosciutti* yearly, purchasing the hams in the

fall, curing them in the special climate of San Daniele, without air-conditioning. They'll sell you a whole *prosciutto* or just enough for lunch.

PROSCIUTTO

Prosciutti Daniel
Via Venezia 148
☎0432.957-543
Closed Saturday and Sunday

This factory makes over 100,000 *prosciutti* yearly, but most work is still done by hand. Their *prosciutto* is aged for up to fourteen months, hung in rows on stainless-steel S-hooks in rooms with controlled humidity and temperature and vents to let in the local winds. You can buy a whole *prosciutto* at the plant, or else head for the Bottega del Prosciutto, via Umberto 1 (closed Monday and Wednesday afternoon), to purchase a smaller amount of Daniel's fine product.

San Floriano del Collio

HOTEL-RESTAURANT

Golf Romantik
Via Oslavia 2
☎0481.884-051
Fax 0481.884-052
All credit cards • expensive

The Golf Romantik, in the heart of the Collio winegrowing district, is one of the few four-star hotels in Friuli. Two restored houses of the village of Castello Formintini are furnished with seventeenth- and eighteenth-century furniture and prints. There's a swimming pool, a nine-hole golf course, and two tennis courts. Each of the ten rooms bears the name of a grape varietal. The large, dark-wood, beamed-ceiling, stone-walled restaurant serves mostly traditional cooking, and makes a perfect setting for the Saturday night medieval banquets. Two sentries in armor greet guests, waiters are costumed, there's Renaissance music and medieval cooking served on big wooden platters—eat with your hands.

San Giovanni al Natisone

HOTEL

Wiener
Via Stazione 68
☎**0432.757-378**
Fax 0432.757-359
All credit cards • moderate

RESTAURANT-HOTEL

Il Campiello
Via Nazionale 40
☎**0432.757-901**
Fax 0432.757-426
Closed Sunday
All credit cards • high moderate
The hotel, modern, efficient, air-conditioned, is a perfect base for touring the region, but the restaurant is worth a visit even if you're not spending the night in one of the sixteen rooms or two suites with Jacuzzis. The *cucina* is based on fresh fish flavored with first-rate local ingredients, a nice change for those who have eaten too much traditional cooking. The menu changes seasonally and may include scallops wrapped in cabbage leaves, *risotto* with vegetables or *scampi, tagliolini* with squid and artichokes, ravioli stuffed with beets, savory poppy-greens strudel. Carnivores will enjoy the roast veal shin or mallard, deer fillet sauced with currants and red wine, or pheasant with braised cabbage. Desserts are extravagant, worth the calories. The wine list is excellent, well priced, focusing on the wines of Friuli, Veneto, and Trentino–Alto Adige. A fine selection of distillates and *grappe* will tempt diners, especially those spending the night at the hotel.

AGRITOURISM

Casa Shangri-La
Frazione Bolzano
☎**0432.757-844**
Fax 0432.746-005
American Express, Visa • inexpensive
This working farm has a swimming pool, tennis, horseback riding, restaurant, and six rooms with private bathrooms, TV, frigobar—a far cry from Old MacDonald. And they take credit cards, too.

GELATO

La Tavernetta
Via Roma 35
No phone
Closed Tuesday
La Tavernetta is a simple modern bar where owner Richetto makes a few seasonal flavors of first-rate *gelato*. The *gelateria* across the street has a bigger selection but uses prepared mixes. Richetto makes each flavor from scratch daily. Visit early in the day or he might not have any left. Custard flavors dominate in the winter, fruit flavors in the summer; either is worth a detour.

San Michele del Carso

HOTEL
See Gradisca d'Isonzo or Gorizia

RESTAURANT

Gostilna Devetak
San Michele del Carso 48
☎**0481.882-005**
Fax 0481.882-488
Closed Monday, Tuesday
All credit cards • moderate
This *gostilna* (*trattoria* in Slovenian) is hard to find but well worth the search, one of my new favorites in the region. The Devetak family has been running their *trattoria* for over 100 years, and the *cucina* is based on, but not tied to, local tradition. Game is an

important element, a perfect excuse to drink big red wines from one of the most impressive wine lists that I've ever seen, assembled by Agostino Devetak. His mother, Michela Devetak, and wife Gabriella Cottali are in the kitchen preparing unusual food, based on herbs and vegetables from their own garden, while Agostino and Merina Devetak bustle through two attractive, rustic, but redecorated dining rooms. The menu, in Italian and Slovenian, changes monthly; diners should look for the savory tart of *speck* and onions; game pâté; rolled, herbed *frittate* filled with herbed cheese; mixed *prosciutti* of pork, turkey, deer, goose; or better yet, the *assaggi di Gabry,* a sampler of appetizers. Homemade pasta is sauced with game or *porcini* mushrooms in season; barley is paired with vegetables, utilizing the same technique as *risotto; gnocchi* are stuffed with red currants instead of the more usual plums. Undecided diners should order the *assaggini di Gabry.* Continue with wild-boar chops, braised hare. Save room for the *gibanica* soaked with *grappa,* sprinkled with sugar, *mascarpone,* and coffee custard or a chocolate and whipped-cream confection. Vegetable lovers will appreciate the vegetarian tasting menu. Nonsmokers (the menu kindly asks diners not to smoke during service) will appreciate the smoke-free air. Dine outside in the summer. The wine list is a joy, well priced, worth a voyage for serious enophiles. Agostino has plans to build a few guest rooms—I can't wait.

San Quirino

RESTAURANT-INN
La Primula
Via San Rocco 35
☎0434.91005
Fax 0434.919-280
Closed Tuesday and August
All credit cards • high moderate restaurant, low moderate hotel

The kitchen of La Primula is staffed by Lidia, Daniela, and Andrea—mother, aunt, and son. Father and son, sommeliers Roberto and Sandro, are in charge of the dining rooms. Traditional and modern *cucine* are beautifully prepared—vegetables are green and crunchy, silky homemade pasta is simply sauced, fish from the nearby Adriatic is perfectly cooked. Fresh herbs and extra virgin olive oil flavor many dishes. The desserts and after-dinner pastries are worth leaving room for. The *menu degustazione* presents a selection, more traditional in the winter months, of dishes paired with wines chosen by Sandro to complement Andrea's cooking. The Canton family has been serving food in the same location since 1875, a fact that leaves me breathless.

Sant'Andrat del Judrio

HOTEL
See San Giovanni al Natisone

RESTAURANT
Osteria all'Armistizio
Piazza Zorutti 7
☎0432.759-017
Closed Monday and August
No credit cards • inexpensive

Lunch at Armistizio is always the same: spaghetti with chicken-liver sauce and *fogolar*-grilled meat or chicken, washed down with mediocre Tocai. A few seasonal specialties are also offered in this authentic classic, a tiny lunch-only *osteria* with a diner atmosphere.

Sauris

RESTAURANT-INN
Pà Krhaizar
Lateis 5
☎/Fax 0433.86165
Closed Wednesday
No credit cards • inexpensive

This incredible inn is difficult to get to, on a twisting mountain road, but it's worth the schlep for lovers of peace, quiet, traditional rustic decor, and the fantastic food of Carnia. Bill Favi, the vice director of the local tourist board, bought an abandoned farm and transformed it into a seven-room inn that feels more like a home than a hotel, with authentic antique furniture, wooden floors, a small dining room with a *fogolar* fireplace. Chef Giorgio Cattarinussi cooked with Carnia's greatest chef, Gianni Cosetti (see page 197) and, like his maestro, his *cucina* is based on impeccable local ingredients. Some items on the limited but excellent menu may be unfamiliar, but there's no risk involved. Appetizers include Sauris *prosciutto* and *speck,* served with wild greens or rose-hip preserves. *Polenta,* nettle or silene (*sclopit* in Friulan dialect) *gnocchi,* pasta made of buckwheat flour, dressed with butter and ricotta, or ravioli are first-course options. Local mushrooms are offered in season. Desserts are based on mountain berries, apples, and walnuts. The all-Friuli wine list is wonderful. Breakfast, of *prosciutto,* homemade bread, preserves, local butter from cows grazed in alpine pastures, is splendid. And the entire experience is inexpensive, one of the great bargains in Italy, a just reward for navigating the road to Sauris.

SMOKED AND CURED MEATS

Prosciuttificio–Salumificio Wolf Petris
Via Dante Volvan 8/F
☎0433.86054

Wolf Petris, located in the Carnia Alps, smokes up to 35,000 cured hams with juniper and beech. Their once small-scale artisanal output has been increased by popular demand, and they now make a selection of good, traditional *salumi* in addition to their smoky *prosciutto.*

Spilimbergo

RESTAURANT-INN

Da Afro
Via Umberto I 14
☎0427.2264
Closed Tuesday
All credit cards • moderate

Dario Martina's traditional *osteria,* in the center of town, feels just right, with locals at the bar or playing *bocce.* The place has been recently restored, but the cooking remains traditional, prepared by Dario, his mother, Adele, and wife, Iliana. Dario and his daughter Elena bustle between the kitchen and dining rooms with plates of *frico,* barley and bean soup, *brovada con musetto, salame* cooked with vinegar, and their signature dish, a medley of boiled meats. Vegetables get more attention in the spring and summer—look for wild greens, *sclopit* (silene), in *frittate* or *risotto.* Mushrooms are featured in season. Six different house wines from first-rate local producers are highly satisfying, although the wine list is extensive, offering regional, national, and international wines, well priced. Stay in one of the seven rooms upstairs.

SALUMI

Salumificio Lovison
Via U. Foscolo 18
☎0427.2068
Fax 0427.3299
Closed Monday and Wednesday mornings, and Saturday afternoon

The Lovison family have been making fantastic *salumi* for four generations, and their production has a cult following. Look for sausage, *musetto, soppressa,* lard, jowl, but expecially the *salame* known as *punta di cotello* because it's chopped with a knife, not ground with a grinder as almost all *salame* are.

Stregna

HOTEL

See Cividale

RESTAURANT

Sale e Pepe

Via Capoluogo 19

☎0432.724-118

Closed Wednesday

No credit cards • low moderate

Teresa Covaceuszach defines her cooking with pride as *Benecjana,* firmly based on local roots within sight of the Slovenian border. Diners will be hard-pressed to understand, not to mention pronounce, the names of the dishes on the menu, for example, *bizna is kampiri plicnjaki* or *plucince.* Trust her husband, Franco Simoncig, to guide you through a reasonably priced tasting of Teresa's cooking. Game lovers should definitely plan a winter visit for the wild boar served with buckwheat *polenta* or deer cooked with *grappa.* Desserts are traditional; the wine list is limited, but the house wine is worth drinking.

Tavagnacco

HOTEL

See Udine

ASPARAGUS

Agricoop Asparagi

Via dell'Asilo 1

☎0432.650-054

Over forty members of this cooperative grow large, tender white asparagus, sold throughout the region in the spring. They're available from the end of March to the end of May along the road that goes from Udine to Tricesimo or in the market in Udine. During the last two weekends of May, Tavagnacco holds an asparagus festival, and every evening asparagus can be tasted at stands in the center of town. Contact Signor Abramo at the Pro Loco, tel. 0432.660-648, for the dates.

RESTAURANT

Furlan

Via Nazionale 130

☎0432.572-895

Closed Sunday

All credit cards • moderate

The Furlan family—Vincenzo on the *fogolar* grill, wife Nella in the kitchen, and daughter Nicoletta as sommelier—join forces in their home-style *trattoria,* easily recognized in the daytime by a small group of knee-high red plastic mushrooms with white spots on the front lawn. The menu is traditional. The house specialty, during the spring and fall, weather permitting, is a wide variety of mushrooms (*funghi*) cooked in an equally wide variety of dishes. Regional wines are the best choice on the well-priced wine list.

RESTAURANT

Al Grop

Via Matteotti 7

☎0432.660-240

Fax 0432.650-158

Closed Thursday evening, Friday, and July

All credit cards • moderate

Al Grop is nothing to write home about—unless you show up in the spring, when homage is paid to the asparagus in practically every course of the meal, not counting dessert.

Tolmezzo

Tolmezzo is the largest city in the Carnia and the gateway to this mountain area north of the Tagliamento River, which shares its Alps with Austria. The breathtaking natural beauty of this region, largely ignored by tourism, is enhanced by a wealth of artisanal crafts and a mountain *cucina* of alpine dairy products, smoked meat and cheese, and sweet and sour flavors.

RESTAURANT-HOTEL
Albergo Ristorante Roma
Piazza XX Settembre
☎**0433.2081**
Fax 0433.43316
Closed Sunday evening, Monday
All credit cards • low expensive

Gianni Cosetti *is* the *cucina* of the Carnia. Many of the dishes he serves in his restaurant have names like *toc in braide, sope di urties e cais,* and *pita,* offering not a hint of their contents. The only thing I could understand when he handed me a menu, hand-printed on a wafer-thin slice of bark, was the wine list. The flavors are simple; the raw materials are the best that the Carnia can produce (and that only Gianni can track down). A sense of traditional pride enriches this rustic, beautifully executed *cucina* with an elegance few restaurants ever achieve. Dining at the Albergo Roma used to be by reservation only in a back room with all the charm of a high school gym. Recently Gianni has removed the gas stoves, replacing them with wood-burning ones (which cook better, he says), and in remodeling has created a one-room, seven-table restaurant next door to the unchanged bar, where the pattern in the floor tiles has been worn away by Friulani serious about their drinking. The hotel is clean, undistinguished, inexpensive, and convenient. The breakfast of local specialties is superlative, especially the fresh sweet butter. I couldn't imagine staying, eating, or breakfasting elsewhere in the Carnia.

Tricesimo

RESTAURANT
Boschetti
Piazza Mazzini 9
☎**0432.851-230**
Fax 0432.851-216
Closed Monday and January
American Express, Diners Club, Visa • expensive

Boschetti, the restaurant that put Friuli on the gastronomic map, is rightfully considered a temple of regional *cucina.* The food is good. The ambience is formal. Spacious damask-covered tables are decked out with seasonal centerpieces. The menu is composed of traditional specialities and local bounty—game and Adriatic seafood, a specialty of chef Vinicio Dovier. Past tendencies toward nouvelle cuisine have disappeared, replaced by simple dishes, beautifully executed—like pasta and bean or barley soups, or *polenta, ricotta e tartufi,* a world-class dish. The smaller dining room with its hearth is used during the winter; otherwise dining is in a large, formal, round, air-conditioned, chandeliered room with endless curtains. The wine list concentrates on quality local producers, but also includes many fine wines from other regions, as well as France and the U.S. Conclude your meal with a distillate from the large collection of *grappe,* Scotch whisky, or Cognac. The hotel was closed at the time this book went to press, and they weren't sure when it would reopen. Fax for information.

Trieste

Trieste is a port that looks longingly to the east, at the land it ceded to the former Yugoslavia. The *cucina* of this province, known as Venezia Giulia, closely relates to that of Venezia, with its Adriatic seafood, eastern spices, coffee, and Austrian desserts. Coffee is stronger, fuller-flavored, in Trieste, home of Illy Caffè, one of Italy's finest commercial coffee roasters.

HOTEL
Duchi d'Aosta
Piazza dell'Unità d'Italia 2
☎**040.760-0011**
Fax 040.366-092
All credit cards • expensive

HOTEL
Italia
Via della Greppia 15
☎040.369-900
Fax 040.630-540
All credit cards • moderate

BAR-CAFFÈ
Caffè degli Specchi
Piazza Unità 7
☎040.60533
Closed Monday

Trieste's best bar is Caffè degli Specchi, which has tables outside on piazza Unità for the best people-watching in Trieste, and interesting pastry. Try the *lettera d'amore* ("love letter"), two sheets of fried pastry with a whipped-cream filling.

BAR-CAFFÈ
Bar Tergesteo
Piazza Borsa 15
☎040.60827
Closed Tuesday

The best coffee in Trieste is found at the Bar Tergesteo, in an arcade near the Stock Exchange. If you want a *cappuccino*, ask for a *cappuccino grande*, or you'll receive a cup of espresso with a bit of foamy milk added.

FISH MARKET
Pescheria
Riva Sauro
Closed Sunday and Monday

Early risers may want to check out the 6:30 or 7 A.M. auction of the day's catch at Trieste's fish market, next to the Aquarium on the Riva Sauro. The market is open in the morning only.

BUFFET
Pepi Sciavo
Via Cassa Risparmio 3/B
☎040.68073
Closed Sunday
No credit cards

The *buffet* is Trieste's version of Venezia's *osteria*—the traditional place to stop off for little snacks and a glass of wine. The specialty of Pepi Sciavo is pork (*maiale*), either cooked or cured San Daniele, served with sauerkraut (*crauti*), mustard, and freshly grated horseradish (*cren*). Locals stop in for a midmorning snack, a light lunch, or a glass of wine before heading for home—it's open from 9 A.M. to 9 P.M.

PASTRY
La Bombπoniera
Via XXX Ottobre 3
☎040.632-752
Closed Sunday afternoon, Monday morning

Trieste's best pastry is found at La Bomboniera. The black-and-white–tiled shop, dating from 1850, bakes velvety cakes of Hungarian inspiration, and many of their tasty *torte* are sold by the slice. The six-layer *dobos torta* is a specialty, as are the homemade chocolates and marzipan.

GELATO
Zampolli
Via Ghega
☎040.364-868
Closed Wednesday
Piazza Cavana 6
☎040.303-280
Closed Monday

Two Zampolli *gelaterie* are separately owned by a family member; each makes its own *gelato*, has its own following of adoring Triestini, and closes from December through February.

RESTAURANT
Suban
Via Comici 2
☎040.54368
Closed Monday lunch, Tuesday
All credit cards • high moderate

Since 1865, five generations of the Suban family have served the traditional *cucina* of

Trieste in this suburban *trattoria*. Taste the *jota*, a soup with the Slavic flavors of cabbage, ham, and caraway, or the *palacinche* dessert crepes. Grilled meats are served with bell pepper sauce. *Strucolo* is the local version of strudel. In the summer, dine on the terrace overlooking Trieste and its urban sprawl. The house wines are pleasant, although the wine list has an interesting selection of fine regional, and some nonregional, wines. Italian families, at least two but sometimes three generations, populate the tables of this Trieste institution.

R E S T A U R A N T

Al Bagatto

Via F. Venezian 2

☎ **040.301-771**

Closed Sunday

All credit cards • moderate

Al Bagatto is the best fish restaurant in Friuli. The decor is understated, the wine list adequate, the service fine. Sautéed mixed mollusks, classic pasta preparations, *risotto*, and poached, grilled, or baked fish are perfectly executed. However, the reason why this restaurant merits a pilgrimage by true fish lovers is the fantastic mixed fish fry. Owner Gianni Marussi defines his *frittura* as *mondiale*, world-class, and he's definitely right. Superfresh fish and seafood from the gulf of Trieste—like tiny squidlets, even tinier gray shrimp, and mullet—are crisp, greaseless, fried in extra virgin olive oil that's used only once. Finish with classic Italian desserts or fresh berries.

E S P R E S S O   C O F F E E ,
C U P S ,   A N D   M A C H I N E S

Illy Caffè

Via Flavia 110

☎ **040.389-0111**

Fax 040.389-0490

Closed Saturday, Sunday

I consider Illy the finest coffee in Italy, due to the almost obsessive attention of the Illy family. In the early 1900s founder Francesco Illy had the brilliant idea of packaging coffee in pressurized cans. His son Ernesto focused on the painstaking selection of the finest *arabica* coffee beans and modern roasting techniques, and is currently assisted by his sons Riccardo and Andrea. Coffee lots are purchased only after tasting, not the usual method by which coffee brokers describe each lot. All beans are sorted by computerized sensors—one by one, 400 beans per second—and rejects are sold to less scrupulous producers. The roasting and packaging operation is high-tech, with rooms of huge machines, computers, terminals, sensors, scales, conveyor belts, operated by workers in smocks and caps.

Different roasts are produced for different areas of Italy, since a deeper roast is preferred in southern Italy. Coffee is sealed in pressurized cans, ripened for twenty days to exalt flavors, and is available throughout Italy in groceries and bars that proudly display the Illy logo. Illy has created a foolproof system for making espresso that eliminates all the inaccuracies of measuring and pressing coffee. Compressed single-dose pods of exactly the right amount (6.8 gr) of perfectly ground coffee in filter paper are produced in strips, to be utilized in special espresso machines for the home, restaurant, or bar. Many domestic and commercial espresso machines use the Illy pods. Contact Annamaria Visini for more information.

Riccardo's brother Francesco has produced a series of stylish espresso cups with fanciful designs by noted artists in limited series each year, created "to bring a smile to your face," a terrific idea. And they work, too. They're sold in stores that sell the coffee.

Illy collaborates with a producer of semi-industrial machines, for offices, small restaurants, and the espresso-obsessed (like me!).

Udine

HOTEL
Astoria
Piazza XX Settembre 24
☎**0432.505-091**
Fax 0432.509-070
All credit cards • expensive

HOTEL
Sport Hotel
Via Podgora 16
☎**/Fax 0432.235-612**
All credit cards • low moderate

BAR-CAFFÈ, GELATO, PASTRY
Volpe Pasini
Via Rialto 12
☎**0432.505-191**
American Express
Closed Sunday
The Volpe Pasini shop specializes in *delizie*, which is translated in my dictionary as "delights." And the vast assortment of products in the shop are truly delightful. The bakery has at least ten kinds of bread and homemade breadsticks, and the pastry shop's fresh cakes and cookies are tasty. There's a fine selection of different brands of coffee at the bar, and the specialty section sells quality extra virgin olive oil, preserves, pasta, honey, chocolates, and life-size, realistically painted Sicilian marzipan fruit. The well-stocked *enoteca* sells fine wine by the glass, bottle, or case. *Gelato*, made with fresh fruits and natural flavors, is sold in the summer.

MARKET
Piazza Matteotti and piazza S. Giacomo
To understand what the *frittata alle erbe* is all about, visit the piazza Matteotti market, where women under multicolored beach umbrellas sell field greens and herbs out of attractive (and unavailable) bent-wire bas-

kets. Piazza S. Giacomo is also known as piazza delle Erbe.

CHEESE
La Baita Formaggi
Via delle Erbe 1/B
☎**0432.204-276**
Closed Monday afternoon and Wednesday afternoon
Visa
La Baita has a nice selection of local cheeses—*latteria*, Montasio and *ricotta affumicata*. The nonlocal *parmigiano-reggiano* is first-rate. In this region where almost no one takes credit cards, they take Visa.

FRUIT
Emporio Frutta
Riva Bartolini 9
☎**0432.501-234**
Closed Monday afternoon and Wednesday afternoon
The Emporio Frutta sells a large assortment of attractive fresh, exotic, and dried fruit and nuts.

SPECIALTY FOODS
Tami Galliano
Riva Bartolini 10
☎**0432.502-198**
Closed Monday afternoon and Wednesday afternoon
Across the street from the Emporio Frutta, this shop sells smoked Sauris *prosciutto*.

RESTAURANT
Al Vecchio Stallo
Via Viola 7
☎**0432.21296**
Closed Wednesday
No credit cards • low inexpensive
Al Vecchio Stallo was once a stable for mail carriage horses; it was converted into a wine bar in the 1920s, then into a charming *osteria*. The beamed dining rooms with wooden floors, wooden tables, old photographs of Udine on the walls are crowded

with students and families who flock to this *osteria* for the well-priced food. The menu is traditional, divided between fish and meat preparations. *Prosciutto, salame,* and mixed-seafood platters are the best appetizers. Follow with bean and barley soup or *cjalcions,* skip the pastas, and continue with main-dish offerings like *frico,* served with potatoes or *polenta; salame* cooked with vinegar; *brovada e musetto;* or sardines with onions, raisins, and pine nuts. Cheese is local. Conclude with *gubana* doused with *Sliwovitz,* or strudel. The house wine, Tocai, is acceptable, but there's also a fine wine list. Dine in the courtyard when the weather is nice. The fixed-price lunch is a bargain.

RESTAURANT
Alla Vedova
Via Tavagnacco 8
☎0432.470-291
Closed Sunday night, Monday, and August
No credit cards • moderate

Part of the charm of Alla Vedova is the decor: antler chandeliers and an attractive *fogolar* (hearth) and *spolerts* (brick oven for cooking traditional grilled meats). The squash or chestnut *gnocchi* are outstanding, but the rest of the menu is uninspired and the wine is mediocre to poor. However, this *trattoria* remains a favorite with locals from Udine, especially for dining outside in the summer. Don't miss the extensive collection of African hunting trophies upstairs.

Verzegnis

TABLEWARE
Roberto Marzona
Via degli Artigiani 6
☎0433.43076
Closed Sunday
No credit cards

Roberto Marzona works with seventy-seven local woods, forming them into plates, bowls, serving pieces, cutting boards, sugar bowls, and the *piattaia,* a traditional wooden dish rack. All pieces are handmade and signed.

Villa Santina

TABLE LINENS
Carnica Arte Tessile
Via Nazionale 14
☎0433.74129
Closed Sunday
No credit cards

Carnica Arte Tessile makes traditional hand-loomed tablecloths and napkins, as well as bedspreads, towels, and sheets, in cotton or linen.

Zompitta

HOTEL
See Boschetti in Tricesimo

RESTAURANT
Da Rochet
Via Rosta Ferracina 8
☎0432.851-090
Closed Tuesday
MasterCard, Visa • low moderate

Follow the scent of barbecue and cross a little wooden footbridge over a clear stream to enter the world of Da Rochet. It's dominated by the sizzling music, the smoky perfumes, the choreography of the brothers and their wives—of Santina and Tite tending the sausage, pork, veal, trout, and chicken on one of Friuli's best hearth grills. The *salumi* and *risotto* (with mushrooms or asparagus in season) are good, but the star here is grilled meat or poultry, perfectly prepared. The mixed salad is a welcome sight. The house condiment is vegetable oil, although if you ask they'll bring olive oil. Dine outside under the trees in the summer, or in one of the cozy dining rooms. The wines could be better.

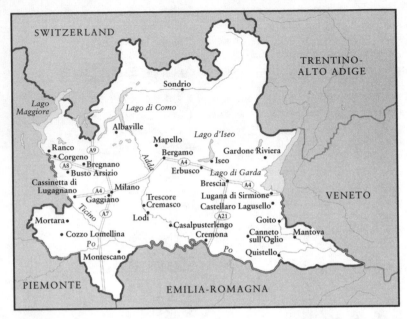

SWITZERLAND

TRENTINO-
ALTO ADIGE

Sondrio

Lago
Maggiore

Lago di Como

Albaville

Mapello *Lago d'Iseo*

Ranco (A9)
Corgeno
(A8) Bregnano
Busto Arsizio
Cassinetta di
Lugagnano (A4) Milano
Gaggiano

Bergamo Gardone Riviera
(A4) Iseo
Erbusco *Lago di Garda*

Brescia (A4)

Adda

VENETO

Trescore
Cremasco

Lugana di Sirmione
Castellaro Lagusello

Ticino (A7)
Mortara

Lodi (A21) Goito

Casalpusterlengo
Cozzo Lomellina Cremona Canneto Mantova
sull'Oglio
Po *Po* Quistello
Montescano

PIEMONTE EMILIA-ROMAGNA

Landlocked Lombardia extends from the Alps
to the fertile plains of the Po River, from
Lago Maggiore to Lago di Garda. Mountains
prevent the cold northern European weather
from penetrating the lakes region, where
Mediterranean vegetation—palms, oleanders,
olive and lemon trees—thrives within sight of
snow-capped peaks.

Lombardia

Caught up in a continuing reshuffling of the political deck, Lombardia was part of the Roman *Gallia Cisalpina*, which included much of northern Italy, despoiled by barbarian tribes, united under the Longobards (Lombards), ruled by the Franks, reunited in the Lombard League, redivided among powerful provincial families—Visconti, Sforza, Gonzaga, Pallavincini, Scaligeri—invaded by Venezia, France, and the Spanish Hapsburgs, transferred to Austria, and absorbed by the Napoleonic Cisalpine Republic until the Austrians came back for another round!

Politics, and the thick fog that blankets and isolates much of Lombardia during the winter months, helped to maintain the separateness of each provincial *cucina*. Rice and *polenta* from the alluvial plains, butter, cream, and cheese from the moun-

tain pastures, are the common denominators in what many people think of as northern Italian cooking. Pasta is fresh, and stuffed with fillings of winter squash, meat, cheese, spinach, or even raisins, candied fruit, and crumbled almond cookies. *Polenta* is made with cornmeal or buckwheat flour (*grano saraceno,* "Saracen grain"). Pork, veal, and cheese play an important role in the *cucina* of Lombardia. Vegetables rarely achieve stardom, although asparagus freaks will delight in the Lombardia spring. Traditional desserts are found in pastry shops, but rarely on restaurant menus. Don't miss *torta di tagliatelle,* a crunchy cake made with fresh egg pasta, almonds, and cocoa, or Mantova's *torta sbrisolona* ("big crumb"), a buttery, cookielike cake made with cornmeal and almonds.

The Menu

Salumi

Bresaola: cured dried beef, dried in the mountain air, served sliced wafer thin, dressed with olive oil and pepper

Cotechino: cooked pork sausage

Salame di Milano: fine-grained pork salami

Antipasto

Nervetti in insalata: cold salad of calf's foot

Sciatt: buckwheat cheese fritters (from the alpine valley of the Valtellina)

Primo

Agnolini: fresh pasta stuffed with meat, Parmesan, and spices

Buseca or busecca: Milanese tripe soup

Casonséi: ravioli stuffed with sausage, Parmesan, and bread

Pizzoccheri: buckwheat pasta served with potatoes, cabbage, butter, cheese, and sage

Polenta alla bergamasca: *polenta* baked with sausage, tomato sauce, and cheese

Polenta e osei: *polenta* sauced with small game birds, butter, and sage

Polenta taragna: buckwheat *polenta* with butter and cheese

Ris e càgnon: boiled rice with butter, Parmesan, and sage

Ris e coràda or riso con coratella: rice and veal lung

Ris e ran: soup with rice and frogs' legs

Ris e spargitt: soup with rice and asparagus

Riso al salto: crispy pancake of *risotto* sautéed in butter

Risotto: short-grained rice, sautéed, then cooked with broth and any number of enrichments

Risotto alla certosina: with freshwater fish, shrimp, and sometimes frogs, peas, mushrooms, and rice

Risotto alla mantovana: with sausage and onion

Risotto alla milanese: with onions, saffron, and beef marrow

Risotto alla pilota: with sausage

Risotto alla valtellinese: with beans and cabbage

Tortelli di zucca: fresh pasta filled with winter squash, *mostarda* (similar to chutney), and almond cookies, served with butter and Parmesan

Zuppa pavese: broth containing a poached egg on fried or grilled toast, sprinkled with Parmesan

Secondo

Asparagi alla milanese: boiled asparagus served with a fried egg, Parmesan, and melted butter (a kind of do-it-yourself Hollandaise sauce)

Cassoeula or cazzoeula: various cuts of pork—usually sausage, ribs, feet—stewed with cabbage, served with *polenta*

Costoletta alla milanese: breaded veal chop fried in butter, served with a lemon wedge

Foiolo: tripe cooked with butter and onions, served with grated cheese

Mondeghili: breaded meat croquettes fried in butter

Ossobuco: braised veal shank sprinkled with *gremolata* (chopped parsley, lemon peel, and garlic)

Rostin negaa: veal chops braised in white wine

Formaggio

Bagoss: hard, aromatic, grainy

Bitto: soft and rich

Crescenza: soft, creamy, mild

Gorgonzola: rich, creamy, blue-veined, pungent, intensely flavored and scented

Grana padana: tasty, grainy texture, nutty flavor, similar to Parmesan

Mascarpone: rich, sweet, triple cream, white to pale yellow

Quartirolo: mild, soft, smooth

Robiola: soft, creamy, rich, eaten fresh or aged

Stracchino: smooth, soft, full-flavored (from *stracco*, dialect for "tired") made from the milk of cows weary from their long trek from alpine pastures **Taleggio:** smooth, soft, ripe; similar to *stracchino,* but riper, more ample

Dolce

Busecchina: boiled chestnuts and cream

Colomba pasquale: dove-shaped sweet yeast cakes with almonds, raisins, and candied fruits, found at Eastertime

Pan de mei *or* man de mej *or* meini: cornmeal yeast buns

Panettone: sweet yeast cakes with raisins, candied citron, orange, and lots of eggs, traditional at Christmastime

Polenta e osei: simple cake layered with apricot preserves, covered with almond paste, and decorated to resemble an unmolded bowl of *polenta,* topped with little chocolate game birds

Torta di tagliatelle: crunchy cake made with fresh egg pasta, almonds, and cocoa

Torta paradiso: delicate sponge cake

Torta sbrisolona: "big crumb" of cornmeal, almonds, and butter, more like a cookie than a cake

The Wine List

The fertile plains and mild climate of the lakes region aren't ideal wine-growing country, although there are areas of Lombardia that do make fine wine. Locals, and especially the Milanese, tend to drink wines produced in other regions—reds from Piemonte and Toscana, whites from Friuli and Trentino–Alto Adige. But some of the sparkling wines are among Italy's best, and are easy to find in better restaurants.

The **Franciacorta** DOC includes red, white, rosé, and sparkling wines, produced south of Lago Iseo in the province of Brescia. The **Pinot Bianco di Franciacorta** is a still, dry white, fruity and elegant, at its best with *antipasti,* fish, and vegetables, made with Pinot Bianco and Chardonnay grape varieties. The **Franciacorta Rosso,** ruby red, mellow, and dry, is made from a blend of Cabernet Franc and Sauvignon, Barbera, Nebbiolo, and Merlot, and is best served with regional *cucina* and meat. Quality producers are Fratelli Berlucchi, Ca' del Bosco, Cavalleri, and Bellavista.

The **Spumante,** which can be white or rosé, and made from Pinot Bianco, Nero or Grigio, and Chardonnay, is one of Italy's finest sparkling wines. Look for sparklers by Cornaleto, Monte Rossa, Enrico Gatti, Brut, Crémant, and Gran Cuvée by Bellavista; Brut, Pas Dosé, and Millesimé by Cavalleri; or Brut, Dosage Zéro, Crémant, Rosé, or gold-labeled Brut Millesimato by Ca' del Bosco, Italy's finest sparkling wine-maker.

Oltrepò Pavese is a DOC that includes fifteen different wines—a large range of whites, reds, rosés, and sparkling wines—for the most part named after grape varieties. Reds **Barbacarlo, Barbera,** and **Rosso** are better than most, go well with the regional *cucina,* and are produced by Ca' Longa, Maga Lino, Le Fracee, Tenuta Mazzolino, and Monsupello.

Riviera del Garda Bresciano is a large DOC zone near the Brescia side of Lago di Garda that includes red **Rosso** and **Chiaretto** rosé wines, both made from

Gropello, Sangiovese, Barbera, and Marzemino grapes. They are served to advantage with first-course dishes and regional *cucina*. Top producers include Costaripa, Comincioli, Cascina La Pertica, and Andrea Pasini.

Nontraditional Wines Some of the *vino da tavola* produced in Lombardia is among the finest wine being made in Italy. Rich, elegant whites to be served with first-course dishes, fish, seafood and poultry, and luxurious reds, a fitting accompaniment to meat and sauced dishes, are a pleasure for

all the senses. Ca' del Bosco makes complex, smoky Chardonnay; splendid red Maurizio Zanella, a blend of Cabernet Sauvignon, Franc, and Merlot, a rich, harmonious red; and rich and full red Pinero, from Pinot Nero—all gems. Tenuta Mazzolino makes barrel-aged Noir from Pinot Nero, Bellavista makes Uccellanda, an elegant oaky Chardonnay, and Casotte and Solesine, both wood-aged reds of finesse. Fine non-DOC spumante are made by Carlo Zadra and Guido Berlucchi.

Regional Specialties

Goose Salami and Prosciutto. The goose presents farmers of the Oltrepò, "the area beyond the Po," with a shortcut version of pork *salumi*, which is made during the fall slaughter of the pigs, after the harvest. Geese are low-maintenance birds and fatten up quickly. The full-flavored meat is well suited to the traditional treatment for pork products such as salami and *prosciutto*. See page 241 for a source—and a goose festival.

Risotto. Rice dominates the first course of Lombardia's menu. It is served in soups but reaches gastronomic glory as *risotto* (see page 212). This dish, which demands much stirring and fussing, the slow addition of broth, and a final enrichment of butter and *parmigiano*, is always served slightly *al dente* ("firm under the tooth"); each grain of rice remains separate. One of my favorite brands of rice comes from the rich rice-growing flatlands southeast of Milano.

Polenta. *Polenta* is the Italian version of cornmeal mush (similar to grits), made of cornmeal, salt, and water cooked to the consistency of breakfast cereal in a traditional copper pot (*paiolo*) and stirred con-

stantly for thirty minutes with a long-handled wooden spoon. Nontraditionalists in a hurry use instant *polenta*, which cooks up in five to ten minutes—not exactly instant. *Polenta* is served freshly cooked as a side dish, or cooled, sliced, and reheated with sauce as a first or main course. (See page 218 for a fine producer.)

Gorgonzola. Gorgonzola—ivory colored, run through with bluish mold, strongly scented—is one of Lombardia's greatest cheeses. It is made in a traditional, naturally fermented version as well as a sweeter, creamier, less aggressive style (*dolce*) that has fermented more quickly and is considered more palatable than the classic Gorgonzola, said by detractors to smell like an adolescent's sneakers. See page 211 for a fantastic producer (Casalpusterlengo).

Bresaola. *Bresaola*, a specialty of the Valtellina area, made of lean beef, lightly salted, marinated with wine and spices and aged, was once upon a time made from deer. It used to be subjected to long aging, but is now eaten much fresher, sliced thin like *prosciutto*, dressed with extra virgin olive oil, lemon juice, and pepper. It's low in fat, light, and has become so popular that it's most often found produced industrially, although artisans in the Valtellina still make traditional *bresaola*. Alfonso Boscacci (via Peccedi 20, Bormio, tel. 0342.903-382, closed Thursday afternoons in winter) makes fine *bresaola* of both beef and deer. His shop has a wonderful selection of local cheese as well as first-rate *salumi*. Industrially produced *bresaola* is found throughout Italy in groceries, served in restaurants as an appetizer, or tucked into new-wave sandwiches.

Sturgeon and Caviar. It's been quite a while since sturgeon swam from the sea up the rivers of the Po Valley, but Agroittica Lombarda has created an industry from a fading local tradition. Sturgeon as well as trout, salmon, and eel are farmed in water from deep artisanal wells, in large outdoor tanks that reproduce a natural environment. Fish are harvested, filleted, cured, and packaged at the modern factory. Agroittica's fresh sturgeon fillets are found in fish shops and restaurants throughout Italy. Smoked sturgeon, sold whole or presliced, is sold in groceries and some supermarkets. Agroittica Lombarda has also started to produce caviar, lightly salted, large (2 to 3 mm) pasteurized gray eggs classified as malossol, sold in upscale groceries in late November. For more information write, call, or fax Agroittica Lombarda, Viadana di Calvisano (Brescia), Italy 25012, tel. 030.968-6991, fax 030.968-433.

Taleggio. Taleggio, from the provinces of Bergamo, Milano, Brescia, Cremona, and Pavia, can be one of Italy's best cheeses. It's made of raw cow's milk, ripened in a warm, damp environment, salted, then aged in cool, humid rooms (replacing the grottoes of tradition) for a month or two on straw mats, turned, and brushed frequently to remove surface mold. Industrial producers use pasteurized milk and higher temperature to coagulate the milk and the results just aren't the same. The Consorzio Tutela Taleggio stamps four circles on the surface of the cheese, three with the letter "T" and one with the number of the dairy that it's from. Numbers have been given out at random so you can't tell the producers from the original Bergamo province from the rest. A well-aged raw-milk Taleggio is hard to find but worth the search, buttery and oozing, luscious. To visit a Taleggio producer, contact Massimiliano Pagani at the Consorzio (piazza Caldara 4, Milano, tel. 02.551-88563, fax 02.551-93153). Cheese master Alberto Marcomini in Padova distributes the best Taleggio I've ever tasted, from a tiny dairy in the Valsassina outside Bergamo.

Mostarda. Once upon a time *mostarda* was made at home, with fruit, sugar, grape must, and mustard oil—a dangerous ingredient, the same stuff that mustard gas is made of. In Lombardia, Mantova and Cremona each make a distinct product called *mostarda*. I spoke to Nadia Santini, one of the great chefs of Italy (see page 210), about Mantova-style *mostarda*, which she makes for her restaurant. She told me that it used to be made with unripe *campanile* apples, but that this apple cultivar has completely disappeared, replaced in the Canneto area *mostarda* recipe with *anguria bianca* ("white watermelon"), a variety grown locally by around twenty people. The Cremona area makes its *mostarda* of whole candied fruits— cherries, apricots, peaches, pears, figs, pumpkin, and citrus fruits, soaked in a sugar syrup zapped with mustard oil. This is a complicated procedure to do artisanally, so Cremona *mostarda* is produced industrially nowadays. See page 213 for a fine source. Or proceed to Dal Pescatore to taste Nadia's homemade version. *Mostarda* is usually served with boiled meats or cheese. The pungent flavor of the mustard oil fades with time, and a container of *mostarda* that's been open for months will lose its bite.

Cities & Towns

Albavilla

RESTAURANT-INN

Il Cantuccio
Via Dante 34
☎031.628-736
Fax 031.627-189
Closed Monday, Tuesday lunch
MasterCard, Visa • high moderate

Il Cantuccio is in a beautifully restored farmhouse with a granite fireplace that blazes on winter evenings. Owner Angelo Foresi has created an elegant ambience for his wife Rosangela Masciardi's cooking, classic and innovative, paired with the best wines of Italy and beyond. *Risotto* is perfectly prepared, pasta is homemade, local freshwater fish, as well as the best seafood that the Milan market has to offer, are always on the menu. Meat and game are featured in the winter, delicately sauced. Dessert lovers will enjoy Rosangela's artistry, especially the buckwheat cake with berry preserves or the superior strudel, served with cinnamon *gelato*. Plan to spend the night in one of Il Cantuccio's four comfortable rooms and dig deep into Angelo's wine list, concluding the meal with some of his amazing selection of *grappe* and distillates.

Bergamo

Medieval Bergamo Alto, of pink-paved piazzas, and Bergamo Basso, which seems to be paved with parked cars, is only fifty kilometers (thirty miles) from Milano. Restaurants in the upper city tend to cater to tourists; lower-city restaurants seem to have abandoned tradition for fresh fish from Milano's market; and almost all restaurants in both parts of town are closed on Monday.

HOTEL

Excelsior San Marco
Piazza della Repubblica 6
☎035.366-111
Fax 035.223-201
All credit cards • expensive

HOTEL

Agnello d'Oro
Via Gombito 22
☎035.249-883
Fax 035.235-612
All credit cards • inexpensive

RESTAURANT

Taverna del Colleoni
Piazza Vecchia 7
☎035.232-596
Fax 035.231-991
Closed Monday
All credit cards • low expensive

I met Pierangelo Cornaro through Tony May, owner of the restaurant San Domenico in New York, who knows just about every important restaurant in Italy. He encouraged me to visit Pierangelo's Taverna del Colleoni and, as usual, Tony's advice was worthwhile. The restaurant, located in a palace attributed to Bramante, is formal, elegant, with incredible vaulted ceilings. Pierangelo's almost exasperating efforts to supply the kitchen with the best ingredients that money can buy and the pure professionalism of the staff are the keys to the Taverna del Colleoni's success. Local *salumi* and cheese are first-rate, often ignored by diners who are wowed by chef Odorico Pinato's delicate dishes of super-fresh fish and seafood from Milano. But humble ingredients like *baccalà* are also treated with respect. Pasta is homemade. Deer is slowly braised with Amarone, served with *polenta gnocchi*. Desserts, like chestnut Montebianco served in a puddle of chocolate sauce, are tempting. The wine list is ample, with a fine selection of Italian and French wines. Dine outdoors in one of the world's most beautiful piazzas when the weather is nice.

CHEESE
Ol Formager
Piazza Oberdan 2
☎035.239-237
Closed Sunday and Monday

Giulio Signorelli comes from a family of cheesemongers. His grandfather, Alessandro, sold cheese from a horsedrawn cart; his father, Luigi, continued the tradition; and now Giulio, assisted by his son Simone, sells some of the best cheese in Italy. Giulio buys directly from artisanal cheesemakers and ripens cheese in a mountain hut. The selection at this cheese lover's paradise includes artisanally made Taleggio and Gorgonzola, both worth a detour, in guidebook language. The *formai de mut*, made from raw milk of cows grazed in alpine pastures, *bitto*, and Asiago are also superlative. Giulio is a sommelier and can recommend wines to pair with cheese. The shop is in the modern part of Bergamo near the stadium.

GELATO
Golosia
Via Broseta 57/D
☎035.253-439
Closed Monday and November to March

Golosia is in the lower, modern, unattractive part of Bergamo but worth a visit. Master *gelataio* Dario Epis, who worked for eight years on cruise ships and speaks perfect English, closes during the winter and takes off for warmer climates. But during the spring, summer, and fall, his *gelateria* is always crowded from noon till around 11 P.M. Dario uses no artificial colors or flavorings. His fruit flavors, made without dairy products, are delicious, made with ripe, seasonal fresh fruit or frozen fruit

when fresh isn't available. White chocolate, *stracciatella, torrone* are among the more than twenty varieties available in season.

INN
Vigneto
Capriate San Gervasio (close by)
☎02.909-39351
Fax 02.909-0179
American Express, MasterCard, Visa • moderate

WINE BAR
Vineria Cozzi
Via Colleoni 22
☎035.238-836
Closed Wednesday
Visa • inexpensive

In Bergamo Alto I head for the Vineria Cozzi for a sandwich (*panino*) prepared with interesting combinations like cured beef with walnuts, oil, and vinegar on a toasted roll, and I wait for owner Leonardo Vigorelli to surprise me with a wonderful local wine I've never heard of. Bentwood chairs, wine-bottle–lined walls, and locals in berets—serious about their drinking—make up the ambience of this old-fashioned authentic wine bar. Fine wine by the glass, freshly made sandwiches, and Leonardo's hospitality make this the best meal in town. And there's even outdoor dining, on the iron bench in front of the Vineria Cozzi.

Bregnano

SILVERWARE
Sabattini Argenteria
Via Don Capiaghi 2
☎031.771-019

The fluid, exquisitely executed, award-winning silver objects, bowls, carafes, and serving pieces of Lino Sabattini are a pleasure to look at and to use. His designs are in the grand tradition of the table, executed in extra-heavy silver alloy. Sabattini lives, writes poetry, and works his metal magic in Bregnano, not far from Como, but his work can also be seen at his Milano showroom in via della Spiga (02.798-449).

Busto Arsizio

Stuck at the Milan airport with a big delay or layover? Head for nearby Busto Arzizio and stop in either or both of these shops, and you'll actually be pleased that your flight was late.

CHEESE
Casa del Parmigiano
Via Tosi 2
☎**0331.635-745**
Closed Monday afternoon

Giovanni Frati's grandfather was a cheese-maker, and cheese is the center of Giovanni's life. He hunts down the best dairy products in Italy and his selection, of over 350 different kinds of cheese, is over-whelming. Extra-aged *parmigiano stravec-chio*, cheese from Friuli and Valtellina, Fontina from Valle d'Aosta, fresh buffalo-milk mozzarella, sheep's milk *pecorino* are all made by artisans. Buy some fresh to eat on the flight back, and/or ask Giovanni to vacuum-seal anything aged over a month, a splendid culinary souvenir.

ENOTECA
Enoshop Bar Franco
Via XX Settembre 8
☎**0331.631-713**
Closed Sunday

Stop at Franco Bozzetti's bar, in the center of town, for a glass of wine and purchase a bottle for the flight. It's perfectly legal to drink your own wine on international flights, although the flight attendant may insist on pouring it, as the law demands.

Canneto sull'Oglio

HOTEL
Margot
Via Tazzoli 22
☎**0376.709-011**
Fax 0376.723-961
All credit cards • inexpensive

RESTAURANT
Dal Pescatore
Via Runate 13
☎**0376.723-001**
Fax 0376.70304
Closed Monday, Tuesday, the first half of January, and the second half of August
All credit cards • expensive

Dal Pescatore seems to be doing everything right, with Bruna and her gentle daughter-in-law Nadia in the kitchen, Giovanni taking care of the provisions and the grill work. His son Antonio hustles between the kitchen, cantina, and dining room, judiciously choosing wines to complement the *cucina* of the Santini women, which is deeply rooted in the local traditions. The elegantly appointed rustic stone farmhouse has three intimate dining rooms with large, well-spaced tables set with damask, silver, and crystal. Logs burning in the brick fire-place and indirect lighting create a feeling of warmth. Local ingredients of the highest quality—*salumi*, sturgeon from a pool in the back, freshwater fish from nearby rivers, and barnyard poultry—are the basis of the *cucina*, which combines tradition and intelligence. Homemade pasta, almost orange with duck eggs; *risotto* properly *al dente*; eel and *provolone* cheese, both grilled over wood; a flavorful chunk of country-style duck—all sit nicely on the plate, without the artistic excess of some fine restaurants. Save room for the fine desserts, especially the buttery almond *torta di amaretto*. The wine list, like almost everything else here, is a joy.

Casalpusterlengo

CHEESE
Angelo Croce
Via Battisti 69
☎0377.84236
Closed Monday afternoon

Gorgonzola fans should make the pilgrimage to Casalpusterlengo to taste the especially fine *gorgonzola malghese naturale* made by the Croce family. They use milk from cows grazing in alpine pastures, and ferment their Gorgonzola naturally (unlike most industrial producers), producing a full-flavored, complex cheese that's a pleasure to eat. The no-nonsense dairy store in Casalpusterlengo also sells smooth soft Taleggio, mild *quartirolo,* packets of sweet fresh butter, and grainy-textured *grana,* sectioned into wedges with a wire cutter. There's no sign on the store; look for pale green Venetian blinds in the window.

Cassinetta di Lugagnano

HOTEL
Albergo Italia
Piazza Castello 31
Abbiategrasso (close by)
☎02.946-2871
Fax 02.946-2851
All credit cards • high moderate

RESTAURANT
Antica Osteria del Ponte
Piazza Negri 9
☎02.942-0034
Fax 02.942-0610
Closed Sunday, Monday, and August
All credit cards • expensive

The Antica Osteria del Ponte—a small, rustic, charming Lombard country house on the banks of the Naviglio Grande, a thirteenth-century navigation canal—is the setting for the new Santin family gastronomic dynasty. Ezio and his wife, Renata, opened their restaurant with no previous experience, but quickly acquired, through passion and intelligence, a sense of professionalism and a style of understated opulence. The triple taste sensation of white truffles, farm-fresh eggs, and foie gras typifies Ezio Santin's *cucina,* combining flavors and nearby Milano's market bounty to great advantage. At times the food gets a little too nouvelle for me, but the excellent cheese tray makes my doubts disappear. Desserts are amazing, the artistry of son Maurizio, a rising star in Italy's culinary lineup. Wines, both French and Italian, are more than up to the rest of the experience.

Castellaro Lagusello

HOTEL
Antico Borgo
Via Castello
☎0376.88978
MasterCard, Visa • inexpensive

HOTEL
See Verona

ENOTECA-RESTAURANT
La Dispensa
Via Castello 21
☎0376.88850 or 045.795-1070
Open Friday and Saturday evenings,
all day Sunday
No credit cards • low moderate

Just across the border of Veneto, not far from Verona, in the medieval village of Castellaro Lagusello, La Dispensa is open on weekends only, hard to find but definitely worth a visit. The wine shop, grocery, and tiny one-room restaurant up a steep wooden staircase are powered by the Zarattini family—Sergio and his wife, Nicola, and their sons Leonardo and Simone. Check out the bottles in the wine shop and the grocery's selection of *salumi,* cheese, breads, exceptional *grissini,* and tempting products like caper and anchovy-stuffed cherry peppers, and you'll know what to ask for when you're seated upstairs. Hope that Nicola has made her incredible *tortellini* in broth, or *tortelli* stuffed with squash, or any kind of *risotto.* Boiled meats, stuffed quail, roast duck breast are second-course options. Fine goat cheeses from Artogne, fresh, aged, herbed or peppered, are fantastic. Conclude with homemade desserts like *torta sbrisolona.*

Corgeno

RESTAURANT-INN
La Cinzianella
Via Lago 26
☎0331.946-337
Fax 0331.948-890
Closed Tuesday and January
All credit cards • high moderate, rooms
moderate

The Gnocchi family's restaurant keeps on improving. The *cucina* is light and innovative, composed of fresh, local, seasonal ingredients. Homemade pasta, *risotto,* lake fish, and Cinzia's homemade bread and pastry are well prepared. Her brother Maurizio, a champion sommelier, keeps enlarging the wine list, and his selections complement the *cucina.* Their father, Alfio, makes sure that everything runs smoothly. Save room for a taste of local, and impossible to find, Corgena *formaggina* cheese. Peaches from nearby Monate are some of the finest in Italy. Those spending the night in one of La Cinzianella's ten rooms may be tempted to do a tasting from the *grappa* collection.

Cozzo Lomellina

RESTAURANT-INN
Castello di Cozzo
Via Castello 20
☎0384.74298
Closed Tuesday, August, and January
No credit cards • expensive

Padre Eligio, a figure of controversy in Italy, founded the Mondo X commune in the 1960s along Franciscan ideals of community and simplicity. His flock of mostly ex–drug addicts restored the abandoned castle, whose origins date from A.D. 800, and created this six-room inn and restaurant with its timeless air. Padre Eligio appreciates fine food and wine, and his disciples have produced some amazing *cucina.* Some dishes seem vaguely French, and plates are seriously stylized. But the *risotto* is first-rate, the homemade pasta is tasty, the dishes are well prepared, and the pastries at the end of the meal are splendid. The wine list offers quality Italian and French wines. Reservations are compulsory.

RICE
Filios Fratelli
Via Mulino 3
☎0384.74112
Superfino Baldo, a new hybrid developed by the Italian Rice Board, is a rising star in the Italian rice lineup and a pleasure to cook with. It holds up under the tooth and contains just the right amount of starch for a perfect *risotto,* but is equally suited to salads, molded rice timbales, and soups. It has a full, grainlike flavor.

The Filios brothers produce six fine varieties of rice, but the best is their Superfino Baldo, which is almost impossible to find outside the tiny village of Cozzo Lomellina. But I spotted the Filios' attractive mill-end plaid fabric sack of Baldo in some of the region's best restaurants, and even outside the borders of Lombardia. Their rice can be purchased at the farm from Tina or her sister-in-law, who are always around, or can be ordered (within Europe) by phone.

Cremona

HOTEL

Impero

Piazza della Pace 21
☎0372.460-337
Fax 0372.458-785
All credit cards • moderate

HOTEL

Astoria

Via Bondigallo 19
☎0372.461-616
Fax 0372.461-810
All credit cards • inexpensive

RESTAURANT

Cerasole

Via Cerasole 4
☎0372.30990
Fax 0372.458-718
Closed Sunday evening, Monday, and August
All credit cards • high moderate

Medieval Cremona, with its Stradivarius Museum—testimony to the workshops producing superior stringed instruments—and charming piazza del Commune, is home to Cerasole. This unusual restaurant is run by Rino Botte, from Basilicata, a region of southern Italy wedged between Puglia and Calabria. His wife, Lucia, and sister-in-law Anna are in the kitchen, cooking up regional Lombard cooking as well as the Mediterranean tastes of their homeland. The menu offers goose liver pâté, *culatello* (the heart of the *prosciutto*), traditional stuffed pasta, and trendier sea bass ravioli, nicely cooked fish and vegetable combinations, and typically Cremonese stuffed duck. Cheese is care-

fully chosen and aged. Desserts, especially the unusually moist walnut cake served with a red wine and citrus parfait, are definitely worth saving room for. The well-selected all-Italian wine list contains some surprising gems.

GROCERY

Sperlari

Via Solferino 25
☎0372.22346
Fax 0372.33644
Closed Monday

Torrone, Sperlari, Mostarda are written in gold letters above the Art Nouveau façade of Sperlari, over two large display windows lined with bottles, boxes of confections, baskets of wrapped candy. Look for typical products from Cremona like *torrone* and the finest *mostarda*, known as "extra-extra," perfect, whole candied fruits in a mustard-oil sauce, sweet and spicy, and made by quality industrial producers Vergani, Dondi, and Sperlari. The shop also sells boxed almond cakes, wines and liqueurs, chocolate-covered maraschino cherries, and a wide range of wrapped candies.

Erbusco

RESTAURANT-HOTEL

L'Albereta

Via Vittorio Emanuele 11, Bellavista
☎030.776-0550 (hotel)
☎030.776-0562 (restaurant)
Fax 030.776-0573
Closed Sunday evening, Monday
All credit cards • moderate fixed-price lunch, otherwise very expensive; expensive hotel

Gualtiero Marchesi, the first Italian chef to be awarded three stars by the Francophile Michelin guide, saw the writing on the wall and closed his restaurant in Milano before political scandals emptied expensive eateries in the city. He moved to Erbusco, where the Bellavista winery restored a villa to create the luxurious hotel L'Albereta and a restaurant with a view for Gualtiero. He's the Armani of Italian cooking, balanced, stylish, innovative, with roots in the Lombard and middle European traditions, influenced but not overwhelmed by nouvelle cuisine and its techniques. Gualtiero's *cucina* is personal, at times provocative, highly professional, but he's doesn't spend much time at the burners anymore, and although the food is well executed it doesn't seem as thrilling as it used to. The setting of his new restaurant is a glassed-in frescoed *loggia* with a view of gardens and countryside, urban sprawl blocked by hedges. There's a moderately priced business lunch and an informal oyster-and-foie-gras bar for elegant snacks, but those who have made the trek to Erbusco dine in the evening.

The à la carte menu is basically the same as it was at Gualtiero's original restaurant, with dishes like *raviolo aperto;* bright yellow Milanese rice, rich with lots of real saffron garnished with a square of gold leaf, and classic Milanese breaded veal chop. *Baccalà,* foie gras, sturgeon and its eggs turn up as appetizers; fish is fresh, lightly sauced. Meat and poultry dishes lack the excitement of the rest of the menu, but the cheese selection is worth saving room for. Local *stracchino, quartirolo,* and Taleggio are at their best, joined by a superstar selection of the greatest cheeses of Italy—Gorgonzola, *parmigiano, pecorino,* goat cheese, and more. The tasting menu offers a panorama of Gualtiero's vision of Italian cooking.

The pricey wine list is arranged by varietal, the house wine is Bellavista, definitely worth drinking, although there's an ample selection of other Franciacorta producers as well as Italian and international wines of distinction.

The hotel, with twelve suites, twenty-seven junior suites, covered pool, tennis courts, sauna, and golf at the local Francia-

corta club, is a perfect place to relax for a day or two, and is actually one of the least expensive luxury hotels around. Don't fail to visit Il Volto in Iseo—see page 216 for more information.

E N O T E C A

Le Cantine di Franciacorta

Via Iseo 56

☎**030.775-1116**

Closed Tuesday

All credit cards

Check out this *enoteca* for an overview of enological Franciacorta; it has a really fine selection of well-priced wines, local, national, and beyond. Local wines are available for tasting by the glass, and although they serve no food at the *enoteca* there are always a few slices of *salame* to sample.

Gaggiano

H O T E L

See Milano

T R A T T O R I A

La Fratellanza

Piazza Vittorio Veneto, San Vito di Gaggiano

☎**02.908-5287**

Closed Tuesday

American Express, Visa • moderate

A young American chef doing a stint in a nearby three-star kitchen told me about this wonderful country *trattoria* where the restaurant staff used to eat on their day off. The De' Lazzari family have been running La Fratellanza for three generations, and the cooking is pure tradition. There's no menu, but Ferdinando will tell you what his brother Luigi has prepared. Begin with *salumi* and *sottaceti* pickled vegetables, continue with *minestrone,* served tepid in the summer, or crispy *riso al salto.* Perfectly prepared *cotoletta alla milanese* and *pollo alla diavola* are always on the menu. Winter diners should look for *cassoeula*—pork ribs, ears, and skin stewed with cabbage. There's no wine list, but there are a few choice bottles for exigent enophiles. Eat outside under the pergola in the summer.

Gardone Riviera

RESTAURANT-INN

Villa Fiordaliso

Via Zanardelli 132

☎0365.20158

Fax 0365.290-011

Closed Sunday evening, Monday, January, and February

American Express • expensive

Villa Fiordaliso, probably the most romantic hotel in Italy, is a turn-of-the-century villa (a favorite of Clara Petacci, Mussolini's girlfriend) decorated with mosaic tiles, patterned marble, alabaster, inlaid wooden floors, Murano glass chandeliers, and columns everywhere. Diners have a view of a peaceful garden and the shores of Lago di Garda, where an occasional *bisse*—traditional flat-bottomed boat powered by four standing rowers—crosses. The *cucina* is delicate, flavored with herbs and extra virgin olive oil from the Garda area. *Risotto,* homemade pasta, grilled or sauced meat and lake fish are well prepared, but the desserts look better than they taste. Presentations here are somewhat formal, served by black-uniformed waitresses with white eyelet aprons. The wine list offers an impressive selection of local wines, as well as a separate well-chosen listing of Italian and a few French wines. Spend the night in one of Villa Fiordaliso's four rooms, possibly with a columned and mosaic-floored balcony overlooking the lake, for fantastic breakfasting on homemade croissants and *cappuccino.* Dine in one of the four intimate dining rooms or on the lakeside terrace.

Goito

RESTAURANT-INN

Al Bersagliere

Via Goitese 258

☎0376.688-399

Fax 0376.668-363

Closed Monday, Tuesday lunch

All credit cards • expensive food, inexpensive rooms

A small shrine here commemorates Sergeant Antonio Pacinotti, who, in 1859, on a site behind the restaurant Al Bersagliere, near the chicken coops, invented the electromagnetic ring, prototype of the dynamo, transforming the current of the Mincio River into electricity. Possibly he celebrated his discovery at the Ferrari family restaurant, which had already been serving fine food for twenty years. The latest generation of Ferraris, brothers Massimo in the kitchen and sommelier Roberto, have continued the family tradition, with the same regional emphasis. Homemade *salumi;* hand-rolled pasta, almost orange with duck eggs; *risotto;* freshwater fish; and poultry are perfectly cooked, elegantly presented. Save room for the appealing desserts and fresh, buttery small pastries. The ambience is warm and inviting, the dishes intelligently prepared, and Roberto ably pairs wine from the extensive cellar with Massimo's *cucina.*

Iseo

HOTEL

See Erbusco

HOTEL

Hotel Milano

Lungolago Marconi 4

☎030.980-449

Fax 030.982-1903

MasterCard, Visa • inexpensive

RESTAURANT

Il Volto

Via Mirolte 33

☎**030.981-462**

Closed Wednesday, Thursday lunch, and July

No credit cards • moderate

The smallest kitchen of all the restaurants listed in this book belongs to the Osteria Il Volto in sleepy Iseo, which seems less serious about its tourism than other larger lakes in Lombardia. A genuine tavern, its two small dining rooms furnished with rustic furniture and tables covered in blue-and-white–striped ticking, it's run by a group of friends—Roberto Sgarbi and his sister Anna Maria, Vittorio Fusari, and Mario Archetti. Armed with passion and an idea, the four friends have created a comfortable place to hang out, to eat something of quality made with fresh local ingredients, combined with simplicity, and paired with amazing local or Italian wines discovered during excursions to interesting wineries. A glass of Ca' del Bosco *spumante* will put you in a good mood while you examine the small but well-composed menu of delicate lake fish, steamed or combined with fresh pasta, country-style meats and poultry, and desserts like tart, cloudy, flowery-tasting strawberry gelatin, the essence of berry, or smooth, elegant *panna cotta* custard, or buttery, crumbly *sbrisolona*. Ask to see the wine cellar of this tiny gem of a restaurant.

Lodi

HOTEL

See Milano

BOOKSTORE WITH MAIL-ORDER CATALOG

Biblioteca Culinaria

Viale Genova 2/B

☎**0371.412-684**

Fax 0371.413-287

Closed Saturday

MasterCard, Visa

This is, without a doubt, Italy's best cookbook store. Gianpiero Zazera and his American wife, Liz, and their friend Eugenio Medagliani collected antique cookbooks and had a hard time locating books. They started a mail-order business in 1990, selling mostly reprints of antique cookbooks, and responded to market demands by adding modern Italian and foreign cookbooks. Recently they moved their mail-order catalog sales outlet to an actual shop, worth a visit just to see everything in one place. They've got new cookbooks, wine books, and some guidebooks, reprints of old cookbooks, and recent releases. Liz will attempt to find anything in print and will suggest books that may be of interest. Books can be charged and sent. Liz will recommend a nearby restaurant for anyone who makes the trip to the Biblioteca Culinaria.

Lugana di Sirmione

HOTEL

Villa Cortina

Via Grotte 12

Sirmione

☎**030.990-5890**

Fax 030.916-390

All credit cards • high luxury

HOTEL

Hotel Sirmione

Piazza Castello 19

☎**030.916-331**

Fax 030.916-558

MasterCard, Visa • moderate

RESTAURANT

Vecchia Lugana
Via Lugana Vecchia
☎030.919-012
Fax 030.990-4045
Closed Monday evening, Tuesday, and January
All credit cards • high moderate

The Vecchia Lugana, Pierantonio Ambrosoli's fine restaurant, is a rustic, carefully restored, old-style lakefront *trattoria* with some new ideas about cooking and wine. Traditional ingredients are given a lightened-up preparation, or are grilled over wood; pasta and pastry are homemade and hand-rolled; even simple dishes like *pasta e fagioli* soup are skillfully prepared. The menu changes with the seasons, and shows the influence of nearby Veneto. Help yourself to a colorful display of fresh appetizers, but don't skip the velvety pasta, prepared by Pierantonio's mother, Alma. Regional cheeses and elegantly presented desserts, including fresh fruit ices, are delightful. The wine list and the incredible list of distillates and liquors clearly display Pierantonio's personal commitment to the Vecchia Lugana experience.

Mantova

Mantova, surrounded on three sides by the Mincio River, which widens enough to be called a lake, is the center of one of the major expressions of Italian regional *cucina*. Rich in courtyard animals and rice, influenced by nearby Emilia and Veneto, *la cucina mantovana* combines a wealth of flavors.

HOTEL

San Lorenzo
Piazza Concordia 14
☎0376.220-500
Fax 0376.327-194
All credit cards • expensive

HOTEL

Mantegna
Via Filzi 10
☎0376.328-019
Fax 0376.368-584
All credit cards • moderate

RESTAURANT

Trattoria dei Martini
Piazza Carlo d'Arco 1
☎0376.327-101
Fax 0376.328-528
Closed Monday, Tuesday, and most of August
All credit cards • moderate

Tano and Alessandra Martini felt that fewer customers were looking for a formal expensive dining experience and so they downgraded their restaurant to a *trattoria*. But the Martinis haven't lowered the level of their food, just eliminated the trappings of fine dining that capture the fancy of important guides and food critics. Tables in the sixteenth-century palace are set closer together, the menu is more limited, and the prices are much lower. Don't look for lobster or foie gras or a huge wine list. Alessandra prepares fantastic *tortelli* stuffed with squash and *amaretti* cookies; *bigoli*, extruded pasta sauced with beans and *pancetta; polenta* with melty herbed lard. Freshwater fish like carp and pike, capon salad, tripe and boiled meats from the cart, served with Mantova-style *mostarda*, are some of the fine main-course offerings. The *sbrisolona* is still irresistible. The wine list is short, well priced, with a more expensive selection of around twenty world-class wines, many French, for those who want to splurge.

RESTAURANT

Aquila Nigra
Vicolo Bonacolsi 4
☎/Fax 0376.327-180
Closed Sunday, Monday
All credit cards • high moderate

Aquila Nigra, on a side street near the Palazzo Ducale, is an elegant restaurant with wooden-beamed ceilings, pink and white marble floors, and frescoes in a fourteenth-century convent. Owners Giorgio Bini and his wife, chef Vera Caffini, have created an eatery worthy of the Gonzagas, refined, based on traditional flavors and impeccable raw materials, utilized by Vera with skill. Both humble and noble ingredients are treated with respect. *Prosciutto* with *mostarda* made from almost-impossible-to-find *campanile* apples; deep-fried *saltarelli* freshwater shrimp and zucchini, crispy and greaseless; marinated eel; and local *salame* are among the starters. Continue with *risotto* with frogs or *porcini* mushrooms in season, nettle *gnocchi*, *maccheroni* with pork rind, and beans or fantastic squash *tortelli*. Main-course options include stuffed pheasant leg, herbed snails with grilled *polenta*, sturgeon with capers and oregano, sea bass baked in a salt crust. The cheese selection is superb—save room for the world-class Taleggio, Gorgonzola, or grilled *tomino*. Desserts, like *sbrisolona*, *torta di tagliatelle*, vanilla *gelato* with warm sour-cherry sauce, fruit sorbet, or *miascia*, a fifteenth-century recipe for bread pudding, are well prepared, well presented. The Italian and French wine list has something for every palate; *grappa* and distillates are well chosen.

RESTAURANT

L'Ochina Bianca

Via Finzi 2

☎/Fax 0376.323-700

Closed Monday, Tuesday lunch

MasterCard, Visa • low moderate

Gilberto and Marcella Venturini's L'Ochina Bianca ("The White Goose") usually cooks for the Slow Food Osteria at the VinItaly wine fair in Verona, and their food impressed me enough for a visit. Their restaurant is decorated with modern sculptures, images drawn from Mantuan fables. Mustachioed Gilberto has an evolutionary idea of regional cooking, so the menu is both traditional and territorial. The menu changes frequently, is contained, and the emphasis is on what's seasonal and regional. Locally produced *salumi* are always available. Hope that they've got the freshwater shrimp *frittata* or the bitter wild salad greens dressed with *pancetta* and balsamic vinegar. Proceed with classics like *tortelli di zucca, riso alla pilota,* catfish *risotto*. Main-course offerings include braised beef cheeks, stewed donkey, or well-prepared freshwater fish. Cheese like *parmigiano* or *mascarpone* is served with *mostarda*. Conclude with pound cake–like *torta sabbiosa* with *zabaione* or *panna cotta*. The wine list pays attention to the best vintages; distillates and *grappa* are well chosen.

Mapello

GRISTMILL

Azienda Agricola Scotti

Via Matteotti 16

☎035.908-115

Baronessa Scotti's farm in Mapello produces grain and corn to be stone-ground in a seventeenth-century watermill in nearby Zogno. The old-fashioned method of milling between two stones produces a coarser, fuller-flavored flour filled with bits of bran. The yellow *farina per polenta* makes a nutty, nicely textured *polenta*, and the whole-wheat *farina integrale* is fine for bread baking. An appointment can be made to view the mill in Zogno.

Milano

Milano, capital of the western Roman Empire and center for the new Christian religion, autonomous municipality, dominion of the Visconti and Sforza families, capital of the dukedom of Milano and subject to the European chessboard of power, ruled by the French, Spanish, Hapsburgs, and the Austro-Hungarian empire, has a true melting-pot mentality. The dynamic financial capital of Italy, Milano has a strong provincial *cucina,* but it's the only city in Italy where restaurants serve many kinds of foods, from American-style hamburgers to Japanese sushi, Neapolitan pizza, Tuscan *trattoria* offerings, and Sicilian seafood. The bounty of a metropolitan marketplace and its international point of view are combined with Old World or new-wave creativity, resulting in dishes that may range from misconceived to miraculous. Prices in Milanese restaurants tend to be higher than in the rest of Italy.

Milano has adopted the sandwich (*panino*) with true inventive style, and locals lunch on made-to-order grilled vegetable or goat cheese and smoky *Speck* combination fillings, perfect for the work-conscious out for a quick lunch. The noontime one-dish meal or fixed-price lunch presents a few different tastes or interesting specials, a light meal, and is offered by some restaurants whose business-oriented clientele doesn't want rich, heavy, sleep-inducing meals.

Dinner is the meal to unwind over after a hard day at work, but reservations are a must, especially since mysterious trade fairs may book up every hotel and restaurant in the city. Beware of the Milanese custom of abandoning town on the weekends, heading for the countryside. Most restaurants in the city close on Sunday, and you may be hard-pressed to find a place to eat. The restaurants that do stay open are indicated here.

DRIVER

Maurizio Avanzi
☎0337.284-421
Fax 02.990-25001
It's not easy to get around Milano, and visitors with many stops to make will find it

easier to deal with a car and driver than with Milanese cabs. Maurizio speaks English, has an air-conditioned Mercedes, knows his way around, and will work by the hour or the day. I couldn't have revised this chapter without him.

MARKET

Mercato Comunale
Piazza Wagner
Closed Monday afternoon,
open 8 A.M.–1 P.M., 4 P.M.–7:30
The Mercato Comunale is the largest daily market of central Milano. Check out the outdoor stands that ring the market for seasonal and exotic fruit, vegetables, mushrooms, or head inside for bread, cheese, meat, and fish. There's even a health food stand, plus a large selection of produce, flowers, and more.

HOTEL

Four Seasons
Via Gesù 6/8
☎02.77088
Fax 02.770-8500
All credit cards • high luxury

HOTEL

Grand Hotel Duomo
Via San Raffaele 1
☎02.723-141
Fax 02.864-60861
All credit cards • luxury

HOTEL

Diana Majestic
Viale Piave 42
☎02.295-13404
Fax 02.201-072
All credit cards • expensive

HOTEL

Ariosto
Via Ariosto 22
☎02.4817-844
Fax 02.498-0516
American Express • high moderate

HOTEL

Hotel Sunset

Via Giuseppe Colombo 14

☎02.701-09561

Fax 02.761-10496

All credit cards • moderate

Italy's only bio-ecological hotel—and in a city that could use a moderately priced hotel.

HOTEL

Gran Duca di York

Via Moneta 1/A

☎02.874-863

Fax 02.869-0344

American Express, MasterCard, Visa • moderate

BAR-CAFFÈ

Biffi

Corso Magenta 87

☎02.480-06702

Closed Monday

Biffi serves one of Milano's best breakfasts: a perfect, foamy *cappuccino* (or *cappuccio,* as it's often called locally) and a warm croissant. They also make one of the city's best *panettone.* The visit is a Sunday tradition.

BAR-CAFFÈ

Cova

Via Montenapoleone 8

☎02.760-00578

Closed Sunday

Cova isn't only a famous tearoom, coffee bar, and meeting place on fashionable via Montenapoleone, where white-aproned, black-tied barmen serve chic Milanese at the stainless-steel bar. Cova also makes fine chocolates, gumdrops, hazelnut chocolate *gianduia,* and *fruttini*—sugared fruit shapes that are elegantly boxed, hand-wrapped, and tied with a velvet ribbon. Austrian-influenced pastrywork, including *sacher torte, rerhuken,* and *dobos,* and one of Milano's best traditional *panettone,* is gift-wrapped in brocade and silk for Christmas but is available year-round. Bring your own surprise to insert in one of Cova's custom-made Easter eggs. Prices are scaled to the rest of elegant via Montenapoleone.

BAR-CAFFÈ

Sant'Ambroeus

Corso Matteotti 7

☎02.760-00540

Closed Monday

Sant'Ambroeus is Milano's most traditional tearoom, with homemade pastry and chocolates to go elegantly wrapped in tulle. The golfball-size chocolate truffles and the ridged *sacher torte* are a chocoholic's dream, but skip the insipid, soft tea sandwiches. Black-bow–tied, white-jacketed bartenders preside over the shiny dark wood, lace-edged, doily-lined bar. The *cappuccino* is creamier than most.

BAR-CAFFÈ

Roffia

Via Turati 3

☎02.657-2523

Closed Monday

All credit cards

Antonino Crinò has always baked fantastic pastry at his shop on via Ripamonti (see page 226), but has now opened a bar, along with his son Fabio, in the center of town. They sell the same stuff as Pasticceria Massimo, but there's a bar and eight small tables for lunchtime dining with food from the *tavola calda.* Visit Roffia for a perfect breakfast, light lunch, or snack of stuffed *focacce* or sandwiches. Be prepared for crowds after 12:30 because locals are onto a good thing. Purchase a *panettone* or tray of mignon pastries for a Milanese friend.

BAR-CAFFÈ

L'Antica Arte del Dolce

Via Anfossi 10

☎/Fax 02.551-94448

Closed Sunday afternoon and Monday

THE EMPIRE OF PECK

The golden sun—symbol of the Peck emporiums, reign of the four Stoppani brothers—never sets on the empire (they have a boutique in a department store in Tokyo). Their top-of-the-line outposts include Gastronomia Peck, Casa del Formaggio, Bottega del Maiale, Rosticceria, and La Bottega del Vino. The jewel of the empire, simply called Peck, is a restaurant located in a series of rooms under the Bottega del Vino.

Pastry chef Ernest Knam has worked in some of Europe's finest restaurants, won awards at the Swiss Toque d'Or pastry competition, and is now making some of the finest baked goods in Milano. Visit his shop for classic and innovative creations, like *panettone;* pear and Gorgonzola, chocolate, and pumpkin tarts; superior cookies; personalized cakes for birthdays and banquets; six flavors of *gelato;* and shelves stacked with homemade preserves. One of Ernest's thirty different chocolate cakes will delight chocoholics.

TEAROOM
Tecoteca
Via Magolfa 14
☎02.581-04119
Closed Monday
Tea from all over the world, and soothing herbal tisanes, are a specialty at the Tecoteca, a quiet tearoom in the Left Bank ambience of the Navigli area of Milano.

BAR-CAFFÈ
Taveggia
Via Visconti di Modrone 2
☎02.760-21257
Closed Monday
The morning ritual of coffee and *brioche* (and croissants) fresh from the oven, afternoon teatime, and pastries from Taveggia, with its unchanged 1930s decor, are classics in tradition-bound Milano. Open Sunday!

SPECIALTY FOODS
Gastronomia Peck
Via Spadari 9
☎02.864-61158
Closed all day Sunday and Monday afternoon
American Express, Diners Club, Visa
This is a food shop to stroll through slowly, inhaling deeply. A triangular stand between the front doors sells almost 500,000 pounds of one of the store's specialties, *parmigiano-reggiano* cheese—golden, perfectly aged, with tiny crunchy crystals and rich, ample flavor. I never leave without a little chunk. Two massive display cases run the length of the shop, filled with a synopsis of all the Peck stores: platters of cold salads, aspics, pâtés, seafood, freshly made egg pasta in a variety of shapes, a butcher shop, take-out section, cheese, salami, and cured meats from all over the world, candy, cakes, coffee, and much more—an overwhelming array of edibles. An extensive selection of Italian and French wines and spirits downstairs completes this gastronomic panorama. A self-catered meal from Peck always makes life a little easier and the flight home a little less sad.

CHEESE
Casa del Formaggio
Via Speronari 3
☎02.864-60104
Closed all day Sunday and Monday afternoon
American Express, Diners Club, Visa

Remo Stoppani selects over 350 different types of cheese from all over the world—in wheels, wedges, loaves, teardrop-shaped globes tied with cord hanging from the ceiling, smoked brown circles, snow-white cones, flattened disks, balls soaking in whey—many almost impossible to find outside their areas of production. This is a cheese lover's paradise, part of Peck's gastronomic contribution.

SALUMI

Bottega del Maiale
Via Victor Hugo 3
☎02.805-3528
Closed all day Sunday and Monday afternoon
American Express, Diners Club, Visa

Angelo Stoppani is in charge of Peck's Bottega del Maiale, specializing in fresh and cured pork products. Festoons of salami; dozens of varieties of sausage; flat and rolled *pancetta* (bacon); *prosciutto* from Parma, Prague, and San Daniele; rendered, fresh, and flavored lard; smoked and fresh meats; and even snout, feet, and ears are sold in this "pig heaven."

ROTISSERIE TAKE-OUT

Rosticceria Peck
Via C. Cantù 3
☎02.869-3017
Closed Sunday afternoon and Monday
American Express, Diners Club, Visa

Slowly spinning rows of poultry, quail, pigeon, duck, pheasant, chicken, and guinea hen rotate on the rotisserie under a wide copper hood, tanning in front of a wood-burning fire at the Rosticceria Peck. *Risotto,* baked pasta, roast meats, even whole pig, are portioned out to take away or to eat at the counter. The fryer section deep-fries poultry, meat, vegetables, *polenta,* and Sicilian rice balls. Pizza is sold by the slice. Avoid the 12:30 to 1:30 tidal wave of locals out for a fast lunch.

STAND-UP CAFETERIA

La Bottega del Vino
Via Victor Hugo 4
☎02.861-040
Closed Sunday
American Express, Diners Club, Visa

The Bottega del Vino is a Milanese version of what fast food should be like, quality cafeteria-style. An interesting selection of hot dishes, cold salads, and freshly made sandwiches, displayed in a long, wide glass case, can be accompanied by one of over 200 fine wines, ordered by the glass or bottle from the extensive list chosen by Mario Stoppani, the family wine expert. Wine can also be purchased by the bottle or case. Avoid the 12:30 to 1:30 lunchtime rush.

PRODUCE

L'Ortolano di via Spadari
Via Spadari 9
☎02.866-063
Closed Monday afternoon

L'Ortolano, on via Spadari, Milano's most elegant food street, sells every imaginable fruit, in and out of season, and a huge variety of salad greens and herbs, all casually but artfully arranged. Choose from untranslatable exotics like *alkikinger, mangoustan, carubi, cirimoia, stachis, corbezzoli,* and fresh dates.

MUSHROOMS AND TRUFFLES

Casa del Fungo e del Tartufo
Via Anfossi 13
☎02.546-5666
Fax 02.546-6801
Closed Sunday, Monday afternoon
All credit cards

It's easy to figure out the specialties of Maurizio Vaglia's House of the Mushroom and Truffle. Fresh white truffles from Piemonte in the late fall and early winter, black truffles from Norcia in the winter and summer, frozen, canned truffles, truffle paste and truffle oil the rest of the year, and one of Milano's best mushroom selections—look for *porcini,* chanterelles, and *ovoli* (golden agarics) in season, preserved frozen, under oil in jars, or dried the rest of the year. Russian caviar and Sardinian *bottarga* (pressed mullet roe) are always available. Maurizio will package fresh truffles to bring home, a wonderful (but expensive) souvenir of a stay in Italy. He recommends wrapping each truffle in paper towels, placing them in an airtight container in the refrigerator. Use as soon as possible or change the paper towel daily.

BREAD

Garbagnati
Via Victor Hugo 3
☎**02.875-301**
Closed Monday afternoon
The Garbagnati bakery, flanking part of the Peck empire, sells tasty bread, rolls, and pastry in this convenient location.

BREAD

Cantoni
Piazza Giovane Italia 2
☎**02.498-7561**
Closed Saturday and Monday afternoons
The authentic turn-of-the-century family bakery of Bianca and Luigi Cantoni makes Milano's best whole-wheat bread, as well as home-style cakes and *panettone.*

ENOTECA

Enoteca Cotti and La Frasca di Cotti
Via Solferino 42
☎**02.290-01096**
Closed Sunday, Monday morning
The Enoteca Cotti and its annex, La Frasca, in the heart of the Brera section of town, feel more like a neighborhood hangout than a wine store. Locals drop in for a chat with Luigi Cotti and a glass of wine before purchasing a bottle for lunch or dinner.

Monthly wine tastings, featuring a winemaker and his or her wines, draw an interested group of Luigi's client-friends.

ENOTECA

Emporio Solci
Via Morosini 19
☎**02.551-95725**
Closed Mondays
All credit cards
The Emporio Solci has an impressive selection of over 1,000 Italian, French, and even some Californian and South American wines, a number of quality extra virgin olive oils from different regions, balsamic vinegar, honey, and a wide range of *grappe* from all over Italy. They will send purchases anywhere in Europe.

ENOTECA

Ronchi
Via San Vicenzo 12
☎**02.894-02627**
Closed Sunday, open 9 A.M.–1 P.M., 3 P.M.–8 P.M.
MasterCard, Visa
Ring the ER bell at via San Vicenzo 12, follow the red carpet, turn left, and go downstairs to Maria Luisa Ronchi's *enoteca,* packed with a truly impressive collection of wines and specialty foods. Maria Luisa was Italy's first woman sommelier and comes from a family that has been in the wine business for five generations. Look for older vintages of Piemontese and Tuscan wines, as well as national and international wines worthy of attention. Thursday wine tastings, each featuring the products of an interesting winery, are held in October and November, from March through June, from 6:30 to 9 P.M., and readers who purchase a bottle of wine are invited to join Maria Luisa's clients. Enophiles should make an appointment to see the Ronchi wine library with bottles that date from 1790.

ENOTECA

Vino Vino

Via Speronari 4

☎**02.864-64055**

Closed Sunday and Monday, open 9 A.M.–2 P.M.,
3:30 P.M.–7:30 P.M.

MasterCard, Visa

In the heart of Milano's gourmet gulch, the tiny *enoteca* Vino Vino has a wonderful floor-to-ceiling selection of wines, distillates, and extra virgin olive oils. Around fifteen wines are available for tasting by the glass. They can't send wine to the U.S., but are willing to ship olive oil.

SUPERMARKET

Esselunga ("Long S") has locations throughout the city. It's the best American-style supermarket in Milano, stocked with fine Italian and some imported products. Prices are reasonable, wines can be excellent, and the delicatessen (*gastronomia*) offers a wide range of *salumi*, marinated salads, cheese, and olives. The small housewares section is well stocked with basics. Esselunga is studded with interesting inexpensive items like Domopak's baking-boiling bags, Frio's Ghiaccio Pronto—disposable plastic bags for making ice cubes—tubes of tomato paste, whole nutmeg sold with a tiny grater, instant aspic, Fini balsamic vinegar, and extra virgin olive oil. Closed Monday afternoon.

SANDWICH BAR

Paninoteca Bar Quadronno

Via Quadronno 34

☎**02.583-06612**

Closed Monday

The rebirth of the sandwich as the *panino* took place at the Bar Quadronno, a gastro-

nomic event of historic importance, especially for flocks of sandwich-eating teenagers, known as *paninari*, who dress like yuppies in designer sweatshirts, jeans, and Timberland shoes. This sandwich shrine won the Oscar of the sandwich world for its special *panino*, the "golden palm" (*palma d'oro*), which is stuffed with cured beef (*bresaola*), pressed mullet roe (*bottarga*), pâté, and Russian dressing. Dagwood would approve.

Bar Quadronno is open from 7 A.M. to 2 A.M.

SANDWICH BAR

Barba del Corso

Corso Vittorio Emanuele 5

☎**02.804-692**

Closed Sunday

Navigating the crowd of coffee drinkers to get to the sandwich station in the back of this anonymous bar isn't easy, but it's worth the effort. Fresh rolls (*panini*) are stuffed with over forty different meat, cheese, fish, or vegetable fillings. Simple classics like *prosciutto* or salami, as well as double-deckers, extra-large (*robusti*), and sometimes bizarre combinations, are Barba del Corso's specialty. There's an extra charge for service at the tables outside, under the arcade. The bar is open from 8:30 A.M. to 1:30 A.M.

SANDWICH BAR

Bar de Santis

Corso Magenta 9

☎**02.875-968**

Closed Sunday

Roberto de Santis specializes in grilling French bread rolls filled with mild goat cheese flavored with either wine, onions, basil, or chile pepper. Other imaginative

---

Fine pastry and *panettone* can also be found at Cova, Taveggia, Biffi, and Sant'Ambroeus, listed as *bar-caffès*.

THE MILANESE SANDWICH

Milano has created its own version of the sandwich (*panino*) as a snack or a lunch for those who can't take the time for a classic Italian meal. The *paninoteca* ("sandwich shrine") phenomenon began in Milano and has spread throughout Italy. Vegetable, cheese, fish, and cold-cut combination fillings are stuffed into partially cooked French bread rolls, then grilled to complete the cooking and to heat or melt the filling. Shrimp and crabmeat *panini* are often paired with Russian dressing (*salsa rubra* or *aurora*).

combinations and fillings, including tasty smoked herring, are stuffed into rolls in this popular *paninoteca*, but Roberto's cheese sandwiches are the new Milanese classics. De Santis is open from 10:30 A.M. to 1:30 P.M., and from 6 P.M. to 1:30 A.M.

SANDWICH BAR
I Panini della Bagi
Corso Vercelli 23
☎02.481-4032
Closed Sunday, open 8 A.M.–8 P.M.
Luigina Nicchio's nickname is "Bagi" (Venetian dialect for peanuts, her childhood passion), and she's been making wonderful sandwiches at her bar for more than twenty-four years. Sandwiches are fresh, stacked in baskets on one side of the bar. Look for *Cocodè*, ham with tuna mousse and hard-boiled eggs; Buffalo Bill, made of beef and green peppercorn mayonnaise; *Profumo di Bosco*, ham with *porcini* mushrooms; and much, much more. Simple first-course *primi* and main dishes are available at lunchtime. Finish with homemade strudel, apple, lemon, or yogurt cake.

SANDWICH BAR
Panino Giusto
Corso Garibaldi 125
☎02.655-4728
Piazza Beccaria 4
☎02.760-05015
Closed Sunday, open 12–3 P.M., 6:30 P.M.–1 A.M.

There's a crest of John, Lord de Montagu, Earl of Sandwich, 1718–1792, above the door at both locations of Panino Giusto. The decor is vaguely English—dark wood counters with stools, one room of tables, a bar with brass fittings, and a display case packed with cooked and cured *prosciutto*. There's a list on the wall of first-rate pricey Milanese sandwiches that includes the Giusto, cooked ham, tomato, mozzarella, and anchovy; Old Turkey, turkey breast, tomato, rucola, and tuna sauce; as well as dozens of other combinations. They've also got simpler sandwiches of cured *salumi*, vegetable *tartine*, and basic desserts. Both shops are packed at lunchtime.

PIZZA BY THE SLICE
Ecopizza
Via Cesare Battisti 1
☎02.760-22257
Closed Sunday, open 10 A.M.–3 A.M.
Buono e Sano ("Good and Healthy") reads the sign of Ecopizza, where all pizzea, *schiacciate*, and *panzerotti* are made with organic ingredients. The selection is large, with around twelve different kinds of pizza to choose from. Drink water, soda, ice tea, or beer.

PASTRY, MARZIPAN
Freni
Corso Vittorio Emanuele 4
☎02.804-871
Closed Wednesday

The Freni window is a joy to behold. Miniature mushrooms, watermelon, fruit, vegetables, salami, cacti, rolls, frying pans with eggs, little animals—all are made from the Freni family's marzipan recipe, sculpted, and hand-painted with vegetable-based dyes by a staff of Sicilian marzipan artists. But the real reason for a pilgrimage to Freni is to taste the warm scallop-shaped *sfogliatelle* (ricotta-filled flaky pastry), a rich, elegant southern specialty.

PASTRY

Massimo di Crinò

Via Ripamonti 5

☎02.55139

Closed Monday

Antonino Crinò named his pastry shop after his infant son for good luck, but luck has nothing to do with the splendid desserts that he turns out. He's been baking since he was thirteen, and his professionalism, dedication, and passion for quality are responsible for the excellent *panettone*, the best I've ever tasted. The secret is in the all-natural ingredients–first-rate raisins, candied orange peel, egg yolks, Italian butter, less sugar than most, and forty hours of work from the dough to the final product. *Panettone* is baked from the end of September through March, when Antonino bakes *colomba*, dove-shaped Easter cakes, for two weeks. *La veneziana*, similar to *panettone* but topped with almonds and sugar, is available the rest of the year. No preservatives are added to these tasty cakes, and I imagine that they won't last as long as more commercial versions, but in my home they disappear so quickly that they don't have time to grow stale.

PASTRY

Marchesi

Via Santa Maria alla Porta 13

☎02.862-770

Closed Monday, except before Christmas

A visit to Marchesi, with its Old World ambience of lace-trimmed aprons, silver, and doilies, where everything is a classic, feels like a time warp. Nothing has ever changed. The chocolates and the pastry are wonderful, but rich yeast breads, like springtime *colomba* or winter *panettone*, are Marchesi's specialty. The traditional Christmas chantilly-cream–stuffed *panettone* is a Milanese classic.

GELATO

Gelateria Ecologica

Corso di Porta Ticinese 40

☎02.835-1872

Closed August and November through February

There's no sign outside Gelateria Ecologica but it's easy enough to find, with its permanent cluster of fans outside eating *gelato* with multicolored plastic spoons. All their *gelato* is made with seasonal organic fruit and natural ingredients. Daily specials are listed on a blackboard and may include date, rhubarb, and honey sesame. The *gelateria* is open from 1 P.M. to midnight, seven days a week.

GELATO

Passerini

Via Victor Hugo 5

☎02.800-663

Closed Wednesday

Passerini, on via Victor Hugo in the heart of gastronomic Milano, founded in the 1920s, is the city's most elegant ice cream parlor. Classic flavors of *gelato* are rich and creamy; the *gianduia* (chocolate hazelnut) is outstanding. Hollowed-out fruit is stuffed with frozen sherbet. *Gelato* snowmen and Santas, and thick hot chocolate topped with whipped cream, are winter specialties. Open from 7:30 A.M. to 8 P.M.

GELATO

Gelateria Umberto

Piazza Cinque Giornate 4

☎02.545-8113

Closed Sunday

Only seven kinds of *gelato,* all exquisite classic flavors, are prepared daily at Gelateria Umberto. Personal favorites are the smooth creamy hazelnut, the intense coffee parfait, the *cassata alla siciliana* (a layered ricotta, candied fruit, and sponge cake dessert), and the white wine and candied fruit *sorbetto Romanov,* which must be ordered in advance. Free delivery, almost unheard of in Italy, is available for orders of more than 300 grams (about 10 ounces). Umberto is open from 9:30 A.M. to 7 P.M.

CANDIED CHESTNUTS
Giovanni Galli
Via Victor Hugo 21
☎02.864-64833
Closed Sunday afternoon
This shop with its turn-of-the-century decor has been around for more than 100 years. It is *the* place to go for *marrons glacés,* almond-paste confections, fruit pralines, fruit jellies, and *boeri,* candied cherries covered with bittersweet chocolate. Chic Milanese do their Christmas shopping at Galli, gifting friends with elegantly wrapped boxes or baskets of perfectly candied *marrons glacés.*

CHOCOLATE
Neuhaus Maître Chocolatier dal 1857
Via San Vittore 6
☎02.720-000-096
Closed Monday morning
How typically Milanese to ignore the fine Italian chocolate tradition and open a shop that sells Belgian chocolates. But Neuhaus chocolates are wonderful. Select from ninety-six different varieties—I love the look of the sleek chocolate cones with piped chocolate filling, chocolate mussels, and dipped cherries with stems. Or choose the chocolate alphabet letters, sold individually, in a box of three. Elegantly wrapped chocolate Easter eggs are another specialty.

The gift baskets and boxes are important-looking, expensive. Fans of chocolate-covered ice cream bonbons should plan to visit Neuhaus for the bite-size bitter-chocolate–coated *gelato* cubes in flavors like mint, chocolate, coffee, or cinnamon.

RESTAURANT
Aimo e Nadia
Via Montecuccoli 6
☎02.416-886
Fax 02.483-02005
Closed Saturday lunch, Sunday, and August
American Express • expensive
A lengthy cab ride to a suburb that looks like Yonkers is the prelude to the privilege of dining at Aimo e Nadia. The decor is modern without being sterile, softened by tones of brick, pale peach, and pink-flecked granite. Lighting, linens, flatware, glassware, and flower arrangements are discreet, complements to rather than distractions from the food. The team work of husband and wife—Aimo procuring the finest raw materials and Nadia at work in the kitchen—is a lesson in harmony and respect. The *cucina* is composed of strong, decisive flavors spiked with herbs, taking full advantage of the best and freshest possible local ingredients, lightly cooked, simply combined. A seasonal vegetable, such as asparagus, zucchini flowers, mushrooms, or truffles, may dominate the menu during its brief period of excellence, weaving its flavor through many courses of the meal, appearing in an *antipasto* salad, as *risotto* or with pasta, or combined with fish or meat. The cheese selection is the essence of Lombardia. The wine list is somewhat confusing, with many French and unknown Italian wines, reflecting the personal taste of the sommelier. The strength and sincerity of Aimo and Nadia Moroni and their *cucina* make dining at their restaurant an exceptional experience.

RESTAURANT

Alfredo Gran San Bernardo
Via Borgese 14
☎02.331-9000
Fax 02.655-5413
Closed Sunday, December 20–January 20,
mid-July through August
No credit cards • high moderate

An extensive menu exists in this classic Milanese restaurant, but if you look at the other tables on your way to be seated, you'll notice that almost everyone is eating the same things: golden-yellow *risotto alla milanese*, or *riso al salto*, a crispy pancake of *risotto* sautéed in butter; the "true" *costoletta alla milanese*, a large pounded, breaded veal cutlet with the bone; and *cazzoeula*, a stew of pork sausage, ribs, forehead, and feet, stewed with cabbage, served with *polenta*. Most diners conclude with the soufflé, which is covered with chocolate sauce. The white-jacketed waiters are impatient, probably because they know what you're going to choose, and the service is speedy. The wine list offers a selection of fine wines as well as plonk.

RESTAURANT

Al Pont de Ferr
Ripa di Porta Ticinese 55
☎02.894-06277
Closed Sunday and two weeks in August,
open evenings only
MasterCard, Visa • moderate

This restaurant's name is Milanese dialect for the iron bridge that spans the nearby Naviglio Canal in the newly gentrified, once-bohemian quarter of town. Local enophiles stop in for dinner, a snack, or a glass of wine from the selection of over 200 quality wines. Owner-sommelier Maida Mercuri is every bit as beautiful as her wine list. The food is simple, the *salumi* are fine, cheese is selected with great care. Swift service is not the highlight of this restaurant,

but the genuine ambience, reasonable prices, and Maida's unfailing palate keep me coming back.

RESTAURANT

Al Porto
Piazzale Generale Cantore
☎02.894-07425
Fax 02.832-1481
Closed Sunday, Monday lunch, and August
All credit cards • expensive

Anna in the kitchen and husband Domenico Buonamici in the dining rooms of Al Porto prepare and serve some of the freshest fish in Milano. The classic *cucina* of this ex-tollhouse on the docks of Porta Ticinese, decorated with maritime paraphernalia, offers few surprises and no disappointments, just fish and seafood, fresher than in restaurants on the coast, simply cooked in traditional Italian style. The *tiramisù* is delicious, although some diners prefer to conclude their meal with a *gelato* at nearby Gelateria Pozzi. Italian, and some French, wines are featured on the fine wine list. Outdoor dining in the warm weather months. Reservations should be made a few days in advance.

RESTAURANT

Asso di Fiori–Osteria dei Formaggi
Alzaia Naviglio Grande 54
☎02.894-09415
Closed Saturday lunch, Sunday, and August
All credit cards • moderate

The informal Asso di Fiori ("Ace of Clubs") in the charming Naviglio Canal section of Milano serves close to 200 different types of Italian cheese, including fresh mozzarella and *burrata* that arrive daily from the south. Order the *degustazione*, a tasting of fifteen difference cheeses, and choose from the interesting selection of fine Italian wines.

R E S T A U R A N T
Aurora
Via Savona 23
☎02.894-04978
Closed Monday
American Express, Diners Club • high moderate

Mushrooms, truffles, and Piemontese cooking are the specialties of this turn-of-the-century restaurant. Tasty *bagna cauda* (raw vegetable dip), *risotto*, homemade pasta, boiled meats with a variety of sauces, salads dressed at the table with your choice of a large selection of olive oils and flavored vinegars, and homemade desserts and *gelato* are served to Aurora's chic Milanese clients. Cheese and wine are mostly Piemontese. The fixed-price menu at lunch and dinner offers a reasonably priced (for Milano) five-course meal, including wine. Drink the Ceretto Dolcetto. Lawn bowling (*bocce*) and garden dining under the trees make Aurora even nicer in the warm months. Open on Sunday.

R E S T A U R A N T
Calajunco
Via Stoppani 5
☎02.204-6003
Closed Saturday lunch, Sunday, and August
All credit cards • expensive

Off the coast of Sicilia, on the Eolian island of Panarea, is a tiny bay called Calajunco, where Renato Carnevale used to dive for fish. His elegant restaurant, named after the bay, serves the *cucina*, lightened up for the modern palate, of Sicilia and Renato's islands. A hollowed-out mini-mozzarella filled with tomato and basil and dressed with olive oil, eggplant salad (*caponata*), and a fried rice ball (*arancino*), or another trio of tasty *antipasti*, will be served while you wait for your order in the evening, or can be your whole meal at lunchtime. Milano's fresh fish is served up in salads, with perfectly cooked spaghetti, and

grilled, delicately fried, or sauced. The sliced fresh fruit makes a light conclusion to the meal, but it may be hard to resist the tiny ricotta-filled fried pastry. Choose from an ample selection of wines.

R E S T A U R A N T –
S A L A D   B A R
Cucina delle Langhe and Insalatiera delle Langhe
Corso Como 6
☎Restaurant:02.655-4279
☎Salad bar:02.659-5180
Closed Sunday
All credit cards • high moderate restaurant, moderate snack and salad bars

The menu is mostly Piemontese, with *tajarin* pasta; *bagna cauda*, garlic and anchovy dip served with raw vegetables and fantastic (and expensive) truffles in season (30,000 lire for a grating); *risotto* with Barolo; *vitello tonnato;* or beef braised with Barolo. The wine list predictably focuses on Piemonte, although wines and foods from other regions are available. The salad bar next door is far more casual, and will appeal to those who want a quick light lunch, dinner, or late snack. Over twenty-five different salads and most of the dishes from next door are available. A note on the menu gently asks diners to refrain from smoking.

R E S T A U R A N T
Da Giacomo
Via Pasquale Sottocorno 6
☎02.760-23313
Closed Monday
All credit cards • high moderate to low expensive

A Milanese friend told me about this terrific fish restaurant, unmentioned in any guidebooks, and it's become a favorite of mine, too. The decor is turn of the century, with painted wainscoting, ceiling fans, old-fashioned light fixtures, and plenty of charm. Owner-chef Giacomo is originally from Toscana, so the menu is studded with Tuscan preparations like *panzanella* (bread salad), Viareggio fish soup, red gurnard Livorno-style with tomato sauce, Florentine steak, or tripe. But don't miss perfectly executed classics like seafood soup or salad, spaghetti with tiny clams, or *risotto* with seafood or mushrooms. Homemade pasta is sauced with *porcini* mushrooms, squid, and rucola or, best of all, deboned scorpion fish. Seafood lovers should try *spaghetti allo scoglio*, with mixed clams, mussels, prawns, shrimp, and much more, a one-course meal for some diners. Second-course offerings are simple: skewers of prawns and squid, sea bass baked in salt, or simply grilled mullet, tuna, jumbo shrimp, or bream. Mushrooms are served in season, raw in salad, grilled, or fried. Finish with a dessert from the cart, homemade *sorbetto* or, in the winter, sample unsweet, slightly smoky *castagnaccio* made with chestnut flour, a Tuscan tradition and probably an acquired taste. Giacomo's daughter Tiziana, born after the family move to Milano and whose Italian is without a Tuscan accent, works the dining room and is well informed about wines from the small but well-chosen list.

RESTAURANT

Da Ilia

Via Lecco 1
☎**02.295-21895**
Closed Friday, Saturday lunch
All credit cards • high moderate

Da Ilia serves classic Italian home-style cooking in an informal ambience. Ceiling fans whirl in warm-weather months, fine art prints line the walls in the dining rooms, which are always packed in the evening with locals looking for well-priced, well-prepared food. Check out the *antipasto* display in the entrance, which may be an entire meal for those who want to eat light. Or begin with hand-sliced *pro-*

sciutto, fine *salumi*, or mushroom salad. Continue with pasta sauced with raw tomato sauce or *pappardelle* with meat sauce and mushrooms, well-made *risotto*, or simple soups like *pasta e fagioli*. Main-dish offerings include the new-wave *cotoletta alla carrettiera* topped with tomatoes, grilled chicken, superfresh fish preparations. Desserts from the cart, *gelato* with wild berries or drowned with whiskey or vodka conclude the meal. The wine list is small with a few bargains. Dine outdoors in the garden when the weather is nice. Luckily, Ilia is open on Sundays.

RESTAURANT

Don Lisander

Via Manzoni 12/A
☎**02.760-20130**
Fax 02.784-573
Closed Saturday evening, Sunday, and most of August
All credit cards • expensive

Don Lisander, elegant and modern, with a beautiful garden dining area in the summer, feels like a patrician Milanese palace. The *cucina* of Maria Bani is Tuscan, sparked by her creativity. Husband Gioacchino Coppini supplies her with the best ingredients that the city has to offer, and she does them justice. Pasta is hand—not machine—rolled. Fish, game, and the best Florentine-style steak in Milano are cooked to perfection, flavored with fresh herbs. Desserts and *gelato* are homemade. Service is swift and formal. A wide selection of quality extra virgin olive oils are available, and the wine list offers some gems.

RESTAURANT

Dorina–Il Pontremolese

Via Pepe 38
☎**/Fax 02.606-340**
Closed Saturday lunch, Sunday, and August
All credit cards • high moderate

Tuscan restaurants with undistinguished food abound in Milano, but this restaurant is an exception. Dorina, expert sommelier, serves the *cucina* from Pontremoli, close to the border between Toscana, Liguria, and Emilia-Romagna, showing the influences of all three regions with strong, determined flavors like *pesto*, whole kernels of wheat, and chestnut dominating the menu, accompanied by a wide selection of extra virgin olive oils, and a fine wine list of Tuscan and Italian gems.

RESTAURANT

Franca, Paola e Lele
Viale Certosa 235
☎02.380-06231
Closed Saturday, Sunday, Monday evening, and August
American Express, MasterCard, Visa • expensive

The damask tablecloths and a few trendy diners are the only hints that there is more to this one-room *trattoria* than meets the eye. Owner Lele, white-aproned and suspendered, is clearly proud of each dish that comes out of his wife's kitchen, and with good reason. Home-grown vegetables, poultry, eggs, and lightly salted homemade *salumi*, all from Paola and Lele's own farm outside Piacenza, are cooked with simplicity and artistry—no flowers, stars, braids, or trellis arrangements on the plates. The country-style *cucina* of *salumi*, fine pâté, home-style chunky soups, duck, goose, but especially chicken that really tastes like chicken, plus *gelato* rich with orange egg yolks, is accompanied by classical music and quality local and often unusual wines. Lele's enthusiasm is infectious, and makes dining in this *trattoria* in suburban Milano a treat.

RESTAURANT

Grand Hotel
Via Ascanio Sforza 75
☎02.895-11586
Evenings only, closed Monday
American Express, Visa • moderate

Named after the film starring Greta Garbo and not part of a fancy hotel, this restaurant is open evenings only, but is worth a visit for the well-priced food and the wonderful wine list—the pride of owners Fabrizio Paganini in the dining room and Stefania Zari in the kitchen. The dining room is comfortable, with pink walls and a large pub bar. *Salumi* are first-rate; lard fans should order the tasting plate of lard from Valle d'Aosta, Toscana, and Piemonte. The menu offers interesting pasta dishes, like Tuscan *testaroli* sauced with *pesto* or walnut sauce, winter squash *tortelli*, wide strips of *pappardelle* sauced with wild boar or hare. *Porcini* mushrooms are served in season. Roast lamb, veal shank, or braised beef with *polenta* are among the main-course offerings. The cheese selection is small but well chosen. Choose from desserts like *panna cotta*, chocolate mousse, or fruit bavarians. Eat outside under the ancient wisteria pergola near the *bocce* courts in the summer, a typical Milanese experience.

RESTAURANT

Il Sambuco
Via Messina 10
☎02.336-10333
Fax 02.3319425
Closed Sunday
All credit cards • expensive

I was enthusiastic about Achille Maccanti's restaurant in Porto Garibaldi for its fantastic fish and seafood. Achille sold his restaurant on the Adriatic coast and has now opened Il Sambuco in the Hermitage Hotel. I'm wilder about the food than the decor, with floral print carpet, roses on the curtains and decorating the walls, red velvet chairs, and banquettes. The tables are elegantly set, service is professional. Achille selects the best fish and seafood from the most important and well-supplied sources in Milano. Carnivores should dine elsewhere, but fish lovers will find some of the best cooking in the city. Begin with appetizers like razor clams steamed in white wine, tiny shrimp with tiny salad greens, monkfish and asparagus salad, raw marinated fish, smoked sturgeon, and swordfish. Or choose classics like spaghetti with tiny clams or mixed-seafood sauce, white *risotto* with squid and baby cuttlefish or black *risotto* with cuttlefish ink; or creations like sea-bass ravioli with fresh sheep's-milk cheese, *orecchiette* sauced with prawns, tomato, olives, and capers. Fish soup is cooked to order for at least two diners, but the forty-minute wait is worth this one-dish meal, packed with the bounty of the Adriatic sea. Sea bass, bream, red mullet, scorpion fish, gurnard are treated with respect, simply sauced. Options from the grill include turbot, sole, scallops, prawns, little cuttlefish, and monkfish, which are cooked to order (20 to 30 minutes warns the menu). Il Sambuco's fried-fish medley is one of the best I've ever encountered— light, barely floured, greaseless baby cuttlefish, tiny shrimp, prawns, whitebait, and more, and they'll serve half-portion tastes. Homemade lemon *sorbetto,* caramel or vanilla *gelato,* or fresh-fruit salad will please diners who like to conclude with something sweet. The wine list is impressive, prepared with the consultation of wine expert Alberto Brovelli, heavy on Italian and French whites with a small selection of light reds, a few heavy hitters like Sassicaia and Gaja reserve Barbaresco, and an ample choice of dessert wines.

HOTEL-RESTAURANT

Il Teatro and La Veranda del Hotel Four Seasons

Via Gesù 8

☎02.77088

Il Teatro, evenings only, closed Sunday

La Veranda, 7 A.M.–11 P.M., nonstop •

high expensive

I greatly admired chef Sergio Mei's cooking at the Casanova Grill at the Palace Hotel. He's moved on to the Hotel Four Seasons,

and his food is better than ever, another reason to visit or stay at Milano's best hotel. It's newly rebuilt, incorporating remains of the original fifteenth-century convent into the stylish decor. The Four Seasons puts all the other fancy hotels in Milano to shame. Concierges actually smile and welcome guests, not always the case in many of the city's luxury hotels. The rooms are luxuriously appointed, bathrooms have separate tubs and showers, mirrors are steam resistant. It could be that this is the only hotel in Italy with room service (swift) twenty-four hours a day. The Four Seasons Hotel is in the heart of Milano's shopping district—more designer shopping bags across the lobby than in any other location in the city.

The food at both hotel restaurants is delicious and the service superior. La Veranda is a casual restaurant, in a glassed-in verandah overlooking the hotel's cloistered courtyard garden. Breakfast, lunch, dinner, or snacks are available all day long and are actually reasonably priced for Milano, a perfect stop for weary shoppers. Choose from the appetizers, salads, or light meals, like fried prawns with green beans, *bresaola* with lettuce, apples, and *pecorino* cheese or grilled vegetables. Or first-course *risotto* with watercress and scallops, homemade pasta or spaghetti, sauced with fresh tomato and basil, simple but fantastic. Fresh fish or Milanese cutlet topped with tomato and rucola are among the main-dish offerings. Fine pastry, homemade *gelato* and *sorbetto* are tempting conclusions, or they can be ordered as a snack between meals. The wine list is small but well chosen, with many wines available by the glass.

Il Teatro is a far more formal restaurant, with an important wine list, leather-upholstered walls, oak-plank floors, large flower arrangements, well-appointed tables. Fresh pasta, seasonal vegetables, fresh fish, Tuscan *Chianina* beef are perfectly cooked, elegantly sauced. Marinated rabbit, black pasta with scallops and zucchini, scorpionfish soup, roast lamb are among the fine selections. I'm skeptical about some dishes, classic flavor combinations that appear in a course where they don't belong. Desserts like crème brûlée with lemon balm and raspberries, homemade *gelato* and *sorbetto*, and a lovely selection of pastries are worth saving room for. Service is flawless, and the sommelier is actually helpful. Four Seasons' alternative-cuisine dishes with lower calories, cholesterol, sodium, and fat and a vegetarian menu are available on request at both restaurants.

RESTAURANT
Joia
Via Panfilo Castaldi 18
☎02.295-22124
Fax 02.204-0244
Closed Saturday lunch and Sunday
All credit cards • high moderate

Vegetarians, vegans, and vegetable lovers will appreciate the efforts of Swiss chef Pietro Leemann, author of *Alta Cucina Vegetariana*. He was greatly influenced by Gualtiero Marchesi, and prepares innovative, experimental dishes with the freshest ingredients that Milano has to offer. The restaurant is modern and elegant, and Pietro's partner, Nicla Nardi, presides in the dining rooms. Many dishes are prepared without eggs or dairy products (marked with an asterisk on the menu), and fish has recently been added. The menu is complicated to order from, but three vegetarian tasting menus and one of fish will help simplify things. All items on these menus can also be ordered à la carte. Appetizers or main dishes can be interchanged, salads can substitute for a main course, or diners can focus on pasta. Herbs play an important part in Pietro's cooking, and it's easy to

see that he's spent time in Asia by elegant presentations like gold-leaf–wrapped chickpea puree and the presence of ginger in many dishes. Pasta is homemade and satisfying—look for buckwheat *tagliolini* with fresh tomato sauce; whole-wheat pasta with *porcini* mushrooms and tender baby spinach or shrimp, potatoes, green beans, and black truffle; or *trenette* with a mild garlicless *pesto*. Main courses include potato *tortino* with yogurt sauce and summer truffle, steamed eggplant with chanterelles and ginger, or sea bass and eggplant skewers served with sautéed tomatoes and basil. Cheese and desserts are worth saving room for, especially the *gelato* gratin, a tasting of three different custards, or the warm fig and almond tart served with cinnamon *gelato*. The wine list is small but well chosen, with Italian and French selections, some organic wines, cider, organic juices, beer, and Plose mineral water, one of my favorites. Miraculously for Italy, there's even a no-smoking dining room.

RESTAURANT
La Latteria
Via San Marco 24
☎02.659-7653
Closed Saturday and Sunday
No credit cards • low moderate

The walls of this ex-*latteria* are completely covered with paintings and prints of roses, the passion of Arturo Maggi. His wife, Maria, is in the kitchen, cooking up comfort food for a crowd of regulars who appreciate home-style cooking. The menu is small and changes daily, but always begins with rustic legume and grain soups. Main courses are based on fish, meat, and lots of seasonal vegetables. Fruit desserts like *crostata* or mousse are homemade. The house wine is simple—search elsewhere for enological thrills. Conclude your meal with the house specialty, Arturosa, a rose-petal tisane.

RESTAURANT

L'Ami Berton

Via F. Nullo 14

☎02.713-669

Closed Saturday lunch, Sunday, Monday lunch, and August

All credit cards • expensive

L'Ami Berton, with its Art Nouveau greenhouse decor, beautiful brown-tendriled marble-chip floor, and planters separating the tables, creating a feeling of intimacy, serves nontraditional, light, simply prepared fish, seafood, and vegetables (meat dishes are a minority on the menu), coupled with a lovely selection of Italian wines. The homemade pasta is fabulous. Desserts are well made, but save room for the small chocolate-covered cube of intense coffee ice cream, served after coffee. Roberto Berton and his wife, Pia, in the kitchen (he's from Veneto, she's Tuscan) are the driving force behind this fine restaurant. In the summer you can dine outside, on the awning-covered sidewalk.

RESTAURANT

La Milanese

Via Santa Marta 11

☎02.864-51991

Closed Tuesday

American Express, Diners Club, Visa • high moderate

It's almost impossible to find a Milanese restaurant open on Sunday, but this typical *trattoria* is the exception to the rule. Giuseppe Villa prepares traditional dishes, his wife, Antonella, and a staff of waiters bustle through three crowded dining rooms lined with still-life paintings. Begin with a salad of *nervetti*, pig's-trotter strips with onion, or *bresaola;* continue with *minestrone,* served tepid in the summer; *risotto alla milanese* or *al salto.* Traditional main courses include tripe (*foilo*), *cotoletta alla milanese, porcini* mushrooms, *ossobuco. Cassoeula, polenta* with Gorgonzola, or

braised meats are offered in the winter. Vegetables are overcooked in the home-style tradition. Always available are basic desserts such as fresh berries, pineapple, or fruit salad. The house wine is Barbera, but there's a limited selection of wines from the Oltrepò and Piemonte.

RESTAURANT

La Rondine

Via Spartaco 11

☎02.551-84533

Closed Sunday

No credit cards • moderate

This is the Alice's Restaurant of Milano, with an almost endless list of anything that anyone would want. Choose from Milanese and classic Italian preparations—over fifteen different *antipasti;* thirty different pasta dishes; *risotto;* soups; endless meat, poultry, and fish dishes, every possible seasonal vegetable. Mushrooms and truffles, never inexpensive, are available in season. Finish with fruit or typical desserts like *panna cotta, gelato* "drowned" with coffee, *crème caramel della casa.* Service is quick, prices are low for Milano, and most tables are occupied by regulars, fans of the home-style cooking. Most drink the house wine, although there's a limited selection of bottled wines.

RESTAURANT

L'Osteria

Alzaia Naviglio Grande 46

☎02.837-3426

Closed Tuesday, open 8 A.M.–2 A.M., Saturday and Sunday 12:00 noon–2 A.M.

No credit cards • low moderate

L'Osteria is a characteristic stucco-walled, marble-countered wine bar in the Naviglio section of Milano. There are over 200 types of wine from all over Italy—with a few French, Alsatian, and even American wines available—to drink with the *salumi,* smoked game, salads, raw vegetables (*pinzimonio*) to be dipped in extra virgin olive oil, and cheese. Desserts, mostly fruit tarts, cakes, and *semifreddo*, are unexciting.

RESTAURANT

Masuelli
Viale Umbria 80
☎/Fax 02.551-84138
Closed Sunday
American Express, MasterCard, Visa •
low moderate

The Masuelli family have been operating this authentic *trattoria* in viale Umbria since 1930, serving the *cucina* of their native Monferrato, in Piemonte, along with Milanese specialities. Pino Masuelli works the two dining rooms, and his wife, Tina, is kept busy in the kitchen. The ambience is typical *trattoria*, with an old-fashioned metal-topped bar and wooden wainscoting. Each day of the week has its own special—Monday, mixed boiled meats; Tuesday, chick-pea soup with ribs, or Milanese meatballs (*mondeghili*); Wednesday, tripe and onion stew; Thursday, pork and cabbage stew; Friday, *polenta* and cod; Saturday, *gnocchi*. The Masuellis used to produce and bottle simple wine from their native Piemonte, but the wine list is expanding and a small, everchanging selection of fine, reasonably priced wines is offered. Reservations are a must, and are not easy to come by for this wonderful *trattoria*.

RESTAURANT

Nino Arnaldo
Via Carlo Poerio 3
☎02.705-981
Closed Saturday lunch, Sunday, and August
Visa • expensive, moderate lunch

Nino Arnaldo's minimalist Milanese decor is warmed by an enormous antique print of Roma, soft modern lighting, transparent wine coolers, and elegant locals dining on creative *cucina*, guided by Nino's wife, Lucia. Seasonal pan-fried flans (*frittate*),

homemade pasta or ravioli stuffed with a meat, vegetable, or fish filling, main-course meat and vegetable combinations and a few simple fish dishes, fine *gelato* and fruit ices, all with well-balanced flavors, are well prepared. Truffles and mushrooms are a specialty in season. The wine list is adequate.

RESTAURANT

Osteria dei Binari
Via Tortona 1
☎02.894-09428
Fax 02.894-07470
Closed Sunday and August
All credit cards • high moderate

Near the Porta Genovese train station (hence *binari*—railroad platforms or tracks), this neighborhood *osteria* with its old Milano ambience serves mixed regional *cucina* with a bit of nouvelle tossed in. Piemonte, Liguria, and most of all Lombardia influence the menu of Osteria dei Binari, where bread, pasta, and desserts are homemade, the wine list wonderful, and the service swift. Lawn bowling (*bocce*) and garden dining under the trees are pleasant in the warm-weather months.

RESTAURANT

Osteria di Porta Cicca
Ripa di Porta Ticinese 51
☎/Fax 02.837-2763
Closed Sunday
MasterCard, Visa • low expensive

Claudio Sadler's talent grew too large for his small Naviglio restaurant, and so he's opened a new one, leaving his *osteria* in the capable hands of chef Pierluigi Squazzini and Sandro Dal Zuffo, in the dining room. The ambience here is not really *osteria*like, prices are lower, more in key with the informal Naviglio area. The menu is creative, combining seasonal ingredients with restraint. Begin with rabbit terrine or smoked-fish rolls, proceed with homemade pasta like goat-cheese ravioli with marjoram, wide pasta strips sauced with seafood, or *maccheroncini* with *porcini* mushrooms. Meat and fish preparations are elegantly sauced—look for duck breast with sweet peppers, veal with sage and hazelnuts, turbot braised with potatoes and *porcini* mushrooms. Or opt for an *insalatone* ("big salad"), in fish, meat, or vegetarian versions. The dessert menu ranges from light to caloric with fruit salad, berries, *gelato*, bavarians, fruit or custard tarts, all homemade, appealing. The wine list is short but sweet, of mostly affordable young wines.

RESTAURANT
Sadler
Via Troilo 14
☎02.581-04451
Fax 02.581-12343
Closed Sunday and lunch
All credit cards • high expensive

At last Claudio Sadler has a restaurant with a kitchen where he can really cut loose. The decor is cool, with wooden floors, modern lighting, simply set, well-spaced tables. Claudio, as usual, works with the finest raw ingredients that money can buy, combining them within the framework of classic and innovative dishes. The menu changes often and offers thrills for carnivores, fish lovers, and vegetarians. Appetizers include seared sole fillets with *ovoli* mushrooms, raw turbot with celery and *bottarga*, squidlets and fennel dressed with extra virgin olive oil. Pasta, *risotto*, and soups are well prepared. Claudio uses the exceptional single-wheat variety of Latini pasta known as *Senatore Cappelli*, sauced with fresh tomato, watercress, and *pecorino* cheese. Choose from main-dish offerings like deep-fried zucchini flowers stuffed with turbot and black truffle, crispy amberjack with shrimp and vegetables, baked pork shin glazed with chestnut honey, guinea hen with balsamic vinegar, baked *porcini* mushrooms with melted cheese and herbs. Desserts are worth the calories—berry gelatin is like

grown-up Jell-O, caramelized fresh figs are served with dried-fig *gelato*, pears stuffed with cinnamon mousse and glazed with white chocolate. Diners who can't make up their minds can do it all with the "*gran dessert*." The tasting menu is, according to the menu, "a platform of known successes and consolidated performances where the kitchen expresses the maximum of fantasy and creativity." The wine list is personal, offering gems from Italy and beyond.

RESTAURANT
Peck
Via Victor Hugo 4
☎02.876-774
Fax 02.860-408
Closed Sunday and the first three weeks in July
All credit cards • high moderate

This restaurant is the jewel in the crown of the Peck empire (see page 221). Quality ingredients procured by the four Stoppani brothers, the princes of Peck, are used to full advantage. Needless to say, *salumi* and cheese are excellent, and the wine list is a joy to read. The six-course traditional Milanese tasting menu is reasonably priced; the *menu degustazione* offers somewhat fancier, although well-made, creative *cucina*. The ambience is modern and unpretentious.

RESTAURANT
Savini
Galleria Vittorio Emanuele
☎02-720.03433
Fax 02.864-61060
Closed Sunday and August
All credit cards • expensive

Savini, decorated with brocade, gilt mirrors, crystal chandeliers, and plush red velvet banquettes—the most elegant and traditional of Milanese restaurants—has been frequented by royalty and stars from the nearby La Scala opera house for over a hundred years. The *cucina* is continental, from the days of the Grand Tour, featuring smoked salmon or sturgeon, Iranian caviar, and superb *salumi*. All pasta is hand-rolled daily by a special pasta roller (*la pastaia*), not a machine. Milanese, Italian, and international classics like chateaubriand with béarnaise sauce and sole Mornay are listed on the menu, which varies daily, but this is the kind of restaurant that will make anything that you want. Vegetables will probably be overcooked. The wine list is wonderful, but only for those for whom price is no object.

RESTAURANT
Sciuè Sciuè
Via Solari 6
☎**02.480-03029**
Closed Monday, Tuesday lunch, and August
American Express, Diners Club • moderate

Sciuè Sciuè may look unpronounceable (say shoo-ay, shoo-ay) but it's worth the effort, because this inviting southern Italian restaurant, with its colorful seafood *antipasto* display, serves perfectly cooked spaghetti, grilled meats and fish, and wonderful pizza. Conclude your meal with the *pastiera napoletana*, a whole-wheat–kernel, ricotta, and candied-fruit flan. The wine list has its highs and lows. Sciuè Sciuè is open on Sunday.

RESTAURANT
Trattoria La Veneta
Via Giusti 14
☎**02.342-881**
Closed Monday
American Express • moderate

What's the 1948 Benelli motercycle doing at the bar-entrance of this *trattoria*? It's on display, Giovanni Pauletto told me proudly. Giovanni is from Treviso and serves the classic *cucina* of Veneto, with a few dishes from neighboring Friuli, in a simple no-frills neighborhood restaurant—two dining rooms almost always packed with locals, conveniently open on Sunday. Begin with grilled Treviso radicchio served with

crispy fried-cheese *frico* and fine *prosciutto* or *soppressa* salami. First-course possibilities include four different bean soups, *bigoli* pasta sauced with anchovy, *tagliatelle* with poppy seeds. *Risotto* with Treviso radicchio is prepared for at least two diners. Look for Venetian specialties like liver, fresh sardines *in saor* with onions and vinegar, *baccalà*, salt cod, either whipped or braised with cabbage. The dessert specialty is called Bomba; it's a custard *gelato* with liquor-soaked ladyfingers, sliced banana, hot chocolate sauce, and coffee. Strudel is cooked to order (a twenty-minute wait), but I can't resist the *sgroppino alla trevisana* (defined in parentheses as a beverage)— lemon *sorbetto* whipped with vodka and Prosecco wine and served in a flute glass. The small wine list is all from Veneto and Friuli. Prices are reasonable, and La Veneta is open on Sunday.

RESTAURANT
Vecchio Porco
Via Messina 8
☎**02.313-862**
Closed Sunday lunch and Monday
All credit cards • moderate

Porcophiles should plan to visit this crowded *trattoria-pizzeria*, frequented by models, soccer players from the Milan team, and journalists, for the first-rate *salumi* and decor featuring their favorite animal. The ambience is homey, cluttered with pork-related prints, framed pig-printed T-shirts and boxer shorts, and a display case with hundreds of pig statuettes. *Vecchio e bello, porco e meglio* ("Old is beautiful, pig is better") is written large on the wall of one dining room. Begin with first-rate *prosciutto, culatello, salame* from Felino, lard from Cavour, or aged *pancetta*. First-course options include Milanese *risotto*, fresh pasta sauced with prawns and squid or with sausage and beans, hearty soups like barley-lentil, *rigatoni* with tomato sauce. Sea bass is grilled or baked in a salt crust; steak, Cornish hen, kidneys, or baby lamb chops are also grilled. *Ossobuco* is served with *risotto alla milanese.* Owner Gerry Mele is from Sardegna and with advance notice will prepare some of the island's specialties like *porceddu,* roast suckling pig with an irresistibly crunchy skin, or *seadas,* deep-fried sheep's-milk cheese ravioli sauced with bitter honey. Pizza fans won't be disappointed with classics or new-wave *pizze* combinations like *scamorza* and rucola, Gorgonzola, or ricotta, fresh tomato, and olives. The wine list is small but well chosen; it even offers a few French wines. Dine outside under the pergola when the weather is nice. There's a private dining room in the wine cellar for small groups.

PIZZA

Pizzeria Il Mozzo
Via Ravizzi 1
☎02.498-4676
Closed Wednesday and August
No credit cards • low moderate

A genuine Napoletano pizza chef and a large wood-burning oven are a guarantee of this pizzeria's quality.

PIZZA

Vecchia Napoli da Rino
Via Chavez 4
☎02.261-9056
Closed Sunday lunch, Monday, and August
MasterCard, Visa • low moderate

Father and son pizza makers Rino and Massimo Francavilla, who consistently place in the European World Pizza Chef competition, prepare fragrant original pizzas in their two wood-burning ovens.

> A pizzeria is only as good as its pizzaiolo, the freewheeling professional pizza chef whose artistic temperament may frequently influence the quality of his pizza.

HOUSEWARES

Medagliani
Via San Gregorio 43
☎02.669-83073
Fax 02.670-1113
Closed Saturday
All credit cards

Medagliani has moved to a bigger location. Walk through the mall at via San Gregorio 43, and you'll find it on the left-hand side. The selection of professional kitchen equipment is better than ever, with over 6,000 items on two floors. There's every possible size of every possible object that can pass through a kitchen. Handmade copper pots, flattened sauce spoons, uniforms, carts, cleavers, cruets, meat hooks, *prosciutto* vises, roasters, sifters, ladles, rolling pins, wooden spoons, pizza peels, buckets, bowls, serving dishes, the Fuf spit roaster, KitchenAid mixers and Cuisinarts for Italian current, and much, much more. Eugenio Medagliani, chemical engineer, painter, philosopher, historian, dreamer, and third-generation restaurant supplier, has combined his spheres of interest as designer of the *pentapiatto,* a white plate with a design of ridges that creates five separate sections, each to be filled with foods that balance harmoniously, both to the eye and the stomach. Check out the display of Eugenio's antique cooking tools and mold collection. Medagliani now takes credit cards and will, as usual, send purchases anywhere.

PAPER ITEMS
Tipographia Lucini
Via Piero della Francesca 38
☎02.314-508
Fax 02.349-0257
Closed August
No credit cards

Giorgio Lucini prints the menus of Italy's gastronomic stars. For over sixty years the Lucini *tipografia* has been printing books, art prints, and more basic everyday jobs. But since Giorgio and his wife, Clara, are devout gastronomes, he prints wine lists and menus for friends who own restaurants. He chooses from over 400 types of paper, many handmade, and works with his clients to come up with a practical object. His eye for color and texture is as perceptive as his palate for taste. His work—books, prints, wine labels, menus, and wine lists—is simply beautiful. Giorgio has promised to design and print up menu forms, to be filled in for special meals, or place cards, or guest or recipe books, for those who would appreciate the work of a man I consider a print and paper artist in the grand Italian artisanal tradition. He does not accept any new work between October and January.

PUBLISHER
Carlo Ferrero
Via Madonnina 9
☎02.866-665
By appointment only
No credit cards

Carlo Scipione Ferrero and his collaborator, Maria Paleari Hennsler, used to sell old-to-ancient cookbooks and culinary memorabilia in his shop, now closed. His archive of gastronomic images has been moved. But he continues to do culinary research and publish an occasional book, beautiful editions on wonderful paper, a joy to own. The remains of Carlo's collection can be purchased through a friend's catalog.

Carlo is handsome, tall, charming, still a whirlwind of ideas, worth a visit for anyone who speaks Italian and is interested in Italian culinary history. Contact Carlo for information on his databank of culinary images.

TABLEWARE
G. Lorenzi
Via Montenapoleone 9
☎02.760-20593
Fax 02.760-03390
Closed Monday morning
All credit cards

Coltellinaio—one who makes, sells, or repairs knives and other cutting tools—is how the Lorenzi family define their profession. They've been supplying Milano with cutlery since 1919, from their Montenapoleone location since 1929, always selling nothing but the finest. Ivory and horn specialty sets—a pineapple carving set consisting of a corer of two knives; a truffle set of slicer, brush, and glass bell jar; or an elegant pair of chopsticks in an equally elegant case—are displayed like jewelry in glass cases. How have you lived without a *prosciutto* vise, *polenta* knife, sea-urchin opener, sardine shovel, a set of horn *osso buco* spoons for digging out marrow, or a mother-of-pearl caviar set, with serving pieces and individual spoons and knives? The knife selection is excellent. I love the look of the stainless-steel mesh glove, perfect for clumsy oyster shuckers or knife wielders. And amid all this elegance, the Lorenzi family still repairs and sharpens knives.

TABLEWARE
Richard Ginori
Corso Matteotti 1
☎02.760-08526
Closed Monday morning
All credit cards

The well-equipped Richard Ginori store on the corner of corso Matteotti sells a complete line of Ginori china, as well as silver and crystal by leading Italian and European manufacturers.

TABLEWARE

La Botteguccia

Via della Pergola 11

☎02.688-7580

Closed Monday

No credit cards

The Botteguccia sells Ginori seconds and leftovers at highly reduced prices, although savings will be minimized by the cost of shipping.

HOUSEWARES

Picowa

Piazza San Babila 4/D

☎/Fax 02.794-078

Closed Monday

All credit cards

Picowa has more than 3,000 objects for the kitchen on three floors filled with crystal, china, stainless steel, wood, and plastic— furnishings for the kitchen, dining room, and garden.

COOKWARE

Alessi

Corso Matteotti 9

☎02.795-726

Open 10 A.M.–7 P.M.

All credit cards

A classic postwar industrial success story, a blend of Italian technology, ingenuity, and design, Alessi has taken stainless steel and worked with it the way a sculptor works with marble. From Carlo Alessi's 1945 chrome-plated tea and coffee set, through Richard Sapper's cooking utensils created with the consultation of Europe's great cooks, a list of who's who in Italian design has shaped Alessi's tools for cooking and serving. Two exceptional books mark the Alessi commitment to the kitchen: The *Pastario* ("Pasta Atlas"), in Italian and English, with its meticulous and delightful illustrations of pasta, was published by Alessi when they introduced their pasta cooker-steamer. *La Cintura di Orione* is a chronicle of an encounter between design and function, a history of cooking from the equipment point of view, illustrated with an unbelievable richness of images of cooking utensils, with recipes by the cooks who consulted with Richard Sapper in the design of this series of elegant, expensive pots and pans.

The entire Alessi line is available in the Milano showroom, but many items are sold in housewares stores throughout Italy.

GLASSWARE

Vetrerie di Empoli

Via Pietro Verri 4

☎02.760-21656

Closed Monday

No credit cards

The lovely rustic mouth-blown glassware, plates, bowls, platters, goblets, tumblers, and decorative pieces are just part of the pleasure of this wonderful shop, with its eighteenth-century frescoes from the school of Tiepolo. Shipping can be arranged.

GLASSWARE

Venini

Via Montenapoleone 9

☎02.760-00539

Closed Monday morning

All credit cards

If you can't make it to Venezia for glass, head for via Montenapoleone, one of Milano's most elegant shopping streets, where Venini's modern mouth-blown colored glass, each piece a work of art, is sold.

GARDEN SUPPLIES

Centro Botanico

Via dell'Orso 16

☎02.864-64474

Closed Saturday, Sunday, and Monday

All credit cards

Be careful or you'll miss the entrance to the Centro Botanico, hidden in the Brera neighborhood. Walk through the courtyard and small garden, and up the stairs to the first floor, where you'll find frescoed rooms filled with books, plants, seeds, herbal creams, floral essences, dried flowers, tea, and honey. This shop offers gardening courses and caters to the needs of the urban gardener.

Montescano

INN

Il Castello di San Gaudenzio

Via Molino 1
Cervesina (close by)
☎0383.3331
Fax 0383.333-409
MasterCard, Visa • low expensive

RESTAURANT

Al Pino

Strada per Santa Maria della Versa
☎/Fax 0385.60479
Closed Tuesday and Wednesday
American Express, Diners Club • moderate

A small house in the middle of Oltrepò Pavese vines, south of Pavia, is the setting for this tiny restaurant with the huge fir tree in the front yard. Pavese chef of worldwide experience Mario Musoni, his English wife, sommelier Patricia, and their son Ivan team up to produce some of the best *cucina* in the province. Nontraditional, simply conceived dishes, usually an encounter between two distinct flavors, hallmark Mario's menu. Fresh-tasting *risotto*, probably one of the best in Italy, and a balanced menu of meat offerings and fresh fish from the Milano market on Fridays are perfectly cooked. Cheese fans will thrill to the taste of the rich, mottled blue Gorgonzola, aged *parmigiano*, and goat cheese with basil. Local wines of La Muiraghina complement the amazing, unheralded *cucina*.

Mortara

HOTEL

Bottala

Corso Garibaldi 1
☎0384.99021
Fax 0384.91593
American Express, MasterCard, Visa • inexpensive

RESTAURANT

Trattoria Guallina

Via Molino Faenza 19, Guallina
☎0384.91962
Closed Monday, Tuesday lunch
American Express, MasterCard, Visa • high moderate

The rustic Trattoria Guallina is hard to find, outside Mortara in the middle of the Lomellina-area rice fields. Owners chef Edoardo Fantasma and Rita Resente in the dining room know what they're doing and draw from fine seasonal products. In the fall and winter, goose is served in practically every course. Begin with the goose *salumi*, continue with *risotto* flavored with goose *salame* and black-eyed peas, goose liver, or braised goose. Or opt for classic *risotto* with frogs from the rice fields. Desserts include *panna cotta*, chocolate mousse, or strudel. The wine list is well chosen, focusing on reds from Piemonte and Toscana, whites from Friuli and Trentino. Stop in for a glass of wine with *salumi* and *formaggio*, a less expensive option than a whole meal.

SALUMI

Gioacchino Palestro

Via Sforza Polissena 27
☎/Fax 0384.93570
Closed Monday afternoon

Gioacchino Palestro transforms goose into salami, sausage, *prosciutto*, pâté, cracklings, and raw foie gras in Mortara, the goose capital of Lombardia, southwest of Milano. His pork products, raw salami, *zampone* and *cotechino* sausages, and Piemontese lard-preserved sausage (*salam d'la duja*) are first-rate. But it is Gioacchino's goose products that have made him famous in the wine world. Coupled at wine fairs with La Monella, a hearty red produced by a friend, these excellent *salumi* have always been the tastiest bite around. Gioacchino has won the Premio Gancia di Gancia, awarded yearly to an artisan and his products of gastronomic excellence.

Mortara's goose salami festival, held the last Sunday in September, begins with a procession of 500 locals in medieval costumes, representing the court of Lodovico il Moro (who used to hunt in the area), followed by a monumental *gioco dell'oca*, a traditional board game played, for this occasion, with human pawns. Traditional goose products are sold at stands.

Quistello

HOTEL

See Mantova

RESTAURANT

L'Ambasciata
Via Martiri di Belfiore 33
☎0376.619-003
Fax 0376.618-255
Closed Wednesday, Thursday lunch, and August
All credit cards • expensive

South of the mighty Po River, tucked in the village of Quistello, L'Ambasciata ("The Embassy") looks like a typical countryside *trattoria*. But look more carefully at the license plates on the cars in the parking lot and you'll notice that diners have come from all over Italy to sample the *cucina* of the Tamani family. The restaurant's decor is busy, with Oriental rugs, copper pots, murky paintings, and elegantly turned-out tables. Mama prepares luxurious traditional dishes, and wine-steward brothers Romano and

Francesco pamper diners and pour splendid regional and Italian wines. The menu changes with the seasons, and features local *salumi* (served with sweet and spicy *mostarda*, a regional version of chutney), *tortelli di zucca* (squash-stuffed hand-rolled pasta), sturgeon from the nearby Po, local duck, pheasant, guinea hen, and capon. Caviar and Scotch salmon are offered for Italians bored with regional family-style *cucina*, which is elevated to an art form at L'Ambasciata. Conclude your meal with the rich, deep orange–colored *zabaione* and the *torta di tagliatelle*.

Ranco

RESTAURANT-INN

Del Sole
Piazza Venezia 5
☎0331.976-507
Fax 0331.976-620
Closed Monday evening and Tuesday
All credit cards • expensive

Ristorante Albergo del Sole seems too good to be true. The domain of the perfectionist professional Brovelli family, husband and wife Carlo and Itala, and their son Davide, this small, comfortable nine-room inn faces Lago Maggiore, twenty minutes from Milano's inconveniently located Malpensa airport. The *cucina* can be inspirational. Diminutive Carlo and his son work magic with local lake ingredients and the bounty of both Milano and nearby Piemonte, turning out both traditional and creative *cucina*, lightened up and artistically arranged. Two tasting menus and a small, well-chosen seasonal à la carte menu are offered. Don't miss the local white peaches of Monate and the exceptional little pastries. The wine cellar, under the able guidance of sommelier Itala, contains a personal selection of fine Italian, French, and even some American wines. Warmweather dining on a terrace overlooking

gardens and the lake is an unforgettable experience. One of the world's finest breakfasts is served in the morning.

Trescore Cremasco

HOTEL

Ponte di Rialto
Via Cadorna 5/7
☎0373.82342
Fax 0373.83520
American Express, MasterCard, Visa • moderate

RESTAURANT

Trattoria Fulmine
Via Carrioni 12
☎/Fax 0373.273-103
Closed Sunday evening, Monday, and August
All credit cards • high moderate

What happened to turn this Lombard village *trattoria,* inconspicuously hidden behind what appears to be a neighbor-hood bar, into a culinary rising star? Gianni Bolzoni serves his wife's well-made traditional *cucina,* based on the freshest local ingredients in an area of rich, fertile farmland. The menu features fine *salumi* (including *culatello,* the heart of the *prosciutto*), homemade pasta, and vegetable soups. Farm-raised goose and duck are cooked with their livers and served with *polenta.* Gianni manages to procure the impossible-to-find *salva* cheese, made with spring milk and aged two months. Desserts are splendid, especially the custard *gelato* and the egg-yolk–rich *zabaione* served with *sabbiosa* (sand cake). The personal wine list offers Italian and French quality wines that make this well-prepared food taste even better. On a recent visit I watched as three priests (said to be knowledgeable about where to eat well) removed their collars and proceeded to accompany Fulmine's tasty home-style *cucina* with Italy's finest wines. Divine providence.

South of the river Po, bordered by the
Apennine Mountains and the Adriatic Sea,
Emilia-Romagna is a crazy quilt of provincial
spheres of influence. It's joined together by
the Roman road, the via Emilia, a vital line of
communication built by Marcus Aemilius
Lepidus in A.D. 187.

Emilia-Romagna

Dominated by ever-changing powers—Etruscans, Romans, barbarians, Guelph-Ghibelline factions, Milanese, Venetians, the Este family, the papal state—the provinces of Emilia-Romagna maintained distinct gastronomic tradi-

tions, linked by a theme as important as the via Emilia: pasta. In this region pasta making has become an art form; not only is it homemade, it is *tirata a mano*, hand-stretched (or rolled or thrown, depending on how you interpret the verb *tirare*). This is accomplished with a two-foot–long wooden rolling pin, not a metal machine. The resulting *sfoglia*, a yellow egg-yolk–rich, almost paper-thin translucent sheet of pasta, is sliced into thin or wide noodles, triangles, squares, curled around a special comb, or cut and stuffed with meat, cheese, or vegetable fillings that vary from village to village. Pasta is served in broth or simply sauced, to allow the unmasked flavors to stand out.

Both Emilia and Romagna maintain their distinct traditions in spite of their hyphenated union. Emilia's *cucina* is characterized by richness and wealth, the product of a gastronomic paradise with fertile plains of fruit trees and grazing land for livestock, resulting in cream, butter, cheese, and *salumi*. Romagna, in the southeast, has a dual personality of Adriatic seafood and Apennine Mountains grilled foods that relate closely to the *cucina* of nearby Toscana.

The Menu

Salumi

Coppa: salt-cured boneless ham from Piacenza

Culatello: the heart of the prosciutto, made from the choice rump, boned, cured for a year; precious, rare, and costly

Fiocco or fiocchetto: cured ham made from the boneless round, left over after taking out the rump for culatello

Mortadella: large, sometimes huge, smooth pork sausage studded with cubes of fat and whole peppercorns

Prosciutto di Parma: salt-cured ham from a limited area near Parma, cured for at least ten to twelve months

Prosciutto Langhirano: salt-cured ham, aged in a specific area within the geographic boundaries of Parma ham

Salame di Felino: fine-grained salami from the village of Felino

Spalla cotta di San Secondo: cured cooked shoulder ham from the village of San Secondo Parmense

Zampone, cappello da prete, cotechino, salama da sugo: cooked pork sausages, which change name and shape in each province

Antipasto

Bocconotti: vol-au-vents filled with chicken livers, sweetbreads, and sometimes truffles

Burlenghi: pan-fried unleavened pastry covered with a lard, rosemary, and garlic spread

Gnocco: deep-fried pastry, served with prosciutto, culatello, or fresh cheese

Piadina: thin rounds of stone-grilled bread dough, served with prosciutto

Scarpazzone or erbazzone: flan containing spinach, onion, and Parmesan cheese

Tigelle: yeast dough rolled into thin circles and deep-fried or grilled; served at times with a lard, garlic, and rosemary spread

Primo

Bomba di riso: baked rice mold with a filling of pigeon, in a rich mushroom sauce

Cappellacci: fresh pasta stuffed with winter squash and cheese

Cappelletti: fresh pasta shaped like an alpine soldier's hat, stuffed with rich meat and Parmesan cheese

Garganelli: homemade egg pasta formed into ridged quill shapes

Lasagne: homemade pasta layered with meat sauce, béchamel sauce, and Parmesan cheese

Lasagne verdi: lasagne made with fresh homemade spinach pasta

Passatelli: strand-shaped cheese and egg dumplings, served in broth

Pasticcio: baked pie crust filled with pasta and various sauces

Pisarei e fasò: tiny bread dumplings sauced with tomatoes and beans

Tagliatelle: flat strips of homemade egg pasta

Tagliatelle alla romagnola: with fresh tomato sauce

Tagliatelle con ragù or alla bolognese: with rich, lusty meat sauce

Tortelli: fresh homemade egg pasta stuffed with cheese and spinach, or with winter squash

Tortellini: fresh homemade egg pasta rings stuffed with meat and cheese, served in broth or with butter and cheese

Secondo

Baccalà alla bolognese: salt cod cooked with garlic, parsley, and lemon

Bollito misto: mixed boiled meats: beef, pork sausages, tongue, pig's foot, and capon, all served with green sauce and mostarda, a fruit chutney

Brodetto: Adriatic fish stew

Capretto alla piacentina: kid cooked in white wine sauce

Costoletta alla bolognese: breaded veal scallop baked with prosciutto, Parmesan cheese, and tomato or meat sauce

Lumache alla bobbiese: shelled snails cooked with celery, leeks, carrots, and wine

Salama da sugo: aged sausage made from various cuts of pork, served with mashed potato purée

Stracotto: pot roast

Trippa alla bolognese: tripe cooked with bacon, garlic, and Parmesan cheese

Zampone: pig's-foot sausage, cooked and served with mashed potatoes or lentils, or with a sauce of whipped egg yolks with balsamic vinegar

Contorno

Asparagi alla parmigiana: asparagus served with Parmesan cheese and butter

Cardi alla parmigiana: cardoons served with Parmesan cheese and butter

Tortino di patate: baked layers of mashed potato, Parmesan cheese, and butter

Formaggio

Mascarpone: rich, triple sweet cream

Parmigiano-reggiano: the king of Italian cheese, straw-colored, nutty, and unique

Pecorino: fresh or aged sheep's milk cheese, distinct

Ricotta: soft, mild fresh cheese made from whey

Squaquarone: fresh, soft, sometimes liquid

Dolce

Bensone: simple lemon cake sprinkled with almonds

Burricchi: puff pastry squares with almonds

Pan speziale: Christmas dessert of candied and dried fruits, nuts, and spices

Savor: mixed fruit—apples, pears, peaches, quince—and squash, cooked with unfermented wine

Spongata: traditional Christmas cake of nuts, honey, and raisins, enclosed in a pie crust

Torta di taglierini: crunchy cake made with fresh egg pasta, almonds, and candied fruit, in a pastry shell

Zuppa all'emiliana or **zuppa inglese:** rum-soaked sponge cake, layered with custard, preserves, and chocolate

The Wine List

Wine production in Emilia-Romagna has traditionally aimed for quantity, turning out beverages of little significance; but wineries Terre Rosse and Castelluccio are producing extraordinary wines, and others are taking notice. The region's most interesting wines are *vini da tavola*, not DOC.

Albana di Romagna is a delicate white, either dry or semi-sweet (*amabile*), and sometimes sparkling. It is Italy's first DOCG white wine, and is made from the Albana grape in the area east of the *via Emilia*. The dry white is well suited to first-course dishes, fish, and seafood. The *amabile* is served with dessert. Top producers include Fratelli Vallunga, Fattoria Paradiso, Tre Monti, and especially Fattoria Zerbina with extraordinary Scaccomatto.

Colli Bolognesi is a DOC zone outside Bologna, where eight different wine varieties are made. The best are fruity **Riesling Italico** and full, dry **Sauvignon,** both whites, and **Cabernet Sauvignon,** an elegant dry red from the Monte San Pietro area, made by Terre Rosse.

The **Colli Piacentini** DOC zone, south of Piacenza, includes eleven wines, most named after grape varieties. Best among them are **Gutturnio,** a dry red served with rich regional dishes, and white **Sauvignon,** paired with first-course pasta and soups. Top producers are Count Otto Barattieri, La Stoppa, La Tosa, and Vigerani.

More than 50 million liters of **Lambrusco,** purplish-red and sparkling, dry or semi-sweet, are made in four different DOC zones. The best are considered to be **Lambrusco di Sorbara** and **Lambrusco Grasparossa di Castelvetro.** I have tried to learn to love Lambrusco, and have been defeated. Locals seem to feel it's the best wine for their hearty rich *cucina,* and they're right—rich wines compete with the food. Top producers of Lambrusco are Cavicchioli, Francesco Bellei, Manicardi, Graziano, Moro, Villa Barbieri, and Contessa Matilde.

Pagadebit is a delicate dry white made from the nearly extinct Pagadebit grape in the province of Forlì, served with first-course dishes, and ably produced by Fattoria Paradiso.

Sangiovese di Romagna is a dry, grapy red made from the Sangiovese grape in a large area between Bologna and the coast. It is usually paired with rich first-course pasta and sauced meats. Top producers include Fratelli Vallunga, Fattoria Paradiso, Spaletti's Rocca di Ribano, Fattoria Zerbina, (and their reserve Pietramora), Cesari, Colombina, Stefano Ferrucci, Uccellina, and Tre Monti.

Nontraditional Wines. Some of the best wines produced in this region come under the classification of *vino da tavola.* Exemplary reds and whites are made by innovative winemakers. Fattoria di Paradiso makes rich red Barbarossa di Bertinoro. Terre Rosse by Vallania makes Malvasia and Chardonnay, elegant whites. Castelluccio di Gianmatteo Baldi makes Ronco Casone, Ronco dei Ciliegi, Ronco delle Ginestre, all complex reds, and Ronco del Re, a full, rich white, expensive and almost impossible to find. Fratelli Vallunga makes elegant red Rosso Armentano. Conte Otto Barattieri makes sparkling white Chardonnay and red Rosso di Vignazzo. Stoppa makes rich red Rosso di Rivergaro. Tre Monti makes Boldo and Favagello, both Cabernet-Sangiovese blends, and Tarsallo, a dry sparkling white.

Regional Specialties

Pasta. La *sfoglia* ("the sheet"), golden egg-yolk–rich pasta, translucent, paper-thin, elastic and resilient, with an almost leathery texture, achieves glory in the *cucina* of Emilia-Romagna. Sliced into thin or wide noodles, curled around a special comb, or cut and stuffed with meat, cheese, or vegetable fillings, pasta attains true stardom in this region. Is the special quality of this pasta attributable to the body English of the pasta roller (known as the *sfoglina*), a talent acquired with decades of experience? Or to the effect of the porous wooden pin and board, or of the air in which it's made? I am still researching the question, with joyful dedication, every time I cross the gastronomic frontiers of Emilia.

Balsamic Vinegar. Balsamic vinegar, *aceto balsamico,* is made from the juice of Trebbiano grapes, evaporated and concentrated in cauldrons directly over fire, and aged in progressively smaller casks of oak, chestnut, cherry, ash, and mulberry. Lengthy aging— anywhere from 12 to over 100 years—in attic storerooms exposed to winter cold and summer heat causes further evaporation.

REGIONAL PRODUCERS OF
ACETO BALSAMICO

Italo Pedroni	Mirella Leonardi Giacobazzi	Consorzio Produttori Aceto
Via Risaia 2	Via Provinciale Ovest 43	Balsamico Tradizionale di
Nonantola	Nonantola	Modena
☎ 059.549-019	☎/Fax 059.549-065	c/o Camera di Commercio
Fax 059.547-514		Via Ganaceto 134
	Cav. Ferdinando Cavalli	Modena
	Scandiano	☎ 059.236-981
	☎ 0522.983-430	Fax 059.242-565

The result is deep brown, almost syrupy, rich, aromatic, sweet and sour, almost sherrylike in flavor, and costly, at least around $80 for a tiny 100-gram bottle (less than 4 ounces). Less expensive, younger balsamic vinegars are thin, lacking the traditional richness that this unique product acquires with barrel aging. It is meant to be used sparingly, by the drop, on meat, eggs, and *parmigiano*. Local balsamic freaks drink a small amount as a *digestivo*, claiming that it stimulates digestion.

Two main groups, each claiming to be the best, attempt to ensure the quality of *aceto balsamico*. Commissions from the Consorzio of Modena and the Confraternita of Reggio examine balsamic vinegars produced within their specific geographic zones that have aged for at least twelve years, and only those that qualify carry the numbered Consorzio or Confraternita seals. A third group, the Consorteria of Spilamberto, holds a yearly competition to determine the best *aceto balsamico*.

Parmigiano-Reggiano. *Parmigiano-reggiano*, the king of cheese, has been made the same way and in the same area for over 700 years. In the *Decameron* Boccaccio describes Bengodi, a make-believe paradise with a mountain of grated *parmigiano*, topped with people making pasta and rolling it down the slopes to coat it with the cheese.

Each wheel of *parmigiano* is made from around 640 liters (170 gallons) of fresh milk from two successive milkings (the evening milk is skimmed, but the morning milk is added whole). The milk is heated in copper cauldrons, stirred, drained in cheesecloth, pressed into a circular wooden mold to shape the cheese, and finally removed. The newly made cheeses are then soaked in brine and placed on wooden shelves to ripen. After a year the cheese is usually sold to an intermediary for further aging in special rooms that may hold up to 200,000 precious wheels of *parmigiano*. These cheese vaults are frequently managed by banks, which may loan money to the dairy or intermediary against eventual profits. Expert cheese testers tap the wheels of *parmigiano* with a hammer, and the resulting thuds sound out defects to the professional ear. Perfect *parmigiano-reggiano* is firm-textured, straw-colored with pale flecks, fragrant but not pungent, delicate, nutty, studded with crunchy granules (a product of the aging process), and unique. It is in no way related to the hyper-processed foul-smelling stuff that comes pre-grated in a jar, a state in which no cheese can survive naturally. Each dairy that makes *parmigiano-reggiano* stamps its number, assigned by geographical location, on the cheese it produces. Lower numbers are closer to the original production zone between Parma and Reggio, although the one- and two-digit dairies are no longer in existence.

TOP PORK PRODUCERS IN EMILIA

Consorzio del Prosciutto di Parma
Via Marco dell'Arpa 8/B
Parma
☎0521.243-987
Fax 0521.243-983

Ermes Fontana
Via per San Vitale 145
Sala Baganza
☎0521.835-631
(*prosciutto, coppa, sahuni*)

Peppino Cantarelli
San Busseto
☎0524.90133
Closed Sunday, open shop hours
(*culatello* and other regional salumi)

Salumificio Boschi
Via G. Verdi 21
Felino
☎0521.835-801
(*spalla di San Secondo* and *salame di Felino*)

Garetti
Piazza Duomo 44
Piacenza
☎0523.322-747
Closed Thursday afternoon
(*coppa*)

Some Pig! Pork Products from Emilia.
Curing pork is an art form in Emilia and, typically enough, each town and province is convinced that its special pork product is superior. Neutered pigs feed on the whey left over from making *parmigiano-reggiano* in addition to their usual grain diet, which makes them fatter and sweeter than those of other regions. *Prosciutto di Parma*, probably the most famous of Italy's cured pork products, is made in a specific geographic area around Parma, of whole thighs that by law may come from only four regions (Emilia-Romagna, Lombardia, Veneto, and Piemonte). *Prosciutto di Langhirano,* produced in a DOC zone south of Parma, gets less attention but can be equal in quality. Fresh pork thighs are massaged with salt and hung to age in open-windowed rooms, basking in special local air, said to be the key to the unique flavors of this legendary cured ham.

True porcophiles should seek out *culatello,* considered to be the finest pork product of the region, made from the hind muscle of a boned pork thigh. Leftover parts are used to make *fiocchetto* and *capello da prete. Culatello* is far more expensive than *prosciutto,* produced illegally by artisans, with far less success by industrials. The heart of the thigh is lightly salted and spiced, tucked into a bladder, tied with string in a weblike

pattern, dried in a well-aired environment for two to three months, then transferred to a dark, humid cellar with packed dirt floors and old brick walls, for five to twelve months of damp aging. It loses about half its weight in the aging process, leaving the string web hanging like old clothes on a successful dieter. Local health authorities have decided that the traditional environment is unsanitary and want *culatello* makers to tile their cellars, eliminating the natural humidity that seeps up from the underground lagoon. Industrial producers have complied with the law, but artisans still make *culatello* on the sly; it's rarely found in commercial outlets but is available at many fine restaurants in the region. See page 271 for the ultimate *culatello* tasting in San Secondo.

Pork lovers should also try to taste other fine products, like *coppa Piacentina,* made from the neck; *fiocchetto,* of the shoulder or the lower part of the thigh; *gola,* of the throat, tied and pressed between boards; *salame di Felino, salame* from the hills outside Parma; *spalla di San Secondo,* cured and cooked; *mortadella* of finely ground scraps studded with cubes of lard and cooked. Seek out *salame da sugo, cotechino, capello da prete,* and *zampone,* all subjected to slow, lengthy cooking in regional restaurants in the winter. Rendered pork cracklings—called *grassoli* or *greppole* regionally, *ciccioli* in Italian—are sold in food shops.

Formaggio di Fossa. "Cheese from a ditch" is made in Romagna, beginning like a conventional *pecorino* but aged with a highly unusual process. Supposedly, the inhabitants of Sogliano hid their just-made cheese in ditches outside town during a lengthy invasion, and when the coast was clear, they dug up their cheese, transformed to a far better bite than the cheese they had interred. It's not that easy to find, still aged in communal four-meter–deep cylindrical ditches lined with straw. Cloth sacks of cheese are stacked in the ditches in mid-August, sealed for three months, covered with a wooden lid topped with sand, to be opened on November 25, the festival of Saint Catherine. The cheese can be found in groceries and restaurants in the region. Three generations of the Mengozzi family have aged cheese in veterinarian Dott. Rossi's ditch in Sogliano. Cheese lovers can call or fax to peer into the empty ditch, and they may be able to purchase a cheese after the ditch is opened in late November (via Pascoli 8, tel./fax 0541.948-009).

Flatbreads. I've never been able to work up any enthusiasm for the bread of Emilia and Romagna with its smooth, thin, tan hard crust and cottony white fluff inside, in spite of entertaining shapes like the four-legged *coppia*, "couple." Focus instead on wonderful regional flatbreads like *tigelle, borlengo, piadina, crescentina,* or *gnocco ingrassato.* They're baked in the oven or on griddles, terra-cotta rounds, or pans over hot coals. I'm wild about *gnocco fritto,* a hollow puff of fried dough, found in many Emilian restaurants. Most of these flatbreads are eaten as a snack, plain or paired with *prosciutto* or lard.

Nocino. Green unripe walnuts are harvested on June 24, the feast of San Giovanni, infused in alcohol and sugar for forty days,

then aged for a year to produce *nocino,* inky-brown, sweet, and potent. Many restaurants throughout the region make their own *nocino,* served after coffee as a digestive. Fans can purchase first-rate *nocino* from Giusti in Modena (see page 264) or beg a favorite restaurant for a bottle.

Pasta Rolling Pin. The one-handled wooden rolling pin (*matterello*), traditional in parts of Emilia for pasta making, can be found in housewares stores in the Bologna area. But this object will have no meaning for you until you have seen an actual demonstration of pasta rolling, a manual ballet performed with pasta, pin, and board, gestures executed with a familiarity that comes with a lifetime of experience. In Bologna the wielders of the rolling pin roll out a circle of pasta; in Modena they form an oval.

Crafts. Linen cloth is decorated with traditional designs in parts of Romagna, and made into tablecloths, napkins, kitchen towels, aprons, bedspreads, and curtains. A paste of minerals, flour, and vinegar is applied to wood blocks, and then pressed onto natural, off-white, coarse linen. Indelibly printed red, green, blue, and most of all, rust-colored country-style patterns of grapes and grape leaves, griffins, roosters, fruits, and flowers, which are among the traditional designs. See page 263 for one source.

The glazed, richly colored earthenware pottery known as *faience* (French for Faenza) has been produced in Faenza since the end of the thirteenth century. Periods of glory for this majolica (*maiolica*) center were the sixteenth century for decorative items, and the eighteenth and nineteenth centuries for tableware. See page 261 for a museum, an exposition, and a source of reproductions.

Cities & Towns

Alseno

HOTEL
Cortina
In Cortina
☎0523.948-101
All credit cards • inexpensive

RESTAURANT
Da Giovanni
Cortina Vecchia
☎0523.948-304
Fax 0523.948-355
Closed Monday evening and Tuesday
All credit cards • high moderate

Da Giovanni is a destination for food lovers. It's comfortable, with intimate antique-filled dining rooms with fireplaces burning during the cold weather months, and a rustic pergola on the site of what was once a *bocce* court, with cane ceilings and walls and stone floors covered with Oriental carpets for dining the rest of the year. The restaurant was founded by Giovanni Besenzoni, who's still in the kitchen, with his son Renato in the dining room. The large menu offers a lovely selection of traditional and creative dishes. Begin with first-rate *salumi* like *culatello, coppa, gola,* and *salame,* paired with a glass of local sparkling wine. All pasta is hand-rolled—look for hard-wheat *cavatelli* sauced with lamb *ragu,* ravioli stuffed with nettles, fantastic *pisarei e fasoi,* pasta and bean soup. Main-course options include stuffed boned duck, spit-roasted pork, guinea-hen breast with *renette* apples, or fish like sturgeon or salmon. Choose the regional tasting menu for traditional dishes or the squab-stuffed ravioli to be rewarded with a Buon Ricordo souvenir plate. Desserts like homemade *sorbetto, latte in piede* custard, bavarians,

and *sbrisolona* are worth saving room for. Finish with a taste of the fine cookies and meringues. The wine list is simply amazing—enophiles will have a field day with older vintages, although I enjoyed the Besenzoni family's own production, which paired well with their food.

RESTAURANT-ROOMS
Boschi
Cortina di Alseno
☎0523.948-102
Closed Wednesday
MasterCard, Visa • moderate restaurant, inexpensive hotel

Burton Anderson told me about the hotel-restaurant Boschi, owned by a *culatello*-and-*salumi* expert. The six-room hotel is inexpensive, the restaurant unmentioned in any guidebooks, but the locals have no problem with Boschi's lack of fame. As would be expected, *salumi* like *prosciutto* and *culatello* are superb. Fresh *porcini* mushrooms are served in all courses when they're in season or preserved under oil the rest of the year. Pasta is homemade, stuffed with *porcini* or winter squash. *Risotto alla parmigiana* is rich, flavored with first-rate *parmigiano.* Grilled mushrooms or guinea hen baked in clay are main-course offerings. Desserts are simple.

Argelato

HOTEL
See Bologna

RESTAURANT
L'800
Via Centese 33
☎/Fax 051.893-032
Closed Sunday evening and Monday
MasterCard, Visa, Diners Club • moderate

Franco Martelli and his wife, Loredana, are proud of their daughters. Both Deborah and Jessica are professional sommeliers (as is Dad), and Jessica works magic in the kitchen along with Deborah's fiancé Alessandro Formaggi. The family restaurant, a building from the 1800s (hence the name), specializes in dishes made with snails, frogs, mushrooms and black truffles, and all fine local products. Franco Loredana and Deborah bustle through two attractive dining rooms filled with gastronomes from Bologna who are onto a good thing. Jessica makes the dough for pasta by hand, rolls it out on a wooden board, and creates ethereal *tortellini*, *tortelloni*, and *tagliatelle*. Main course options include rabbit fillet, radicchio dressed with *guanciale* pork jowl, and filet mignon. Save room for the grilled *pecorino* with bitter honey and desserts like seasonal fruit bavarians, custard gelato with caramelized figs, or fruit sorbet. Keep decisions to a minimum with one of the bargain-priced tasting menus featuring mushrooms, snails, or black truffles. As would be expected from a family with so many sommeliers, the wine list is a sheer joy, with lots of unheard of but splendid local wines, as well as a selection of Italian and foreign gems.

Bagno di Romagna

HOTEL-RESTAURANT
Paolo Teverini
Piazza Dante 2
☎0543.911-260
Fax 0543.911-014
Always open
All credit cards • high moderate

Chef-owner Paolo Teverini's restaurant has been a favorite for years of those who love creative cooking, and he and his wife, Giordana, have brought a new twist to their successful formula of elegant restaurant next to an attractive hotel with a pool. They've added a health club called Gaia Teverina,

and Paolo has created a series of diet menus in a region known not to take anything seriously that doesn't have at least three forms of cholesterol in it. Gaia Teverina is probably the only place in the entire region, and one of the few in Italy, where losing weight isn't a painful (and expensive) experience. Those who are on the protein diet can drink from Paolo's extensive wine list.

Bibbiano

CHEESE
Dairy 193–Nuova Barco
Giancarlo Grisendi
Via 24 Maggio 56
☎0522.875-182

A visit to Nuova Barco is an instant lesson in *parmigiano*. If you're interested in seeing the cheesemaking process, plan to arrive early in the morning. All visitors can purchase a chunk for less than store price, and the dairy's always open, Giancarlo told me, because the cows don't go on vacation.

Bologna

Bologna, the heart of Emilia (or of all Italy, according to locals) beats strongly, in spite of the cholesterol content of the extra-rich Bolognese *cucina*. This is the birthplace of the oversized *mortadella*, pink sausage studded with creamy cubes of pork fat; of *tortellini*, forcemeat-stuffed fresh pasta rings; and of *ragù alla bolognese*, richer and headier than a meat sauce—all triumphs of meat and spice, symphonies of flavors. The Bolognese seem to have been impressed by nouvelle cuisine, and many famous restaurants serve "creative" dishes. They are not mentioned here. The splendid medieval towers, Gothic churches, pleasant arcades, and eleventh-century university are a delightful setting for one of Italy's major pasta cults.

HOTEL

Grand Hotel Baglioni
Via Indipendenza 8
☎051.225-445
Fax 051.234-840
All credit cards • luxury

HOTEL

Al Capello Rosso
Via Fusar 9
☎051.261-891
Fax 051.227-179
All credit cards • expensive

HOTEL

Touring
Via de' Mattuiani 1/2
☎051.584-305
Fax 051.334-763
All credit cards • moderate

BAR-CAFFÈ, PASTRY

Roberto
Via Orefici 9/A
☎051.232-256
Closed Friday

Smoking is not allowed in Roberto's wonderful *bar-pasticceria*. A glass of sparkling water, served on a coaster, is offered to all clients at this always crowded bar near the market. The coffee is wonderful, triangular sandwiches (*tramezzini*), fresh, glossy miniature rolls filled with quality *salumi*, are tasty snacks, pastry is well made, and the service is rapid and friendly. And all these wonders are available in a smoke-free ambience, rare indeed in Italy. Hooray for Roberto!

Market. The Bologna market is too dynamic to limit itself to a single piazza like most Italian cities. It sprawls through the streets—via Orefici, via Mercanzie, via Capraie, via Drapperie—perfumed with produce, packed with residents pinching, poking, sorting, intent on selecting the best before someone else grabs it up. The fruit is especially fine. Mornings only.

CHEESE

La Baita Freo
Via Pescherie Vecchie 3/A
☎051.223-940
Closed Thursday afternoon

La Baita Freo has the best selection of cheese in Bologna. Look for *squaquarone*, a fresh, soft, sometimes liquid cheese, and *parmigiano-reggiano*. Nonregional gems include three different ripenesses of Gorgonzola, a wide selection of *pecorino* sheep's-milk cheeses, at least ten kinds of mozzarella, and layered cream cheese and salmon or herb *torte*.

SPECIALTY FOODS

Salsamenteria Tamburini
Via Caprarie 1
☎051.234-354
Fax 051.232-226
Closed Thursday afternoon

The windows and glass display cases of Tamburini are a monument to the *cucina bolognese*, a triumph of local products, and contain the ingredients for an instant banquet. Butter, cheese, and yogurt made from water buffalo (*bufala*) milk are all first-rate. The selection of *salumi* is overwhelming—choose from over thirty different *prosciutti di Parma, culatello*, and *coppa*. Salami, *zampone* ("big paw") sausage packed in a pig's shin and foot, and various sausages (*insaccati*, "sacked meats") are made by Tamburini using quality meat, salt, and pepper—no extraneous herbs or spices to distract from their intensely porky flavor. The cannon-size *mortadella* sausage is world-class. Thousands of golden handmade *tortellini* in various sizes flank a wood-burning fireplace, where chicken, quail, and large cuts of meat turn on a vertical merry-go-round of spits. The take-out section has over seventy-five prepared dishes and salads. Tamburini is irresistible.

BAKERY

Panetteria e Pastificio Atti

Via Drapperie 6, via Caprarie 7

☎051.220-425

Closed Thursday afternoon

Atti's windows are lined with breads in all sizes, shapes, and hues of golden brown, plus homemade pasta, *tortellini, tagliatelle,* and vol-au-vents. Handwritten notes extoll the virtues of these fine products. Cookies, pastries, spiced *pan speziale, torta bolognese di tagliatelle, tagliatelle* cake, and apricot "ravioli" are among Atti's tempting specialties. A second location at via Caprarie 7 sells the same fine products.

FRUIT AND VEGETABLES

Fratelli Fortuzzi

Via Castiglione 91

☎051.332-692

Closed Thursday and Saturday afternoons

Primizie, the first examples of seasonal fruit and vegetables, are a specialty of this shop, along with fresh herbs and practically every exotic import available in Italy. Mushrooms and truffles are available in season.

CHOCOLATE

Majani

Via Carbonesi 5

☎051.234-302

Closed Thursday afternoon

Majani, founded in 1796, is a legendary chocolate shop. The specialty is the Fiat *cremino,* first created in 1911, a creamy, square, squat two-tone layered hazelnut and chocolate confection, sold throughout Italy. The shop, which opened in 1834, is the only place to get Majani's *cannellini,* crispy cookie tubes stuffed with the Fiat filling. Roman ruins have been discovered under this historic chocolate shop; they've been restored but still aren't on view. Maybe by the time this book comes out things will have changed. Chocoholics will want to visit Majani just to be sure.

RESTAURANT

Diana

Via Indipendenza 24

☎051.231-302

Fax 051.228-162

Closed Monday

All credit cards • high moderate

Marcella and Victor Hazan recommended the Diana to me and, as usual, their advice was right on target. The restaurant serves classic Bolognese cooking at its very best, with a few concessions for locals bored with traditional fare. Eros Palmirani runs a tight ship; service is swift and professional in the large dining room, with outdoor dining on a side street when the weather is nice. I usually focus on the appetizers, eat multiple pasta courses, and never get around to the rest of the menu—who could resist perfect *tortellini, passatelli,* green *lasagna* or hand-rolled *tagliatelle,* sauced with *ragù? Porcini* mushrooms and white truffles are paired with pasta in season. Those with culinary stamina can continue with roast meats or *bollito misto* from the cart, served with *salsa verde,* green sauce, or *mostarda,* sort of like a whole-fruit chutney. Game is prepared in season. The dessert cart is laden with classics that seem attractive enough although I've never been tempted. The wine list has its highs and lows—exigent palates should drink anything from the nearby Vallania winery.

RESTAURANT

Antica Osteria Romagnola

Via Rialto 13

☎051.263-699

Closed Monday, Thursday lunch, and August

All credit cards • high moderate

The Antica Osteria Romagnola feels like a local tavern, with marble tables, a wine-bottle–lined bar, and an attractive red and chrome slicing machine—in use, but displayed like a jewel. Owner Antonio Amura is from Napoli, and his *cucina* is a blend of sturdy Bolognese with southern-style vegetables and herbs. The vast *antipasto* of vegetable salads using seasonal bounty will probably be a complete meal for most diners. Eggplant fans will find their favorite purple-skinned vegetable treated with respect in practically every course. Meat, and fish on Friday, are nicely sauced; desserts are well done and not excessively sweet. The wine selection is good, and even the Lambrusco is drinkable.

RESTAURANT
Da Sandro al Navile
Via Sostegno 15
☎051.634-3100
Fax 051.634-7592
Closed Sunday and August
American Express, Diners Club, MasterCard •
high moderate

Sandro Montanari's restaurant is in a farmhouse on the banks of the Navile Canal in suburban Bologna. His wife, Silvana, rules in the kitchen and prepares all the pasta, a task of great importance in Bologna. The ambience is country, with low beamed ceilings, and walls covered with *trattoria* art, gastronomic awards, bottles, and lamps. The tables are set with salmon-colored tablecloths and the heaviest service plates I've ever seen, over six pounds of distressed

bronze. Appetizers are interesting, but I can't resist concentrating on the pasta, tasting two or three traditional offerings, each one perfection. The main course is anticlimactic, but the *parmigiano* is worth saving room for. Sandro makes all the desserts—including sweet and gooey triflelike *paciugo* or simple *ciambella*, a lemony ring-shaped cake. The wine list offers many older Tuscan, Piemontese, and French wines in addition to a few local gems.

HOUSEWARES
Aguzzeria del Cavallo
Via Drapperia 12
☎051.263-411
Closed Thursday afternoon
No credit cards

Knives and unusual kitchen accessories are sold in this charming wooden-floored tack shop perfumed with leather and wax. Riding, hunting, and fishing gear are also sold, and have been for the last 205 years, by the Bernagozzi family.

COOKWARE, TABLEWARE
Schiavina
Via Clavature 16
☎051.223-3438
Closed Thursday afternoon
American Express, MasterCard, Visa

It seems only logical that the Bolognese would furnish their kitchens and set their tables with the finest. Schiavina has an interesting selection of Italian and imported cookware, crystal, wooden objects, china, and accessories.

Brisighella
HOTEL
Terme
Viale delle Terme 37
☎/Fax 0546.81144
No credit cards • low moderate

HOTEL

Relais Torre Pratesi

Cavina 11, Fognano

☎**0546.84545**

Fax 0546.84558

All credit cards • low expensive

Letizia and Nerio Raccagni of La Grotta fell in love with a medieval tower and farmhouse not far from their restaurant, but it was too large for two so they created a delightful hotel in addition to their own residence. Set amid olive trees and grapevines that produce extra virgin olive oil and wine for the restaurant, the farmhouse is impeccably restored, with only four tastefully furnished rooms and three apartments with modern lighting and large bathrooms with fantastic amenities. The breakfast is one of the best in Italy, more like a brunch: *salumi, frittate,* just-baked cookies and cakes, vegetables preserved under oil, toast, homemade preserves, fruit salad, and more.

RESTAURANT

La Grotta

Via Metelli 1

☎**0546.81829**

Fax 0546.84558

Closed Tuesday and January

American Express, Diners Club, Visa •

inexpensive to moderate

La Grotta is located in a genuine stone grotto, a spectacular backdrop for a special restaurant. The *cucina* is original, the result of a collaboration between owner-sommelier Nerio Raccagni, who reminds me of a munchkin, and his son, chef Pierluisi. Nerio speaks rapid-fire Italian, as if he can't communicate his passion for everything local fast enough. Three fixed-price menus change daily, offering traditional, light, or more complex meals, created with the best fresh seasonal produce, meat, and fish. The simple, beautifully prepared dishes that exit

from the minuscule kitchen are tasty. Nerio seems to know the name of each farmer responsible for each item in the restaurant. The dishes are beautiful hand-painted Faenza pottery (see page 261), and the place mats are rust-dyed, from Gambettola (see page 263). Save room for some of the special cheeses, unavailable elsewhere. Most people seem to enjoy the cereal coffee, which tastes like dirty water to me. Wines are wonderful, beautifully selected, and enhance the *cucina*—especially those of Castellucio.

OLIVE OIL

Cooperative Agricola Brisighellese Frantoio Sociale per Olive

Via Firenze 30/A

☎**0546.81103**

Cholesterol-loving Emilians practically scorn the use of full-flavored extra virgin olive oil, but it is used to advantage in the cooking of Romagna. A small amount of quality oil is produced in the Brisighella area by a local farmers' cooperative. It can be purchased here or at La Grotta.

Cafragna

HOTEL

Cavalieri

Fornovo di Taro

Frazione Salita

☎**0525.3100**

Fax 0525.400-100

No credit cards • inexpensive

HOTEL

See Parma

RESTAURANT

Trattoria di Cafragna

Cafragna

☎**0525.2363**

Closed Sunday evening, Monday

Diners Club, MasterCard, Visa • moderate

Cafragna isn't on my most detailed maps and may be difficult to find since there are few signs, although the drive is lovely and the food, wine, and ambience at the *trattoria* at the end of the road are definitely worth seeking it out. Take the Collecchio–Fornovo road from Parma, turn left at Ponte Scodogna, and turn right at the woods of Carrega, passing farms and rich cultivated countryside. The paved road stops, and the only building around is this simple *trattoria* with a small grocery and wine shop in the entrance. Adele Camorali enthusiastically welcomes diners, and her husband, chef Giancarlo Camorali, rewards them for their navigational skills with some of the best traditional food in the area. The ambience is cozy, with wooden wainscoting, attractive flower arrangements, a fire-

place that blazes in the winter. *Salumi,* especially *prosciutto, culatello, gola,* and salami are first-rate, not to be missed. Butter and superior *parmigiano-reggiano* are the condiments of choice for homemade *tagliatelle* and ravioli. The house specialty, *risotto* with local white truffles, is rich and creamy. Giancarlo prepares interesting second courses like veal shank with rosemary, braised pork ribs, rabbit, duck, guinea hen for those with hearty appetites. His supplier of *parmigiano* knows that a defective cheese will be sent back, and diners should save room for a taste of this superlative cheese. Homemade tarts, cakes, and chocolate mousse will satisfy dessert lovers. The house wine is worth drinking, although Adele has a fine, well-priced wine list.

ESPRESSO MACHINE

In my quest for the perfect espresso maker I've built up quite a collection. The oldest piece is a moka, the classic Italian burner-top coffee-maker, low-tech, easy to use, but the results are nothing like an espresso at a bar. I graduated to my first electric machine, a Pavoni, with an impressive-looking chrome column, black plastic knobs, and a pressure gauge. It never made great coffee although it steamed milk well. I moved on to a Saeco which I disliked—sloppy, spattering coffee all over, and steam wasn't sufficient to properly foam milk. I bought a Krups espresso machine made for Illy Caffè, utilizing ground coffee or Illy's prepackaged pressed pods of coffee, which make espresso-making effortless. But the Krups was slow to make more than two coffees and I called Illy to ask what the best machine for home use was. They got me in touch with Euromatik, a company that makes espresso machines for offices and small restaurants. I ordered their best model, Espresso Steam, which now sits on my counter, winking its red light at me, signaling that it's ready to make a perfect espresso.

I'm in love. The machine is imposing, sturdy, rectangular, chrome and black with red switches and lights. It uses the Illy pods, more expensive than ground coffee but they eliminate messy (and possibly inaccurate) measuring. An Illy pod is placed on the filter, locked firmly in place by a lever, a button is pushed to force hot water under high pressure through the pod. The results are a flawless espresso, almost syrupy in texture, topped with crema, a burnished foam that's usually achieved only with professional machines. The steaming wand is powerful; it foams milk for cappuccino to perfection. The Euromatik is expensive, around $600, but worth it if you're looking for the ultimate espresso machine. Contact Euromatik, via Parini 10, Castelecchio di Reno, tel. 051.613-0752, fax 051.590-136 for more information.

Casalecchio di Reno

HOTEL

See Bologna

RESTAURANT

Biagi

Via Porettana 273

☎**051.572-063**

Closed Sunday evening and Tuesday

No credit cards • moderate

The Ristorante Biagi, just off the Casalecchio exit of the *autostrada,* a few minutes south of Bologna, looks like an annex of the AGIP gas station next door. The decor is quintessential *trattoria,* tidy, with small copper kettles of flowers on the tables. The *cucina* is classic, pure Bolognese, perfected by years of experience. Stick to the local specialties and do not miss the exquisite tiny *tortellini* (ten to the soupspoon), served in a tasty broth that lets the splendid tastes and textures of this dish sing out. The *cotechino* or *zampone* (cooked pork sausages) and the *costoletta alla bolognese* (breaded fried veal topped with melted cheese, wrapped with *prosciutto*) are served with mashed potatoes that are the essence of comfort food. Finish your meal with the superb homemade *gelato,* either egg-yolk–rich custard (*crema*) for the intrepid, or light lemony ice (*sorbetto di limone*) for the fainthearted. Wines aren't up to the rest of the experience. Postcard collectors will be thrilled by the souvenir card of Ivano Biagi in the kitchen with his *tortellini* crafters.

Castelfranco Emilia

RESTAURANT-INN

Villa Gaidello

Via Gaidello 18

☎**059.926-620**

Closed Sunday, Monday, and August

All credit cards • moderate

Villa Gaidello is three rustic apartments in a restored farmhouse plus a reservations-only fixed-menu restaurant, all on a working farm in the flat Emilian countryside, owned and run by Paola Bini. The restaurant is in a carefully restored hayloft, and the setting is perfect for the meal that unfolds, with its family-type service and home-style *cucina.* Rustic unpuréed soups and pasta are delicious. Featherweight *gnocco* and *crescentina* (fried breads) are served with tasty *salumi* and onions marinated in balsamic vinegar. Chicken, rabbit, guinea hen, vegetables, and fruit all come from the farm and are full-flavored. Fresh fruit tart and *frutta sotto spirito* (liquor-soaked cherries, grapes, and apricots) are topped with whipped cream. Wines are from the farm, and not up to the quality of the *cucina.* The apartments are an ideal base for touring the area, and you'll be close to Nonantola, home of one of the area's great restaurants (see page 265).

Castelvetro

HOTEL

See Modena or Vignola

HOTEL

Green Park

Via Giardini 440

Casinalbo (close by)

☎**059.511-200**

Fax 059.511-306

Diners Club, Visa • low moderate

RESTAURANT

Al Castello

Piazza Roma 7

☎**/Fax 059.790-276**

Closed Monday, January

American Express, Diners Club, MasterCard • high moderate

Located in a castle, this restaurant serves classic regional *cucina* with a Modenese accent. The *salumi* are served with whole-wheat fried pasta pillows (*crescenta fritta*) and crunchy purple pickled onions, a sensational trio of tastes. Homemade pasta is fine, especially the *tortellini*. The *fritto misto*—a procession of deep-fried seasonal vegetables, meats, flowers, and even a fried rice pudding—is nicely done. Meat dishes are anticlimactic, but the *parmigiano* is splendid. Finish with strawberries and balsamic vinegar, a local classic combination, made with owner Mario Pelloni's vinegar. Visit the attic across the street, where he makes his wonderful vinegar, for sale—along with preserves, pickled onions, and other fine homemade products—in La Vecchia Dispensa ("The Old Pantry"), adjacent to the restaurant. Local wines are disappointing, and the nonlocals are expensive. Dine under canvas umbrellas on the terrace when the weather is nice.

Castrocaro Terme

HOTEL

Prati
Via Samori 6
☎**0543.767-531**
Fax 0543.766-034
All credit cards • low moderate

RESTAURANT

La Frasca
Via Matteotti 34
☎**0543.767-471**
Fax 0543.766-625
Closed Tuesday, January, and part of September
All credit cards • expensive

La Frasca is considered one of Italy's gastronomic temples, but I found Gianfranco Bolognesi's restaurant a series of contrasts, not all of them harmonious. The intimate rustic stone dining rooms have odd touches of sophistication. The table is set with silver candelabra, long-stemmed glassware, and Faenza pottery dinnerware.

The tone is hushed and formal. The *cucina* has, until recently, been exclusively creative, composed of overly delicate perfumes, occasionally using quality local products. Large and small tasting menus give a perspective of this inventive, somewhat bland, but perfectly executed *cucina*. The third and newest of the fixed menus is called *Sapore di Romagna*, "The Tastes of Romagna," and it features samples of hearty regional food, professionally prepared. Enjoy *garganelli* (handmade pasta with a rich, velvety *ragù* sauce), stuffed rabbit, and other decisively flavored dishes. The cheese is especially fine, and desserts are beautifully presented. Gianfranco's wine cellar is one of Italy's finest, and his regional selections are impeccable. A small gift shop sells beautiful rust-stamped table linens and Faenza ceramics.

Cavriago

HOTEL

Posta
Piazza Cesare Battisti 4
Reggio nell'Emilia (close by)
☎**0522.432-944**
Fax 0522.452-602
All credit cards • expensive

HOTEL

Reggio
Via San Giuseppe 7
☎**0522.451-533**
Fax 0522.452-602
All credit cards • moderate

RESTAURANT

Picci
Via XX Settembre 2
☎**0522.371-801**
Fax 0522.577-180
Closed Monday, Tuesday, and August
All credit cards • low expensive

Raffaele Piccirilli, known as Picci, is crazy

about mushrooms and goose. He has composed a menu based on his passions, with three tasting meals. Two are studies in monomania, devoted to mushrooms and goose products, which turn up everywhere but dessert. The third menu is seasonal. They are all good excuses for avoiding the seemingly exhaustive options of Picci's five-page menu. *Salumi* are first-rate, and mushroom dishes, usually available spring through fall, are well done. Grilled lamb chops with Picci's own balsamic vinegar are a splendid combination. The wine list is as exhaustive as the menu, and Italian, French, and even Californian, but especially regional, selections are fine, although the Lambrusco is, as usual, disappointing.

Collecchio

HOTELS

See Parma

RESTAURANT

Ceci

Villa Maria Luigia

☎**0521.805-489**

Fax 0521.805-711

Closed Thursday, most of August, and January

American Express, Diners Club, MasterCard •

expensive

Villa Maria Luigia, surrounded by manicured lawn and massive trees, is an elegant restaurant in the grand Parma tradition. The daily menu is aimed mainly at locals bored with familiar dishes, but the regional *cucina* is well done. *Culatello*, the heart of the *prosciutto*, is pale pink, sweet, and delicate. The homemade stuffed pasta—*tortelli* and *anolini*—are glorious, and the *stracotto* (beef braised for two days in red wine) is tasty. A nontraditional "fantasy" of grilled vegetables was a welcome sight in this region that regards anything without cholesterol with suspicion. The *parmigiano-reggiano* is fantastic. Desserts are

hyper-caloric, although the small pastries (*piccola pasticceria*) are irresistible. The wine list is strong on Friulan white wines and Piemontese and Tuscan reds.

Faenza

MUSEUM

Museo Internazionale della Ceramica

Via Campidori 2

☎**0546.21240**

Closed Monday

The Museo Internazionale della Ceramica documents the history of the ceramic arts of all ages and countries, and its fine collection includes beautifully displayed examples of prehistoric, pre-Columbian, Italian Renaissance, and Faenza pottery as well as more modern pieces by Chagall, Matisse, and Picasso.

EXPOSITION

Manifestazione Internazionale della Ceramica d'Arte Contemporanea/Mostra Antiquariato di Ceramica

Palazzo Esposizioni

Corso Mazzini 92

☎**0546.22294**

Faenza hosts one of Europe's most important modern ceramics competitions in July (odd-numbered years) and an antique ceramics exposition in late September (even-numbered years). For more information call the Palazzo Esposizioni.

TABLEWARE

Gatti di Dante Servadei

Via Pompignoli 4

☎**0546.30556**

No credit cards

The best reproductions of traditional *faenza* pottery are made by Dante Servadei. The Gatti studio, where he has always worked, was founded in 1928, and all work is still done by hand. Traditional designs from the eighteenth century are beautifully executed; the carnation (*garofano*), acorn (*ghiande*), and vine-leaf (*foglio di vite*) patterns are personal favorites. Dante welcomes visitors to his workshop-showroom, so that they can see the process involved in the creation of his lovely *faenza* pottery. The store in piazza della Libertà (closed Monday) doesn't have the same selection and lacks the excitement of the workshop.

Ferrara

HOTEL

Ripagrande
Via Ripagrande 21
☎**0532.765-250**
Fax 0532.764-377
All credit cards • expensive

HOTEL

Europa
Corso Giovecca 49
☎**0532.205-456**
Fax 0532.212-120
All credit cards • moderate

RESTAURANT

La Provvidenza
Via Ercole d'Este 92
☎**0532.205-187**
Closed Monday
All credit cards • moderate

La Provvidenza is on a charming, river-rock–paved road in the center of town. Chef Claudio Schiappapietri makes both regional and Italian classics, Germana Moretti makes the desserts, Alessio Magri rules in the rustic but well-appointed dining rooms. Choose appetizers from the extensive buffet of platters or order garlicky *salame* or fine *prosciutto*, served with melon in season. Pasta is homemade, dressed with classic and innovative sauces based on vegetables, which aren't usually taken too seriously in Emilia. *Cappelletti* are served in broth. *Porcini*

mushrooms are offered in season. Traditional dishes like *salama da sugo* with mashed potatoes; greaseless *fritto misto all'Italiana*, a lightly breaded sweet-and-savory medley; duck breast with balsamic vinegar; and baked veal shin as well as grilled meats are second-course possibilities. The dessert cart, especially the *torta di tagliatelle*, may tempt those with a sweet tooth. The wine list is ample, studded with gems.

Forlimpopoli

HOTEL

Hotel della Città
Corso della Repubblica
☎**0543.28297**
Fax 0543.30630
All credit cards • moderate

RESTAURANT

Al Maneggio
Selbagnone
☎**/Fax 0543.742-042**
Closed Monday
American Express, Diners Club, MasterCard • low expensive

Forlimpopoli is the birthplace of Pellegrino Artusi, the Italian Fannie Farmer. And even though Artusi's house has been turned into a bank, the gastronomic reputation of the city lives on, thanks to Bruna Sebastiani in the dining room and her husband, Giorgio, in the kitchen and in the cellars of this seventeenth-century countryside villa. The menu takes advantage of the finest products that Romagna has to offer and treats them with respect. The home-style salami is wonderful. Homemade pasta, especially with field greens like *strigoli* (poppy stems), is a treat to find, a sign of Giorgio's dedication to his regional *cucina*. The *manzetta brasata* (braised beef) is tasty, and the cheese is a hard-to-find local treasure. Wines are a complement to the *cucina*, and include fine regional and Italian selections.

Gambettola

TABLE LINENS
Antica Bottega Pascucci
Via Verdi 18
☎0547.53056
No credit cards

The Pascucci family has been hand-stamping cloth for seven generations in Gambettola. The workshop smells decidedly of the vinegar used in the printing process (see page 251). The shop has a fine selection of ready-made items, but you can also special-order a hard-to-find size or a pattern chosen from their collection of antique hand-carved pearwood blocks. A small catalog, with designs numbered for easier identification, is available.

Imola

HOTEL
Villa Bolis
Via Corriera 5
Barbiano di Cotignola, near Lugo (close by)
☎0545.79347
Fax 0545.78859
American Express, Diners Club • moderate

RESTAURANT
San Domenico
Via Sacchi 1
☎0542.29000
Fax 0542.39000
Closed Monday
American Express, Diners Club, Visa •
very expensive

In spite of chef Valentino Mercatilii's expertise and Gianluigi Morini's splendid cellars, I didn't like dining at San Domenico. It seemed so formal, smug, and condescending, so unlike what I look for in a restaurant, that I never went back for a second try. The menu proudly declares its dedication to the "culinary traditions of the antique noble families of Italy," who, Mr. Morini informed

me, ate the best, most luxurious food that money could buy, paying no attention to region or season. I found the food insipid, a bit too precious. Breads and pastry, baked twice daily, were the high points of the meal. The wine list is one of Italy's finest—incredible wines at incredibly high prices.

RESTAURANT
Osteria del Vicolo Nuovo
Via Codronchi 6
☎0542.32552
Closed Monday
Diners Club, MasterCard, Visa • moderate

Lack of pretension and an excellent, extensive, well-priced wine list attracted me to the unknown Osteria del Vicolo Nuovo. The *cucina* is creative, which seems to be a tradition in Imola, but the *salumi*, cheeses, sandwiches, and soups are tasty. The daily six-course tasting menu is reasonably priced, and the wine suggestions are interesting.

Marano sul Panaro

HOTEL
See Bologna or Modena

RESTAURANT
Da Pastore
Via Fondovalle 5406
Casona
☎059.703-026
Closed Monday and Tuesday
No Credit Cards

Da Pastore is an unassuming *trattoria* in the hills beyond the village of Vignola on a road flanked by the Panaro River. Owners Gastone Mazzi and his wife, Graziella Tirelli, dropped out in the seventies, became shepherds, made sheep's milk cheese, and sold it at their bar. Graziella started to make a few dishes and the bar slowly evolved into a *trattoria* that was so successful that they gave up their sheep. The decor is strange, one wall covered with a huge photograph of woods, stream, waterfall, and mill, blond wood wainscoting and rattan lampshades overhead. There's one dining room, no menu or wine list, but Gastone knows just what you want to eat. You'll begin with platters of tortelloni stuffed with creamy ricotta, potatoless gnocchi of spinach or winter squash, pasta with ricotta-enriched tomato sauce. Next comes a bread basket of warm tigelle flatbreads, the size of hockey pucks to be split open and sandwiched with condiments like lardo salt pork, herbed goat cheese spread, grated Parmigiano, or grilled vegetables. Grilled cheese is served with honey or balsamic vinegar; a sweet ricotta cream is paired with wild berries. Eat outdoors on the patio overlooking the Panaro when the weather is nice.

Modena

Modena, the epicenter of the *cucina emiliana*, makes a perfect base for touring the area. It's close to Nonantola, Castelfranco, Castelvetro, Rubbiera, Reggio, and Soliera. Modena offers an incredible culinary tradition and plenty to do between meals. There's an important Romanesque Duomo, and the Estense Museum, Gallery, and Library. Plus the Giusti grocery beckons, a perfect one-stop shopping for culinary souvenirs.

HOTEL

Canalgrande
Corso Canalgrande 6
☎**059.217-160**
Fax 059.221-674
All credit cards • low expensive

HOTEL

Rechigi Park Hotel
Via Emilia Est 1581, Fossalta
☎**059.283-600**
Fax 059.283-910
All credit cards • expensive

HOTEL

La Torre
Via Cervetta 5
☎**059.222-615**
Fax 059.216-316
All credit cards • inexpensive

HOTEL

Castello
Via Pica 321, 3 km from Modena
☎**059.361-033**
Fax 059.366-024
MasterCard, Visa • inexpensive

GROCERY-RESTAURANT

Giusti
Via Farini 75; *osteria* **at vicolo del Squallore 46**
☎**059.222-533**
Closed Thursday afternoon; *osteria* open for lunch only, closed Sunday, reservations required
MasterCard, Visa, American Express • *osteria* high moderate

Porcophiles should plan a pilgrimage to the hosteria Giusti, the *trattoria* of my dreams, Modena-style, with only four tables. The official address is vicolo del Squallore 46, almost impossible to find, but owner Nano Morandi will wait outside the door of the Giusti shop on via Farini 75, to usher diners through a room perfumed with *prosciutto* and *parmigiano*, with bottles of youthful, adolescent, and ancient balsamic vinegars displayed in a case, and shelves and stacks of foodstuff to examine: Carnaroli rice, Sicilian belly tuna. Later. Walk through a hallway lined with crates and bottles from impressive wineries. You are now primed for lunch. Drink the house wine or check out the cellar across the alley from the dining room for something more important. Nano's wife, Laura Galli, is a phenomenal cook and rolls all pasta by hand. Carnivores will have a good time; vegetarians or those on a low-cholesterol diet should probably dine elsewhere. Begin lunch with *gnocco fritto*, a hollow, featherweight pastry pillow, paired with the sweet porky flavors of *prosciutto* or, even better, *culatello*. It's hard to resist the superb tiny *tortellini* in capon broth, and Nano always brings everyone a serving of deep-fried *minestrone* fritters. Taste the capon salad drizzled with ancient *balsamico* to understand what this special condiment is all about. Pork fans will appreciate the wide range of main dishes that Laura cooks with skill and respect. Nano forced me to try the *panna cotta*, served with *sapa*, cooked grape must, without a doubt the best I've ever had, although the homemade cakes are hard to resist. Anyone who fondly remembers the Restaurant Cantarelli will probably enjoy lunch at Giusti, open for lunch Monday through Saturday. Reservations are a must.

RESTAURANT

Osteria Francescana
Via Stella 22
☎059.210-118
Closed Saturday lunch, Sunday
All credit cards • high moderate

I was reluctant to try Osteria Francescana because a friend told me they had *piatti Americani* but I couldn't find anything else interesting that was open on Monday and, to my surprise, fell in love. The restaurant has American plates but not American food because owner-chef Massimo Bottura spent a year in New York, fell in love with the dishes at Fishs Eddy and bought them for the restaurant he opened in Modena. Osteria Francescana is attractive, with beamed ceilings, modern halogen lighting, local modern art on the walls, simply set tables, fine crystal, and nontraditional breads served in wooden bowls. Local clients aren't really interested in regional cooking and the menu is inspired by seasonal produce handled with respect. Begin with first-rate *salumi* and *culatello* or a featherweight lightly smoked ricotta and parmigiano mold. Pasta is hand-rolled daily, a gastronomic thrill. Tiny *tortellini* are served in broth or coated with a creamy yet cream-less Parmigiano-Reggiano sauce. Cotechino is steamed over Lambrusco, paired with extra virgin olive oil–enriched mashed potatoes. Poultry and seafood are well prepared. Desserts like classic *tiramisù*, custard *gelato* with candied orange peel and citrus caramel, and *panna cotta* flavored with cardamom, drizzled with *balsamico* are tempting. Co-owner Luca Gabrielli's wine list is well chosen and priced.

ENOTECA

Compagnia del Taglio
Via del Taglio 12
☎059.210-337
Closed Monday
Diners Club, MasterCard, Visa • low moderate

The wine selection is fantastic, with fine local, national, and international wines, available by glass or bottle. The saber hanging on the wall, with dozens of decapitated Champagne bottlenecks, corks still inserted, shows that this *enoteca* takes sparkling wine seriously, but also that patrons and clients enjoy a good time. *Salumi*, local and French cheeses are served with flatbread. Their own production of *torta Barozzi* is sold by the piece or whole. The assortment of *grappa* and distillates, especially fine single-malt Scotch, is simply incredible.

Nonantola

HOTEL

See Modena or Soliera

RESTAURANT

Osteria di Rubbiara
Via Risaia 2
Rubbiara
☎059.549-019
Closed Sunday and Thursday evenings, Tuesday, and August
American Express, MasterCard • moderate

It's impossible to hide my enthusiasm for the Osteria di Rubbiara, opened in 1862 by host Italo Pedroni's great-great-grandfather. I love the little grocery store out front, the *acetaia* next door, where Italo makes some of the best balsamic vinegar in Emilia (winner of the Spilamberto Palio in '77, '79, and '81), and the room downstairs where he makes eleven different types of fruit *liquore*, following Grandmother Claudia's recipes. The kitchen is powered by his wife, Franca, and his mother, Irma, who roll out some of the tastiest pasta I've ever eaten—alone worth the trip. Italo served his last *antipasti* five years ago, he told me, because they were ruining appetites, detracting from the stellar first courses. Mom's paper-thin hand-rolled pasta is simply treated to butter and a sprinkling of *parmigiano*, or elegantly dressed with a *ragù* that's more than just another meat sauce. Meats are anticlimactic, but don't skip the *frittata all'aceto balsamico* or the plain boiled potatoes, elevated to glory by Italo's balsamic vinegar. Clean your plate or Mom will be upset, and watch out for the bathrooms: *Dann'* is for women, *Ann'* is the men's room. Italo's own wines are well suited to the *cucina*, but a small selection of more elegant wines is also available. Reservations are a must.

Parma

Parma, important jewel on the necklace of the *via Emilia*, greatly influenced culturally and artistically by France, had moments of glory as the dukedom of Maria Luigia, ex-empress, wife of Napoleon II. Pastry, *prosciutto*, *parmigiano*, and pasta are the essence of Parma's gastronomic tradition. The *parmigiana* treatment—sprinkled with grated *parmigiano-reggiano* cheese and butter, and baked until brown and crisped—is given mostly to worthy vegetables. Unfortunately, some restaurants in town seem to be thriving on past laurels.

HOTEL

Grand Hotel Baglioni
Viale Piacenza 12/C
☎0521.292-929
Fax 0521.292-828
All credit cards • expensive

HOTEL

Park Hotel Stendhal
Piazzetta Bodoni 3
☎0521.208-057
Fax 0521.285-665
All credit cards • expensive

HOTEL

Button
Borgo Salina
☎0521.208-039
Fax 0521.238-783
All credit cards • moderate

PASTRY AND CHOCOLATE

Pasticceria Torino
Via Garibaldi 61
☎0521.235-689
Closed Monday

This is the best pastry shop in Parma, almost 100 years old, heirs to the secrets of the chefs of Duchess Maria Luigia, the bride of Napoleon who infused the *cucina* of Parma with a sophisticated Franco-Austrian influence. Check out the *torta duchessa* and *torta della nonna*, recipes that owner Dino Paini got from court cookbooks with the help of a client-historian. Spinach *tortelli* in sweet pastry, a dessert version with the secret ingredients of the classic pasta dish that was a favorite of the duchess. Giuseppe Verdi fans will want to buy a chocolate bust of the composer.

MARKET
Piazza della Ghiaia

Open weekday mornings, and all day Saturday

The components of Parma's elaborate *cucina* can be found in the exciting outdoor and covered market in piazza della Ghiaia and in the nearby grocery shops, festooned with fragrant *salumi* and decked out with shining chubby forms of *parmigiano-reggiano*.

GROCERY
Gastronomia Garibaldi

Via Garibaldi 42
☎0521.235-606
Closed Monday morning
MasterCard, Visa

A perfect stop for gastronomic souvenirs and picnic ingredients like cheese and *salumi*. They can vacuum-pack purchases, convenient for those who want to bring back first-rate *parmigiano*, one of the greatest reminders of a trip to Parma.

PROSCIUTTO CONSORTIUM
Consorzio del Prosciutto di Parma

Via Marco dell'Arpa 8/B
☎0521.245-987
Fax 0521.243-983

Interested in knowing more about *prosciutto* and learning how this world-class product is made? Fax Dott. Montuschi at the Consorzio for an appointment to visit a factory to see the whole production cycle and to thrill to the sight of rooms with floor-to-ceiling rows of *prosciutto* thighs maturing.

FOOD FAIR
Cibus

Via Fortunato Rizzi 67/A, Baganzola
☎0521.9961
Fax 0521.996-270

The food fair Cibus is held in Parma in even-numbered years in early May. A massive enterprise, with thousands of stands filled with fine (and less fine) Italian food products. There are a few jewels in a sea of industrial production for those who have the patience to "work" a big fair. Contact Signora Margaritelli for information about events and dates. Hotel rooms will be hard to find.

CHEESE
Otello dall'Asta

Via E. Copelli 2/E
☎0521.233-788
Closed Thursday afternoon

Otello dall'Asta sells lovely *parmigiano-reggiano*, selected from different dairies. He usually has three or four different years of cheese available, as well as *tenero*, which is unripened, fresh, sweet *parmigiano*, found only in this area. Although they're probably wonderful, Otello's other cheeses seem like a distraction from his splendid, fragrant *parmigiano-reggiano*, which is what this shop is all about.

RESTAURANT
Cocchi

Via Gramsci 16
☎0521.981-1990
Fax 0521.292-606
Closed Saturday and August
All credit cards • high moderate

Ristorante Cocchi serves classic regional *cucina* with a Parma accent. *Salumi*, especially *culatello* and *spalla di San Secondo* (cooked shoulder ham), are wonderful. Homemade, hand-rolled pasta is well done, and second-course *trippa alla parmigiana* (Parma-style tripe) and *bollito misto* (mixed boiled meats), served at lunch only, are tasty. Salads are dressed with a selection of extra virgin olive oils. Corrado Cocchi and son-sommelier Daniele preside in the dining room, and the wines they offer are fine, well suited to this typical restaurant.

RESTAURANT
La Greppia
Strada Garibaldi 39
☎**0521.233-686**
Fax 0521.235-021
Closed Thursday, Friday, and July
All credit cards • expensive

The menu of Maurizio Rossi's restaurant, La Greppia, is filled with nouvelle-inspired inventions for locals bored with the same old home-style cooking. But the regional dishes that I'm looking for are also prepared here. Choose the excellent *culatello* (heart of the *prosciutto*) or any of the handmade stuffed pasta. *Stracotto* (braised beef, cooked for eight hours) can be cut with a fork. The wide selection of vegetables is a welcome surprise in this meat-oriented region. Desserts are interesting, especially the green tomato tart, and the wines are fine.

RESTAURANT
Antica Osteria Fontana
Via Farini 24/A
☎**0521.286-037**
Closed Sunday and Monday
Visa • inexpensive

Join the students and locals at the bar, or sit down at the tables of the Antica Osteria Fontana and order some of their first-rate *salumi* tucked into tasty sandwiches. The *principe,* "prince," sandwich of young *grana* cheese and *prosciutto* is a popular choice. Quality wines, reasonably priced, are sold by the glass or the bottle.

TOSCANINI MUSEUM
Casa di Toscanini
Via R. Tanzi 13
☎**0521.35964**
Closed Monday

One of the few calorie-free experiences in Emilia. For a nice pause from eating, visit the birthplace of Arturo Toscanini, a small museum filled with souvenirs and relics of the grand *maestro*'s musical career.

Piacenza

Piacenza is a lively, bustling agricultural center south of the mighty Po River, on the gastronomic frontier that divides Emilia from neighboring Lombardia. Rose-colored brick piazza dei Cavalli, with its equestrian statues and impressive town hall, Il Gotico, is worth a visit. *Pisarei,* tiny dumplings dressed with beans and tomato sauce, are a local specialty not to be found elsewhere. The market, held on Wednesday and Saturday mornings in piazza del Duomo, hums with a special excitement and seems to electrify the whole city.

HOTEL
Grand Albergo Roma
Via Cittadella 14
☎**0523.323-201**
Fax 0523.330-548
All credit cards • high moderate

BAR-CAFFÈ-PASTRY
Pasticceria Daniel Durand
Corso Vittorio Emanuele 82
☎**0523.324-758**
Closed Sunday

The pastry in my favorite bar in Piacenza is made by Frenchman Daniel Durand, a fan of bicycle racing and a friend of American cyclist Greg LeMond. This explains the miniature bicycle on the bar and the French and American flags in the entrance. The croissants (*cornetti*) are always fresh, and the tiny two-bite sandwiches are irresistible.

SPECIALTY FOODS
Garetti
Piazza Duomo 44
☎**0523.322-747**
Closed Thursday afternoon

The Garetti brothers and their wives proudly make and sell tasty *salumi*. Their sausage, *prosciutto*, and *pancetta* are first-rate, but gastronomic heights are reached with their splendid *coppa*, made from a cut of pork near the neck, and their *salame piacentino*, a special family recipe created three generations ago by the founder of their gastronomic dynasty. Take-out cold salads are interesting.

RESTAURANT

Antica Osteria del Teatro
Via Verdi 16
☎0523.323-777
Fax 0523.384-639
Closed Sunday and August
American Express, Diners Club, MasterCard •
expensive

The Antica Osteria del Teatro has always been a duet featuring host-sommelier Franco Ilari and his former chef, Georges Cogny. A brilliant French chef who paired with Franco for the first years of the restaurant, Monsieur Cogny added a decidedly Francophile spirit to the menu. But he has since moved to Farini, where he has founded a place of his own, Locanda Cantoniera. The kitchen at the Antica Osteria del Teatro is now headed by co-proprietor Filippo Chiappini-Dattilo, who is young, local, intelligent, and highly skilled, and who has brought a breath of life to this formal (but not uncomfortable) restaurant. The 1400s palace setting has been carefully restored, revealing wooden ceilings, stone, and brick. Honey-colored walls, indirect lighting, and modern but comfortable seating in three dining rooms create an intimate ambience. The à la carte menu features a perfectly executed innovative *cucina*, a bit precious at times. A tasting menu has been joined by a regional menu, cooked with professionalism. Cheese is local, and fine. Desserts are memorable. Franco Ilari's wines, especially the unknown, hard-to-find locals, are a pleasure.

Reggio nell'Emilia

CHEESE

Dairy 122–Due Madonne
Sesto Dallari
Via Abramo Lincoln 3
☎0522.512-151

Outside the city of Reggio nell'Emilia, at the end of a dead-end street with no street signs, Sesto Dallari's dairy makes and sells quality *parmigiano*. Prices are reasonable and they're always open.

Rubiera

RESTAURANT-HOTEL

Arnaldo–Aquila d'Oro
Piazza XXIV Maggio 3
☎0522.628-686
Fax 0522.628-145
Closed Sunday and August
American Express, Diners Club • moderate

It's hard to resist a restaurant that subtitles itself a *clinica gastronomica*. Housed in a fifteenth-century gem of a country house, with wooden beams, terra-cotta floors, and frescoed friezes, Ristorante Arnaldo offers a charming setting for a marathon of a meal. Regional *cucina* triumphs, hearty and heavy. The *salumi* are tasty, especially the *prosciutto di Parma* and *mortadella*. *Tortellini*, served in a purist's broth, and the morel-mushroom *lasagna* are specialties. A serving cart is crowded with a selection of six or seven different roast meats, including guinea hen (*faraona*) cooked in a strange red crust. The *bollito misto* (mixed boiled) meats are served with green sauce and *mostarda*—spicy pickled whole fruit, an acquired taste. The vegetable cart, with its bowls of raw and cooked seasonal produce, to be dressed with olive oil and vinegar, is a welcome sight. Desserts may tempt the intrepid, and the *spazzacamino* ("chimney sweep") tisane guarantees that you'll digest everything you've eaten. Choosing a fine wine may be difficult. Thirty-six reasonably priced, attractive, modern, air-conditioned rooms make this "clinic" a comfortable base for touring the area.

Sala Baganza

HOTELS
See Parma

RESTAURANT
Da Eletta
Via Campi 3
☎0521.833-304
Closed Monday, Tuesday, and the second half of August • high moderate

Eletta Violi, who cooked at Cantarelli continues with her impeccable *cucina* in Sala Baganza. Husband Ivan selects fine local *salumi* from farmers working with traditional methods: *culatello, spalla di San Secondo,* Langhirano *prosciutto,* and salami from Felino. Pasta is rolled out by hand, and the *cappelletti* and *anolini* (stuffed pastas) and *tagliatelle* are worth a detour. Meats are cooked home-style, with rich, earthy sauces. Save room for dessert. The great difficulty of dining at Trattoria da Eletta is deciding what to skip—I always want to taste practically everything. The wines are an asset to the meal, and reservations are a must.

San Busseto

HOTEL
I Due Foscari
Piazza Carlo Rossi 15
Busseto
☎0524.92337
Fax 0524.91625
All credit cards • moderate

SPECIALTY FOODS
Cantarelli
Località Samboseto
☎0524.90133
Closed Sunday
No credit cards

Peppino Cantarelli created a legendary restaurant here, one of the first to emphasize quality wines with simple home-style regional Italian cooking, prepared by his wife, Mirella. They officially closed the restaurant at the end of 1982, but Peppino still sells his excellent *prosciutto, salame di Felino,* and *parmigiano,* as well as his own wine. Taste the *culatello* and you'll begin to understand why this unassuming grocery store still attracts a faithful following, who return to stock up on Peppino's fine regional products and to get a glimpse of the restaurant, looking somewhat diminished, that formed some of Italy's finest palates.

RESTAURANT-INN
Palazzo Calvi
Via Samboseto 26
☎0524.90211
Fax 0524.90213
Closed Monday, Tuesday lunch
All credit cards • high moderate restaurant, moderate rooms

Palazzo Calvi is a rising star in Emilia's gastronomic scene, with Rita Demontis in the kitchen and her husband, Roberto Morsia, in the elegantly appointed dining rooms. They're part of the dynamic Young Chefs of Italy group, and the *cucina* is a blend of traditional and innovative dishes that draw on first-rate ingredients. Begin with *salumi,* continue with hand-rolled pasta, paired with vegetables and seafood. Meat and fish are lightly sauced, desserts are beautifully presented, little cookies are irresistible. The aged *parmigiano* is worth a voyage, the wine list is ample, and the distillates will tempt those who choose to stay in one of Palazzo Calvi's eight rooms or suites.

San Secondo

HOTEL

Sant'Angelo
Via Garibaldi 128
☎0521.873-246
All credit cards • low moderate

CULATELLO COMPETITION

Arcisodalizio per la Ricerca del Culatello Supremo
Castello di San Secondo
☎0336.565-011

The Sala dei Rossi in the Castle of San Secondo is the setting for an incredible competition. It's held the last Saturday of March, dedicated to researching the supreme *culatello*, as the name of the fraternal association attests. Lino Pezzarossa is in charge and guests are welcome. Write or call for more information.

Soliera

RESTAURANT-INN

Da Lancellotti
Via Grandi 120
☎059.567-406
Fax 059.565-431
Restaurant closed Sunday and Monday
Diners Club, MasterCard, Visa • moderate
restaurant, inexpensive rooms

The town of Soliera is easy to find, although the Restaurant Lancellotti isn't. But it's worth a detour for food lovers, in spite of the nondescript decor and modern building. This restaurant is propelled by family power, with Angelo Lancellotti in the kitchen assisted by his wife, Zdena. Mom deftly rolls out pasta with a yard-long, slim, one-handled rolling pin, and Dad cooks it. Brothers Emilio and Francesco and Angelo's daughter Ida cover the dining room. Angelo doubles as gardener in the Lancellotti's organic herb and vegetable garden outside town.

Aromatic herbs and greens stud the menu at Lancellotti, a surprise in a region that doesn't take anything without cholesterol too seriously. *Culatello, prosciutto, coppa, salame,* and incredible herb-infused *lardo* (less cholesterol than butter), as well as fruit and wild-greens salads, dressed with real traditional *balsamico,* are among the tasty appetizers. Pasta is elevated to an art form—it's hard to choose among the quintessential *tortellini* in broth; *farfalle* (butterfly pasta), dressed with angelica and *prosciutto* and homemade on a comb; or *maccheroni* sauced with squab. Herbs flavor all the second-course offerings, like marinated *baccalà* with chives and sweet cicely, and duck breast with "perfumes from the garden." Vegetables are simple and invite the addition of *Aceto Balsamico Tradizionale di Modena* for an extra charge of 3,000 lire, definitely worth the expense. Salad lovers will be in heaven with the *mischianza,* a mix of dozens of cultivated and domesticated wild greens, herbs, and flowers, just picked from Angelo's garden—rucola (*Diplotaxis tenufoglia,* not the usual *Eruca sativa* found worldwide), chicory, dandelion, oak leaf and lamb's lettuces, chervil, lovage, brunet, chives, bronze fennel, nasturtium, and borage flowers. Herbs and greens change with the season. Conclude with a taste of a tart filled with unbaked, barely sweetened ricotta topped with currants or, in the winter, the *torta al savor,* made with cooked wine must. Herbal infusions or

grappa conclude the experience. Although Lancellotti's rooms aren't luxurious, they're clean, modern, comfortable, and well priced. I can't imagine staying elsewhere.

Trebbo di Reno

HOTEL

See Bologna

RESTAURANT-HOTEL

Il Sole–Antica Locanda del Trebbo
Via Lame 67
☎**051.700-102 or 700-290**
Fax 051.701-138
Closed Sunday
All credit cards • high moderate, inexpensive rooms

Il Sole, also called Antica Locanda del Trebbo, is a rising star on Emilia's restaurant scene. The 120-year-old inn has recently been restored by new owners, experienced professionals who seem to be doing everything right. Beamed ceilings and terra-cotta floors are a pleasing backdrop for the *cucina* of regional and innovative specialties. *Salumi* are well chosen. All pasta is hand-rolled daily. Thursday's menu is devoted to beautifully prepared fish at its freshest. Desserts and *gelato* are homemade, and hard to resist. Chef Francesco Guerra prepares traditional specials at lunch, but cuts loose in the evening with

dishes of his own invention in addition to the classics. His partner, Guido Paolato, complement the well-prepared *cucina* with wines of distinction, both local and from the rest of Italy. Dining outdoors is a pleasure in the summer. Sample the *grappa* collection, and then spend the night in one of Il Sole's twenty rooms.

Vignola

HOTEL

Eden
Via C. Battisti 49
☎**059.772-847**
Fax 059.771-477
All credit cards • low moderate

RESTAURANT

Antica Osteria da Bacco
Via Selmi 3
☎**059.762-560**
Closed Tuesday
All credit cards • moderate

It's a simple *enoteca,* a perfect stop for a simple glass of wine from a fine but limited selection selected by sommelier Renato Clo. It's an even better choice for a fine meal of traditional cooking in the dining room in the back, prepared by his wife, Maria Teresa Broli, and her son Massimiliano. *Gnocco fritto* and *salumi* are typical starters, homemade pasta and *tortellini in brodo*, simple main dishes like rabbit, lamb, grilled meat, *torta di tagliatelle, benzone,* and *torta Barozzi* from Gollini. A complimentary bowl of cherries is served to diners during the June cherry festival. Conclude with *nocino* walnut liqueur.

RESTAURANT

La Bolognese
Via Muratori 1
Closed Saturday
MasterCard, Visa • low moderate

La Bolognese is close to the house where Ludovico Antonio Muratori, father of modern historiography, was born. Owner-cook Elda Franceschini, whose parents were from Bologna, respects culinary history, and the menu is pure tradition. Pasta is hand-rolled, sauced home-style in *ragù* that has simmered for hours. Look for *tortellini* and *tortelloni*, roast or boiled meats, *cotoletta alla bolognese*, simple desserts like *tiramisù* and crème caramel, and incredible local fruit. Drink Lambrusco.

CHERRIES

Consorzio della Ciliega Tipica di Vignola

Via Barozzi 2
☎**059.771-207**
Fax 059.773-645

Cherry lovers should plan to visit Vignola in June, when the local *durone* cherry season is celebrated with musical and theatrical per-formances, as well as initiatives that pro-mote the healthy virtues of cherries. Visit the cherry market the first week in June and check out via Mazzini, lined with 200 meters of tables covered with cherry tarts— ask for a free taste. Call or fax the consor-tium, which comprises over 800 cherry growers in the area, for more information.

PASTRY

Pasticceria Gollini

Piazza Garibaldi 1
☎**059.771-079**
Closed Monday

Worth a detour in tour-guide language, Pas-ticceria Gollini is *the* source for two incredible cakes. *Torta Barozzi* gets all the press, named after home boy Iacopo Barozzi, an important Renaissance architect known as Vignola. The *torta* is a buttery, rich, flat chocolate cake fla-vored with almonds, coffee, and peanut butter. Chocoholics will probably require the 1.5-kilo size. I prefer the *torta Muratori*, named after another native son, Ludovico

Antonio Muratori, priest, scholar, historian, founder of modern historiography based on scientific and documentary evidence. And the historiographic evidence in my kitchen was that the *torta Muratori*, golden colored, rich with eggs, flavored with sweet almonds and hazelnuts, sprinkled with pine nuts, dis-appeared while the *torta Barozzi*, served to a group of serious eaters, lingered for weeks.

Zibello

HOTEL

Locanda del Lupo

Via Garibaldi 64, Soragna
☎**0524.690-444**
Fax 0524.69350
All credit cards • high moderate

RESTAURANT

La Buca

Via Ghizzi 5
☎**0524.99214**
Closed Monday evening, Tuesday
No credit cards • moderate

Don't look for anything new on the menu of this fantastic *trattoria* in the heart of the foggy lowlands of *culatello* country. Perfectly executed traditional regional cooking is offered as it has been for generations. *Salumi* are first-rate, but *culatello* is in a class of its own. Homemade pasta, boiled meats, tripe, *zampone*, eels, and fried frog's legs. Desserts are almost an afterthought. The house wine is fine, but there's a fine selection for more exigent palates.

On the map (labels):

Pontremoli • Bagnone • Pieve Fosciana • Castelnuovo di Garfagnana • Ponte a Moriano • Abetone • EMILIA-ROMAGNA • LIGURIA • Camporgiano • Colonnata • Pietrasanta • Forte dei Marmi • Camaiore • Viareggio • Bozzano • Ponte Attigliano • Monsummano Terme • Montecatini Terme • Borgo a Buggiano • Lucca • Piteccio • Gello • Catena • Lamporecchio • Agliana • Ponte Attigliano • Prato • Fiesole • Sesto Fiorentino • San Giorgio a Colonica • SAN MARINO • Pisa • Fucecchio • Artimino • Firenze • Bagno a Ripoli • Mercatale • Castelfranco di Sopra • LE MARCHE • Arno • Montelupo • Cerbaia • Impruneta • Strada in Chianti • Anghiari • Sansepolcro • Montefiridolfi • Greve • San Giovanni Valdarno • Montevarchi • Lari • Radda in Chianti • Panzano • Gaiole in Chianti • Arezzo • Villa a Sesta • Castelnuovo Berardenga • Castiglioncello • Colle di Val d'Elsa • Castellina in Chianti • Ponte a Bozzone • Rosia • Siena • Sinalunga • Ligurian Sea • Murlo • Trequanda • Montefollonico • Montepulciano • Montalcino • Pienza • Monticchiello di Pienza • San Vincenzo • Ghirlanda • Bagno Vignoni • Chiusi • UMBRIA • Cetona • ELBA • Saturnia • Fonte Blanda • Montemerano • Porto Ercole • LAZIO • Adriatic Sea

Toscana seems to have the best of everything: art, architecture, archeological wonders, soft rolling countryside, mountain forests, and pastures—all less than a couple of hours from the coast and the Tyrrhenian Sea. Three tonalities of green—olive, cypress, and grapevine—color the landscape, mostly unchanged from the background of Renaissance paintings. Political loyalty is a temporary sentiment in Toscana.

Toscana

Beginning with the Etruscan Confederation in the eighth century B.C., a series of invasions, power struggles, and alliances by Romans, Lombards, Medici, Guelphs (backed by the Vatican), and Ghibellines (backed by the emperor) kept the Tuscan provinces suspicious and separate, alike only in their accent, with its aspirated "c," and in their condiment of choice, *olio d'oliva extra vergine.*

The *cucina toscana* is dominated by bread and oil. Bread appears in every course, from appetizer to dessert, even as a snack. *Schiacciata,* literally "crushed," is flattened dough baked with olive oil, or in the fall, sweetened with sugar and studded with purple wine grapes, just as it's depicted in Etruscan frescoes. Bread is also enriched with egg yolks and orange rind, and dusted with a heavy layer of powdered

sugar, for a carnival dessert. Unsalted country loaves are paired with *companatico,* defined as anything that's eaten with bread, from *prosciutto* to preserves. Bread is sliced into thick slabs, grilled, rubbed with garlic, and dipped into extra virgin olive oil, or skewered between pieces of sausage and pork liver punctuated with bay leaves. *Ribollita* and *pappa,* hearty country soups, are thickened with stale bread.

All through Toscana the olive trees are growing back, after the disastrous freeze of 1985, hand-harvested in the late fall, stone-crushed, and pressed between woven mats, transformed into murky green extra virgin olive oil, peppery tasting and almost effervescent when fresh, more transparent and less pungent when the sediment filters out after a month or two. The flavor of this special oil is felt throughout the *cucina toscana*.

Prosciutto, salami, or sausage made from pork or wild boar, and *crostini* (liver-pâté appetizers) start off most traditional meals in Toscana. Meat and poultry are either roasted, grilled, or fried, and the accompanying lemon wedge is the Tuscan idea of a sauce. Vegetables are simply cooked or eaten raw, but always dressed with extra virgin olive oil. Traditional desserts are uncomplicated cakes and cookies flavored with spices, nuts, or dried fruit, served with a glass of *vin santo*, an aromatic dessert wine.

I live in Toscana, and I love the proud simplicity of its *cucina*. I am captivated by the Tuscans, the countryside, the light, and the oil. Living and traveling in Italy, I've discovered new foods—some so elegant, harmonious, and beautifully prepared that I've wondered what can I possibly eat at home after this kind of experience? Simple: bread and oil.

The Menu

Salumi

Finocchiona: pork sausage flavored with fennel seeds
Prosciutto di cinghiale: salt- and air-cured wild boar ham
Salame toscano: pork sausage studded with pepper and cubes of fat
Salsicce fresche (or secche): fresh (or dried) sausage of pork or wild boar
Soprassata *or* soppressata: head cheese; cooked sausage made from pig's head, with spices and lemon peel

Antipasto

Crostini: traditional minced chicken-liver canapés
Crostini di milza: canapés of minced sautéed spleen

Donzelle *or* donzelline: fried dough balls
Fettunta *or* bruschetta: slab of toasted country bread rubbed with garlic and dipped in tasty extra virgin olive oil, sprinkled with salt and pepper

Primo

Acquacotta: vegetable-mushroom soup served over toasted bread and topped with a poached egg
Cacciucco: coastal fish stew with tomatoes, chile pepper, and red wine
Carabaccia: onion soup
Cavolo con le fette: cooked black cabbage on garlic bread, moistened with cabbage broth and liberally dressed with olive oil
Garmugia: springtime vegetable soup made with tender fava beans, peas, artichokes, asparagus tips, and bacon

Gnocchi di ricotta: dumplings filled with ricotta and spinach
Infarinata: vegetable soup thickened with cornmeal
Minestra di farro: emmer and bean soup
Panzanella: summer salad of tomatoes, basil, cucumber, onion, and bread, dressed with olive oil
Pappa col pomodoro: tomato soup thickened with bread, enriched with olive oil at the table
Pappardelle sulla (*or* alla) lepre: homemade egg pasta noodles with a wild rabbit sauce
Penne strascicate: quill-shaped pasta "dragged through" a meat sauce
Pici: hand-rolled egg pasta that looks like thick, short spaghetti
Ravioli *or* tortelli: ravioli filled with spinach and ricotta

Ribollita *or* **minestra di pane:** hearty winter vegetable soup thickened with bread, enriched with olive oil at the table

Risotto nero: rice cooked with cuttlefish and its black ink, and, at times, Swiss chard

Zuppa di fagioli: vegetable soup dominated by beans

Secondo

Arista: roast pork loin with garlic and rosemary

Asparagi alla fiorentina (*or* **alla Bismark):** asparagus topped with melted butter, a fried egg, and cheese

Baccalà alla livornese: salt cod cooked with garlic, tomatoes, and parsley

Bistecca alla fiorentina: T-bone steak at least two inches thick, charcoal-grilled

Cibreo: stew of chicken livers, unlaid eggs, and cockscomb

Cieche (*or* **cèe) alla pisana:** tiny baby eels cooked with garlic and tomatoes, served with Parmesan cheese

Fritto misto: mixed fried foods, usually chicken, rabbit, or lamb chops, and vegetables: zucchini, zucchini flowers, artichokes, potatoes, winter squash, green or ripe tomatoes, mushrooms, and *polenta*

Lombatina: veal chop, usually grilled

Peposo: peppery beef stew

Pollo alla diavola *or* **al mattone:** chicken flattened with a brick, grilled with herbs

Scottiglia: mixed stew of veal, game, and poultry,

cooked with white wine and tomatoes

Spiedini di maiale: pork loin cubes and pork liver spiced with fennel, skewered with bread and bay leaves, and grilled or spit-roasted

Stracotto: pot roast

Tonno con fagioli: tuna served with white beans and raw onion

Totani (*or* **seppie) all'inzimino:** cuttlefish (or squid) cooked with Swiss chard and tomatoes

Triglie alla livornese: red mullet cooked with tomatoes, garlic, and parsley

Trippa alla fiorentina: tripe cooked with tomatoes, served with Parmesan cheese

Contorno

Fagioli al fiasco: boiled white beans (once cooked in a *fiasco,* wine flask, slowly, in the ashes of the country hearth)

Fagioli all'olio: white beans served with olive oil

Fagioli all'uccelletto: white beans cooked with tomatoes, garlic, and sage

Frittata (*or* **tortino) di carciofi:** pan-fried (or oven-baked) artichoke flan

Pinzimonio: raw seasonal vegetables dipped in lively extra virgin olive oil, salt, and pepper

Formaggio

Pecorino: fresh or aged, made from sheep's milk

Raveggiolo: soft, fresh, made from sheep's-milk

whey, delicate and hard to find

Ricotta: soft, fresh, mild, made from whey

Dolce

Biscottini di Prato *or* **cantucci:** dried almond cookies, served with dessert wine

Bongo: filled cream puffs with chocolate sauce

Brigidini: anise wafer cookies

Buccellato: simple anise raisin cake

Castagnaccio: baked unleavened chestnut-flour cake containing raisins, walnuts, and rosemary

Cavallucci: spiced cookies

Cenci: "rags" of fried dough dusted with powdered sugar

Frittelle di riso: rice fritters

Meringata: frozen meringue with whipped cream and chocolate chips

Necci: chestnut-flour crepes baked in special terra-cotta forms

Panforte and panpepato: medieval candied fruit, nut, and spice cakes

Ricciarelli: marzipan almond cookies

Schiacciata alla fiorentina: orange-flavored cake covered with powdered sugar, found at carnival time

Schiacciata con l'uva: grape- and sugar-covered bread dessert of Etruscan origin, served in the fall

Zuccotto: chocolate and whipped-cream–filled sponge cake dome

The Wine List

The wines of Toscana are dominated by Sangiovese, a local grape that forms the backbone of traditional reds: Chianti, Brunello di Montalcino, Vino Nobile di Montepulciano, and Carmignano. Wine in Toscana is red; white wines have never been given much consideration. But modern winemaking techniques have drastically improved the quality of many whites, including traditional Vernaccia di San Gimignano and Bianco di Montecarlo. Many wineries are making high-quality non-DOC whites, although there is also a tendency toward dry, insipid wines to drink chilled in the summer.

Innovative Tuscans and non-Tuscans (it seems as if all the enologists responsible for interesting new wines are from outside Toscana) are experimenting with traditional grapes as well as nontraditional Cabernet Sauvignon, Chardonnay, and Sauvignon. They are using the French technique of *barriques,* 225-liter oak casks, for aging both reds and whites. The results are largely positive, and have contributed to a renewed interest in both traditional and innovative wines of quality.

Bianco di Pitigliano is a clean, delicate, dry white DOC from the south of Toscana, made of Trebbiano, Greco, Verdicchio, and Malvasia grapes. It is served with fish and the coastal *cucina* of southern Toscana. The best, La Stellata, is produced by Lunaia and Provveditore.

Bianco Vergine della Valdichiana is a soft, dry white DOC, made of Trebbiano, Malvasia, and Grechetto grapes south of Arezzo. Served with fish and vegetable dishes, it's at its best produced by Fattoria di Manzano and Avignonesi.

Bolgheri is a newly created DOC from an area known for its *vino da tavola.* White,

made from mostly Trebbiano and Vermentino, is produced by Grattamacco, Le Macchiole, and Michele Satta; rosé from mostly Sangiovese. Reds are made with Cabernet Sauvignon, Sangiovese, and Merlot, divided into **Rosso** (young and fresh) and **Rosso Superiore** (aged in barriques), with a special category, **Rosso Sassicaia,** for Tenuta San Guido's eponymous wine. Look for wines from Antinori's Tenuta Belvedere, Le Macchiole, Tenuta San Guido, Tenuta dell'Ornellaia, Tenuta Belvedere, Le Macchiole, and Grattamacco, a personal favorite worth hunting for.

Brunello di Montalcino, a DOCG from south of Siena, is made of the Brunello or Sangiovese Grosso grape. It's a full, harmonious red and one of Italy's finest wines—served with meat, fowl, game, and mixed grills. Top producers are Altesino, Case Basse, Cerbaiona, La Chiesa di Santa Restituta, La Casa by Tenuta Caparzo, La Gerla, Lisini, Poggio Antico, Poderi Emilio Costanti, Tenuta Caparzo, Tenuta Il Poggione, Mastrojanni, and Castello Banfi. Also, Due Portine, Ciacci Piccolomini, Casanova di Neri, Argiano, Col d'Orcia, Fattoria dei Barbi, Lisini, Poggio Antico, Fuligni, La Poderina, and Talenti.

Carmignano, a DOC zone west of Firenze, produces **Carmignano,** a dry, elegant red, served with meat and regional *cucina,* and **Vin Ruspo,** a fresh, fruity rosé, served with appetizers and first-course dishes. Both wines are made with Sangiovese, Canaiolo, Cabernet, and a small percentage of Trebbiano and Malvasia grapes. Top producers are Fattoria Ambra, Fattoria di Bacchereto, Podere Lo Locco, Capezzana, and Villa di Trefiano.

Chianti is made of Sangiovese, Canaiolo, Malvasia, and Trebbiano grapes in seven distinct zones that cover most of central

Tuscany. Over 1,000 wineries produce Chianti, ranging from simple rustic table wine to elegant balanced dry reds well worth aging. The DOCG (*denominazione di origine controllata e garantita*) sticker on the neck of the bottle guarantees the wine's quality. Chianti is served with regional *cucina,* and with meat and poultry dishes.

Chianti Classico, produced in the area between Siena and Firenze, is the most famous of the seven Chianti zones. Members of a powerful consortium of producers label the neck of each bottle with a black rooster (*gallo nero*) as a further guarantee of quality. But the "G" of DOCG stands for "guaranteed," and the consortium's role has been partially superseded by government-appointed commissions. Not all wineries in the Classico area have chosen to join the consortium, and the lack of a *gallo nero* doesn't mean that a wine isn't good. The best wines in Chianti Classico are produced by Badia a Coltibuono, Capannelle, Casa Emma, Carobbio, Castellare, Castell'in Villa, Castello di Cacchiano, Castello di Fonterutoli, Castello di Gabbiano, Castello di Paneretta, Castello di Querceto, Castello dei Rampolla, Castello di Volpaia, Colle Bereto, Fattoria di Felsina, Fattoria Querciabella, Fattoria di Vistarenni, Fontodi, Castello di Ama, which makes special crus *Bellavista, San Lorenzo, Casuccia, Bertinga,* and Le Filigare, Podere Il Palazzino, Isole e Olena, Monsanto, Monte Vertine, Pagliarese, Peppoli, Podere Capaccia, Poggerino, Poggio al Sole, Poggio Bonelli, Giorgio Regni, Riecine, Savignola Paolina, San Felice, San Giusto a Rentennano, San Polo in Rosso, Terrabianca, Vecchie Terre di Montefili, Villa Antinori, Villa Cafaggio, Villa Calcinaia, and Viticcio.

Chianti Colli Aretini is made in the hills outside Arezzo, and produced by Villa Cilnia and Villa La Selva.

Chianti Colli Fiorentini is made to the south and east of Firenze, and is produced by Fattoria Il Corno, and Lanciola II.

Chianti Colli Senesi is made in a large area from San Gimignano southward, and produced by Boscarelli, Castello di Farnetella, Falchini, Fattoria L'Amorosa, Il Poggiolo, Montenidoli, Pacina, Parizza, and Pietraserena.

Chianti Montalbano is from the area where Carmignano is grown, west of Firenze, and produced by Fattoria di Artimino, Fattoria di Bacchereto, and especially Tenuta di Capezzana by Contini-Bonacossi.

Chianti Rufina is made east of Firenze, produced by Castello di Montesodi, Castello di Nipozzano, Tenuta di Pomino, Remole, and Selvapiana.

Galestro is a recently created summer white wine, made with Trebbiano and Malvasia grapes, light and dry, at its best chilled and served with light pasta, vegetable, and fish dishes. It is produced by Marchesi Antinori, Marchesi de' Frescobaldi, and Ruffino.

Montecarlo, a DOC from outside Lucca, is a white made of Trebbiano, and a wealth of French and Italian grapes, is elegant, full, and dry, one of Toscana's finest whites. It is served with fish in all courses. There's also a red based on Sangiovese, served with meat. Top producers are Fattoria del Buonamico, Carmignani, and Romano Franceschini.

Morellino di Scansano, a DOC, is made near Grosetto from Morellino, a strain of the Sangiovese grape. It is an elegant, balanced red, served with meat, game, and regional *cucina.* Top producers are Erik Banti, Sellari Franceschini, Le Pupille, and Moris Farms.

Rosso delle Colline Lucchesi (*or* Colline Lucchesi), a DOC from east of Lucca, is made of mostly Sangiovese grapes. This dry, lively red is served with meat and hearty regional *cucina.* The best is produced by Fattoria di Fubbiano, Tenuta Maria Teresa, Tenuta di Valgiano, and La Badiola.

Rosso di Montalcino *or* Rosso dei Vigneti di Brunello is a DOC from the Montalcino area, made from the Brunello grape and aged less than noble Brunello di Montalcino. It's a full-bodied, lively red, served with meat, poultry, and regional *cucina*. Top producers are Altesino, Case Basse, La Chiesa di Santa Restituta, Lisini, Mastrojanni, Poggio Antico, Tenuta Caparzo, Tenuta Il Poggione, Val di Suga, and Castello Banfi. Also, Argiano, Ciacci Piccolomini, Casanova di Neri, Col d'Orcia, Fattoria dei Barbi, Lisini, La Poderina, and Talenti.

Dry sparkling **Spumante** is a break from Tuscan tradition. Using the *champenoise* or *charmat* method and Pinot and Chardonnay, or local Brunello, Vernaccia, or other native grape varieties, the following wineries have come up with a quality product. Marchesi Antinori makes Antinori Brut Nature, Tenuta Caparzo makes Caparzo Brut Rosé, Guicciardini-Strozzi makes Cusona Brut, Teruzzi e Puthod makes Sarpinello, and Contini-Bonacossi's Villa di Capezzana makes Brut di Capezzana.

Vernaccia di San Gimignano is a DOC from the hills of San Gimignano, made with the Vernaccia grape. This traditional Tuscan white is subtle and dry, served with fish and shellfish. Top producers are Falchini, Fattoria di Pietrafitta, Guicciardini-Strozzi, Montenidoli, Pietraserena, and Ponte a Rondolino.

Vino Nobile di Montepulciano is a DOCG from the hills outside Montepulciano, south of Siena. Prugnolo Gentile, a clone of Sangiovese, is the backbone of this full, elegant red, served with meat, poultry, and game. Top producers are Avignonesi, Bindella, Contucci, Boscarelli, Dei, Poliziano, Valdipiatta, Fassati, and Tenuta Trerose.

Vin Santo Toscano is a lively aromatic wine, usually made from semi-dried Malvasia or Trebbiano grapes, sealed in small casks for at least three years. The resulting wine may range from dry to sweet, and is usually served for dessert. Fine *vin santo toscano* is produced by Avignonesi, Artimino, Castellare, Castello di Ama, Fattoria del Buonamico, Castello di Volpaia, Badia a Coltibuono, Tenuta di Capezzana, Frescobaldi, Isole e Olena, Poggio al Sole, Pomino, and Santa Cristina by Antinori.

Nontraditional Wines. Tuscan winemakers, not content with the traditional DOC wines, have turned to making *vino da tavola* to express themselves. Usually complex, many are aged in small oak casks and are frequently made with familiar grapes.

Chardonnay seems to be the white grape of the moment in Toscana, and many wineries have come out with interesting and very different Chardonnays. Castello di Ama makes Colline di Ama, a crisp white Chardonnay, and Bellaria from Pinot Grigio. Ruffino makes Cabrèo, a rich oaky Chardonnay. Tenuta di Capezzana makes a crisp, fruity Chardonnay. Castello Banfi makes Fontanelle Chardonnay, elegant and silky. Marchesi de'Frescobaldi makes Il Benefizio with Pinot Bianco and Chardonnay grapes, an elegant, smoky white. Podere Capaccia makes Spéra, a Tuscan "sunbeam" of a white. Teruzzi e Puthod makes oak-aged Terre di Tufo. Avignonesi makes Marzocco, a rich Chardonnay, one of Toscana's best whites. Fontodi makes Meriggio, a well-made Chardonnay; Vecchie Terre di Montefili makes Vigna Regis, an interesting, mouth-filling blend aged in oak; and Tenuta Caparzo makes Le Grance, a balanced Chardonnay.

Sangiovese, also called Sangioveto, is the most Tuscan of grapes, and is used alone or blended with nontraditional varieties in the red *vino da tavola*. Almost all are aged in new

French oak. Vecchie Terre di Montefili makes Bruno di Rocca from Cabernet Sauvignon and Sangioveto, a rich, dry red. Tenuta Caparzo makes Ca' del Pazzo from Cabernet Sauvignon and Brunello, a Sangiovese clone. Ruffino makes Cabrèo from Cabernet Sauvignon and Sangiovese. Isole e Olena makes Borro Cepparello, an all-Sangiovese rich red, and a Syrah called L'Eremo. San Polo in Rosso makes Cetinaia with only the red grapes of Chianti, Canaiolo, and Sangiovese, and the result is a complex lively red. Fattoria di Vistarenni makes Codirosso with all Sangiovese. Castello di Volpaia makes Coltassala with Sangiovese and Mammolo. Castello di Fonterutoli makes Concerto, a blend of Sangiovese and Cabernet. Fattoria di Felsina makes Fontalloro, a rich, ripe Sangiovese. Fattoria di S. Giusto a Rentennano makes Percarlo, a red of unusual proportion and finesse. Fontodi makes Flaccianello della Pieve, a highly successful all-Sangiovese red. Contini-Bonacossi makes Ghiaie della Furba of Cabernet Sauvignon, Franc, and Merlot, a rich fruity red. Avignonesi makes Grifi with Sangiovese-clone Prugnolo and Cabernet. Podere Il Palazzino makes all-Sangiovese Grosso Senese. Castellare makes single-vineyard I Sodi di San Niccolò from Sangioveto, Canaiolo, and Malvasia grapes. Monte Vertine makes Le Pergole Torte, one of Toscana's first all-Sangiovese reds aged in French oak. Altesino makes elegant Palazzo Altesi with Brunello or Sangiovese Grosso, and Alto Altese, made with the addition of Cabernet. Podere Capaccia makes Quercia Grande, an all-Sangiovese wine of promise. Fattoria del Buonamico makes Rosso di Cercatoia from Sangiovese blended with other grapes. Badia a Coltibuono makes a long-lived Sangioveto from all Sangiovese. Castello dei Rampolla makes Sammarco, a heady blend of Cabernet and Sangiovese. Marchesi Antinori makes Solaia from mostly Cabernet with a little Sangiovese. Castello Banfi makes Tavernelle from Cabernet Sauvignon. Marchesi Antinori makes elegant, harmonious Tignanello from Sangiovese blended with Cabernet. Tenuta di Ghizzano makes Veneroso from Cabernet. Tenuta di Bagnolo makes Pinot Nero from Pinot Noir. Querciabella makes Querciabella from Cabernet, Sauvignon, and Sangiovese. Podere Poggio Scaletta makes Carbonaione from Sangiovese. Tenuta di Ornellaia makes Masseto from Merlot.

CYCLING IN TOSCANA

Cicloposse Rental Bike
Via dell'Opio nel Corso 18
Montepulciano 53045
☎/Fax 0578.716-392

There are many organized cycling tours in Tuscany. Marco Tornaghi rents lightweight mountain bikes and hybrids (a cross between road and mountain bikes) by the day or week, providing helmets, water bottles, bike adjustments, maps with measured distances, routes for different levels of cycling. Bilingual guides can accompany cyclists; picnic lunches are available; wine tastings can be incorporated into the day. Marco knows the countryside around Pienza and Montalcino well, and his tours pass through vineyards, olive groves, pastures of wild flowers. He'll also help with local B&B and restaurant reservations. Prices are inexpensive.

Regional Specialties

Extra Virgin Olive Oil. Quality *olio extra vergine di oliva*, extra virgin olive oil (see page 303), is a Tuscan specialty. The olive trees' silver leaves and gnarled trunks dominate the landscape of much of Toscana, although many trees were turned into shrubs by the freeze of 1985. The finest oil is made with hand-picked olives, quickly transported to the olive mill, where they are washed, picked over, crushed with millstones, and separated. There are distinct zones with individual taste characteristics. The oil of the Lucchesia, the area surrounding Lucca, is golden, delicate, fruity, and well suited to fish and lightly flavored dishes. The oil from the Carmignano area is green, full-flavored, balanced, and a personal favorite. I also love the oil from the Chianti area, green, intense, mouth-filling, to be used as a dressing. The oil of the Valdarno area is strong, green, and peppery. The southern part of Toscana yields a dark, strongly flavored oil that is best used uncooked. The southern coastal area produces a delicate golden oil with a peppery aftertaste.

The olive trees in most of Toscana have recovered from the 1985 freeze. Genuine Tuscan olive oil should have *prodotto e imbottigliato*, "produced and bottled," written somewhere on the label, which means that the olives are grown by the oil producer, a guarantee of quality. All oils with only *imbottigliato* on the label can be made with olives from other regions, or other countries, and are not necessarily Tuscan.

F R A N T O I O   D I   S A N T A   T E A
Santa Tea
☎055.868-117
Piero Gonnelli's family has milled olives at their *frantoio* in Santa Tea near Reggello, for over 400 years. In 1962 they were the first olive mill to experiment with a system of centrifugal pressure. For three years oil was made with both the traditional press and the newer method; today only the latter is used. Green olives, which can't be pressed effectively with the older system, are used in the Santa Tea's extra virgin olive oil, which is green, fruity, and peppery when fresh.

The oil can be purchased directly from the mill.

G I O V A N N I   G I A C H I
Via Campoli 31
☎055.821-082
Alberto Giachi, a third-generation olive oil merchant from San Casciano, in the heart of Chianti, works with his brother Francesco and his uncle Renato, selecting olives from local farmers. Their oil is considered one of the best reasonably priced quality extra virgin olive oils made. The Giachi label states *selezionato e imbottigliato*, "selected and bottled," because they choose, but do not raise and harvest, their own olives.

Bread. Tuscan bread, sold throughout Italy, is made without salt. When freshly baked, the crust is crisp and the inside (*midolla*) is moist. Wood-burning ovens traditionally were used to bake bread in the country, and they weren't fired daily, so the bread had to last. *Pane toscano* is at its best after a day, actually improving in texture and flavor. There are many different theories to explain the unusually fine breads baked in some areas— better water, special microclimates, the material or shape of the oven, the type of wood firing the oven, and the type of flour are some of the rationalizations for particularly fine breads. Of course, nothing has ever been proved scientifically.

Chestnut Flour. Chestnut flour (*farina di castagne*) is used in many Tuscan desserts. Some of the best flour is made in the Garfagnana area, north of Lucca. Chestnuts from high-altitude forests are placed on straw mats in drying rooms and subjected to a smoking-drying process that lasts thirty to forty days. The chestnuts are then stone-ground to produce an extremely fine flour. Many of the mills in the Garfagnana region are still water powered.

Pecorino. *Pecorino* is the most Tuscan of cheeses, a tradition going back over 500 years, when shepherds crossed the region with their flocks, moving them between mountains and valleys according to the seasons. *Pecorino* is made with all sheep's milk, or with a combination of cow's and sheep's milk. Freshly made cheese called *marzolino* ("little March") or *pecorino fresco* is sold in the spring and is often eaten with raw fava beans (*bacelli*). Cheese held for aging is frequently rubbed with tomato or ashes, coloring the rind orange or dark gray. The combination of pears and *pecorino* is considered so great that a local saying warns about telling the farmer how well they go together, for fear he'll never part with them again.

Salumi. Tuscan bread is said to be saltless in order to accommodate the savory tastes of the full-flavored local *salumi*. Fennel is an important ingredient in *finocchiona*, a specialty of the Chianti area. It was often served by farmers when prospective buyers came to taste their new wine, because Italians rarely drink without eating something, and fennel alters the palate, enhancing many flavors. The verb *infinocchiarsi*, to "fennel up" or cheat, comes from this palate-confusing custom of the cunning Tuscan farmers.

Chianina Beef. Texas has its longhorns, and Toscana's best beef comes from *la Chianina*, a local breed of large white cattle. The perfect Florentine T-bone (*bistecca alla fiorentina*), at least two inches thick, should be grilled over a wood or charcoal fire, and ideally will be *Chianina* beef. But this prized cut of a prized breed of cattle isn't easy to find.

Farro. Use of the grain called emmer, *farro* in Italian, *triticum dicoccum* in Latin, dates from the Neolithic era in central Italy. It's an early form of wheat, boiled whole or milled, to make flour. Etruscans ate emmer. Emmer fueled the Roman legions, and its use spread throughout the Roman empire but is now substituted in northern regions

---

OIL-PRODUCING WINERIES

Olive trees grow well in the same climate as grapes, and fine oil is made by many wineries, including Antinori (Pèppoli), Castello di Ama, Castello di Volpaia, Castello Banfi, Grattamacco, Podere Le Boncie, Tenuta di Capezzana, Tenuta di Valgiano, and Fattoria Mansi-Bernardini.

Antinori (Pèppoli)	**Castello Banfi**	**Tenuta di Capezzana**
Piazza degli Antinori 3	Piazza Mincio 3	Via di Capezzana 100
Firenze	Roma	Seano di Carmignano
☎055.23595	☎0577.840-111	☎055.870-6005
Castello di Ama	**Grattamacco**	**Tenuta di Valgiano**
Lecchi in Chianti	Castagneto Carducci	Valgiano (Lucca)
☎0577.746-031	☎0565.763-840	☎0583.402-271
Castello di Volpaia	**Podere Le Boncie**	**Fattoria Mansi-Bernardini**
Radda in Chianti	Castelnuovo Berardenga	Segromigno Monte
☎0577.738-066	☎0577.359-116	☎0583.928-014

by barley. Emmer is often confused with spelt, triticum monococcum, a less-evolved grain with a smaller kernel.

Emmer's flavor is somewhere between barley and wheat, sweet with light starch, almost nutty. The use of emmer is common in the Garfagnana area of Tuscany, north of Lucca, used in a soup paired with beans, *minestra di farro*, ground into flour for pasta or cookies, boiled and dressed like a salad. There's lots of spelt and wheat being sold as emmer since it's recently become quite fashionable.

Brigidini and Berlingozzo. *Brigidini* cookies and ring-shaped *berlingozzo* can be found at most fairs in Tuscany and even beyond, sold at stands that sell candy, gummies, and nut confections. They're both from the village of Lamporecchio, south of Pistoia, the creation of the nuns of Santa Brigida of San Baronto, who made communion wafers as well as *cialde profane*, wafers sweetened with honey, substituted over time with sugar and enriched with eggs and anise. They were traditionally cooked between two long-handled heated disks of iron. *Berlingozzo* is made of almost the same dough, formed into a ring, and baked in the oven. See page 321, Lamporecchio, or page 325, Montecatini, for two wonderful sources.

Gelato. Did the Tuscans really invent *gelato* as they claim? Bernardo Buontalenti, Mannerist architect, artist, poet, late Renaissance man, is said to have built an ice cave in Boboli for Medici Grand Duke Francesco I and churned milk flavored with egg yolks and Malvasia wine over ice, the first example of milk-based *gelato*. Tuscan *gelato* makers have named a flavor after Buontalenti, rich and eggy with a secret ingredient that I suspect is probably Malvasia. See page 305, Firenze, and page 341, San Giorgio a Colonica, for two terrific sources of *Buontalenti*. It's easy to find the small-scale industrial products of the Gelateria Versilia on the coast near Viareggio. I'm wild about the *coppa versilia*, a frozen confection of sponge

cake, vanilla *gelato*, and Marsala that, when inverted on a plate, is topped with chocolate sauce. See page 289, Bozzano, for more information. Along the Tuscan coast to the south, in Castiglioncello, Dai Dai is another small-scale industrial *gelato* producer specializing in bite-size chocolate-coated *gelato* cubes as well as frozen truffles. See page 294 for more information.

Vin Santo Toscano. Concluding a meal with a glass of amber-colored, aromatic, velvety Vin Santo is a local tradition that's easily adopted. The Tuscan dessert wine was supposedly given its name by Cardinale Bessarione, who, when served a glass after a banquet in 1440, was so impressed that he declared, "*Questo è Xanto!*" ("This is holy!") and ever since it's been known as Vin Santo. To make this special wine, grapes are partially dried on straw mats, or hung from rafters, then pressed and sealed in small barrels for at least three years in attics exposed to the summer heat and winter cold. Exactly what goes on in the wooden casks is unknown, but the resulting wine—sweet, semidry, or dry—may range from dreadful, when made by unscrupulous wineries, to glorious.

The best Vin Santo, precious and difficult to find, is made by Avignonesi, Isole e Olena, and Castello di Ama. Other fine winemakers also make this delightful finish to a meal, a bit less successfully.

Crafts. Rustic pottery is found throughout Toscana. Industrially manufactured or handmade by artisans, terra-cotta clay dinnerware and cooking utensils are produced in a wealth of traditional patterns and shapes. See pages 297, 313, and 314 for sources.

Large terra-cotta jars—four feet high, unglazed on the outside—are the traditional storage containers for olive oil in Toscana. The village of Impruneta is famous for its pots (see page 320). The wide-mouthed, top-heavy *orcio*, either plain or festooned, is kept in a cool, dark room, and the oil is ladled out when needed.

Cities & Towns

Abetone

RESTAURANT-INN

La Capannina
Via Brennero 256
☎0573.60562
Fax 0573.606-926
Closed Tuesday evening and Wednesday
American Express, Diners Club, MasterCard • moderate

Restaurants in mountain resorts tend to confuse quantity with quality, and most famished skiers or hikers don't seem to mind. However, at La Capannina, Luigi Ugolini and Romea Politi don't make that mistake—or many others for that matter. Their *cucina* is based on the bounty of the forest and mountains— mushrooms, chestnuts, freshwater fish, herbs, and splendid cheeses. The fresh ricotta, of an unbelievable richness and natural sweetness, is served for dessert with chestnut-flour crepes (*necci*), an acquired taste. Some dishes tend toward nouvelle and are less successful than the home-style cooking. Olive oils and wines are wonderful. La Capannina has seven modestly priced rooms, convenient for a stay in the mountains.

Agliana

Even my most detailed guidebook, which lists every unheard-of wonder in every unknown village in Toscana, makes no mention of Agliana. But this place merits a pilgrimage, especially for chocolate, and wine lovers. The stars of Provincial Highway 376, which connects Pistoia and Prato, are a master chocolate maker and a wine shop called Lavuri down the road. Fine Tuscan bread, tasty *salumi,* and quality *gelato* are also made in this village of gastronomic significance.

HOTEL

Richard Hotel
Via Giovanni XXIII
☎0574.751-192
Fax 0574.751-381
Diners Club, MasterCard, Visa • moderate

RESTAURANT

Ovidio
Via Roma 83
☎0574.718-065
Closed Saturday, Sunday, open for lunch only
No credit cards • moderate

I love this no-frills *trattoria,* a local hangout, always crowded at lunch. Owner Ovidio Sgatti is practically retired and sits in the front room chatting with clients while his two daughters, Miria and Alessandra, bustle between the kitchen and the dining room, serving home-style Tuscan food—classic starters, like *ribollita* in the winter, *panzanella* in the summer, wide strips of pasta sauced with game or springtime vegetables. Look for roast meat, stewed duck, mushrooms in season, fish on Friday, like *baccalà* Livornese-style, *cacciucco,* fish soup, or mixed fry. Desserts are simple. Due to the influence of the nearby Enoteca Lavuri, there's a wonderful wine list studded with well-priced wines.

ENOTECA

Lavuri
Via Provinciale 154/G
☎0574.751-125
Fax 0574.751-366
Closed Sunday
American Express, MasterCard, Visa

Carlo Lavuri bought Andrea Trinci's *enoteca* and the tradition of wonderful wine in Agliana continues. Look for well-priced bottles from all over the world, with an especially strong Tuscan and Piedmont red selection. Rare distillates, single varietal *grappe,* coffee, and Italian regional cookies and sweets are also available.

CHOCOLATES

Roberto Catinari
Via Provinciale 378
☎0574.718-506
Closed Sunday and Monday
MasterCard, Visa

The first time I tasted Roberto Catinari's innocent-looking chocolates I took a delicate bite and dribbled the entire liquid center all over my sleeve. I selected a different shape the next time around, and once again was surprised by a liquid filling, the specialty of Italy's best chocolate artisan. *Maestro* Roberto fills many of his chocolates, each differently shaped, with *grappa, vin santo,* and fruit liqueurs. Once you've learned to pop the whole *cioccolatino* into your mouth, you'll be in for a treat. The rich, almost smoky-flavored chocolate shell is coated inside with a crunchy, wafer-thin layer of crystallized sugar that contains the liquid center—not strong enough to be intoxicating, but exhilarating due to the pure quality and intense flavors of the ingredients. The covered cherries are exceptional. Chocolate hazelnut creams (*gianduja*), a large variety of all-handmade chocolates, and a small selection of chocolate keys, tools, and horseshoes are also for sale. Easter eggs and Christmas *panforte* are available in season.

BREAD

Castino
Via Calice 18
☎0574.711-433
Closed Sunday

Angelo Giusti, known as "Castino," is a wonderful baker perennially dusted with a coat of flour. His bread is sold in an anonymous grocery store, owned by his family, next door to his oven, and the scent of fresh bread perfumes the air. His wood-burning oven is over 100 years old, and the bread baked in it, fragrant and wheaty, is made from Tuscan flour, starter, and a small amount of yeast. Bread rises in a room over the still-warm oven. On Saturdays bread is baked three times to satisfy the local demand, since Castino's bread is known to last longer and taste better than most.

SALUMI

Macelleria Marini
Via Selva 313, Ferruccia
☎0574.718-119
Closed Monday, Tuesday, Wednesday, and on Thursday afternoons

Adriano and Patrizia Marini make some of the finest *salumi* in the area. Locally grown pigs are transformed into tasty *prosciutto,* salami, *finocchiona,* and fantastic spiced *pancetta.* The wonderful *coppa,* a smaller version of the chunky pork sausage called *soprassata,* is not for the squeamish—it's made from head. All products are made by hand and contain salt, spices, and meat. *Prosciutto,* hung upstairs in well-aired rooms, ages for a year if Adriano and Patrizia aren't sweet-talked into selling it earlier.

GELATO

Bar Anisare
Via Roma 93
☎0574.718-490
Closed Tuesday

Surely all the people seated at the sidewalk tables or milling outside the Bar Anisare can't be local. The reputation of "Il Cinese," who is not from China and doesn't even look Oriental, has traveled because his *gelato* is made from all-natural ingredients. Most colors are pale, but the flavors are intense. The largest selection is available on summer weekends, with a splendid assortment of fresh fruit flavors. Nut, banana, and citrus fruits, plus a rich, egg-yolky custard (*crema*) and a slightly gummy, almost black, dark chocolate will thrill winter *gelato* fans.

Anghiari

INN
See Sansepolcro

AGRITOURISM
Ca'Faggio
Sucignano 42
☎**0575.749-025**
No credit cards • low moderate

RESTAURANT
Castello di Sorci
Via San Lorenzo 21
☎**0575.789-066**
Closed Monday • inexpensive
Located in a farmhouse outside the Castello di Sorci ("Mouse Castle"), this archetypal *trattoria* serves an astounding inexpensive fixed-price meal. Diners are served, or assaulted on Sundays and holidays, with an *antipasto* of *salumi* and chicken-liver canapés (*crostini*). Pace yourself for two *primi*, usually pasta and a soup or *gnocchi*, and a main dish of roasted meat, served with vegetables. Desserts, if you're still interested, are homemade. All the mediocre red and white wine you can drink, mineral water, and even an after-dinner *caffè* and a *digestivo* are included in the price.

Arezzo

HOTEL
Continental
Piazza Guido Monaco 7
☎**0575.20251**
Fax 0575.350-485
All credit cards • moderate

RESTAURANT
L'Agania
Via Mazzini 10
☎**0575.25381**
Closed Monday
American Express, MasterCard, Visa •
moderate

The ambience is typical *trattoria*, there's no wine list—only mediocre house wine, but L'Agania is my favorite place to eat in Arezzo. The menu is short but sweet, with classics like *ribollita* in the winter, pasta sauced with rabbit or duck sauce, stewed main courses like tripe, *grifi in umido*, stewed veal snout, rabbit roast in the style of *porchetta*, grilled meats.

Artimino

HOTEL
Paggeria Medicea
Viale Papa Giovanni XXIII
☎**055.871-8081**
Fax 055.871-8080
All credit cards • high moderate

RESTAURANT
Da Delfina
Via della Chiesa 1
☎**055.871-8119**
Fax 055.871-8175
Closed Sunday evening, Monday, and August
No credit cards • high moderate
Delfina was the cook at the hunting lodge of Artimino, and when sportsmen were lucky, she turned their bounty into tasty Tuscan *cucina*. She still presides in the kitchen at her rustic country-style restaurant, but her son Carlo has taken over most of the work—with great skill, enthusiasm, and intelligence. The *cucina* is strictly local, tied to seasonal ingredients from the vegetable garden, courtyard, and fields. Wild herbs and flowers play an important role in Delfina's dishes. The vegetable soup is thickened with bread (*ribollita*) and then is pan-fried, an unusual treatment that Carlo says is the "real" way. Call the chestnut-flour dessert by its dialectical name, *ghirighio* (pronounced GHEE-REE-GHEE'-OH), and Carlo will jump for joy. The wines are local, from one of the great winemaking areas of Toscana. The lusty Carmignano reds are wonderful.

Bagno a Ripoli

HOTEL
See Firenze

RESTAURANT-APARTMENTS

Centanni
Via di Centanni 7
☎055.630-122
Fax 055.630-533
Closed Saturday lunch and Sunday
All credit cards • high moderate

I love Centanni, located in the Florentine countryside, ten minutes from the city. Matriarch Silvana Burgassi, who comes from a family of restaurateurs and salt-cod importers, rules the restaurant, assisted by her husband, Giovanni Bianchi, sons sommelier Silvano and Nicola, whose specialty is desserts, and chef Danilo Bini in the kitchen. The restaurant is a bit overmodernized, but I've got no complaints about anything else. Tables are simply set, service is superprofessional, the menu changes often, reflecting seasonal produce. *Antipasti* choices include classics like *prosciutto* and *crostini;* the Burgassi cured fish, tasting of anchovies, herring, and tuna; vegetarian *carpaccio,* and *salumi.* Continue with traditional Tuscan soups, homemade ravioli or pasta sauced with meat or vegetable sauces, or *risotto.* Fried chicken or rabbit, grilled beef or veal, braised squab in the winter are tempting main dishes. Look for first-rate salt-cod dishes in the winter months (it's impossible to properly reconstitute salt cod in the summer, says expert Silvana). *Porcini* mushrooms are featured in many courses during their spring and fall seasons. Conclude with homemade *gelato, sorbetto,* fruit bavarian creams, or tasty tarts. Silvano is positively obsessed about wine, has a wonderful palate, and hunts down well-priced enological gems that spark the wine list, a thrill to drink from. The family has just restored a huge farmhouse across the street, creating ten apartments (one or two bed-

rooms each) that can be rented daily, weekly, or monthly. Dine outdoors on the terrace overlooking olive trees and the lights of Firenze.

Bagno Vignoni

HOTEL

Posta Marcucci
Via Ara Urcea 43
☎0577.887-112
Fax 0577.887-119
All credit cards • moderate

RESTAURANT

Osteria del Leone
Via dei Mulini 3
☎0577.887-300
Closed Monday
MasterCard, Visa • moderate

Most visitors come to Bagno Vignoni, with its steaming thermal pool substituting for the usual town piazza, to bathe in the waters. But the Osteria del Leone, a charming, rustic *trattoria,* is another good reason to visit this village. Meals begin with *bruschetta,* dressed with local extra virgin olive oil, and *salumi.* Hearty soups, homemade *pici* with meat sauce, braised rabbit or duck, and *pecorino* are perfect for tasting Brunello, Rosso di Montalcino, or Vino Nobile di Montepulciano. Finish with custard or homemade *crostata.* The wine list is well priced, with a fine selection of Tuscan gems.

Bagnone

RESTAURANT-INN

Locanda La Lina
Piazza Marconi 1
☎/Fax 0187.429-069
Closed Thursday
MasterCard, Visa • inexpensive rooms, low moderate restaurant

It's impossible to hide my enthusiasm for this wonderful *locanda,* five bedrooms and two dining rooms in a tiny turn-of-the-century noble palace in the untouristed village of Bagnone. Lina closed her old restaurant and opened the inn seven years ago with her daughter Francesca and son-in-law Walter, a wine maniac/sommelier. The rooms are furnished with old-fashioned furniture, comfortable beds, modern bathrooms at bargain prices. Lina's cooking is home-style, simple; the menu is short but sweet, with more dishes available on the weekend, although *testaroli* sauced with *pesto*, fantastic ravioli, and hand-rolled pasta are always served. Hope that Lina's made *torta d'erbe*, a savory tart of wild greens or Swiss chard. Mushrooms and artichokes are prepared in season. Main-course offerings include chicken, rabbit, or breaded lamb chops, perfectly deep-fried. Local *pecorino* offers a perfect excuse to drink big from Walter's well-chosen but personal wine selection—there's no list, but his advice is on target. Finish with home-made *canestrelli*, a rustic cake.

Borgo a Buggiano

HOTEL
See Montecatini

RESTAURANT
Da Angiolo
Piazza del Popolo 2
☎**0572.32014**
Closed Monday, Tuesday, and August
All credit cards • high moderate

Luckily the food is far better than the coral, white, and olive-green decor of this gem of a fish restaurant nowhere near the coast. Angelo is in the kitchen, and his partner, sommelier Roberto, presides in the dining room. Almost everything on the extensive menu is made without sauce, and the clean, extra-fresh taste of the shellfish and fish, treated with respect, is a treat. Carnivores will be content with the meat selection. Desserts are simple, and the wine list is wonderful.

Bozzano

HOTEL
See Viareggio

GELATO FACTORY
Gelateria Versilia
Via Francalanci
☎**/Fax 0584.93043**
Closed Sunday afternoon

The Gelateria Versilia, small-scale industrial *gelato* producer, was founded in 1968 by Aurelio Angeli, now joined by his sons, making quality products that are easily found in bars on the coast near Viareggio. I'm wild about the *dessert versilia*, a frozen confection of sponge cake, vanilla *gelato*, rum or Marsala, and chocolate sauce that's served inverted on a plate. And I love the fifties-style graphics of a bathing beauty on a boat. To visit the factory, contact the Angeli family by fax or phone.

Camaiore

HOTEL
Villa Iolanda
Viale Pistelli 127
Lido di Camaiore (nearby)
☎**0584.617-296**
Fax 0584.617-295
All credit cards • moderate

HOTEL
Villa Ariston
Viale Colombo 355, Lido di Camaiore
☎**0584.610-633**
Fax 0584.610-631
All credit cards • expensive

HOTEL
Gigliola
Via del Secco 23
☎**0584.617-151**
Fax 0584.617-172
All credit cards • moderate

RESTAURANT

La Dogana

via Sarzanese 442, Capezzano Pianore

☎**0584.915-159**

Closed Wednesday

All credit cards • moderate

La Dogana is a new favorite, propelled by hyperenthusiastic Vittoriano Pierucci and his wife, Lida, in the kitchen, *simpatico* sommelier son Daniele in the dining rooms. The experience begins at the bar in the entrance with a glass of wine and a taste of *salumi* or deep-fried mini-whitebait called *avanotti* in season. Once seated, simply choose between fish or meat and let Vittoriano decide the menu. I've never been disappointed. Daniele ably pairs wines with his parents' cooking—the selection is personal, ample, well priced, and studded with lots of unknown gems. Hooray!

MEAT

Danilo Bonuccelli

Via Vittorio Emanuele 9

☎**0584.989-680**

Closed Wednesday afternoon

Danilo Bonuccelli is known beyond the borders of Toscana for his *salumi*. His specialties include local versions of *soprassata* and *biroldo* (blood pudding). Best of all is Danilo's *lardo* (unrendered lard), tasty pork fat barely streaked with meat, more flavorful than butter, to be served in thin slices on saltless Tuscan bread, a treat for those who fear no cholesterol. (Note that local residents call via Vittorio Emanuele, via de Mezzo.)

WINE BAR

Enoteca Nebraska

Via Nocchi 72/C

No phone

Closed Tuesday and November

No credit cards • inexpensive

The Enoteca Nebraska is unique. The unheated, unrestored farmhouse opens around 5 or 6 P.M. and quickly fills up with locals who look like Hell's Angels, and who come to taste the reasonably priced, unusual selection of wines that Tiziano Franceschini has to offer. They mix with sophisticated summer people who come over from the nearby fashionable beach resorts, and everyone hangs out over stemmed glasses until 2 A.M. The *salumi* (served on paper plates) are quality, and the local extra virgin olive oil is light but olivey. "Nebraska," one of the original owners, has left to open a wine shop with regular hours, but Tiziano seems to be managing.

RESTAURANT

Emilio e Bona

Via Lombricese 22

Località Candalla

☎**0584.989-289**

Closed Monday

All credit cards • high moderate

Overlooking a woodsy ravine by a mountain stream, Emilio e Bona looks like the kind of place where Snow White would hang out. Three large millstones dominate the dining room of this former olive oil mill where Luigi (Emilio was his father) and his wife, Bona, serve simple, well-prepared food. Start with *polenta* tiles served with a rabbit mousse. I love the greaseless mixed fry (*fritto misto*) of bread dough, sage leaves, potato croquettes, and chicken, rabbit, or lamb chops. Freshly made *bomboloni* (light, hole-less doughnuts), served with hot chocolate sauce, are my son's favorite dessert anywhere. But if perfectly fried food isn't your style, try *pasta alla Bona* (creamy ricotta-and-spinach–dressed homemade pasta), *carpaccio* (thinly sliced raw beef served with wild mushrooms, artichokes, or truffles), roast veal, or anything grilled over the wood-burning fire in Bona's spotless kitchen. Luigi will bring you a glass of sparkling wine while you wait for your meal, and will help you to choose from the mostly Tuscan wine selection. This is home-style cooking at its best.

Camporgiano

**AGRITOURISM-
RESTAURANT**

Mulino del Rancone
Camporgiano
☎**0583.618-670**
Fax 0583.644-146
Closed January, February
MasterCard, Visa • inexpensive

I'm wild about Mulino del Rancone, a one-time mill and adjacent farm on the banks of the Serchio River, converted into a restaurant, inn, and camping facility by Gabriele Bertucci. The restaurant is undistinguished-looking, two dining rooms decorated with maps and photos of the area on the walls, terra-cotta floors, paper tablecloths. The *cucina* makes up for any deficits in decor, with Gabriele's mother, Elda, assisted by Franca and Oriana, preparing traditional food of the Garfagnana area. Legendary Tuscan pastry chef Enzo Pedreschi has retired from his shop in Castelnuovo, but makes all the desserts, utilizing local cornmeal, chestnut flour, *farro* (emmer). Begin with an unusual *antipasto* of savory pastry. Move on to classic emmer and bean soup or hand-rolled pasta made of emmer and wheat flours—*tordellacci*, stuffed with meat, or *maccheroni strappati,* "ripped" pieces of pasta. Braised pork is served with chestnut-flour *polenta* in the winter, lamb is usually on the menu, trout from the Serchio are prepared with butter and almonds, mushrooms are available in season. The house wine is fine, but there's also a small selection of bottled wines. The Molino del Rancone sells *farro,* chestnut flour, dried chestnuts, cookies, and an eggy raisin cake wrapped in butcher paper, tied with red ribbon. Stay in one of eight inexpensive rooms, all with private bath. There's a train from Lucca that stops in Camporgiano, 200 meters from the Molino—a wonderful way to see the Garfagnana area for those without cars.

Castelfranco di Sopra

HOTEL

See Firenze

HOTEL
Villa Casagrande
Via Castel Guinelli 84
Figline Valdarno (nearby)
☎**055.954-4851**
Fax 055.954-4322
All credit cards • moderate

RESTAURANT
Vicolo del Contento
Via Mandria 38
☎**055.914-9277**
Fax 055.914-9906
Closed Monday, Tuesday, and August
All credit cards • high moderate

The Vicolo del Contento is a food lover's "easy street." Angelo and Lina Reditti have moved from the village to a carefully restored brick barn in the neighboring countryside, and the improved setting makes dining even more pleasant. Angelo's *cucina* is based on the best ingredients that his father can get his hands on. In the kitchen, together with his mother, who makes all the pasta and pastry, Angelo works wonders. Quality meat and super-fresh fish are simply cooked and graced

with impeccable vegetable sauces that are bright and full-flavored. *Gnocchi* made with vegetables, fish, or ricotta, are ethereal. The olive oils are the best that Toscana has to offer. Lina gracefully suggests and serves wines from their wonderful selection. Desserts are well prepared, but I like the homemade *gelato* best, and the cookies that Mom makes are irresistible.

Castellina in Chianti

HOTEL

Salivolpi
Via Fiorentina 89, Salivolpi, outside Castellina in Chianti
☎0577.740-484
Fax 0577.740-998
All credit cards • low moderate

RESTAURANT

L'Albergaccio
Via Fiorentina 35
☎0577.741-042
Fax 0577.741-250
Closed Sunday
No credit cards • low expensive

L'Albergaccio ("The Ugly Hotel") is an attractive rustic restaurant located upstairs in a restored farmhouse. Chef Sonia Visman interprets Tuscan cooking with skill, depending on fresh herbs and local ingredients. Francesco Cacciatori hustles through the dining room, explaining the small but exciting menu, pairing Sonia's food with fine Tuscan wines. Begin with local *salumi* or squab pâté with *porcini* mushroom salad. Look for rustic grain or legume soups, homemade pasta or *gnudi* ("naked") ravioli, poached greens and ricotta *gnocchi*. It's difficult to resist the perfectly grilled *bistecca* or fried chicken, lamb and brains, stewed boar with greens. Save room for aged *pecorino* or fresh goat's-milk cheese.

Desserts are interesting, like rice pudding, hazelnut pudding, fresh fruit tarts.

RESTAURANT

Antica Trattoria La Torre
Piazza del Comune 13
☎0577.740-236
Closed Friday
All credit cards • moderate

This hyper-Tuscan *trattoria* is in the middle of town, run by the Stiaccini family for over 100 years, preserving the *cucina* of Chianti territory. The wine list focuses on local production, but even the house wine is worth drinking. Don't look for surprises on the menu—just perfect *salumi, fettunta* (garlic bread), classic Tuscan soups, or baked pasta. The grilled *bistecca* is worth a trip, although stewed *cinghiale* (boar) and braised squab are tempting. *Pecorino* cheese is first-rate. Finish with fresh fruit, cookies and Vin Santo, or *tiramisù*.

Castelnuovo Berardenga

HOTEL-RESTAURANT

Relais Borgo San Felice
San Felice
☎0577.359-260
Fax 0577.359-089
All credit cards • expensive

San Felice is a perfectly restored hamlet in one of the sweetest corners of Toscana. It's home to the fine San Felice wines, olive groves, a Relais & Chateaux hotel and restaurant. The style is gentrified rustic, with comfortable floral-print sofas in the living rooms, old-fashioned furniture, terra-cotta floors. The restaurant, Poggio Rosso, is decorated in the same style, with important crystal glasses, well-appointed tables, professional service. The menu is a blend of classic and creative cooking, based on quality ingredients. Some dishes are a bit too far out for my taste, and the one-dish salads on the lunch menu are overpriced, overingrediented. Simple pastas, fish soups, anything with *porcini* mushrooms and grilled meat or poultry are probably the best options. Desserts are delicious, non-Tuscan, and *gelato* and *sorbetto* are homemade. A wide range of wines and vintages from San Felice and Campogiovanni, an estate owned by San Felice that makes wonderful Brunello, make dining at Poggio Rosso a pleasure.

AGRITOURISM

Felsina
Strada Chiantigiana 484
☎0577.355-117
Fax 0577.355-651
MasterCard, Visa • moderate to expensive
Five apartments on the estate of a fantastic winery right outside Castelnuovo.

RESTAURANT

Da Antonio
Piazza Marconi
☎0577.355-321
Closed Monday, open evenings only except Sunday
MasterCard, Visa • expensive
What's a fish restaurant doing in the landlocked Chianti area, and where does the fish come from? Owner Antonio Farini is from the Tuscan coast, decided to open a restaurant inland, and shops the markets in Viareggio and Piombino for the freshest local fish and seafood he can get his hands on. There's no written menu, and the endless *antipasto* of perfectly cooked dishes changes constantly, followed by a pasta sauced with seafood, simply grilled fish, *gelato*, or fresh fruit, paired with offerings from the super wine list. This is one of the best fish restaurants in Toscana. Dine on the terrace when the weather is nice.

RESTAURANT-WINERY

Castell'in Villa
Castell'in Villa
☎/Fax 0577.359-356
Fax 0577.359-222
MasterCard, Visa • moderate
Dynamic Princess Coralia Pignatelli is a born-again Tuscan, her winery makes first-rate Chianti, and now she's opened a wonderful restaurant on her estate. Look for fine cooking that's innovative but Tuscan in spirit, paired with Castell'in Villa's fine wines. Seasonal vegetables and fresh herbs are used to advantage to flavor meat and poultry. The menu changes weekly—diners should hope that ricotta-stuffed zucchini flowers are offered. Continue with warm barley salad or flat pasta sauced with arugula, walnuts, and *pecorino*. Lamb, squab, or roast suckling pig are all perfect excuses to drink the *riserva*, but non–meat eaters can quaff it with the fine *pecorino* cheese (either fresh or aged). Vegetarians will do well dining on pasta and side dishes. Desserts are worth saving room for.

Castelnuovo di Garfagnana

HOTEL

Da Carlino
Via Garibaldi 13
☎0583.62616
Fax 0583.62616
Visa • inexpensive

ENOTECA

Vecchio Mulino
Via Vittorio Emanuele 12
☎0583.62192
FAX 0583.62616
Closed Sunday, open 7:30 A.M.–8 P.M.
MasterCard, Visa • low moderate
Vecchio Mulino is, in guidebook language, worth a detour, a three-star experience. It's an old-fashioned bar; locals stop in at all

hours for a coffee, glass of wine, or snack. But there's also an amazing selection of wine and local products, well chosen by Andrea and Cinzia Bertucci. Stop in for a snack of first-rate *salumi*, cheese, marinated vegetables, or anchovies served with green sauce, paired with one of the well-priced wines sold by the glass. Buy emmer, chestnut flour, beans, extra virgin olive oil, and wine, all perfect gastronomic souvenirs of a visit to the Garfagnana area. Hang out at one of the tables and observe the local action.

EMMER CONSORTIUM
Consorzio Produttore di Farro della Garfagnana c/o Communità Montana della Garfagnana
Via Vittorio Emanuele 7
☎0583.644-911
Fax 0583.644-901
Twenty-five small producers of emmer have banded together in this newly founded consortium to defend their hyper-traditional local product. Due to the current popularity of *farro*, lots of people are getting spelt (an inferior product utilized for animal food) and emmer from other regions (or countries) and packaging them. All of the consortium's *farro* is grown and milled locally, and they've just been granted a DOC for this traditional grain. Contact Pierluigi Angeli at the Communità Montana, across the street from Vecchio Mulino for more information.

TABLE LINENS AND MORE
Artis
Via Vannugli 61
☎0583.62015
Fax 0583.62174
No credit cards
Maria Grazia hand-looms fabrics on thirteenth-century looms, of hemp, linen, cotton, silk, and cashmere. Look for tablecloths, bedspreads, towels, and fashionable scarves and shawls of superior

quality and brands that can't be mentioned in print.

Castiglioncello

GELATO
Dai Dai
Via del Sorriso 8
☎0586.752-754
Fax 0586.751-653
Open 8:30 A.M.–5 P.M., closed Saturday and Sunday
Dai dai, the Italian equivalent of "giddiap," were the words used to by Signor Tancredi to incite the mule who pulled the cart from which he sold *gelato* in the pinewoods of Marradi. Bite-size *bocconi*, cubes of vanilla, coffee, chocolate and, best of all, pine-nut *gelato*, are coated with bittersweet chocolate, wrapped in foil-lined brown paper. The *bocconi* are often served in fine restaurants along with an espresso, but those who want to go to the source should visit Dai Dai. Antonio Bartoletti purchased the *gelateria* a few years ago, production has increased, and is now distributed nationally, but the *gelato* is still wonderful. Look for frozen confections like *mattonella* ("tile"), *trancio* ("slice"), *cassatina*, frozen chocolate truffles, or *sorbetto*.

Catena

HOTEL
See Firenze or Carmignano

RESTAURANT-HOTEL
La Bussola
Via Vecchia Fiorentina 382, Catena
(between Firenze and Pistoia)
☎0573.743-128
Fax 0573.744-591
Closed Saturday lunch, Sunday
Visa, American Express • inexpensive hotel, moderate restaurant
I'm wild about La Bussola, an enlightened *trattoria* outside Poggio a Caiano, on the

border between the provinces of Firenze and Prato. I met pony-tailed owner Moreno Janda at a wine auction a few years ago buying up old vintages and decided I had to check out his *trattoria*. The decor is rustic, a collection of old rifles on the wall hints that someone was interested in hunting and that game is served. Rosalba Coveri rules in the kitchen, assisted by a staff of women cooks and her sommelier son, Moreno, who shuttles between the kitchen and dining rooms with his wife, Franca, and Mary. Most diners start with a basket of slice-it-yourself *salumi* or appetizers like *fettunta* topped with white beans and truffles, Colonnata *lardo,* vegetable salads, *tonno di coniglio,* rabbit marinated in oil like tuna. Homemade pasta is sauced with truffles, seasonal vegetables, game, or chicken innards, all tasty options. The main-course specialty is roast suckling pig, but game like mallard and wild boar are worth tasting. Mushrooms and truffles are available in season. The dessert selection is small but well executed, and there's usually something delicious made by Roxanne Edwards, a skilled pastry chef who lives nearby. The wine list makes me jump for joy; it's packed with bargains, young inexpensive wines and impressive older vintages at unbelievably low prices.

Cerbaia

HOTEL
See Firenze

RESTAURANT
La Tenda Rossa
Piazza del Monumento 9/14
☎**055.826-132**
Fax 055.825-210
Closed Wednesday
All credit cards • expensive
La Tenda Rossa is a family-run restaurant obsessed with quality. Capable sommelier Silvano Santandrea and his wife, assisted by

a host of in-laws and offspring, offer one of the Florentine countryside's most interesting nontraditional dining experiences. The decor is modern, with diffused lighting, planter-dividers that create intimate dining zones, and tables elegantly set with silver, crystal, china, and linen. The menu is innovative. Goose liver, lightly cooked fish, and tasty local meats are well prepared, flavored with lots of fresh herbs, local extra virgin olive oil, and white truffles in season. Pasta is homemade and tasty. Mushrooms are always splendid. Alas, there are too many concessions to puréed mousse cuisine, and some dishes tend to get faddish. The wine list is a personal favorite; there's always something new and wonderful that Silvano ably pairs with his wife's *cucina.*

Cetona

RESTAURANT-INN
La Frateria di Padre Eligio
Convento di San Francesco
☎**/Fax 0578.238-015**
Closed Tuesday and January
American Express, MasterCard, Visa • expensive
The Frateria was created by Padre Eligio, a controversial priest who has probably cured more drug addicts than anyone else in Italy, but who has a penchant for fine wine and red underwear. His hardworking flock has restored both the Castello in Cozzo Lomellina in Lombardia, and La Frateria di Padre Eligio, and they now staff both restaurants. La Frateria is located in a spectacular thirteenth-century Franciscan convent with stone walls, brick floors, and vaulted ceilings. Walnut tables are set with hand-embroidered linens; the menus are hand-painted. The total effect is mystical, special, otherworldly. The *cucina* has its roots in Toscana, based on excellent local ingredients produced by the restaurant's working farm, but the menu is hardly regional. The olive oil is one of the area's finest, the preserves are tasty, and the pastry

is first-class. Prices are high, more acceptable as a charitable contribution than as payment for a meal. (Note: Credit cards are not accepted at the inn.)

Chiusi

HOTEL

Il Patriarca
Stada Statale 146, Querce al Pino
☎**0578.273-400**
Fax 0578.274-594
Visa, American Express • moderate

RESTAURANT

Osteria La Solita Zuppa
Via Porsenna 21
☎**0578.21006**
Closed Tuesday
Diners Club, MasterCard, Visa • moderate

La solita zuppa is an expression of derision for the kind of cooking that's boring, "the same old soup." But there's nothing boring about the food at this *osteria*, which offers seasonal Tuscan cooking from a wood-burning oven served with enthusiasm by Roberto and Luana. Look for soups like *cipollata*, onion; bean and emmer; chickpea and mushroom, or hand-rolled pasta like *pici*. Continue with roast pork, stewed wild boar, or *pane del garzone*, stuffed veal. Desserts aren't as exciting as the rest of the menu, but I wouldn't let that stop me from returning to La Solita Zuppa. There's a reasonably priced tasting menu with local specialties and a short but sweet wine list, although the house wine is worth drinking.

Colle di Val d'Elsa

RESTAURANT-HOTEL

Arnolfo
Via XX Settembre 52
☎**/Fax 0577.920-549**
Closed Tuesday and January 10–February 10
All credit cards • low expensive

Chef-owner Gaetano Trovato's tiny restaurant is named after Colle di Val d'Elsa's native son Arnolfo di Cambio, architect and sculptor. The *cucina* is as original as Arnolfo's work must have seemed in the thirteenth century. Based on tradition but highly creative, some of the finest food between Firenze and Siena is prepared by Gaetano with the best and freshest ingredients that his territory can provide. Pasta is homemade, soups are stellar, and hard-to-find *Chianina* beef is always on the menu. Cheese fans should leave room for the sheep's-milk ricotta. Desserts are tempting. The wine list is a true joy and enhances the dining experience at Arnolfo, always a pleasure.

RESTAURANT

L'Antica Trattoria
Piazza Arnolfo 23
☎**0577.923-747**
Fax 0577.921-635
Closed Tuesday
All credit cards • low expensive

L'Antica Trattoria is in Colle's main piazza, an old *trattoria* that evolved into a fine restaurant. The decor is modern, with hardwood floors, imitation antiques, brick walls studded with bits of an older edifice. The *cucina* is Tuscan and outer-regional, with typical *salumi* and *crostini* to start with, then homemade pasta sauced with seasonal vegetables or soups like *farinata* with black cabbage or chick-peas with clams. Squab braised with Vino Nobile di Montepulciano wine is the house specialty. Desserts are tasty, nontraditional, perfect for those who have tired of *cantucci*. The wine list is

impressive, with lots of Tuscan and Piemontese reds and a large selection of *grappa* and distillates. Dine outdoors overlooking the piazza when the weather is nice.

POTTERY

Vulcania
Via Mason 42
☎**0577.920-089**
Fax 0577.923-530
Closed Saturday and Sunday
No credit cards

Traditional dark brown casseroles and pans with a lighter brown interior, as well as matching or bright red dinnerware, are manufactured by Vulcania in Colle di Val d'Elsa and sold directly from the factory. The pottery is available in most housewares stores, as are their bean pots (*fagioliere*).

Colonnata

HOTEL

Villa Irene
Via delle Macchie 125, Ronchi (nearby)
☎**0585.309-310**
Fax 0585.308-038
No credit cards • low expensive

HOTEL

Hotel Residence Tropicana
Ronchi (nearby)
☎**0585.309-041**
Fax 0585.309-044
All credit cards • expensive in July and August, high moderate the rest of the year

RESTAURANT

Da Venanzio
Piazza Palestro 3
☎**0585.758-062**
Closed Sunday evening, Thursday
Visa • high moderate

Venanzio Vannucci put *lardo di Colonnata* on Italy's culinary map. His restaurant is rustic, but the *cucina* is worth a detour for Tuscan cooking at its best. I can't imagine a

visit to Venanzio's without a taste of homemade *lardo*, although other first-rate *salumi* are available, and Venanzio is presently brine-aging *Chianina* beef. His wife, Lena, makes pasta like ravioli stuffed with vegetables or wild greens, *lasagnette* made with borage or spinach, sauced with mushrooms or wild asparagus in season. Main-course offerings include kid stewed with juniper berries, lamb flavored with rosemary, snails cooked with sausage, perfectly fried rabbit, grilled *Chianina* steak. Vegetable *contorni* are called "trimmings" on the menu. The cheese selection is important and always includes local *pecorino*, made by a shepherd who summers his flock near Colonnata. Finish with homemade *sorbetto* or *gelato* in the summer, or figs and prunes cooked in spiced wine, or rice-pudding cake made by Venanzio's daughter Elisabetta. The wine list is impressive, reasonably priced, although the house wine is worth drinking. Purchase *lardo* from Lena's mother, Fernanda, at her *alimentari* across the piazza from the restaurant.

Fiesole

HOTEL-RESTAURANT

Villa San Michele
Via Doccia 4
☎**055.59451**
Fax 055.598-734
All credit cards • high luxury and beyond

This luxury hotel is simply spectacular, set above the hills north of Florence, a world away from the smog and bustle of the city. Formal gardens, frescoed halls, impeccable service, linen sheets, antique furniture, rooms and suites with prices for those who don't count the zeroes on Italian banknotes. The restaurant serves lightened-up Tuscan food and classics from other regions, but some dishes sound better than they taste while others seem to have too many trendy ingredients. Avoid lobster (it's from Maine) and anything that sounds pureed, and stick to the basics like nicely done homemade pasta, *Chianina* beef, grilled fish. Desserts may be the best part of the meal, with homemade *gelato,* perfect pastry, wild berries, or creamy spoon desserts like *panna cotta* and fruit bavarians. The wine list is choice but pricy, as would be expected. Dine outdoors on the *loggia* overlooking Firenze when the weather is nice.

STAYING IN A FLORENTINE VILLA

The Florentines built beautiful villas in the surrounding countryside to escape the city's sweltering summers. Some have been turned into lovely small hotels, perfect as a base for touring the region and for excursions into Firenze. Most are expensive, but less costly than comparable accommodations in the city.

Villa Casalecchi
Castellina in Chianti
☎ 0577.741-111
Fax 0577.741-111
Closed November through March
All credit cards • expensive

Villa Casalecchi, with sixteen rooms, a suite, and three apartments in the former stables, is furnished in Tuscan style and surrounded by a magnificent park.

Villa Le Barone
Via San Leolino 19
Panzano
☎ 055.852-621
Fax 055.852-277
Closed November through March
All credit cards • expensive

The sixteenth-century Villa Le Barone has twenty-five rooms and a beautiful pool in a large park with a spectacular view. Guests are required to eat at least one meal a day at the villa's restaurant.

Villa Rigacci
Strada Rigacci 76
Vaggio
☎ 055.865-6718
Fax 055.865-6537
All credit cards • moderate

More like a friend's country house than a hotel, the Villa Rigacci's ten rooms are tastefully furnished. Horseback riding in the Tuscan countryside or hanging out at the pool may distract you from visiting the city.

Villa Sangiovese
Piazza Bucciarelli 4
Panzano
☎ 055.852-461
Fax 055.852-463
American Express • expensive

The restored Villa Sangiovese has sixteen rooms, and there are three apartments in the farmhouse next door to the nineteenth-century villa.

Suzanne Pitcher
Via M. Buonarroti 8
Firenze
☎ 055.234-3354
Fax 055.234-7240

Suzanne Pitcher rents villas, farm houses, and apartments in Florence and Tuscany in a wide range of prices and styles, from humble to palatial.

Firenze

Firenze was founded in hilltop Fiesole by Etruscans who seem to have known better than to settle in the Arno Valley, with its frigid winters and torrid summers. The Romans colonized the city on the banks of the silver Arno. From the *comune's* founding in 1115, Firenze flourished for over 500 years as a center of art, architecture, finance, and culture. Etruscan frescoes and excavations have revealed many details of daily life, including the use of utensils like the rolling pin, pasta strainer, and cheese grater, and typical dishes that are still part of the Florentine menu: wide pasta, grilled meats, and *schiacciata con l'uva* (a grape and honey cake). By the year 1200 the character of the Florentine *cucina* was already dominated by bread, in the form of *panunto* or *fettunta* (garlic-rubbed bread dipped in olive oil), early versions of bread-based soups, and *schiacciata alla fiorentina* and *pan di ramerino*, two dessert breads. Renaissance feasts for kings, popes, and the Medici family became food marathons. Catherine de' Medici, a true gourmand, took her own cooks and a supply of local ingredients to a distant and uncivilized France when she married Henry II. She also took another local invention, *la forchetta*, a two-tined instrument adapted from the Roman *lingula*, a spearlike utensil used to transfer food from serving dish to plate, and refined by the already famous Florentine goldsmiths. But the food found in most restaurants today isn't that of kings or the Medici but of the *contadini*, the farmers or peasants—simple, austere cooking that reflects the Tuscan emphasis on bread, beans, and olive oil. Soups, especially the trio of *pappa*, *ribollita*, and *panzanella*, dominate the first courses, while meats are usually grilled or fried. *La Fiorentina* can refer to the local soccer squad or to a T-bone steak at least two inches thick, charcoal-grilled rare. The Florentines,

insultingly called "bean eaters" by their neighbors, are said to lick plates and ladles when beans are served. The *pinzimonio* style of eating raw vegetables dipped in fresh, peppery extra virgin olive oil, salt, and pepper is generally limited to the winter. All other vegetables in Firenze will be deep-fried or overcooked. Traditional desserts are a bit austere, but fine non-Tuscan desserts and *torte* are found in most restaurants.

The city is currently attempting to deal with a traffic problem—a siege of buses, cars, and pigeons—struggling against those who'd like to turn this unique Renaissance gem into a polluted parking lot. Tourism has spawned pizza-by-the-slice stands and restaurants that dish out mediocre food and crummy wine for a clientele who will never return. I haven't been thrilled by too many eateries in the city. But don't get me wrong—I live in Firenze, and I love it. Note: Street numbers of commercial establishments appear in red; this is indicated by an "r" (*rosso*, red) in the address.

HOTEL-RESTAURANT
Helvetia e Bristol
Via dei Pescioni 2
☎**055.287-814**
Fax 055.288-353
All credit cards • luxury

HOTEL
Principe
Lungarno A. Vespucci 34
☎**055.284-848**
Fax 055.283-458
All credit cards • expensive

HOTEL
Bellettini
Via dei Conti 7
☎**055.213-561**
Fax 055.283-551
MasterCard, Visa • low moderate

HOTEL

Torre Guelfa

Borgo SS. Apostoli 8

☎055.239-6338

Fax 055.239-8577

MasterCard, Visa, American Express • low moderate

HOTEL

Torre di Bellosguardo

Via Roti Michelozzi 2

☎055.229-8145

Fax 055.229-008

All credit cards • low luxury

HOTEL

Loggiato dei Serviti

Piazza SS. Annunziata 3

☎055.289-592

Fax 055.289-595

All credit cards • high moderate

HOTEL

Park Palace

Piazzale Galileo 5

☎055.222.431

Fax 055.220-517

American Express • low expensive

BAR-PASTRY

Dolce Dolcezza

Piazza Beccaria 8/r

☎055.234-5458

Fax 055.234-6698

Closed Monday

Giulio Corti and his wife, Ilaria, make some of Firenze's finest (and most expensive) desserts. The shop is elegant, illuminated with chandeliers, glass display cases filled with tempting *crostate*, tarts of lemon, pear, or fruit-topped custard. The flourless chocolate cake and the chocolate hazelnut *torta Ilaria* will thrill chocoholics. Miniature versions of almost everything allow visitors to taste it all. Individually portioned bavarian creams come in a wealth of flavors, like coffee, mint, seasonal fruit, and

even rose petal (in May). Fine coffee from local roaster Piansa is served at the bar.

BAR-CAFFÈ, PASTRY, LIGHT LUNCH

Caffè Italiano

Via della Condotta 56/r

☎055.291-082

Closed Sunday

No credit cards • moderate

Umberto Montano, owner of Alle Murate (see page 306), has created a wonderful bar that looks old-fashioned, like it's been there forever, just steps from piazza della Signoria. He's paid attention to all the details, as usual, and serves a special roast of coffee made just for him, first-rate pastry made in his laboratory downstairs, and a refreshing, lightly carbonated, and sweetened drink called *acqua antica*, served plain or with the addition of fresh fruit puree. Sit at one of the tables next to the window or climb the stairs in the back to a large room upstairs, perfect for loitering after a shopping spree. Caffè Italiano serves a simple well-priced lunch from a limited menu, and diners have the option of ordering just one dish or a whole meal.

BAKERY–SNACK BAR–ENOTECA

Cantinetta dei Verrazzano

Via de' Tavolini 18/20

☎055.268-590

Closed Sunday, open 8 A.M.–8 P.M.

American Express • inexpensive to low moderate

Although it looks like an unassuming bakery from the street, the Cantinetta dei Verrazzano is one of the best stops in Firenze for a snack. Head past the display cases to the back, check out the elegant copper espresso machine and the wood-burning oven where pizza and *schiacciate* (what we think of as *focaccia*) are used to sandwich vegetable, meat, and cheese fillings. Diners can order from a blackboard menu in a room on the left, choosing from fine *salumi* from Falorni in Greve (see page 320), assorted *crostini,* or adorable truffle-paste sandwiches. The wine comes from the Ver-razzano estate in Greve, and the selection is wonderful. Finish a light lunch with *biscotti* and *vin santo.*

SNACK BAR
Oliandolo
Via Ricasoli 38–40/r
☎**055.211-296**
Closed Sunday
No credit cards • low moderate

Another perfect choice for a snack or light lunch in the area of the Duomo. Owner Bep-pino Mazzanti is a professional whose expe-rience at the restaurants Angiolino and Acquacotta (see page 306) has paid off with this winning formula. *Salumi, crostini,* sand-wiches, *bruschetta,* cold salads, and cheese are served at wooden tables. There's a small selection of wines (including those of neigh-bor Marchese Pucci), beer, and soft drinks.

SNACK BAR–LUNCH AT CENTRAL MARKET
Nerbone
Via San Casciano in the Mercato Centrale
☎**055.219-949**
Closed Sunday, open 7 A.M.–2 P.M.
No credit cards

Nerbone is one of the culinary jewels of the city, tucked into the San Lorenzo central market. The building, all glass and cast-iron, was designed by Giuseppe Mengoni (who also did *gallerie* in Milano and Napoli), built in 1864 during an urban-renewal project. The aisles are named for nearby towns, and Nerbone is located on via San Casciano, on the periphery of the ground floor. It's an attractive area, with a dark green old-fashioned sign, handsome white-tiled walls, and Chianti bottle decor. Easy to spot because there's always a swarm of locals at the cash register, and waiting in

front of the counter for a boiled-beef sand-wich, the specialty of the house. A black-board shows daily specials and there are a few marble-topped tables across the aisle for a real meal, but I can never resist the world-class boiled-beef *panino.* Pay first, then order, opting for a dry or "wet" (*ba-gnato*) roll (wet is considered the best choice), with or without *salsa verde,* green sauce. Drink a *gotino,* shot glass, of Chianti Classico. Nerbone offers one of the great bargains of Italy and sums up the joy of Tuscan food—but it's not for vegetarians.

BAR·CAFFÈ
Rivoire
Piazza della Signoria 5/r
☎**055.214-412**
Fax 055.211-302
Closed Monday

Rivoire is the best of the people-watching bars in Firenze, with indoor seating as well as outdoor tables in the piazza della Signo-ria, one of the world's most beautiful squares. The sandwiches are fresh, the pas-try is fair, and the chocolates are wonderful, especially the bitter chocolate rectangles individually wrapped in royal blue paper and tin foil. The chocolate Easter eggs, cus-tom-stuffed with a surprise of your own choice, are the best in Firenze. Thick hot chocolate (*cioccolata calda*) topped with whipped cream is a winter specialty.

BAR·CAFFÈ
Giacosa
Via Tornabuoni 83/r
☎**055.239-6262**
Closed Monday

Giacosa, under the same ownership as Rivoire but with a different pastry chef, serves the same fine coffee and chocolates. Florentines flock here for the quick stand-up lunch (*pranzo in piedi*). Counter service is crowded, elbow room only. The Negroni, a Campari and gin cocktail named for the count who loved them, was invented at Giacosa, and is still in demand during the cocktail hour.

SPECIALTY FOODS
Procacci
Via Tornabuoni 64/r
☎055.211-656
Closed Sunday

Procacci's window display of miscellaneous Anglo-Saxon expatriate items like English tea tins and jars of Scotch marmalade doesn't even hint at the specialty items in this understated shop. Delicate oval glazed rolls are spread with salmon or anchovies, but the cognoscenti turn up here for the truffle sandwiches (*panini tartufati*). Help yourself from the glass display case and sip a glass of white wine or *spumante* at the bar. Weary shoppers can recover at one of Procacci's two tiny tables.

MARKET
San Lorenzo Market
Piazza del Mercato Centrale
Open Monday through Saturday mornings, and Saturday from 4 to 8 P.M.

The ground floor of the huge nineteenth-century cast-iron San Lorenzo market is filled with stalls, most selling perishables that need refrigeration. Meat, poultry, fish, and general grocery (*alimentari*) stalls abound.

Mario Conti (banco 300, tel. 055.239-8501) is one of the stars of the ground floor, with his fabulous, and expensive, selection of the first early vegetables and fruits of the season, known as *primizie*. In general, his fruits and vegetables are the biggest, best, and most exotic. Mushrooms and a wide range of wild salad greens, herbs, and exotic fruit are beautifully displayed along with sidelines of beans, olives, and nuts. His stall faces Luciano Baccetti, whose selection of well-priced quality cheeses always draws a crowd. Nearby, Signora Panerai, the cookie lady, sells *biscotti* of every shape and size, including crispy

chocolate-cream–filled logs that thrill my son Max.

Gianni Fancelli (upstairs at banco 16, tel. 055.263-028) has the best selection of fresh herbs and salad greens, both wild and cultivated, and berries, all highly seasonal. It's a pleasure to see so many different baskets of fresh, lively-looking, unfamiliar types of salad.

MARKET
Mercato di Sant'Ambrogio
Piazza Ghiberti
Open Monday through Saturday mornings

Medium-size Sant'Ambrogio is a gem. The building, with its iron trim and more stainless steel than marble, houses the perishables and an inexpensive take-out stand. The outdoor market sells some of Firenze's finest produce, piled up in mounds, as well as clothes, housewares, plants, herbs, and vegetable seedlings. Teresa Dutto's corner stand sells fresh produce from her family's farm, and has for more than fifty years.

MARKET
Santo Spirito
Piazza Santo Spirito
Open Monday through Saturday mornings

Piazza Santo Spirito has a small neighborhood market. Four large fruit and vegetable stands sell a wide range of produce at one end of the piazza, while at the other end, closer to the Santo Spirito church, four or five farmers set up tables, offering their seasonal harvest of fruit, vegetables, herbs, and flowers.

Valerio is my favorite farmer here. No strawberries in December, no grapefruit from Israel, just peak-of-the-season, fresh-from-the-garden vegetables, fruit, eggs, chicken, and rabbits to order, all raised by the Innocenti family. The flavors aren't as good as they used to be because the land has been ruined by chemicals, says this farmer with a palate that remembers, but his produce is among the best in Firenze. As if all this weren't enough, Valerio also provides excellent, original advice on how to cook everything he sells.

SPICES
Bizzarri
Via della Condotta 32/r
☎**055.211-580**
Closed Wednesday afternoon

Bizzarri, founded in 1842, sells chemical supplies, no-frills cosmetics, and spices, whole or ground. It's always a thrill to breathe the strangely scented air in this shop with its huge, dark, glass-doored wooden cupboards.

WINE
Alessi
Via dell' Oche 27/r
☎**055.214-966**
Closed Wednesday afternoon
MasterCard, Visa

Alessi's *enoteca* is hidden downstairs, behind their floor-to-ceiling assortment of candies, cookies, and seasonal sweets like Easter *colomba* and chocolate eggs and Christmas *panettone* and *panforte*. The back room is dedicated to fruit syrups, liqueurs, *grappa,* and sparkling wines. But the best part of the shop is downstairs, where wine is displayed according to region. Some areas are smaller than they should be, but the Toscana room is terrific, and features a large range of Chianti Classico, Brunello, and the new-style Tuscan table wines. Not all the wines are fantastic, but the selection is the best in Firenze.

WINE AND OIL
Vino e Olio
Via de' Serragli 29/r
☎**055.298-708**
Closed Wednesday afternoon

This neighborhood wine and olive oil shop is a personal favorite. Wines are well priced, and the Tuscan selection is wonderful. There are usually at least five or six different

extra virgin olive oils for sale. Informal Saturday afternoon wine tastings are casual, attended by locals.

SUPERMARKET
Esselunga
Via Pisana 130
☎**055.706-556**

Viale de Amicis 89/b
☎**055.604-442**
and other locations
Closed Wednesday afternoon

Esselunga ("Long S") is the best American-style supermarket in Firenze, stocked with fine Italian and some imported products.

TRIPE
Pinzauti
Piazza Dante
☎**No phone**
Closed Wednesday afternoon

Boiled tripe (*trippa*), looking very much like a worn-out bathing cap, is sold warm at stands in strategic locations in Firenze, ready to be turned into Florentine-style tripe or stuffed into a crispy roll. Major stainless-steel stands are to be found at the San Lorenzo central market, the Porcellino market, and best of all, at the corner of via Tavolini and via dei Cerchi, at piazza Dante, manned by Signor Pinzauti. Open from 9 A.M. to 1 P.M., and from 5 to 7:30 P.M.

PIZZA
Pizzeria alla Marchigiana
Via del Corso 60/r
☎**055.214-961**
Closed Tuesday

Warning! Most street pizza is tourist food, and to be avoided. But high-quality pizza-by-the-slice possibilities do exist in Firenze. Pizzeria alla Marchigiana, for example, serves squares of tomato, mozzarella, mushroom, or *prosciutto* thick-crust pizzas. The house beverage is *spuma,* a locally produced carbonated drink of uncertain and undistinguished flavor. The wad of paper napkins they place your slice on provides inadequate insulation from the hot molten cheese when this pizza comes straight from the oven. Open from 9 A.M. to 2 P.M., and 3:30 to 9 P.M.

BREAD, PASTRY, PIZZA
Forno Sartoni
Via dei Cerchi 34/r
☎055.212-570
Closed Wednesday afternoon

The Forno on via dei Cerchi sells bread, rolls, sandwiches, and pastry, all baked on the premises. The crowd in the back is waiting for pizza or *schiacciata*—flat pizza crust dressed with a bit of oil, a local favorite—to come out of the oven, and it is well worth the mob scene and the wait.

ENOTECA-WINE SHOP
Fuori Porta
Via Monte alle Croci 10/r
☎055.234-2483
Fax 055.234-1408
Closed Sunday
All credit cards • low moderate

Rocco Ascani and his friends Andrea Conti and Angelo Carciola own the *enoteca* Fuori Porta, my favorite wine bar in Firenze, outside the fourteenth-century San Niccolò gate. The ambience is rustic, with a bar in the entrance, three rooms of dark wood tables, wooden stools and wainscoting, typical wine-related posters on the walls, shelves of bottles. The wine list is one of the best in town, affordable, with in-depth coverage of Tuscan reds as well as an impressive selection from the rest of Italy and beyond. Since Italians don't drink wine without eating, there's a menu of savory snacks like *crostoni*, open-faced sandwiches, *salumi*, and cheese. At lunch they offer a first course like soup, *panzanella*, or pasta sauced with vegetables or meat. Visit Fuori Porta when the weather is nice and

sip wine at an outdoor table overlooking Florence's medieval walls.

ENOTECA
Volpe e l'Uva
Piazza de' Rossi
☎/Fax 055.239-8132
Open 10 A.M.–8 P.M., closed Sunday
American Express, MasterCard, Visa • low moderate

Named for Aesop's Fox and Grapes fable, this *enoteca*, steps from the Ponte Vecchio, is a perfect choice for a snack or light meal in the center of town; worth a visit for Emilio Monechi and Riccardo Comparini's original selection of wines from small producers all over Italy. Two semicircular marble counters with stools aren't terribly comfortable but worth the inconvenience for enophiles. Interesting wines are served by the glass or bottle, and sandwiches, first-rate *salumi*, and domestic and imported cheese are displayed in a glass case. Sample wine and snacks outdoors at a wooden bench next to the *enoteca* or sit in the piazza at tables covered with grape-cluster–patterned cloths when the weather is nice.

WINE, SANDWICHES
Vini e Panini i Fratelli
Via dei Cimatori 38/r
☎055.296-096
Closed Sunday

This closet-size hole in the wall is the original Florentine version of fast food. Crummy Chianti by the short, squat *osteria* glass, essential sandwiches of *salumi*, and chicken-liver *crostini* are the unchanging menu for a stand-up lunch or snack. Hanging out on the corner of Firenze's main pedestrian drag substitutes for decor.

PASTRY
Pasticceria Sarti
Via Senese 147/r
☎055.232-0024

Closed Sunday, Wednesday afternoon, and most of August

Sarti makes the best "squashed" desserts in Firenze. The *schiacciata alla fiorentina*, an orange-and-egg–flavored pre-Lenten cake coated with a generous layer of powdered sugar, is excellent. So is the *schiacciata con l'uva*, bread dough baked with grapes and sugar, a dessert of Etruscan origins.

P A S T R Y
Gualtieri
Via Senese 18/r
☎**055.221-771**
Closed Monday

The *torta iris* isn't made with iris corms, bulbs, leaves, or even flowers, but the moist, delicate crumb of this white iced loaf cake makes it a favorite at this fine *pasticceria*.

G E L A T O
Carabè
Via Ricasoli 60/r
☎**055.289-476**
Closed Mondays, always open May to September, completely closed mid-November to mid-February

When I saw a bowl of lumpy lemons, a Sicilian cart, and a ceramic plate depicting the *trinacria*—Medusa with three bent legs angling from her head to represent the three corners of the triangular island—at Gelateria Carabè in Florence, I knew I was going to be happy. Owners Antonio and Loredana Lisciandro are from Patti, on the north coast of Sicily in the province of Messina. They make Firenze's best *gelato* and *sorbetto*, but best of all is their sublime *granita*, prepared Messina style, smooth and silky, not in the Palermo or Catania styles, which are granular.

Antonio taught me how to eat the Sicilian "Breakfast of Champions," coffee *granita* in a drinking cup topped with barely sweetened whipped cream, served with a warm brioche roll on the side. Dig

the spoon into the corner of the whipped cream, exposing the *granita*, taste the whipped cream, reinsert the spoon deeply, and gently mix, creating a kind of frozen *cappuccino*. Break off a piece of the brioche and dip it into the cup, scooping up as much of the *granita* mixture as possible. Eat this over the cup!

I'm wild about Carabè's *gelato, sorbetto,* and *granita* made with Sicilian products like pistachios, hazelnuts, almonds, and bumpy lemons, which Antonio has shipped from Sicily weekly. *Gelato* mavens should plan daily visits to Carabè while staying in Firenze, but bear in mind that it closes from November to the middle of February.

G E L A T O
Badiani
Viale dei Mille 20/r
☎**055.578-682**
Closed Tuesday

Badiani is the original Florentine source for fabulous *Buontalenti*, the egg-yolk–rich flavor named for Francesco de' Medici's personal *gelato* maker. Fruit flavors are good, but the rich chocolate, smoky, intense nut, and combination flavors are fantastic. The location is a bit out of the way, but this is one of the best *gelaterie* in Firenze.

R E S T A U R A N T
Acqua al Due
Via della Vigna Vecchia 40/r
☎**055.284-170**
Closed Monday
No credit cards • moderate

There's always a crowd waiting for a seat at one of Acqua al Due's communal tables and a crack at this ex-vegetarian restaurant's two different tastings. Start with the *assaggio di primi,* a series of first courses, usually four pastas and a rice dish, and conclude with the *assaggio di dolci,* a tasting of desserts including fruit tarts, fudgelike chocolate cake, and *tiramisù*. The wines could be better.

RESTAURANT

Acquacotta
Via dei Pilastri 51/r
☎055.242-907
Closed Wednesday
MasterCard, Visa • low moderate

Acquacotta is a simple, home-style *trattoria*. The food is reasonably priced and well prepared. The house specialty is *acquacotta*, rich vegetable soup served over toasted bread and topped with a poached egg. Some, but not too many, of the wines are wonderful.

RESTAURANT

Alle Murate
Via Ghibellina 52–54/r
☎055.240-618
Fax 055.245-474
Closed Monday, open evenings only
All credit cards • high moderate

Those who are tired of classic Tuscan should head to Alle Murate for a taste of southern Italian hospitality; it's the domain of multilingual Umberto Montano and his ex-wife, Giovanna Iorio, from the region of Basilicata. The restaurant's logo, an empty birdcage with an open door, evokes the nearby (and now defunct) prison of the same name and liberation from local tradition. The decor is modern, with jazz music playing softly, and beautifully appointed tables. The menu features southern Italian classics like Basilicata *lasagna*, fava-bean puree topped with cooked chicory, *orecchiette* sauced with broccoli, along with creative (but restrained) dishes. Homemade ravioli, vegetable-sauced pastas, simple soups are beautifully prepared. Meat dishes like braised beef, lamb with artichokes, or fish poached *acqua-pazza*–style are among the main-course selections. Most diners finish with a dessert called Armstrong

(named after Louis)—a large, warm chocolate-chip cookie topped with unsweetened whipped cream. The wine list is wonderful, personal, studded with gems—enophiles will definitely want to visit the cellar. Umberto serves a limited (and lower-priced) menu at the jazz club/wine bar next door, where diners can stop in for a glass of wine and dessert if they don't want a full meal.

RESTAURANT

Angiolino
Via Santo Spirito 36/r
☎055.239-8976
Closed Monday
All credit cards • moderate

Everything is always the same at Angiolino. Waiters, decor, wine, and *cucina* are Tuscan. Stick to the regional *salumi*, *crostini*, and soups—skip the pasta, which is overcooked in true Florentine fashion. Tripe fans will be in heaven, but demanding enophiles will have a hard time with the wines.

RESTAURANT

La Baraonda
Via Ghibellina 67/r
☎/Fax 055.234-1171
Closed Sunday, Monday lunch
American Express, Diners Club • high moderate

The name means "convivial chaos," but there's nothing chaotic about the home-style cooking or service in this restaurant. There's a marble butcher's counter in the front dining room, with two smaller rooms beyond. Owner Duccio Magni explains the menu in Italian or English (with a Scottish accent), and after some difficult decision-making a platter of goat cheese or black olive-paste *crostini* is served. Begin with *risolata*, a romaine lettuce *risotto*, pasta, or simple soups. Second courses always include Baraonda's signature dish, veal meat loaf, served with *salsa verde*, grilled *tomino* cheese on a bed of cooked greens, and daily specials. The dessert selection is simple but worthy: caramelized apple tart, *gelato* with chocolate sauce, pastry cream with berries or chocolate and nuts. The wine list is short, mostly Tuscan.

RESTAURANT
Belle Donne
Via delle Belle Donne 16/r
☎**055.238-2609**
Closed Saturday and Sunday
MasterCard, Visa • low moderate

Right in the center of town, inconspicuous except for the knot of people waiting outside for a vacant seat, the Belle Donne is a favorite with many Florentines, especially for lunch. Marble tables seat four, place mats are made of coarse ocher-colored butcher paper, and service is unfriendly at times. The blackboard menu is below the window, and it's wise to take a look before you're seated. The *cucina* is Tuscan, with a few concessions for locals bored with home-style dishes. The mixed green salad and interesting vegetables will please most diners. Desserts are simple, homemade, and tasty. Mario Bussi always promises that he'll improve the wines.

RESTAURANT
Osteria de' Benci
Via de' Benci 13
☎**055.234-4923**
Closed Sunday
American Express, MasterCard, Visa •
moderate

This restaurant has been around forever, but has been given a face-lift by the current owners, Marco Meneghini and Nicola Schioppo. The dining rooms are attractive, with green-stenciled wainscoting, ceiling fans, terra-cotta tiled floors, butcher paper place mats, bright yellow paper napkins, and friendly service. The menu is interesting: Vegetarians will have an easy time with dishes like the mixed-

vegetable *carpaccio* topped with arugula and *parmigiano* or grilled red radicchio, but carnivores will be even happier with first-rate *salumi* and *Chianina* beef from Falorni in Greve (see page 320). Desserts are from Dolce Dolcezza. The wine list is small but original, well priced—check out the selection over the bar in the front room for late arrivals that haven't made it onto the list.

RESTAURANT
Bibe
Via delle Bagnese 1/r
☎**055.204-9085**
Closed all day Wednesday and Thursday lunch
American Express, MasterCard, Visa •
high moderate

Outside the city, on the Bagnese River, Bibe has grown a bit more sophisticated with the latest generation, the fifth of the Scarselli family to reign in this typical Tuscan *trattoria*. They now make original herbal liqueurs, preserved fruits, and improved desserts, but otherwise the menu is unchanged. Classics are executed with time-honed expertise, and beautifully made country soups, grilled or fried poultry, meat, and nontraditional desserts are always tasty. The wine list is well thought out and includes wonderful Tuscan wines. The charming country store entrance is filled with groceries as well as fine local cheeses and *salumi*. The fish tank with the piranha will entertain children of all ages waiting for their food.

RESTAURANT
Cantinetta Antinori
Piazza Antinori 3/r
☎**055.292-234**
Closed Saturday and Sunday, holidays, and August
All credit cards • high moderate

Cantinetta Antinori, in the beautiful fifteenth-century Palazzo Antinori, was created as a showplace for the Antinori wines. The simple *cucina* is mostly Tuscan, with some concessions for the Florentine regulars who frequent this restaurant. Some dishes are splendid, especially the *pappa al pomodoro* and *ribollita* bread soups, stellar tripe, and *calamaretti all'inzimino* (squid stewed with Swiss chard), served on Fridays. *Pecorino* and *caprino* cheeses and extra virgin olive oil from the Antinori estates are first-rate. Conclude your meal with Mattei's authentic *biscotti di Prato* (rich almond cookies) or the nontraditional, beautifully prepared cakes and other desserts. The Antinori family has been making wine for over 600 years, and the Cantinetta's all-Antinori wine list is wonderful. All wines are available by the bottle or the glass.

RESTAURANT
La Casalinga
Via dei Michelozzi 9/r
☎055.218-624
Closed Sunday
MasterCard, Visa • low moderate

La Casalinga is my favorite neighborhood *trattoria*, serving home-style food, as its no-frills name declares. It's frequented by locals, students, workers in overalls, businessmen in suits, elderly women in slippers. Portions are large, the *cucina* is hearty, classic Tuscan. Look for *ribollita*, vegetable soup, and a pasta or two for starters. Stewed meat or fish dishes are the best choice for a

main course; the mixed salad is large; vegetable side dishes are boiled or served raw. Finish with *tiramisù* or *"crem caramel."* Most diners drink the house wine, but a limited selection of bottled wines is available—check out the display behind the bar where Paolo presides in the entrance.

RESTAURANT-TRATTORIA-BAR
Cibreo
Via de Verocchio
☎055.234-1100
Fax 055.244-966
Bar 055.234-5853
Closed Sunday and Monday
All credit cards • expensive in the restaurant, moderate in the *trattoria* and bar

Cibreo is my favorite restaurant in Firenze, the brainchild of Fabio Picchi and Benedetta Vitali; it's more than just a restaurant, it offers three differently priced alternatives for the best food in town. Everything comes out of one kitchen, located between the restaurant and the less expensive *trattoria* around the corner. The bar across the street houses the pastry kitchen, serves sandwiches, a few simple dishes, salads, and makes a mean espresso. The ambience in the restaurant is understated, elegant, with well-set tables and stemware; the *trattoria* is tiled, with communal dining at place-matted tables; the bar is attractive, old-fashioned, with wooden wainscoting, wooden ceilings, tiny round tables indoors and outside when the weather is nice, perfect for hanging out.

Cibreo doesn't serve pasta or grilled meat, which are easy enough to find elsewhere. The *cucina* is high-spirited, lusty, flavored with garlic and spice. Meals begin in the front room with *antipasti* (not available in the *trattoria*) like spicy tomato aspic, marinated tripe, liver *crostini*, ricotta *sformato*. *Polenta* sauced with herbs and butter, savory potato cheesecake, traditional soups, like *pappa al pomodoro* or *ribollita*, and house specialties like creamy (yet creamless) bell-pepper, mushroom, zucchini or winter-squash soup, always topped with a drizzle of extra virgin olive oil, are among first-course options. The long list of main courses is divided between meat and fish. Look for chicken and ricotta meatballs with tomato sauce; sliced, boned, and stuffed duck; peppery sausage and beans; braised beef or veal's foot. I'm wild about the *inzimino*, a spicy stew of cuttlefish and spinach, the marinated anchovies, and *palombo* baked in tomato sauce; there's a wonderful version of eggplant *parmigiano* that will please vegetarians and eggplant lovers. Tasty side dishes like beans, braised cauliflower, spicy stewed potatoes, cooked vegetable compote come with all main courses. Benedetta's desserts—*panna cotta*, fruit-studded bavarians, and cheesecake topped with bitter orange preserves—are worth the calories. Chocoholics will be thrilled with a wedge (or two) of flourless chocolate cake. The wine list is well chosen but not well priced. Exigent enophiles should ask handsome sommelier Alfonso about older vintages and wines that aren't on the list.

RESTAURANT
Enoteca Pinchiorri
Via Ghibellina 87/r
☎055.242-777
Fax 055.244-983
Closed Sunday, Monday lunch, and August
All credit cards • very expensive

The Enoteca Pinchiorri is considered by many to be Italy's brightest gastronomic star. It's a beautiful, tasteful restaurant that seats fifty, with all the trappings of elegant dining—hand-painted Richard Ginori china, Riedel crystal, damask tablecloths, attentive service. But the *cucina*, either innovative or *ritrovata* ("found again"— who lost it?), has never swept me away.

Although the food is skillfully prepared by chef Annie Feolde and a large staff of young professionals, I have never eaten anything truly memorable here. The spectacle of waiters whisking domed silver covers from plates in front of diners, in unison, strikes me as silly.

The best part of the meal is the wine, every drop a pleasure. Unless you have a specific preference from the wine books (surely they are too big to be called lists), your sommelier will serve you the wine that he, or Giorgio Pinchiorri, feels you merit. Important people drink better wines at the Enoteca. Giorgio is passionate and obsessive about his collection. Some of his wines can't be found elsewhere, and the cellar, which he owns privately, is absolutely breathtaking, with a vast and truly impressive selection of vintage Italian, French, and Californian wines. The Sauterne room, the Romanée-Conti hand-numbered double magnums, and the stacked pyramids of stupendous Tuscan wines can bring enophiles to their knees. If this sounds like your idea of fun, reserve a table, grab a gold credit card or a pile of cash, and hustle off to the Enoteca Pinchiorri.

RESTAURANT
Oliviero
Via delle Terme 51/r
☎055.287-643
Fax 055.230-2407
Closed Sunday, open evenings only
All credit cards • low expensive

Chef-owner Francesco Altomare is an experienced professional who's taken over Oliviero, which has a long tradition for sophisticated dining in Firenze. The *cucina* is innovative Tuscan, with classic flavors and ingredients combined with restraint. Gina Martinelli has been checking coats in the entrance since 1962 (she's taken wraps from Ava Gardner, Sophia Loren, Humphrey Bogart, Fred and Ginger, Maria

Callas, and more during the restaurant's heyday). The ambience is refined, with elegantly set tables, important stemware, low lighting. The menu is seasonal and draws on local specialties like *rigatino* (similar to *pancetta*), Sorana beans, *Chianina* beef, *raveggiolo* cheese, and fish from the coast. Begin with a tasty octopus salad or first-rate *salumi*. Try homemade pasta like seafood ravioli or Mugello-style *tortelli* stuffed with potato, sauced with rabbit *ragù*, tempting options as well as classic Tuscan soups. Main-course possibilities include *baccalà* stewed with leeks, tripe with artichokes, perfectly fried chicken and assorted vegetables, and one of the best Florentine steaks in the city, grilled over olive-wood charcoal. The freshest fish Francesco can find is prepared grilled or baked with potatoes, filleted at the table by skilled professional waiters. *Porcini* mushrooms are used to great effect during their season. Desserts are worth saving room for—look for homemade *gelato, sorbetti, necci* (chestnut flour crepes) with ricotta and chestnut honey, but chocoholics will be delighted by the horizontal chocolate tasting. The wine list is ample, well priced, with mostly Tuscan reds and fine whites from other regions.

RESTAURANT

Omero

Via Pian dei Giullari 11/r

☎ **055.220-053**

Closed Tuesday and August

All credit cards • high moderate

A five-minute cab ride up a narrow winding road leads to the hamlet where Galileo Galilei was exiled. His house is across the street from Omero, a quintessential Florentine country *trattoria*, with a quintessential Tuscan view of olive trees, cypresses, and hills. The *cucina* is home-style, pure, and never strays from the simple Florentine specialties. *Salumi* are local and tasty. First-

course stars are bread soups (*ribollita* in the winter and *panzanella* in the summer), homemade ricotta and spinach-filled ravioli, and *pappardelle*—wide strips of pasta sauced with wild boar or wild rabbit. Meats, chicken, and rabbit are grilled over a real charcoal fire or deep-fried in fresh oil. Omero prepares the Florentine specialty *bistecca alla fiorentina* to perfection—charcoal-grilled T-bone steak at least two inches thick, and rare. Seasonal vegetables are eaten raw (*in pinzimonio*) or deep-fried. Ask for *carciofi senza pastella*, featherweight artichokes fried without batter. *Pecorino* cheese, fresh or aged, is always a good choice, an excuse to dig into Omero's stellar wine list of Tuscan reds. Desserts are lackluster, although the *meringata* is tasty and sweet. On your way out, buy a piece of first-rate *pecorino* or *salumi* from Alvaro, the small grocery store in the entrance.

RESTAURANT

Pandemonio

Via dei Leoni 50/r

☎ **055.224-002**

Fax 055.289-712

Closed Sunday

All credit cards • low expensive

Rolando Brogi has a leather-goods business, but always wanted a restaurant to show off the cooking of his wife, Giovanna Biagi. They decided to call it Pandemonio because they enjoy a bit of informal confusion, evident when the restaurant is packed and service seems to grind to a halt. The menu is Tuscan in spirit, with extra virgin olive oil playing a major role in most dishes. Begin with tomato *crostini, bottarga* with beans, or salami with figs in season. Continue with fresh pasta, sauced with seasonal vegetables, *porcini* mushrooms, *bottarga*, or seafood. Main dishes are equally divided between fish and meat—octopus dressed with oil, fish soup, fish cooked with garlic and tomatoes (called *guazzetto*), or boned and fried chicken and vegetables, breaded veal topped with tomatoes, tripe, or classic *bistecca alla Fiorentina.* Conclude with homemade desserts like *panna cotta,* cheesecake, fresh berries, or seasonal fruit. The wine list is small, heavy on Tuscan reds, with a few whites from other regions.

RESTAURANT

Da Ruggero
Via Senese 89/r
☎**055.220-542**
Closed Tuesday, Wednesday
American Express, MasterCard, Visa •
moderate

I've been going to this quintessential *trattoria* for years, but they begged me not to list them in the first edition of this book. "We've got too many regulars, and foreigners tend to linger, which means we can't turn over the tables," Anna explained. But her son Riccardo feels differently, and I'm thrilled to be able to include this Florentine favorite in the revised edition. Ruggero's still in the kitchen, his wife, Anna, son Riccardo and daughter Paola work two crowded dining rooms decorated with undistinguished paintings and prints. A display of seasonal produce at the bar—asparagus, *porcini* mushrooms, artichokes, stuffed vegetables, and berries will prepare diners for the experience of reasonably priced hyper-Tuscan cooking at its best. Begin with *salumi* and *crostini,* or head straight for rustic soups like *ribollita* and *pappa al pomodoro* in the winter, *panzanella* in the summer, and pasta sauced with meat or vegetables, although I can never resist the *spaghetti alla carrettiera,* with spicy, garlicky tomato sauce. Meat like *arista,* grilled pork chops, or Florentine steak, *bollito misto,* served with tangy green sauce, are among the main-course offerings. Vegetarians will have an easy time with seasonal produce. Conclude with simple desserts like *crème caramel,* or *biscotti*

served with Vin Santo or seasonal fruit. There's no wine list—check out the shelves over the bar or drink the house wine. A large table in the corner is reserved for single diners.

RESTAURANT

Tranvai
Piazza Torquato Tasso 14
☎**055.225-197**
Closed Saturday, Sunday
MasterCard, Visa • inexpensive

Tranvai is probably the tiniest eatery in the city, one narrow room roughly the size of a cable car, for which it's named. The decor is inspired by the same theme, with framed pictures of trams, headlight on the bar, metal flooring, always packed with locals, just like the public transportation system. Prices are low, cooking is traditional, prepared by Nanda Vanni. Look for pasta sauced with meat, tomatoes, or leeks; boiled beef with onions, stuffed cabbage, and tripe, *lampredotto* (similar to tripe, another stomach lining), or *budellino,* intestines, for intrepid eaters. Drink the house wine; dine outdoors when the weather is nice.

RESTAURANT

Trattoria Antellesi
Via Faenza 9/r
☎**/Fax 055.216-990**
Always open
All credit cards • moderate

Enrico Verrecchia and his brothers own lots of restaurants in Firenze, but Trattoria Antellesi is my favorite; Enrico runs it with his American wife, Janice. Two small dining rooms, with wooden tables and simple glassware, are always packed with locals and students of Janice's wine classes. Service is quick, professional; the menu offers many Tuscan classics and daily specials. I almost never resist the *spaghetti chiantigiana,* sauced with diced Chianti-stewed beef, although ravioli or rustic soups are also fine. Look for seasonal vegetables from the nearby San Lorenzo market, braised or grilled meats, and poultry. Vegetarians will have no problem with the menu, dining on dishes like *pecorino*, arugula, and pear salad, or simply grilled vegetables. Desserts are also simple but tasty—*panna cotta, tiramisù, crème caramel,* or chestnut *budino.* Janice is wild about wine, teaches classes to American-semester-abroad university students, and has a small but wonderful wine list, on which there are always a few new unlisted gems that she's willing to share.

RESTAURANT

La Vecchia Bettola
Viale Ariosto 32/34
☎055.224-158
Closed Sunday, Monday
No credit cards • moderate

It's called "The Old Dive," but La Vecchia Bettola hasn't been around for that long and it's not really rundown. One large tiled dining room with paper place–matted marble tables; bench and stool seating is always crowded with locals who appreciate the rustic cooking. The menu is handwritten, hard to decipher, and changes daily. *Salumi* and *crostini* are the usual starters, followed by hearty soups, pasta like tomato and vodka-sauced *penne* or *gnocchi,* called *topini.* Second-course meat options include braised boned rabbit, roast pork *arista,* grilled chops, or Florentine steak. Vegetables are almost an afterthought—vegetarians will probably be happier elsewhere. Desserts are simple, like *biscotti* paired with *vin santo* and *tiramisù.* There's no wine list—check out the small but fine selection displayed behind the counter—most customers drink the house wine. Dine outside when the weather is nice.

RESTAURANT–TAKE-OUT

La Pentola dell'Oro
Via di Mezzo 24/r
☎055.241-821
Closed Sunday
No credit cards • inexpensive

Giuseppe Alessi, who used to own a highly rated restaurant outside Firenze and has written an Etruscan cookbook, has opened a take-out diner with tiny marble-topped tables not far from Santa Croce. His sign defines the *cucina* as old-fashioned, rustic, and Tuscan, but the food is mostly undistinguished, as are the wines. Cheese, however, is local and wonderful. Prices are low.

RESTAURANT PIZZERIA

Baldovino
Via San Giuseppe 22/r
☎/Fax 055.241-773
Closed Mondays from spring to October
All credit cards • moderate

David Gardner, handsome Englishman and his wife, Catherine, took over an undistinguished *trattoria,* redecorated it with taste, and the results are wonderful. Three attractive dining rooms are usually filled with young Florentines and hip tourists dining at wooden tables with place mats. The *cucina* is light, modern, and simple, using fresh fish, Chianina beef, and porcini mushrooms. There's a wood-burning oven and a pizza chef from Naples, who turns out some of the city's best pizzas. Splurge for the mozzarella di bufala for an extra charge or share a focaccia with fresh tomato to begin with. Look for Catherine's desserts like apple pie with pine nuts and raisins or Swiss chocolate cake and stellar gelato from Carabe. The wine list is short and well priced. For a light snack, check out David's recently opened caffè-enoteca next door (at Via San Giuseppe 18/r) for a great selection of wines, as well as tasty salads and sandwiches.

PIZZERIA
Il Pizzaiuolo
Via de' Macci 133/r
☎055.241.171
Closed Sunday
MasterCard, Visa • moderate

"Mozzarella, tomato sauce, heart and hard work," written in Neapolitan dialect on the business cards of this pizzeria, account for the success of Il Pizzaiuolo. Owner Carmine Calascione presides at the cash register, pizza-cook Ciro di Roberto performs at the counter in the rear, in front of the oven, preparing the best Neapolitan-style pizza in the center of Florence. Two rustic dining rooms with wooden tables set with place mats are always packed in the evening—it's easier to get a table at lunch or after 10 P.M. The rest of the menu is strictly Neapolitan, but nothing is as worthy as the pizza. Carmine has modified the restaurant's knives, cutting off the tips and sharpening the edge for optimum pizza cutting. Drink beer.

PIZZERIA
Pizzeria Firenze Nova di Fratelli di Giacomo
Via Benedetto Dei 122
☎055.411-937
Closed Monday, open for lunch from Tuesday to Friday • low moderate

Inconvenient to get to, but this is the best pizzeria in town. It's located in the unattractive modern suburbs of Firenze, but worth a visit for pizza lovers. The ambience is quintessential pizzeria, large, well lit, a bit seedy, with coatracks on the wall and a TV in the corner. Check out the wood-burning oven near the entrance and the old-style open kitchen and counter display. Some diners begin with the sautéed clams and/or mussels, but I head straight for anything with fresh mozzarella or smoked *provola* delivered daily, baked with tomatoes in the

oven or topping first-rate pizza. Choose a classic *margherita* or the *margherita DOC* made with superrich buffalo mozzarella. Other original options are tempting—for example, *biancaneve* ("Snow White") with mozzarella, cheese and basil; "lunatic" with tomato, mozzarella, mushrooms, artichokes, *prosciutto*, and red pepper; *completo* with tomato, mozzarella, ricotta, *prosciutto*, and red pepper; *fantasia* is a surprise, which I've never tasted. The house wine is an undistinctive Chianti and there's also a house white—I usually opt for beer on tap.

TABLEWARE
Richard Ginori
Via Rondinelli 17/r
☎055.210-041
All credit cards

This is the biggest and best of the Richard Ginori shops. Two large windows on via Rondinelli formally display the latest output of the nearby Sesto Fiorentino factory (see page 343). Inside, the complete Ginori production is displayed: place settings of seventeenth-century, Empire, Art Nouveau, and modern porcelain dinnerware. Reproductions of architect Gio Ponti's designs are stunning. The shop also sells Murano glass, Broggi and Ricci silver, some Alessi stainless steel, and many fine non-Italian items, like Riedel and Baccarat crystal.

BOOKSTORE, WINE AND FOOD SHOP
Pitti Libri e Gola
Piazza Pitti
☎/Fax 39-55-212-704
Closed Sunday, Monday morning
American Express, MasterCard, Visa

Cecilia Bandini bought the bookstore in piazza Pitti, across the street from the eponymous fifteenth-century Florentine palace, and shifted the focus from art to *gola,* gluttony, and the wine cellar. Her approach is both didactic and practical, with books about Tuscan wine and food, posters and guidebooks, and shelves from floor to ceiling, filled with first-rate wine and nonperishable food products. Pitti Gola e Cantina sells the region's best wines, *grappa,* olive oil, preserves, wild honey, Latini pasta, Riedel crystal wineglasses, and more. And they'll send purchases home.

SILVER AND TABLEWARE
Pampaloni
Borgo SS. Apostoli 47/r
☎**055.289-094**
Fax 055.232-1277
Closed Monday morning
All credit cards

Those who appreciate fine silver should head straight for Pampaloni, Florentine silversmiths since 1902. The shop sells beautiful objects for the table, including handcrafted silver tableware, frames, and decorative objects, both modern and traditional, most of them created in the workshop outside town. Some items are sold at Tiffany's in the U.S. The best reason to visit is to view (and possibly purchase) reproductions from an incredible book. The National Library of Firenze contains a 1604 codex by Giovanni Maggi, Roman artist, entitled *Bichierografia,* a collection of 1,600 drawings of extravagant goblets, fountains, vases. Stemmed goblets are fanciful—a heart pierced by an arrow, a cup with legs, single or double snail shells, columns, alphabet letters, a cow's head are just some of the shapes. They were meant to be executed in glass in the workshops of the grand dukes Francesco I and Ferdinando de' Medici. Gianfranco Pampaloni was fascinated by the codex and decided to reproduce some of Maggi's goblets in silver and glass. Starting in 1992, he adds a few pieces every year, and is now making a limited production of 180 silver and 20 glass goblets, expensive, handcrafted, using tradi-

tional artisanal techniques. Look for the whole collection and a reproduction of a part of Maggi's book in Pampaloni's shop.

HOUSEWARES
Viceversa
Via Ricasoli 53/r
☎**055.239-8281**
Fax 055.216-175
All credit cards

This is my favorite designer housewares shop in Firenze. The staff is friendly, they're willing to order, wrap, and ship, and the selection is vast. The entire Alessi line is well displayed (I couldn't live without their designer pasta pot, although it's priced beyond extravagant), and they're willing to order anything they don't have. There's a large, well-displayed assortment of attractive plastic items by Guzzini, Venetian and Tuscan glassware, tableware, new-wave designer espresso pots, fireplace tools, high-tech juice squeezers, wall-mounted corkscrews, sturdy British toasters, and best of all, the Illy espresso machines in both designer domestic and chrome semiprofessional models in 220V (although they're willing to order 110V). And all down the street from my favorite *gelateria.*

LINENS
Tessilarte
Via Toselli 100
☎**055.364-097**
Fax 055.365-182
By appointment only, closed August
MasterCard, Visa

Paolo Martinetti's linen factory has been a personal favorite for years, and now that they take credit cards I feel that I can write about them. I've become addicted to Tessilarte's fine sheets, in linen, cotton-linen blends, or the softest silky cotton I've ever slept on. Flip through cards of sample fabrics and colors for custom sheets or choose from made-up samples that cost less. Tessilarte's sheets aren't cheap, but they're sold in the U.S. for at least triple the factory price. Table linens were once woven on looms upstairs but are now made elsewhere, and are available in solid colors with jacquard designs, embroidered or in bold geometric weaves. Tablecloths and napkins can be made up in any size or shape. Those who have unusually sized tables should bring measurements.

PERFUME ARTISAN
Lorenzo Villoresi
Via de' Bardi 14
☎055.234-1187
Fax 055.234-5893
By appointment only, closed August
American Express, MasterCard, Visa

Lorenzo Villoresi is a "nose," a creator of perfumes, a blender of scents, an artisan who deals with his craft like a Renaissance master. "My perfumes are eclectic, born of many influences. My essences speak of faraway places." Lorenzo's atelier, open by appointment only, has a living room and office with a heartbreaking view of the city, and a workshop with a desk flanked by thousands of blue-labeled bottles, essences, and concentrates in a variety of permutations. A bookcase next to the entrance holds scented candles; seed, leaf, and pod-studded potpourri; linen sachets; and a shelf of ambience perfumes in brown-stoppered glass bottles with typed labels—jasmine, amber, citrus, spice—I'm wild about the bottle that smells like the sea. Prepared scents are sold in attractive hexagonal bottles—look for perfume, cologne, bath oil, shampoo, olive oil soap, and more. Silk moirè or molded leather cases for the most precious items are handcrafted, simply exquisite. The ultimate (and costly, beginning around $100 or more depending on ingredients and time) experience in this atelier is a custom-made perfume created for its wearer by Lorenzo. The session resembles analysis. Clients are asked to describe agreeable

scents, sniffing thin strips of paper dabbed with essences and extracts that Lorenzo blends in a glass beaker, creating an exclusive fragrance that can be reordered by mail. But whether readers buy a bar of olive oil soap, Mediterranean sachet, pepper potpourri or personalized perfume, a visit to the atelier is a treat—and one of the few no-calorie experiences in this book.

HOUSEWARES
La Ménagère
Via dei Ginori 8/r
☎055.213-875
All credit cards

La Ménagère has the best selection of quality housewares in Firenze. Founded in 1896, it looks like an old-fashioned general store, with wooden floors, long counter, and tall cabinets filled with stainless-steel cookware. La Ménagère is such a gold mine that it will take a while to examine all the rooms, shelves, stands, racks, and display cases filled with mostly Italian products. Choose from Richard Ginori porcelain, Bellini ceramics, Sambonet and Alessi stainless, IVV glassware, Guzzini plastics, Style picnic sets, Montana knives, and a wide assortment of rolling pins, sifters, wooden spoons, custom doormats, tin olive oil cans, pasta guitars and hand-cranked machines, a windup spit rotisserie, and every nonelectric *caffettiera* imaginable. The selection of cookware is exceptional, in copper, stainless, iron, enamel, and practically every other heatproof material known to man. They won't ship, but they will pack your purchases for shipping. La Ménagère's wonderful ornate 1914 cash register is reproduced on their sturdy plastic bags.

POTTERY
Sbigoli
Via San Egidio 4/r
☎055.247-9713
All credit cards

Sbigoli sells a wonderful selection of terra-cotta pottery, in a wealth of sizes and shapes. Unglazed garden pots, rustic no-lead bakeware, and a lovely selection of hand-decorated dinnerware, pitchers, egg cups, mugs, and attractive serving pieces that are reasonably priced and hard to resist. I love the green and white, or green and yellow, spatterware, "blessed" with a sprinkling of color. Choose from traditional patterns, or create your own with owner Valentino Adami. Shipping makes this pottery more convenient to purchase, but less of a bargain.

TABLE LINENS

Loretta Caponi
Piazza Antinori 4/r
☎055.213-668
Fax 055.293-118
All credit cards

If you've always dreamed of owning heirloom linens but no one has left you any, head for Loretta Caponi. The selection of hand embroidery is unique, exceptional, eccentric, and justly expensive. Loretta loves the creativity of custom orders and has designed table linens to match her clients' whims, from dinnerware and wallpaper to villa gardens. Place-mat sets known as *servizi all'americana* are embroidered and appliquéd with hunting, fishing, fruit, or floral themes, each mat and napkin decorated with a different scene or design. A lemon series uses at least ten shades of green and yellow, depicting lemons in bloom, on the branch, and sliced into halves, quarters, wedges, and slices. Brightly colored waterfowl and marine-life sets are also knockouts. Linen tablecloths can be ordered with hand fagoting, handmade lace inserts, or trimmed with hand embroidery. Damask cloths can be made in any size up to almost 24 meters (80 feet) long. The three-dimensional mimosa-pattern cloth with a scalloped hem is a classic. Practical Loretta says that almost all her linens can be machine-washed. Prices are steep. A visit to the new larger shop is amazing—a must for those who appreciate linens, lace, and much more.

SILVER TABLEWARE

Argenteria Il Leone
Via San Giovanni 13–15/r
☎055.233-7848
Fax 055.220-415
No credit cards

Until recently, Il Leone had no showroom, and orders were taken in a corner of the workroom, over the racket of tiny hammers pounding away. But the fourteenth-century building's ground floor has been restored, revealing brick arches and beamed ceilings, creating a labyrinth of workrooms, each devoted to a different phase of the silversmithing craft. Lathes for shaping and buffers for polishing are used on Il Leone's silver and silver-plated pieces, but all other work is done by hand. The showroom is filled with glass display cases of plain, hammered, and chiseled trays, serving pieces, bowls, ice buckets, leaf-shaped candy dishes, and decorative items, but Walter Caselli assured me that he will custom-make or reproduce practically anything. His prices are the lowest in Firenze.

TABLEWARE

Parenti
Via Tornabuoni 93
☎055.214-438
Fax 055.268-519
All credit cards

Parenti, founded in 1865, has an interesting selection of tableware and silver. Many items are secondhand—not old enough to be antique, the granddaughter of the original, Parenti told me. But I was impressed by silver or silverplate knife trays, berry spoons, potato rings, oyster forks, lamb bone holders, *osso buco* marrow scoops, sugar tongs, tea strainers, grape shears, and champagne stirrers.

BOOKS
BM Bookshop
Borgo Ognissanti 4/r
☎**055.294-575**
All credit cards

The BM Bookshop carries only new books, both hardcover and paperback, and has a wide variety of beautiful photographic books on Italy. They also sell English-language cookbooks and wine books, and can be counted on for the latest edition of Burton Anderson's wine guide.

BOOKS
Paperback Exchange
Via Fiesolana 31/r
☎**055.247-8154**
All credit cards

The Paperback Exchange sells some new paperbacks and accepts used paperbacks in exchange for credit on used-book purchases. They also sell English-language regional Italian cookbooks.

ESSENCES
Officina Profumo–Farmaceutica di Santa Maria Novella
Via della Scala 16
☎**055.288-657**
No credit cards

The chapel entrance of the Officina Profumo–Farmaceutica di Santa Maria Novella sets the stage for the pharmaceutical-herbal-floral essence specialties, displayed in tall, dark oak cabinets. A visit to what feels like a medieval drugstore is a most astounding experience, and is accompanied by a unique, haunting scent. Fainting salts, strange tasting *liquore* and digestive tonics, as well as skin creams, soaps, shampoos, and potpourri are all made with original seventeenth-century formulas.

Fonte Blanda

HOTEL
Corte dei Butteri
Via Aurelia Nord, km 157
☎**0564.885-546**
Fax 0564.886-282
American Express, Visa • luxury

AGRITOURISM
Club "Le Cannelle"
Talamone (nearby)
☎**0564.870-068**
Fax 0564.870-470
No credit cards • moderate

RESTAURANT
Bar Trattoria Uccellina
Via Aurelia, km 163.2
☎**0564.596-000**
Closed Wednesday
MasterCard, Visa • moderate

SHIPPING SERVICE

Fracassi International Forwarders
Via Santo Spirito 11
☎**055.283-597**
Fax 214-771

And now that you've bought it all and can't even bear to think about packing it up and dragging it home, call Fracassi. They will pick up your purchases, pack them, and ship them home, by air or sea. Their service may be costly, but everything will arrive intact.

The truckers whose rigs fill the parking lot of the Bar Trattoria Uccellina along the via Aurelia share this restaurant in the summer with tanned tourists visiting the coast or one of Toscana's most beautiful parks. The *cucina* is uncomplicated and abundant. Pasta is homemade, and toothsome spaghetti is laced with a meaty sauce of wild boar (*cinghiale*). Pork ribs or chops are tasty, roast meats are generally overcooked, game is offered in season, and vegetables are lackluster. Finish your meal with seasonal fruit or ice cream bars. The coppery-colored white wine, sold by the carafe, won't satisfy exigent palates, but it slips down nicely in the summer.

Forte dei Marmi

HOTEL

Augustus
Viale Morin 169
☎0584.787-200
Fax 0584.787-102
All credit cards • luxury

HOTEL

Astoria Garden
Via Leonardo da Vinci 16
☎0584.787-054
Fax 0584.50176
All credit cards • moderate

RESTAURANT

Lorenzo
Via Carducci 61
☎/Fax 0584.84030
Closed Monday, November and December, and
for lunch during July and August
All credit cards • expensive

Reservations are hard to come by in Lorenzo Viani's restaurant in Forte dei Marmi. The light, well-prepared fish dishes are as elegant as the clientele. Lorenzo painstakingly hunts down the freshest seafood, which the kitchen treats with respect. Pasta and *risotto* are nicely cooked.

Seasonal vegetables and herbs flavor most dishes. Desserts are simple, and the wines, the best in fashionable Forte, are worthy of the *cucina*.

Fucecchio

HOTEL

See Firenze

RESTAURANT

Le Vedute
Via Romana-Lucchese 121
Ponte a Cappiano
☎0571.297-498
Fax 0571.297-201
Closed Tuesday and most of August
American Express, Diners Club • moderate

Le Vedute is where the managers of all the tanneries in the Arno Valley take their important guests. It's a large classic restaurant, but the *cucina* is mostly fish and shellfish, decidedly unusual for inland Fucecchio. Most food is simply treated. Pasta is homemade and nicely cooked, and mushrooms are served in season. The menu is interesting, and dishes are well prepared. The wine list is wonderful, and a joy to find in a restaurant like this. Watch out for weddings and communions on Sundays, when service may suffer a bit.

Gaiole in Chianti

HOTEL

See Radda

RESTAURANT

Badia a Coltibuono
☎0577.749-424
Fax 0577.749-031
Closed Monday
American Express, MasterCard, Visa • high moderate

The estate of Badia a Coltibuono, known for its wine, oil, and cooking school, has revamped its restaurant. It's now a family affair, directed by Paolo Stucchi with food prepared from his mother's (Lorenza de' Medici) recipes. Seasonal produce and fresh herbs flavor many dishes, fresh pasta, local *Chianina* beef, and cheese are featured on the menu. Begin with assorted *antipasto* plates or herring and orange salad. First-choice possibilities include chick-pea and emmer soup, *pappardelle* with duck sauce, lemon *risotto,* or ravioli with black truffles. Grilled Florentine steak, lamb chops, or squab stuffed with pears are perfect paired with Coltibuono's red wines. Vegetable side dishes are more exciting than usual. Conclude with local sheep's or goat's milk cheese, desserts like rice pudding with wine syrup, custard *gelato* with chestnut honey, or my favorite, Roberto Catinari's chocolates. The wine list offers local wines, but logically focuses on Coltibuono's production, with older vintages and reserves that are hard to find elsewhere.

Gello

HOTEL

Il Convento

Via San Quirico 33, Pontenuovo (nearby)

☎**0573.452-651**

Fax 0573.453-578

MasterCard, Visa • moderate

RESTAURANT

La Limonaia

Via di Gello 9 (outside Pistoia)

☎**0573.400-453**

Closed Monday evening, Tuesday

All credit cards • moderate

La Limonaia is an outbuilding on an estate outside Pistoia in which lemons were once stored in the winter. The building is long and narrow with large windows and a rustic decor of oxen yokes, cart wheels, decorative plates, photographs, and awards. Mamma Annarosa is in the kitchen making Tuscan classics served by her son Ilario.

Look for chick-pea and mushroom or emmer soups, ravioli with wild greens, or homemade *gnocchi.* Main-course options include kid, prepared *dolce forte,* slightly sweet and sour; roast pork *arista;* grilled beef, lamb, pork, or chicken. Finish with *zuppa alla Limonaia,* baked meringue-topped trifle, or the *cornuto* ("cuckold"), chocolate and *amaretti* custard served with wafer cookies.

Ghirlanda

HOTEL

Il Sole

Corso della Libertà 43, Massa Marittima (nearby)

☎**0566.901-971**

Fax 0566.901-959

All credit cards • inexpensive

RESTAURANT

Bracali

Via Ghirlanda

☎**0566.902-318**

Fax 0566.940-302

Closed Tuesday

All credit cards • high moderate

The name of this restaurant tells what it's all about—the Bracali family, Francesco in the kitchen, Luca and Luciano in the dining room, have created the quintessential restaurant evolved from a *trattoria.* Local ingredients of superior quality are used with great skill and paired with fine wine. The dining room is large, comfortable, service is efficient, wineglasses are important. The menu changes daily, tied to the season and there's a well-priced *menu degustazione.* Diners may find semolina *gnocchi* sauced with mushrooms, homemade vegetable ravioli, *tagliolini* with spinach and crunchy pasta threads. Look for herbed lamb with seasonal vegetables, braised *Chianina* beef *stracotto,* bell-pepper pudding with *parmigiano* sauce. Save room for cheese, a perfect excuse to drink a big red from the wonderful wine list. Dessert lovers will be in heaven with options like fresh fruit tarts, ricotta timbale with rhubarb compote, citrus terrine, chocolate puff pastry with acacia honey and pine nuts. The wine list is wonderful, the selection of *grappe* and distillates ample. Check out the *enoteca* selling wine, distillates, honey, preserved vegetables, and Tuscan extra virgin oils from the Maremma as well as oils from Liguria and Umbria.

Greve

HOTEL

Dal Chianti
Piazza Matteotti 86
☎055.853-763
Fax 055.853-764
All credit cards • moderate

HOTEL

See Firenze or Montefiridolfi

RESTAURANT

Giovanni da Verrazzano
Piazza Matteotti 28
☎055.853-189
Closed Sunday evening and Monday
All credit cards • moderate

Rossella Rossi cooks classic Tuscan *cucina—salumi*, hearty soups, meat-sauced pastas, roast meat, and simple desserts, offering no culinary thrills but no disappointments either. Probably the best part of this restaurant is sitting on the terrace when the weather is nice, overlooking the main piazza of Greve. Drink Chianti.

THREE-STAR PORCHETTA

Giovanni
Piazza Matteotti
No phone
Open Saturday morning at the Greve market

There are two stands that sell *porchetta*, roast pork, at the Greve market, held Saturday mornings. One is practically empty, the other

has a long line of customers waiting patiently while Giovanni handcrafts his sandwiches. He's not in a hurry and can't be rushed no matter how large the crowd. There are only a few variables—"Want some liver? Or some *droga?*," the pungent salty spice mixture, a secret blend of wild herbs and seasonings that flavors Giovanni's *porchetta*. This sandwich is worth a detour, a three-star experience and one of Italy's great culinary treats.

SALUMI

Macelleria Falorni
Piazza Matteotti 69
☎055.853-029
Fax 055.854-4531
Closed Monday, Wednesday, and Thursday afternoons
MasterCard, Visa

After a drive on the via Chiantigiana, south of Firenze, with its breathtakingly beautiful countryside and vineyards that produce Chianti Classico wines, stop off in Greve for a stroll around piazza Matteotti. The shops are unexciting: The wine shop staff is surly and unhelpful, and the basket shop is half-filled with Oriental merchandise. The clear star of the piazza is the Macelleria Falorni. They butcher all the meat that goes into their fine *salumi*. Pork *salame*, fennel-laced *finocchiona*, crumbly *sbriciolona*, giant *soprassata*, and peppery *pancetta* are among their tasty homemade products. Another specialty is wild boar (*cinghiale*), black-bristled with dark maroon meat, sold fresh or cured as *salsiccie* (sausages), *salamino* ("little salami"), or *prosciutto*.

Impruneta

POTTERY

Fornance Ugo Poggi
Via Imprunetana 16
☎055-201-1077
Fax 055.231-3852
Closed Sunday and Saturday afternoon
No credit cards

Fornace Ugo Poggi's artisanal production is wonderful. Each piece of pottery is hand-crafted. The spectacular terra-cotta production is small, traditional, and Poggi's daughters Licia and Lilliana run the show, in charge of 12 potters who handcraft the entire production. Super-large pots are a specialty.

Lamporecchio

COOKIES

Pioppino
Piazza Berni
☎**0573.82177**
Closed Wednesday

Brigidi, anise-flavored eggy crisps cooked on flat irons, were created in the convent of Santa Brigida by nuns. The cookies are made industrially with electric molds, found throughout Tuscany, but are at their best freshly made by Pioppino. Check out their other specialty, *berlingozzo*, a flat round ring made with the same ingredients as *brigidini* but baked. They also sell classic pastry and *cantucci*, almond cookies. But anyone who goes to Lamporecchio should focus on the local specialties.

Lari

PASTA

Pastificio Martelli
Via San Martino 3
☎**0587.684-238**

Pasta isn't a particular specialty of Toscana, and it is frequently overcooked in this region. In spite of this, Italy's best dry pasta comes from the tiny Tuscan village of Lari.

What makes Martelli pasta so terrific? The factory is owned and run by the Martelli family, brothers Dino and Mario and their wives, Lucia and Valeria. The secret of their pasta isn't in the water, or the 100 percent Canadian hard wheat (the best), ground into *semola*, the hard-grain equivalent of flour.

Their pasta is extruded through bronze dies, which produce a rougher surface that holds on to sauce better—but many pasta makers use bronze dies. The secret of Martelli pasta is time. The pasta-making machines are never pushed to the maximum; the dough is kneaded gently and extruded with less pressure, leaving more air in the pasta. Most spaghetti are slowly dried for eight hours, but the Martelli pasta is dried for fifty hours, maintaining more of the grain flavor. The resultant golden rough-textured pasta, which looks as if it's been sanded, is produced in only four shapes. Spaghetti and thinner spaghettini are dried on rods, forming foot-long narrow U's. The barely ridged *maccheroni* are a tribute to Napoli, the birthplace of pasta, and the *penne* (quill-shaped pasta) are smooth, without the usual deep ridges necessary for most *penne* to hang on to the sauce. They all need to cook in more water than most pasta, Dino warned me, but the instructions are in Italian and English on the package. In the best Italian family tradition, twelve Martellis sit down to a bowl of pasta together every day. A visit to the factory is most fun on Wednesdays and Fridays, when extra-long spaghetti are made.

Lucca

Surrounded by intact Renaissance ramparts, Lucca is a jewel of a city, with medieval monuments, Romanesque churches, and nearby villas in the green countryside. Garden fans shouldn't miss a visit to Villa Reale, Villa Torrigiani, and Villa Mansi.

HOTEL

San Marco
Via San Marco 368
☎**0583.495-010**
Fax 0583.490-513
All credit cards • moderate

HOTEL
Piccolo Hotel Puccini
Via di Poggio 9
☎0583.55421
Fax 0583.53487
All credit cards • low moderate

HOTEL
Villa Rinascimento
Via del Cimitero, Santa Maria del Giudici (nearby)
☎0583.378-29
Fax 0583.370-238
All credit cards • low moderate

RESTAURANT
Buatino
Via Borgo Giannotti 508
☎0583.343-207
Closed Sunday
No credit cards • inexpensive

I'm wild about Buatino, a no-frills *trattoria* located outside the walls of Lucca, frequented mostly by locals. Paper place mats on wooden tables, paintings by local artist-clients, simple glasses, house wine. Traditional dishes like emmer and bean soup, *farinata*, vegetable *polenta*, and *torta d'erbe con i becchi*, a Swiss chard–custard-tart dessert, are always on the menu along with classics like pasta sauced with tomato, stewed rabbit, and grilled meat. The salad of bitter wild greens is tasty. Owner Giuseppe Ferrua

is a jazz fan and hosts live concerts Monday evenings from October through May.

RESTAURANT
Da Leo
Via Tegrimi 1
☎0583.492-236
Fax 05831/405321
Closed Sunday
No credit cards • inexpensive

A friend from Lucca recommended Da Leo, his favorite place to eat in town. It's a typical *trattoria*, run by the Buralli family, with a classic Lucchese menu. Begin with *crostini* or *salumi*, or go straight for hearty first courses like *minestra di farro*, meat-stuffed *tordelli* pasta, fresh pasta *tacconi* sauced with *ragù*. Continue with fried chicken, grilled or roast meats, stewed rabbit, or tripe. *Tiramisù* and Lucca specialty Swiss chard–custard-tart are always on the menu. Wines are from the area, although most of the locals who frequent this *trattoria* drink the house wine.

RESTAURANT
Giulio in Pelleria
Via delle Conce 45
☎/Fax 0583.55948
Closed Sunday, Monday, August, and Christmas
All credit cards • moderate

Giulio in Pelleria is a classic *trattoria*. The *cucina* is regional, home-style, unpretentious, and fantastic. Emmer (*farro*), a wonderful wheaty grain, is cooked in bean soup. I find it hard to resist the *farinata*, a vegetable soup thickened with cornmeal. Meats, stewed for hours, are tasty. The horsemeat tartare will appeal to the intrepid, but isn't as bad as it sounds. Desserts are traditional, but the flan of candied fruit and Swiss chard is strange. Wines are from the Lucca area and not too exciting. The strictly local crowd of workers and families who pack this restaurant for lunch and dinner are onto a good thing.

PASTRY

Pasticceria Marino Taddeucci
Piazza San Michele 34
☎0583.44933
Closed Wednesday

Buccellato, a specialty of Lucca, is surely one of the world's most austere desserts: simple bread dough enriched, but not too much, with raisins, anise, and a bit of sugar. I haven't been able to work up too much enthusiasm for this ring-shaped cake, but the best version is produced by Marino Taddeucci. Look for Life Saver *buccellato* next to the bakery's sign.

CEREALS AND SEEDS

Cereali Sementi Marcucci
Via Santa Lucia 13
☎0583/343-747
Closed Wednesday afternoon

Cereal, seeds, soap, and dog food are the unlikely combination of wares sold in this *simpatico* store. Large burlap sacks are filled with beans in different sizes, shapes, and colors, lentils from Castelluccio, rice, *polenta* flour, and most important, emmer (*farro*) for the Lucca area's fantastic bean and emmer soup. The large sack of brownish pasta at the end of the row is made especially for dogs—it seems only logical that Italian canines would have a pasta all their own.

Mercatale

HOTEL

See Firenze or Montefiridolfi

AGRITOURISM

Salvadonica
Via Grevigiana 82
☎055.821-8039
Fax 055.821-8043
American Express, MasterCard, Visa •
moderate

RESTAURANT

Il Salotto del Chianti
Via Sonnino 92
☎/Fax 055.821-8016
Closed Wednesday
All credit cards • high moderate

"The Chianti Living Room" is charming, intimate, well appointed, as a living room should be, with two banquettes that run the length of the room, simply set tables, modern lighting, good acoustics, and a bar in the back stacked with cases of wine. The *cucina* is innovative but not weird, Tuscan in spirit. Chef-owner Marcello Crini is passionate about wine and pairs his cooking with the finest wines of Toscana. The menu changes every two weeks and is based on fine seasonal and local ingredients. Look for appetizers like first-rate *salumi,* marinated fish, vegetable timbales, deep-fried sage leaves. Look also for fresh pasta sauced with vegetables, like asparagus-stuffed *agnolotti* with *parmigiano* sauce. For a main course I usually opt for squab, kid, or lamb, perfect for pairing with big Tuscan reds. Save room for the lovely selection of Italian cheese. Desserts are worth writing home about, often created by Roxanne Edwards, an expert English pastry chef who's worked in Toscana for more than a decade. The wine list is loaded with the region's best wines at affordable prices; the *grappa* and distillate selection is impressive. Dine outdoors on a terrace behind the restaurant when the weather is nice.

Monsummano Terme

HOTEL

Grotta Giusti
Via Grotta Giusti 171
☎0572.51165
Fax 0572.51269
All credit cards • high moderate

COFFEE AND CHOCOLATE
Slitti Caffè e Cioccolato
Via Francesca Sud 246
☎/Fax 0572.640-240
MasterCard, Visa
Closed Sunday

The Slitti family is into caffeine, and their shop outside the village of Monsummano Terme is a worth the voyage for coffee and chocolate lovers. Luciano, who studied coffee roasting with a legendary Florentine roaster, began his own business in 1969. He's been joined by his son Daniele, and their coffee is rich, ample, a full roast of *arabica* beans. Taste a perfect espresso at the bar and purchase coffee to take home. Luciano's son Andrea got interested in chocolate, took courses in France and Switzerland, and in 1988 began making and selling chocolate at the family store. The extra-bitter chocolate, a blend of Belgian, French, and Italian brands, is a super-Tuscan flavor—intense, austere, with a long finish, 73 percent cocoa, an extremely high proportion. All hazelnuts used in the chocolate are from Piemonte; almonds come from Puglia. Look for elegant boxes of assorted chocolates, chocolate hazelnut cream, chocolate keys and tools, chocolate nut *tortine,* and impossible-to-resist cocoa-dusted chocolate espresso spoons sold in boxes of six. Chocolate-covered *arabica* beans are the best I've ever tasted. Easter eggs are elevated to an art form.

Montalcino

HOTEL
Casanova Hotel Residence
Strada Statale 146, San Quirico d'Orcia (nearby)
☎/Fax 0577.898-177
All credit cards • moderate

AGRITOURISM-RESTAURANT
Taverna dei Barbi
Fattoria dei Barbi
☎0577.848-277
Restaurant 0577.849-357
Fax 0577.849-356
Restaurant closed Wednesday
MasterCard, Visa • high moderate

The Fattoria dei Barbi produces wonderful wine and has two attractive apartments that can be rented by the week or month on the estate. Regional cooking reigns at the restaurant Taverna dei Barbi. *Salumi,* homemade *pici* and pastas, hearty soups, stewed and grilled meats, first-class *pecorino* cheese, basic desserts always satisfy, the kind of simple local cooking that a visitor would want. The Barbi wines complete the menu, with older vintages available.

RESTAURANT
Poggio Antico
Poggio Antico, outside Montalcino
☎/Fax 0577.849-200
Closed Monday
No credit cards • low expensive

Chef Roberto Minetti and his wife, Patrizia, used to own a restaurant in Roma but moved to Montalcino a few years ago, lured by the sweetest countryside in Toscana, pulled by Roberto's Tuscan roots. Their restaurant is on the estate of Poggio Antico, a leading producer of Brunello, with elegant, well-spaced tables set with simple china, large wineglasses, silver. Roberto's cooking concentrates on regional flavors, and quality ingredients are used with creativity and style. Begin with variations on classics like chicken-liver parfait with Moscadello sauce, *raveggiolo* mousse, *polenta* with melty Taleggio and grilled radicchio. *Farro* (emmer) is paired with fish in soup, fresh pasta is delicately sauced, potato *gnocchi* are topped with white truffles in season. Second-course offerings like beef, lamb, or squab are just right for Brunello di Montalcino drinkers. Save room for cheese—local, Italian, and French. Desserts are as exciting as the rest of the meal—look for toasted almond parfait or frozen *zabaione gelato* with hot chocolate sauce. The wine list has been expanded to include Brunello from other estates as well as Poggio Antico and wines from other regions.

ENOTECA
La Fortezza
Piazzale della Fortezza
☎**0577.849-211**
Always open
All credit cards

Mario Pianigiani and Marzio Gianelli's *enoteca*, located in the Fortezza, offers the biggest, best collection of local enological jewels from over 100 producers, concentrating on young Rosso di Montalcino, a vast choice of Brunello, super-Tuscan table wines, Vin Santo, and Moscadello. There's also a fine selection of local products such as extra virgin olive oil, *grappa, pecorino, salumi,* honey, and cookies like *ossi di morto,* made with *mandorle* and egg whites. Most wines are available for tasting, paired with *salumi,* cheese, and bread. This was the first *enoteca* to receive the *Leccio d'Oro,* an award for superior Brunello wine service, proudly displayed by Mario and Marzio.

RESTAURANT AND ENOTECA AWARD
Leccio d'Oro
Consorzio del Vino Brunello di Montalcino
Costa del Municipio 1
☎**0577.848-246**
Fax 0577.849-425

Montalcino's ancient name was *Monte Ilcinus,* Holm Oak Mountain, since the holm oak dominated the nearby forests. The tree has been adopted as the symbol of the Brunello Consortium, which hosts a three-

day event focusing on its wines the first weekend in February. An international jury, appointed by the Consortium, awards the *Leccio d'Oro* ("Golden Holm Oak") yearly to an *enoteca* and restaurant with the best Brunello service in the world. Valentino in Los Angeles and Enoteca Pinchiorri in Firenze are past winners in the restaurant category; Enoteca Brantl in Munich and the Enoteca La Fortezza in Montalcino in the *enoteca* category. Tastings of the recent vintages and previews of the latest harvest, dinner at Castello Banfi, a presentation in the adorable Teatrino (little theater) of Montalcino are packed into three days that focus on my favorite wine in the world. Phone or fax the consorzio if you would like to attend.

Montecatini Terme

Montecatini, known to Americans for a line of beauty treatments, is famous in Italy for its waters, unpleasant tasting but remarkably laxative. The spa town, with its Belle Epoque architecture, is a pleasant place to recover from the rigors of gastronomic Italy, although it's not without its own temptations.

HOTEL
Grand Hotel & La Pace
Via delle Torretta 1
☎**0572.75801**
Fax 0572.78451
Closed November to March
All credit cards • luxury

When I think of spas, cures, and taking the waters, I think of the Grand Hotel & La Pace, with its century-old trees, park, swimming pool, tennis, fully equipped health center, greenhouse filled with orchids, and Belle Epoque ambience. Mud or ozone baths, seaweed treatments, massages, and saunas are all available at this luxury, truly "grand" hotel.

HOTEL-RESTAURANT
Croce di Malta
Viale IV Novembre 18
☎0572.75871
Fax 0572.767-516
All credit cards • high moderate,
moderate off season

The Croce di Malta isn't the most famous hotel in Montecatini, but it's my favorite, thanks to director Giuseppe Mazza, who runs a tight ship. Service is impeccable, the location is ideal for touring Tuscany, and the restaurant serves nicely prepared food, far better than anything offered in Montecatini's other hotels, which cater to tourists suffering from digestive problems visiting the city to take the waters.

RESTAURANT
Enoteca Giovanni–Cucina da Giovanni
Via Garibaldi 27
☎0572.71695
Closed Monday
All credit cards • Enoteca, expensive; trattoria, high moderate

Sommelier Giovanni Rotti's two side-by-side establishments offer a culinary diversion for those who come to Montecatini to drink the waters with their curative (and laxative) powers. His full-fledged restaurant serves creative cucina with a faint Tuscan accent, pasta, meat, and fish cooked with style. The trattoria next door has a much more traditional menu, with dishes like pappa al pomodoro, ribollita, grilled meats, and the same desserts as the enoteca. The wine selection in both eateries is first-rate, as would be expected from a professional sommelier like Giovanni.

PASTRY
Ditta Stefano Desideri
Via Gorizia 5
☎0572.71088
Closed Monday; always open in winter

Wafer cookies (cialde) are a specialty of Montecatini. A simple batter is poured, cooked, and pressed in a metal mold; two rounds of wafer thus produced are filled with a mixture of crushed almonds and sugar, and then recooked. Each of Montecatini's pasticcerie has its own design stamped on these seven-inch disks. I love the pattern on Desideri's cialde, the best in Montecatini: a heron and spitting-toad fountain. Brother and sister Stefano and Maria Grazia Desideri also make wonderful brigidini—eggshell-thin cookies delicately flavored with aniseed—without the usual dose of artificial coloring that most brigidini makers use.

Montefiridolfi

INN
Il Borghetto
Via Collina San Angelo 23
☎055.824-4442
Fax 055.824-4247
Visa • low expensive

What's better than having a home in the Tuscan countryside? Visiting someone else's place, especially if it's as wonderful as Il Borghetto, an eight-room inn in a restored fifteenth-century farmhouse complex set in the hills amid olive trees and vineyards. Rosy Cavallini and her husband, Roberto, bought the property twenty years ago, restored a summer home for themselves, and created Il Borghetto, which opened in 1994. The ambience is informal, the decor impeccable, rooms scattered with objects from Rosy's world travels. She wisely hired Florentine superchef Francesca Cianchi to manage the property. Francesca cooked at Mezzaluna in New York for eight years, moved back to Florence, and is now cooking at Il Borghetto.

Francesca has an aromatic herb garden, buys vegetables from a nearby farmer, picks fruit from trees on the property, makes tomato sauce and preserves and some of the finest unfussy Tuscan food I've ever had. Like a recent summer lunch, served on the shaded terrace, of first-rate local salami and figs; *prosciutto* and melon; perfectly cooked spaghetti with tomato sauce, flavored with Sicilian capers and oregano; summer vegetable compote seasoned with herbs and Il Borghetto's extra virgin olive oil; creamy young and tangy aged *pecorino* cheese; and just-picked superripe peaches and pears for dessert. Or a dinner of Francesca's own version of *acquacotta*, made with Swiss chard and *porcini* mushrooms, roast pork, ending up with perfect *tiramisù*. The wine list is short but sweet. Francesca teaches her inspired Tuscan cooking in one-week hands-on cooking sessions for a maximum of eight students in the spring and fall.

Montefollonico

RESTAURANT-INN
La Chiusa
Via Madonnina 88
☎0577.669-668
Fax 0577.669-539
Closed Tuesday except in August and
September, and January through March
All credit cards • expensive

Although it's difficult (impossible at night) to find La Chiusa, a farm-complex-turned-inn, it is worth the effort. The setting is breathtaking. Owner Dania Lucherini is beautiful and hospitable, and she can cook. The restaurant is small but spacious, beautifully restored in Dania's personal style. The *cucina* is revisited Tuscan, with vegetables from the La Chiusa's garden and local ingredients treated with the utmost respect. They make their own extra virgin olive oil, and Dania's husband, Umberto, searches out fine cheeses and wines. I have never ordered a meal here, but let Dania compose a series of *assaggi* ("tastes") and tell Umberto when you've had enough, a diffi-

cult decision. Flavors are intense, Tuscan, and combined with restraint. Mushrooms are the best I've ever had, firm and tasting of forest. Desserts are good, but I always finish with the *pan di caffè*, a spongy coffee custard. Eight rooms for overnight guests are special, decorated with farmhouse furniture, equipped with the most fabulous bathrooms ever. Eating and staying overnight at La Chiusa is my idea of a treat!

Montelupo

POTTERY
N.D. Dolfi
Via Tosco-Romagnola 1
☎/Fax 0571.910-116
Always open
American Express, Visa, MasterCard

Guido Dolfi makes wonderful majolica dinnerware and terra-cotta cookware. The patterns are traditional, the pottery is handmade, and the charming yellow and blue Montelupo bird pattern, usually so poorly executed, is the best I've seen.

Montemerano

HOTEL
See Saturnia

AGRITOURISM
Pian dei Casali
Via Pian dei Casali 23, Pianetti
☎0564.602-0625
Fax 0564.602-627
No credit cards • inexpensive

RESTAURANT
Da Caino
Via Canonica 3
☎0564.602-817
Fax 0564.602-807
Closed Wednesday, Thursday lunch
All credit cards • expensive

Da Caino, tucked in the medieval village of Montemerano, is a classic example of a family *trattoria* grown into an elegant restaurant. Hard-working owners chef Valeria Piccini and her husband, sommelier Maurizio Menichetti, have upgraded the Tuscan dining experience: fine linens, crystal, professional service in refined yet rustic dining rooms with stone walls, beamed ceilings, terra-cotta floors, and featuring a *cucina* based on first-rate ingredients used with wisdom. Valeria learned to cook from her mother, although her approach has expanded to include new ideas and cooking techniques. The menu changes with the seasons, and is based on local produce, meat, herbs. Warm lamb liver with artichokes, hand-rolled pasta sauced with a light meat sauce, boned rabbit with wild fennel, game and wild boar in the winter. Mushrooms and truffles are used with abandon in season. The cheese selection is important; desserts are worth the calories. The wine list is spectacular, with wines from Italy and beyond that represent the world's best enological offerings, which Maurizio ably pairs with Valeria's cooking.

ENOTECA-GROCERY

Perbacco
Via della Chiesa 8
☎0564.602-817
Fax 0564.602-807
All credit cards

This *enoteca*-grocery is owned by Valeria and Maurizio (see above), and shares the same phone and fax, although not the same location as their restaurant, Da Caino. They sell a wonderful selection of extra virgin olive oil, homemade fruit preserves, olive pâté, game sauces, vegetables preserved in oil, and over 500 wines from all over the world. Check with the restaurant if the shop is closed, and someone will open it.

Montepulciano

HOTEL
Il Borghetto
Borgo Buio 7
☎/Fax 0578.757-535
MasterCard, Visa • moderate

AGRITOURISM
Macchione
Via Gaggiole 1
☎/Fax 06.980-3226
or 0578.716-010
No credit cards • low moderate

RESTAURANT
Diva e Maceo
Via Gracciano nel Corso 92
☎0578.716-951
Closed Tuesday
No credit cards • moderate

This typical *trattoria* is in the center of Montepulciano and serves traditional food of the area, prepared by Diva. *Pici*, homemade *tagliatelle*, grilled and roast meat, simple desserts are served by sommelier Maceo. His wine list focuses on Nobile di Montepulciano, paired perfectly with the local *cucina*.

Montevarchi

HOTEL
See Firenze

AGRITOURISM
Fattoria Petrolo
Mercatale Valdarno, Bucine (nearby)
☎**055.991-1322**
Fax 055.992-749
No credit cards • inexpensive

RESTAURANT
Osteria di Rendola
Rendola 76–81
☎**055.970-7490**
Fax 055.970-7491
All credit cards • high moderate
Alberto Fusini's restaurant is wonderful, a welcome addition to the Tuscan restaurant scene. The ambience is restored rustic, with nicely set tables, modern lighting, soft music. Chef Francesco Berardinelli has cooked his way around some of the best restaurants in Italy, including nearby Vicolo del Contento (see page 291), and has developed a healthy respect for seasonal produce and traditional flavor combinations. Begin with classic Tuscan *salumi* and *crostini, tonno di coniglio* (rabbit poached and marinated under oil like tuna), served with beans, or *capocollo* with whipped eggplant. First-course options include soup, *risotto,* classic spaghetti with tomato sauce and basil, homemade *pappardelle* sauced with chicken liver and beans. *Secondi,* like guinea hen with lentils, pork braised with prunes and tarragon, or simply grilled *costata* steak for two, are perfectly prepared. The wine list is small, with mostly non-Tuscan whites, and a more interesting selection of Tuscan reds, with a few well-chosen outer-regional wines for bored locals. Homemade desserts like lemon-flavored ricotta topped with seasonal fruit compote are worth saving room for, although those with a sweet tooth should opt for the dessert sampling.

PRADA OUTLET
Prada
Levanella
Montevarchi
☎**055.978-9188**
All credit cards
Call for hours
Diners will have to pass the Prada outlet if they're going to Osteria di Rendola. Men's and women's shoes, clothes, luggage, umbrellas, and more are sold at discounted prices. The sign reads Pellettieri d'Italia and isn't easy to locate.

Monticchiello di Pienza

INN
L'Olmo
Podere Omio 27
☎**0578.755-133**
Fax 0578.755-124
MasterCard, Visa • high moderate
The Lindo family has restored a typically Tuscan seventeenth-century country house, with five luxurious suites and one single, furnished with antiques, canopy beds, superior bathrooms, cable TV. Guests can opt for bed-and-breakfast or half-pension, which includes a candlelight dinner of local cooking—discuss the menu with Francesca Lindo, who runs the inn. The wine list is small, with a few sparkling wines and expensive Champagne along with a well-priced local white and reds like Brunello and Rosso di Montalcino, Vino Nobile, and Rosso di Montepulciano.

Murlo

HOTEL
Albergo di Murlo
Via Martiri di Rigosecco 1
☎**0577.814-033**
Fax 0577.814-243
All credit cards • inexpensive

AGRITOURISM

Podere Vignali

Outside Murlo (call for directions; it's not easy to find)

☎0577.814-368

No credit cards • inexpensive

RESTAURANT

La Befa

Località La Befa (nearby)

☎0577.806-255

Closed Wednesday

No credit cards • low moderate

La Befa, in the tiny eponymous hamlet, is a *trattoria* caught in a time warp. There's no sign—look for a few tables in front of a bar where locals hang out, walk through the bar to one of two small no-frills dining rooms. Rosa's in the kitchen, hand-rolling pasta, preparing simple dishes that are served by her son Brunello. Mushrooms and game like wild boar are offered in season. The house wine is no thrill. Vegetarians and enophiles should probably dine elsewhere, but I love the food and feeling of a meal at La Befa.

ETRUSCAN MUSEUM AND DINNER

Museo Etrusco

in center of Murlo

☎0577.814-099

Fax 0577.814-246

In the heart of the village of Murlo, located in the Bishop's Palace, the Etruscan museum is a jewel. Worth a detour are the roof and pediment of a building that dates back to the fifth century B.C. On the first Saturday in September, the village hosts an Etruscan dinner, and although it's not 100 percent authentic it's plenty of fun. Tables are set up in a main piazza, with candles and torches illuminating the square. Slides of Etruscan pottery depicting food-related subjects are shown. There's a reproduction of an Etruscan brazier where some (but not all) food is cooked. There's lots of wine,

although most diners don't mix it with water the way the Etruscans did, and the meal usually includes olives, *farro*, rustic pasta, wild boar, grilled and braised meats flavored with local juniper berries, and whole-wheat hazelnut cake for dessert. Contact the museum for more information.

Panzano

Panzano is the culinary epicenter of the Chianti territory, a *"paese dei golosi* [a village of gourmands]," according to Dario Cecchini. His butcher shop is the heart of Panzano, a place to stop off to find out what's going on—parties, concerts, festivals, markets, and more. Vineyards and olive trees surround the village, supplying their bounty to its restaurants, wine shops. The bakery has a wood-burning oven and makes superior bread and *schiacciata con l'uva*. There's a nearby cheesemaker of *pecorino* and ricotta. Two *frantoii*, olive oil mills, make oil in the late fall. The Sunday-morning market is wonderful, all the stores are open, and everyone in town hangs out.

MASTER BUTCHER

Dario Cecchini

Via XX Luglio 11

☎/Fax 055.852-020

Closed Sunday afternoon and all day Wednesday

It's only fitting that Panzano begin with Dario Cecchini, a legend locally and far beyond. His shop is the Uffizi of Meat, Dario the Michelangelo of *macellaii*, butchers, worth a pilgrimage for true carnivores. His *macelleria* performs the function that a bar does in most towns. Locals stop in to chat (Dario knows everyone and what's going on in town) and buy meat, but there are usually visitors from the world beyond Panzano (I've met Italians from north to south, Scandinavians, Germans, Americans, British, French, Dutch, Austrians, Australians, Asians, Africans, and more) who've come for a taste of Dario's *salumi,* meat and veracious *chiantigiano* hospitality. Spotless, white-tiled walls are laden with strands of *peperoncini* (red peppers), cured pig's feet, and *guanciale* (cured jowl). Attractive, no-nonsense displays of raw and prepared meats line the glass-fronted counter. Dario, assisted by his wife, Laura, presides behind the counter, exiting to greet friends. Check out the meat locker through a window: sides of real *Chianina* beef and Tuscan lamb on stainless-steel hooks. There's a high-fidelity system playing classical music, jazz or blues, a culinary library next to bookshelves of spices, and a sofa, because this is a shop where people hang out. Vegetarians lapse. Buy some *salumi* for a picnic (see below for the best bread and wine). Anyone with a kitchen to cook in should plan to purchase Dario's quintessential *Chianina* steak, the finest I've ever come across. My husband, Massimo, can't resist the *pancetta fresca,* slices of pork belly rubbed with vinegar, then herbed and spiced with artistry, to be grilled at home over a wood-burning fire in our hearth.

HOTEL

Villa Sangiovese

Piazza Bucciarelli 5
☎055.852-461
Fax 055.852-463
All credit cards • low expensive

AGRITOURISM

Casaloste

☎/Fax 055.852-725
high moderate
Three apartments in a building in an organic vineyard that produces a wonderful extra virgin olive oil.

**FARMHOUSE
RENTALS-WINERY**

Fontodi Winery

Casa La Rota

☎/Fax 415.925-0322 in the U.S.
(November–March)
☎/Fax 055.852-817 in Italy
☎ 055.852-005
Fax 055.852-537 (March–November)
expensive

Fontodi's farmhouse rentals are as fine as their first-rate wines. Choose from three beautifully restored, well-equipped houses with gardens, swimming pool, and views of vineyards and olive trees responsible for this winery's fine products. Rentals are weekly or monthly, more expensive from June 15–September 15 and two weeks around Easter.

RESTAURANT

Il Vescovino

Via Ciampolo da Panzano 9
☎/Fax 055.852-464
Closed Tuesday, Wednesday lunch
All credit cards • low expensive

Chef-owner Domenico Baldi and his wife Arianna's restaurant offers another excuse for a visit to Panzano, one of my favorite spots in Toscana. Traditional Tuscan dishes and innovative cooking share space on the menu. Look for smoked salmon, *bruschetta al pomodoro,* classic *salumi* or *crostini* to start. First courses include bread soups like *ribollita;* fresh pasta sauced with seafood, meat, or vegetables; or tasty lasagna, followed by delicately sauced fish, hearty poultry, or grilled-meat main dishes. Local cheese and homemade desserts conclude the meal. The wine list is stellar, well priced, inviting diners to drink big. Dine on the terrace overlooking the countryside of olive trees, vineyards, villas, and farmhouses when the weather is nice.

RESTAURANT

Oltre il Giardino

Piazza Bucciarelli 42
☎055.852-828
Closed Tuesday
MasterCard, Visa • moderate

Oltre il Giardino (literally "beyond the garden," but also the Italian title of the film *Being There* with Peter Sellers) was just about to open when I was wrapping up this edition of my book, but I have every confidence that I'll love the restaurant. Giulietta and Stefania are in the kitchen—they've done catering in Panzano and I'm wild about their cooking. Stefano Cozzi and Lucrezia have a farm outside town that provides extra virgin olive oil and produce for the restaurant. Meat is supplied by master butcher Dario Cecchini, the wine list is impressive, focusing on Tuscany but with a strong selection of wines from other regions. Judging from the enthusiasm of everyone involved with this *trattoria*, it's going to be a winner.

ENOTECA
Enoteca Baldi
Piazza Bucciarelli 25
☎055.852-843
Open 9:30 A.M.–10:30 P.M. daily, closed for a few weeks in February
MasterCard, Visa • moderate
Domenico Baldi and his wife, Arianna, of Il Vescovino (see above), also own the Enoteca Baldi, a wine bar with a wonderful selection of Tuscan, Italian, and foreign wines. Stop in for a glass of wine or purchase a bottle for a picnic. Snack on *salumi*, cheese, or a light dish or two at one of the tables. Finish with cookies and a glass of *vin santo*.

WOOD-BURNING OVEN BAKERY
Adriano Badii
Via Santa Maria
☎055.852-132
Closed Sunday afternoon and Wednesday
A classic Chianti bakery that's worth a detour for fragrant Tuscan bread baked in a wood-burning oven. Fans claim it tastes even better the next day. Look for the *schi-*

acciata con l'uva, made with wine grapes in season and raisins the rest of the year.

Pienza

Pienza, named for Pope Pio II, born there as Enea Silvio Piccolomini, is a jewel of a city. It was transformed (in only three years, from 1459 to 1462) by Florentine architect Bernardo Rossellino and the Pope, who turned the rustic hamlet of Corsignano into a graceful Renaissance town.

HOTEL
Il Chiostro di Pienza
Corso Rossellino 26
☎/Fax 0578.748-400
All credit cards • moderate

BED AND BREAKFAST
La Saracina
Strada Statale 146, km 29.7
☎0578.748-022
Fax 0578.748-018
All credit cards • expensive

WINE AND SPECIALTY FOODS
Club delle Fattorie
Piazza dei Martiri della Libertà 2
☎/Fax 0578.748-150
Closed Wednesday afternoon, and November, January, and February
All credit cards
The Club delle Fattorie, founded in 1969, offers a unique service. In a country known for its highly irregular postal service, Alberto del Buono has created a mail-order food and wine business that actually works. The catalog features quality wines and special regional products not usually available outside their own areas, often packaged especially for the Club delle Fattorie. The selection of rare aged single-malt Scotch whiskies—twelve-year-old Lochnagar, sixteen-year-old Laphroaig, eighteen-year-old Tamnavulin, and a Macallan 1937 among

others—is impressive. Dried *porcini* mushrooms, capers, balsamic vinegar, extra virgin olive oil, pasta, preserves, candied fruit, honey, cookies, chocolates, and natural cosmetics are all offered in the illustrated catalog mailed to club members. The shop in Pienza sells all items listed in the catalog. Prices are high. Mail and phone orders are accepted, and the club will ship, although due to difficult customs regulations they won't send alcoholic purchases to the U.S.

Pietrasanta

HOTEL
Palagi
Piazza Carducci 23
☎**0584.70249**
Fax 0584.71198
All credit cards • moderate

HOTEL
See Lido di Camaiore

RESTAURANT
Sci
Vicolo di Porta a Lucca 3–7
☎**0584.790-993**
Closed Sunday
No credit cards • inexpensive
There are three tables in the dining room and two outside for lunch when the weather is nice. But the most important table is the one in the kitchen where the women work, preparing the home-style *cucina* that the local stoneworkers and sculptors adore. The food is unpretentious and gutsy, and the *fritto* of chicken and rabbit is fried in an iron frying pan. Vegetables, in true Tuscan style, are tasty but overcooked. When the food runs out, this *trattoria* closes, so be prepared to arrive early. Wines are not up to the rest of the delightful experience. Sci is open for lunch only.

Pieve Fosciana

HOTEL
See Castelnuovo di Garfagnana or Camporgiano

GRISTMILL
Ercolano Regoli
Pieve di Sotto
Pieve Fosciana
☎**0583.666-095**
Ercolano Regoli is a miller (*mugnaio*). His mill, where he stone-grinds corn, wheat, and smoked chestnuts, is powered by the swift-flowing Esarulo River. Ercolano's chestnut flour is intense, with a rich smoky flavor, ground as fine as baby powder. His wheat flour and cornmeal are also first-rate.

Pisa

Pisa, onetime powerful maritime republic on the shores of the Arno River, offers much more than the Leaning Tower. Architectural wonders stud the city, the botanical garden is fantastic, and the university has a world-class science department. Pisa also has a young group of noncompetitive wine-conscious restaurant owners who hang out together. They have made the city a haven for food lovers, and have earned praise for their dedication and passion.

HOTEL
Royal Victoria
Lungarno Pacinotti 12
☎**050.940-111**
Fax 050.940-180
All credit cards • moderate

HOTEL
Villa di Corliano
Rigoli, outside San Giuliano Terme (close by)
☎**050.818-193**
Fax 050.818-341
Visa, MasterCard • moderate

RESTAURANT

Lo Schiaccianoci

Via Vespucci 104

☎050.21024

Closed Monday and most of August

All credit cards • high moderate

Carlo Silvestrini inherited the name of his restaurant, Lo Schiaccianoci, "The Nutcracker," from the previous owner, but the *cucina* is original. Carlo sets out for the market each morning, ready to be inspired. And each day he returns to his restaurant, inspired, and composes a menu that takes advantage of the regional bounty that he's unearthed. Fish and seafood are nicely cooked, and flavors are balanced. The fish soup is intense and boneless; fried fish is lightly crisped and greaseless. The *cee* (young eels), raw and squirming in a plastic bin, won't appeal to the squeamish, but they are stellar—cooked in a tomato sauce, served with *parmigiano* cheese, a dish that breaks all the rules and succeeds. Seasonal desserts are creative and well prepared. Wines, reflecting the dedication of one of the young Pisan restaurateurs, are wonderful.

RESTAURANT

Al Ristoro dei Vecchi Macelli

Via Volturno 49

☎050.20424

Closed Wednesday, Sunday lunch, and August

All credit cards • expensive

The formula is a classic in Italy. Miranda Vanni presides in the kitchen, and her son,

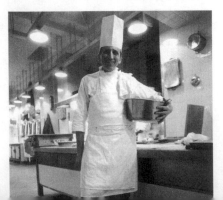

sommelier Stefano Vanni, in the dining room. Their restaurant serves light, fresh-tasting *cucina* based on quality fish and seafood from the coast, inland wild boar or pigeon, all perfumed with herbs or seasonal vegetables. Save room for the homemade desserts. Wines are wonderful.

RESTAURANT

Taverna Kostas

Via del Borghetto 39

☎050.571-467

Closed Monday and August

No credit cards • inexpensive

Kostas Touloumtzis created this wonderful "taverna," a simple, inexpensive student cafeteria at lunchtime, offering a fixed menu. He's returned to Greece and the tradition is being maintained by Mario and Federico Ferrò. The wines, available anytime, have always been superb. I hope that the Ferrò brothers keep it up.

RESTAURANT

La Mescita

Via Cavalca 2

☎050.544-294

Closed Saturday lunch and Sunday

All credit cards • moderate

La Mescita, once a simple wine bar, was transformed by its current owner, Marco Griffa, into a charming *trattoria* with vaulted brick ceilings, terra-cotta floors, and friendly ambience. It's close to Pisa's market, and therefore utilizes the freshest, best ingredients in town. The menu is simple, well priced, and the dining room is always packed with university professors and locals. Look for nontraditional but mostly interesting dishes, based on fresh seasonal vegetables. Dine on vegetable pastas or *sformati, baccalà* with chick-peas, roast chicken. The fine cheese selection is a great excuse to drink a big red from the interesting wine list that features the superstars of Tuscan enology.

Piteccio

HOTEL

See Montecatini

APARTMENTS

Residence il Castagno
☎/Fax 0573.42193

No credit cards • moderate

Weekly rentals in modern apartments with a swimming pool.

RESTAURANT

Il Castagno
Via Castagno 46/B
☎/Fax 0573.42214

Open evenings only except Sunday,
closed Monday

MasterCard, Visa • high moderate

Pierangelo Barontini moved from Montecatini to the middle of nowhere, outside Pistoia on a road that winds through woods and over streams. He's toned down his culinary act, and I'm wild about the transformation. Il Castagno is casual, gentrified country-style, and the *cucina* reflects the ambience. Pierangelo has trained in France, traveled widely to hone his skills, and is passionate about cooking. Ingredients are first-rate, local whenever possible, utilized with restraint. Mushrooms, often from the surrounding chestnut woods, are worth a voyage during their season. Deep-frying is an art form for Pierangelo—he fries in extra virgin olive oil, and the results are extraordinary as diners will learn when they begin with *pasta fritta*, fried dough balls. The menu is composed of Tuscan classics, some with a twist (like *panzanella* done with cous-cous) and creative dishes that combine traditional flavors, like bean-stuffed ravioli with *amatriciana* sauce. Quality *salumi* and cheese are worth tasting. Among the simple but tempting desserts are custard and nut-stuffed *torta*

mantovana and flawlessly executed *cenci*, deep-fried cookies. The wine list is wonderful, well chosen, and not overwhelmingly huge. Hooray for Pierangelo.

Piteglio

AGRITOURISM-NECCI

Lucia Andreotti
Piteglio, località Lolle
☎0573.69135

No credit cards • inexpensive

Lucia Andreotti and her husband, Giorgio Maffucci, sell *necci*, chestnut-flour crepes, in Florence but "at home we make them the real way," she explained to me. This is done by sandwiching the batter between chestnut leaves on sandstone disks that have been heated over a wood-burning fire. Lucia and Giorgio have an organic farm in the almost-impossible-to-find area of Lolle, outside Piteglio, northwest of Pistoia. They rent two rooms to tourists, and will make lunch or dinner, including *necci*, for guests who reserve in advance, for 30,000 lire, a wonderful reward for those who make it to Lolle.

Ponte a Bozzone

HOTEL

See Siena

RESTAURANT

Osteria Ponte a Bozzone
On Strada Statale 408 toward Gaiole,
southeast of Siena
☎0577.356-809

Closed Sunday

Diners Club, MasterCard, Visa • high moderate

This *osteria* is a well-kept secret, unmentioned in most guides. It's outside Siena on the road to Gaiole, next to a bridge that crosses the Bozzone stream. Two tiny dining rooms (and outdoor tables when the weather is nice) are filled with locals. Cinzia Certosini in the kitchen, husband Gianfranco Frenci bustles between tables. The menu is small but interesting, with homemade pasta, soups, simple meat preparations like braised rabbit with olives, and rustic desserts. The wine list is ample, featuring lots of Chianti Classico as well as reds from the north and abroad, and whites from Veneto and Trentino.

Ponte a Moriano

HOTEL

See Lucca

RESTAURANT

La Mora

Via Sesto di Moriano 104
☎**0583.406-402**
Fax 0583.406-135
Closed Wednesday evening and Thursday
All credit cards • high moderate

La Mora began over 100 years ago, as a stopping-off point for mail, a resting place for horses, and a tavern serving local wine and fried fish from the Serchio River. Times have changed, but Sauro and Angela Brunicardi's restaurant is still firmly traditional. Sommelier and able host Sauro serves straightforward *cucina* based on the seasons, regional comfort food prepared by his wife, Angela, and chef Bruno Ercoli. *Salumi* are local, but I can never resist the *delizie del Serchio*, delicate, crispy, deep-fried whitebait that even fish haters usually enjoy. The *minestra di farro*, emmer and bean soup, is a five-star dish, worth a gastronomic detour. Pasta is homemade, meats are grilled or roasted with herbs, and cheese is local. Extra virgin olive oil is the house dressing, delicate yet full-flavored, olive-y and green. Basic desserts are somewhat anticlimactic after La Mora's hearty *cucina*, and the *buccellato*, containing

raisins with serious pits, is a bit austere but goes nicely with *vin santo*. Wines are splendid, and sommelier Sauro has one of my favorite selections of local, Tuscan, Italian, and foreign wines and spirits, all of impeccable quality. The *enoteca* in front of the restaurant sells wine and regional products of excellence. Whenever I asked other chefs or restaurateurs in Toscana where they liked to eat on their days off, the response was almost always La Mora. I agree.

Ponte Attigliano

BREAD

Forno Agnese

Via G. Braga 360
☎**0574.620-081**
Closed Sunday

One of my favorite breads comes from the Agnese family bakery in Ponte Attigliano, near Poggio a Caiano. Signora Agnese baked her bread, which has a kind of cult following in the area, until recently. Her daughter-in-law and grandson now run the bakery, everything is done the same way. The bread is made from Tuscan flour and starter. The oven is fired with wood, bread is placed on the oven's stone floor, the heavy iron door is plugged into the opening, and when it is time (something the Agneses know), the bread is done. On Saturdays bread is baked three or four times to satisfy the local demand. The Agnese bread is heavy—a 1-kilo loaf looks half the size of a normal loaf of Tuscan bread. It's dense, wheaty, a bit sour, complex, and gummy when fresh. Agnese's bread is at its best one day old, barely toasted over a fire, rubbed with garlic, dipped in extra virgin olive oil, and sprinkled with salt and pepper.

Pontremoli

HOTEL
Golf Hotel
Via Pineta
☎0187.831-573
Fax 0187.831-591
American Express, MasterCard, Visa •
inexpensive

AGRITOURISM
Costa d'Orsola
Orsola (outside Pontremoli)
☎0187.833-332 or 055.280-539
No credit cards • low moderate

RESTAURANT
Da Bussè
Piazza Duomo 31
☎0187.831-371
Closed Friday, open for lunch only on weekdays,
and Saturday and Sunday dinner
No credit cards • low moderate

Da Bussè is a genuine old-fashioned *oste-ria*—one room, one large table with ten seats, for locals stopping in for a glass of wine and a taste of Antonietta Bertocchi's home-style cooking. Look for *testaroli* sauced with *pesto;* chestnut-flour *gnocchi; torta di erbe* made with potatoes, chard, and leek; *bardella*, baked *polenta;* stuffed vegetables; *polpettone*, meat loaf; rabbit *cacciatora;* and fine local *salume* and cheese. Conclude with simple desserts like *crostate, zuppa di mascarpone*, berries, or seasonal fruit. There's no written menu, dishes are seasonal, the house wine (everyone drinks the white) will disappoint enophiles. Check out the rack behind the bar that holds decks of cards that belong to regulars who stop in for a game and a glass of wine after lunch.

BAR-CAFFÈ-PASTRY SHOP
Caffè degli Svizzeri
Piazza della Repubblica 7
☎0187.830-160
Closed Sunday afternoon and Monday

Overlooking Pontvemoli's main piazza with its Wednesday and Saturday morning markets, the Caffè degli Svizzeri is an Art Deco jewel, with attractive lamps, wooden wainscoting, marble-topped tables, chairs, and woodwork trim. The specialty is *amor*, a wafer cookie stuffed with a fluffy icinglike filling that's probably an acquired taste.

GROCERY
Salumeria Angella
Via Garibaldi 11
☎0187.830-161
Closed Wednesday afternoon

Local products like *testaroli, pesto*, and dried *porcini* mushrooms are specialties of this unassuming shop run by Angela and Armando Angella, but a slim horse's bone next to the *salumi* was the tip-off that someone was really into cured pork. The bone is used by experts, who insert it into *prosciutto*, then extract and sniff it, since the porous bone absorbs the scent. Armando learned how to make *salumi, spalla cotta*, cooked shoulder, *capocollo*, and a local version of *mortadella*, from his father, Osvaldo, and he will show those who are interested the basement rooms where he ages his fine *salumi*.

MUSEUM
Museo delle Statue Stele Lunigianesi
Castello del Piagnarro
☎0187.831-439
Closed Monday, open 9 A.M.–12 noon, 4–7 P.M.
in the summer; 9 A.M.–12 noon, 2–5 P.M. in the
winter

I'm wild about this small, rather shabby, but wonderful museum with a fantastic bookstore containing area guidebooks and souvenirs in a castle that overlooks the city of Pontremoli. It's filled with rooms of *stelae*, late-prehistoric stone slabs that represent "large-breasted mothers" or warriors from a civilization that pre-dates the Romans by 2,000 years.

Porto Ercole

HOTEL-RESTAURANT

Il Pellicano

Sbarcatello (outside town)

☎0564.833-801

Fax 0564.833-418

All credit cards • luxury, expensive out of season

Il Pellicano is a jewel of a Relais & Chateaux luxury hotel, a little chunk of paradise on the Tuscan coast. This is what informal elegance is all about, with beautifully appointed rooms, tasteful prints, fine linens, unobtrusive, efficient service, terraces that lead down to the pool and the sea, and a wonderful restaurant. Owner Roberto Scio is the quintessential host, looking after details, making sure that his guests are perfectly content. Don't expect these delights to be reasonably priced. The restaurant is unpretentious, well appointed, but most diners prefer to eat outside on the terrace when the weather permits. The menu concentrates on fish and seafood, beautifully prepared, simply presented. Start with steamed prawns, or paper-thin slices of smoked swordfish and tuna on a bed of tiny salad greens, or marinated rabbit loin with truffle oil and herbs. Pasta is often homemade, sauced with fish, herbs, or seasonal vegetables like mushrooms or ripe summery tomatoes. Main-course options include fresh local fish, simply sauced or grilled to perfection, boned at the table by the skilled staff. Local *Chianina* beef fillet with black truffle and red wine sauce, or roast rack of lamb will please car-

nivores. Conclude with a selection of local cheeses or tempting "spoon desserts," such as frozen *zabaione* served with wine and honey-poached cherries, caramelized lemon cream, yogurt bavarian with fruit sauce, and seasonal *sorbetto* and *gelato*. The wine list is wonderful, personal, ample, an impressive selection of Italian gems, lots of French Champagne, and even a few American wines although prices are high. The only other hotel that comes close to rivaling the elegance of Il Pellicano is its sister, La Posta Vecchia, in Palo Laziale, twenty minutes from the Rome airport, run by Roberto's son Harry.

Prato

Industrial Prato, considered an ugly duckling by the Florentines, is worth a visit, and has earned a place in the gastronomic hall of fame with their perfect *vin santo* cookie, unequaled elsewhere, and wonderful bread.

HOTEL

See Firenze

HOTEL

Villa Santa Cristina

Via Poggio Secco 58

Prato (close by)

☎0574.595-951

Fax 0574.572-623

All credit cards • moderate

PASTRY

Mattei

Via Ricasoli 2

☎0574.25756

Closed Monday

The quintessential *biscotti di Prato*, called *biscotti di mattonella* by the locals and *cantuccio* by those outside the city of Prato—an egg-yolk–rich almond cookie far superior to all others—is produced by the Forno Mattei. They also bake a companion cookie, *brutti e buoni* ("ugly and good"), a squat, truncated cone of ground almond and egg white, clearly a move by the frugal Pratese to use the egg whites left over from making *biscotti di Prato.* The ladyfingers are the best for making *tiramisù,* and their *torta con canditi,* a loaf studded with candied cherries and with a streusel topping, is a winner.

BREAD
Loggetti
Via Matteotti 13
☎0574.25267
Closed Sunday

Is it the water, the flour, the air, or the oven that makes Prato's bread so special? Saltless, made with a starter, flour, water, and yeast, it serves as a contrast to other foods, both in taste and texture. Most Pratese feel that the best *pane* is produced by Loggetti, founded in 1921. The secret of the high quality, explained bakers Mario and Angelo, is in the mixture of local and imported flours, and the natural starter, used in combination with yeast. Each bread is signed, branded with the letters "BL," for Logetti and his partner-cousin Bigalli, founders of this essential bakery.

BREAD
BAKERY-GASTRONOMIA-
RESTAURANT
Barni
Via Ferrucci 24
☎0574.607-845; bakery 0574.33835
Bakery closed Wednesday afternoon
Restaurant closed Saturday lunch, Sunday, and Monday evening
All credit cards • inexpensive

I love the bread from Barni, considered one of Prato's best bakeries, delivered to Florence daily. Giovanni Barni learned to bake from his father Luciano, who's known as "Trentino." The bread is baked in a wood-burning oven with all-Italian flour, natural yeast, and some hand-rolling. Saltless Tuscan loaves are almost triangular, with an almost cookielike crispy crust when just baked—dense, firm, and tasty for up to a week, perfect for all the Tuscan stale-bread preparations. Giovanni's son Angioli is passionate about food and wine, has traveled in France, and has broadened the operation to include a well-supplied shop, wine store, and restaurant. In the shop look for a fantastic selection of imported, domestic, and local *salumi,* cheese, and wine as well as Barni's bread. A tiny restaurant used to be located in the back, but has now expanded next door and is well worth a visit for beautifully prepared nontraditional but well-thought-out dishes and a taste of the fine products sold next door. The wine list is amazing, with Italian and French bargains begging to be opened, and fine wine is served by the glass.

CAFFÈ-LIGHT LUNCH
Caffè Giulebbe
Via Piave 24–28
☎0574.605-370
Closed Monday
No credit cards • low moderate

Dynamo Osvaldo Baroncelli has expanded his culinary empire and opened a *caffè* that's already become a classic. Marble tables with wrought-iron legs are perfect for lingering over a snack or a light lunch accompanied by fine wine by the bottle or glass. Osvaldo's own selection of fine foods like imported and local cheese, *salumi,* and wine are also sold at the *caffè.*

CONTEMPORARY ART
MUSEUM
Museo Pecci
Via Baldanzi 16
☎0574.570-620
Fax 0574.572-604
Open 9 A.M.–7 P.M. daily; shows are closed Tuesday

One of the few lively modern art museums in all Italy, the Pecci offers a wonderful cultural justification to sample the gastronomic wonders of town.

R E S T A U R A N T

Osvaldo Baroncelli
Via Frà Bartolomeo 13
☎0574.23810
Fax 0574.605-370
Closed Saturday lunch, Sunday evening, and August
All credit cards • high moderate

Owner-sommelier Osvaldo Baroncelli seems to have made a wise choice when he hired chef Marisa Lucchesi, because the regional *cucina* they've produced is inspired. The appetizers are tasty, especially the *frittatine*—tiny pan-fried flans made with seasonal vegetables. First-course soups and homemade pasta are traditional; second-course meats are nicely done and flavored with herbs. Finish with seasonal *gelato*. Wines complement the *cucina*, and the local selections of Carmignano are a welcome sight.

Radda in Chianti

H O T E L

Vescine
☎0577.741-144
Fax 0577.740-263
All credit cards • expensive

G R O C E R Y

Porciatti
Piazza IV Novembre 1
☎0577.738-055
Closed Wednesday afternoon and Sunday
All credit cards

Porciatti is the best grocery in Radda, with a fine assortment of products, including *pecorino*, bread, pasta, rice, and homemade *salumi* like *prosciutto*, *salame*, *finocchiona*,

and *soppressata* along with such household necessities as soap and toilet paper. There's a small selection of prepared foods, perfect for picnic fans. The wine selection focuses on the surrounding area of Chianti Classico.

C E R A M I C S

Ceramica Rampini
Casa Beretone di Vistarenni
☎0577.738-043
Closed Sunday afternoon, but someone's usually around
American Express, MasterCard, Visa

The entire extended Rampini family are responsible for some of the Chianti area's best ceramics. Tiziana and her brother Romano design and execute pottery, which is decorated with the help of a squad of assistants. Romano's companion, Jessica (from Britain), works in the shop and takes care of orders, packing, and shipping. Look for attractive modern and traditional designs. Shipping makes this pottery pricy, but it's probably worth the extra expense.

Rosia

H O T E L

Borgo Pretale
Borgo Pretale, near Sovicille
☎0577.345-401
Fax 0577.345-625
All credit cards • expensive

H O T E L

Borgo di Toiano
Toiano, outside Sovicille
☎0599.314-639
Fax 0577.270-596
All credit cards • low expensive, moderate off season

H O T E L

See Siena

RESTAURANT

La Torre di Stigliano

Piazza Grande

Stigliano, outside Rosia

☎0577.342-029

Closed Monday

Visa • high moderate

Giancarlo Gianelli is passionate about Tuscan cooking—he and his wife, Adriana, run this rural but sophisticated restaurant. Giancarlo hunts for the best ingredients from nearby farms and woods—expect wonderful seasonal vegetables, mushrooms, truffles, poultry, rabbit, and game. Begin with deep-fried sage leaves, or mushroom, chicken-liver, or tomato *crostini*. Pasta and *gnocchi* are homemade, sauced with game, mushrooms, or vegetables. Second-course options include grilled beef, veal, rabbit, flattened chicken *al mattone* or mushrooms, roast suckling pig, *porchetta*-style duck, or rabbit braised with grapes. Vegetarians will be happy with classic seasonal preparations. Finish with local *pecorino* or homemade desserts like *schiacciata* made with wine grapes, *gelato* sauced with chocolate or fruit, or *tiramisù*. The house wine is local, although exigent enophiles will find better wines from the mostly Tuscan list of reds and whites from Veneto and Fruili.

San Giorgio a Colonica

GELATO

Bar Pasticceria San Giorgio

Piazza San Giorgio 13

☎0574.542-491

Closed Monday

Realmo Cavalieri and his sister Maria Teresa make Toscana's finest *gelato*, always fresh, light, and creamy, worth a pilgrimage for true fans of this delectable frozen treat.

All flavors are created with natural seasonal ingredients, and colors are pale, with no artificial colorings added. The summer selection of around twenty flavors does justice to ripe local fruit, especially berries and melon. Only ten flavors are available in the winter, when *gelato* is decidedly less popular with Italians and the varieties of fruit are more limited. Heady chocolate, caffeine-rich coffee, smoky hazelnut, and tangy lemon, tasting of lemon and not peel, are all memorable, but many people come from far away to taste the splendid *Buontalenti*, a superrich custard *gelato* flavored with secret ingredients and named after Francesco de' Medici's *gelato* maker.

San Giovanni Valdarno

GLASSWARE

IVV

Lungarno Guido Reni 60

San Giovanni Valdarno

☎055.942-619

Fax 055.942-003

Closed Monday morning

MasterCard, Visa

The IVV glass factory in the Val d'Arno makes jars, dishes, vases, glassware, and pitchers—all mouth-blown. The lines are simple and modern. A small IVV shop by the side of the road sells part of their attractive production for less than the normal retail prices. Some items are irresistibly inexpensive, although you'll have to ship them yourself.

Sansepolcro

RESTAURANT-INN
Ristorante Paola e Marco
Via Palmiro Togliatti 66
Pieve Vecchia
☎0575.734-875
Fax 0575.735-051
Closed Sunday, open evenings only
All credit cards • inexpensive rooms, low expensive meals

The restaurant started off as an ambitious pizzeria in a hayloft, but Marco and Paola Mercati's enthusiasm has since transformed the adjacent farmhouse into one of Toscana's gastronomic luminaries. The dining rooms have been carefully restored and have terra-cotta floors, exposed brick and beamed ceilings, country-style furniture, and handmade lace doilies. Marco and Paola have studied with stellar chefs, in both Italy and France, and their *cucina* is based on impeccable local ingredients, nicely cooked and formally presented. Two fixed-price menus—a five-course "territorial" of local ingredients and a seven-course "creative"—include aperitifs and first-rate after-dinner pastries. Mushrooms and truffles are served to advantage in season. Marco is seriously interested in wine, and his growing cellar of reasonably priced selections is a pleasure to drink from. He hosts special evenings, inviting fine winemakers to make a statement and show their wines. The combination of *cucina*, wines, and guests leads to a better understanding of a winery and its products, and is usually lots of fun. Spend the night in one of Paola and Marco's nine newly remodeled, inexpensive rooms, and check out the choice Piero della Francescas at the Pinoteca communale, the local museum.

San Vincenzo

HOTEL
Villa Marcella
Via Palombo 1, Conchigli (nearby)
☎0565.701-646
Fax 0565.702-154
All credit cards • moderate

WINERY–AGRITOURISM
Grattamacco
Podere Santa Maria, Castagneto Carducci
☎/Fax 0565.763-840
No credit cards • moderate

RESTAURANT
Gambero Rosso
Piazza della Vittoria 13
☎0565.701-021
Fax 0565.704-542
Closed Tuesday and November
All credit cards • expensive

Fulvio Pierangelini is the owner, chef, and able purveyor of Gambero Rosso. The ambience, stemware, silver, and flowers are formal, and the creative *cucina* is carefully structured and personal. The raw materials are flawless—fresh fish that's known no ice, tender vegetables. Poultry, local lamb, and game dishes have been added to the menu, widening Fulvio's horizons beyond seafood and lightness. Desserts and *piccola pasticceria* are made by Fulvio's wife, Emanuela. Extra virgin olive oils and an exhaustive selection of wines are focused on areas of interest to Fulvio, and are nicely paired with the *cucina*.

Saturnia

SPA HOTEL
Terme di Saturnia
☎0564.601-061
Fax 0564.601-266
All credit cards • luxury

If, after a few weeks of serious eating and drinking, you're having trouble fitting into your clothes, head for the Terme di Saturnia. Mud, massages, the health club, and the fitness program will get you back into shape. The spa's pool of sulfurous waters and their special line of cosmetic treatments will make your skin feel like a baby's.

RESTAURANT

Ai Due Ceppi

Piazza Vittorio Veneto
☎**0564.601-074**
Fax 0564.601-207
Closed Tuesday and January
No credit cards • high moderate

Another husband-and-wife team, Aniello and Bianca Michele, prepare and serve Tuscan *cucina* but add a little something of themselves in each dish. *Acquacotta* (veg-

etable soup), homemade pasta, suckling pig, game, fresh mushrooms and truffles in season are prepared by Bianca with respect for tradition. Finish with ricotta mousse or *vin santo* and cookies. Choose from the nice selection of mostly quality Tuscan wines.

Sesto Fiorentino

TABLEWARE

Richard Ginori (factory)

Viale Giulio Cesare 50
☎**055.420-491**
Fax 055.420-4953

Richard Ginori is Italy's finest producer of porcelain. Located in Sesto Fiorentino, outside Firenze, the company was founded in 1735 on the Doccia estate of the Ginori marquises, and fused with the Richard

---

THE SENESE SWEET TOOTH

Three candied-fruit-and-almond cakes, *panforte, panpepato,* and *torta margherita,* and two nut cookies, noble *ricciarelli* and rustic *cavallucci,* have satisfied all classes of Senese from the thirteenth century to the present. *Panpepato,* first mentioned in a document dated 1205, is made of honey, almonds, candied fruit, lots of spices, pepper, cocoa, and a caramelized sugar syrup that gives this medieval dessert a more complex, less sugary flavor. *Panforte,* with spices but no pepper and a simple sugar syrup, is a more modern creation, and *torta margherita* is even more delicate—barely spiced, named in honor of Queen Margherita (of pizza fame, see page 313) but not taken too seriously by real *panpepato* fans. The lozenge-shaped almond-and-honey *ricciarelli* cookies are now made with honey and sugar. The *cavallucci,* made with ingredients that farmers had on hand—walnuts, honey, and aniseed—were originally jawbreakers to be dipped in *vin santo,* but have been softened up for modern tastes.

Nannini—Conca d'Oro	Nannini	Factory—Zona Industriale
Via Banchi di Sopra 23	Piazza Salimbeni	Isole d'Arbia
☎0577.41591	☎0577.281-094	☎0577.395-380
Closed Tuesday	Closed Sunday	

Nannini, with two shops in Siena and a factory on the outskirts of town, is the best commercial producer of the traditional Senese sweets. Their all-Italian almonds from Bari are tastier than the imported almonds most of the other producers use.

PALIO DINNERS

The *Palio*, Siena's medieval bareback horse race, complete with flag tossing and costumed pageantry in the Campo, the main square, occurs twice a year, on July 2 and August 16. The center field of the Campo and all the windows and balconies overlooking the course are packed with fans from the city's *contrade* (neighborhood associations), cheering for one of the ten horses, each representing a *contrada*.

The associations hold a number of dinners each year, with long tables set in the streets and flags with the symbol of their *contrada* festooning the neighborhood. The food served may not be the finest in Toscana, but it's a rare experience. Dinners are also held the night before the race, in each of the ten *contrade* racing in the next day's *Palio*. The victory dinner, held for the victor two months after the race, and the *cena del piatto*, held in the spring, present more opportunities to attend these Senese street suppers.

Tickets may be purchased directly from the *contrade* for all celebratory dining with local revelers. For more information, contact the Siena Tourist Information (tel. 0577.280-551), to find out who won the *Palio* if you're interested in the victory dinner then contact the individual *contrada*—the following list is only partial—to get tickets.

Della Nobil Contrada del Bruco
Via Comune
☎0577.286-021

Società Civetta Cecco Angiolieri
Via Angiolieri
☎0577.285-505

Società della Giraffa
Via Verine 18
☎0577.287-091

Società del Nicchio
Via Pispini
☎0577.286-021

Società Trieste—Contrada dell'Oca
Circolo Recreativo 55
☎0577.280-003

company of Milano in 1896. The factory is large, modern, and manufacturers over five million pieces of fine china annually. But in the midst of their mass production, small pockets of workers utilize traditional techniques, meticulously crafting and painting dishes by hand. These artisans, some wearing stereo headsets, deftly embellish plates with bands of color, golden borders, or intricate designs, repeating the same movements and patterns with an individual flourish that I found moving.

SIENA COUNTRYSIDE HOTELS

Borgo Pretale
Borgo Pretale, near Sovicille
☎0577.345-401
Fax 0577.345-625
All credit cards • expensive

La Suvera
Pievescola, near Casole d'Elsa
☎0577.960-300
Fax 0577.960-220
All credit cards • expensive

Le Piazza
Outside Castellina in Chianti
☎0577.743-190
Fax 0577.743-191
All credit cards • expensive

Borgo di Toiano
Toiano, outside Sovicille
☎0599.314-639
Fax 0577.270-596
All credit cards • low expensive, moderate off season

Casafrassi
Via Chiantigiana 40, Cassafrassi,
near Castellina in Chianti
☎0577.740-621
Fax 0577.740-805
All credit cards • low expensive, moderate off season

Salivolpi
Via Fiorentina 89, Salivolpi, near
Castellina in Chianti
☎0577.740-484
Fax 0577.740-998
All credit cards • low moderate

MUSEUM

Museo di Doccia
Via Pratese 31
☎055.420-4952
Closed Sunday, Monday, Wednesday, Friday, and holidays

The Doccia Museum, next to the Ginori factory, is a gem, a must for porcelain collectors and lovers of the finely set table. It traces the history of Richard Ginori from its founding to the present day, with over 5,000 examples of the porcelain from all periods. Some of the museum's most exciting pieces—a swan's-neck teapot, a pedestal candle holder, a wavy-edged glass chiller, an oval bowl with gold-leafed wild fruits, a water lily Art Nouveau candy dish, and Milanese architect Giò Ponti's bowl, tortoise paperweight, and cachepot—have been reproduced in limited numbers, for Richard Ginori's 250th anniversary.

TABLEWARE

La Botteguccia
Viale Giulio Cesare 19
☎055.421-0472
Closed Monday
All credit cards

Across the street from the Doccia Museum, La Botteguccia sells Ginori seconds and close-outs, straight from the factory. Luck will determine the selection on any given day, but shipping costs will make your finds less of a bargain. Not all items can be charged.

Siena

The food in most of Siena's restaurants is miserable and locals rarely dine out, preferring the neighborhood dining clubs in their contrada.

Most tourists who come to Siena stay for only a few hours, and restaurants haven't gone out of the way to make this brief stay memorable. Visitors would be wise to snack on the traditional cakes and cookies, or to picnic in the spectacular countryside outside the town.

HOTEL

Santa Caterina
Via A. Piccolomini 7
☎0577.221-105
Fax 0577.271-087
All credit cards • moderate

HOTEL
Piccolo Hotel Etruria
Via Donzelle 3
☎0577.288-088
Fax 0577.288-461
All credit cards • inexpensive

RESTAURANT
Osteria Le Logge
Via del Porrione 33
☎0577.48013
Closed Sunday
All credit cards • high moderate

Le Logge, on a little street off piazza del Campo, is the best place to eat in Siena. Owner Gianni Brunelli is wild about Tuscan food and wine, and his enthusiasm is contagious. The *trattoria* is rustic, an ex-hardware store with wooden shelves, scale, and old price lists from when a few lire actually bought something. Wonderful watercolors of vegetables hang on the walls and illustrate Gianni's cookbook, available in Italian, German, and English. Look for classic Tuscan *salumi; gnudi,* spinach and ricotta *gnocchi;* basic pasta; hearty soups; and anything dressed with Gianni's extra virgin olive oil. The wine list is small, mostly Tuscan, and includes Gianni's own production of Rosso and Brunello di Montalcino.

WINE BAR
Il Grattacielo
Via de' Pontani 8
☎0577.289-326
Closed Sunday, open 8 A.M.–2 P.M., 5–8 P.M.
No credit cards • inexpensive

Il Grattacielo ("The Skyscraper"), a tiny low-ceiling *mescita* wine bar, is a local hangout, not a real restaurant, that serves simple wine and some food to accompany it. *Prosciutto,* tripe, or *condito,* dressed tomatoes and tuna, or roast pork accompany the lackluster house red. Those in search of an authentic but no-frills snack should plan a visit. It's close to impossible to get a table at lunch—stop in before noon if you want to have something to eat.

ENOTECA
San Domenico
Via del Paradiso 56
☎0577.271-181
Fax 0577.309-074
Open 9 A.M.–8 P.M. daily
American Express, MasterCard, Visa

For those who love *ricciarelli,* paradise is located on via del Paradiso at the Enoteca San Domenico. These cookies, a specialty of Siena, are usually hard, but those of Betti e Sinatti are soft, with an intense almond flavor, the best I've ever tasted. To visit the factory, fax San Domenico's owner, Francesco Bonfio. But San Domenico sells more than just cookies—look for the best wine, *spumante, grappa,* and distillate selection in town. It's a perfect stop for a gastronomic souvenir of Tuscany: extra virgin olive oil, pasta like *pici,* dried *porcini* mushrooms, local honey, and more.

SPECIALTY FOODS
Morbidi
Via Banchi di Sopra 73/75
☎0577.280-268
Closed Wednesday afternoon

The best picnic possibility in Siena is Morbidi, with a selection of prepared dishes, cold salads, and typically overcooked vegetables to go, as well as bread, quality wine, first-rate *salumi,* and fine local *pecorino* cheese.

Sinalunga

RESTAURANT-INN
Locanda dell'Amorosa
L'Amorosa
☎0577.679-497
Fax 0577.678-216

Closed Monday, Tuesday lunch, and mid-January through February

American Express, Diners Club, MasterCard • expensive

The Locanda dell'Amorosa is in a spectacular setting, two kilometers (about a mile and a quarter) from Sinalunga. The long cypress-lined drive is a passage that leads to another world, a stone-walled hamlet of the 1300s, with its graceful arches, frescoed church, and stone-and-brick restaurant. The *cucina* used to reflect the ambience— refined, rustic, and Tuscan—but at times it strays a bit too far from its traditional roots. Many dishes are puréed and insipid, but the homemade pasta, thrush pâté, grilled eel, and wonderful *Chianina* beef steak are full-flavored and well prepared, nicely accompanied by the much improved house wines. Desserts, especially the simple country *torte*, a kind of cross between a cake and a pie, are irresistible, and fruit *sorbetto* and *gelato* are nicely done. Stay overnight in one of the seven rooms or in the apartment, and bask in the most Tuscan of experiences. Go for a drive along the road to Siena in a landscape that's an emotional experience in all seasons.

Strada in Chianti

HOTEL

See Firenze

GELATO

Gelateria Cabane
Via Mazzini 32
☎055.858-8659
Fax 055.852-0482
Open 4 P.M.–midnight, closed Monday in the winter

Gelateria Cabane is, in the language of guidebooks, worth a detour for *gelato*-holics. Alessandro Rossini makes some of the finest *gelato* in Italy, with flavors like *stracciatella*, studded with shreds of bitter-

sweet chocolate; tangy yogurt; rich eggy custard; *bacio*, chocolate hazelnut. The *pistacchio* is grayish, made from the finest-quality Sicilian pistachio nuts, without the artificial green coloring that lesser *gelaterie* use. Fruit-flavored *sorbetti* are made with seasonal fresh fruit from Alessandro's own farm in Panzano—look for berry, peach, apricot, and more. Cabane also makes their own fine pastry, but although it looks wonderful I've never tasted it because I simply can't resist the *gelato*.

Trequanda

CHEESE AND MEAT

Azienda Agricola Belsedere
☎0577.662-137
Closed during mass on Sunday

Belsedere, the working farm (almost impossible to find) of Countess de Gori Pannilini, makes superb *pecorino* from 100 percent sheep's milk. They also produce large and small salami, *prosciutto*, sausages, and *peposo*, a boneless cured ham rolled in pepper. If you visit the farm in the sweet countryside south of Siena, you can purchase fresh or aged *pecorino*, whole cold cuts, or freshly made ricotta directly from the spry, bright-eyed, octogenarian countess.

Viareggio

Viareggio, a turn-of-the-century seaside resort, is a favorite with vacationing Italians, especially in August, when the beach appears to be standing-room-only. Umbrella-covered beach chairs can be rented by the day, week, month, or season. Two wonderful wine bars, and a restaurant that knows what to do with fish, lure me to the Tuscan coast, but not at the height of the season.

HOTEL

Plaza

Piazza D'Azelio 1

☎0584.44449

Fax 0584.44031

All credit cards • luxury, moderate off season

HOTEL

Mirage

Via Zanardelli 12

☎0584.322-22

Fax 0584.484-46

All credit cards • moderate

WINE BAR

La Taverna dell'Assassino

Viale Manin 1

☎0584.45011

Closed Wednesday

American Express, Visa, MasterCard • low moderate

The Taverna dell'Assassino combines maritime decor with the paraphernalia of wine lovers—bottles, cases, crates. I need no excuse to skip dinner to snack on the fine *salumi*, or to stop in for a glass of wine before or after dinner. A lively crowd of vacationers and locals keeps gentle Alberto Montalbano busy from 7 P.M. until he feels like closing, and many local restaurant owners finish the evening at his wonderful *enoteca*. The wine selection is astounding, a reasonably priced thrill for enophiles.

WINE BAR

Il Punto di Vino

Via Mazzini 229

☎0584.31046

Closed Monday and January

All credit cards • moderate

Il Punto di Vino is a wine bar with a seasonal, mostly regional menu of three or four simple dishes that change daily. *Salumi* and cheese are tasty. The wine selection is formidable. Stop in for a glass of wine, a snack, or a full meal.

RESTAURANT

Romano

Via Mazzini 120

☎/Fax 0584.31382

Closed Monday and January

All credit cards • expensive

Romano and Franca Franceschini's modern, air-conditioned restaurant is one of the gastronomic peaks of the Tuscan coast. Franca's *cucina* is prepared with fresh, mostly local fish and shellfish, simply prepared, elegantly presented on large white plates. The flans of tiny pan-fried baby clams (*frittatine*), perfectly cooked spaghetti sauced with seafood, and turbot baked with potatoes or mushrooms are all delicious. *Calamaretti*—thumbnail-size squid—are poached in a wonderful garlicky soup or lightly fried to a golden delicate crunch. The extra virgin olive oil and house wine come from nearby Montecarlo and are highly suited to the classic *cucina*. The tasting menu offers a reasonably priced series of mostly creative seafood dishes. Romano ably pairs wines from his personal quality selection with Franca's tasty food. Desserts are generally anticlimactic. Service tends to be slow during the crowded summer season.

RESTAURANT

La Darsena

Via Virgilio 172

☎0584.392-785

Closed Sunday, Monday evening

Diners Club, MasterCard, Visa • high moderate

La Darsena ("The Dock") is one of the few authentic *trattorie* left in a town that's been overcome by seaside tourism. Owner Giulio Baroncini works hard in his one-room locale behind the bar. Look for large portions of superfresh seafood, prepared in classics like spaghetti with clams, or assorted seafood and a first-rate grilled fish, or *fritto misto di pesce*. Desserts aren't worth saving room for. Drink Giulio's own production of

Montecarlo, or choose something more important from the small wine list.

RESTAURANT

Calimero

Viale Europa
Torre del Lago Puccini (close by)
☎0584.340-264
Closed Monday
American Express • high moderate

Signora Dani is in the kitchen, and her husband, Marco Pardini, efficiently runs the dining rooms in this family restaurant, which specializes in fresh local fish and seafood. The *antipasto* is one of the best, and most ample, on the Tuscan coast. You'll be presented with a series of eight or nine simply prepared seafood dishes—delicate marinated raw fish, shrimp and beans, and mushrooms and fish combinations in season are just a few of the highlights. Pasta and second courses appear to be well made; each time I go I promise to pace myself, but I never make it past the appetizers. I've never even tried a dessert, but always have room for a *bocconcino Dai Dai,* an ice-cube–sized chocolate-coated vanilla *gelato.* There's no wine list, and waiters aren't too well informed—you'll have to check out the glass-fronted refrigerators to see what's available.

Villa a Sesta

HOTEL

See Castelnuovo Berardenga

AGRITOURISM

Borgo Villa a Sesta
☎/Fax 0577.359-014
or 0577.734-0064
Cellular 0335.221-646

RESTAURANT

Bottega del Trenta

Via Santa Caterina 2
☎/Fax 0577.359-226
Closed Tuesday, Wednesday, and lunch except on weekends and holidays
No credit cards • low expensive

Franco Camolia is a monomaniac whose obsession is his restaurant, which is artfully restored in a perfectly rustic locale on the edge of the village of Villa a Sesta, surrounded by olive trees and vineyards. He presides in two attractive dining rooms with stone walls and beamed ceilings, his wife, Helene Stoquelet, rules in the kitchen, preparing elegant Tuscan food that draws heavily on first-class local ingredients. Start with *bruschetta, salumi,* assorted *crostini,* or grilled vegetables, but don't miss the *raveggiolo,* a creamy-custardy sheep's-milk cheese, served with a tender salad. First-course possibilities include ravioli stuffed with spinach and ricotta, *pappardelle* with a piquant porky sauce, spaghetti with seasonal vegetable sauces, or hearty soups based on beans or chick-peas. Stuffed rabbit or anything braised (poultry, beef, lamb, or possibly game) are usually served as a second course, although I can't resist the tasty squab. Helene's desserts are worth saving room for. The wine list is limited but offers a fine selection of Tuscan reds and whites from northern Italy. Dine outdoors under the *loggia* next to the courtyard when the weather is nice. Helene and Franco have a new cooking school—contact them for all the details.

TOSCANA

LE
MARCHE

•Gubbio

Isola Maggiore

San Feliciano sul Trasimeno

Bastia Umbra •Ponte Valleceppi

*Lago
Trasimeno* Perugia • Torgiano

Tevere

A1

•Deruta •Spello
Bevagna • Foligno

Pettino• Preci

Pigge•

Orvieto • Todi Spoleto Norcia•

Lago di Corbara
•Baschi Scheggino

Arrone
Terni • •

Narni • • •Piediluco
Stroncone

LAZIO

Coastless Umbria is in the center, the heart of Italy, a land of mountains, hills, valleys, lakes, and rivers, colonized by an ancient race, the Umbri. And after the Umbri came the Etruscans, Romans, Goths, Byzantines, Longobards, various noble families and republican regimes, and finally the Vatican, in a series of power struggles, bloodbaths, and disasters that taught the occupants of each village how to run for the fortress (*rocca*) that dominates each medieval hill town in the region.

Umbria

The *cucina*, if not the politics or history, reflects the gentle simplicity of Saint Francis of Assisi. Umbrian dishes seem rarely to contain more than three or four ingredients, each one tasting like itself—plain, sauceless, minimalist cooking with the backdrop of an open fire for spit-roasting or grilling, and a wood-burning oven for baking the fragrant, wheaty bread. Tasty extra virgin olive oil is the regional condiment. Homemade hand-rolled pasta is dressed with the black winter truffle's evanescent earthy perfume. Grains play an important role, with ancestral flatbreads made from stone-ground flour and water cooked on the hearthstone. Emmer (*farro*), the wheat-flavored grain that fed the Roman legions, is widely found in southern Umbria, cooked in soup, or ground and rolled into a substantial pasta known as *stringozzi, ceriole,* or *manfrigoli.* Spit-roasted suckling pig (*porchetta*) and game *salumi* made by artisan butchers are seasoned with herbs. Fish and eel from the lakes of Trasimeno and Piediluco and freshwater shrimp from the Tevere and Nera rivers grace the Umbrian table. Desserts are sweetened with honey, chestnuts, pine nuts, hazelnuts, and especially almonds. *Fave di morti* cookies and *serpentone* ("big snake"), a coiled cake with coffee bean eyes and a cherry tongue, are both based on the almond. All these foods seem to depend on the simple elements of Umbria for their flavors, and most are unavailable outside the region's borders.

It seems fitting that local artisans work with a material as basic as clay, making terra-cotta pottery in Deruta. The Museo del Vino in Torgiano has a fine collection of medieval, Renaissance, and baroque wine containers, from Deruta and other regions.

The Menu

Salumi

Prosciutto di Norcia: *prosciutto* from Norcia

Salsiccia di cinghiale: wild boar sausage

Antipasto

Bruschetta: garlic toast made with country bread and olive oil

Schiacciata: flatbread, similar to pizza crust, baked with olive oil or enriched with onions or cooked greens

Torta al testo: flat unleavened bread baked on a slab of stone

Primo

Manfrigoli, stringozzi, *or* **ceriole:** homemade rustic pasta dressed with garlicky tomato sauce

Minestra di farro: soup of tomatoes, vegetables, a *prosciutto* bone, and emmer

Spaghetti alla norcina: spaghetti with an oil-based sauce of black truffles, garlic, and anchovies

Secondo

Anguilla alla brace: grilled eel

Anguilla in umido: eel cooked with tomatoes, onions, garlic, and white wine

Frittata di tartufi: black truffle omelet

Gobbi alla perugina: deep-fried cardoons baked with meat sauce

Lepre alle olive: wild hare cooked with herbs, white wine, and olives

Mazzafegati: pork sausages with raisins and pine nuts

Palombe *or* **palombacci:** wood pigeon, usually spit-roasted

Pollo in porchetta: chicken cooked in same manner as suckling pig

Porchetta: small suckling pig baked in a wood-burning oven with wild fennel, garlic, wild mint, and rosemary

Regina in porchetta: carp from Lago di Trasimeno, cooked in same manner as suckling pig

Salsiccia all'uva: fresh pork sausage cooked with grapes

Tegamaccio: mixed lake-fish stew, with white wine and herbs

Formaggio

Ricotta: soft, fresh, mild, made from whey

Pecorino: fresh or aged, sheep's milk, distinct

Dolce

Cialde: paper-thin sweet cookies, cooked on the embossed disks of a long-handled iron tool

Fave di morte: almond cookies

Pinoccate: pine-nut cookies

Serpentone, torcolato, *or* **torcolo:** almond-and-dried-fruit dessert formed like a coiled snake

The Wine List

Until fairly recently, Umbrian wines were pleasant, drinkable, and poor travelers. The only wine of note was golden semisweet Orvieto, a favorite of princes and popes. In the early 1960s the Lungarotti winery, under the leadership of Dr. Giorgio Lungarotti, concentrated its efforts on quality, and the resulting wines, especially Rubesco Riserva and San Giorgio, rich complex reds, and Torre di Giano Riserva, an elegant, smooth white, are among the best in Italy. New-style wines are crisp, the product of the latest technology. Most quality Umbrian wines are the result of the efforts of a few dedicated winemakers.

Cabernet Sauvignon di Miralduolo is an ample, dry red, almost purple, from Torgiano, made with Cabernet Sauvignon grapes. It is served with meat and poultry, and produced by Lungarotti.

Chardonnay di Miralduolo is a smooth, dry white, made with Chardonnay grapes from Torgiano, aged in wood. It is served with fish and poultry, and produced by Lungarotti.

San Giorgio is a rich, full-bodied red, made in Torgiano of Sangiovese grapes enriched by Cabernet Sauvignon. It is served with meat and game, and produced by Lungarotti.

Solleone is amber, dry, and sherrylike, made from Grechetto and Trebbiano grapes. It is a perfect aperitif, and is produced by Lungarotti.

Cervaro della Sala, made mostly from Chardonnay and Grecchetto and aged in French oak, is produced by Castello della Sala.

Pinot Nero from the Consola vineyard is produced by Castello della Sala.

Muffato della Sala, a botrytised sweet white, is said to resemble sauterne, and is produced by Castello della Sala.

Decugnano dei Barbi is a fresh, fruity red, made of Montepulciano and Sangiovese grapes grown near Lago di Corbara. It is served with meat and poultry, and produced by Decugnano dei Barbi.

There are two DOC **Montefalco** wines, both reds from the Todi area. The **Rosso** is a soft, dry red made from mostly Sangiovese grapes, and is served with meat and poultry. The **Sagrantino,** made with the Sagrantino grape, is a full-bodied, rich, dark purple wine, either dry (*secco*), sweet (*passito*), or lightly sweet (*abboccato*). Look for wines by producers Adanti and Val di Maggio, A. Caprai.

Orvieto is probably Umbria's most famous DOC wine, a dry, light white, or a lightly sweet dessert wine (*abboccato*). Antinori, Barberani, Brugnoli, Palazzone, and Decugnano dei Barbi produce the best dry Orvieto, served with fish and vegetable dishes, and Antinori and Barberani's lightly sweet wine is perfect with simple desserts. Decugnano dei Barbi's minute production of Orvieto Classico Pourriture Noble, made in the style of a sauterne, is worth looking out for.

The **Torgiano** DOC, south of Perugia, includes both red and white wines. The white **Torre di Giano,** made from Trebbiano and Grechetto grapes, is fresh, fruity, and dry, served with first-course dishes, fish, and shellfish. The **Torre di Giano Riserva,** from the Il Pino vineyard, is aged in wood and gains elegance with aging. Red **Rubesco,** made from Sangiovese and Cannaiolo grapes, is balanced, full, and dry, served with meat, fowl, and game. The **Rubesco Riserva,** from the Monticchio vineyard, is one of Italy's finest red wines. All are produced by Lungarotti.

Spumante is mostly based on the Chardonnay grape and makes a lovely aperitif. It is well made by Decugnano dei Barbi and Lungarotti.

Vin Santo is a sweet or semi-sweet dessert wine made from partially dried Trebbiano, Malvasia, and Grechetto grapes, and aged in small barrels. It is served with simple desserts or cookies, or between meals. Top producers are Adanti and Lungarotti.

Regional Specialties

Bread. Umbria is one of the few regions where bread still tastes like wheat and natural yeast. Flatbreads are baked on an open hearth, in front of the embers of a wood fire where meat and poultry are cooked. Vaulted brick and stone ovens are fueled by wood, and the bread and cookies that exit from them have a crispness, a friability, that is unique. See page 366 for one such bakery.

Extra Virgin Olive Oil. Ancient olive trees (mostly *Moraiolo, Leccino,* and *Frantoio* olives) are an almost constant presence in the Umbrian landscape, and golden green and fruity olive oil is an important ingredient in the *cucina umbra.* The delicate, clean, and decidedly olivy flavor will probably convert most holdouts to the world's finest condiment.

The Umbrian Lentil. Are the small lentils (*lenticchie*) from the area of Castelluccio, outside the city of Norcia, tastier than all others? Yes, says the cooperative of thirteen growers from two plains located outside the hill town of Castelluccio (altitude, 1,453

meters) and I agree. The lentils are tiny, not uniform in color, higher in iron than other lentils. They don't require soaking and should be simply boiled twenty to thirty minutes. Most lentils sold in Italy are from Turkey, and Castelluccio is the only geographical area designated with a lentil of its own. See page 361 for a source.

Caciotta. *Caciotta* (*piccoli caci,* small cheeses) is the regional cheese of Umbria. It's made of 70 to 80 percent sheep's milk blended with 20 to 30 percent cow's milk and ripened for a month. *Caciotta* is eaten fresh, not aged, and it is soft and delicately flavored.

The Legendary Butchers of Norcia. In Umbria, meat shops are called *norcinerie* and butchers are called *norcini,* both names deriving from the name of Norcia, a town famous for its highly skilled butchers who used to specialize in castrating and curing pigs and did a bit of surgery on the side. *Prosciutto, pancetta, guanciale, coppa, spalla,* sausage, and more are displayed like crown jewels in meat shops throughout the region. It's a dying art, and those who would like to learn about pork butchering from a master *norcino* should turn to page 366.

Emmer.   Most people have never heard of emmer. In Italian it's *farro* (*Farrum triticum* in Latin), often erroneously translated in English as spelt. Emmer is an ancient form of wheat often found in the *cucina* of regions conquered by the Roman legions. It looks like dark barley and has a rich, nutty flavor and a nice *al dente* consistency.

Truffles.   Umbria is world-famous for its black truffles (*tartufi neri*). Hunted by dogs in the forests, they flavor, but only slightly, many dishes in the fall and winter. For more information on truffles, see page 367.

Pasta.   Pasta in Umbria isn't paper-thin, egg-yolky, rich, and elegant, as it is in Emilia-Romagna, but rather an essential Umbrian interpretation; stone-ground grain and water, rib-sticking, and a hearty first course. Spigadoro (page 357) makes quality pasta industrially, an evolution of the Umbrian tradition.

Perugina Chocolates.   Perugina is an Umbrian success story. Founded in 1907 by the Buitoni and Spagnoli families with the intention of manufacturing sugar-coated almonds (*confetti*), it rapidly expanded. The company moved in 1913, added candies and chocolates to its products, and in 1922 introduced the *bacio* ("kiss"), invented and named by the off-spring of Perugina's founders. They were an instant success. The center, made of ground hazelnuts and chocolate, is topped with a whole hazelnut looking decidedly nipplelike, and covered with chocolate. Perugina currently produces 200 million *baci* a year, making their own chocolate

from beans. The hazelnuts are mostly Turkish, which cost less than the *tonda gentile delle Langhe*. The traditional star-covered aluminum-foil wrappers hold a piece of waxed paper, printed with a romantic quotation. Perugina also makes many other chocolate products, including a seasonal output of over three million gaudily wrapped and ribboned hollow chocolate Easter eggs ranging in size from three ounces to nine pounds. Each contains a surprise of dubious value. The factory is in Perugia (see page 364), and of course the candies are available worldwide.

Deruta Pottery.   Glazed majolica pottery has been made in Deruta since the twelfth century. Early designs were simple, and grew more colorful and elaborate with the passage of time. The village of Deruta has a ceramics museum, located in the medieval Palazzo Comunale, and a state ceramics school, which ensures the future glory of the local artisanal tradition. The streets of Deruta are lined with factories and shops selling reproductions of this traditional glazed pottery (see page 357).

Flatbread Griddle.   The traditional flat-bread of Umbria, *torta al testo*, is cooked on a flat griddle (*testo*) originally made of sandstone, but now found in terra-cotta, cast iron, aluminum alloy, and even cement. They can be found in most house-wares stores in Umbria, or on the steps of the Duomo in Perugia at the Tuesday and Saturday morning pottery market.

Cities & Towns

Arrone

HOTEL
Fonte Gaia
Racognano, beyond Arrone from Terni
☎**0744.388-621**
Fax 0744.388-598
American Express, Visa • moderate

RESTAURANT
Trattoria Rossi
Località Casteldilago
☎**0744.388-794**
Closed Friday
No credit cards • inexpensive

This is the essential Umbrian *trattoria,* located in the breathtaking valley of the Nera River known as the Valnerina. The *cucina* is composed of purely local ingredients, like lamb, game, trout, and freshwater shrimp. Most dishes are dressed with herbs or truffles, pasta and desserts are homemade, and wines are local.

Baschi

HOTEL
Villa Bellago
Strada Statale 448
☎**0744.950-521**
Fax 0744.950-524
All credit cards • moderate

RESTAURANT
Vissani
Strada Statale 448, Civitella del Lago
☎**/Fax 0744.950-396**
Closed Sunday evening, Wednesday, and July
All credit cards • expensive to outrageous

The perfectly executed dishes of Gianfranco Vissani are those of a genius, idiotsavant, or idiot, depending on your point of view, and have little to do with Umbrian, Italian, or any other cuisine eaten on the face of this earth. The influence appears to be French, as are many of the ingredients and wines. If *porcini* mushrooms stuffed with blueberries, cooked in grape leaves, and served with a champagne sauce, or a foie-gras scallop sauced with mussels and black truffles, or steamed salmon with strips of pork tripe in a lemon-marjoram sauce sound interesting, this may be the place for you. A different bread, probably the best part of the meal, is served with each course. The *menu degustazione,* six or seven courses and five breads, is less expensive, the combinations more adventurous than the à la carte menu, but a selection or two from Vissani's beautifully chosen list of Italian and French wines will add more to your bill than you expected. There's also a cigar list, and a music list, although I don't know what happens if diners are of different musical inclinations. The decor is dreary but fancy, with big plants, heavy drapes, and important china, silver, crystal, and orchids adorning the tables. Evidently Gianfranco Vissani has been to France and has been greatly moved by the experience. Intrepid explorers may find his personal vision of cuisine of interest. It seems fitting that this restaurant is situated on the shores of an artificial lake.

Bastia Umbra

HOTEL

Lo Spedalicchio

Piazza B. Buozzi 3
Ospedalicchio (nearby)
☎/Fax 075.801-0323
American Express, Visa • moderate

PASTA

Spigadoro (factory)

Via IV Novembre 2/4
☎075.80091
Closed Saturday and Sunday

The Spigadoro factory in Bastia Umbra, with its all-Italian high-tech pasta machinery, spits out 2,000 quintals, or 441,000 pounds, of pasta a day. Their dried and packaged pasta is made from 100 percent durum wheat, usually Canadian or American, ground in the Spigadoro mill. This medium-size pasta factory also produces a small quantity of high-gluten pasta, extruded from bronze dies, which create a rougher surface that holds on to the sauce better. Added gluten increases elasticity, and cooked gluten pasta remains *al dente* longer. It also contains more protein. Simonetta Crociani, who speaks perfect English (she grew up in Australia), will show you around the factory if you call or write in advance.

Bevagna

HOTEL

Villa Pambuffetti

Viale della Vittoria, Montefalco (nearby)
☎0742.378-823
Fax 0742.379-245
All credit cards • expensive

HOTEL

See Foligno

RESTAURANT

Ottavius

Via Gonfalone 4
☎0742.360-555
Closed Monday
All credit cards • moderate

Located in the center of the medieval village of Bevagna, in the onetime cellars of Palazzo dei Consoli, Ottavius looks the way a typical Umbrian *trattoria* should, with stone walls, terra-cotta–tiled floors, a fireplace ablaze in the winter, simply set tables. The *cucina* reflects the austerity of the ambience, with basic Umbrian dishes flavored with herbs. Truffles are available most of the year. Look for pasta like *tagliatelle* or *stringozzi* or potato *gnocchi,* all made by Signora Lisetta. Meat is local, farm-raised—lamb with wild herbs and juniper berries, braised pheasant or anything on the grill, including vegetables. Legumes like beans, lentils, and chick-peas are usually on the menu. Finish with cookies or classic desserts like *millefoglie,* flaky pastry layered with custard. The wines are local, well chosen.

Deruta

HOTEL

See Perugia or Torgiano

POTTERY

Ubaldo Grazia (factory)

Via Tibertina 181
☎075.971-0201
Fax 075.972-018
Closed Sunday

Ubaldo Grazia's family has been making majolica since the fifteenth century. He has the best selection of attractive, authentic-looking Deruta patterns, some dating from the sixteenth century, a particularly rich period for this pottery. Plates, bowls, espresso cups, crescent-shaped individual salad or vegetable dishes, pitchers, canisters, vases, egg cups, ashtrays, and mugs are stacked in piles in a jumble of rooms on the ground floor of this factory. Ubaldo works with some famous shops—the plate you pick up may have been made for Saks, Neiman Marcus, or Barney's. Artists also work with Ubaldo and his artisans, creating modern dinnerware with Umbrian materials. Paula Sweet's patterns are stylish, original, and can be ordered. Her crescent-shaped side dishes are a personal favorite. If you don't see anything you like, or if the colors are wrong for your dining room, Ubaldo will work with you to design something to suit your taste. Prices are reasonable, except for custom-designed work, but don't forget to add on shipping costs, which will make this hand-painted pottery less of a bargain. No credit cards are accepted, but they'll take checks, personal or traveler's, and will ship.

Foligno

Foligno, which is situated on the banks of the Topino River, is home of the first printed edition of Dante's *Divine Comedy*, and the Giostra della Quintana, a traditional tournament of costumed cavaliers from the ten neighborhoods of the city, held the second and third Sundays in September. Each neighborhood tavern (*osteria*) serves simple Umbrian dishes from the 1600s and local wines during the festival. For more information, contact the Foligno Tourist Information Center (Azienda di Turismo di Foligno, Porta Romana 126, tel. 0742.60459).

RESTAURANT-INN
Villa Roncalli
Via Roma 25
☎/Fax 0742.391-091
Closed Monday and most of August
All credit cards • rooms, low moderate; restaurant, high moderate
Villa Roncalli is a small private villa on the outskirts of the city, a ten-room guest house with a restaurant that serves magnificent Umbrian family-style cooking. The restaurant is powered by three generations of the Scolastra family. Sandra, in the kitchen with her mother, prepares all the pasta and sauced dishes, and bakes bread in the wood-burning oven. Husband Angelo pampers meat, poultry, and game at the grill of a wood-burning fire, and sommelier–dessert creator daughter Luisa takes care of the two frescoed dining rooms. Vegetables receive special attention, and all dishes are dressed with tasty local extra virgin olive oil. Angelo Scolastra produces a pleasant Sagrantino, a rich red wine that suits the elemental Umbrian *cucina* of Villa Roncalli, and the wine list offers a lovely selection of quality regional and Italian wines.

ENOITECA
Il Bacco Felice
Via Garibaldi 73
☎0742.231-019
Closed Monday
No credit cards • low moderate
Surely Bacchus would be happy at Salvatore Denaro's wine bar–*osteria* in the center of Foligno. It's a long, narrow room with vaulted ceilings, a modern fresco of Bacchus, a wall full of travel, food, and wine books, and wines from the world, served with enthusiasm at four tables. The entrance display of wine and *grappa* should thrill lovers of the grape. Salvatore tracks down first-rate local products like *prosciutto* and *pecorino* cheese, fantastic bread, extra virgin olive oil. A daily soup made with local legumes and salads is also available; all courses are accompanied by fine, well-priced wines. This is a perfect place to stop for a light meal, but bear in mind that Salvatore "hates teetotalers and smokers." Water is the only nonalcoholic beverage served, and there's no smoking at Baccho Felice.

BUTCHER AND FANTASY
Macelleria e Fantasia
Via Garibaldi 41
☎0742.350-974
Closed Thursday afternoon
Sandro Santacroce's shop displays meat like jewels, but also has fine homemade *salame* and prepared dishes, perfect for a picnic.

BAKERY
Panetteria San Feliciano
Via XX Settembre 4
☎0742.357-236
Closed Thursday afternoon
This centrally located bakery sells fine bread baked in a wood-burning oven; pizza by the slice, *pane pasquale*, bread enriched with eggs and *pecorino*, and simple Umbrian desserts, excellent choices for picnic shoppers.

Gubbio

HOTEL
Bosone Palace
Via XX Settembre 22
☎075.922-0688
Fax 075.922-0552
All credit cards • moderate

RESTAURANT-INN
Villa Montegranelli
Monteluiano (nearby)
☎075.922-0185
Fax 075.927-3372
All credit cards • high moderate

RESTAURANT
Taverna del Lupo
Via G. Ansidei 6
☎075.927-4368
Fax 075.927-1269
Closed Monday
All credit cards • low expensive
When Rodolfo Mencarelli was a village doctor he used to trade recipes with his patients, until he found his true calling and opened the Taverna del Lupo with his wife, Elisa, in a building from the thirteenth century with vaulted stone ceilings. The restaurant is large, with elegantly set tables, sober lighting, and artfully displayed Umbrian pottery. Truffles, grilled meat, *bruschetta*, and regional specialties are joined on the menu by hard-to-find dishes like *bustrengo*, fried dough served with appetizers; *imbrecciata*, soup made with ten different legumes; or tasty stuffed pigeon. Diners who choose the rabbit *alla taverniera*—boned, stuffed with wild fennel and braised with white wine—will be rewarded with a Buon Ricordo souvenir plate. Rodolfo is a sommelier and will suggest appropriate wines from his ample list.

TRUFFLES AND MUSHROOMS
Buca del Tartufo
Via XX Settembre 33
☎075.927-4922
Always open
The Bartolini family shop in the center of town is a great place to buy the perfect culinary souvenir of a stay in Umbria. Black or white local truffles, truffle paste, or dried *porcini* mushrooms are lightweight, easy to pack, worth bringing home.

Isola Maggiore

RESTAURANT-INN
Sauro
Lago di Trasimeno
☎075.826-168
Fax 075.825-130
Closed January and February
All credit cards • low moderate
Sauro, a modestly priced, simple inn with eleven neat, basic rooms, is a perfectly peaceful getaway. It's located on the prettiest island in Lake Trasimeno, accessible by boat or ferry from Passignano sul Trasimeno. The restaurant's *cucina* is simple, home-style, composed of hand-rolled pasta sauced

with fish, grilled meats, local lake fish and eel, and rich desserts like *zuppa inglese,* all prepared by Signora Lina. Mostly local wines are offered, including some gems.

Narni

RESTAURANT-HOTEL

La Loggia–Hotel dei Priori

Vicolo del Comune 4

☎0744.726-843 and 726-844 (hotel)

Fax 0744.717-259

Closed Monday and the second half of July

All credit cards • moderate

Medieval Narni is perched on a hilltop dominating the plain of Terni. It has a fortress from the 1300s, and a Ghirlandaio fresco in the middle of the town council meeting room. La Loggia and the adjacent Hotel Priori are located on a tiny cobblestoned side street. The *cucina* is mostly Umbrian, with some pasta like *bigoi* and the presence of *risotto,* both hints at the chef's Veneto origin. Emmer, a traditional Roman grain, is prepared like pasta, with a spicy *amatriciana* sauce, or ground into flour for the doughy homemade *manfrigoli,* or even made into *polpette* (grain cakes). Trout is served with a bowl of summer truffle sauce. Game—wild boar, deer, hare—is braised and served with *polenta.* A self-service buffet of *antipasti* could make a complete meal for many. The wine list is a major surprise, offering all the great local wines plus a few well-chosen selections from other regions. In the summer, dine under large off-white umbrellas in a geranium-draped stone courtyard.

COVERED MARKET

Loggiato of Palazzo dei Priori

Open Monday–Saturday mornings

Local produce is sold under the arcade of the Palazzo dei Priori. Look for wild greens, local mushrooms, chestnuts, and farmers selling their wares.

GROCERY

Antichi Sapori

Via Garibaldi 10

☎0744.717-362

Closed Thursday afternoon

Vanessa and Melissa Cagliesi's shop sells fine local cheese, *salumi,* bread from a wood-burning oven, and pizza by the slice as well as take-out items like roast chicken or pork, seasonal vegetables, and mixed fish fry on Fridays. Some fancy gourmet products are also available.

BAKERY

Pasticceria Evangelisti

Piazza Garibaldi 25

☎0744.715-2560

Closed Tuesday

Best pastry in Narni doesn't sound like much of a compliment, but Evangelisti deserves a visit for their ricotta or Nutella-stuffed ravioli and crescent-shaped pastries. Cookies, *crostate,* and freshly made pastry make this the best place to have breakfast or a snack in Narni.

Norcia

Although Norcia is famous as the hometown of Saint Benedict, founder of Christian monasticism, and his twin sister Scolastica, it's worth a detour for its culinary interest. Carnivores, especially porcophiles, should plan to visit this town to take a look at what remains of the tradition of pork butchers, called *norcini.*

HOTEL

Grotta Azzurra

Via V. Alfieri 12

☎0743.816-504

Fax 0743.816-513

All credit cards • low moderate

LODGINGS
Monastero delle Benedettine di San Antonio
Via delle Vergini 13
☎/Fax 0743.828-208
No credit cards • low inexpensive

No-frills rooms, simple meals, the nuns' own production of honey and homemade pasta, and possibly the lowest prices in Umbria for food and lodging.

BUTCHER
Norcineria Asuini
Via Anicia 105
☎0743.816-643
Closed all day Wednesday

Even though you can't take any of the Norcineria Asuini's products back to the U.S., check out the beautifully displayed *salumi*, sausage, *prosciutto, pancetta*, and cured pork made from local pigs. Buy enough *affettati* for a sandwich.

LENTIL COOPERATIVE
Cooperativa della Lenticchia di Castelluccio
Via del Lavoro (in the industrial area)
☎/Fax 0743.828-174
Around twenty lentil growers from Castelluccio have formed a cooperative and sell their lentils in Italy through their distributor, Natura Dist. To visit a member of the cooperative, learn all about Castelluccio's special lentils, or purchase some from the source, contact Sante Coccia at the cooperative.

Orvieto

HOTEL
La Badia
Orvieto Scalo
☎0763.90359
Fax 0763.92796
Closed January and February
American Express, MasterCard, Visa • low expensive

HOTEL
Maitani
Via Lorenzo Maitari 5
☎0763.42011
Fax 0763.42013
All credit cards • moderate

HOTEL
Villa Ciconia
Via dei Tigli 69
Orvieto Scalo
☎0763.92982
Fax 0763.90677
All credit cards • moderate

ENOTECA
Enoteca Barberani
Via Michelangeli 14
☎0763.341-532
Open most of the year, 10 A.M.–12:30 P.M., 2:15–5:30 P.M.; summer hours, 9 A.M.–8 P.M.
All credit cards

In the center of town, the Barberani *enoteca* sells wonderful wine and extra virgin olive oil from their own estate. Maurizio Castelli, enologist and olive oil master, consults for Barberani, which may explain why their products are so good. Anise- and wine-flavored *biscotti* and preserves are also sold. Typical Umbrian products like truffles, Castelluccio lentils, local honey, and liqueurs are also sold. Wines can be tasted so customers know what they're buying.

BAR-CAFFÈ
Montanucci
Corso Cavour 21/23
☎0763.341-261
Closed Wednesday
Locals stop in to chat with the sassy cashier-owner at the Bar Montanucci. The coffee is the best in Orvieto, but most people are attracted by the ambience. Wooden sculptures by the Michelangeli family and a vast variety of hard candies are displayed with almost equal zeal.

WINE, SANDWICHES
Cantina Foresi
Piazza del Duomo 2
☎0763.341-611
Closed Tuesday and January

Cantina Foresi is a perfect place to stop for a snack. Sandwiches (*panini*), local wine, cheese—including Castello della Sala goat cheese—and soft drinks are sold from 8 A.M. to 8 P.M.

SALUMI
Dai Fratelli
Via del Duomo 10
☎0763.343-965
Closed Wednesday afternoon, all day Sunday (winter), Sunday afternoon (summer)

Dai Fratelli makes some of the best *salumi* in the region, especially *prosciutto,* sausages, and salami made of wild boar (*cinghiale*). The meat of the Umbrian wild boar is said to be tastier than that of other regions because of its diet of truffles, plentiful in its natural forest habitat. Emilio and Filippo Patalocco hunt for boars in the area of Civitella del Lago, to supply their shop with meat cured according to methods learned from their father. The shop is filled with festoons of sausage, piles of salami, black-bristle–covered *prosciutto,* bottles of green Umbrian extra virgin olive oil, woodsy-scented dried *porcini* mushrooms, and an embalmed boar, just in case you haven't caught on to what most of the local specialties are made of.

GELATO
Gelateria del Duomo
Piazza del Duomo 14
☎0763.341-034
Closed mid-December to mid-February

The Gelateria del Duomo makes all the classic flavors of *gelato.* Chocolate and hazelnut are intense, and fruit flavors are all natural, made with seasonal fruit.

RESTAURANT
Antica Trattoria dell'Orso
Via della Misericordia 18/20
☎0763.341-642
Closed Monday evening, Tuesday, and mid-January to mid-February
All credit cards • moderate

The restaurant's sign shows a bear holding a wine bottle and glass on a tray, and the interior is decorated with wooden and ceramic sculptures by local artists. So why are all the locals, and the chic Romans up for the weekend, eating in this unprepossessing *trattoria,* in the non-touristy part of Orvieto? Because Gabriele di Giandomenico serves fresh-tasting country *cucina* spiked with fresh herbs. The summery vegetable-filled *frittate* and the local lamb are well prepared. Richard takes care of the wines, drinkable enough, but Gabriele's *cucina* deserves more. Finish your meal with coffee at Montanucci and a *gelato* near the Duomo.

TABLE LINENS
Maria Moretti
Via Maurizio 1
☎0763.341-714
MasterCard, Visa
Always open

Signora Moretti sells hand-embroidered linens and lace—including place mats, tablecloths, and centerpieces—in her tiny shop on the corner of piazza del Duomo.

CRAFTS
Michelangeli
Via Gualltieri Michelangeli 3
☎0763.342-660
Closed Sunday afternoon
American Express, MasterCard, Visa

Simonetta, Donatella, and Raffaella Michelangeli have maintained the artisanal shop founded by their sculptor father, where wood is turned into fanciful sculptures, objects, and tables. Sit on the wooden benches outside the store, or on the horse if you're young enough, and enjoy the Michangeli pieces even if you don't buy one. The charming barnyard animals would make fun Christmas tree ornaments. The store is on the way to the Antica Trattoria dell'Orso.

Perugia

Perugia, with its Etruscan and medieval origins, imposing walls, and subterranean escalators that go under and through the walls at the Rocca Paolina, the fortress, is home to one of the major universities in Italy, with a substantial non-Italian student body. In fine weather it seems as if all of Perugia, not just the foreign students, strolls down Corso Vanucci and loiters in front of shop windows or in piazza IV Novembre with its cathedral, Palazzo dei Priori, and Maggiore fountain.

HOTEL
Brufani Palace
Piazza Italia 12
☎**075.573-2541**
Fax 075.572-0210
All credit cards • luxury

HOTEL
Castello dell'Oscano
Strada della Forcella Cenerente (nearby)
☎**075.690-125**
Fax 075.690-666
All credit cards • expensive

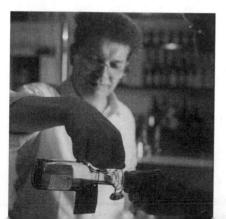

FARMHOUSE RENTAL
Borgo Il Poeta
Montecastelli di Umbertide (outside town)
☎**02.294-01801**
Fax 075.941-0589
No credit cards • low expensive

HOTEL, RESTAURANT, ENOTECA, FOOD SHOP, ART GALLERY, AND MORE
Hotel Gio' Arte e Vini
Via Ruggero d'Andreotto 19
☎**/Fax 075.573-1100**
Restaurant closed Sunday evening and Monday lunch
All credit cards • moderate

This modern hotel, right outside town, lacks Old World charm but offers plenty for modern art fans, enophiles, crafts and food lovers, swimmers, and those with a car. They've got a well-supplied wine shop and gastronomic emporium, an art gallery, and an exhibition of local crafts, a swimming pool, and private parking. Each of the hotel's 100 rooms is named for an Italian winery, and 5 wines from that particular estate are displayed in the room, available for tasting. Choose to stay in the room of your favorite winery. The restaurant serves classic Umbrian cooking, the wine list is massive, over 800 well-priced wines, inviting diners to drink big.

INTERNATIONAL CHOCOLATE SHOW
Chocolate
Via Ruggero d'Andreotto 19
☎**075.573-2625**
Fax 075.573-1100
It seems fitting that Perugia, home of Perugina chocolates, would host an international chocolate show, with one week of workshops, tastings, concerts, art exhibitions, special dinners, and the Grand Prix Chocolate awards. Participating bars and restaurants feature desserts made with chocolate. Chocolatiers and chocoholics

should contact the fair for dates, prices, and a full list of events and workshops.

CHEESE STORE
Casa del Parmigiano
Via San Ercolano 36
☎**075.573-1233**
Closed Sunday except for the third Sunday of the month
MasterCard, Visa

The owner of this terrific shop, Clelio Corradi, is from Parma and, as would be expected, he has a sublime selection of aged *parmigiano-reggiano* cheese. Casa del Parmigiano is worth a visit for its local sheep's, cow's or goat's milk cheese. Regional and national Italian cheese and *salumi* are sold, and they'll even Cryovac your purchases, making this a great stop for culinary souvenirs. But who'd ever expect over 700 products for Asian cooking? The shop is open on the third Sunday of the month for the flower market.

CHOCOLATE
Spagnoli Confiseur
Via San Donato 6, Fontana (outside town)
☎**075.517-1710**
Fax 075.517-8442

This chocolate factory has an artisanal feeling and makes first-rate products. I'm wild about the chocolate-covered cherries as well as the chocolate Easter eggs in sizes that range from miniature to massive. Spagnoli welcomes visitors, but not on weekends—fax if you'd like an appointment.

BAR-CAFFÈ, PASTRY
Pasticceria Sandri
Corso Vanucci 32
☎**075.572-4112**
Closed Monday

Sandri, with its frescoed ceilings and no-nonsense red-jacketed bartenders, is the best choice in town for traditional desserts, especially the *rocciata*, a powdered-sugar–covered swirl of a cake, and nontraditional

chocolate *torta*. Skip the leaden rice pudding—candied fruit cake. A hot table (*tavola calda*) in the back of the shop offers prepared foods, which can be eaten off of tiny cramped tables or at the crowded bar.

LENTILS
Giuliano Finetti
Via Danzelli 1
☎**075.528-7790**

Giuliano Finetti's shop sells the special organic lentils from Castelluccio (see page 361) in 500-gram packages (just over one pound).

CHOCOLATES
Perugina
Via M. Angeloni 59
☎**075.52761**
Fax 075.527-6666

For a description of Perugina candies, see page 355.

Perugina is now part of Nestlé, the behemoth multinational corporation. Chocoholics interested in visiting the Perugina chocolate works should contact Dott. Saverio Ripa di Meana.

RESTAURANT
Cesarino
Via della Gabbia 13
☎**075.573-6277**
Closed Wednesday
All credit cards • moderate

This typical Umbrian *trattoria* around the corner from charming piazza IV Novembre serves well-made traditional *cucina*. The open kitchen is the domain of two white-capped, rosy-cheeked women, who roll out the house pasta and prepare the tasty chicken livers in tomato sauce zapped with a bit of chile pepper, and who do all the stove cooking. The open hearth, with its spits and grills of roasting lamb, poultry, and sausage, is the province of a white-aproned man in careful attendance. *Torta al testo*—flat, unleavened bread baked on a slab of stone, split, and stuffed with arugula and a bit of cheese—is a splendid starter. Vanilla custard *gelato* is homemade, and the wine list is mostly local, with some pleasant surprises. Dine outside under an awning in the spring and summer, or downstairs in the winter.

Pettino

HOTEL
Vecchio Molino
Via del Tempio 34, Pissignano (nearby)
☎0743.521-122
Fax 0743.275-097
All credit cards • moderate

RESTAURANT
Pettino
Pettino Colle 31
☎0743.276-021
Closed Wednesday
No credit cards • moderate

The curving mountain road that leads to the Trattoria Pettino doesn't discourage local diners who make the trek for family-style Umbrian mountain food prepared by Mama Marsilia and her daughter-in-law, Caterina, served by her son Giovanni. Truffles are available year round and flavor many dishes. Start with *bruschetta*, truffled *frittata*, *prosciutto* and *salame*, which are local; pasta like *stringozzi* and *tagliatelle* are homemade, game is braised and used to sauce pasta. Main-course meats are grilled, and mushrooms are served in season. Look for wild asparagus in the spring, sheep's milk ricotta and *pecorino*, and simple homemade desserts like fruit *crostate*. Local wines from the limited list are the best choice.

Piediluco

On the road from Terni to Piediluco, the world's fifteenth-tallest waterfall, the *Cascata delle Marmore*, fuels an important hydroelectric plant. The dammed-up falls are unleashed for tourists on Sundays and holidays only.

RESTAURANT-HOTEL
Albergo Lido
Piazza Bonanni 2
☎/Fax 0744.368-354
No credit cards • moderate

The Albergo Lido, on the shores of Lago di Piediluco, has the kind of restaurant that Italians love to celebrate in. Weekend revelers of at least three generations, seated at tables laden with bottles of mineral water and wine, baskets of rolls and breadsticks, are served from long stainless-steel platters piled with predictable regional specialties. Your menu will probably include *carbonetti* (grilled lake fish), freshwater shrimp in herb sauce, homemade pasta, salmon trout and salmonlike *coregoni* fresh from the lake, and *tiramisù* for dessert. Owner Renzo Bartolucci's wines include some pleasant surprises, and more than a few disappointments. The experience on Saturday and Sunday, when huge banquets of up to 750 diners invade this otherwise peaceful lakeside restaurant, may not be your idea of fun.

Pigge

HOTEL
Vecchio Molino
Via del Tempio 34, Pissignano (nearby)
☎0743.521-122
Fax 0743.275-097
All credit cards • moderate

RESTAURANT
La Taverna del Pescatore
Strada Statale Flaminia, km 130
☎0742.780-920
Fax 0742.381-599
Closed Wednesday
All credit cards • moderate

It's hard to hide my enthusiasm for Claudio and Katia Menichelli's restaurant, Taverna del Pescatore, set in the countryside outside Trevi. Claudio is passionate about the history of Umbrian cooking and works the dining room. His wife, Katia, is in the kitchen, preparing fine regional cooking that draws on local ingredients like freshwater fish; legumes like lentils, *cicerchia* (chickling vetch), and chick-peas; mushrooms and truffles in season; first-rate Umbrian extra virgin olive oil. The gentrified rustic ambience is reflected in the menu, offering simple dishes like homemade *stringozzi*, pasta sauced with *guanciale, pecorino* cheese, and onion; goose cooked with Sagrantino and chestnuts; grilled pork liver, lamb, squab or hard-to-find beef from *Chianina* cattle, which Claudio insists is really Umbrian, not Tuscan as most people believe. Trout, freshwater shrimp, eel, and frog's legs are usually on the menu. Claudio's garden provides much of the produce for the restaurant. The wine list is worth a detour for enophiles—wines at bargain prices, just begging to be ordered. The restaurant doubles in size in the summer with outdoor dining on a terrace.

Ponte Valleceppi

BREAD

Forno Faffa

☎**075.692-0122**

Closed Sunday

At Faffa, a family-owned and -run bakery established in 1851 outside Perugia, baking is done in an oven fueled by wood. All whole-wheat flour is stone-ground, and the resulting bread—made by hand with such special flour, with a starter to make it rise, baked in a traditional wood-burning oven—is fragrant, redolent of wheat. Specialties include *schiacciata*, flatbread similar to pizza crust (mornings only), *ciaramicola*, a liquor-soaked mountain of a cake, topped with meringue and colored sprinkles, and around twenty different kinds of cookies, traditional to Umbria and other regions as well. Luigi Faffa, great-grandson of the founder, presides behind the counter of this historic bakery.

Preci

AGRITURISMO AND PORK-BUTCHERING COURSE

Il Collaccio

Castelvecchio di Preci

☎**0743.939-084**

Fax 0743.939-005

Closed November to March

American Express • inexpensive to moderate

Il Collaccio, the Baldoni family's Umbrian *agriturismo* farm, has accommodations for every budget—rooms with bunk beds, a four-bedroom chalet with a kitchen, or double rooms with private baths in a *locanda*, reasonably priced meals by reservation, a swimming pool, and tennis. Il Collaccio is best known for its pork-butchering course, held annually from December 26–January 2. "*Viene a fare il porco da noi*" entices the brochure, a play on words that takes advantage of the multiple meanings of the verb *fare*. Hence the invitation to get or make or act like a pig. Each participant receives half a pig, then carves up and cures the various cuts under the supervision of skilled *norcino* Salvatore Loreti. Do-it-yourself butchers get to keep their finished products. Those not interested in butchering will enjoy the rest of the program, which includes baking bread in a wood-burning oven, stalking wild greens and herbs in the countryside, and visits to the nearby medieval village of Preci. Contact Enzo Baldoni in Milano, tel. 02.480-00072, fax 02.481-94601, for more information.

San Feliciano sul Trasimeno

OLIVE OIL

Alfredo Mancianti

Frantoio San Feliciano sul Trasimeno

☎**0576.849-617**

Faliero Mancianti bought the Frantoio San Feliciano in 1952 and produces fine extra virgin olive oil here. Son Alfredo has always felt strongly about the Umbrian land, the olive trees, and the stone mill where their olives are crushed, producing some of Umbria's finest olive oil. The Manciantis make two special oils from designated geographic areas, *San Feliciano* and *Monte del Lago*. They also make *Affiorato*, of the lightest oil that floats to the surface of the newly pressed oil. It's skimmed off the top, and is intensely olivy and costly. The Mancianti olive paste is also fine.

Mancianti can also be reached at via Poggibonsi 14, Milano, tel. 02.407-8461.

Scheggino

TRUFFLES

Urbani Tartufi (factory)
Sant' Anatolia di Narco
☎0743.613-171
Fax 0743.613-036
Closed Sunday

The Urbani Tartufi factory in Scheggino, truffle capital of Umbria, is the world's largest producer of truffle paste, *pasta di tartufo*. Black and white winter truffles and black summer truffles are collected around the world, cleaned, graded, and sold fresh, preserved whole in cans or jars, or puréed with oil or thrush pâté and packed in tiny tubes. For a visit to the factory, which is open year-round but works hardest in the early winter months, call, fax, or write for an appointment.

Spello

HOTEL

Palazzo Bocci
Viale Cavour 17
☎0742.301-012
Fax 0742.301-0464
All credit cards • moderate

RESTAURANT-INN

Il Cacciatore
Via Giulia 42
☎0742.651-141
Fax 0742.301-603
Closed Monday
All credit cards • inexpensive rooms, moderate dining

Assisi should be seen—but not experienced at great length unless hordes of pilgrims, their buses, and souvenir shops are your idea of fun. The hotels and restaurants, like those of many villages that live on tourists who visit once, never to return, aren't exactly motivated to serve the most inspirational food. When visiting Assisi I like to stay, and eat, at the Cacciatore, an archetypal Umbrian *trattoria* in nearby Spello. Everything is plain, no frills, but the perfumes coming out of Signora Bruna's kitchen will make you overlook the lack of decor, and if you're lucky enough to show up on a calm evening in the spring or summer, you can sit on the terrace, with its quintessentially Umbrian view. All pasta is hand-rolled, truffles are fresh, meats and poultry are local—simply roasted, stewed, or grilled—and there's game in the winter and tasty local *pecorino* cheese from Monte Subasio. Golden, glossy fruit tarts (*crostate*) made with homemade preserves are hard to resist. Drink Lungarotti's Rubesco or Torre di Giano, or the simple house red, which is better than the white. Some of the hotel's eighteen rooms have the same breathtaking view as the terrace.

Spoleto

Spoleto is a typical Umbrian town, but it's invaded by tourists of all nations who come for its Festival of the Two Worlds, featuring theater, concerts, and ballet in June and July. Some of Spoleto's restaurants are decorated with autographed photographs of the stars who have dined there, a warning that almost everyone else will be treated like second-rate citizens, with fixed tourist meals, sloppy service, and more expensive prices.

H O T E L
Eremo delle Grazie
Monteluco
☎**0743.49624**
Fax 0743.49650
All credit cards • luxury

H O T E L
San Luca
Via Interna delle Mura 21
☎**0743.223-399**
Fax 0743.49866
All credit cards • moderate

R E S T A U R A N T
Pecchiarda
Vicolo San Giovanni 1
☎**0743.221-009**
Closed Thursday, always open in summer
No credit cards • low moderate

Renato Rivoli, assisted by his brother-in-law Franco, runs the Trattoria Pecchiarda, the oldest in Spoleto, with his sister Silvana, wife, Adua, and daughter-in-law in the kitchen. Renato's son Gianni works the family farm in Uncinano, supplying the *trattoria* with extra virgin olive oil, superfresh produce, and Sangiovese wine, an unbeatable combination. Look for home-style offerings like stuffed *gnocchi*, *stringozzi*, simple pasta and soups, grilled meats, stewed game, lentils cooked with pork rind, and stuffed chicken, the house specialty. Dine under the pergola in the summer.

R E S T A U R A N T
Il Pentagramma
Via T. Martani 4
☎**0743.223-141**
Closed Monday
Diners Club, MasterCard, Visa • high moderate

Il Pentagramma, with its quintessential red-and-white–checked *trattoria* tablecloths, serves hearty, well-priced food. Mirella and Manola prepare a menu of all-Umbrian classics, like *bruschetta; stringozzi,* homemade pasta; hearty soups of emmer, lentils, chickling vetch (*cicerchia*), or chick-peas; or multigrain and legume *imbrecciata.* The menu is set up like a concert, with *ouverture* appetizers, *sinfonie* pasta, *concerto grosso* main courses, *balletti* grilled dishes, and a few *concerti di sapori umbri* tasting menus. In spite of this silliness I like this restaurant. Main-course dishes are minimalist, like lamb chops *scottadito* and local trout. Roast lamb will probably be well done, no longer pink. Look for wild asparagus and summer truffles in season and first-rate local cheese. Most diners will be happy to drink from the fine selection of Umbrian wines, although the rest of the list is well chosen, reasonably priced.

Stroncone

H O T E L
See Terni

R E S T A U R A N T
Taverna de Portanova
Via di Porta Nuova 1
☎**0744.60496**
Closed Wednesday, open for dinner and Sunday lunch
MasterCard, Visa • moderate

Stroncone may seem like just another tiny stone medieval hill town in Umbria, but it's worth a detour for the ambience and style of Taverna de Portanova, opened "as a joke, on the weekends," Enzo Vierucci told me, in what was once the cellars and pantry of a convent. His wife, Milly, her sister Elisa, and Elisa's husband, Davide, joined forces with Enzo, dishing out home-style traditional cooking based on local ingredients like chestnuts, mushrooms, legumes, wild greens, and extra virgin olive oil. The setting is rustic, with terra-cotta floors, whitewashed walls, fourteenth-century wooden ceilings, brick arches, and a blazing hearth, where Davide grills meat and heats terracotta disks to make flatbreads (*pizza sotto lu focu*) which are stuffed with vegetables, sausage, *prosciutto,* or cheese. Look for appetizers like local *prosciutto,* grilled vegetables, legumes dressed with oil. Davide learned about the Franciscan tradition of soup served in a bowl made of bread from Sister Anita, a nun from the convent, and has named the daily soup after her—a nearby bakery makes the bread in which the soup is served. Handmade *ciriole,* flour-and-water pasta, are served with mushrooms; pasta and emmer (*farro*) are dressed with truffles. Lamb, veal, and sausage are grilled in the fireplace, and there's a large selection of seasonal vegetables. Save room for the lightly grilled *scamorza* or *pecorino* cheese, or finish with homemade *tiramisù,* *zuppa inglese* (trifle), or cookies and wine. Enzo and Davide are interested in wine, and their regional selection will satisfy most diners.

Terni

H O T E L

See Narni

H O T E L
Valentino
Via Plinio il Giovane 5
☎**0744.402-550**
Fax 0744.403-335
All credit cards • high moderate

B A K E R Y
Panificio La Spiga
Via del Serpente 14
☎**0744.426-042**
Open mornings only
La Spiga, on a winding back street, is a shop with a display case, bins of bread, large baskets filled with cookies. Enrico Altei has been baking traditional Umbrian breads

and sweets for eighteen years. He's known for his *pizza rustica,* rich with eggs and chunks of *pecorino* cheese, and *ciambelline,* ring-shaped cookies, flavored with wine, milk, or anise. If you'd like to check out the baking in the back room, ask Enrico.

E X T R A   V I R G I N   O L I V E O I L   A N D   ''M I D N I G H T S A U C E ''
Azienda Agricola dei Conti Possenti Castelli
Via Cavour 16
☎**/Fax 0744.428-170**
Local archives document the replanting of the Possenti olive groves in 1640 after a severe frost. They're still producing extra virgin olive oil, and have added a line of aromatic oils flavored with herbs, garlic, *porcini* mushrooms, or truffles. Most aromatic oils are made with inferior olive oil and artificial flavorings, but Countess Maria Possenti Castelli, a class act, insists on using first-rate extra virgin and fresh herbs. She also sells natural unrefined honey; truffle, *porcini* mushroom, and olive pâté; asparagus cream; and preserves. My favorite product is called *salsa di mezzanotte* ("midnight sauce"), a puree of black olives, sun-dried tomatoes, capers, hot *peperoncino,* and extra virgin, of course. It makes a wonderful spread for *bruschetta* or a sauce for pasta. Don't wait until midnight to try it. The countess is elegantly restoring five rooms with private baths in the family palace in Terni, which should be ready for guests by the time this book is published. Call or fax for more information.

W I N E ,   O L I V E   O I L
Vino Vino
Corso Vecchio 201
☎**0744.406-683**
Fax 0744.813-885
Closed Monday morning
No credit cards

Vino Vino is one of the oldest stores in Terni, specializing in spices, nuts, paper cups, ruffled candy papers, and, as its name indicates, wine. Renzo and Gigliola Franceschini have assembled an impressive selection of Italian, and especially Umbrian, wines. Renzo also produces his own stone-ground extra virgin olive oil, *Colle dell'Oro,* from the northern hills outside Terni. Lucia makes original *bonboniere*—individual packets of tulle-wrapped candy-coated almonds given away at weddings, communions, and anniversaries. If you ask, they'll take you around the corner to a bakery that makes its breads and cookies in a wood-burning oven.

Todi

HOTEL
Fonte Cesia
Via Lorenzo Leony 3
☎**075.894-3737**
Fax 075.894-4677
All credit cards • high moderate

HOTEL
Residenza di Campagna
Via Asprili 7, Poggio d'Asproli (nearby)
☎**/Fax 075.885-3385**
Visa • moderate

RESTAURANT
Ristorante Umbria
Via San Bonaventura 13
☎**075.894-2737**
Closed Tuesday
All credit cards • high moderate

The Ristorante Umbria, run by the Todini family for more than forty years, with Maurizio in the dining room, his brother Fausto in the kitchen, has something for everyone. The view from the terrace is quintessential Umbria, the *cucina* offers regional and Roman dishes (Todi is only 130 kilometers from Rome, and Romans might not be able to live without *pasta alla carbonara* or *all'*

amatriciana), Italian classics like *vitello tonnato,* lamb in many forms, including *coratella,* innards, and the usual grilled meats. The list of *contorni,* side dishes, will satisfy vegetarians who generally won't have an easy time in this region. The wine list is ample; enophiles will want to visit the Enoteca dell'Accademia dei Convivianti next door.

Torgiano

RESTAURANT-INN
Le Tre Vaselle
Via Garibaldi 48
☎**075.988-0447**
Fax 075.988-0214
All credit cards • expensive

Like Dallas, with its Ewings and its oil, Torgiano is home to the Lungarotti family, producers of fine wine, creators of Italy's best wine museum, and owners of Le Tre Vaselle, a beautifully restored forty-seven-room country inn, part of the Relais & Chateaux chain of luxury hotels. The restaurant serves some of the finest *cucina* in Umbria. Enjoy a glass of the Lungarotti sparkling *spumante,* accompanied by bread rounds (*crostini*) spread with olive paste, in front of the fireplace in one of the comfortable sitting rooms. The *cucina* reflects the gracefully underrestored rustic simplicity of the hotel. Linen, silver, and crystal stemware seem natural rather than opulent, just as ingredients like mushrooms and truffles are presented as everyday fare rather than luxury items. Olive oil and balsamic sauce are the house dressings. Pasta is homemade, grill work is beautifully executed, vegetables are perfectly cooked. Hard-to-find cheeses are tasty and local. Desserts are traditional. Don't skip the *cialde,* paper-thin wafers cooked on the medieval Umbrian version of the waffle iron, served with custard *gelato.* The Lungarotti-only wine list offers some amazing gems. What a joy to stay in one of the simply appointed rooms of this hotel.

**BALSAMIC SAUCE,
OLIVE OIL**

Lungarotti Osteria
Corso Vittorio Emanuele 33
☎075.80069

Lungarotti's *salsa balsamica di mosto* is not a traditional Umbrian product. It's a dark brown sauce made from must, the unfermented juice of freshly pressed grapes, and undergoes the same production process as balsamic vinegar. But since it's made outside the limited geographic area of production in Emilia, it can't be called *aceto balsamico*. The tasty, sherrylike Lungarotti sauce is made with a 100-year-old balsamic culture, aged in casks of seven different woods, packaged in a lovely glass cruet, and expensive.

The same interest in quality guarantees the fine Lungarotti extra virgin olive oil, produced with local olives.

Next door to the *osteria* is the Lungarotti Wine Museum. Both are open seven days a week, but closed at lunch.

MUSEUM

Museo del Vino
Corso Vittorio Emanuele 33
☎075.988-0200

The Museo del Vino offers a global vision of wine. It traces the history of wine, from its Middle Eastern origins, through its evolution as a part of the meal, as a medicine, and in myth. An impressive collection of wine containers—Cycladic pitchers, Hittite jars, Attic wine containers, Etruscan bronzes, Roman glassware, and local wine-making utensils, beautifully displayed, make this the most attractive wine museum in Italy.

CRAFTS

La Spola
Via Garibaldi 66
No phone
American Express, Diners Club, MasterCard

La Spola's name, "The Shuttle," is a direct reference to its focus. The shop sells a variety of quality Umbrian handcrafts, but specializes in hand-loomed traditional and contemporary fabrics. Embroidery, metalwork in copper and iron, baskets, terracotta majolica from Deruta and Gubbio, and other Umbrian pottery are also sold here. Ask the concierge at Le Tre Vaselle to open the store for you if it is closed.

PORCHETTA, ROAST PORK

Luigi Lunghi
Via Bettona 5, Costano (nearby)
☎075.800-2121
Open 9 A.M.–1 P.M., 4–8 P.M., closed Sunday, Monday morning, Thursday afternoon

The town of Costano is known for its *porchetta*, roast pork, said to be the best in Umbria. Luigi Lunghi apprenticed with *porchettari*, pork roasters, and learned their ancient recipes. He's been making *porchetta* for more than thirty years, carefully selecting local pigs that weigh less than a quintal (220 pounds). Pork is boned, dressed with garlic, wild fennel, salt, pepper, and a secret mixture of herbs, then baked over a wood-burning fire. Porcophiles should plan a visit.

FLATBREAD FAIR

Pro Loco
Pila (nearby)
☎75.774-241

The flatbread tradition is celebrated for ten days at the end of June in Pila, at the Sagra della Torta al Testo. Large disks of unleavened wheat flour or cornmeal are baked on a hearth heated with local oak, served plain or topped with herbs, *prosciutto*, or spicy, "angry style." Pasta and stewed boar are also sold from stands in the garden of Villa Umbra. Although the fair is dedicated to flatbread, the evening activities include music, dancing, theater, and soccer matches. Call Enrico Bonelli, president of the Pro Loco, for the exact dates.

Map labels:
EMILIA-ROMAGNA
SAN MARINO
Pesaro
Fano
Adriatic Sea
Calcinelli
Metáuro
A14
Cesano di Senigallia
TOSCANA
Senigallia
Falconara Marittima
Acqualanga • Cartoceto
Ancona
Pergola   Jesi   Osimo   San Lorenzo in Campo
Serra San Quirico
A14
Fabriano
Macerata •
Tolentino •   Porto San Giorgio
Campofilone •
Grottamare
UMBRIA
A14
Ascoli Piceno •
ABRUZZO

Le Marche is divided from neighboring Romagna, Umbria, Toscana, Lazio, and Abruzzi by mountains and hills, crossed by parallel rivers that flow east to the Adriatic and the modern umbrella-paved seaside resorts. It's a region with a history of changing alliances, of separate states.

Le Marche

The political cast of powers includes Gauls to the north and the Piceni to the south of the Esino River, Romans, Longobards, noble families, and the Vatican. It gets its name from the *Marca* of Ancona, Camerino, and Fermo, three border provinces, each governed by a marquis or margrave.

The *cucina* of Le Marche draws its inspiration and its ingredients from two main sources. Inland mountain dishes are based on freshwater fish, mushrooms, truffles, *marchigiana* beef, lamb, and *pecorino* cheese. Coastal shellfish and fish—prawns looking like mini-lobsters and delicate, almost opalescent, six-inch sole—are the bounty of the Adriatic, and are simply grilled with fresh bread crumbs. The olives of Ancona are pitted, stuffed with a rich filling, breaded, and deep-fried—surely a labor of love. Le Marche produces extra virgin olive oil, and Cartoceto's fruity olives are gently cold-pressed, producing a special extra virgin olive oil. A return to the use of grain, like barley and tasty emmer, found where the Roman legions marched, is under way, assisted by Massimo Schiavi's excellent products. Traditional desserts of cookies, served with a glass of dessert wine, aren't always easy to find in restaurants.

Most tourists come to Le Marche for the Adriatic seaside, lined for miles with row after row of chairs, beach umbrellas, and changing cabins. The beach isn't hard to find, because it's parallel to the road and the railroad tracks, backed by a solid mass of hotels. But Le Marche offers far more than a strip of sand to get tan on. Pesaro's wonderful Art Nouveau Villa Ruggieri and Ceramics Museum, Ancona's Roman triumphal arch, medieval Ascoli Piceno, Fabriano, Fermo, Jesi, and Gradara, fifth-century Osimo, Renaissance jewel Urbino, the religious shrine of Loreto, and Numana with its Greco-Roman past all present an alternative to the beach.

The Menu

Antipasto

Olive ripiene (or all'ascolana): pitted giant green olives, stuffed with meat and Parmesan cheese, and deep-fried

Pizza al formaggio: yeast bread cooked with Parmesan and other cheeses

Pizza alla campagnola: flatbread enriched with lard and pork cracklings

Primo

Passatelli: strand-shaped cheese and egg dumplings

Vincisgrassi: rich *lasagna* with meat sauce, béchamel sauce, chicken livers, and black truffles

Secondo

Brodetto: fish stew, made with a wide variety of Adriatic fish and shellfish

Coniglio in porchetta: roast rabbit with wild fennel, garlic, and bacon

Moscioli or muscioli: mussels, usually steamed, and baked or grilled with bread crumbs and herbs

Porchetta: suckling pig roasted with wild fennel, garlic, rosemary, and white wine

Potacchio: a stew of tomato, chile pepper, white wine, and herbs applied to either fish, lamb, poultry, or rabbit

Sarde alla marchigiana: fresh sardines, marinated in olive oil and herbs, then grilled, with bread crumbs

Stocco or stoccafisso all'anconetana: salt cod, layered with olive oil and tomatoes, stewed with white wine

Formaggio

Pecorino: fresh or aged, made from sheep's milk

The Wine List

The simple wines of Le Marche don't seem to have traveled well, although they are lovely with the regional *cucina* of seafood and sauced poultry. Few wineries aim at quality, but those that do are worth seeking out. Some wines, like those of Bucci, are easier to find outside their native region.

Rosso Cònero is a robust dry DOC red, made from Montepulciano and Sangiovese grapes grown south of Ancona, on the hills near Monte Cònero. It goes well with meat, fowl, and regional *cucina,* and is produced by Garofoli, MecVini, Moroder, Le Terazze, Serenelli, and Umani Ronchi.

Rosso Piceno is a grapey dry DOC red, made from Montepulciano and Sangiovese grapes in the Ancona, Ascoli, and Macerata areas. It is served with sauced meat and fowl, and is produced by Cocci Grifoni and Villamagna.

Verdicchio dei Castelli di Jesi is a fresh, dry white DOC wine, made from Verdicchio blended with Trebbiano and Malvasia grapes in the Castelli di Jesi area, west of Ancona. It is at its best with fish and seafood, in any course, and can be one of the region's best wines. Top producers are Fattoria Coroncino Brunori, Garofoli, Umani Ronchi, and Bucci, whose Villa Bucci Riserva is splendid, unusually elegant, and impossible to find regionally.

Vernaccia di Matelica is a delicate dry white DOC wine, made in the Matelica area, west of Ancona. It is served with fish and seafood, and is at its best produced by Fratelli Bisci Fattoria dei Cavalieri, Enzo Mecella, and La Monacesca.

Vernaccia di Pergola is a rich dry red made of local Balsamina grapes in the inland hills of Pergola. It is served with roast and sauced fowl, and ably produced by Ligi-Montevecchio.

Vernaccia di Serrapetrona is a sparkling DOC red—dry (*secco*), semisweet (*amabile*), or sweet (*dolce*)—made from the Vernaccia di Serrapetrona grape. It can be served with practically any course of a meal, depending on its sweetness. Top producers are Attilio Fabrini and Raffaele Quacquarini.

Nontraditional Wines. Vino da Tavola is made by most of Le Marche's leading wineries. Enzo Mecella makes white, oaky Antico di Casa Fosca. Bucci makes rich, elegant red Pongelli. Massimo Schiavi's wines frequently change names, but look for Gallia Togata, Jubilè, and San Secondo, all interesting whites by Fattoria di Montesecco.

Regional Specialties

Extra Virgin Olive Oil. A small amount of dense, green extra virgin olive oil is produced in Le Marche, primarily from *Raggiolo, Frantoio,* and *Leccino* olives.

Villa Bucci
Via Cona 30
Ostra Vetere
☎**071.964-179 (or in Milano**
☎**/Fax 02.655-4470)**

Villamagna
Contrada Montanello 5
Macerata
☎**/Fax 0733.492-236**
Olive trees often grow well in the same climate as grapes, and some of Le Marche's top olive oil producers—such as Villa Bucci and Villamagna—are also winemakers. The quality of their wines serves as a guarantee for their olive oil.

Ciauscolo. *Ciauscolo* is a cured pork *salame*, soft, spreadable, almost impossible to slice, easily found in Le Marche and Umbria. It's made from pork, ground fine, flavored with salt, pepper, garlic, juniper berries, and wine or cooked wine must, stuffed into a casing, and lightly smoked. *Ciauscolo* is served as an appetizer in restaurants and sold in most groceries and butcher shops.

Prosciutto. Although it's not as famous as that of Parma or San Daniele, fine *prosciutto* is made in the area of Carpegna. The curing technique is basically the same, although locals feel that their air produces a superior product. For information contact Carpegna Prosciutti, via Petricci, Carpegna, tel. 0722.77521.

Salame di Fabriano. Fabriano *salame* is easy to find throughout central Italy. It's made with finely ground lean pork and cubes of lard, seasoned with salt and pepper, packed into a casing, and aged for a few months. Local producers point with pride to a letter dated April 22, 1881, from Giuseppe Garibaldi to his friend Benigno Bigonzetti, thanking him for the gift of precious and welcome Fabriano *salame*. See page 381 for the best version of this tasty product.

Ascolano Olives. The *Ascolana tenera* olive is classified as an eating olive, as it's not really suitable for making oil. But the olive is essential in making a fantastic, labor-intensive snack that's popular in the area of Ascoli-Piceno and beyond, and is even sold frozen in supermarkets throughout Italy. Green olives are pitted, stuffed with a meat filling similar to that of *tortellini,* floured, dipped in beaten egg, coated with bread crumbs, and deep-fried, a lot of work for a tasty little bite.

Pasta. Two important pasta traditions rule in Le Marche. The village of Campofilone is famous for its *maccheroncini,* superskinny *tagliatelle* made with hard wheat and eggs. They're found in many restaurants and groceries in the region. Fresh-pasta freaks might want to visit Campofilone for the annual pasta festival in August. See page 379 for more information. My favorite dried pasta is made in Osimo by Latini from hard wheat and water pasta. See page 385 for more information.

Formaggio di Fossa. "Cheese from a ditch" is made in Le Marche, beginning like a conventional *pecorino,* aged with a highly unusual process. Not that easy to find; the cheese is still aged in humid cylindrical ditches lined with barley straw. Cloth sacks of cheese are stacked in the ditches, layered with straw, covered with a wooden lid topped with dirt, to be opened 100 days later. Some groceries and restaurants in the region carry *formaggio di fossa.* See page 378 for a fantastic source.

Salame di Fichi, Fig "Salame." The flavors of this "*salame*" are strictly Mediterranean—figs, anise liqueur, walnuts, and cooked grape must, pressed into a *salame* shape and wrapped with fig leaves, tied with string, then aged in a wooden cask for a month. It's sliced thin, just like *salame,* and eaten as a snack or paired with cheese.

Look for *salame di fichi* in fancy food shops and upscale restaurants that are reviving a disappearing tradition. See page 378 for a source.

Visciolato, Wild Cherry Wine. *Visciolato* is a dark red dessert wine made with an infusion of wild cherries, *Prunus cerasus.* It almost never appears on wine lists because it's classified as a flavored wine and therefore requires a special authorization that most producers don't bother with since they only make small quantities. Cherries are harvested in July, dried in the sun, ground up, mixed with red wine, sugar, cinnamon, cloves, and lemon peel. The mixture is then refermented, and alcohol is added to stabilize the product. Ask for *visciolato* in restaurants and *trattorie* in the region, but don't expect to find it in a shop or on a wine list.

Mistrà. Anise-flavored liqueurs, known for their digestive benefits, are popular in central and southern Italy. Their usual role is as an *ammazzacaffè* ("coffee killer"), a shot of liqueur consumed after a coffee or mixed with it at the end of the meal. In Le Marche, wild anise, *Pimpinella anisum,* grows in the area of the Sibilline mountains and is used to produce *mistrà.* The name probably comes from Misithra, a Byzantine city from which the Venetians imported anise liqueur. Homemade versions may include wild fennel as well as anise, and are almost impossible to find. However, Varnelli *mistrà* can be found everywhere in Le Marche. The company was founded by herbalist Girolomo Varnelli, who wanted to create a liqueur that was more refined than the homemade version, and Varnelli still uses his formula for *mistrà.* Varnelli also produces *Amaro Sibella,* made from bitter roots and herbs from the Sibilline mountains, sweetened with honey and *persico,* an alcoholic infusion of peaches. For more information on Varnelli's liqueurs, contact

Simonetta Varnelli, piazza V. Veneto 13, Pievebovigliana, tel. 0737.44101, fax 0737.44333.

Truffles. Three kinds of truffles are found in Le Marche. Summer (*Tuber aestivum*) and winter (*Tuber melanosporum*) are black truffles. The glorious *Tuber magnatum* are early winter white truffles. They are all found in oak forests of the Apennine mountains in the Acqualagna area. The black truffles are inexpensive, almost tasteless, and not in the same league as the white truffles, found from October through December. Truffles are hunted with dogs in Italy, not with pigs.

Crafts. Pesaro has been an important center for the production of majolica since the sixteenth century. Majolica tiles, pharmaceutical jars, decorative pieces, and dinnerware with intricately hand-painted designs are a specialty of this city. The Ceramics Museum (see page 386) houses some lovely pieces, mostly from Umbria, Le Marche, and Romagna, and G. Molaroni produces fine reproductions.

Cities & Towns

Acqualagna

TRUFFLES

Truffa e C.
Via Pole 26/A
☎072.799-065
Fax 0771.797-259
Closed Saturday and Sunday

Truffa e C. sells fresh and preserved *tartufi neri* and *bianchi*—black and white truffles. They also sell truffle paste, bottled sauces, cheese, boar sausage, chick-peas, and oil, all under the intoxicating effect of the truffle.

Ancona

HOTEL

Il Fortino Napoleonico
Via Poggio, Portonovo
☎071.801-124
Fax 071.801-314
All credit cards • low expensive

HOTEL

Grand Hotel Roma e Pace
Via G. Leopardi 1

☎071.202-007
Fax 071.207-4736
All credit cards • moderate

AGRITOURISM FARM

La Giuggiola
Frazione Angeli di Varano 204/A
☎071.804-336
No credit cards • inexpensive

RESTAURANT

Osteria Teatro Strabacco
Via Oberdan 2
☎071.54213
Fax 071.720-7629
Closed Monday
All credit cards • high moderate

It's not the most famous eatery in Ancona, but it's my favorite—tiny, rustic, propelled by the enthusiasm of owner-sommelier-chef Danilo Tornifoglia and his wife, Grazia. Traditional cooking rules, although there are a few innovative dishes for locals tired of home cooking. Pasta and bread made from emmer are homemade. Begin with local *prosciutto* or stuffed mussels, or head straight for *primi* like pasta sauced with nettles, broccoli rabe, or radicchio in season. Main-course offerings include stuffed mussels, grilled sardines, fish *brodetto,* Ancona-style *stoccafisso* (air-dried, not salt-cured cod), nicely grilled or fried fish. Carnivores can opt for grilled lamb or steak; vegetarians won't have anything to complain about. Finish with cookies and dessert wine. The selection of extra virgin olive oils is impressive. The wine list is ample, but the house wine is worth tasting. Jazz lovers should plan to visit from October through March, when live concerts are held in the restaurant. Fax Danilo for the schedule.

CHEESE STORE

Il Re Formaggio
Via Kennedy 10
☎071.201-771
Closed Thursday afternoon

Antonio Budano's shop is called "The King of Cheese," and logically enough *parmigiano-reggiano,* considered the "king of Italian cheeses" is given the attention it deserves, with aged *parmigiano* from 1990, 1991, and 1992 on sale. Antonio's selection of other cheeses is impressive, with *formaggio di fossa,* Umbrian and Tuscan *pecorino,* fresh buffalo mozzarella, *burrata* from Puglia, and more. *Salumi,* pasta, *ventresca,* belly-meat tuna, and fine extra virgin olive oil complete the picture.

Ascoli Piceno

HOTEL

Gioli
Viale A. De Gasperi 14
☎/Fax 0736.255-550
All credit cards • moderate

RESTAURANT

Osteria Enoteca Kursaal
Via Mercantini 66
☎/Fax 0763.253-140

Closed Sunday
All credit cards • inexpensive to moderate

Lucio and Simona Sestili's *osteria* hasn't been open long, but it's quickly become a local favorite. There are two dining rooms—one with a limited, less expensive menu, the other with a more ample menu and a complete wine list. Chef Giacinto Biagini prepares regional cooking for both. Look for fried stuffed olives, or pasta with Ascolano olives, tuna, and anchovies. Main-course possibilities include cuttlefish with potatoes, turkey cooked like suckling pig, and fine *fritto misto* with lamb and artichokes. Finish with *pecorino* cheese or desserts like *crostate* (tarts), chocolate or coffee mousse, or *zuppa inglese.* The wine list is vast, with something for everyone including some blockbuster wines and unexpected distillates that will make enophiles go wild.

GREAT GROCERY, TAKE-OUT, AND THE BEST FRIED ASCOLANO OLIVES

Migliori
Piazza Arringo 2
☎0736.250-042
Fax 0736.256-611
Closed Sunday afternoon and Monday •
No credit cards

The dynamo behind this fantastic food shop, a temple of Ascoli Piceno's gastronomic products, is Nazareno Migliori, known as "Zè" by everyone. He started a crusade to preserve the true Ascolano olive against the invasion of less expensive imports, and he sells the *Ascolana tenera* olives in brine or stuffed and deep-fried at the take-out counter, definitely worth a detour for fans of this labor-intensive snack. Look for all the products mentioned in this chapter, like *salame di fichi, mistrà,* and a fine selection of outer-regional foodstuffs.

Calcinelli

HOTEL

See Fano or Pesaro

RESTAURANT
La Posta Vecchia
Via Flamina Vecchia
☎**0721.897-8000**
Closed Monday and November
American Express, MasterCard, Visa •
low moderate
Pinetto ("little Pino") Pompili, his wife,
Ivana, and their sons are responsible for the
success of this totally anonymous *trattoria*
with its decor of white stucco walls; circular
neon-tube lighting in mustard-colored
fringed, domed shades, wine-filled refrigerator, and brick pizza oven. The *cucina* is
simple, home-style, based on Pinetto's
scrupulous search for quality ingredients,
especially fresh mushrooms, and on Ivana's
traditional mentality. *Salumi* are local,
pasta is homemade, poultry and meat are
nicely cooked, but the specialty here is
mushrooms—cooked with pasta, in salads
with arugula and cheese, grilled, studded
with chunks of garlic, or deep-fried. Pizza
and *piadine*, flatbreads, are baked in the
wood-burning oven in the evening. From
September to January they serve local white
truffles. Munch on a portion of *olive all'ascolana* (deep-fried stuffed olives) while
waiting for your food to arrive, and drink a
bottle of Jubilè, the best of the local wines.
Ivana's anise cookies are lovely.

Campofilone

HOTEL
San Marino
Via San Marino 2, Pedaso (nearby)
☎**0734.931-241**
No credit cards • inexpensive

HOTEL
See Porto San Giorgio (nearby)

PASTA FACTORY
Spinosi
Via XXV Aprile 23
☎**0734.932-196**
Fax 0734.931-663
Closed Saturday afternoon
Vincenzo Spinosi's factory makes a first-
rate commercial pasta product based on
the local tradition of the hand-rolled egg
pasta known as *maccheroncini,* narrow
strips. Machines do all the work here, but
have been specially designed to reproduce
the effects of hand-rolling. His pasta is
found in fine shops throughout the area.
Fax if you're interested in a visit.

ARTISAN PASTAMAKER
Sabina Salvatori
Contrada Santa Maria 7
☎**0734.932-850**
Closed at lunch
Sabina Salvatori hand-rolls *maccheroncini*
as Campofilone's tradition demands, but
under her apron she is dressed with style,
decked out with gold jewelry but no rings,
which would interfere with her rolling. She
and her family live above the laboratory
and sell their pasta seven days a week. Call
ahead if you're planning a visit on Sunday.

PASTA FESTIVAL
Campofilone salutes its pastamakers at a
three-day festival, usually held the first
weekend in August. Over 1,000 pounds of
maccheroncini are sauced with over 3,000
pounds of meat sauce—"Our pasta
absorbs a lot of sauce," I was told. Fresh-
pasta freaks should plan to attend.

Cartoceto

HOTEL

See Pesaro or Fano

RESTAURANT

Symposium
Via Cartoceto 38
☎0721.898-320
Fax 0721.898-493
Closed Sunday evening and Monday
All credit cards • high moderate to expensive

Pinetto Pompili practically dragged me to Symposium to taste the *cucina* of his younger brother, Lucio. In the hills outside Cartoceto, in a former farmhouse surrounded by olive trees, Lucio prepares a professional, personal *cucina* based on the four seasons and his region's finest ingredients. He's close to both mountains and coast, and grows one of the most complete restaurant herb gardens in Italy. The decor is original, and tables are set with antique tablecloths and extra-large, hand-fagoted, handkerchief-quality linen napkins. Red-haired, freckled Lucio, continually dashing out the backdoor to pick some herbs, carefully contrasts and balances flavors with skill, and each dish makes sense. *Salumi* are homemade, pasta is hand-rolled, and barley is cooked like *risotto—al dente*, a revelation of a dish. Fresh fish, country meat, and just-picked produce are all beautifully prepared. Local *pecorino* is splendid, and desserts—traditional regional cookies, fruit ices, and especially custard *gelato* served with preserved wild cherries (*visciole*)—are tasty. After a *caffè* go native, rinsing out your coffee cup with anise liqueur. Local wines of quality help make the meal a memorable experience. Outdoor dining is under large canvas and wood umbrellas in the summer.

OLIVE OIL

Frantoio della Rocca di Vittorio Beltrami
Via Umberto I 21–23
☎0721.898-145
Closed Sunday afternoon

Vittorio Beltrami is a wine salesman with a passion for the olive tree, and for the process for turning its fruit into oil. Olives are washed, pitted, crushed with a pink Verona granite wheel, and pressed between mats to extract the oil in Vittorio's beautifully, respectfully restored olive oil mill, Frantoio della Rocca. He also makes *mono olivo* oil, using olives of one type only, and special olive oil from a particularly good area. Oil is stored in a grotto, in large traditional terra-cotta containers (*orci*). His oil can be tasted in the area's best restaurants, but the only place to buy it is straight from Vittorio. A visit to the mill is a treat.

Cesano di Senigallia

HOTEL

See Jesi

RESTAURANT

Da Pongetti
Statale Adriatica 96
☎071.660-064
Closed Sunday evening and Monday
Diners Club, MasterCard, Visa • high moderate

Four generations of the Pongetti family have worked in their restaurant, founded in 1888. Luigi Pongetti is at the helm of this Adriatic seafood restaurant, with his wife, Alda, and stepmother in the kitchen. What started out as an *osteria* for teamsters has evolved, but not too much. Every dish on the menu is a classic, and succeeds because of the absolute freshness of the Adriatic-only fish and shellfish: fish salad *antipasti*, homemade *tagliatelle* or *risotto* sauced with fish or clams, traditional *brodetto* (fish stew). Their fish tastes like the essence of the sea, sweet and squeaky. Practically everything is grilled, crunchy deep-fried, or simply poached, the latter served with a homemade mayonnaise yellow with egg yolks. The house wines are passable, but could stand some improvement.

Fabriano

HOTEL
Janus
Piazzale Matteotti
☎0732.4191
Fax 0732.5714
All credit cards • high moderate

AGRITOURISM FARM AND MUSEUM
La Ginestra
Via Serraloggia
☎0732.3182
No credit cards • inexpensive
La Ginestra is a working farm that rents three rooms with private bath, and three bedrooms that share two bathrooms. Meals are not provided, but there's a kitchen where guests can cook. And there's a small museum exhibit of farm tools from the past.

RESTAURANT
Marchese del Grillo
Rocchetta Bassa 73 (outside town)
☎0732.625-690
Fax 0732.627-958
Closed Monday
All credit cards • high moderate
The Marchese del Grillo—wealthy, eccentric, libertine gastronome of the seventeenth century—according to legend retired from a career in the papal court to Fabriano, where he built a villa outside town on a hilltop. Lanfranco D'Alessio and his wife, Emanuela,

bought the villa in 1987, restored it, and opened their restaurant, named after the Marchese. The restaurant is attractive, with vaulted ceilings, terra-cotta floors, peach-colored tablecloths, and important wineglasses, a tip-off that the wine list is important too. Lanfranco is a sommelier, Emanuela presides in the kitchen. Two seasonal menus combine tradition and innovation, but utilize quality ingredients, local whenever possible. There's fresh fish from the coast, when it's available, but Fabriano lamb and almost-impossible-to-find *marchigiana* beef are always on the menu. Begin with a *bruschetta* tasting, or *sfilacci di puledro*, shredded cured horse. Rustic soups like barley and pea, pasta and bean, or emmer and chick-pea; homemade pasta like *tagliatelle* or *malfatte* (green *gnocchi*) are simply sauced. Boned rabbit cooked like suckling pig (*in porchetta*) with wild fennel, *fritto misto*, grilled meats, or fish are each served with a seasonal vegetable. Cheese lovers should taste the *formaggio di fossa*, served with apple slices and green-tomato preserves or the goat cheese with alfalfa honey. Desserts like *tiramisù*, fruit tarts, bavarians, *semifreddo*, and sliced fresh fruit conclude the meal. Sommelier Lanfranco's wine list is wonderful, strong on regional wines and *grappa*. Look for truffles and mushrooms in season.

GROCERY
Caio Bilei
Via Cialdini 5
☎0732.3418
Closed Thursday afternoon
The Bilei family have been making *salumi* for 150 years, which may be why their *salame di Fabriano* is the best in town. Look for excellent pork products like *salame lardellato*, rolled *pancetta*, cured loin, sausage, and more—all made without preservatives or chemicals. The shop also sells a nice selection of Italian products like olive oil, pasta, simple desserts, and more.

SMOKED TROUT

Acquarello
Via Campodiegoli 33/d
☎0732.72003

Smoked trout isn't a traditional Marchigiano product. But there was a clear, cool mountain spring for raising trout and pike, and an abundance of the aromatic woods, herbs, and berries needed for the smoking process. The Cooperativa Agroittica Fabrianese had tasted smoked fish from other countries and decided they could do as well. They make smoked trout, eel, and pike, smoked over hardwoods, juniper, bay leaves, and coriander, all vacuum packed.

Falconara Marittima

HOTEL

Monteconero
Monte Conero
Sirolo (close by)
☎071.933-0592
Fax 071.933-0365
All credit cards • moderate

RESTAURANT-INN

Villa Amalia
Via degli Spagnoli 4
☎071.916-0550
Fax 071.912-045
Closed Tuesday except in summer,
and January 5–20
Diners Club, MasterCard, Visa • high moderate

Amelia Ceccarelli knows what to do with local fish and seafood. Her villa in Falconara Marittima has been turned into an intimate three-room restaurant. Son-sommelier Lamberto pairs fine wines with his mother's cooking. The *cucina* is based on fine local ingredients, treated with a creative touch. Spend the night in one of the villa's seven rooms and taste some of Lam-

berto's fine selection of *grappa* and whiskey.

RESTAURANT

Da Ilario
Via Tito Speri 2
☎/Fax 071.917-0678
Closed Sunday evening, Monday, and June
All credit cards • moderate

Ilario Berardi is the chef, sommelier, and animator of this restaurant. The *cucina* takes advantage of fresh seafood, local lamb and pork, and a wide selection of vegetables. Salads are dressed with extra virgin olive oil—local, Tuscan, or Ligurian. The cheese selection is wonderful, but desserts are less interesting. Ask Ilario to let you see his wine cellar, stocked with well-priced regional gems, and he'll jump for joy.

Fano

HOTEL

Hotel Angela
Viale Adriatico 13
☎0721.801-239
Fax 0721.803-102
All credit cards • low moderate

HOTEL

See Pesano

RESTAURANT

Pesce Azzurro
Viale Adriatico 48
☎0721.803-165
Closed Monday, and September 1–April 30
No credit cards • least expensive meal in the book

I thought of Calvin Trillin when I stumbled upon Pesce Azzurro while looking for Trattoria Da Quinta and decided that a five-course fish dinner served with bread, water, and wine for less than 10,000 lire (under $10) couldn't be passed up. The fixed meal of this cafeteria, operated during the tourist season by the fishermen's cooperative, changes daily, and always includes two appetizers followed by a pasta course. You'll receive two kinds of fish for a second course, made from either local clams or *pesce azzurro*, literally "blue fish," the term used to indicate anchovies, sardines, mackerel, and a few other related fish. Pay for your meal, get a tray, and join the line. "Please hold plate of pasta with two hands," the sign on the wall commands with the voice of experience. Eat your meal outside under the pergola, or inside when it rains (a bit more claustrophobic), at the long, sticky, blue and white plastic-covered communal tables. The wine is miserable, but forgivable under the circumstances.

R E S T A U R A N T
Trattoria Da Quinta
Viale Adriatico 42
☎0721.808-043
Closed Sunday and August
No credit cards • low moderate

Quinta Darpetti cooks the best fish in Fano. Her *trattoria*, next door to Pesce Azzurro, is across the street from the commercial, big-business industrial port, the antithesis of a fishing village scene. Da Quinta is always filled with fishermen and locals who enjoy her specialties: marinated anchovies, *risotto* or *tagliatelle* sauced with seafood, grilled and deep-fried fish. The waitresses are in a hurry, and not noted for their patience. Wines are unfortunate, and detract from Quinta's *cucina*.

Grottamare

H O T E L
Parco dei Principi
Lungomare De Gasperi 70
☎0735.735-066
Fax 0735.735-080
All credit cards • moderate, higher in the summer

R E S T A U R A N T
Osteria dell'Arancio
Piazza Peretti, Grottamare Alta
☎0735.631-059
Open evenings only, closed Wednesday, open every evening in the summer
No credit cards • high moderate

I'm enthusiastic about Osteria dell'Arancio, a rustic new-wave *trattoria* in a charming piazza in Grottamare Alta, away from the bustle of the touristy coast. The ambience is rustic, with yellow butcher paper place mats and important wineglasses, a hint that owner-host-sommelier Michele Alesiani really cares about wine. Chef Ciccio Fannella's creative cooking is based on fine local ingredients. The menu changes constantly, but *bruschetta* and *salumi* like homemade *salame lardellato*, liver and orange rind sausage, and *ciascolo* are always available. First-course offerings may include legume soups, fresh pasta dressed with fish or rabbit, pasta with green tomato sauce and pungent *ricotta marzotica*, a fermented cheese from Puglia. Guinea hen, roast kid, braised rabbit, or goose are well prepared. The cheese selection is wonderful, local, and outer-regional artisanal varieties that Michele has hunted down. Finish with homemade pastry or "spoon desserts" like ricotta pudding, orange *semifreddo*, or mousse. The tasting menu, paired with three wines, is a

bargain. Many clients stop in after dinner for a snack of *salumi*, cheese, dessert, always accompanied by a glass of fine wine. The wine list is fantastic, reasonably priced, packed with regional, national, and international jewels. Enophiles should plan a detour.

Jesi

HOTEL
Federico II
Via Ancona 100
☎0731.211-079
Fax 0731.57221
All credit cards • moderate most of the year, expensive in the summer

ENOTECA
La Serva Padrona
Piazza Pergolesi 1
☎0731.212-550
Closed Sunday
MasterCard, Visa
The best wine selection in the area, sold by the bottle, with many wines available for tasting by the glass. Snack on *salumi*, cheese, sandwiches, or cold dishes. Fine pasta and nonperishables like Mongetto stuffed red peppers, Latini pasta, coffee, balsamic vinegar, extra virgin olive oil, and jarred truffle products are also sold. La Serva Padrona is a wonderful stop for breakfast and serves a perfect *cappuccino* accompanied by a *cornetto* pastry.

GELATO
Gelateria Carlo Casoni
Corso Matteotti 42
☎0731.64472
Closed Tuesday
Carlo Casoni only makes nine flavors of *gelato*, but each is worth sampling, as all are made with fresh seasonal fruit and first-rate fresh ingredients. Other *gelaterie* in Jesi have a larger selection, but Carlo's *gelato* is the best in town.

Macerata

HOTEL
Hotel Claudiani
Via Ulisse 8
☎0733.261-400
Fax 0733.261-380
All credit cards • moderate

HOTEL
Villa Quiete
Valle Cascia
Montecassiano (close by)
☎/Fax 0733.599-559
All credit cards • moderate

RESTAURANT
Floriani
Borgo Compagnoni 9
Montanello (close by)
☎0733.492-792
Closed Monday
No credit cards • low moderate
Carla and Andrea Cesanelli's Ristorante Floriani serves an enlightened version of *cucina marchigiana* with country elegance, in a setting of vineyards and olive trees. Some of their rustic traditional dishes are difficult to find elsewhere. The menu shows signs of careful research, and Carla and Andrea frequently experiment with recipes from the 1600s. Andrea is a sommelier and can offer splendid local wines, but the wines of Villamagna, their own production, are fine with the *cucina*. Extra virgin olive oil is also produced by Villamagna. Finish your meal with the fennel *grappa*.

Osimo

HOTEL
Grand Hotel Cristoforo Colombo
Strada Statale 16, km 310 plus 400 meters on the state highway
☎071.710-8890
Fax 071.710-8994
All credit cards • moderate

PASTA
Latini
Via Jesi 186
☎/Fax 071.717-587

Latini pasta, artisanally produced by Carlo and Carla Latini, is my favorite in Italy. They're the only pastamakers who grow their own wheat, Italian durum cultivars, including higher-protein Senatore Capelli. The wheat is milled into semolina flour, *farina di semola di grano duro*, kneaded mechanically with water, extruded from hand-turned bronze dies, and slow-dried for over twenty-four hours. Artisanally produced pasta tastes better; it has a sweet semolina flavor, cooks to a firmer *al dente*, and presents a rough golden surface that looks sanded. The pasta is high in gluten and glutamic acid, directly metabolized by the brain, heightening mental activity. Pasta also contains thiamine or vitamin B_1, which regulates carbohydrate metabolism and has a positive effect on mental attitude. Therefore, eating pasta makes you smart and happy! And Latini pasta makes you smarter and happier, and tastes better than any other brand I've ever sampled. Fax for an appointment if you'd like to see the wheat fields or the new mill that Carlo and Carla are building.

Pergola

HOTEL
Silvi Palace
Piazza Brodolini 6
☎/Fax0721.734-724
All credit cards • inexpensive

EMMER
Fattoria di Montesecco di Massimo Schiavi
Via Montesecco 149
☎0721.778-277
Always open

Winemaker Massimo Schiavi organically cultivates barley (*orzo mondo*), a tasty variety of hard wheat called *grano d'or*, and my favorite, emmer (*farro*). It's a rich nutty-tasting grain that the Roman legions planted to feed their troops, and that has become part of the gastronomic tradition of many regions. Massimo sells whole emmer, to be cooked in soups or like rice for a less starchy, more flavorful *risotto*, and stone-ground emmer, a whole-wheaty, bran-studded *farina* to be used in combination with other flours in baking and pasta making. Massimo also grows bean sprouts, and it's easy to tell which local restaurants are serious about what they're doing by the presence of these decidedly beany-tasting sprouts in their dishes.

Pesaro

The summer beach scene in Pesaro is as umbrella-studded as its neighbors, but the city's wonderful Art Nouveau Villa Ruggeri, Ceramics Museum, the house where Rossini was born, and the gardens and fountains of Villa Caprile may tempt you to visit—but not in August, I hope.

HOTEL
Villa Serena
Via San Nicola 6/3
☎0721.55211
Fax 0721.55927
All credit cards • moderate

RESTAURANT-HOTEL
Hotel Principe–Da Teresa
Viale Trieste 180
☎0721.30096
Fax 0721.31636
Closed Monday and November
All credit cards • moderate

The Hotel Principe is decidedly unattractive. But the vacationing families who book here year after year, and who eat twice a day in the dining room, know that an attractive edifice is pleasant but not necessary. The dining room has a one of the nicest views in Pesaro of the unique Art Nouveau gem, Villa Ruggieri. After a look at the interesting menu and even better wine list, you probably won't mind the lack of architectural distinction or ambience. Sommelier Otello Renzi selects wines from his splendid collection (stop in for a late-night glass of wine in the *enoteca* downstairs even if you don't eat here) and pairs them with his mother's *cucina,* composed of the best, freshest local ingredients Otello can get his hands on. Pasta is homemade and ethereal, sauced with fish; second courses are inventive, grilled or delicately floured and deep-fried. Finish with a refreshing fruit *sorbetto* or one of the rich but somewhat sweet desserts.

P O T T E R Y

G. Molaroni
Via Luca della Robbia 17/19
☎0721.33181
Closed Monday morning
No credit cards

The best ceramics in Pesaro are produced by Molaroni. Since 1880, four generations of this family have been involved in the creation of hand-painted majolica tiles, vases, ornamental plates, pharmaceutical jars, soup tureens, platters, and dinnerware. Traditional designs are lovely and include the Pesaro rose pattern (*rosa di Pesaro*), a floral (*fiori Pesaro*), and my favorite, a striking black and white design of rampant lions and oak leaves known as *querciato.*

M U S E U M

Museo delle Ceramiche
Piazza Toschi Mosca 29
☎0721.31213 or 6971
Closed Sunday afternoon and Monday

The Museo delle Ceramiche houses a well-presented collection of Renaissance and Baroque ceramics, mostly from Umbria and Le Marche.

Porto San Giorgio

R E S T A U R A N T - H O T E L

David Palace Hotel and Ristorante Davide
Via Lungomare Gramsci Sud
☎/Fax 0734.676-848
Closed Monday
All credit cards • high moderate restaurant, moderate hotel

Davide Scafa's restaurant used to have an anonymous ambience with a squalid little hotel next door, but they've both moved to a new site on the coast. Don't expect anything rustic or traditional in this modern but ugly edifice except for the menu of well-prepared *cucina marchigiana* and seafood classics. Look for *gnocchi* sauced with mussels, pasta sauced with crab, seafood *risotto,* and the Buon Ricordo special—fresh egg pasta with prawns, squid, cuttlefish, clams. Main-dish options include Ancona-style cod, mixed fried fish and seafood, simply grilled fish, all paired with fine wines, mostly whites, by Davide's son Luciano, a sommelier. Luciano is interested in culinary history, reads ancient texts on the subject, and is concerned with maintaining regional traditions. The hotel has its own private beach, pool, parking, and garden.

San Lorenzo in Campo

R E S T A U R A N T - H O T E L

Il Giardino
Via Mattei 4 (outside town)
☎0721.776-803
Fax 0721.776-236
Closed Monday
All credit cards • high moderate restaurant, moderate hotel

I'm wild about Il Giardino and Efresina Rosichini's cooking. Her son Massimo Biagiali, sommelier, and his Canadian wife,

Patrizia, bustle through the dining room, serving Mom's food, making sure everything is running smoothly, helping diners choose something suitable from the fantastic wine list studded with bargains. Impeccable local ingredients are combined with wisdom and restraint. Look for lamb, fish from the Adriatic, dishes flavored with wild fennel, mushrooms and truffles in season, superfresh vegetables supplied by a nearby farmer. Begin with fine regional *salumi* like *ciasculo,* Carpegna *prosciutto,* home-cured *salame,* or appetizers based on vegetables like eggplant stuffed with flavored ricotta. Pasta is homemade, sauced with fish and vegetable combinations. *Passatelli,* normally served in broth, are prepared like pasta, dressed with white truffle. Look for simple fish preparations, herbed lamb, braised squab. Tasting menus offer a sampling of Efresina's cooking at bargain prices. Homemade desserts are worth saving room for, especially the *gelato* and tiny pastries. Massimo's collection of *grappe* and distillates is noteworthy, and will be greatly appreciated by those staying at the hotel. Rooms are clean, modern, functional, plus there's a pool.

BAKERY

Pasticceria Leila
Piazza Verdi 5
☎0721.776-909
Closed Wednesday

Head to the Pasticceria Leila for traditional cookies, simple pastries, and the best *pizza di formaggio,* a briochelike egg dough enriched with sheep's milk cheese. Leila's version is made with olive oil instead of butter. I love the look of the "fake peaches," two small rounded cakes glued together with a custard filling, drenched with *Alkermes,* a red liqueur, and coated with sugar for a peachlike appearance.

MUNICIPAL MUSEUMS

Ethnographic Museum
Paleontological Museum
Postage Stamp Museum
Pro Loco
Via San Demetrio 3
☎0721.776-915
Fax 0721.776-479

I visited San Lorenzo in Campo with intrepid researcher-author Carol Field. We were invited to visit the town's museums by a proud local and just couldn't say no. We were given a tour by someone from the mayor's office and tried to be interested and enthusiastic about the Ethnographic Museum—relics brought back from Africa by Dr. Giorgio Gello, and the Paleontological Museum—Roman artifacts and rocks, but I tried my hardest to avoid the Postage Stamp Museum, envisioning an endless display of stamp albums. Instead, it was one of the highlights of the trip. Local artist Zingaretti (no one could remember his first name) completely covered the walls of a tiny room with over 97,000 stamps, used like tiles in a mosaic, to depict Romulus and Remus, the official San Lorenzo in Campo crest, and a map of Italy, with each region in a different color. The museums are open by appointment only—contact Lorenzo Bonafede at the Pro Loco tourist office for more information.

Senigallia

HOTEL

Duchi della Rovere
Via Corridoni 3
☎071.792-7623
Fax 071.792-7748
All credit cards • moderate

RESTAURANT

Riccardone's

Via Rieti 69

☎071.64762

Closed Monday except summer, and mid-November to mid-December

All credit cards • moderate

Riccardone ("Big Riccardo")—friendly, bearded, and *simpatico*—serves minimalist Adriatic seafood in his two-room restaurant. The emphasis on quality is evident in the entranceway display of extra virgin olive oils, local wines, aged balsamic vinegar, and chocolates from Roccati, all products that are up to Riccardone's high standards. Begin with the *antipasto misto* of fresh local fish, served with garlic bread (*bruschetta*) made with local extra virgin olive oil. Homemade pasta and *al dente* spaghetti are sauced with fish, and grilled shellfish and fish, including sweet six-inch sole (*sogliole*), are given the traditional bread crumb and parsley treatment. Riccardone has his own ideas about what you should eat, and he probably won't let you order, but it shouldn't be a problem. The desserts and *sorbetti* are homemade, and the selection of local wines is impressive. The bathroom is one of the most attractive in the region.

Serra San Quirico

HOTEL

See Fabriano or Jesi

HOTEL

K 3

Via Piedastri 1

☎0731.86063

No credit cards • inexpensive

RESTAURANT

Le Copertelle

Via Leopardi 3

☎0731.86691

Closed Tuesday

All credit cards • moderate

It's impossible to hide my enthusiasm for Le Copertelle, a rustic restaurant on the main drag of the village of Serra San Quirico. Felice Orazi greets diners, ushers them into one of four small dining rooms decorated with cork wainscoting, a few freshwater shrimp hanging out in an aquarium. The menu is exciting, filled with traditional dishes made with wild greens, herbs, mushrooms and truffles that Felice and his friend Raul Ballerini (see following) stalk in the nearby mountains. Fixed tasting menus—truffle or organic—are reasonably priced, although I'd rather let Felice serve what he wants to. Hope for preserved mushrooms, *bruschetta* with wild herbs and hot *peperoncino*, herb *frittate*, and *calcione*, pastry filled with fresh *pecorino* cheese and a hint of lemon peel. *Risotto* or *farro* (emmer) is flavored with wild greens (called *consigli* in dialect), potato *gnocchi* are sauced with *formaggio di fossa*, and spaghetti with freshwater shrimp. Main-course choices include local kid, squab, partridge, snails, grilled *porcini* mushrooms in season. Conclude with excellent *formaggio di fossa*, paired with *sapa*, cooked wine must. Simple desserts complete the menu. The wine list is short but sweet, focusing on terrific, affordable regional wines. Finish with a glass of *visciolato*, or rosehip liqueur.

HERB AND MUSHROOM STALKER-RESTAURANT

La Pianella

Via Gramsci

☎0731.880054

Closed Monday

All credit cards • moderate

I met Raul Ballerini when I asked too many questions about the wild greens served at Le Copertelle. Felice knew all the answers in dialect, but Paula Wolfert and I wanted to know the names in Latin so that we could identify them in English. So Raul was called, and he brought a book with plant pictures identified in Latin. He said that he'd love to take anyone interested in hunting for wild herbs, greens, and mushrooms on his forays in the mountains. However, those who are interested in simply eating the bounty of his hunts can stop at La Pianella, Raul's new restaurant: one large dining room downstairs, a private dining room upstairs, and tables outside in the garden when the weather is nice. Most of the best wines of the region are on the list; *visciolato* is served, although it's not on the list.

Tolentino

I didn't stick around town long enough to dine, but enjoyed the Ex-voto Museum so much (as did Carol Field) that I decided to include this entry, even though it has no culinary implications.

FRESCOES, CERAMICS, AND VOTIVE OFFERING MUSEUM
Basilica di San Nicola
☎0733.969-996
Open 9 A.M.–12 noon, 3:30–7 P.M.

Pilgrims have always flocked to this sanctuary dedicated to local saint San Nicola, a miracle worker of the fourteenth century. Check out the restored frescoes from the school of Giotto, considered one of the greatest in Le Marche, the ceramic collection donated by Cardinal Giovanni Tacci. But don't miss the Ex-voto Museum containing hundreds of hand-painted wooden panels depicting supplicants to San Nicola in their moment of need. Sick men, women or children in bed, a child run over by a cart, prisoners in jail, a roof caving in on a family, a man falling down the stairs twice are assisted by San Nicola, floating in clouds in a corner. Those who love folk art should definitely plan a pilgrimage.

La Festa Continua

And now that your vacation has slipped by too quickly, and you have fallen in love with Italy, pasta, *prosciutto*, and *parmigiano*, and with the plains of the Po or the hills of Toscana or the villas of Veneto or the truffles of Piemonte, and you're already thinking about when you can get back and where you'll go, how can you incorporate the Italian festival that you have experienced into everyday life at home? The following books capture the spirit of the Italian table.

Marcella Hazan's *Essentials of Classic Italian Cooking* is written from a practical Italian traditionalist point of view, with general information on basic ingredients like rice, extra virgin olive oil, pasta, and balsamic vinegar and where to get them, and with recipes that range from simple everyday dishes to complicated holiday preparations. The world awaits the revision of Victor Hazan's book about Italian wine.

Carol Field's award-winning *The Italian Baker* is one of the few cookbooks that I actually use. It is a personal favorite, not only for its useful hints and wonderful recipes for breads, pizza, cakes, and cookies, but for its scholarly research of regional Italian baking and modern approach to reproducing traditional food with everyday ingredients and equipment. Look for *Celebrating Italy, Italy in Small Bites,* and anything else written by rabid Italophile Carol Field.

Burton Anderson's *Pocket Guide to Italian Wines* is compact, precise, perfect for liquor-store reference when shopping for wine. *Vino, The Wines and Winemakers of Italy* offers more in-depth coverage of the wines, and contains informative interviews with some of Italy's finest vintners, who discuss personal winemaking philosophy with the author, Burton Anderson, considered the leading Italian wine expert by Italians and Americans alike. And look for his *Italian Wine Atlas.*

Leslie Forbes's *A Taste of Tuscany,* with its charming colored-pencil illustrations of the Tuscan table and authentic recipes from fine restaurants that prepare genuine food, is a visual treat that never fails to transport me to the countryside of Toscana.

For a good drool, nothing is finer than Giuliano Bugialli's *Foods of Italy,* with its double-page color plates of *prosciutto* and luscious purple-skinned fresh figs, net-draped olive trees awaiting harvest, rows of golden traditional Mantovano desserts in the Palazzo Ducale in Mantova. The recipes seem overly complicated, calling for hard-to-find ingredients, but the photographs, too beautiful to risk the dangers of the kitchen, are guaranteed to stimulate your salivary glands.

My own cookbook *Red, White and Greens* is about the true Italian approach to vegetables.

Read anything that Nancy Harmon Jenkins and Corby Kummer have to say about Italy. Both are knowledgeable about all things Italian.

So put a large pot of water on to boil, uncork a bottle of fine Italian wine, and get out your maps. *La festa continua.*

Glossary

This glossary provides translations of Italian terms that appear frequently in *Eating in Italy* or on menus. It is not a complete "food dictionary." Dishes of specific areas are described under "Menu" and "Regional Specialties" for each region.

Don't be thrown by variations in endings. Italian nouns can end in *a, o,* or *e,* the plurals in *e* or *i,* according to their gender; and adjectives will have corresponding endings.

acciughe: anchovies
aceto: vinegar
aceto balsamico: balsamic vinegar
acqua del rubinetto: tap water
acqua minerale: mineral water; either *gassata* (fizzy) or *naturale* (still)
acqua non potabile: "water not fit for drinking"; sign may appear on fountains
affettato: sliced salami
affumicato: smoked
aglio: garlic
agnello: lamb
agnolotti: pasta stuffed with meat, egg, and cheese
agretti: a green that resembles chives and has a pleasant (not oniony) sour taste
agrodolce: sweet and sour
albicocca: apricot
al dente: just slightly chewy; applies to pasta and rice
alici: anchovies
alimentari: general grocery store
alla spina: on tap (beer)
allodole: larks

alloro: bay leaves; also called *lauro*
amabile: semi-sweet; used to describe wines
amaretti: sweet and bitter almond cookies
amaro: bitter
analcolico: nonalcoholic
ananas: pineapple
anatra: duck
anguilla: eel
anguria: watermelon
animali da cortile: "courtyard animals": chicken (*pollo*), squab or pigeon (*piccione*), quail (*quaglia*), guinea hen (*faraona*)
animelle: sweetbreads
antipasto: appetizer
antipasto misto: assorted appetizers
aperitivo: aperitif, believed to stimulate the appetite
aperitivo della casa: house cocktail, usually made with white wine or *spumante,* bitters, and a mystery ingredient
apribottiglia: bottle opener
aragosta: lobster
arancia: orange

aranciata: orange soda
arrosto: roast
arsella: wedge-shell clam; also called *tellina*
asiago: a hard, sharp, dry cow's-milk cheese
asparagi: asparagus
assaggi: "tastes"; a series of dishes, a tasting, of desserts (*di dolce*), of first courses (*di primi*)
astice: lobster

baccalà: dried salt cod
bacelli: fava beans (Tuscan)
baci di dama: chocolate-covered almond cookies
bagoss: a hard, aromatic, grainy cheese
bar: café serving alcoholic drinks, coffee, *gelato,* snacks, breakfast; also the place where you may find a public telephone, read the newspaper, listen to a sports match
barbabietola: beet
basilico: basil
beccaccia: woodcock
beccafico: fig pecker, warbler

Bellini: Prosecco and peach juice cocktail

bel paese: a soft, mild cheese

besciamellé: béchamel sauce

bianchetti: tiny anchovies; also called *gianchetti, schiuma di mare*

bianco: white

bicchiere: drinking glass

bietole: Swiss chard

bigoli: pasta made with a special press

birra: beer; may be *nazionale* (from Italy) or *estera* (imported); *alla spina* means on tap

biscotti, biscottini: cookies

bistecca: beef steak

bitto: a soft, rich cheese

bollito misto: mixed boiled meats

borragine: borage

bottarga: pressed dried mullet roe

bottega: shop

boudin: potato-based blood pudding or sausage (*salumi*)

branzino: sea bass

brasata: braised

bresaola: cured dried beef, sliced thin like *prosciutto* (*salumi*)

brioche: croissants; also called *cornetti*

brodeto, brodetto: fish soup

brodo: broth

bruscàndoli: wild hops

bruschetta: garlic bread

buridda: fish stew

burrata: fresh cheese stuffed with cream and mozzarella threads

burro: butter

cacciagione: game

cachi: persimmon

caffè: espresso coffee, served in a demitasse cup; also called *espresso; ristretto* means stronger, *lungo* means weaker; *corretto* means "corrected" with a shot of brandy or liquor; see also *Hag*

caffè d'orzo: coffee made from barley

caffè latte: *cappuccino* made with extra milk, served in a large cup

caffè macchiato: espresso "stained" with a little milk

caffettiera: espresso pot

calamaro or **calamaretto:** squid

caldo: hot

camomilla: chamomile tea

camoscio: châmois

cannellini: white beans; see also *piattellini*

cannolicchio: tube-shaped razor-shell clam

cantina: cellar

capesante: scallops

capitone: large eel

caponata: eggplant salad

cappa santa: scallop

cappelletti: stuffed pasta

capperi: capers

cappone: capon

cappuccino: coffee topped with foamy steamed milk, the classic breakfast drink; also called *cappuccio;* see also *marocchino, caffè latte*

cappuccio: see *cappuccino*

capretto: kid

caprino: a cream cheese, sometimes made with goat's milk

capriolo: venison

carciofi: artichokes

cardi: cardoons, thistlelike vegetable

carpaccio: thinly sliced raw beef

carta da musica: "sheets of music": unleavened wafer-thin flat disk of cracker bread, from Sardinia

cartoccio: baked in parchment paper

casalinghi: combination hardware/housewares store

cassa: cashier

castagne: chestnuts; see also *marroni*

castelmagno: a rich-flavored mountain cheese, fresh or aged, rare

cavallo: horse

cavatappi: corkscrew

cavolo: cabbage

ceci: chick-peas

cee: elvers (young eels); see also *cie, ciechi*

cena: dinner; see also *colazione, pranzo*

chiuso: closed

ciabatta: crusty flat "slipper" loaf of bread

cicchetti: "pick-me-ups"; little snacks served with a glass of wine (Veneto)

cie, cieche: eels; see also *cee*

ciliegia: cherry

cinghiale: wild boar

cioccolata: chocolate

cioccolata calda: hot chocolate; at its best, hot, thick, almost black bitter chocolate; served *con panna* (with unsweetened whipped cream)

cipolla: onion

cocomero: watermelon

colazione: breakfast (also called *la prima colazione*); lunch; see also *pranzo*

colomba: wood pigeon
coltello: knife; *per parmigiano:* special knife for breaking off chunks of Parmesan cheese
congelato: frozen
coniglio: rabbit
conto: bill
contorno: third course, a side dish of vegetables or a green salad
coperto: cover charge, a fixed charge added to the bill in most restaurants
coppa: cup; also a salt-cured boneless ham (*salumi*), or a large rough-textured pork sausage
corbezzolo: fruit of the Mediterranean strawberry tree
coregoni: a salmonlike fish
cornetti: croissants; also called *brioche*
costoletta *or* **cotoletta:** chop or cutlet
cotechino: cooked pork sausage
cozze: mussels
crauti: sauerkraut
crema: custard
cren: horseradish
crescenza: a soft, creamy, mild cheese
crocchette: croquettes
crostata: open-faced fruit tart
crostini: canapé, often with pâté
crudo: raw
crumiri: *polenta* butter cookies
cucchiaio: spoon
cucina: cuisine, cooking, cookery, dishes

culatello: the heart of a *prosciutto crudo,* from the Parma area (*salumi*)
cuore: heart

dattero di mare: date-shell clam
degustazione: a tasting
delizie: "delights"; specialty foods
distilleria: distillery
DOC: "Denominazione di Origine Controllata"; applies to wines controlled by laws determining geographic origin, grape variety, character, yield, and aging requirements
DOCG: "Denominazione di Origine Controllata e Garantita"; applies to wines controlled and guaranteed by laws determining geographic origin, grape variety, character, yield, and aging requirements
dolce: sweet
dragoncello: tarragon
droghe: spices; also called *spezie*

edicola: newsstand
enoteca: wine shop
erbe: herbs
espresso: see *caffè*
estera: imported

fagioli: beans
faraona: guinea hen
farina: flour
farina di castagne: chestnut flour
farro: emmer, a grain with a wheaty taste
fave: fava beans
fegatelli: pork liver
fegatini: chicken livers

fegato: calf's liver
fetta: slice
fettunta: Tuscan garlic bread
fichi: figs
fichi d'India: prickly pears
fiera: festival, fair
filetto: fillet
finanziera: stew of chicken livers and sweetbreads
finocchio: fennel
finocchiona: fennel-laced sausage (*salumi*)
fiocchetto: the part of the *prosciutto* other than the heart (*culatello*); also called *fiocco*
focaccia: a flatbread; naked pizza
fogolar: open hearth, traditional in Friuli–Venezia Giulia
fonduta: creamy melted *fontina* cheese, milk, and eggs, served with *polenta* or toast rounds
fontina: a delicate buttery-flavored cheese, compact and smooth
forchetta: fork
formaggella: a fresh cheese
formaggetta: small, soft tasty rounds of white cheese made from a mixture of cow's and ewe's milk
formaggio: cheese
formaggio di malga: a cheese made from the milk of cows grazing in alpine pastures
fragoline: tiny wild strawberries
frantoio: olive oil mill
freddo: cold
friggitoria: fry shop

frittata: pan-fried egg flan; resembles an unfolded omelet
frittelle: fritters
fritto: fried
fritto misto: a variety of deep-fried foods, including meat, vegetables, fruit
frutta: fruit
frutta cotta: seasonal fruit cooked with wine and spices
funghi: mushrooms
fusilli: see *pasta corta*
fuso: melted

galletti: chanterelles
gallina: hen
gamberetti: little shrimp
gassosa, gazosa: sweetened mineral water, sometimes with a slight lemon flavor
gastronomia: grocery store
gelateria: shop selling *gelato*
gelato: frozen confection; not to be confused with the American product
germano: mallard duck
ghiaccio: ice
gianchetti: see *bianchetti*
gianduja, gianduia: combination of chocolate and hazelnut; specialty of Piedmont
ginepro: juniper berry
gnocchi, gnocchetti: potato dumplings
gorgonzola: a rich, blue-veined cheese
gorgonzola dolce: sweeter, creamier, and less aggressive than the classic blue cheese
grana: a grainy cheese with a nutty flavor, similar to *parmigiano*

granchio: crab
granita: water ices
grappa: alcoholic spirit distilled from pomace, the grape skins and pits left after the winemaking process
grappa monovitigno: *grappa* distilled, from a single grape variety
gratella: rectangular cast-iron pan for stovetop grilling; also called *griglia*
grattata: grating; truffles are often sold by the *grattata*
grattugia: cheese grater
griglia: grill
grissini: breadsticks
groviera: Italian gruyere cheese

Hag: brand name of Italy's most popular decaf; used to mean decaffeinated coffee in general

insaccati: sausage and salami
insalata: salad
integrale: whole wheat

lampone: raspberries
lardo: salt-cured lard streaked with pork (*salumi*)
latte: milk
latte fritto: cinnamon-spiced deep-fried custard
latteria: store selling dairy products; also a cheese made from cow's milk, mild when fresh, more intense when aged
lattuga: lettuce
lauro: laurel; also called *alloro*
lenticchie: lentils
lepre: wild hare

lesso: boiled
limone: lemon
liscio: neat, as in a drink with no ice
locanda: inn
lombatine: veal chop
lumache: snails

maccheroni: macaroni; pasta
macchinetta da caffè: espresso maker
macedonia: fresh fruit salad, served for dessert
maggiorana: marjoram
maiale: pork
mais: corn
mandorle: almonds
manzo: beef
mare: sea
marinato: marinated
marocchino: strong, dark *cappuccino*, made with less milk than usual
marroni: chestnuts; richer and more flavorful than *castagne*
marzolino: freshly made *pecorino* cheese; also called *pecorino fresco*
mascarpone: a rich, sweet triple-cream cheese
mattarello: rolling pin
mela: apple
melanzana: eggplant
melacotogna: quince
melagrana: pomegranate
melone: cantaloupe
menta: mint
merenda: snack
merluzzo: cod
mezzaluna: crescent-shaped double-handled rocking knife
mezzo: half
midolla: the inside of a loaf of bread

miele: honey
milza: spleen
minestrone: vegetable soup
mocetta: *prosciutto* made from chamois; now more commonly made of beef (*salumi*)
moleche: soft-shelled crabs
montasio: a mild, smooth cheese made from cow's milk
montone: mutton
mortadella: large smooth pork sausage studded with cubes of fat and whole peppercorns (*salumi*)
moscardino: small, curled octopus
mostarda: chutney-style condiment
mozzarella: fresh, white, elastic cheese, made from buffalo's milk (*di bufala*) or cow's milk (*fior di latte*)

nazionale: domestic, made in Italy
nespolo: loquat, a small tart orange fruit
noce: walnut
nocciola: hazelnut

oca: goose
olio d'oliva: olive oil
oliva: olive
ombra: glass of wine enjoyed at midday along with some *cicchetti*—a Venetian term
orata: gilt-head bream
orzo: barley
osei: small game birds
osteria: inn, restaurant
ostriche: oysters
ovoli: agaric mushrooms

padella per castagne: chestnut-roasting pan; looks like a long-handled frying pan with holes in the bottom
palombo: a tasty, medium-size sharky-looking fish
pancetta: salt-cured bacon (*salumi*)
pane: bread
panettone: sweet yeast cake with raisins, candied citron, orange, and eggs, traditional at Christmastime
panino: sandwich
paninoteca: sandwich shop
panna: cream
panna cotta: rich cream dessert
papavero: poppy seed
parmigiano: Parmesan cheese; see *parmigiano-reggiano*
parmigiano-reggiano: a firm, straw-colored cheese with pale flecks, fragrant, delicate, and nutty, studded with crunchy granules
pasta: dough; pastry; pasta
pasta corta: short lengths of pasta, such as *penne, fusilli, rigatoni*
pasticceria: pastry shop
pecorino: distinctly flavored all or part sheep's-milk cheese, fresh or aged
pecorino fresco: freshly made *pecorino* cheese; also called *marzolino*
penne: quill-shaped pasta
pepe: pepper
peperoncini: chile pepper
peperoni: bell peppers
pernice: partridge
pesce: fish
pescespada: swordfish

pesche: peaches
pescheria: fish market
pesto: sauce made with crushed basil
petto: breast
piastra di terracotta refrattaria: terra-cotta pizza stone; simulates an Italian brick pizza oven in the home oven
piattellini: white beans
piatto: plate
piatto unico: one-course meal
piccione: squab or pigeon
piccola pasticceria: "little pastries" or cookies, served after dessert in formal restaurants
piedini: feet
pinoli: pine nuts
pinzimonio: raw vegetables dipped in olive oil
pizza: pizza
polenta: ground cornmeal (either white or yellow) cooked slowly with salt and water; served freshly made as a side dish, or cooled, sliced, and reheated with a sauce; frequently grilled in Veneto
polipo: octopus; also *polpo, moscardino*
pollastro: young chicken
pollo: chicken
polpettone: meat loaf
polpo: octopus; also called *polipo, moscardino*
pomodoro: tomato
porcini: a type of mushroom
porri: leeks
porzione: portion
posate: flatware
pranzo: dinner; lunch; see also *cena, colazione*

pranzo in piedi: quick stand-up lunch

prezzemolo: parsley

prezzo da vedere: "price to be seen," meaning you are charged according to the amount you eat

primizia: the earliest, and tiniest, produce of the season

primo: first course, usually pasta, rice, or soup

prodotto e imbottigliato: "produced and bottled"; guarantee of quality on a bottle of olive oil

prosciutto cotto: cooked ham (*salumi*)

prosciutto crudo: salted air-cured ham (*salumi*)

provolone: a smooth cheese, delicate to zesty, fresh or aged

prugna: plum; also called *susina*

pure: mashed potatoes

quaglia: quail

quartirolo: a mild, soft, smooth cheese

rabarbaro: rhubarb

radicchio: red chicory, served both raw and cooked

ragù: meat sauce

ramerino: rosemary; also called *rosmarino*

rape: turnip, turnip greens

raschera: a hearty, smooth cheese

ravanella: radish

raveggiolo: a soft, fresh cheese made from sheep's-milk whey, delicate and hard to find

reblec: a fresh curdled cream cheese

ribes: currants

ricotta: a soft, fresh, mild cheese made from whey

rigatoni: see *pasta corta*

ripiene: stuffed

riso: rice; *originario* is the shortest grain, followed by *semifino, fino,* and *superfino,* the largest

risotto: rice toasted in butter, then cooked in broth, which is added gradually; served with butter and grated Parmesan cheese

robiola: a soft, creamy, rich, delicate cheese made from cow's or sheep's milk

rombo: turbot

rosette: "little roses"; hollow, all-crust rolls

rosmarino: rosemary; also called *ramerino*

rospo: monkfish

rosso: red

rosticceria: rotisserie take-out store

sagra: festival

salamino: small-size salami

salame, salami: raw salt-cured pork sausage (*salumi*)

sale: salt

salsiccia: sausage

salumeria: store selling cold cuts or cured meats (*salumi*)

salumi: general term for cured meats, such as *prosciutto,* salami

salvia: sage

san marzano: plum tomato

sarago: sea bream

sarde: sardines

sbriciolona: a crumbly sausage

scamorza: a firm, buttery, pear-shaped cheese

scampi: prawns

schiacciata: a flatbread

schiuma di mare: larval anchovies; also called *bianchetti, gianchetti*

secco: dry

secondo: second course, usually fish or meat

secondo quantità: "according to the quantity," meaning you are charged according to the amount you eat

sedano: celery

selezionato e imbottigliato: "selected and bottled"; appears on bottles of olive oil where the makers do not raise and harvest the olives themselves

seltz: soda water

selvaggina: game

semi: seeds

semifreddo: *gelato* with whipped cream folded in

semola: flour made of duram wheat

senape: mustard

seppia: cuttlefish

servizio: percentage for service automatically added to the bill in restaurants, in addition to the *coperto*

setaccio: sifter

sfoglia: sheet of egg-rich pasta, which is made into noodles or filled with various stuffings

sfogliatelle: ricotta-filled flaky pastry

sogliola: sole

soprassata: cured raw ham, or large rough-textured pork sausage

(*salumi*); also called
soppressa, coppa
soppressa: see *soprassata*
sorbetto: fruit sorbet
sottaceti: pickles
Speck: ham marinated in
brine with herbs and spices,
then cold-smoked and aged
(*salumi*)
spezie: spices; also called
droghe
spigola: sea bass
spremuta di arancia:
freshly squeezed orange
juice
spremuta di pompelmo:
grapefruit juice
spugnoli: morels
spumante: sparkling wine
squaquarone: a fresh, soft,
sometimes liquid cheese
stracchino: a smooth, soft,
full-flavored cheese
stracotto: braised beef
strutto: lard
succo di frutta: fruit juice
sugo: sauce
surgelato: frozen
susina: plum; also called
prugna

tabacchi: tobacco shop—
the place where you can buy
cigarettes, matches, salt,
stamps, bus tickets; often
also a *bar-caffè*
tacchino: turkey
tagliatelle: flat strips of egg
pasta
tajarin: a type of egg pasta
taleggio: a smooth, soft,
ripe cheese, similar to
stracchino but more ample
tarocco: blood orange
tartufo: truffle; either black
(*nero*) or white (*bianco*)
tartufo di mare: venus

clam
taverna: inn, restaurant
tavola calda: hot table,
take-out, or counter service
for prepared dishes
tellina: wedge-shell clam;
also called *arsella*
thè, tè: tea; served *al latte*
(with milk) or *al limone*
(with a slice of lemon)
tiramisù: a rich
mascarpone dessert
tirata a mano: hand-
stretched; used to describe
hand-rolled pasta
tisana: herbal tea
toast: grilled ham and
cheese on American-style
bread
tome: a smooth, firm
cheese, with some small
holes
tomini: small rounds of
goat or mixed-milk fresh
cheese
tonno: tuna
topinambur: Jerusalem
artichoke
tordo: thrush
torrone: nougat candy
made of hazelnuts, honey or
sugar, and egg whites
torta: cake
tortellini: fresh egg pasta
rings filled with a stuffing
tostapane: bread toaster
consisting of a hole-
punctured stainless-steel
square topped with a wire
grid screen, with a U-
shaped metal handle
totano: flying squid
tovagliolo: napkin
tovagliolo di carta: paper
napkins
tramezzino: sandwich
trattoria: restaurant

triglia: red mullet
trippa: tripe
trota: trout
tucco, tocco: sauce
tuorlo: egg yolk

un'etto: 100 grams,
around 4 ounces
uova: egg
uova da bere: extra-fresh
eggs
uva: grape, white (*bianca*)
or purple (*nera*)

vassoio: tray
vendemmia: harvest of
wine grapes
verdure: vegetables
verza: cabbage
vezzena: a smooth, fatty,
bland cheese
vigneto: vineyard
vino: wine; white is *bianco*,
red is *rosso*
vino da tavola: table wine
vino della casa: house
wine; also called *vino sfuso*
vin santo: aromatic dessert
wine
visciola: wild cherry
vitello: veal
vongola verace: carpet-
shell clam

zabaione: a dessert of egg
yolks whipped with sugar
and wine, served with
cookies or as a dessert sauce
zafferano: saffron
zampone: cooked pork
sausage packed in a pig's
shin and foot
zenzero: ginger; chile
pepper
zucca: squash
zuppa: soup

Index